KU-455-637

THE HAMPSHIRE HEARTH TAX ASSESSMENT, 1665

WITH THE

SOUTHAMPTON ASSESSMENTS FOR 1662 AND 1670

Edited by

Elizabeth Hughes and Philippa White

ISBN 1 873595 085

ISSN 0267 9930

General Editors

C. M. Woolgar : R. C. Dunhill : M. W. Doughty

Graphics Adviser

C. Heywood

HAMPSHIRE COUNTY LIBRARY

929 - 84227

1873595085

C002876954

PORTSMOUTH DIVISION

AUG 1993

Typeset and Printed by Hobbs the Printers of Southampton

CONTENTS

PREFACE

The hearth tax assessment for the year and a half ending Michaelmas 1665 for the county of Southampton, was primarily chosen for publication to complement the edition of the Hampshire Lay Subsidy rolls of 1586 (Hampshire Record Series, Volume IV, 1981). Both sources can be regarded as directories of the county for their respective periods. The 1665 county assessment was chosen, rather than any of the other surviving hearth tax assessments for the county, as it is the most complete and legible.

The whole document has been reproduced apart from the section relating to the Isle of Wight which has already appeared in print.[1] The assessment does not include the town of Southampton for which a separate assessment was invariably drawn up. The Southampton assessment for 1665 does not survive, therefore assessments for 1662 and 1670 are reproduced instead. The former survives locally amongst the Southampton City archives in Southampton City Records Office (SRO). The other assessments are held by the Public Record Office (PRO).

---

1. Russell, P. D. D., *The Hearth Tax Returns for the Isle of Wight, 1664 to 1674* (Isle of Wight Records Series Volume I, Isle of Wight County Record Office, 1981)

ACKNOWLEDGEMENTS

It is difficult, when work on a volume has been undertaken over a period of many years, to remember everyone who has helped with its production, and we can only apologise if we have omitted anyone.

Thanks are due first of all to Miss Margaret Cash, who was General Editor of the Hampshire Record Series when the project started, and to the Hampshire Record Series Editorial Panel both for suggesting it to us and for its encouragement to complete it. We are particularly grateful to Miss Rosemary Dunhill, the County Archivist, for her help and advice as General Editor. We also owe both her and Mrs Gina Turner an incalculable debt for their help with the formidable task of compiling and typing the indexes, introduction and appendices. A number of other people were roped in to help and we would therefore also like to thank Michael Hughes for identifying some of the obscurer place names and the staff of Hampshire Record Office for patiently sorting index slips.

The Hampshire hearth tax assessment of 1665 and Southampton assessment of 1670 are Crown Copyright and are reproduced with the permission of the Controller of Her Majesty's Stationery Office. The Southampton assessment of 1662 is reproduced with the permission of the Southampton City Records Office. We are grateful to the staff of the Public Record Office and the Southampton City Records Office for their help and co-operation.

Elizabeth Hughes and Philippa White
Hampshire Record Office

March 1991

INTRODUCTION

The hearth tax

The hearth tax was introduced in 1662 in an attempt to alleviate Charles II's financial difficulties. At the time of the Restoration in 1660, Parliament had calculated that the King needed an income of £1,200,000 a year in order to run the royal household and the country during peacetime. The failure of the financial settlement to produce the required amount, led to the need for supplemental taxation. After considerable debate, a tax on hearths was proposed. Although the idea of taxing hearths was new to England and Wales, it had precedents abroad. It was supported by Sir William Petty, the leading English political economist of his day, who commented that it was "easie to tell the number of Harths, which remove not as Heads or Polls do".[1]

The original hearth tax bill had a relatively rapid passage through Parliament, receiving its first reading in the House of Commons on 1 March and its third reading in the House of Lords on 19 March 1662. The bill received the royal assent on 19 May 1662 under the title, "An Act for establishing an additional Revenue upon his Majestie his heires and successors for the better support of his and their Crown and Dignity" (14 Car. II c.10).

The Act created an annual levy of two shillings, payable on every firehearth or stove within all dwellings, houses, edifices or lodgings, to be paid half-yearly in equal parts at Michaelmas (29 September) and Lady Day (25 March); the first payment was due at Michaelmas 1662.

To begin with, the bill had not distinguished between the liability of landowners or occupiers, nor did it exempt anyone from paying the tax. A series of amendments remedied these defects. The tax was charged only on the occupier and not on the landlord, making the basic unit of taxation the household or family rather than the house. Those who did not pay poor or church rates were exempt, as were those who inhabited a house worth less than 20 shillings a year on the full improved rent, and who did not occupy land or tenements of a greater value than 20 shillings a year, or possess, or have held in trust for them, lands, tenements, goods or chattels of the value of £10. The latter required an exemption certificate signed by the minister and one of the churchwardens or overseers of the poor of the parish, certified by two Justices of the Peace (JPs). The tax was not payable on private ovens, furnaces, kilns and blowing houses, or on hearths within hospitals or almshouses for the relief of the poor, whose endowment and revenue did not exceed one hundred pounds a year.

The Act was amended twice. From 1663 (15 Car. II c.13) the assessments were required to list the names and hearths of the non-liable as well as the liable. In 1664 (16 Car. II c.3) everyone with more than two hearths was made

---

1. Quoted in Beckett, J. V., "Restoration Taxation", in Alldridge, N., *The Hearth Tax: Problems and Possibilities* (Hull, 1983) and in Beckett, J. V. and Barley, M. W., Introduction, *Nottinghamshire Hearth Tax, 1664-1674* (Thoroton Society Record Series, Vol. XXXVII, 1988)

liable even if they were otherwise exempt. The owner also had to pay the tax if he let lands or buildings separately from any house to which they had formerly belonged, divided a house into several dwellings, or let these out to persons exempt by reason of their poverty.

The Crown's financial difficulties continued throughout the 1660s, 1670s and 1680s, exacerbated by the two Dutch wars and preparations for war with France. As a result, the hearth tax, originally a temporary expedient, continued until 1689 when it was abolished following the Revolution of 1688, as one of the first acts of the reign of William and Mary. The tax had always been unpopular and the Government never seemed to be satisfied with the way it was administered, changing the system of administration several times between 1662 and 1689.

The administration of the hearth tax

The sheriffs' administration, 1662-1664

The administration of the hearth tax falls into several distinct periods. From 1662 until 1664, the tax was administered by the ordinary machinery of local government. The petty constables and tithingmen were responsible for making the lists of the hearths in their area. Initially, these assessments were based on information supplied by the occupants of houses. Later, the constables were empowered to enter houses, along with two substantial inhabitants of the parish, to check the numbers of hearths. The assessments were forwarded to the Clerk of the Peace for enrolment at the next Quarter Sessions. The Clerk of the Peace also had to provide the Exchequer with a duplicate. The petty constables then had to collect the money within six days of Michaelmas or Lady Day and send it within 20 days to the high constables along with lists of defaulters. The high constables had ten days to pass the money and lists to the Sheriff or his specially appointed deputy, who had 30 days to make a return to the Exchequer. The Sheriff submitted his return in a bag of particulars of account containing all the vouchers necessary to justify his statements of what money had been collected and what had not. Each official was allowed a poundage or a fixed amount out of each pound that passed through his hands: two pence for petty constables, one penny for high constables and three pence for the Sheriff. There were also fines for both officials and householders who failed to comply with the regulations.

Within the period two assessments were prepared. The first, compiled in the summer of 1662, was used for the Michaelmas 1662 and both the 1663 collections, and listed taxpayers only. The second was prepared in the autumn and winter of 1663 to 1664 and was used for the Lady Day 1664 collection; this assessment listed both taxpayers and the exempt.[2] There is no surviving copy of the 1662 assessment for the county of Hampshire, although the assessment for

---

2. This, and all following general information about the compilation and survival of hearth tax documents, comes from Meekings, C. A. F., Introduction, *The Hearth Tax, 1662-1689* (Public Record Office, 1962)

the town of Southampton has survived locally and is reproduced in this volume (SRO SC14/2/32b). The assessment for Lady Day 1664 has survived and is probably a revision of the earlier assessment (PRO E179/375/32). The sheriffs submitted three bags of particulars of accounts: one for Michaelmas 1662, one for both 1663 collections and one for Lady Day 1664. Only documents from the Lady Day 1664 collection have survived for Hampshire (PRO E179/176/564).

The yield of the hearth tax in the first year was disappointing; only a little over a third of the anticipated yield of £300,000 came into the Exchequer.[3] The Government thought the shortfall was due to problems with assessment rather than collection, hence the revising act of 1663 (15 Car. II c.13) which gave constables power to enter houses and laid down that both liable and non-liable hearths had to be recorded. However, these measures did not improve matters and increased the unpopularity of the tax. By 1664, the sheriffs' administration was judged to be inefficient and unequal to the task. It was not only that the amount collected was low (an average annual income of £115,000 for the period as a whole[4]), but that the administration was slow.

The first receivers, 1664-1665

From Michaelmas 1664 until Michaelmas 1665, the hearth tax was administered by receivers, popularly called chimney men. They were assisted by sub-collectors, who in turn were helped by the petty constables. The revising act which set up this machinery (16 Car. II c.3) allowed the sub-collectors and petty constables to enter property to ascertain the numbers of hearths. The Clerk of the Peace continued to draw up a duplicate of the assessment to send it up to the Exchequer, and parish officials and JPs carried on making out the exemption certificates. Anyone refusing to pay could have their goods to the appropriate amount seized; the sealing of chimneys to avoid the tax was discouraged by double rating when the chimneys were uncovered.

The receivers were appointed in the summer of 1664. Their first assessment was probably a revision of that of 1662, made out after the collection of Michaelmas 1664 in the autumn and winter of 1664 to 1665. Such an assessment does not exist for Hampshire. A further assessment was made for one or both of the 1665 collections. These assessments, being usually drawn up after collection, were largely assessment and return in one. The surviving assessment for the county of Hampshire for this period covers the year and a half ending Michaelmas 1665; it is reproduced in this volume (PRO E179/176/565). Bags of particulars were submitted by the receivers for their single account for the year and a half ending Michaelmas 1665. None such survives for Hampshire.

---

3. Beckett, and Beckett and Barley, *op. cit.* Also Tom Arkell, "A Student's Guide to the Hearth Tax: Some Truths, Half-Truths and Untruths", in Alldridge, *op. cit.*
4. All figures for the average annual yield of the hearth tax cited come from Chandaman, C. D., *The English Public Revenue 1660-1688* (Oxford, 1975) p. 322 quoted in Beckett and Arkell, *op. cit.*

Extract from the Hampshire hearth tax assessment for 1665 (PRO E179/176/565 *fol. 59r*). *See* section 293. Crown copyright. Reproduced with the permission of the Controller of Her Majesty's Stationery Office

The first farm, 1666-1669

In March 1666, with little warning, the government decided to farm out or lease the tax to three City of London merchants. The expected improvement in the amount collected had not occurred (the average annual yield had fallen to £112,500 for the period of the receivers' administration) and dislike of the hearth tax had continued to grow. The merchants agreed to take a seven year lease of the tax for an advance of £250,000 and a rent of £145,000 a year for the first five years, £150,000 for the sixth year and £170,000 in the final year, with an option to surrender the lease after three years.[5]

Little is known about the administration of the tax during this period as few records survive. It is known that the tax for Lady Day 1666 was managed by sub-farmers. They acted as receivers for this collection and had a staff of sub-collectors who were helped by the petty constables. The sub-farmers were appointed in the summer of 1666 after the instalment became due. Their paper books were made out after the collection and were an assessment and return in one. These books, or copies of them, were submitted for audit in the Exchequer through the central Hearth Office. However, later accounts of the sub-farmers were not audited in the Exchequer and none are known to survive.

The farmers' administration failed, largely because the rent had been fixed at a higher figure than the yield from the tax justified. During the period of the farm, the average annual income was only £103,228. It was also at this time that popular hatred of the tax reached its peak, and an attempt by Parliament to abolish the tax in October 1666 provoked widespread riots. The merchants surrendered the farm at the earliest opportunity following the collection of Lady Day 1669.

The second receivers, 1669-1674

A report on how the collection of the hearth tax could be better administered recommended a return to the earlier system of receivers, but with improvements. The receivers, with a staff of sub-collectors helped by the petty constables, came under a small central office, independent of the Treasury, called the Agents for the Hearth Tax; receipt and audit remained the business of the Exchequer. There was a steady increase in the efficiency of the collection in this period helped by a detailed instruction manual for the receivers, who were renumerated at a higher rate, and printed exemption forms. The average annual yield rose to £145,000.

The receivers were not appointed until the summer of 1670 which meant that the collections of Michaelmas 1669 and Lady Day 1670 were already outstanding. The first assessment for Michaelmas 1669 and up to two succeeding years (for the year and a half ending Michaelmas 1670) was made in the summer and autumn of 1670. It was enrolled after collection and was a combined assessment and return, as were all the assessments of this period. The last assessment under this administration was for the year ending Lady Day 1674.

5. Beckett, *op. cit.*

The number of assessments in between varied from area to area. No assessment survives for the county of Hampshire for the year and a half ending Michaelmas 1670, although there is an assessment for the town of Southampton which is reproduced in this volume (PRO E179/247/29). County assessments exist for the year and a half ending Lady Day 1673 (PRO E179/176/569) and the year ending Lady Day 1674 (PRO E179/247/30). The receivers' bags of particulars of accounts were usually full of exemption certificates. These survive for Hampshire for the whole of this period (PRO E179/176/568, E179/330/1, E179/176/570).

The final administrations, 1674-1689

Government policy changed again in 1674 and, despite the increased efficiency under the receivers, reverted to farming the hearth tax. From Michaelmas 1674 the tax was farmed out on two successive five year contracts. Despite opposition to this method of administration, the yield from the tax continued to rise. The average yield between 1674 and 1679 was £144,495 rising to £156,862 between 1679 and 1684. When in 1684 it appeared that the farmers were making excessive profits, the farm was ended and the administration was placed in the hands of a special commission set up to manage both the excise and the hearth tax. The yield continued to increase, reaching an average yield of £216,000 a year between 1684 and 1688. Despite this, the tax was abolished by William and Mary after the Revolution of 1688 in order to win popular support. The act which abolished the tax (1 Gul & Mar c.10) described it as "not only a great oppression to the poorer sort, but a badge of slavery upon the whole people". The last collection was made at Lady Day 1689. No detailed records survive from this period.

The records

Nearly all of the surviving detailed hearth tax documents come from the two periods, Michaelmas 1662 to Lady Day 1666 and Michaelmas 1669 to Lady Day 1674, when the tax was levied directly involving the machinery of local government, and when detailed accounts were sent for audit to the Exchequer. These detailed lists, such as assessments, returns and exemption certificates, were preserved in the Exchequer's general secretariat, the King's Remembrancer's Office, together with the material generated by the auditors in the course of preparing the accounts. All of these records are now held by the Public Record Office. The detailed records are amongst a collection entitled Exchequer King's Remembrancer Lay Subsidy Rolls (E179). The hearth tax accounts are mostly in the portfolio of the class of Pipe Office Declared Accounts (Taxes) (E360). Some assessments have survived locally, usually amongst Quarter Sessions records.

Very few records survive for the periods when the hearth tax was farmed (Michaelmas 1666 to Lady Day 1669 and Michaelmas 1674 to Lady Day 1684) and when it was collected directly by a special commission (Michaelmas 1684 to Lady Day 1689). During these administrations, the detailed accounts of the

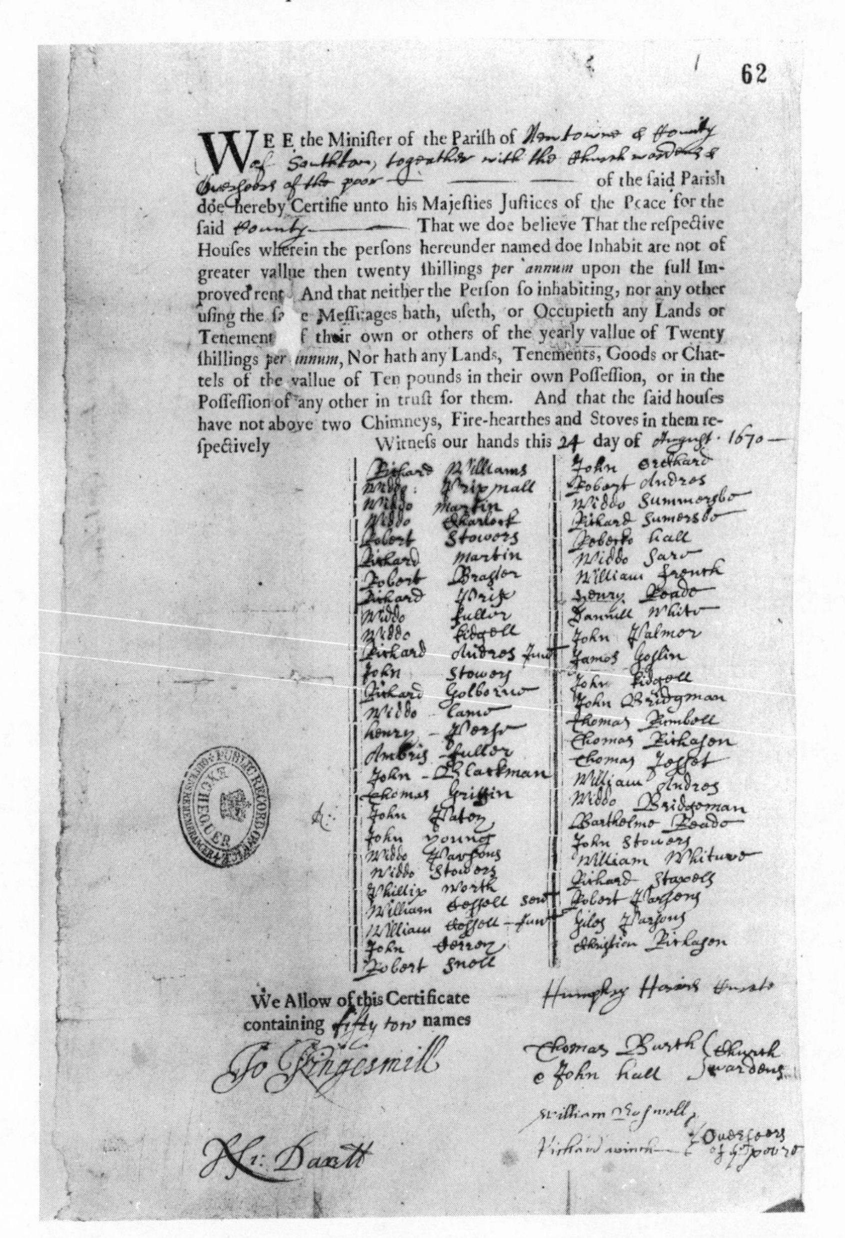

62

WEE the Minister of the Parish of Newtowne & County of Southton, together with the Church wardens & Overseers of the poor — of the said Parish doe hereby Certifie unto his Majesties Justices of the Peace for the said County That we doe believe That the respective Houses wherein the persons hereunder named doe Inhabit are not of greater vallue then twenty shillings *per annum* upon the full Improved rent And that neither the Person so inhabiting, nor any other using the same Messuages hath, useth, or Occupieth any Lands or Tenements of their own or others of the yearly vallue of Twenty shillings *per annum*, Nor hath any Lands, Tenements, Goods or Chattels of the vallue of Ten pounds in their own Possession, or in the Possession of any other in trust for them. And that the said houses have not above two Chimneys, Fire-hearthes and Stoves in them respectively Witness our hands this 24 day of August 1670

Richard Williams	John Orchard
Widd: Wigmall	Robert Andros
Widdo Martin	Widdo Summersbe
Widdo Charlott	Richard Sumersbe
Robert Stowers	Roberte Hall
Richard Martin	Widdo Saro
Robert Brastor	William French
Richard Wright	Henry Roade
Widdo Fuller	Dannill White
Widdo Ridgoll	John Palmer
Richard Andros junr	James Gosling
John Stowers	John Ridgoll
Richard Golborne	John Bridgman
Widdo Lamo	Thomas Kimbell
Henry Worth	Thomas Richason
Ambris Fuller	Thomas Jossot
John Blackman	William Andros
Thomas Griffin	Widdo Bridgman
John Haton	Bartholmo Roade
John Younge	John Stowers
Widdo Parsons	William Whitwood
Widdo Stowers	Richard Staroll
Phillip Worth	Robert Parsons
William Gossell senr	Giles Parsons
William Gossell junr	Christian Richason
John Sorroy	
Robert Snell	

We Allow of this Certificate containing fifty two names

Jo Kingesmill

H: Dartt

Humphry Hains Curate

Thomas Burth & John Hall Church wardens

William Bosswell, Richard winch Overseers of the poore

Exemption certificate for the parish of Newtown (Burghclere), 1670 (PRO E179/176/568/62). Crown copyright. Reproduced with the permission of the Controller of Her Majesty's Stationery Office.

sub-farmers or collectors responsible for local areas were not audited in the Exchequer, but at the central Hearth Office (apart from those for Lady Day 1666). None of the records held by this office are known to survive. The grand farmers and the commissioners had their accounts audited in the Exchequer, but their supporting vouchers did not include detailed lists from the local areas.

All the surviving detailed hearth tax documents for Hampshire are listed in Appendix 1 and are referred to above.

The uses of hearth tax records

The hearth tax records are an invaluable source for social and economic historians, and local and family historians, alike. The records which give detailed lists of names are most useful and of these the hearth tax assessments are particularly important. The assessments are primarily directories of the people resident in a given community towards the end of the 17th century. However, they can also be used to calculate population size, density and distribution, to assess mobility and social structure and to investigate the distribution of wealth and poverty, on both a local and national scale.

The value of the hearth tax assessments rests on their completeness. The revising act of 1663 required all householders to be listed, including those exempt from paying the tax, so in theory they provide a record of every household in a locality. However, there is some uncertainty as to whether in practice all households were recorded. It is possible that the very poorest people were omitted and there is debate over the amount of evasion.[6] The accuracy of the information recorded probably varies from area to area. Also, the assessments do not give much information beyond a list of householders' names and numbers of hearths. Sometimes an indication of the householder's status is given, such as esquire, gentleman or widow, but rarely an occupation. On the face of it, therefore, the assessments would not seem to be very helpful in providing biographical details or information about economic or social structure. Nevertheless, used in conjunction with other sources, particularly parish registers and records, and probate records, they have an important role to play.

The use of hearth tax assessments as a source for population size has been much debated. The main problem is to decide what multiplier to use in order to convert the number of householders into the number of people. The size of households probably varied greatly determined by such things as location, the degree of urbanization of the area and the wealth of the households (which might include servants as well as family members). A generally accepted multiplier is 4.5, although numbers as low as 3.7 and as high as 6.8 have been suggested.[7]

---

6. Husbands, Chris, "Hearth Tax Exemptions Figures and the Assessment of Poverty in the Seventeenth Century Economy" in Alldridge *op. cit.* and Patten, John, "The Hearth Taxes, 1662-1689" (*Local Population Studies*, No. 7, Autumn 1971)
7. Howell, Roger, "Hearth Tax Returns" (*Short Guides to Records*, 7, reprinted from *History*, vol. 49, 1964) and Patten, *op. cit.*

Although it may be difficult to use the assessments to obtain accurate population figures, they can be used to indicate the relative size of the population in various areas and to give an idea of the distribution of the population and relative density within an area. Comparison between assessments and other sources for different dates can yield information on changes through time, not only with regard to size, distribution and density, but also in relation to mobility, social structure and the distribution of wealth.

The use of the assessments, together with other hearth tax records such as the exemption certificates, to investigate the distribution of wealth and poverty has also been a subject of debate. It is generally assumed that the more hearths a household had, the wealthier the householder was. Classifying the households in groups determined by the number of hearths can reveal a pattern of wealth and poverty. It has been suggested that the most useful groupings are householders with a single hearth, those with two, those with three to five, those with six to nine and those with ten or more. Less than three hearths denotes a degree of poverty while more than ten denotes considerable affluence.[8] It is also useful with larger areas to calculate the average numbers of hearths for each smaller unit to reveal information about the settlement pattern; this can be particularly valuable with urban areas.[9] Recent studies have emphasised the need to use hearth tax records in conjunction with other sources to build up an accurate picture.

The hearth tax records are an indispensable source to the historian. In importance, as a source of basic information about a given community, they have been placed on a par with parish registers and 19th century census returns.[10] They provide full, versatile and comparable information in an easily accessible form, more so when they appear in print. Of course, they have their limitations and there are problems associated with their use, some of which have been mentioned above. Many of the problems can be minimised if they are used in conjunction with other sources. This is true whether the records are being used in a detailed analysis of a community or to help complete a family tree.

8. Patten, *op. cit.*
9. Howell, *op. cit.*
10. Alldridge, N., Introduction in Alldridge, *op. cit.*

The Select Bibliography gives a more extensive list of useful works on hearth tax records.

THE DOCUMENTS

The hearth tax assessment for the year and a half ending Michaelmas 1665 (county of Southampton) (PRO E179/176/565)

The assessment is made up of 106 parchment membranes (approximately 22 × 81 cm) sewn together at the head. The membranes have been sewn into a cloth cover and have been consecutively numbered with a stamp on the bottom right hand corner on the front of each. They are written on both sides in a double column arrangement. The assessment is written in a uniform hand throughout with some exceptions (*see* Editorial Practice). The language of the document is English apart from a few place names. The condition and legibility is generally good, although there is some damage at the feet of the membranes and the head of the first skin is badly discoloured. This means that the preamble to the assessment, the heading and first few entries are completely illegible and that some other entries are completely or partially illegible. The assessment is therefore almost complete. It relates to the whole county, apart from the town of Southampton, and includes the Isle of Wight. The assessment is arranged by division. Within the divisions it is divided into hundreds and liberties and then into parishes and tithings. For each place there is a list of personal names with the numbers of hearths on which the tax is chargeable followed by a list of names with the numbers of hearths on which the tax is not chargeable. Total numbers of hearths chargeable and not chargeable are given for each place, hundred or liberty and division. These totals are not always accurate. There is a microfilm copy of the assessment in the Hampshire Record Office (HRO M362).

The hearth tax assessment for Michaelmas 1662 (town of Southampton) (SRO SC14/2/32b)

This is the original assessment prepared by the local officials in Southampton which was sent to the Clerk of the Peace to be copied out and sent to the Exchequer. It consists of seven folded paper sheets (15 × 39 cm), one for each parish assessed, which have been gathered into one booklet with a cover. The assessment is written in single columns, on both sides of the paper where the assessment for a parish is a long one. It is written in English in a uniform hand except where the beadles or tithingmen have signed, or set their mark, at the end of each parish assessment. The condition and legibility are good, although the top of the final return has been slightly damaged and this has resulted in a small loss of information. Each parish assessment gives names and numbers of hearths. There are no separate lists of hearths not chargeable. A total of assessed hearths is given for only one of the seven parishes.

The hearth tax assessment for the year and a half ending Michaelmas 1670 (town of Southampton) (PRO E179/247/29)

The assessment is made up of six parchment membranes (approximately 17 × 80 cm) sewn together at the head. The membranes have been consecutively numbered with a stamp in the bottom right hand corner on the front of each in reverse order. They are written on one side only in a single column arrangement in a uniform hand; the language used is English. The condition and legibility are good, although the heading of the document is incomplete and a strip has been cut away from the right hand side of membrane six so removing some of the numbers of hearths. The assessment is otherwise complete and is arranged by wards. For each ward it gives names and numbers of hearths chargeable. A list of those discharged by certificate is given separately. The assessment is signed by the Mayor of Southampton and two Justices of the Peace. The document ends with a certification by the Clerk of the Peace.

EDITORIAL PRACTICE

The county assessment

The text of the Hampshire hearth tax assessment for Michaelmas 1665 was produced from a microfilm copy of the original document at the Public Record Office (E179/176/565). The microfilm is owned by the Hampshire Field Club and Archaeological Society and deposited in the Hampshire Record Office (M362). The original document was consulted with regard to doubtful readings.

The whole document has been transcribed except for membranes 96 to 105 relating to the Isle of Wight for which a transcript already exists (*The Hearth Tax Returns for the Isle of Wight, 1664 to 1674*, P. D. D. Russell, Isle of Wight Record Series Vol. 1, 1981 pp. 63-100). The assessment does not include the town of Southampton for which a separate assessment was invariably drawn up. Unfortunately, the Southampton assessment for 1665 has not survived and therefore assessments for 1662 and 1670 are reproduced instead. The text of these assessments was produced from the original documents. The following details of editorial practice relate to the 1665 county assessment. A brief note of editorial practice as regards these Southampton assessments is given at the end.

The order of the original is followed in the text, but not in the actual arrangement that it is found there. The text should be read down the columns and then across the page from left to right. The original membranes have been consecutively numbered with a stamp in the bottom right hand corner on the front only. They are written on both sides in a double column arrangement. The membrane numbers and columns are given in italics at the appropriate place in the text. The membrane number is followed by an indication as to whether it is the front (*r* for *recto*) or back (*v* for *verso*) of the membrane and as to whether it is the left hand column (*i*) or right hand column (*ii*). Thus the begining of the left hand column of the front of the fourth membrane would be indicated by *4r(i)*.

The document is damaged or illegible in several places, particularly at the feet of some of the membranes. Where readings are doubtful, they are enclosed in square brackets. Where the original cannot be read at all, square brackets enclosing a space of a convenient, but not significant length are used.

Place names are given in their modern form. The original spelling, if it differs from the modern spelling, is given in the footnotes at the end of the text for that place. The places have been consecutively numbered in the text and it is these numbers which are used in the indexes and appendices.

Forenames have been modernised, and abbreviated forenames extended and modernised, wherever possible. An alphabetical list of the modern forms of forenames used in the text together with the abbreviations and forms used in the original is given in Appendix 2. Ambiguous abbreviations and unusual forenames are in the form they appear in the original. Surnames have been spelt as in the original, but an attempt has been made to group variants of names under a common modern spelling in the index of personal names. Abbreviations denoting title or status have been extended and modernised.

The spelling of all other words used in the original has been modernised and abbreviations, including ampersands, extended where this can be done with confidence; punctuation has also been modernised. In places in the original i has been used where the modern spelling would be j and u where the modern spelling would be v. In the text the modern spelling is used in all cases even with surnames. Likewise the use of lower and upper case letters has been rationalised throughout. The headings "Hearths chargeable" and "Hearths not chargeable" are given in that form irrespective of the way they are given in the original.

Roman numerals are invariably used in the original for the numbers of hearths and totals for each place. Arabic numerals are used in the totals for hundreds and divisions. Numbers are written out in the margins and with some numbers added later. In the text all these are given as arabic numerals. It should be noted that the total numbers of hearths given for each place, hundred or division often do not agree with the figure arrived at when the numbers are added up. No attempt has been made to amend incorrect totals.

Comments in the margin to the right of each column in the original have been placed below the text for each place to facilitate the layout. These are indicated by lower case letters in brackets in an alphabetical sequence to distinguish them from the footnotes proper which use arabic numerals.

The original document is in a uniform hand with a few exceptions. The comments relating to the increase or decrease of hearths found at the end of the "Hearths chargeable" and "Hearths not chargeable" sections in the New Forest division only have all been added later in a different hand. Other comments or alterations added later are indicated in the footnotes.

The Southampton assessments

Editorial practice as regards the use of square brackets, the modernisation of place names, forenames and other spellings, the treatment of marginalia and the use of footnotes is the same as for the county assessment. The following details of editorial practice relate specifically to the Southampton assessments.

The assessment of 1662

The text was produced from the original held at Southampton City Records Office (SC14/2/32b). The single column arrangement of the original has not been retained in the text, which is arranged in two columns. The page numbers allocated by the Southampton City Records Office have been used in the text and are given in italics at the appropriate place. There are a number of blank pages, which have not been noted.

In the majority of cases the names of those assessed are followed in the original by the word "hath". This has been omitted in the text.

The number of hearths is in each case (with the exception of totals) given in letters in the original (for example, "fower", "seven". These have been rendered as arabic numerals in the text.

The assessment of 1670

The text was produced from the original held at the Public Record Office (E179/247/29). The single column arrangement of the original has been retained except for the list of persons discharged which is in two columns. The correct order of the membranes has been followed with the result that the membrane numbers as they appear in italics in the text are in reverse order.

All numbers in the original are arabic numerals, which have been retained in the text. However, single figure assessments are preceded by a nought in the original (for example, 07), which has been omitted in the text. In the case of void assessments, the main assessment column is normally left blank and the void figure is written to the left of it. This arrangement has been retained in the text. A number of other figures, clearly not regarded as void but whose significance has not been established with certainty, also appear to the left of the main column, both in the original and the text. These have been footnoted as such. The totals, sometimes single and including the void totals, sometimes two or three apparently indicating totals of voids, totals of chargeable hearths and totals of all hearths, are rendered as in the original. No attempt has been made to amend apparently incorrect totals.

Marginal notes are written to the left of the column of names in the original manuscript. For ease of layout these have been footnoted in the same way as the marginalia which appear in the county assessment.

LIST OF DIVISIONS AND HUNDREDS

All references are to section numbers

Portsdown Division

New Forest Division

Alton Division

Fawley Division

Kingsclere Division

Basingstoke Division

Andover Division

TEXT OF THE HEARTH TAX ASSESSMENT FOR HAMPSHIRE, 1665

Fol. 1r(i)[1]

1. [PORTSMOUTH]

[Hearths chargeable]

Name	Hearths
[ ]	6
[ ]	2
[ ]	4
[ ]	1
[ ]	2
[ ]	5
[ ]	4
[ ]	2
[ ]	2
[ ]	6
[ ]	4
[ ]	6
[ ]	10
[ ]	5
[ ]	3
[ ]	2
[ ]	6
[ ]	3
[ ] [ ]inder	9
[ ] [A]ine	2
[ ] [Barnes]	2
[ ] [Thomas]	2
[ ] [or]ling	4
[John] [Mi]lls	8
[ ] [Peck]	5
[ ] Sta[r]es	5
[ ] [Barlow]	3
[ ]astine Watts	2
[ ] Gudge	2
Mister John Clements	8
Henry Warren	4
[Thomas] Plower	5
[Mistress Lee] widow	4
[Thomas] Parks	6
Robert Hawkes	6
Philip Elmes	3
George Roach	4
[ ] Baker	8
William L[unne]	4
[ ] Flood	7
Richard Joyce	3
[ ] Cotten	4
Paul Richards	1
John [Dine]	3
[ ] English	7
[ ] Frye	4
[Robert] Upman	8

Fol. 1r(ii)[2]

Name	Hearths
[Mister Francis Nawes]	7
[Widow Taylor]	13
John Woodley	3
Mister William Y[oung]	8
Mister Philip Elmes	4[(a)]
William Hau[ ]	6
Wiliam [White]	5
John [ ]	[4]
Grantha[m] Wy[ ]	9
Mistress James widow	9[(b)]
Sir Philip Ho[p]wood	12
John Scamell	[1]
Edward Wigmore	4
John [Jeffery] & Alexander Watkins	7
Mister William [Tyer]	3
Israel Pownell	10
William Rives	2
Widow Wooll[rid]ge	3
Anthony Seladen	3
William Wheaden	2
John Hunt	2
Nicholas Saunders	4
John Moody	5
Griffin Reads	4
George Plimier	9
Edward Brooker	2
John Wheatland	2
Peter Carter	6
Thomas Symes	5
Robert Wilkins	8
Henry Albin	2
Thomas Channell	4

1. [PORTSMOUTH]—*cont'd.*

Thomas Barnet	3
Thomas Waldren	3
Robert Tippitts	7
Thomas Chillin	4
Richard Blake	1[(b)]
Michael Taylor	1
Andrew Beacham	8
Mister Samuel Williams	7
Richard White	2
William Lunn	4
Walter Thurman	6
Mistress [Brate] widow	9
Mister Charles Chapman	5
John Knight	2
Mister Christopher Brunk[on]	10
Edward Chapman	4
John Barfoot	5
Widow Woadin	2
Dan[iel] Baker	2
John Eastment	7
Thomas Ranffeild	3
James Plover	6
Thomas Barnard	6

Fol. 1v(i)

[ ] Triggs	7
[Mister] John Tawke	7
Isaac Bell	12
Henry Jenner	1
Mister Thomas Mills	5
Mister [Nicholas] Hedger	7
Mister Thomas Butters	9
Mister John Newlock	4
Philip James	6
Mister Thomas Needler	4
Mister Daniel Peck	6
William Collins	5
John Hagben	3
John Lewin	6
Robert Sabin	7
Henry Whitehorne	6
Elizabeth Whitehorne	4
George Garland	5
John Gray	3
John Stone	2
Richard Barnes	4
Thomas Chase	3
Thomas Carter	3
George Barcomb	2
Mistress Stevens widow	9[(c)]
Richard New	6
Justinian Wyatt	5
William Juward	8
William Batton	4
Henry Speering	2
Stephen Rumsey	4
John Leves	2
George Woolfrey	5
John Timbrill	8
Henry Ismonger	5
Thomas Randoll	3
John Voake	3
Robert Grinaway	5
Thomas Watts	4
George White	6
William Potter	5
Zacharias Gray	2
George Moth	2
Andrew Lampson	2
Samuel Ingram	4
Richard James	2
Mister Thomas Mullins	8
John Hubbert	7
Widow Fauvis	4
Nicholas Sellan	4
Edward Goater	5
John Champin	5
Robert Reynolds	5
Widow White	3
John Grinaway	3
Mistress Holt widow	8
John Aldridg	6
William Parker	3
Henry Tarrant	4
Thomas Jenner	5
John Vincent	6
Widow Hawes	6
Widow Biggs	9

William Cooper	3
Henry Goldfinch	3
[ ] Wheeler	3
[ ] Willard	4
John Wattson	3
[Peter Albry]	2
[ ]	8
[ ] Th[rough]good	5
[ ]	2
James [Has]teed	2

Fol. 1v(ii)

William Meade	2
Richard Evans	2
Henry Richards	2
Samuel Smith	4
Francis Triblecock	1
Peter Belbin	3
Mister Henry Peryn	10
William Jenman	3
Daniel Missingham	2
William Turner	3
Stephen Gase	3
Simon Coward	6
Thomas Greenetree	2
Robert Pollard	2
Richard Sparks	5
Mister Stratton	4
James Horwood	2
Mistress Timbrill widow	11
John Cooke	2
John White	2
William Whithead	1
Widow Merrett	4
Edward Cleines	3
Widow Roaker	4
Widow Gostree	5
George Northcott	2
Anthony Coward	1
William Light	2
Thomas Overy	3
Simon Franklin	2
John Addes	3
William Vinning	2
Francis Vining	2
Richard Beckensall	3
Thomas Moss	3
William Holmes	2
John Coles	4
Robert Bridger	2
Matthew Randford	2
Henry Edwards	2
Thomas Leves	2
William Lock	1
Simon Larnam	3
Widow Collins	2
William Saint	4
Owen Simons	3
Robert Philipps	1
James Lloyd	2
James Biggs	2
John Nightingall	1
William Norton	2
Edward Cawt	2
John Perryn	1
John Morley	2
Christopher Carter	2
John Goddard	2
Ambrose Stanford	2
John Bisshopp	2
Judith Musgrave widow	7
Widow Walder	2
Widow Barton	3
Samuel Tackell	2
Joshua Wheate	2
John Poate	5
Thomas Powell	2
William Glaspell	2
Thomas Burry	3
Henry Bisling	5
Henry Waite	3
Widow [Freman]	5
John Ray	1
Richard Bombye	3

Fol. 2r(i)

Thomas Mulford	2
Richard Symes	2
[ ] Goppin	3
Silvester Woodford	2
William Bragg	1

1. [PORTSMOUTH]—*cont'd.*

Widow Jackson	5
Matthew Simons	5
Samuel Smith	6
Thomas Bulbeck	7
John Sharke	3
John Lambert	5
John Arnold	5
Thomas Crosby	2
Stephen Critch	3
John Showell	3
Thomas Feild	3
Richard Appleford	3
Godfrey Floyd	6
Widow Spr[ ]	5
William Tyre	4
Robert Juward	5
Edward Haberden	4
William Shory	5
Henry Galpin	2
Richard Collins	2
Nathaniel Scarlett	2
George Younge	3
Widow Curtis	6
Nicholas Hammon	5
Widow Goddard	4
Joshua Steedman	4
Widow Besten	9
John White	4
Richard White	5
Samuel Worlidge	2
John Puttland	2
Stephen Oldinge	3
Widow Sniller	4
Jacob Stevens	3
Edward Woodnott	6
Richard Mells	2
Widow Dallarose	3
Henry Moser	8
John Bray	3
William Baker	3
James West	5
William Bramley	5
Richard Roberts	2
Thomas Carter senior	4
Richard Childs	3
William Mobery	2
David Goaste	2
Richard Locker	6
William Gold	5
Mister William Steventon	3
Mistress Arundell widow	3
Richard Goldfinch	5
Mister Cropley	4
Joan Humber	6
Matthew Turner	3
John Fussard	7
Richard Parrett	3

Fol. 2r(ii)

Peter Wellbred	2
Thomas Hunt	2
Edward Brinkhurst	1
Richard Barrow	1
Mary Numan	3
Widow Tombs	2
William Prichard	2
John Hall	4
Ralph Ruman	5
Widow Cumfort	7
John Withers	7
Richard Ingram	6
Henry Holester	5
Thomas Mitchener	2
William Buckland	2
Mister Hugh Salisbery	9
John Battell	4
Mister Anthony Haberly	6
Edward Grantham	2
John Lymeburner	2
Thomas Grant	6
Thomas Davis	6
Henry Band	3
Mister Archer	6
George Carde	7
Edward Osgood	2
William Habberly	6
Alexander Eastwood	6

Thomas Stevens	7
Paul Richards	8
John Norton	6
Thomas Roberts	2
Thomas Parker	3
John Chason	2
Samuel Knight	4
Edward Bolter	3
Esardes Porter	2
John Merriott	2
Francis Holes	2
Mister Jerome Country	7
John Edmunds	3
Ralph Butterfeild	3
Thomas Jackson	3
James Blunt	3
Thomas Hills	3
Philip Mansbridg	5
Thomas Poate	5
William Baker	2
Peter Nicholas	2
Edmund Austin	4
Thomas Woolfe	2
John Welch	1
Simon Musgrave	3
Henry Davis	2
John Heyward	2
David Merriweather	2
John Baily	2
James Swann	2
Robert Davis	1
William Mudge	2
Ellis Days	4
William Webb	2
Daniel Gudge	2
Thomas Cooke	2
Thomas Hoare	2
John Austin	2
Thomas Band	1
Robert Eastman	3

Fol. 2v(i)

William Levett	5
William Hunt	2
George Tailor	6
Thomas Carter	6
Isaac Deacone	6
Thomas Paye	2
Richard Deacon	4
John Roe	3
John Leafe	3
Widow Fawley	3
Richard Rose	3
Henry Hunt	3
John Child	3
William Griffin	3
Oliver Hunt	3
Anthony Colebrooke	2
Richard Mittens	2
William Tyer	7
Richard Cleere	2
Thomas Eaton	2
Mister Robert Smith	9
John Day	4
William Waters	2
Henry Vines	2
John Rammer	2
Thomas Grover	2
Edward Goley	2
Thomas Chamberlin	1
Thomas Younge	3
Philip Gascoyne	3
William Davis	3
Roger Start	3
John Knight	3
Lewis Hawkins	3
John Butcher	3
John Hopkins	3
William Cosins	7
Walter Perry	4
Thomas Pydgeon	3
John Reading	3
Mister Binckman	4
Humphrey Jones	3
Edward Wittingham	8
John Roman	3
Anthony Smith	3
Anthony Browne	2
James Holloway	4
Nicholas Hopkins	1
Michael Gray	4

1. [PORTSMOUTH]—*cont'd.*

Edward Ansell	4
Widow Fudger	2
Francis Gray	4
Joseph Biggs	6
Sir John Steventon mayor	8
Mister John Tippetts	9
Richard Perkins	5
Robert Neale	6
Mister Hugh Salisbery	9
Benjamin Johnson	6
Mister Edward Byland	8
Mister Purnell	8
Mistress Steventon widow	5
Mister John Tinker	10
William Kerby	6
Widow Basten	4

Fol. 2v(ii)

Widow Basten	2
John Walcott	2
John Garrett	4
Thomas Browne	7
Robert Bishopp	5
Robert Perryne	2
Nicholas Russell	4
Thomas Hatch	5
Roger Flower	5
Garrett Wright	6
John Ayleward	5
William Martin	3
Stephen Worlidge	6
Widow Daniell	5
James Bartin	2
Edward Blatch[3]	2
John Leach	2
Edward Garrett	2
Thomas Jellett	8
Richard Mills	2
Christopher Stoller	2
Francis Lucas	6
James Austin	5
John Mason	5
John Wyatt	3
Richard Starvill	1
Mister James Lock	9
Robert Parr	6
Edward Garrett	6
John Timbrell junior	9
Robert Reynolds	4
Thomas Gudge	3
John Davis	3
Richard Stone	3
John Sowter	3
Barnard Williams	3
George Hadley	3
Anthony Heyward	3
Andrew Monson	4
Widow Bird	6
John Bird	2
John Martin	4
Richard Newbone	3
James Earlesmore	4
Henry Tovye	4
John Deane	4
John Hunt	6
David Luces	5
Michael Scott	5
Robert Gardner	4
Thomas White	3
Timothy Clungen	3
Thomas Kerby	3
Thomas Addams	5
Thomas Jones	8
Thomas Newbery	8
Christopher Brewer	1
Richard Atkins	2
Sidrach Addams	5
Nicholas Inwood	9
Arthur Smith	4
Robert Giles	6
Robert Butten	3
Thomas Homard	4
James Hewson	2
Edward Smith	3

Fol. 3r(i)

John Doe	3
Patrick Rampkin	3
Joseph Voake	3

James Etherington	7
Mister Nicholas Person	13
Henry Woods	3
John Cardy	3
Philip Godwin	4
George Dickson	5
Robert Start	4
Anthony Haswell	2
John Haswell	2
James Hockley	5
Henry Pressey	4
Robert Kingman	2
George Colson junior	2
George Colson senior	2
Edward Bunckley	2
Thomas Stepto	2
Thomas Whitherly	6
John Parr	3
Robert Seazon	2
Roland Jarves	2
Thomas Clungen	2
John Golden	2
Robert Batt	1
George Moore	2
Daniel Davis	1
Godfrey Morgan	1
Thomas Webb	1
John Pitters	2
Thomas Welsh	3
Thomas Ponte	1
Widow Woolfe	2
James Hooper	1
John Hampton	1
William Knight	2
Widow Dyer	2
George Rogers	2
Richard Tibbs	3
Widow Bissell	5
John Pope	4
Richard West	4
Benjamin Mathews	4
Christopher Peck	7
John Biffin	2
Thomas Burley	3
Richard Clerke	8
William Willis	2
Francis Gardner	2
Henry Acton	4
William Giles	3
Alexander Verrell	3
James Habberly	7
John Beale	2
Francis Hicks	2
George Padding	2
Edward Patricke	4
Joseph Wheate	4
Robert Harford	3
John Thorne	4
Robert Dorrell	1
Richard Gardner	2
Jasper Williams	2
Mark Fowler	3
Thomas Hancock	5
Henry Ransteed	5
Peter Havery	2
John Doneaway	2
Gabriel Jenkins	4
Henry Scott	4
Richard Marks	7
Mister Benjamin Okeshott	5

Fol. 3r(ii)

Robert Parker	4
Francis Hicks	4
John Kent	10
John Heyward	2
Thomas Brewer	5
Richard Thomas	2
Thomas Linsey	2
Philip Hunter	2
Widow Stubber	2
John Woolger	1
James Pope	4
John Baulch	3
Richard Launder	5
Mister William Michell	5
Widow Curtis	1
Peter Steggen	1
Thomas Goldsmith	1
Thomas Morley	2
Ann Aycliff	2

1. [PORTSMOUTH]—*cont'd.*

Arthur Hoptree	2
Thomas Beakon	1
Mister William Hawely	9
Samuel Williams	6
William Clapshaw	4
Thomas Baulch	3
Henry Pelten	1
Thomas Hickman	2
John Benger	4
Richard Potte	2
John Thomas	1
Richard Gruett	4
Nicholas Pryer	1
Thomas Reed	4
William Waller	2
John Bettsworth	2
John Moody	5
John Rockwell	1
Edward Ridge	1
Mistress Gale widow	3
John Ayleward	3
His Majesty's house called Gods House in his own use	26
Sebastian Watts	4(d)
Mister Anthony Haberly	2(d)
Thomas Lotter	3
Edward Ellis	3
Widow Lewes	2(d)
William Benham	4
Thomas Silley	3
Widow King	3
Joan Egerton	3
Mister Anthony Habberly	2(d)
Widow May	3
Widow Basten	2(d)
Henry Johnson	4
William Hardy	3
Robert Hawkes	4(d)
Stephen Caver	3
Lifften Cadman's tenants	9
William Goddwin equire	4(d)
Lifften Cadman	6(d)
hearths	2548

Fol. 3v(i)

Hearths not chargeable

Humphrey Seddall	2
James Humphrys	2
Henry Hare	1
William Reeves	1
James Cannion	2
William Southt	2
Elizabeth Person	2
Widow Tassell	2
Clement Stiller	1
Matthew Baker	2
Zacharias Graye[4]	2
John Williamson	1
Widow Johnson	2
Robert Mott	1
John Brooke	2
Francis Triblock	1
Widow Tompson	2
Robert Willis	2
Thomas Tooker	2
William Light	2
Thomas Francis	2
John Davis	2
William Symes	2
William Knight	2
William Hollard	2
Widow Asker	2
Widow Meakens	2
Thomas Jones	2
Edward Newhooke	2
Widow Cooke	2
Simon Ismonger	2
Richard Carter	2
John Feild	2
William Goddwin	2
Richard Ruffen	2
Thomas Rooke	1
Edward Caute	1
Thomas Wells	2
Jerome Harte	2

Edward Greenaway	1
Charles Cottman	2
Robert Mott	1
John Welch	2
John Webb	1
Thomas Smith	2
William Cock	1
John Wyatt	2
James Larman	1
Widow Ransom	1
John Gunne	2
Thomas Slatterforde	2
John Castell	2
Joseph Taylor	1
Thomas Holland	2
Nicholas Major	2
Robert Stares	2
Thomas Jacobb	2
Thomas Hills	2
William Midleton	2
Barnard Redman	2
John Castleman	1
Widow Heringman	1
John Mills	2
John Hasell	2
Thomas Rowter	2
Abraham Isaack	2
Peter Beatley	2
John Williams	2
Thomas Webb	2

Fol. 3v(ii)

Daniel Davis	2
Widow Clever	2
William Found	2
Thomas Howchins	2
Thomas Body	1
Thomas Vincorne	1
Widow Newman	1
Francis Hicks	2
Thomas Willard	1
Widow Chidley	1
George Stucke	1
Thomas Heath	2
William Badcock	2
Christopher Gransome	2
Christopher Rogers	2
John Oliver	2
Widow Tucker	2
Henry Lipscombe	2
William Palladay	2
Ralph Carpenter	1
Ellis Worth	2
John Pocock	2
Thomas Kinge	2
Nicholas Cake	2
John Bridger	1
Thomas Head	1
John Gilbert	1
Clerk Jackson	2
William Clerke	2
Simon Halcope	2
Andrew Whitman	2
Widow Gunn	1
Edward New	1
William Crobard	1
Widow Treddle	2
John Cooper	1
John Waldron	2
Thomas Leonard	1
John Greffitts	2
William Knight	2
James Jefferys	1
Michael Mills	2
Peter Jackman	2
John Henrys	1
Judith Gredge	2
Widow Casten	2
Five work houses in the cooper's yard	5
hearths	201

(a) 2 pulled down
(b) 1 overcharged
(c) 3 overcharged
(d) void

1. *Much of the top half of the skin is illegible*
2. *Much of the top half of the skin is illegible*
3. *Altered from* Blatck
4. *Altered from* Gaaye

Fol. 3v(ii)

PORTSDOWN HUNDRED

2. SOUTHWICK[1]

Hearths chargeable

Richard Norton esquire	34[(a)]
Thomas Smith	1[(a)]
Henry Greene	1
John Bennett	2
Thomas Warner	1
William Jeffery	4
Thomas Weston	2
Thomas Coles	1
Richard Crocker	2
John Hurlock	4
Edward Collins	2
Roger Greenegoe	3
Mistress Jane Williams	5
Stephen Bevis	4
Widow Hurst	3
Fol. 4r(i)	
Robert Avare	2
Thomas Weston	1[(b)]
Francis Framan	2
Mister Robert Philipps	5
Thomas Bartlett	2
Thomas Shorte	1
William Mersh	2
Mister Thomas Bragne	5
Edward [ ]imple[2]	5
Mister Simons	3
John Steele	2
Thomas Hurlock	2
John Majors	1
Widow Rippin	2
Widow Farly	1
John Bishopp	2
Thomas Woods	1
William Short	2
John Fowley	1
Widow Lock	2
Widow Orpington	2
David Pincke	1
Richard Newell	3
Thomas Carter	2
Edward Clewer	4
William Pratt	1
Richard Taunt	4
John Farly	2
Robert Pincke	2
William Gosling	3
Robert Rolfe	1
Ralph Barrow	2
Richard Pratt	4
Nicholas Clements	2
Lazarus Winn	1
Widow Crasswell	1
William Gruett	2
John Prowling	1
hearths	151

(a) 1 overcharged
(b) 1 taken down
1. Southwicke
2. *Initial letter of surname written over twice. Could be* H, P *or* W

3. WEST BOARHUNT[1]

Hearths chargeable

Thomas Henslow esquire	23
John Barrow	3
Richard Shackleford	1
Mister Harwood	1
Edward Attwood	1
Thomas Russell	2
Brian Earle	1
Mister John Pounds	4
Richard Norton esquire	1
Thomas Pounds	2
Thomas Millett	2
William Abbott	1
William Fisher	6
Henry Mersh	2
John Paford	4
Richard Taunt	2
John Alison curate	1
Fol. 4r(ii)	
Edward Farly	1
George Petteford	2
John Woolger	2
Thomas Gregory	2

Robert Cooke	1
hearths	65

Hearths not chargeable

Henry Deeringe	1
Henry Davis	1
Widow Dunce	1
Thomas Mordant	1
Henry Mathews	1
Thomas Woodnott	1
hearths	6

1. West Burrant

4. OUT PORTCHESTER[1]

Hearths chargeable

Peter Whitinge	2
John Appleford	3
Thomas Wigge	2
Robert Carpenter	2
William Denmeade	1
Widow Beene	1
Richard Baker	1
John Sparks	2
hearths	14

Hearths not chargeable

Robert Barnard	1
Nicholas Broadway	1
hearths	2

1. Out Porchester

5. PORTCHESTER[1]

Hearths chargeable

Mister Henry Selward	7
Mister March	3[(a)]
Widow Abbott	1
John Cheeseman	2
Mister Loader	3
Robert Stevens	1
Richard Whitinge	3
Francis Ireland	2
Widow Inwood	2
Robert Sparks	1
John Tasker	2
John Rowte	1
Richard Whitinge	1
Thomas Henslow	1
William May	2
Ralph Roman	1
Widow Bassett	1
John Whitinge	1[(b)]
John Privett	1

Fol. 4v(i)

Thomas Henslow	2
Lewis May	1[(c)]
Thomas Hillett	1
Stephen Appleford	1
Thomas Boulton	1
Thomas Greene	2
Widow Langford	1
James Tucker	1
Richard Pereman	2
Mistress Pereman	2
Francis Rowte	2
John Rowte	2
John Ham	2
Widow Martin	3
John Gillman	1
John Sutton	2
Thomas Ham	3
Thomas Whitinge	2
Stephen Glass	1
Widow White	2
Richard Whitinge junior	2
John Whitinge	1[(b)]
Stephen Glass junior	1
Thomas Greene	3
Richard Browne	2
Thomas Spencer	1
Mary Pereman	1
Widow Cheseman	1
John Ansell senior	1[(d)]
John Ansell junior	1
Widow Dagwell	1
William Greene	4
hearths	89

Hearths not chargeable

Widow Chapman	1
Robert Whitinge	1
James Beare	1
William Rolfe	2

5. PORTCHESTER—*cont'd.*

Widow Ribread	1
Widow Knight	1
Widow White	1
William Whitinge	1
James Locke	1
Widow Watkins	1
George Bittle	1
Richard Bowen	1
Alice Porter	1
William Dubnell	1
Thomas Chidley	1
Widow Haregood	1
Widow Watkins	1
Francis Allen	1
Robert White	2 } (e)
Thomas Greene	1 }
hearths	22

(a) 4 taken down
(b) 1 overcharged
(c) 1 decreased
(d) decayed 1
(e) burnt down
1. Porchester

Fol. 4v(ii)

6. FARLINGTON AND DRAYTON

Hearths chargeable

Mister Henry Pound	5
William Hammon	4
Henry Garrett	3
John Weeks	4
Widow Pitter	4
William Padden	2
Henry Stradling	5
Mary Love	1
James Younge	3
Thomas Knight	1
Stephen Harding	2
Henry Prior	1
Nicholas Hickman	3
John Binsteed	2
Anthony Ingram	2
Roger Carlington	1
Henry Collins	1
Mister Nelson	4
Edward Smith	4
John Browne	1
Edward Reade	1
Robert Beane	2
hearths	56

Hearths not chargeable

William Seevier	1
Richard Wade	1
John Goodman	1
John Harding	1
Robert Hall	1
Thomas Smither	1
John Browne	1
John Norris	1
George Emery	1
Widow Wright	1
Widow Odums	1
hearths	11

7. WALLINGTON[1]

Hearths chargeable

John Pafford	8
Francis Anthram	3
Widow Smith	3
Edward Powling	2
Widow Norman	2
John Bennett	1
Thomas Pollentine	1
Thomas Saunders	1
William Screvin	4
Timothy Browne	1
John Anthram	5
hearths	31

1. Walton Heath. *A tithing of this name has not been identified, however it is probable that it is* Wallington.

Fol. 5r(i)

8. FRATTON[1]

Hearths chargeable

Matthew Champion	3
Mister John Ridge	4
John Voake	3
Stephen Heyward	3
Mister John Ridge	2
Thomas Baily	3

Thomas Turner	2
Mister John Ridge	4
Eleanor Hellier	2
William Ivy	2
William Porbery	4
John Upsdale	5
Nathaniel Ridge	3
Mister Knowles	4
William Perryne	2
hearths	46

Hearths not chargeable

Thomas Moss	1
John Burrell	1
Robert Smith	1
hearths	3

1. Frodington

9. COPNOR[1]

Hearths chargeable

Mister Burgis	3
William Whitehorne	3
Peter Holmes	4
Thomas Biggs	1[(a)]
Clement Vaughan	2
Thomas Veare	2
hearths	15

Hearths not chargeable

John Stayres	2
William Day	2
Charles Summers	1
hearths	5

(a) 1 overcharged
1. Coppner

10. PORTSEA

Hearths chargeable

Widow Knowen	2
William Playfoote	1
Thomas Baily	1
John Voake	2
Richard Potter	2
Thomas Cosens	2
Henry Passenger	2
Roger Warre gentleman	4
John Batchelor	2
John Farly	4
John Brickinden esquire	7
William Smith	1
John Carpenter	2
Robert Carpenter	1
hearths	33

Fol. 5r(ii)

11. WANSTEAD[1]

Hearths chargeable

The Lady Ployden	11
Thomas Speeringe	1
John Hunt	3
Elizabeth Hurt	3
Edward Smith	2
Andrew Burningfeild	1
Robert Pledger	1
Stephen Parsons	2
John Christian for Plant Farm	2
hearths	26

Hearths not chargeable

John Wards	1
hearths	1

1. Wansteed

12. WALSWORTH

Hearths chargeable

Clement Kent	3
Clement Kent	3
John Bensteed	2
James Penycott	1
George Allen	1
Mister Richard Grivett	2
John Hartly	1
Clement Frowde	1[(a)]
Richard Smith	3
Richard Goddwin	1
Widow Binsteed	1
Thomas Bentley	3
John Heath	4
Widow Frowde	3
hearths	29

(a) 1 taken down

13. EAST BOARHUNT[1]

Hearths chargeable

Thomas Bartlett	3
Thomas Speeringe	3
Thomas Speeringe	2
Thomas Speeringe	4
George Anthram	5
John Nepper	1
Thomas Pollington	3
Widow Rooke	1
William Goslinge	1
hearths	23

1. East Burrant

14. BEDHAMPTON

Hearths chargeable

Richard Cotton esquire	15[a]
Thomas Cooke	6[b]
Mister Luffe	4
Mister Jenman	4
John Weeden	4
John Holt	4[c]

Fol. 5v(i)

Thomas Roodes	3
John Barter	1
Widow Beedle	2
Richard Pincke	2
Widow Cole	3
Thomas Swann	2
William Barling	2
John Fishooke	2
Henry Shephard	2
John Chantrell	3
Mister Nelson	5
William Beedle	6
Henry March	3
hearths	73

Hearths not chargeable

Widow Charlington	1
Thomas Harris	2
Nicholas Drewell	1
William Osier	1
John Waterman	1
Ralph Stane	1
Widow Cooke	1
hearths	8

(a) 1 pulled down
(b) 1 overcharged
(c) decayed 1

15. EAST COSHAM[1]

Hearths chargeable

John Weeks	2
Widow Odums	1
Edward Dyaper	1
Elizabeth Prowtinge	1
Henry Garrett	1
William Orchard	2
hearths	8

Hearths not chargeable

Thomas Appleford	1
William Newman	2
hearths	3

1. East Causum

16. WIDLEY

Hearths chargeable

John Hunt	7[a]
Lancelot Bricknell	1
John Guy	2
Robert Furlonger	1
Robert Nuttyer	2
Henry Bensteed	1
William Barling	1
John Carisbridge	1
Richard Summers	4[b]
John Bonney	1
Thomas Bulbeck	1
Widow Gilbert	2
John Godwin	1
Richard Bulbeck	1
Philip Taylor	1
Mister Richard Grivett	1
hearths	28

Fol. 5v(ii)

Hearths not chargeable

Andrew Williams	1
William Bassett	1
John Carisbridg	1

Philip Tailor	1
Widow Gilbert	2
hearths	6

(a) 2 fallen down
(b) 1 overcharged

17. WYMERING[1]

Hearths chargeable

Mister Michael Bold	5
John Spershott	12
Mister Atherne	6
Mister Atherne	1
Lancelot Bricknell	3
George Acers	6
Robert Gillman	7
Edward Anthram	2
Peter Whitinge	3[(a)]
Edward Anthram	3
Widow Guyer	3
Widow Guyer	1
Robert Cooke	1
Thomas Spencer	1
John Hunt	1
Thomas Knight	1
Robert Lambe	1
Richard Taylor	1
Mistress Gale	3
Thomas Austin	2[(a)]
Thomas Appleford	1
Robert Coles	1
Thomas Spencer	1
Mister Ridge	1
hearths	67

Hearths not chargeable

Nicholas Weilder	1
John Cradock	2
Widow Hills	1
Robert Coles	1
Widow Chaimberlaine	1
Robert Perryn	1
Widow Sherryer	2
Richard Nottam	1
John Bennett	2
Mister Atherne	2[(b)]
Thomas Speeringe	1[(b)]
hearths	14

(a) 1 overcharged
(b) houses down
1. Wimeringe

18. MILTON[1]

Hearths chargeable

Mister Beeston	6
John Higgins	2
John Higgins	1
Richard Harwood	1
Thomas Knight	2
Thomas Younge	3
William Holmes	2

Fol. 6r(i)

Mister Bearde	2
William Pope	2
Anthony Cadman	2
Mistress Ray and Richard Keepinge	4
Richard Sparks	1
William Hackman	2
Nicholas Palmer	1
Nicholas Blunden	2
William Holmes	6
John Sparks	4
hearths	43

1. Meltem

The number of hearths chargeable within the hundred of Portsdown is	797
Not chargeable	82

BISHOPS WALTHAM HUNDRED[1]

19. UPHAM

Hearths chargeable

Doctor Mirth Wafferer	7
Richard Turner	7
Mister Stock	8
John Gass	5
Widow Hicks	5
Henry Leekeblade	3

19. UPHAM—*cont'd.*

Widow Leekeblade	3
William Barton	3
William Crowcher	1
Robert Barton	2
Thomas Lowmer junior	1
Thomas Barton	3
Thomas Barton	4
Thomas Coles	3
Peter Barton	1
Widow Hasler	2
Giles Kinge	5
John Cleverly	2
Thomas Sharp	3
Nicholas Caute	2
Gilbert Turner	2
Richard Pledger	3
Robert Caute	1
Francis Trodd	2
hearths	78

Hearths not chargeable

Elizabeth Beedle	1
Richard Clerke	1
Edward Moores	1
Widow Buck	1
Widow Cames	1
Thomas Wyatt	1
Walter Kernell	2
Nicholas Stubbington	1
Widow Hearecock	1
William Roe	1
Walter Steele	1
Widow Caute	1
hearths	13

1. Waltham Hundred

Fol. 6r(ii)

20. MINCINGFIELD[1]

Hearths chargeable

Widow Hellier	3
Thomas Hewett	3
Robert Goslinge	3
Thomas Collins	3
Mister Peter Hersent	7
Peter White	2
Thomas Mayham	3
Thomas Bensteed	1
George Harmsworth	1
John Ewens	2
William Coles	2
John Hockley	2
William Case	2
Francis Dummer	1
John Stubbington	3
William Jones	2
Mister Peter Hersnett	1
hearths	41

Hearths not chargeable

William Pirce	1
Edward Bensteed	1
Nicholas Singleton	1
hearths	3

1. Minsingfeild

21. SWANMORE

Hearths chargeable

Richard Brewer	4
John Wyatt	3
John Horner	3
John Clever	3
Thomas Clever	3
Widow Britten	3
Widow Strugnell	3
Robert Ryves	5
Henry Prowtinge	4
Mister Henry Collins	4
John Woods	3
John Cleverly	1
Theodore Clapshaw	2
Richard Doe	2
Mister Henry Harwood	8
Richard Prowting	1
William Sharrier	3
German Cleverly	2
Thomas Wassell	1
Richard Knight	3
Edward Jerman	2
Widow Goldfinch	3
Peter Cleverly	3
hearths	69

Hearths not chargeable

Widow Sharpe	1
Thomas Holt	2
Thomas Turner	1
John Brewer	2
Richard Prowtinge	1

Fol. 6v(i)

John Fee	1
Henry Bottome	1
Andrew Strugnell	2
Edward Jerman	2
Thomas West	1
Richard Suatt	1
Nicholas Cradock	1
John Austin	1
John Hatter	1
Bartholomew Cleverly	2
Widow Prowting	1
hearths	21

22. HOE

Hearths chargeable

Robert Burrell	3
Richard Goddwin	3
Robert Woodman	3
Henry Suett	3
John Woodman	4
Thomas Charker	3
Maurice Martin	2
John Woods	3
Ann Cleverly widow	2
Thomas Cosens	3
German Goldfinch	3
Richard Cosens senior	2
Nicholas Cosens	4
John Woodman	2
William Cole	4[1]
hearths	44

Hearths not chargeable

Richard Cosens junior	2
Elizabeth Kerby widow	2
Alexander Roode	2
Ralph Caute	2
Parnel Kerby	1
Thomas Crooke	1
hearths	10

1. *Whole entry in different hand*

23. DROXFORD[1]

Hearths chargeable

Sir Richard Uvedale	15
William Bensteed	10
Mister James Betts	7
John Archer	8
Robert Smith	3
John Potterne	3
Edward Searle	4
William Smith	3
John Wheeler	2
William Bensteed	4
John Boreman	3
Simon Hatch	4
John Sparshott	3
John Prowtinge	3
Richard Hockley	2

Fol. 6v(ii)

John Honyman	3
John Honyman	4
John Addams	3
Stephen Hatch	3
Anthony Wittcombe	2
Edward Hatch	1[a]
Edward Knight	4[b]
Widow Lydalle	3
Thomas Addams	1
Peter Lydalle	1
Richard Smith	1
Daniel Lee	3
Stephen Hatch	4
hearths	107

Hearths not chargeable

William Stevens	1
German Honyman	1
Robert Bensteed	1
Thomas Knowler	1
Francis Conmore	2
Edward Kenwood	2
John Bensteed	2
John Cooke	2

23. DROXFORD—*cont'd.*

Peter Knight	2
Edward Strugnell	2
hearths	16

(a) 1 down
(b) 2 void
1. Drocksford

24. FAWLEY

Hearths chargeable

Richard Strong	3
John Houchins	3
Peter Peale	4
Charles Witherington	2
Charles Witherington	1
Henry Smart	3
David Witherington	2
Richard Cross	2
James Isrone	1
Thomas Noell	1
Thomas Parsonage	5
William Webb	2
John Gage	2
Nicholas Strong	4
Henry Etheridg	3
Henry Toovey	2
Robert Uphill	2
Richard Rill	3
Widow Warwick	2
Thomas Arnold	1
Richard Flight	1
Mister Ralph Robinson	3
Edward Brixey	1
William Bond	3
William Youngs	2
Robert Swann	3
Widow Hooker	4
Robert Carter	1

Fol. 7r(i)

William Ansell	2
Edward Covey	1
Robert Abbott	1
James Osey	3
Widow Flight	1
Roger Skipper	3
John Certter	3
hearths	80

Hearths not chargeable

Almshouse	3
Richard Morris	1
Edward Prince	1
Thomas Morris	1
Richard Parnell	1
Nicholas Chiett	1
Widow Frissell	1
Widow Hussey	1
John Wilson	1
Thomas West	1
Thomas Stoyle	1
Thomas Fryth	1
Martin Weale	1
David Downer	1
Thomas Lovell	1
Robert Brixey	1
Thomas Lovell	1
Henry Edwards	2
Robert Swann	1
George Severton	1
Nicholas Downinge	1
Robert Morton	1
James Harris	1
Widow Bound	1
hearths	27

25. ST. MARY EXTRA[1]

Hearths chargeable

Richard Suett	6
Thomas Dixon	5
Mister Stone	4
William Martin	3
Mister James Mills	11
Mister Mills	3
William Jourd	4
John Gold	2
William Warner	1
Thomas Jourde	1
John Smith	2
John Canterton	1
Mister Higgins	3

Robert Sone	3
John Cooper	3
Robert Longland	3
John Wescombe	3
Mister North	4
Richard Edwards	4
Richard Kent	2(a)
Richard Diaper	3
William Diaper	2
Francis Hickley	3
Mister Fawkner	3(b)
Mister North	3(b)

Fol. 7r(ii)

Nicholas Waterman	2(b)
hearths	84

Hearths not chargeable

Robert Tucker	1
Richard Lyde	1
Edward Guy	1
Widow Kinge	1
Speede	1
Robert Tucker	1
Richard Deane	1
Robert Addams	1
Richard Addams	1
Widow Buttler	1
John Rutter	2
Thomas Tucker	1
Goodman Foster	1
James Dibden	1
Edward Holloway	1
William Corke	1
Richard Savage	1
James Addington	2
Widow Morden	1
Nicholas Feilder	1
Widow Rives	1
George Foster	1
Widow Sceate	1
William Horne	1
Nicholas Hounsom	1
Richard Webb	1
William Feilder	1
Henry Fox	1
Laurence Foster	1
Thomas Fox	1
Widow Wilkins	1
Richard Benny	1
Clement Smith	1
Widow Jourd	1
hearths	36

(a) 1 overcharged
(b) void
1. Weston

26. ASTHON

Hearths chargeable

Richard Suett	4
John Freind	4
Nicholas Harfell	4
John Cleverly	2
Thomas Goldfinch	3
Andrew Freind	3
Thomas Freind	3
Richard Barfoot	2
Robert Barfoot	5
Robert Barfoot	1
David Prowting	3
Henry Friend	3
Richard Caute	2
Richard Warner	1
Widow Barfoot	2
Thomas Cleverly	3
Richard Trodd	4
Ann Freind	2
John Knight	3
Robert Kerbye	4
hearths	58

Fol. 7v(i)

Hearths not chargeable

John Trodd	1
William Mundey	1
John Bray	1
John Stubbington	2
Andrew Trodd	2
Thomas Trodd	1
Edward Babes	1
Richard Trodd	1
David Stubbington	1
Edward Trodd	1
hearths	12

27. BURSLEDON

Hearths chargeable

Richard Wyatt	3
Giles Pullinger	3
John Channell	1
Thomas Straggleford	2
Laurence Chamberlaine	2
Andrew Strugnell	1
Robert Channell	1
Widow Feverell	2
John Shepherd	1
Stephen Parlett	3
Thomas Tucker	1
Robert Ivy	1
Henry Rudd	2
Alexander Fry	1
John Smith	1
Laurence Chamberlaine senior	1
John Kinge	2
William Heath	2
Edward Marks	2
Bartholomew Westcott	2
Mary Cleverly widow	2
Henry Peach	2
Richard Newman	1
William Fry	1
John Chamberlaine	1
Robert Channell	2
hearths	43

Hearths not chargeable

Mary Wigge widow	1
John Castle	2
Henry Chamberlaine	2
Sarah Parlott	1
Robert Kite	1
Thomas Berry	1
Susan Morgan	1
Richard West	1
Moses Parr	1
William Langford	1
John Cleverly	1
Edward Sampson	1
The almshouse	4
John Abraham	1
John Blake	2
Mary Wigge	1
Joseph Wigge	2
hearths	24

Fol. 7v(ii)

28. WOODCOTT

Hearths chargeable

Richard Caute	6
Thomas Cleverly	5
Daniel Bawerstock	4
John Turner	3
Nicholas Harwood	2
Richard Hunt	2
John Stubbington	2
Richard Caute	2
hearths	26

29. BISHOPS WALTHAM[1]

Hearths chargeable

John Pye	3
Thomas Penford	2
John Deane	3
John Grossmith	3
James Hampton	4
Mister Peter Browne	9
Peter Cooke	5
Edward Wheeler	2
John Pryor	3
Richard Lee	2
Mistress Kelsey	5
Doctor Joseph Gulstone	7
Richard Bradsell	7
Cuthbert Dowse	1
Widow Penford	2
James Symes	1
John Bradsell	4
Henry Wilshire	3
Widow Pryor	4
Widow Horner	3
Widow Compton	2
John Horner	4
James Blackly	4
Richard Seale	3

Thomas Cleverly	4
John Newbery	5
John Cole	1
Mister Morrison	6
Edward Goodeve	5
Robert Boshere	3
Richard Prowtinge	3
John Lockett	4
Richard Fawkner	3
Richard Cooke	2
Francis Biggs	4
Richard Hackett	2
John Hackett	3
Widow Freind	4
Thomas Dipnell	3
Thomas Nash	1
Widow Heatherfeild	4
John Hackett	1
William Reeves	2
Thomas Pryor	2
Thomas White	7
Thomas Reeves	3
Richard Mooreing	2
Thomas Lee	4

Fol. 8r(i)

William Barry	2
Thomas Dipnell senior	4
Widow Dipnell	1
John Hockley	1
Francis Hackett	2
Francis Marriner	2
William Bulbeck	1
William Mundey	2
William Mann	2
Richard Hancock	2
Edward Littlefeild	2
Hugh Wheeler	1
Richard Hancock	2
Ralph Peppersele	2
Henry Dipnell	2
Widow Katterell[2]	1
Robert Burrell	2
William Goldinge	3
Thomas Peperinge	5
Peter Babes	5
Henry Peperinge	3
John Elliott	2
Thomas Walker	3
William Peperinge	3
Widow Penforde	2
Thomas Biggs	3
Thomas Addams	4
Andrew Deane	2
John Dipnell	2
William Layne	3
William Wooll	3
Nicholas Bedbrooke	4
George Scragnell	3
Richard Trodd	3
Widow Hampton	3
Peter Boyes	3
Widow Feilder	3
Thomas Godwin	3
Samson Austen	3
Charles Camish	3
Nicholas Skinner	4
Robert Biggs	3
hearths	273

Hearths not chargeable

John Dorsett	2
John Liberd	2
Henry Barfoot	2
Richard Mooringe	1
Widow Allen	1
Widow Barfoott	2
Richard Harfeild	1
Widow Mills	1
James Martyn	2
Robert Caute	1
Cuthbert Penford	2
Henry Barfoot	1
John Tucker	1
Richard Randoll	1
Thomas Nash	1
William Whitcher	1
Richard Gill	1
Widow Bethell	1
Ralph Jennings	1
William Bethell	2

29. BISHOPS WALTHAM—*cont'd.*

Fol. 8r(ii)

Thomas Speede	1
John White	1
Nicholas Bedbrooke	1
Francis Londay	1
Widow Addams	2
Robert Skinner	1
Nicholas Spencer	1
Weames	2
Widow Cooke	1
Widow Adams senior	2
Laurence Adams	1
Widow Williams	1
John Martindale	2
John Woodman	1
Thomas Skynner	2
Widow Restall	1
Widow Adams	2
Thomas Addams	1
Thomas Golley	1
Giles Morley	1
John Peperinge	2
William Wilson	2
Laurence Good	2
Robert Harris	2
Widow Stubbington	1
John Hewes	2
Widow Wiltshire	1
James Wittcombe	1
Widow Waight	1
John Crowcher	2
Arthur Bower	2
John Lee	2
Thomas Fawker	1
Richard Goddwin	2
John Warrene	2
Matthew Barber	1
George Carpenter	2
Andrew Colepis	2
Nyatt Warren	2
Thomas Combs	2
Mary Bower	1
John Roach	2
hearths	88

1. Waltham Episcopi
2. Catterell *changed to* Katterell

30. SHEDFIELD[1]

Hearths chargeable

Thomas Lunn	4
Thomas Burnell	2
Henry Smith	3
Peter Hawksworth	5
Richard Barry	2
Edward Clewer senior	7
Edward Clewer junior	2
William Churcher	2
John Boyes	1
Richard Spershott	6
Richard Freind	4
Thomas Sweet	2
Edward West	3
William Barry	2
Thomas Barry junior	5
Stephen Barry	4
Thomas Barry senior	3

Fol. 8v(i)

Henry Webb	6
James Marks	3
Widow Cosens	3
Henry Barfoot	1
James Jourd	3
John Jonas	3
Richard Rutter	1
Thomas Walter	1
hearths	78

Hearths not chargeable

Richard Kinge	1
Widow Barry	1
James Jourde	2
Widow Woodman	1
Widow Holt	1
Edward Cleverly	1
Andrew Mills	2
Philip Strugnell	1
John Barry	1
Richard Rooder	1
hearths	12

1. Shidfeild

31. HILL

Hearths chargeable

Thomas Knight	4
John Knight	3
Edward Arthur	4
William Cleverly	3
Stephen Bunn	2
Jerome Burnell	4
Nicholas Cleverly	2
Widow Vinden	1
Widow Brewer	2
Richard Fry	2
Richard Jerman	2
Edward Cleverly	4
Widow Fry	4
Nicholas Cleverly	3
Thomas Knight	1
Richard Cleverly	2
hearths	43

Hearths not chargeable

Thomas Wassell	1
William Cooke	1
Philip Smith	1
hearths	3

32. DURLEY

Hearths chargeable

John Hickley senior	3
John Cosens	3
Thomas Mowrton	3
Thomas Benham	2
William Meare	2(a)
William Holt	3
John Hickley junior	3
Thomas Rybeard	3
Henry Glaspoole	3
John Mayle	5
John Staignell	1

Fol. 8v(ii)

Andrew Kent	2
John Freind	3
William Cosens	2
Edward Cripps	6
Edward Cripps	3
Edward Houghton	4
Robert Gregory	2
John Hickley senior	2
Thomas Abraham	2
John Cosens	2
hearths	58

Hearths not chargeable

John Harmsworth	1
Peter Carpenter	1
Richard Aubrey	1
William Scott	1
hearths	4

(a) 1 taken down

33. BITTERNE[1]

Hearths chargeable

Mister Clungeon	4
Mister Robert Richbill	8
Mister Hopgood	2
Mister James Mills	12
Mister Tomlins	4
Widow Dummer	1
Robert Baldrey	2
John Buckland	2
William Bowles	1
Mistress Ann Clerk	2
Ann Burgis	1
hearths	39

Hearths not chargeable

Thomas Paskins	1
William Prowtinge	1
John Gold	1
Thomas Smith	2
hearths	5

1. Bittherne

34. POLLACK[1]

Hearths chargeable

Mistress Ann Clerke	14
Roger Turner clerk	5
George Rapier	3
hearths	22

Hearths not chargeable

Walter Buxey	2
Anthony Barfoot	2
John Asher	1

34. POLLACK—*cont'd.*

Henry Bevis	1
John Kent	1
George Hammon	1
hearths	8

1. Pollacke

Fol. 9r(i)

35. CURDRIDGE

Hearths chargeable

James Marks	3
Peter Russell	3
John Litchfeild	2
Thomas Kingate	7
John Wyatt	5
Reuben Cleverly	3
Matthew Freind	3
Thomas Wyatt	6
John Smith	4
Richard Hackett	3
Thomas Osbourne	6
Edward Barfoot	3
Edward Barfoot	3
Henry Baker	1
Thomas Fawkner	2
William Habben	1
William Stares	7
John Chalcroft senior	1
John Faithfull	2
Stephen Sparkman	2
John Moore	2
Thomas Strugnell	1
John Parker	1
Edward Hackett	6
Widow Penford	5
Mister Peter Ashton	5
John Penford	3
John Chalcroft	2
William Walker	1
hearths	93

Hearths not chargeable

Thomas Weale	2
William Palmer	1
William Fisher	1
John Faithfull	1
William Hunt	1
Christopher Price	1
Widow Terry	1
Stephen Philippe	1
Widow Carter	1
Stephen Hunt	1
Michael Philipp	1
Stephen Dagger	1
Benjamin Fisher	1
Robert Booker	1
Elias Edes	2
Edward Booker	1
Jourd	1
Widow Holt	2
hearths	21

36. WINTERSHILL

Hearths chargeable

Francis Dummer	8
John Cosens	3
John Freind	5
John Colebroke	4
Thomas Barnard	3

Fol. 9r(ii)

William Mattox	4
Robert Pincke	3
Francis Trodd	3
James Parsons	2
Henry Goldfinch	3
James Bone	3
Richard Hasteed	4
Richard Moory	4
Robert Hasler	3
William Chaimberlaine	3
Richard Gill	3
Ogle Riggs	3
Edward Yeomans	2
Richard Barfoot	2
Hugh Tanner	3
hearths	68

Hearths not chargeable

Widow Culver	2
George Page	1
Widow Abraham	1
Widow May	1

William Feverell	1
Richard Crocker	1
John Crocker	1
William Greatham	1
William Sweat	1
Henry Wiltshire	1
William Jones	1
Richard Yeoman	1
John Bone	1
Henry Bone	1
Henry Abraham	1
William Caute	1
Richard Fidler	1
Widow Knight	1
William Cofen	2
Richard Cofen	1
hearths	22

The number of hearths chargeable within the hundred of Waltham is	1302
Whereof for half a year	1[1]
Not chargeable	327

1. *Whole entry added later in a different hand*

ALVERSTOKE AND GOSPORT LIBERTY

37. ALVERSTOKE

Hearths chargeable

Mister John Earlsman	4
Mister William Rolfe	6
Thomas Sayte	2
Thomas Rowte	2
Nicholas Hawkesworth	3
John Stokes	3
Widow Starres	3
William Woodman	1
John Player	3
Robert Hobbs	2

Fol. 9v(i)

John Hamon	3
John Patten	4
Widow Browne	1
Jane Babye	3
William Woodison	3
Widow Jelman	1
Widow Barton	3
Thomas Smith	3
Philip Fowles	2[(a)]
Richard Clewer	3
George Bearde	3[(a)]
Edward Bone	2
John Carter junior	2
Thomas Evens	1
John Forder	3
Widow Hunt	3
Edmund Dummer	1
William Harmsworth	3
John Fuller	3
Thomas Arnold	3
John Ryves	2
Chideock Bucknell	3
Jerome Collins	3
Stephen White	3
John Hobbs	3
William Kingman	2
Richard Eames	2
Francis Bryan	2
Sarah Smith	1
William Arnold	3
John Marshall	3
William Gregory	4
Robert Watts	5
Widow Hobbs	2
Francis Lock	3
Widow Hawksworth	1
John Woodman	3
Richard Lipputt	3
Ralph Heather	4
Edmund Page	3
William Carter	3
Ann Woodman	3
Jame Abraham	3
Edward Palmer	3
hearths	146

Hearths not chargeable

William Bonner	1
Richard Fish	1
Thomas Dibden	2

37. ALVERSTOKE—*cont'd.*

John Baker	1
Widow Crofte	1
Barzillay Avery	1
John Turner	1
Jerome Collins	2
James Money	1
Henry Gisbye	2
William Roodes	1

Fol. 9v(ii)

Nicholas Wheate	1
Widow Hollis	1
John Carter senior	1
Simon Fuller	1
Nicholas Pratt	1
Thomas Durrick	2
John Page	1
William Parker	1
[ ]	[ ][1]
John Powell	2
Sarah Bassett	1
Ann Price	1
Widow Love	2
Widow Abram	1
John Bourne	1
Widow Norris	1
Thomas Slonn	1
Thomas Croft	1
Widow Tire	1
hearths	36

(a) 1 overcharged

1. *Name and number of hearths crossed through. Possibly* Ann Woodman; *number of hearths* 1

38. GOSPORT

Hearths chargeable

Mark Goodinge	4
Quinbanner Mersh	3
Richard Mathews	5
Nicholas Perkins	2
Widow Mills	3
Henry Tilden	4
Robert Frampton	8
Gervase Morlen	3
Thomas Ayliffe	6
John Hollyster	5
Thomas Haregood	5
Thomas Wheeler	2
William Congden	2
Roger Gudgeridge	2
Thomas Lawes	1
William Betts	5
Richard Wise	2
George Reynolds	4
Thomas Kirke	4
James Edwards	2
James Taylor	2
Thomas Shepdam	3
Gabriel Gilles	2
Jonathan Capell	3
Jona[1] Savadge	3
Dorothy Lock	3
John Lowes	4
Boatsman Curtis	3
Peter Sone	2
Abraham Penfold	3
Robert Kinge	3
William Chatram	9
Nicholas Podd	5
John Robbins junior	2
John Edmunds	1
Ann Collins widow	2
Philip Philipps	2
Alice Tasker	5

Fol. 10r(i)

William Evans	5
Peter Pitts	4
Thomas Guyer	6
Edward Bartholomew	2
William Dale	3
Roger Grainger	3
George Dew	3
Thomas Oxford	2
James Elliott	3
Robert Lee	3
John Lilly	2
John Musgrave	3
Timothy Hawkins	2
Thomas Burgis	3
Widow Moncke	4

Thomas Thorne 2
Mister John Pitts 5
Christopher Lidd 2
John Barnaby 2
Thomas Arland 2
Robert Small 3
Francis Lale 2
John Player 4
Thomas Dart 2
Thomas Wilson 3
Edward Furse 2
Richard Symons 5
John Pope 1
William Page 6
James Wise 3
John Softly 2
Thomas Parsons 6
Nicholas Rowland 2
John Collins 2
Widow Risden 3
Edward King 2
Abraham Hewlett 3
Edward Hill 5
Zacharias Leather 7
Samuel Burningham 9
Gregory Peachy 4
William Baily 2
Roger Eastwood 4
Laurence Pamons[2] 4
Widow Pretty 4
John Bremly 9
Rebecca Pope 4
Robert Cowley 9
Richard Bushell 8
Thomas Langley 2
Boyer Deacon 3
Doctor Chamberlaine 2
Newton Newland 4
James Palmer 5
Thomas Bond 2
John Morgan 3
William Gittins 3
William Woodman 3
Robert Driver 9
John Button 3

Fol. 10r(ii)

Robert Bennettland 2
John Stepney 5
Stephen Francis 2
Christopher Elmanston 2
Thomas Hooper 2
Arthur Cleverly 1
Widow Richardson 2
Henry Avis 4
William Hunt 2
Widow Hodges 4
Thomas Lucas 2
Captain Richard Hodges 7
Edward Merrick 6
Edward Hogge 2
Robert Collins 8
Walter Fry 4
George Browne 2
Richard Stedman 4
Thomas Seymore 3
Arthur Baker 3
Widow Taylor 4
Widow Capell 2
Thomas Smart 2
James Howell 2
James Aylinge 2
Thomas Cruys 5
John Ballard 6
William Stakes 5
Thomas Arminer 4
Dorothy Morris 4
Ralph Greenewood 3
William Hodges 3
Thomas Eastwood 5
Theophilus Chiverell 4
Abraham Andsley 4
Edward Pannell 5
Thomas Weight 1
John Robbins senior 2
George Lathum 2
John Cosens 1
John Wassell 1
Daniel Bradley 4
John Oleife 3
Henry Peeke 3

38. GOSPORT—*cont'd.*

George Mersh	2
Nicholas Benson	4
John Benstead	4
William Ballard	3
John Burley	3
Robert Bierd	3
Thomas Pentford	3
Widow Uvedale	3
Widow Wheeler	3
Thomas Bistowe junior	3
Widow Anderson	4
Herbert Batchelor	3
John Burnett's house	4[a]
Thomas Driver's house	7[a]

Fol. 10v(i)

Edward Holt	2[a]
Walter Hill's house	2[a]
Widow Andrews	3
hearths	549

Hearths not chargeable

Roger Veale	2
Hugh Hearne	2
Henry Bushell	1
Laurence Gudgeon	2
Henry Forte	2
Richard Gregory	2
Widow Paulle	2
Stephen Thomas	1
Edward Dixon	1
Thomas Cowdry	2
Edward Powell	2
Widow Caswell	2
John Layman	3
George Warden	2
Samuel Lynne	2
James House	2
John Saintlow	2
John Triver	2
Thomas Hensin	2
Widow Twine	2
Richard Barton	2
Thomas Parker	2
Widow Proper	2
Nicholas Whitley	2
Thomas Woodman	2
Amy Carter	2
John Osborne	2
Widow Perne	2
William Perne	2
Widow Young	2
Maurice White	1
Widow White	2
Widow Marshall	1
Widow Ingram	2
Elizabeth Hancock	2
Robert Browne	2
John Yorke	2
Widow Hasteed	2
Widow Foster	1
Richard Swithingham	2
Widow Andrews	2
James Ricketts	2
John Spencer	2
Thomas Norris	2
John Swithingham	2
Thomas Ralfe	2
John Goddard	2
Thomas Agden	2
Gilbert West	2
Thomas Spooner	2

Fol. 10v(ii)

John Gold	1
Nicholas Foster	2
Roger Lee	1
Widow Pincke	2
John Benjamin	1
Widow Gover	2
Roger Pickett	2
Thomas Bistome	1
John Michill	2
Joan Exceter	1
Widow Trudle	1
John Agden	1
John Johnson	1
Michael Henslowe	2
Leonard Banes	2
Stephen Blitch	2
Joseph Goddwin	1
Geoffrey Sone	2

William Smith	1
John Hewes	2
John Booker	2
Ellis Bishopp	2
Philip Gittins	1
John Hull	2
John Dash	2
Francis Jones	2
Widow Lawes	2
Laurence Anthrum	1
Widow Edwards	1
John Legg	2
William Collins	2
Widow Blake	2
Philip Eames	1
John Brissett	1
John Williams	2
John Prenton	2
Widow Warrell	2
Richard Quallett	2
William Hammon	2
John Biggs	2
Thomas Osbone	2
Andrew Rives	1
Stephen Harman	2
Widow Oliver	2
Edward Denham	2
William Bowers	2
John Morrill	1
Thomas Robbins	1
hearths	173

(a) void
1. *Possibly Jonah* or *Jonathon*
2. *Surname looks like* Paviour *changed to* Pamons

The number of hearths chargeable within the liberty of Alverstoke and Gosport is	695
Not chargeable	209

Fol. 11r(i)

HAVANT LIBERTY

39. BROCKHAMPTON

Hearths chargeable

William Greenefeild	3
Henry Voake	3
Richard Softly	3
Richard Stonard	3
John Smith	1[(a)]
John Sapp	1
Francis Long	2[(b)]
Widow Stone	3
John Catchlove	1
John Jenkins	3
Barnard Smither	2
John Sone	4
John Abery	1
Richard Softly	3
Thomas Hancock	2
Thomas Collins	1
Thomas Boxall	3
John Wassell	4
Henry Woolgar	1
Edward Cole	1
William Kent	2
Edward Ansell	3
Thomas Hancock	2[(c)]
hearths	52

Hearths not chargeable

Richard Stent	1
Robert Boulton	1
Widow Irish	1
Jerome Oliver	1
John Hart	1
John Penfold	2
Arthur Woollgar	2
Samuel Hills	1
William Deane	1
Widow Eldridge	1
Francis Buttler	2
Henry Baker	1
John Booker	1
Matthew Mills	2
Widow Benbery	1
Samuel Lawrence	2
Thomas Paye	2
Henry Winn	1
John Reynolds	2

39. BROCKHAMPTON—*cont'd.*

Gilbert Burch	1
Baker	1
hearths	28

(a) one overcharged
(b) one taken down and one overcharged
(c) void

40. HAVANT

Hearths chargeable

William Woollgar esquire	13
Mister Batten	4
Mister John Batten	4
Thomas Stone	2
Robert Aylmer	4
John Reynolds	2
James Sparkman	5
Widow Parr	1
William Witcher	2
Jethro Bates	3
Stephen Palmer	2
John Evander	3
[Richard][1] Flood	1
John Smith	5
William Cockwell	2
Richard Marriner	4
John Jones	2

Fol. 11r(ii)

William Dallyrose	4
Henry Heather	4
William Norman	6
William Softly	2
William Upman gentleman	5
Henry Wilks	4
Edward Hayter	3
Bartholomew Harrisson	5
John Adrey	5(a)
John Godfrey	3
Robert Cook	2
Richard Parker	3
Thomas Baily	4
Nicholas Loader	4
John Hyde	3
John Price	3
Robert Westbrooke	5
Thomas Catchlove	2
Richard Long	2
Henry Hammon	3
William Bally	2
William Cacknell	2
William Woollgar	4
Mister Streate	5
Bartholomew Mills	3
John Drewett	9
Thomas Maydley	4
Richard Goodfaith	3
John Lunn	3
William Pannell	4
Mister Nathaniel Hammon	4
John Eedes	3
Francis Aylinge	1
Mister Belchamber	8
Francis Stone	2
Arthur Bagshall	3
Arthur Bagshall	1
William Scardefeild	4
Richard Corke	2
James Sparkman junior	3
Widow Marriner	1
Arthur Baily	3
Robert Goter	3
Mister Watson	3
Edward Thorner	3
Widow Shaw	4
William Fuse	3
John Higgins	5
Widow Searle	3
Edward Millard	3
Widow Westbrooke	3
John Dibden	4
Thomas Martin	3
John Dolegarde	4
Widow Carrington	4
Widow Woods	7
William Grigge	3
John Searles	3(b)

Clement Knight	2[b]
John Westbrooke	3[b]
Baylys house	4[b]
John Vaughan	3[b]
John Golding	3[b]
John Dummer	4[b]
Robert Henty	4[b]
Widow Gillingham	3
hearths	[ ]

Fol. 11v(i)

Hearths not chargeable

Thomas Hurlock	2
Thomas Hunt	2
Widow Ewbancke	1
John Neigh	1
Widow Grigg	1
John Browne	2
John Thomas	1
Thomas Prowting	1
Widow Salter	2
John Blanchard	1
Henry Heather	1
Matthew Street junior	2
Widow Buckett	2
Richard Guy	2
Simon Alvin	1
Thomas Greene	2
Richard Dowlinge	2
Thomas Jenkins	2
Francis Kempe	2
Benjamin Chestle	1
Stephen Dam	1
William Browman	1
Widow Fayth[2]	1
Robert Martle	1
Clement Knight	2
Widow Gubbett	2
Widow Grigge	1
John Mason	2
Guy Harper	1
Thomas Heather	2
William Palmer	2
Widow Younge	1
Henry Kempe	1
John Heather	2
Widow Woolston	1
Widow Fowle	1
Simon Freeborne	1
Widow Cole	2
John Gittins	2
Widow Maydman	2
Richard Cockwell	1
Nicholas Rich	1
Bartholomew Harris junior	2
Richard Heale	1
John Higgins	1
Widow Smith	1
Leonard Ellis	1
James Kinge	2
John Palmer	1
hearths	71

(a) 1 down
(b) void
1. *Possibly* Nicholas
2. *Original surname erased and* Fayth *written in*

41. LEIGH

Hearths chargeable

Mister Francis Aylmer	7
John Page	3
Thomas Swann	5
William Pannell	3
Thomas Freeborne	3
John Freland	6
Widow Pledger	1
Francis Ayling	1
John Feilder	2
Thomas Smith	2
John Mariner	2
John Reynolds	1
Richard Marriner	1
Widow Cosens	1
Robert Higgins	3
Mister William Aylmer	1
hearths	42

Fol. 11v(ii)

Hearths not chargeable

John Rowden	2

41. LEIGH—*cont'd.*

Thomas Guy	1
Ann Westbrooke	1
John Pledger	1
Thomas Smith	2
Francis Feilder	2
Robert Reynolds	1
John Williams	1
hearths	11

The number of hearths chargeable within the liberty of Havant is	38
Not chargeable	109

HAMBLEDON HUNDRED

42. HAMBLEDON

Hearths chargeable

Mister Edmund Bewninge	9
Mister Harby	6
Mister Newman	7
John Venable	2
Thomas Tribb	4[a]
John Longrish	3
Arthur Nosse	2
Ann Littlefeild	3
Richard Stent	5
Robert Roe	2
Richard Tribb	3
George Heather	3
William Padwick	3
William Hasler	5
Christopher Bensted	3
Widow Mullings	3
Widow Knight	2
Widow Heather	7
Richard Wyatt	1
Henry Aldridge	3
Thomas Beane	2
Thomas Courtnell	4
John Smith	2
William Smith	2
Robert Sutton	2
Richard Goddwin	2
Thomas Fawchin	3
Thomas Hooker	2
John Fawchin[1]	2
Edward Jaques	5
John Marshall	1
Robert Pincke	1
Thomas [ ]alloway[2]	2
Thomas Martin	2
George Bensteed	1
John Pratt	4
Widow Hills	4
Simon Mullins	6
Widow Fawchin	3
Richard Martin	3
hearths	128

Hearths not chargeable

Richard Fuller	2
Robert Cooke	2
William Mullins	1
Mary Taylor	1
William Mitchell	2
Ellen Pratt	2
Widow Strugnell	1

Fol. 12r(i)

Benjamin Wyatt	1
Thomas Bydinge	2
Daniel Fowle	2
Richard Jenner	1
Richard Elcombe	1
John Ray	2
John Stubbington	2
William Newman	1
Richard Lamboll	1
Widow Aldridge	1
Henry Dudman	1
Widow Pildrim	1
John Holland	1
Widow Jennings	1
Widow Michell	2
Walter Collins	1
Richard Coles	1
hearths	33

(a) 1 overcharged
1. *Possible that originally written as* Fawckin
2. *Originally* Holloway, *first letter altered illegibly*

43. GLIDDEN

Hearths chargeable

Thomas Kinge	4
Stephen Tyre	1
Robert Aldridge	2
Philip Foster	1
Thomas Maydlow	1
William Foster	2
John Tyre	1
Richard Kennett	1
John Aldridge	2
Henry Kennett	6
hearths	21

Hearths not chargeable

Henry Foster	1
John Farly	1
Widow Skinner	1
hearths	3

44. CHIDDEN

Hearths chargeable

Sir Henry Cesar knight[1]	6
John Luffe	6
Nicholas Caute	11
Richard Binsteed	2
Elizabeth Bensteed	4
William Goldsmith	1
Gunner Hobb	5
Thomas Pratt	2
William Ringe	2
Nicholas Foster	3
John Ringe	3
William Pratt	2
Thomas Ringe	3
Thomas Pincke	3
John Mitchener	1
Richard Roudway	2
Stephen Ringe	3
Ursula Turner widow	1
John Mansbridge	1

Fol. 12r(ii)

Thomas Ayleward	1
John Luff junior	3
hearths	66

Hearths not chargeable

Daniel Sherryer	1
William Pincke	2
Margaret Ray widow	1
John Purdue	1
hearths	5

1. knight *added later*

45. ERVILLES[1]

Hearths chargeable

Bartholomew Smith esquire	10
Thomas Pryor	3
William Pratt	4
Anthony Bensteed	3
William Searle	1
Mister Symons	3
William Dunnett	2
William Padwick	1
Edward Allnett	2
Thomas Morlett	3
Widow Gray	3
Nathaniel Hockley	1[(a)]
hearths	36

Hearths not chargeable

Widow Bensteed	1
William Luke	1
German Jolley	1
John Knapp	1
John Spencer	1
Widow Hunt	1
John Reade	1
Thomas Martin	1
Widow Bensteed	2
hearths	10

(a) 1 overcharged
1. Erville

46. DENMEAD[1]

Hearths chargeable

Thomas Laud	5
George Oliver	5
Nicholas Harfeild	6
Thomas Newman	1
William Brewer senior	2

46. DENMEAD—*cont'd.*

Henry Richards	3
Richard Ismonger	3
John Glaspoole	3
John Bassett	4
Edmund Barnard	2
Thomas Brookes	1
John Horwood	3
Nicholas Wheeler	1
Richard Warden	1
Widow Withers	1
Francis Pincke	1
Thomas Mellis	3
Widow Withers	3

Fol. 12v(i)

Edmund Pryor	3
Widow Padwick	4
Anthony Foster	2
Robert Padwick	1
John Foster	3
Nicholas Boyes	3
Henry Harwood	3
Robert Aldridge	2
Richard Baker	1
Daniel Baker	1
Humphrey Padwick	8
John Hooker	2
John Hooker	2
Simon Latter	5
Simon Goddwin	2
Edward Attwood	2
Henry Nosse	3
Philip Reede	2
Nicholas Walker	1
Edward Attwood	2
John Kempe	2
Richard Harwood	2
John Sone	4
John Tomsone	2
William Luttman	2
William Brewer junior	1
Amy Foster	2
Nicholas Tribbicke	3
hearths	118

Hearths not chargeable

Peter Rice	1
John Marriner	1
Widow Blanchard	1
Thomas Gilbert	1
Widow Farly	1
William Bensteed	1
John Holt	1
John Edwards	1
Widow Carter	2
Anthony Smith	1
Humphrey Ayleward	1
Thomas Baker	2
Widow Vengon	1
Widow Person	1
hearths	16

1. Denmeade

The number of hearths chargeable within the hundred of Hambledon is	369
Not chargeable	67

FAREHAM HUNDRED

47. CROCKERHILL

Hearths chargeable

Edward Sparvell	4
John Swann	2
Robert Woolgar	3
Richard Swann	3
Richard Crocker	1
John Holt	2

Fol. 12v(ii)

Humphrey Edwards	3
Goodman Boulton	3
Thomas Bristow	4
Benjamin Bedford	1
Richard Bartholomew	4
Thomas Steele	3
Stephen Percy	3
William Heather	3
hearths	39

Hearths not chargeable

Thomas Cosens	1
Margaret Wassell	1
hearths	2

48. CAMS BISHOP[1]

Hearths chargeable

Sir Thomas Badd baronet	15
Roger Woodman	6
Ralph Holt	3
William Swann	1
Nicholas Weston	2
John Heyter	2
John Mainor	2
Samuel Wyatt	2
Thomas Hasler	1
John Bennett	1
Widow Wassell	1
hearths	36

Hearths not chargeable

Widow Wigg	1
Widow Cocker	1
Thomas Trodd	1
hearths	3

1. Camesbisshopp

49. CAMS OYSELL[1]

Hearths chargeable

William Button	2
Mister William Bennett	6
Mister Nathaniel Wilson	5
William Price	2
Edmund Persons	3
Doctor Stone	2
Thomas Ayers	1
John Hasling senior	1
Thomas Penfold	6
William Hewett	2
Francis Masters	1
Thomas Pye	5
Francis Stevens	4
William Heyter	3
Richard Nunn junior	1
Widow Kinge	6
Mister Pescodd	8
John Firkins	5
William Brooman	1
Richard Nunn senior	1
Robert Grigge	2
John Fowles	3
Edward Cleverly	1

Fol. 13r(i)

Richard Brewcer	1
Widow Perry	4
Nicholas Edwards	2
John Newman	2
Edward Garland	2
Stephen Heale	1
Francis Smith junior	1
George Hockley	2
John Gill	1
John Faythorne junior	2
William Edmunds	1
John Deane senior	1
John Hastling	1
hearths	92

Hearths not chargeable

Widow Tyre	1
John Mansbridge	1
John Bowles	1
Edward Newbery	1
Henry Baker	1
Widow Masters	1
Richard Ackley	1
Widow Hammon	2
Thomas Todd	2
John Parlter	1
William Smith	1
Anthony Slade	2
Robert Mayle	1
Nicholas Cosens	1
hearths	17

1. Camsoysells

50. DEAN[1]

Hearths chargeable

William Hewlett	3
William Woolgar	4

50. DEAN—*cont'd.*

Clement Kent	4
Anthony Swann	3
William Hellier	2
John Fowles	1
Richard Hopkins	2
Richard Prowtinge	1
William Coles	5
William Princke	2
William Bryant	2
John Addams	3
Alexander Swinden	3
Nicholas Stares	2
Henry Sewett	3
Edward Sparvill	3
John Gringoe	1
Roger White	2
William Pincke	4
Edward Cosens	2(a)
James Hassell	3
Richard Barnard	1
Thomas Mourne	2
Henry Reynolds	1
hearths	60

Hearths not chargeable

Widow Heather	2
George Naule	1
Robert Moores	1
John Colles	1
Roger White	1
[ ] S[ ]te	1
hearths	7

(a) 1 overcharged
1. Deane

Fol. 13r(ii)

51. FAREHAM

Hearths chargeable

Mister John Hurst	6
Robert Page	3
John Jacobb	1
Nicholas Harris	1
Widow Page	3
William Ayres	3
Benjamin Jolley	5
Mister John Barton	9
Geoffrey Gray	1
Thomas Powsely	4
James Simpson	3
Andrew Chapman	2
William Bennett	3
William Lee	2
George Abridge	2
Thomas Fowles	2
Widow Hentey	2
Henry Boyes	2
Thomas Fowles	3
Mister Roger Barton	4
Widow Penford	2
Thomas Godwin	4
Thomas Palmer	3
Henry Franklin	4
Andrew Wilkins	2
Henry Stanton	2
Widow New	2
Elizabeth Penford	2
John Ranfeild	1
John Woolls	3
Nicholas Biggs	2
William Hasler	2
Widow Hasler	5
Widow Truddle	1
William Truddle	2
Nathaniel Biggs	2
Nicholas Swann	2
Edward Austen	2
John Holt	1
Mister John Hildropp	5
Widow Barnard	3
John Godwin	1
Thomas Rule	1
William Sabine	2
John Smither	3
Widow Ashton	1
Thomas Philipps	3
Edward Cockwell	2
John Person	4(a)
John Lee	4(a)
Mister John Barton	5(a)
Ralph Codwin	3(a)
hearths	142

Hearths not chargeable

Widow Warner	1
Widow Peake	2
John Uvedale	1
Henry Lunn	1
Edward Stocker	1
Mary Shannbler	2
Bridget Galler	1
Robert Ackland	1
Nicholas Elzey	1
Widow Pye	1
William Burrell	1
Widow Hamon	1
Christopher Pinchin	1
Widow Roy	1
John Hasling	1
Widow Faithorn	2
Thomas [ ]rd	2
Zacharias [ ]e	2
[ ]	1

Fol. 13v(i)

[ ]	1
[ ]	2
[ ]	1
[ ]	1
[ ] Wilkins	1
Henry [ ]	1
Widow Hatter	2
Henry Ackland	2
Henry Leonard	1
Widow Hickman	1
Old Newbery	1
Widow Appleford	1
Thomas Williams	1
Widow Merven	2
hearths	42

(a) void

52. CATISFIELD[1]

Hearths chargeable

Mister James Clerke	3
Nicholas Hammon	3
James Plascott	4
John Trodd	2
William Emery	3
John Overy	3
John Dawkins	1
John Garrett	1
John Princke	1
William Slawter	2
William Potter	1
Anthony Oyliffe	3
hearths	27

Hearths not chargeable

James Bluatt	2
Richard Harris	2
William Slawter	1
Robert Greatham	1
William Potter	1
Nicholas Hurte	2
Widow Eghill	1
Margaret Crowder	1
hearths	11

1. Cattesfeild

53. NORTH FAREHAM

Hearths chargeable

Thomas Hincksman	10
Thomas Hall	4
Thomas Spencer senior	1
John Woollgar	3
John Albeck	1
William Holt	2
William Francombe	1
William Luffder	2
hearths	24

Hearths not chargeable

Richard Spencer	1
John Bensteed	1
hearths	2

54. POKESOLE[1]

Hearths chargeable

Mister Riggs	7
Mister Roger Barton	6
John Osborne	1
Richard Walker	1
Ralph Paye	2
John Palmer	1
William Lyon	3

54. POKESOLE—*cont'd.*

William Route	3
John Heath	1

Fol. 13v(ii)

[ ]	3
[ ]	2
[ ]	3
[ ] Halt[ ]	[ ]
Richard [ ]te	3
Edward Sparfeild junior	3
William Wattson	3
Ralph Holt	1
John Whitinge	2
Edward Whitinge junior	2
Widow Allen	1
Francis Hawksworth	2
William Francombe	3
Thomas Attweeke	2
William Rolfe	3
Christopher Westbrooke	1
Widow Fry	2
John Fauchin	1
Robert Swann	1
Widow Stent	3
Mister Hedger	4
John Woodman gentleman	4
Widow New	1
Thomas Avery	1
hearths	79

Hearths not chargeable

Geoffrey Swann	1
Clement Mayle	1
Anthony Foster	1
Richard Woods	1
Widow Roker	1
hearths	5

1. Puxolls

The number of hearths chargeable within the hundred of Fareham is	499
Not chargeable	95

TITCHFIELD HUNDRED[1]

55. THE BARONEY[2]

Hearths chargeable

Mistress Catherine Lee widow	13
William Churcher	3
William Churcher	1
John Crowcher	3
Henry Lee	5
William Mersh	3
William Crowcher	1
John Cooper junior	3
Jo Crowcher	3
William White	3
Roger Beane	3
John Stoakes	7
John Osmond	3
William Houghton	3
John Osmond	3
Thomas Warner	1
Giles Leach	3
Widow Warner	1
Widow Browne	3
John Waller	3
Henry Randoll	2
John Cooper senior	6
John Cooper junior	4
Henry Legatt	2
John Mansell	2
hearths	84

Hearths not chargeable

Robert Cuttler	2
George Eldridge	1
William Skinner	1

Fol. 14r(i)

John Heyward	1
Widow Cumber	1
John Cumber	1
Widow Austin	1
Widow Luffe	1

William Oslinge	1
Francis Oslinge	1
John Petty	1
William Tryman	1
Widow Longe	1
hearths	14

1. Titchfeild Hundred
2. The Barroney

56. TITCHFIELD[1]

Hearths chargeable

George Mersh	57
More at Siddingworth	6
More at St. Margaret's	16
Mister Tille vicar	9
William Smith	7
Richard Smith	1
Thomas Sandford	1
Thomas Sandford	2
Luke Melsome	2
James Crowcher	4
John Hartwell	3
Richard Batt	3
William Mersh	3
William Swann	3
Widow Lee	3
Laurence Barber	3
Richard Longe	1
Andrew Batt	2
Thomas Plaskett	5
John Page junior	3
John Page senior	1
Isaac Williams senior	2
Richard Cripps	2
Thomas Cleverly	4
Peter Sone	2
Elizabeth Garrett widow	7
Henry Sabine	1
Francis Lunn	3
Peter Price	2
Alexander Spershott	3
William Hacke	5
William Grinedge	2
William Addams	3
William Houghton	3
Philip Houghton	4
Petronella Roy	2
Anthony Barry	2
Henry Roy	1[a]
James Hewett	2
Richard Philipps	5
Thomas Leadwell	2
Widow Scarvill	3
Elizabeth Peirce widow	3
William Angell	4
Christopher Foster	1
Roger Barrey	3
Thomas Mayle	1
John Spershott	2
John Mayle senior	6
Philip Boulton	3
Thomas Reymand	5
Thomas Reymand	5
Mister Henry Gaywood	3
Elizabeth Bensteed widow	4
Mister Hookes	3

Fol. 14r(ii)

Elizabeth Lomday	2
Peter Parsons	2
Thomas Heynes	1
Widow Dummer	1
Robert Bastone	2
Widow Goldfinch	1
John Woods	2
Isaac Williams	1
Robert Spershott	7
Matthew Bristleton	1
John Mayle	2
Richard Diaper	1
Richard Diaper	1
Mister Henry Poulter	5
Richard White	2
William Bryant	2
Robert Chestle	1
Widow Foster	4
Richard Addams	3
hearths	278

Hearths not chargeable

William Parsons	2

56. TITCHFIELD—*cont'd.*

William Godwin	1
William Trivett	1
William Glaspoole	1
William Littlefeild	1
Francis Lock	1
Widow Readall	1
Widow Sommers	2
Widow Ward	1
Edward Cooper	1
Edward Buttler	1
Abraham Bristowe	1
Thomas Wise junior	2
Sarah Bassett	2
John Godfrey	2
William Cleverly	1
Widow Leach	1
Widow Wright	1
William Parsons	2[(b)]
hearths	25

(a) 1 taken down
(b) burnt down
1. Titchfeild

57. SWANWICK

Hearths chargeable

John Freind	3
Francis Harmsworth	1
John Kinge	1
William West	2
John Russell	1
William Colson	1
Peter Price	1
William Gatterell	1
Stephen Waller	2
Widow Chamberlaine	4
Robert Wigge	2
John Hasteed	2
William Kinge	1
William Pewe	2
William Holt	3
Thomas Houghton	1
Nicholas Luffe	2
William Houghton	3
Edward Houghton	2
Philip Foster	2
John Waller	2
John Sutton	1

Fol. 14v(i)

William Feilder	1
Thomas Wigge	1
hearths	42

Hearths not chargeable

Richard Rule	1
Robert Waller	1
John Price	1
Thomas Dawes	1
Valentine Dawes	1
Widow Hollis	1
Widow Hooke	1
Henry Winter	1
William Sweete	1
John Sutton	1
Widow Cleverly	2
hearths	12

58. SARISBURY AND SOUTHBROOKE[1]

Hearths chargeable

John Richards	1
Thomas Wigge	3
Robert Courtnell	1
Giles Leach	3
John Trippett	1
William Knight	1
Richard Sharpe	1
Widow Harris	1
Richard Gatterill	1
Richard Colson	1
Walter Charker	1
Henry Saxey	2
Widow Higgins	2
John Pildrim	1
Widow Shaulle	1
Thomas Smith	3
William Oxford	3
hearths	27

Hearths not chargeable

Widow Trebeck	1
Widow Fletcher	1
Gilbert Millard	1

Sergeant Hamond	2
Thomas Knight	1
Robert Parker	1
hearths	7

1. Carisbery and Southbrooke

59. CROFTON

Hearths chargeable

Anthony Bensteed	4
Mary Clever	2
William Stares	5
Richard Foster	3
Richard White senior	1
Widow Bond	2
Widow Plaskett	3
Widow Bower	3
William White	3

Fol. 14v(ii)

Robert Duke	3
John Marks	1
Thomas Woolgar	4
Robert White	3
William Fry	1
Richard White	3
Thomas Brocke	3
William Gyourne	1
Giles Mann	1
Richard White	1
Peter Baker	2
William Wassell	2
Thomas Hewett	1
Henry Davis	2
Richard Alliston	1
Widow Plaskett	3
Widow Saxey	2
Richard Foster	3
Widow Plaskett	1
William White	1
hearths	65

Hearths not chargeable

Widow Hopley	1
Edward Wordlinge	1
Widow Hartford	2
Henry Davis	1
hearths	5

60. STUBBINGTON

Hearths chargeable

Richard Wilks	5
Thomas White	3
William White	4
Widow Crassman	2
William White	1
John Franklyn	2
William Missinge	4
Thomas Knight	3
William Rives	3
Widow Cosens	1
Richard Longe	2
Widow Shalle	1
Matthew Holt	1
William Stares	4
Laurence Arthur	3
Francis White	1
John Hyde	2
Richard Harwood	2
Edward Gaudey	1
hearths	45

Hearths not chargeable

John Nunn	1
hearths	1

61. PRALLINGWORTH[1]

Hearths chargeable

Stephen Coles	2
Richard Smart	3
William Reed	1
Robert Pinck	1
Richard Goddard	2[(a)]
Elizabeth Tribbick widow	3
John Wigge	2
Francis Waler	1
hearths	15

(a) 1 overcharged

1. Prolingworth

Fol. 15r(i)

62. MEON, BROWNWICH AND CHILLING[1]

Hearths chargeable

Roger Beane	10
John Gatterell	3
Thomas Smith	5
Andrew Mansbridge	2
Robert White	1
Henry Legatt	1
hearths	22

1. Meane, Brownewich and Chilbinge

63. LEE BRITTEN

Hearths chargeable

Luke Feilder	3
James Stares	4
John Seager	1
Richard Martin	2
hearths	10

Hearths not chargeable

William Waller	1
Thomas Franklyn	1
Robert Hewett	1
hearths	3

64. LEE MARKS

Hearths chargeable

William Pafford	3
Thomas Pafford	5
Edward Knight	3
John Legatt	3
Thomas Swann	3
hearths	17

Hearths not chargeable

John Cooper	1
John Bonner	1
hearths	2

65. CHARK[1]

Hearths chargeable

John Feilder	3
Widow Pafford	3
Thomas Cosins	1
Thomas Swettman	2
Richard Wilkes	3
Richard Binsteed	3
hearths	15

Hearths not chargeable

Richard Forder	2
Thomas Churcher	1
Robert Churcher	1
Thomas Eames	2
William Lock	1
Richard Caute	1
hearths	8

1. Charke

66. WEST HOOK[1]

Hearths chargeable

William Osmond	6
George Skinner	2
Joan Hearly widow	1
William Addams	3

Fol. 15r(ii)

Thomas Money	2
Richard Deepe	3
hearths	17

Hearths not chargeable

Richard Caute	1
John Bricknell	1
hearths	2

1. West Hooke

67. WICKHAM BOROUGH[1]

Hearths chargeable

Thomas Clement	4
William Dunce	5
John Person	4
Richard Cleverly	2
John Coote	6
John Smith	5
Richard Callaway junior	4
William Gilbert	1
Thomas Baker	2
Peter Greenegoe	1
John Cosens	1
Robert Dash	2

Henry Lunn	2
Stephen Smith	5
John Chaundler	3
Thomas Atkins senior	3
Edward Holt	1
John Lake	1
William Bensteed	1
Robert Smith	1
Thomas Coles	3
Richard Callaway senior	2
John Hewett senior	4
John Hurst	1
Catherine Eames widow	1
Henry Bedbrooke	1
William Horne	2
John Deane	2
Daniel Crocker	4
Sibyl Michell	3
hearths	77

Hearths not chargeable

Widow Hobbs	1
Tobias Holder	2
John Price	2
John Willmott	2
Mary Hurst widow	1
Dorothy Dyde widow	1
Joseph Smith	1
William Rowse	2
Ann Smith widow	1
John Hewett junior	2
Mary Goodyer widow	1
James Vildew	2
Ann Pawlter widow	2
William Frowde	1
Barnard Perryn	2
William Cosens	2
Joan Persons widow	1
William White	1
Thomas Persons	2
John Bensteed	1
Robert Dash junior	1
Ann Clever widow	1
hearths	32

Fol. 15v(i)

68. WICKHAM

Hearths chargeable

The Lady Uvedale	35
Humphrey Neale clerk	6
William Wither	4
Nicholas Hasler	4
Richard Boyes	2
William Mann	3
Stephen Stainsmore	1
William Knight	1
Richard Bensteed	2
Richard Bensteed	3
Stephen Pirce	4
Richard Bensteed	1
Robert Coles	5
Laurence Brodbridge	1
Thomas Fleete	3
Roger Seager	3
Thomas Bensteed	1
Edward Hurst	2
John Hewett senior	3
John Beane	1
Andrew Mills	1
John Hobbs	1
Robert Willmott	1
Thomas Grasswell	2
Thomas Attkins	2
Robert Franklyn	3
Margery Symes widow	2
William Hewett	3
hearths	100

Hearths not chargeable

Stephen Chacroft	1
Richard Chacroft	1
Widow Foster	1
Thomas Evans	1
Andrew Austin	1
Hills	1
Robert Mills	1
Widow Vinn	1
Widow Waller	1
John Parker	1
Bartholomew Churcher	1
Widow Hall	1

1. Wickham Burrough

68. WICKHAM—*cont'd.*

John Mowdy	1
Edward North	1
William North	1
James Whetter	1
John Caute	1
hearths	17

69. FUNTLEY

Hearths chargeable

Thomas Prowtinge	3
Nicholas Littlefeild	2
John Littlefeild	1
Robert Spershott	7
John Cleverly	1
William Barry	3
hearths	17

Fol. 15v(ii)

70. EAST HOOK[1]

Hearths chargeable

John Stokes	4
William Glaspoole	1
Thomas Money	1
Francis Greatham	1
John Baker	1
William Osmond	1
hearths	9

Hearths not chargeable

Robert Locke	1
Richard Caute	1
John Wastell	1
Widow Glasspool	1
John Kindley	1
Thomas Chidley	1
hearths	6

1. Easthooke

71. ROWNER

Hearths chargeable

Mister William Duncombe	3
Robert Stares	6
John Feilder	3
Robert Brooker	1[(a)]
John Bassett	2
Henry Knell	4
Thomas Brooker	1
Mister William Duncombe	3
Robert Hills	3
George Bearde	3
hearths	29

Hearths not chargeable

Thomas Butterly	2
Widow Spershott	1
hearths	3

The number of hearths chargeable within the hundred of Titchfield[1] is 870

Whereof for half a year 1[2]

Not chargeable 136

(a) 4 overcharged

1. Titchfeild
2. *Whole entry added later in a different hand*

MEONSTOKE HUNDRED

72. MEONSTOKE

Hearths chargeable

Doctor Mathew	9
George Louse	3
William Richards	3
Richard Budd	3
Nicholas Caute	3
Daniel Collins	4
William Wyatt	2
Henry Dash	1
Robert Addams	4
James Doncaster	3
Daniel Budd	3
John Collins	4
Henry Scott	3
Matthew Searle	3
William Lane	3
Richard Crosswell	2
Peter Linter	5

Fol. 16r(i)

Henry Bensteed	1
George Lane	3
Edward Hatrell	2
Henry Doncaster	3
Peter Hatch	3
John Attwood	2
Widow Dash	3
Richard Buxey	3
hearths	78

Hearths not chargeable

John Edwards	2
William Poynter	1
John Mourne	1
John West	1
Widow Maphy	2
John Dash	1
Robert Knight	2
Widow French	2
Robert Potter	2
Thomas Cheeseman	1
John Sherryer	1
Thomas Pincke	1
Thomas Abarrow	2
Peter Heath	1
Henry Bensteed	2
Henry Kempe	2
John Button	1
Thomas Newland	2
John Penycott	1
Mark Button	2
John Jourd	1
Thomas Graunt	2
Goodman Canner	1
John Crickwyre	1
Widow Parsons	1
Alice Ansell	2
Widow Hattrell	1
John Patterne	1
Richard Dyaper	1
John Hoare	1
Richard Daunce	2
John Attwood	2
Richard Reading	1
Samson Poore	1
Edward French	1
Edward Newman	2
hearths	51

73. WESTBURY AND PEAK[1]

Hearths chargeable

Richard Erewaker	12
William White	5
hearths	17

Hearths not chargeable

William Ayleward	1
hearths	1

1. Westbury & Peake

Fol. 16r(ii)

74. LISS ABBAS[1]

Hearths chargeable

Thomas Crosswell	4
Richard Bridger	4
Richard Aslett	3
Richard Ball	3
William Randall	3
Thomas Hersey	2
Richard Bridger	3
Nicholas Chicke	2
hearths	24

Hearths not chargeable

Henry Fey	1
George North	2
John Tipper	1
Thomas Aylinge	2
John Hodges	1
Edward Chacroft	1
Thomas Cover	1
Peter Randall	2
Robert Hounsom	2
Joseph Rickman	2
John Crowcher	1
Richard Woolgar	1
William Blake	1
William Crowcher	1
William Tipper	1
John Parker	2
Matthew Goble	1
hearths	23

1. Liss Abbes

75. WARNFORD[1]

Hearths chargeable

Thomas Neale esquire	20
Benjamin Burnard vicar	5
Ann Boneham widow	5
Andrew Mundey	6
Nicholas Smith	3
William Ratchell	6
Widow Cook	4
John Winter	3
Edward Wyatt	3
Henry Lunn	3
Mary Kettlewell	3
Robert Spencer	3
Thomas Edwards	3
William Bone	3
William Bodycotte	3
Widow Mundey	3
Robert Pincke	3
Martin Filler	2
Francis Goodyer	1
Ellen Garrett	1
William Woodly	1
Richard Pryor	1
Richard Wade	1
Matthew Stokes	8
Robert Othon	4
hearths	98

Fol. 16v(i)

Hearths not chargeable

Mary Farr	2
William Kinge	1
Henry Wiatt	2
Joan Bagine	2
Robert Streets	1
George Earle	1
John Okely	2
George Sutton	1
hearths	12

1. Warneford

76. SOBERTON[1]

Hearths chargeable

Mister Eyre	16
Nicholas Roy senior	3
Nicholas Roy junior	3
John Lyon	3
Robert Smith	4
Thomas Clever	3
Thomas Beane	1
Lionel Ryves	5
Thomas Hatch	7
Edward Nash	7
Richard Hawksworth	2
William Twynham	2
Henry Twynham	1
Widow Hobbs	2
John Roy	2
Richard Knight	3
Henry Richards	2
Daniel Mourne	1
William Edwards	5
Widow Wheatland	2
William Hasler	2
William Hatterell	3
Thomas Bagley	3
John Buttler	4
John Beane	3
John Hall	3
John Buttler senior	5
William Gisbye	2
Mistress Cole	5
Mister John Bright	8
John Goldsmith	4
Widow Arnold	3
Nicholas Russell	3
John Carman	1
Robert Hasler	1
Francis Pratt	5
William Roy junior	1
John Arnold	4
John Gisbye	2
Edward Russell senior	3
Edward Parford	2
Henry Nash	3
William Roy senior	2
Gregory Merriott	1
James Addams	2
Widow Merrett	3

Widow Russell	1
Widow Merriott	3
John Goldfinch	3
hearths	159

Fol. 16v(ii)

Hearths not chargeable

Bartholomew Blake	1
Robert Byam	2
Arthur Goodridge	1
Gregory Hooker	1
John Goldfinch	2
Thomas Murrell	2
Robert Roode	1
John Mowdey	1
John Lowmer senior	1
Widow Wyatt senior	1
Richard Beamon	2
John Beacham	1
John Harford	1
William Cleverly	1
Widow Brewer	1
Widow Wyatt junior	1
John Lowmer junior	1
Widow Hewett	1
William Barber	1
William Arthur	1
Widow Todd	1
Widow Cames	1
Jasper Gregory	1
John Morrack	1
Widow Norris	1
Philip Parford	1
John Knight	1
Widow Allen	1
Widow Courtnell	1
hearths	32

1. Subberton

77. BURWELL

Hearths chargeable

Mister Symons	3
Robert Bower	3
Richard Tribb	3
Thomas Fleete	3
Widow Knight	3
Walter Collins	3
Joan Bensteed	3
Richard Ringe	4
Nicholas Foster	3
Edward Attwood	2
Henry Nosse	2
Widow Ringe	2
John Eyles	2
William Wootheridge	3
hearths	39

Hearths not chargeable

John Barfoot	1
Thomas Parsons	2
John Littlefeild	2
Richard Newman	1
John Baker	1
John Sone	2
William Foster	1
Elizabeth Hunt	1
John Foster	2
Richard Rickman	1
Richard Fuller	1

Fol. 17r(ii)

Elizabeth Selling	1
Barbara Pryor	1
Thomas Foster	2
Humphrey Johnson	1
Stephen Heather	1
Anthony Richman	1
Widow Cleverly	2
hearths	24

78. CORHAMPTON

Hearths chargeable

John Stewkely esquire	17
William Collins esquire	12
Mister William Fisher	6
Widow Fennell	1
Widow Harwood	1
Edward Foster	2
Arthur Taylor	3
Gilbert Caute	3
Widow Wyatt	3
Robert Wyatt	2
John Dyaper	2

78. CORHAMPTON—*cont'd.*

Ambrose Harfeild	1
Edward Sherryer	4
hearths	57

Hearths not chargeable

John Snuggs	1
William Reading	2
Henry White	1
hearths	4

79. EAST HOE

Hearths chargeable

Mister John Styles	11
John Fleete	3
Thomas Chrisbye	2
John Hockely	3
John Paddock	1
John Ballard	1
James Glaspoole	1
Thomas Saunders	1
John Cooper	3
Thomas Hellier	3
John Edwards	3
John Pratt	1
Daniel Arnold	1
Widow Russell	3
hearths	37

Hearths not chargeable

John Dyaper	1
Thomas Collins	1
Philip Richards	1
William Arnold	1
John Franklyn	1
hearths	5

The number of hearths chargeable within the hundred of Meonstoke is	509
Not chargeable	152

Fol. 17r(ii)

BOSMERE HUNDRED[1]

80. WARBLINGTON

Hearths chargeable

The Parsonage	7
William Pannell	4
Richard Trimm	3
Roland Wingham	2
Richard Oliver	3
William Andrews	2
Richard Martin	1
Thomas Sone	4[(a)]
Bartholomew Sone	2
Mister William Taylor	7
Mister John Bexhill	5
Widow Wingham	2
Thomas Richards	3
Philip Pannell	3
Thomas Browne	1
Richard Martin	3
Edward Oughton	1
John Austin	2
Richard Goodeve	2
Thomas Cooke	3
John Oliver	3[(b)]
hearths	63

Hearths not chargeable

Thomas Smith	1
William Hammon	1
John Hammon	1
Thomas Ligge	1
Widow Browne	1
Nicholas Burrell	1
William Mattocke	1
John Harris	2
Edward Fry	1
Widow Brooke	2
Matthew Marriner	2
hearths	14

(a) 1 taken down
(b) void
1. Bosmeere

81. EMSWORTH

Hearths chargeable

Thomas Wheeler	2
John Godfrey	2
Jospeh Longe	2
Jacob Hearsey	2
Thomas Tille	2
John Headger	3

Humphrey Brett	3
James Spriggs	3
Thomas Boyes	2
Thomas Smith	3
John Wingham	3
Anthony Smith	2
John Legatt	2
William Butcher	2
John Wheeler	2
John Hewett	1
John Tille	2
Henry Burrell	1
Widow Smith	2
Widow Wheeler	1
Richard Chapman	2
Nicholas Randell	2
William Spriggs senior	2
Robert Hedger	3

Fol. 17v(i)

William Baily	2
John Moore	2
John Smith	2
William Pragnell	5
John Legatt	1
Richard Hedger	1
Edward Rowland	1
hearths	65

Hearths not chargeable

Widow Woolgar	1
Clement Barnes	1
Thomas Wheeler	1
Thomas Turkett	1
William Palmer	1
Thomas Aslett	1
Francis Smith	1
Richard Fines	2
William Moore	1
Simon Spriggs	1
Jacob Tribb	1
Thomas Manser	1
Thomas Chapman	1
Henry Spriggs	1
Thomas Goodfaith	2
William Lane	2
Nicholas Holloway	1
William Pay	1
William Allen	1
Elias Hills	1
William Spriggs	1
hearths	24

82. NEWTIMBER[1]

Hearths chargeable

Mister Hyde	5
Thomas Sharp	2
Richard Coles	2
Thomas Lambe	2
hearths	11

Hearths not chargeable

John Harris	1
Thomas Prowtinge	1
Daniel Barwick	2
hearths	4

1. Nuttimber

83. SOUTH HAYLING[1]

Hearths chargeable

Nicholas Perringe	6
Nicholas Fry	1
Spinola Dumper	3
Thomas Sone	1
Thomas Perkins	1
William Longe	3
Thomas Vengon	2
James Callaway	1
Andrew Revell	3
Richard Rogers	1
Edward Harte	1
John Carpenter	3
William Smith	3
Thomas Grigge	4
John Carpenter	1

Fol. 17v(ii)

Robert Carter	5
Thomas Vengen	3
John Michell	3
John Guy	3
Robert Baker	1
William Bowles	1
John Whittley	1

83. SOUTH HAYLING—*cont'd.*

John Milles	2
John Browne	3
William Pepson	3
John Browne	1
Edward Langford	2
Philip Bowles	1
Thomas Fawkner	1
Thomas Guy	1
William Rouse	1
William Newman	2
William Newman	1
Nathaniel Sparks	1
William Bowles	4
hearths	74

Hearths not chargeable

William Kemp	1
John Biskin	1
Widow Frogbord	1
Thomas Manser	1
Richard Mosse	1
James Callaway	1
hearths	6

1. Haylinge South

84. NORTH HAYLING[1]

Hearths chargeable

Richard Fisher	8
Thomas Pepson	3
Andrew Colepis	2
John Tombs	1
Thomas Roman	4
Thomas Millard	2
William Pay	6
Thomas Perkins	2
Richard Clever	4
Richard Perkins	3
Richard Belston	3
Andrew Bucknell junior	1
William Pepson	2
Thomas Seire	3
John Reade	1
Widow Rogers	1
Guy Mersh	1
John Almer	2
Francis Browne	4
Andrew Bucknell senior	4
John Blanchard	3
Mister Andrew Revell	1[a]
Arthur Voake	5
William Newman	1
Nicholas Aylinge	1
Widow Newman	3
Stephen Pay	1
John Atherley	2
Thomas Perkins	1
Thomas Mew	2
Widow Backshall	3
Widow Higgins	3
Anthony Farly	3
John Goldinge	3
Thomas Bryant	1
hearths	90

Fol. 18r(i)

Hearths not chargeable

John Edwards	2
Widow Voake	1
Clement Millard	1
John Biggs	2
hearths	6

The number of hearths chargeable within the hundred of Bosmere[2] is	303
Not chargeable	54
The number of hearths chargeable within the whole division of Portsdown is	3278
Not chargeable	1432

(a) 1 taken down
1. Haylinge North
2. Bosmeere

Fol. 19r(i)

NEW FOREST DIVISION[1]

NEW FOREST HUNDRED[1]

85. SOUTH BADDESLEY[2]

Hearths chargeable

Henry Philpott esquire	8

Christopher Carde	2
Kemberlin King	2
John Barnes	2
William Henning	1
Thomas Fisher	2
William King	1
Thomas Cosens	3
Henry Corbin	1
John Jordan	1
Richard Storke	1
Henry Pocock	2
Henry Wright	1
Richard Moore	1
John Pope	4
William Haynes	3
Richard Plowman	1
Barnard Collens	3
Thomas Burgis	1
James Braford	4
Mister Richard Sampson	6
Christopher Stovell	2
Edward Samber	1
John Burgis	1
hearths	54

Hearths not chargeable

Thomas Wright	1
William Hall	1
John Carter	1
Mary Cumell	1
John Card	1
William Fisher	1
John Mellendey	1
Widow Waters	1
Widow James	1
John Penney	1
William Lucas	1
William Baily	1
William Cuffley	1
hearths	13

1. New Forrest Division/Hundred
2. South Badsley

86. PILLEY AND WARBORNE

Hearths chargeable

Henry Bromfeild esquire	15
John Drew	9
Samuel Hoyle	3
Edward Gasteed	2
Arthur Watts	3
Timothy Long	1
John Carter	1
John Tovey	1
Henry Jones	1
William Rashbridg	2
Robert Amon	2
Abraham Watts	1
Farden Watts	1
James Plowman	3
Grace Rickman	2
Edward Reeves	1
John Harris	1
Christopher Caplin	1
Barnard Clements	1
Martin Saunders	1

Fol. 19r(ii)

Thomas Mifflin	1
Edward Reeves	4
Thomas Joyce clerk	5
Ann Marks	1
Peter Gosney	1
William Barges	1
Widow Gost	1
Martha Watts widow	1
hearths	67

Increased 13

Hearth not chargeable

Widow Egger	1
William Hotton	1
Widow Ayles and James Atkins	2
Richard Waterman	1
Widow Semor	1
Henry Semor	1
Widow Henning	1
Richard Rolfe	1

86. PILLEY AND WARBORNE *—cont'd.*

John Lake	1
Widow Slydle	1
hearths	11

87. BUTSASH, HARDLEY AND IPLEY[1]

Hearths chargeable

Ipley Farm	2
John Bradley	1
Butsash[2] Farm	7
Zacharias Steele	1
Andrew Harvie	3
William Cross	2
Richard Dereman	1
John Collis	1
Charles Lyne	1
Widow Collins	1
Henry Nash	2
Thomas Parsons	1
William Heyward	2
Mister Osey	2
John Brooks	1
Robert Shepherd	1
Thomas Steele	1
Richard Cross	2
Thomas Edwards	4
William Crowcher	1
Nicholas Hebert	1
Richard Shepherd	1
hearths	39

Increased 7

Hearths not chargeable

Edward Lowman	1
Widow Bennett	1
John Osman	1
Widow Frolick	1
John Wademan	1
Widow Wademan	1
Widow Freind	1
William White	1
Widow Deekeman	1
Thomas Eatton	1
Robert Bridger	1
Christopher Trimer	1
James Osey	1
Thomas Tefferd	1
Thomas Adams	1

Fol. 19v(i)

John Sewell	1
William Osey	1
Laurence Foster	1
Widow Newne	1
hearths	19

1. Buttesash, Hardly and Ipley
2. Buttesash

88. HOLBURY AND LANGLEY[1]

Hearths chargeable

Mister William Stanley	9
Henry Knight	3
Robert Smith	1
Richard Foster	4
Edward Cuttler	1
Richard Gates	1
James Wakeford	2
John Ryder	6
Henry Coombs	2
John Pinhorne	3
Nicholas Barnard	1
Robert Barnes	1
Cornelius Macco	2
Henry Coombs	1
Robert Lambert	1
Robert Lutter	1
hearths	39

Hearths not chargeable

William Dibden	1
Coxes children	1
Roger Barfoott	1
Robert Warden	1
Christopher Hobbs	1
hearths	5

1. Holbery & Langley

89. BROCKENHURST[1]

Hearths chargeable

Whitley Bridge Lodge	2
Denney[2] Lodge	5

Sir George Carew knight	4
Nicholas Barling	2
Mister Thomas Fitz James	8
John Taplin	2
William Freind	1
Mary Lawrence	2
Richard Penney	1
William Fassett	1
Thomas Williams	1
Widow Cooper	1
Widow Smith	1
Widow Ford	1
John More	1
Thomas Burton senior	2
John Newen	2
Widow Roades	2
Thomas Gretham	1
John Ames	1
Henry Browne	3
William Draper	2
Mister Browne	6
John Lalle	1
Edward Rowland	2
Jane Hobbs	1
Elizabeth Gretham	3
Henry Williams	1
Widow Norton	1
John Paynter	2

Fol. 19v(ii)

Matthew Reynolds	2
John Pillian	1
George Wren	1
William Lucas	3
Thomas Early	3
Richard Roe	3
Mister Michaell	4
Philip More	2
William Hall	1
Thomas Burton junior	2
Richard Stropp	1
Edward Batten	1
John Attwood	3
William Furner	1
Mister William Knapton	11
Widow Powell	1
Joan Hobbs	1
Mister Lukenour Mills	6
John Farthing	1
John Smith	1
Robert Crooke	2
Richard Knapton	3
John Bisse	3
John Oliver	1
Thomas Browne	1
Hercules Masters	1
Thomas Vinson	1
Richard Draper	6
Richard Smith	1
Mister Robert Tuchin	1
Michael Rositer	1
Widow Tarver	1
Mister Bartholomew Knapton	4
Alexander Buttler	1
John Bleatham	2
Roger Hollier	6
Woodhouse	4
Joan Rossiter	1
Edward Bond	1
William Dundee	1
Philip Rossiter and William Furner }	1
Thomas Baker	1
Henry Baker	1
Albin Knapton	4
hearths	162

Increased 21

Hearths not chargeable

John Tarver junior	1
Thomas Stevens	1
William Ames	1
An[3] Wilson	1
William Mitchell	1
John Ward	1
Richard Burte	1
Richard Beale	1

89. BROCKENHURST—*cont'd.*

William Beale and Widow Beale	2
John Tarver senior	1
William Smith	1
Widow Drake	2
Thomas Ames	1
Walter Newman	1
John Strawbridg	1
John Cooper	1
Jane Baker	1
Widow Warwick	1
Elizabeth Russell	1
Widow Deepe	1
William Penny	2
hearths	24

1. Brockenhurst
2. Dinney
3. *Probably* Andrew, *maybe* Anthony *or* Ann

Fol. 20r(i)

90. CADLAND AND STANSWOOD[1]

Hearths chargeable

Mister Andrew Osey	6
Mister Edward Fleet	5
Richard Combs	5
Richard Strode	1
William Andrewes	1
Mister Thomas Lord	8
Mister Peter Peale	4
Robert Terry	2
William Hunt	2
John Lawes	3
Simon Purchase	1
Peter Browne	4
Thomas Holebrooke	3
Richard Andrews	1
Henry Combs	1
John Ryder	1
Richard Legatt	3
Elizabeth Christian	1
Thomas Downer	1
hearths	53

Increased 14

Hearths not chargeable

Ann Elkins	1
hearths	1

1. Cadland & Staneswood

91. BATTRAMSLEY AND WOOTTON[1]

Hearths chargeable

Mister Henry Goddard	4
Robert Fry	4
James Rossiter	3
Thomas Attlane	5
Nicholas Lambert	3
Richard Goste	3
Richard Goste	1
Richard Stote	2
Richard Stote	1
John Chase	4
William Spett	3
Thomas Hopgood	1
Henry Robins	1
Thomas Younges	1
John Thomas	1
John Toms	1
Roger Paynes	1
Peter Penny	1
hearths	40

Decreased 1

Hearths not chargeable

James Warwick	1
Edward Barnes	1
Thomas Wyatt	1
Thomas Smith	1
John Urry	1
William Day	1
Nicholas Tarver	1
Nicholas Burrant	1
Robert Tuffy	1
hearths	9

1. Batremsly & Wootten

92. EXBURY AND LEPE[1]

Hearths chargeable

William Colevrden	6
Francis Stowell	5

Richard Implefeild	2
Francis Lawson	2
Richard Cole	2
Widow Smith	2

Fol. 20r(ii)

John Flye	1
Henry Sish	4
John Hayward	1
John King	3
William Cole	3
Widow Hitchman	3
Edward Stone	2
James Taylor	3
David Wiseman	1
Thomas Salter	1
Andrew Kerrill	1
Henry Stevens	1
Robert Draper	1
Roland Deane	2
Robert Rooke	2
Arthur Gibbs	2
William Bannister	4
Edward Moone	3
Matthew Wilson	1
John Moone	4
Thomas Warne	2
William Bannister	1
John Willmett	4
Benjamin Whitehead	4
David Mills	1
Henry Stemp	4
Edward Baldrey	1
Bartholomew White	1
hearths	80

Increased 11

Hearths not chargeable

John Stowell	1
George Frizer junior	1
George Frizer senior	1
Richard Stevens	1
Richard Perkinson	1
Widow Woodford	1
Philip Hebbe	1
Charles West	1
Joan Keepen	1
Mary Burges	1
William Michell	1
Cuthbert Deluke	1
William Pye	1
Thomas Tee	1
Patience Shepherd	1
Philip Pitt	1
Robert Coleman	1
Widow Cole	1
hearths	18

1. Exbury & Leape

93. CANTERTON AND FRITHAM

Hearths chargeable

Mister Thomas Stanter	1
Mister Thomas Smith	2
Thomas Lock	4
Edward Penton	1
Richard Andrews	4
Mary Andrews	1
Matthew Warde	1
Mister Francis Perkins	5
Alice Lock	1
Walter Coleman	3
John Deale	4
Richard Iremonger	1
John Dove	3
Cosine Reeves	4

Fol. 20v(i)

Mister Andrew Twitchen	6
Ann Archer	2
John Deale	1
Mister Swithun Wells	3
Richard Edwards	2
William Hobbs	2
Robert Burcher	1
Nicholas Hatch	1
William Pincke	1
Benjamin Edwards	3
Robert Andrews	1
George Gauntlett	1
Henry Reade	2
James Eburne	2

93. CANTERTON AND FRITHAM—*cont'd.*

John Barebone	1
Mister Edward Tabut	3[(a)]
John Aldridge	6
James Barrow	3
Richard Bassett	5
John Emblen	3
Edward Yeoman	1
Henry Kinge	1
John Dible	3
Alice Compton	2
William Pinson	1
William Coyte	3
Widow Hoare	1
Thomas Vennor	3
William Hooker	2
Mister Clerke	2
hearths	103

Increased 24

Hearths not chargeable

John Yeoman	1
Henry Reade	1
John Taylor	1
Mary Warden	1
John Hix	1
Widow Warden	1
Clement Hobbs	1
Widow Hatcher	1
John Aldridg	1
Francis Michells	1
Widow Wild	1
John Laughtry	1
Roger Backton	1
William Gregory	1
Widow Andrews	1
John Webb	1
Clement Goast	1
William Trunby	1
Margaret Goare	1
John Edwards	1
Henry Edwards	1
Widow Comley	1
Widow Jackman	1
John Mills	1
Widow Bell	1
John Coles	1
John Morles	1
Elizabeth People	1
Widow Barling	1
Widow Kimber	1
hearths	29

(a) for half a year

Fol. 20v(ii)

94. MINSTEAD[1]

Hearths chargeable

William Royall clerk	5
Robert Cull	4
Richard Hurst	3
William Olding	1
Christopher Stride	1
William Cull	1
John Burden	1
Thomas Soafe	2
Drew Penton	1
John Henvist	1
William Stride	1
Richard Heyes	1
Widow House	2
George House	3
James Philipps	3
Robert Hobbs	1
William Rogers	1
Widow Stride	2
John Pearce	1
John Martin	1
Joseph Stride	1
Clement Morris	4
Widow Lamb	1
Widow Wright	1
John Weshman junior	1
Widow Ansell	1
Thomas King clerk	2
Mister Arthur Jeford	6
Charles Heyward	1
hearths	55

Decreased 2

Hearths not chargeable

Thomas Blake	1

Widow Perkins	1
Thomas Martin	1
Robert Soafe	2
John Reade	1
Andrew Warne	1
Thomas Masey	1
Thomas Price	1
John Right junior	1
John Bromfeild	1
Robert Peckham	1
Thomas Peckham	1
Thomas Buckley	1
Edward Righte	1
Robert Whitehorne	1
John Meshman senior	1
Widow Osmand	1
John Pearle senior	1
John Pearle junior	1
John Stride	1
Widow Spranger	1
Widow Moulton	1
Richard Godden senior	1
John Bargen	1
John Perryer	1
Thomas Godden	1
John Wright senior	1
Thomas Wolfe	1
William Wright	1
Widow Slaskett	1
Widow Heyes	1
Widow Sands	1
Widow Michell	1
Richard Godden junior	1
John Parker	1
hearths	37

1. Minsteed

Fol. 21r(i)

95. BARTLEY REGIS AND LONDON MINSTEAD[1]

Hearths chargeable

Richard Goddard esquire	10
Thomas Knapton	1
William Rogers	1
Thomas Newman	1
Thomas Lovell	2
Edward Hammon	4
Widow Wyatt	2
William Stride	1
William Lansdall	2
Francis Courtney	6
Thomas Ingepenn	2
William Rogers and Cox	3
Robert Over	1
John Chatter	1
William Renger	1
Mistress Browne	2
Robert Hiscock	1
Thomas Cowdry	2
William Gayne	1
John Purcas senior	1
William Powlett esquire	5
John Purcas junior	1
Thomas James	2
William Hooker	3
hearths	62

Increased 5

Hearths not chargeable

John Bidlecomb	1
John Light	1
William Besant	1
Henry Higgens	1
Edward Shepherd	1
Ann Pyball	1
Widow Bulbeck	1
Widow Osmand	1
Blaks cottages	1
Widow Lingham	1
Robert Dible	1
John White	1
Jane Luffe	1
Matthew Wolfe	1
Hugh Pyball	1
hearths	15

1. Barly Regis & London Minsteed

96. LYNDHURST[1]

Hearths chargeable

Sir George Carew	4

96. LYNDHURST—*cont'd.*

George Redney esquire	9
Robert Lambert esquire	9
Mister Edward Fitchett	5
Barnard Legith	5
Thomas Graunt	3
George Brextone	2
William Waterman	4
Widow Phillips	1
William Bright	3
John Willcox	9
John Batchelor	1
Benjamin Barrowe	1
John Gaskin	1
John Hogges	1
Widow Brokenshufe	3
Arthur Harding	1
William Carpenter	2
Thomas Leece	1
James Elcombe	5
Widow Barger	2
Nicholas Phillips	1
Philip Pocock	1
John Morrice	2
John Mortimore	2

Fol. 21r(ii)

John Bucle	4
Henry Bucle	2
Thomas Hall	3
James Philipps	1
Edward Welch	1
William Pocock	3
Richard Game	1
John Gill	1
George Hedger	1
James Harding	1
James Baker	3
John Creed	1
James Price	2
Robert Andrewes	3
John Starks	1
William Thorne	1
John Pocock	1
Edward Stride	1
Henry Batchelor	2
Richard Gaskin	1
John Stote	3
Mister John Jennings	2
Ralph Carter	3
Ralph Buckler	1
The King's House	13
hearths	143

Hearths not chargeable

James Bayly	1
Elton Waterman	1
Richard Packe	1
Widow Tuckle	1
Widow Henvy	2
John Risbrige	1
Widow Ivy	1
Samuel Penfull	1
Henry Randoll	1
John Knight	1
John Pusse	1
Anthony Waterman	1
Henry New	1
John Goff	1
Widow Shilly	1
Widow Kimber	1
Widow Batchelor	1
Edward Shaw	1
William Hancocke	1
John Mooten	1
William Pope	1
hearths	22

1. Lindhurst

97. GODSHILL

Hearths chargeable

Thomas Gray	5
Henry Good	1
William Rooke	5
Henry Herrington	1
Bartholomew Trickhup	1
Henry Froth	1
Thomas Randoll	1
George Coles	3
Richard Pearce	1
Thomas Ealfes	1
Nicholas Percy	1

Thomas Tomer	5
John Scovell	1
Ambrose Broadshaw	1
Widow Whitingstall	1
John Philpott	1
Widow Norris	1
William Sandford	1
William Browne	1

Fol. 21v(i)

Widow Miller	3
Edward Rogers	1
William Whittington	1
Samuel Foule	1
John Saunders	3
Broomy Lodge	5
John Pitt	1
Nicholas Scotcher	1
Ogden Rooke	4
Henry Cosier	1
Henry Rooke	1
Richard Philpott	2
William Dimock	1
Edward Amy	1
John Hyde	1
Widow Bright	3
John Gibbs	2
Thomas Lockett	1
Widow Amey	1
John Weilder	1
hearths	69

Increased 13

Hearths not chargeable

Samuel Gossoe	1
William Witt	1
Thomas Kimber	1
John Kimber	1
Widow Downer	1
Thomas Percy	1
Joseph Eldridg	1
Richard Plinnell	1
John Curtis	1
Nicholas Knightingall	1
William Newman	1
Richard Collens	1
William Scott	1
Widow Ingram	1
Widow Harris	1
Widow Stephens	1
John Stent	1
George March	1
Walter Elkins	1
Thomas Hinton	1
hearths	20

98. BURLEY

Hearths chargeable

George Bright	8
Mister William Batten	6
John Thayne	1
John Godden	1
Thomas Reeks	1
William Rooke	1
Henry Thorne	2
Edward Lynne	2
Thomas Randoll	3
Robert Wells	1
Joseph Coffin	2
William Mist	1
Richard Pitt	1
Jane Bannister	1
Benjamin Mathewes	1
John Younges	1
Edward Burtt	1
Alexander Purchase	1
William Adey	1
Widow Stronge	3
Widow Garrett	3
Henry Swetingham	1
John Warne	1
Henry Etheridg	2
Mary Tarver	3

Fol. 21v(ii)

Christopher Bidlecombe	3
William Adye	2
Edward Pitt	1
William Bence	1
Hugh Tiller	1
Farmer Reeks	1
Anthony Fish	1

98. BURLEY—*cont'd.*

William Etheridge	2
Widow Oliver	1
Thomas Randoll	1
William Reeks	2
Widow Tarry	3
Sarah Brixey	2
James Randoll	2
Christopher Henvill	1
Thomas Rogers	1
William Bidlecombe	1
Widow Younges	1
Elizabeth Waterman	1
hearths	76

Increased 14

Hearths not chargeable

Robert Hellier	1
Richard Buckler	1
Jane Warne	1
John Wiseman	1
Richard Burt	1
Widow Woods	1
Nicholas America senior	1
Nicholas America junior	1
John Woods	1
Thomas Chase	1
William Saunders	1
James Osborne	1
Henry Watts	1
Widow Robbins	1
John Randoll	1
Batten Selfe	1
Peter Blake	1
Widow Wiseman	1
Widow Kyles	1
William Blake	1
hearths	20

99. HYTHE[1]

Hearths chargeable

Benjamin Durrent	3
William Bond	2
Widow Howe	1
Mister Lynne	2
John Serrell	1
Edward Harvy	2
Robert Swayne	3
John Cull	2
John Bradley	4
Richard Abraham	6
Alexander Bornett	2
Nicholas Powell	2
John Alsford	1
Alexander Alsford	1
Thomas Withers	3
hearths	38

Hearths not chargeable

William Withers	1
Stephen Smith	1
John Zelman	1
William White	1
John Dickman	1

Fol. 22r(i)

Christopher Wademore	1
Peter Cull	1
John Harvye	2
Stephen Wheeler	1
Nicholas Potter	1
Richard Tanner	2
Michael Blatch	1
William Luff	2
Edward Evins	1
William Wheeler	2
Joan Sentilo	1
John Dickman	1
Richard Merricott	1
Samuel James	1
hearths	23

The number of hearths chargeable within the hundred of New Forest[2] is 1056

Not chargeable 282

1. Heath
2. New Forrest

RINGWOOD HUNDRED

100. RINGWOOD

Hearths chargeable

Robert Bound	3
Humphrey Bond	2
Widow Chatter	1
Barnard Gold	1
Roger Swayne	1
Christopher Buckland	2
William Chamell	3
Richard Short	2
Joseph Warne	1,
John Stote	2
Mister Philip Percivall	10
Mister Laurence Horne	2
Mister Thomas Harwood	3
Richard Slader	2
Edward Stallard	1
William Bampton	12
Tristram Turgis	3
William Welch	5
Richard Bond	6
John Lynne junior	9
William Lyne	2
Henry Browne	2
James Pope	9
William Buckland	4
John Ayles	6
Arthur Blanchard	6
Thomas Blanchard	4
Thomas Hickman	2
Stephen Martin junior	2
Thomas Bull	3
Martin Taylor	4
Henry Whitemersh	1
James Phetiplace	1
Robert Miller junior	2
Josias Melledge	1
Henry Stote	5
Edward Phetiplace	5
Thomas Elmes	1
Richard Belom	5
John North	2
Robert Miller senior	4
Benjamin Highmore	4

Fol. 22r(ii)

James Willis gentleman	4
John Hill	2
Francis Turgis	6
Felix Wixell	1
John Battson	3
James Ayles	1
Ralph Miller	1
John Wild	2
John Benster	2
William Belbin	2
Stephen Lane	2
Thomas Lane	1
Mary Lane	1
Sarah Godding	1
Hugh Lyne	2
James Hunt	1
James Warne	2
Widow Hattrell	4
John Warne	2
John Barter junior	2
John Lyne senior	1
William Follett	2
Robert Budden	1
Stephen Martin senior	2
Samuel Batter	1
Francis Bull	6
Barnard Coles	1
Peregrine Forrest	1
John Forrest	1
Holden Lyne	2
Philip Chandler	2
Christopher Persons	2
Widow James	1
Joseph Drover	1
Philip Scapland	2
John Street	6
Joseph Welch	2
John Lyne	1
Robert Browne	2
John Bloss	3
Richard Garrett	2
John Warne	1
Thomas Richman	1
Thomas James	2
Thomas Clasby	1

100. RINGWOOD—*cont'd.*

John Lansdale	3
Thomas Coachman	2
Gowen Tremany	5
James Belbin	1
Robert Mesher	1
Anthony Burt	1
John Keepen	1
Richard Thomas junior	2
John Pinhorne	1
Nicholas Streete	4
John Miller	1
John Clasbye	1
Reynold Forrest	5
Hugh Viveash	3
John Iveman	3
John Warne	1
Widow Warne	1
John Livelong	2
Edward Pritchett	2
Widow Stoakes	1
Thomas Lyne	4

Fol. 22v(i)

Widow Iveman	4
Peter Tremaine	1
Widow Batson	2
William Borne	4
William Sibley	1
Philip Prince	1
John Pewsey	1
Alexander Randoll	1
Robert Richman	1
Philip Bence	1
John Melledge	1
William Beasent	1
Anthony Holloway	1
William Etheredg	3
James Gardner	1
Thomas Coffen	2
John Etheridg	1
William Ayles	1
Thomas Clasby	1
Richard Aldridge	4
Richard White	2
Widow Hobbs	1
Timothy[1] Ayles	2
John Whitemersh	1
James Keepen[2]	1
Anthony Wilkins	3
Richard Beachman	1
Richard Brixey	1
Widow Clasby	1
Widow Read	3
Richard Whitmersh	1
Henry Aldridge	1
Widow Bower	1
Widow Lovedy	1
Origen Cottman	3
Thomas Cleaver	2
John Sangar	1
Richard Richman	1
Joseph Coles	4
Richard Livelong	1
Richard Cosh	2
Mary Crisben	2
John Bidlecombe	3
Christopher Brixey	3
Henry Lyne	3
Mister William Trevise	3
Thomas Cheffen	1
John Ayles senior	1
John Ayles junior	2
Stephen Ayles	1
Mistress Clifford	3
Nicholas Ayles	1
John Harris	1
Christopher Cobb	1
John Badripp	1
Mister Samuel Percivall	5
Hugh Slidle	1
Durnford	1
John Newport	1
John Clever	1
James Poole	1
Nicholas Masters	1
Widow Wilkins	1
Widow Zealy	1
Roger Bamister	2
Robert Wixell	1
John Browne	1

Fol. 22v(ii)

Widow Webb	1
Widow King	1
Widow Browne	1
Reynold Batten	2
Martin Bence	1
George Daniell	3
hearths	413

Increased 44

Hearths not chargeable

Widow Harding	1
Joan Swayne	1
Thomas Richards	1
Widow Welsted	1
John Wixell	1
Christopher Bull	1
Vincent Bidden	1
Widow Abbott	1
Thomas Bevis	1
Robert Fryer	1
Widow Martyn	1
Richard Sweetland	1
Richard Hobbs	1
Widow Woodman	1
John Barten	1
John Budden	1
Widow Lane	2
Thomas Mathews	1
Henry Wilkins	1
Widow Okeford	1
Widow Elliott	1
Henry Lyne	1
John Inges	1
Richard Thomas	1
William Peckham	1
Widow Hattrell	1
Thomas Moule	1
Henry Baily	1
Widow Bether	1
John Tapp	1
Jane Cooke	1
Walter Godden	1
Widow Freke	1
Henry Bidle	1
William Tapp	1
William Bunch	1
Hugh Harris	1
William Adcock	1
Henry Woodman	1
Widow Namier	1
Widow Poole	1
Robert Dawe	1
Thomas Streete senior	1
Thomas Streete junior	1
John Carter	1
Hobbs house	1
Thomas Hinton	1
Chappels house	1
Thomas Browne	1
John Wooll	1
William Gage	1
Martin Gates	1
John Currell	1
John Wooll	1
Nicholas Thomas	1
Thomas Martin	1
Richard Elcock	2
Henry Livelong	2
Walters	1
Thomas Collins	1
Peter Bursey	2
hearths	64

1. Thynothy
2. *Originally written* Repen *and altered*

Fol. 23r(i)

101. COLLEGE TITHING[1]

Hearths chargeable

Doctor James Saunders	11
Anthony Brixey	3
Roger Swayne	3
Mary Allen widow	3
Ambrose Forde	6
Christopher Garrett	5
Richard Richman	3
Ann Gosse	3
Hugh Warne	3
John Warne	3
Nicholas Ockford	3
Thomas Melledge	2

101. COLLEGE TITHING—*cont'd.*

Mister John Slade	8
John Chrisben	1
George Chambers	1
hearths	58

Hearths not chargeable

John Luckeham	1
Joan Lake	1
Catherine Angood	1
hearths	3

1. Colledge Tithinge

102. HARBRIDGE[1]

Hearths chargeable

Mistress Bridget Wykes	6
Mister Robert Kinge	5
John Bampton	3
William Cosens	3
Robert Whittington	1
Thomas Keepen	2
Mister Hussey	3
Henry Andrews	2
Henry Bampton	3
Mister William Edwards	1
Mister Postumus Long	4
Mister George Garrett	5
Thomas King	3
Simon Wiseman	3
William Palmer	1
Catherine Stevens widow	3
Margaret Livelong widow	1
Nicholas Plumbly	2
William Northover	3
John Padner	1
Ambrose King	3
Simon Andrews	2
Barnaby Andrews	1
Margery Cox	3
Barnaby Poole	1
Robert Marten	1
John Marten	1
John Warne	2
Richard Livelong	1
Mary Bampton widow	1
Mister Webb	1
William Wiseman	1
Stephen Frampton	1
Widow Guy	1
George Martin	1
Henry Clase	1
Robert Wareham	1
Widow Stent	1
William Warne	1
hearths	80

Increased 10

Hearths not chargeable

Margery Amy	1
John Veale	1
Nicholas Bound	1
John Ederidg	1
Alice Ederidg	1

Fol. 23r(ii)

Ambrose Bond	1
William Martin	1
Edward Witt	1
William Lewis	1
Philip Poole	1
John Scott	1
Widow Witt	1
Widow Stevens	1
Widow Symons	1
William Cross	1
William Allen	1
William Poole	1
Maurice Bound	1
hearths	18

1. Hartbridge

103. BISTERNE AND CROW[1]

Hearths chargeable

Richard Compton esquire	21
Michael Blunn	4
John Justigan	1
Nicholas Rickman	3
Christopher Gold	2

Jonathan Younges	4
William Pitt	1
William Brixey	1
William Rickman	1
Henry Rogers	1
Ann Hinton	2
Richard Lincefeild	1
William Bedlecombe	2
Henry Etheridg	2
John Younges	1
Robert Reade	6
Thomas Keeffen	1
Felix Hinton	1
Joseph Younges	1
William Wagg	3
Henry Rogers	3
Peter Rogers	1
Dorcas Bramly	2
John Walden	1
Mary Churchett	2
Henry Lyne	2
Thomas Taylor	1
John Forde	4
Robert Tompson	2
John Churchett	1
Thomas Manner	1
Thomas Hinton	1
John Bidlecombe	1
Philip Cooke	1
Richard Chappell	1
Bartholomew Forder	2
Widow Owting	1
Widow Slidle	1
Foule Forde	2
Thomas Warne	1
William Bidlecombe	1
Thomas Mannor	1
hearths	92

Hearths not chargeable

Bisterne[2] Lodge house	1
William Davie	1
John Inges	1
John Holmes	1
Philip Gold	1
Walter Gold	1
Nicholas Badripp	1
John Woodman	1
Henry Knight	1
John Tremaine	1

Fol. 23v(i)

Widow Moores	1
Richard Wiseman	1
Thomas Woodford	1
Samuel Yeatmay	1
John Starke	1
John Bidlecombe	1
Widow Penny	1
Felix Gage	1
Widow Gage	1
Widow Maydman	1
John Gosling	1
Widow Gold	1
Henry Whiteash	1
hearths	23

1. Bisthurne & Croe
2. Bisthurne

104. KINGSTON

Hearths chargeable

Philip Lyne	2
Nicholas Boyte	1
Widow Cosens	2
Christopher Lyne	2
Widow Perkins	1
Henry Done	1
John Slidles	4
John Painter	2
James Phelps	1
Widow Elliott	3
Richard Belden	4
Widow Warne	2
Robert Forde	2
John Bidlecomb	4
John Pitt	1
John Goddard	4
Stephen Forde	1
William Lisle	5
William Ivemay	1
Mister Balney	3

104. KINGSTON—*cont'd.*

Richard Elliott	5
John Tremaine	3
Thomas Heyward	2
Robert Durnedall	1
John Marshall	1
James Gatrell	1
Peter Rogers	1
Thomas Glevin	4
Joseph Gray	3
John Rooke	2
Widow Hinton	1
John Walden	1
Thomas Kiffen	6
Thomas Tucker	1
Thomas Warne	3
Widow Moyle	3
Ralph Warne	1
Thomas Barnes	1
Maurice Wagge	2
Maurice Wagge	1
Thomas Wagg	3
James Warne	1
John Lyne	2
John Garrett	2
Ambrose Forde	3
Widow Lyne	3
Michael Barry	1
William Hinton	1
John Perkins	1
Nicholas Mullenox	5
Henry Owting	1
Maurice Lyne	1
John Watten	3
Thomas Warne	2
John Wiseman	2

Fol. 23v(ii)

Widow Brixey	1
William Warne	2
Henry Snelling	1
Edward Gold	1
John Drover	1
Ann Gate	1
John Dover	1
William Pitt	1
John Deeks senior	1
Philip Lyne	1
Richard Brixey senior	1
Richard Streete	2
Widow Spratt	1
Thomas Glevin	3
Mister Heyward	1
Richard Belben	1
Philip Lyne	1
William Warne	2
Ralph Warne	1
hearths	145

Increased 21

Hearths not chargeable

John Sibley	1
Maurice Cosh	1
Margaret Cosh	1
Margaret Manner	1
Thomas Ellis	1
Peter Tibley	1
William Wiseman	1
Joseph Woodford	1
Widow Bowden	1
Henry Graunt	1
Francis Pitt	1
John Pitt	1
Nicholas Masey	1
Francis Dimock	1
Widow Gifford	1
Henry Pitt	1
James Purse	1
Widow Pitt	1
Thomas Ellis senior	1
Henry Spratt	1
Widow Gold	1
Widow Carpenter	1
Robert Gate	1
John Deeke junior	1
William Daniell	1
Thomas Pitt	1
Richard Baker	1
Widow Aldridge	1
Thomas Stevens	1
Widow Wimbleton	1
Widow Cumage	1

John Keepen senior	1
John Keepen junior	1
Robert Wagg	1
Henry Reade	1
hearths	35

105. NORTH IFORD[1]

Hearths chargeable

Charity Whiteway	2
John Mariner	1
hearths	3

1. North Efford

Fol. 24r(i)

106. PENNINGTON

Hearths chargeable

Mister David Wavell	6
William Edwards	4
Bartholomew Harmwood	4
George Johnson	4
John Shepherd	2
Henry Rowe	2
Susannah Shidley	4
Tristram Newell	2
Thomas Bayly	2
George Brent	1
David Dore	1
Richard Bary	2
John Oliver	3
George Palmer	1
Richard Stent	2
Ambrose Phelps	3
George Newell	2
William Weale	3
Robert Newman	2
Stephen Tompson	1
hearths	52

Hearths not chargeable

Joyce Hennard	1
Philip Reade	1
James Pitt	1
Joan Mariner	1
John Merrett	1
George Pearce	1
hearths	6

The number of hearths chargeable within the hundred of Ringwood is	828
Not chargeable	157

FORDINGBRIDGE HUNDRED

107. HALE

Hearths chargeable

Sir John Penruddock	13
Henry Lawes	3
John Eades	3
Henry Norice	1
Widow Chubb	1
Thomas Norice	1
Widow Pascue	1
George Harison	2
Richard Wheatley	1
Andrew Mowland	1
William Richman	1
Matthew Chubb	1
Roger Harrison	1
William Harrison	2
Robert Norice	1
Andrew Richman	1
hearths	35

Decreased 5

Hearths not chargeable

Christopher Jacob	1
Richard Woort	1
John Chubb	1
John Fox	1
John Richman	1
Richard Wheatly	1
[ ] Wheatly	1
hearths	7

Fol. 24r(ii)

108. FORDINGBRIDGE

Hearths chargeable

William Casbert	15
William Waterman	2
Richard Hall	7

108. FORDINGBRIDGE—*cont'd.*

William Pope	2
Thomas Joyce	1
William Hellender and Bartholomew Gibbs	6
Margaret Reade	6
Edward Triphooke	3
Ralph Casbert	3
Andrew Pope	2
John Gifford	3
Richard Waterman	2
Nicholas Norris	1
William Gusse	2
John Fullford	1
Francis Barrowe	2
Ralph Zanger	1
Francis Barrowe senior	3
Samuel Harris	3
John Moores	2
George Summers	2
George Woort	3
Richard Oram	1
Giles Sandford	2
Charles Reade	3
William Hancock	2
Charles Barter	2
hearths	84

Increased 21

Hearths not chargeable

Thomas Smith	1
Thomas Lymington	1
Francis Atlander	2
John Chatter	1
George Thorne	2
William Burte	2
Henry Bestland	1
Widow Phettiplace	2
William Scamull	1
John Bound	2
Henry Dale	1
Charles Burt	1
Mister Ringwood	2
John Siveor	1
Richard Moore	2
Edward Waterman	2
Simon Ashton	1
Robert Light	1
Richard Fullford	1
William Tiler	1
Ralph Casbert	2
Richard Gost	2
Samuel Harris	2
hearths	34

109. MIDGHAM[1]

Hearths chargeable

Mister Blackford	4
John Pinhorne	4
William Miller	1
hearths	9

Hearths not chargeable

Robert Mowland	1
Robert Reade	1
hearths	2

1. Midgcam

110. PROVOST[1]

Hearths chargeable

Mister Hall vicar	4
Henry Barry	5[(a)]
Henry Castle	4
George Hawkins	4
Richard Curtis	5
William Lumbard	1
John Huntly	1

Fol. 24v(i)

[ ]	1
[ ]	4[(b)]
[ ] Curtis	3
Edward Norris	6
Widow Stoakes	3
hearths	44

Increased 21

Hearths not chargeable

Thomas Rumsey	1
Alexander Perry	1
John Blanchard	2
James Michell	1
John Hewlatt	1

John Hobbs 1
Richard Willis 1
Andrew Lester 1
Mister Blachford 3
hearths 12

(a) 4 of half year's standing
(b) for half a year
1. Provist

111. SOUTH CHARFORD[1]

Hearths chargeable

Richard Holloway 5
George Harrison 1
Ralph Harrison 1
John Norris 1
John Chubb 1
Christopher Harrison 1
George Fry 1
Oliver Coward 1
Robert Lansdalle 1
George Fox 1
hearths 14

Decreased 1

Hearths not chargeable

Widow Phillpott's children 1
Widow Jacob 1
Widow Furzby 1
John Gibbs 1
hearths 4

1. South Charforde

112. BURGATE

Hearths chargeable

Mistress Bulkely 15
John Younges 2
William Hall 3
Matthew Stevens 2
John Mist 5
Edward Oram 2
John Cleeves 4
Richard Spickernell 2
Widow Bragg 1
Widow Major 1
Henry Rooke 2
William Trusler 3
Edward Reade 1
Robert Besling 1
Richard Hales 1
John Major 5
Mister Bates 6
William Rooke 2
Mister John Butcher 4
William Casbert 6
Ralph Bessling's house 1
George Gasse 4
Nicholas Barter 2
Robert Harris 2
Mister Talke 3
John Elfes 5
Thomas Bampton 2
Nicholas Gilbert 4

Fol. 24v(ii)

William Kerly 2
Nicholas Reade 1
Nicholas Reade 1
Robert Norris 2
Thomas Cox 3
John Pascue 3
Henry Seager 2
Henry Stamsmore 2
Philip Sex 2
William Newman 1
Peter Reddhead 1
Ogden Rooke 3
Widow Philpott 3
William Jubber 1
Ralph White 1
Richard Sex 3
Walter Barry 2
John Sex 1
Richard Livelong 1
Thomas Winge 1
Widow Chubb 2
John Davis 1
Mister Browne 10
Robert Norris 6
Scutts for Mullens 1
William Frost 5
Francis Barry 4

112. BURGATE—*cont'd.*

William Winge	4
John Cox	1
Henry Wing	2
Ralph Wing	1
Thomas Austin	1
Widow Collins	1
Robert Osgood	3
Peter Curtis	3
Widow Collins	3
Nicholas Dimote	5
Peter Street	1
Anthony Phelps	2
William Baily	1
William Hicks	2
Nicholas Cox	1
Widow Crewis	1
hearths	191

Increased 33

Hearths not chargeable

William Langley	1
Drogg	1
Drogg	1
Henry Blunt	1
John Symes	1
Thomas Cram	1
Morgan Horder	2
Widow Browne	2
John Hudd	2
Thomas Symes	1
John Michell	2
Peter Kent	1
John Moulton	1
John Andrews	1
William Butten	1
John Medhouse	1
John Bishopp	1
Richard Swettingham	2
Edward Tiler	1
Thomas Wittingstall	1
John Saunders	1
Widow Handy	1
Margaret Deane	1
Henry Rogers	1
Widow Addams	1
John Hurst	1
John Harris	1
Thomas Collins	1
John Dowle	1
William Pocock	1
Henry Lane	1

Fol. 25r(i)

John Daniell	1
Abraham Wheeler	1
William Collens	1
Arthur Hendy	1
Widow James	1
Richard Cole	1
Widow Sibley	1
Catherine Aysh	1
Widow Lovedidge	1
Widow Lacy	1
Widow Collins	1
John Shalle	1
Widow Aysh	1
Thomas Kent	1
hearths	50

113. IBSLEY[1]

Hearths chargeable

Sir John Rogers	9[(a)]
Mister Hall	2
Richard Reekes	6
Mister Woolfreys	1
John Martin	1
Nicholas Mist	1
Anthony Dimott	2
Nicholas Dimott	2
Widow Phelps	1
Ambrose Dimott	1
Henry Goodboy	2
Arthur Spratt	1
William Baily	1
William Osgood	4
Widow Odber	3
Widow Bayly	3
William Fisher	4
Dorothy Barnes	1
Robert Bursey	3
Nicholas Stride	2

James Carde	1
William Wigley	1
Thomas Livelong	1
William Garrett	1
Widow Beasling	3
Widow Card	1
Walter Watts	2
William Bayly	2
Ralph Elfes	2
Walter Dimott	2
Robert Bishopp	2
John Bishopp	1
William Garrett	1
Walter Watts	1
Nathaniel Drover	1
Giles Bursey	1
Widow Bishopp	1
Elizabeth Rose	1
John Harvy	1
hearths	67

Increased 1

Hearths not chargeable

Nicholas Dimott	1
Edith Bound	1
Widow Stride	1
John Andrew	1
William Light	1
Nicholas Bayly	1

Fol. 25r(ii)

Edward Kinge	1
Anthony Kinge	1
Widow Stride	1
William Kinge	1
Sir John Roger's house pulled down	9
hearths	21

(a) decreased by pulling down (*added later*)

1. Ibbesly

114. BICKTON[1]

Hearths chargeable

John Davenant	5
John Davenant	2
Widow Beslant	1
Ralph Curtis	2
William Vincent	3
Widow Bolton	1
William Batt	2
Widow Laninge	3
Thomas Gibbs	1
William Curtis	2
Widow Harris	1
Richard Batt	1
William Gilbert	4
Thomas Edmunds	3
William Hooker	2
Widow Coules	1
Widow Bonus	1
John Ransome	1
Henry Moulen	1
hearths	37

Hearths not chargeable

Richard Bound	1
John Hollyer	1
hearths	2

1. Bicton

115. ROCKBOURNE[1]

Hearths chargeable

John Martin	3
Arthur Leach	1
Widow Pope	1
Ambrose Trippocke	1
Thomas Newman	1
Roger Brittany	1
John Newman	1
Edward Trippocke	1
Mister William Meade	4
Richard Penny at the farm	8
Alexander Randoll	1
Ann Poole	1
Anthony Newman	2
Richard House	1
William White	1
Robert Newman	1
Nicholas Fullford	1
William Penney	2
Nicholas Short	1

115. ROCKBOURNE—*cont'd.*

John Triphook	1
Henry Penny	2
John Fullford	1
Alexander Randoll	1
Mister John Haddsly	2
Mister Gabriel Lapp	5
Catherine Holloway	1

Fol. 25v(ii)

Mister James Percivall	5
Andrew Hunt	1
George Mintey	3
Anthony Newman	1
William Mowland	2
William Rooke	2
John Fullford	1
John Tegg	2
Mister Gilbert Pope	3
Matthew Fulford	2
Roger Minty	1
Mister Walter Pope	4
Andrew Holloway	1
Thomas Holloway	1
Henry Dove	2
Ann Fullford	1
William Oates	1
Joseph Barker	1
Rebecca Smith	1
Edward Dyer	1
Mister James Percivall	1
hearths	87

Increased 3

Hearths not chargeable

John Starke	1
Widow Witt	1
Evan Griffin	1
William Hayter	1
Andrew Hescoks	1
Joan Gearne	1
Edward Witt	1
George Sheppard	1
Nicholas Fulford	1
Ann Witt	1
John Vincent	1
William Bayliff	1
John Bush	1
William Bush	2
Amy Bishopp	1
John Dring	2
Edward Triphooke	1
Alice Evans	1
Mary Scott	1
Evan Bush	1
Richard Witt	1
Ambrose Finder	1
John Witt	1
Robert King	1
Edith Drover	1
Robert Oats	1
Ambrose Oates	1
Widow Oates	1
William Tegg	1
John Fursby	1
Matthew Vincent	1
Richard Prover	1
Richard Wareham	1
Richard Dyer	1
Bartholomew Triphooke	1
John Street	2
hearths	39

1. Rogborne

116. NORTH CHARFORD

Hearths chargeable

Robert Sawer	10
Thomas Gauntlett	2
Richard Darrell	1
Susan Elkins	1
hearths	15

Increased 5

Fol. 25v(i)

Hearths not chargeable

Nicholas Thomas	1
William Thomas	1
Widow Thomas	1
hearths	3

117. ELLINGHAM

Hearths chargeable

Mistress Lisle	14
Vincent Goodboddy[1]	1
Thomas Barnes	2
Edward Rooke	1
Thomas Dimott	3
William Coles	1
Francis Street	2
Thomas Combs	2
Thomas Blake	1
Richard Tarver	2
Maurice Ivemay	1
Thomas Richman	2
Thomas Hyde	2
Vincent Goodboddy	1
Philip Hyde	1
John Reade	5
Christopher Coles	1
John Maurice	1
William Badripp	1
Philip Wiseman	1
Humphrey Coles	1
Richard Aldridge	1
Widow Walles	1
Ambrose Coleborne	1
John Bemister	3
John Rooke	3
William Tarver	5
Widow Odber	2
Thomas Mowday	1
Philip Hyde	1
John Wheeler	3
Widow Talbott	1
Henry Gibbs	1
John Tarver	2
Widow Bistone	5
Peter Bemister	5
Thomas Early	1
Giles Bemister	1
John Anngood	1
William Bemister	3
Vincent Wiseman	1
John Bemister	2
Ellingham Farm	11
Mister Harwood	1
John Talbott	2
hearths	105

Increased 22

Hearths not chargeable

John Harris	1
Thomas Pope	1
John King	1
Nicholas Pope	1
John Bemister	1
Richard Houchins	1
Richard Houchins	1
Richard Wareham	1

Fol. 26r(i)

John Penke	1
Widow Gibbs	1
Richard Peace	1
William Carde	1
Thomas Barnes	1
Henry Boulton	1
Henry Wiseman	1
Richard Wiseman	1
Widow Etheridg	1
John Combs	1
James Welch	2
Widow Purcas	2
Mary Bussey	1
Thomas Wallis	1
Richard Barrington	1
Widow Coles	1
hearths	26

1. *Originally* Goodboy

The number of hearths chargeable within the hundred of Fordingbridge is	676
Not chargeable	208

CHRISTCHURCH HUNDRED

118. AVON[1]

Hearths chargeable

Sir Henry Titchborne	13
Widow Lockier	1
Richard Bidlecombe	4

118. AVON—*cont'd.*

John Legg	1
Henry Warne	1
Robert Palmer	2
John Crowcher	3
Mister William Tulse	4
Thomas Saunders	3
William King	1
Jonathan Younges	1
Widow Waterman	5
William Hinton	1
Luke Saunders	1
Thomas Noris	2
Barnard Crowcher	1
Richard Saunders	3
William Brixey	3
John Warne	1
Henry Warne	2
Christopher Moyle	1
John Saunders	4
Mary Pope	3
John Weeke	1
Christopher Wade	1
Widow Jenkins	2
John Snellen	2
William Charke	1
John Zebutt	2
John Perkins	1
Joseph Scott	3
Thomas Bond	3
William Harding	2
James Scott	3
Widow Veeke	3
Widow Bath	1
Widow Moyle	4
John Veeke	1
Robert Dyatt	1
John Saunders	3
Thomas Lane	1

Fol. 26r(ii)

John White	1
Robert Goby	2
Thomas Trim	1
Widow Davie	1
James Jeffery	1
Richard Hopkins	1
Thomas Pope	1
Sir Henry Titchborne	2
Mister William Tulse	1
Thomas Wheeler	2
Susan Clerke	1
Francis Newen	1
Nicholas Greene	2
Laurence Leach	1
Widow Rabbetts	1
Barnard Grosse	1
Widow Atkins	1
Stephen Wheeler	1[a]
Richard Kerly	1
Henry James	1
William Wheeler	2
Widow Crobie	1
Thomas Jennens	1
Widow Saunders	1
William Barnes	1
hearths	135

Increased 18

Hearths not chargeable

John Kerly	1
Thomas Light	1
John Walter	1
George Tilly	1
Edward Tilly	1
Thomas Graunt	1
John Leffe	1
Nicholas Godden	1
Daniel Tilly	1
William Heyward	1
John Younges	1
Edward Tombs	1
William Waterman	1
Thomas Joanes	1
John Waterman	1
James Blanchard	1
Pernasses Persons	1
John Burt	1
John Adlam	1
Richard Tilly	1
Widow Adlam	1
William Blanchard	1

Martin Barnes	1
Thomas Elliot	1
William Parkins	1
John Burt	1
William Deeke	1
Alice Parkins	1
Henry Irish	1
Widow Combe	1
Widow Burtt	1
John Tooke	1
William Winn	2
John Waterman	2
John Davis	1
William Harding	1
Henry Swettingham	1
William Gosling	1
hearths	40

(a) half a year
1. Auen

Fol. 26v(i)

119. WINKTON[1]

Hearths chargeable

Mister Edward Lewyn	6
Mister Edward Westbery	5
Widow Swaine	3
Anthony Kitch	1
James Rowles	1
John Saunders	2
William Dunman	2
William Awner	1
John Cooke	1
Widow Heyward	1
Thomas Dunman	2
John King	1
John Wareham	1
Widow Heale	1
William Winge	1
Elias Emberly	2
John Rickman	6
Stephen Barrowe	2
John Kitch	3
William Boorne	2
William Attlane	3
Joseph Boorne	3
Widow Golding	1
John Dunman	2
Thomas Pack	3
John White	1
Widow Pack	4
William Tuckle	2
Widow Woodcock	1
Robert Dunman	2
Peter Whiteman	3
Widow Moores	1
Nicholas Emberly	1
John Barrowe	3
Barnard Gauntlett	1
Widow White	2
Anthony Norris	1
Richard Hopkins	3
Widow Creed	1
William Creed	1
William Westbery	1
William Darfe	1
Widow Lauder	1
John Jeffery	1
Richard Warren	1
William Trebett	1
Widow Leucar	1
Henry Hopkins	1
Widow Lane	1
Widow Darfe	1
Henry Direshford	1
hearths	98

Increased 19

Hearths not chargeable

James Davie	1
John Holms	1
Peter Baker	1
Thomas Bidlecombe	1
Hugh Attland	1
Giles Smith	1
William Badripp	1
Ann Towlman	1
Henry Aubery	1
William Gatterell	1
Francis Gardner	1
John Parker	1
Widow Mosey	1

119. WINKTON—*cont'd.*

Fol. 26v(ii)

John Notten	1
Edward Sturt	1
Thomas Parsons	1
William Peeke	1
John Sturte	1
hearths	18

1. Winckton

120. HURN[1]

Hearths chargeable

Edward Hooper esquire	15
Elis[2] Prowte	6
William Frampton	5
Widow Smith	3
John Deane	3
Mister John Williams	3
Widow Barnes	1
Bartholomew Pettwyne	1
Richard Bidlecombe	5
William Reade	2
Richard Mann	2
Thomas Warren	2
George Toomer	2
William Lockyer	2
Robert Sleate	2
Widow Doegood	1
Widow Hancock	3
Thomas Florie	1
William Coffin	3
Pittman Blanchard	3
John Farrant	1
John Clapcote	1
Thomas Guilford	1
Henry Gibbs	1
Thomas Gibbs	1
Widow Gay	1
Nathaniel Clerke	1
Thomas Bryant	1
Thomas Trim	1
George Cole	5
Richard Bugby	1
Widow Warren	2
Stephen Doegood	1
Robert Bryant	1
Widow Harben	1
John Keepen	1
Widow Slydle	1
Richard Lockyer	1
Thomas Forde	2
Widow Curtis	1
John Ember	5
Nicholas Pittman	2
James Gibbs	1
Robert Pearce	1
Widow Freeborne	2
Robert Tomes	1
John Kellis	1
Robert Fry	1
hearths	104

Increased 4

Hearths not chargeable

Widow Tomes	1
William Peeke	1
William Hopkins	1
Anthony Randoll	2
Edward Randoll	1
Thomas Randoll	1
Widow Merriott	1

Fol. 27r(i)

Catherine Sibley	1
John Davie	1
Margaret Flory	1
Joseph Jolleffe	1
Martin Sibley	1
James Sibley	1
Widow Sibley	1
Widow Sibley	1
Robert Wyatt	1
William Wyatt	2
Widow Drake	1
Widow Hall	1
William Hardye	1
Nicholas Barrent	1
Richard Gage	1
Robert Kerly	1
Widow Kinge	1
Arthur Bason	1
John Wild	1

Thomas North	1
George Batt	1
Widow Perkins	1
John Phripp	1
hearths	32

1. Hurne
2. *Could be* Ellis *or* Elias

121. BURTON

Hearths chargeable

William Hinton	2
James King	4
Robert Reeks	1
William Burton	1
John Preston	2
Richard Reekes	2
Widow Burton	1
John Hancock	1
Henry Hodges	1
William Etheridg	5
Joseph Preston	2
John Windover	2
Edward Scott	5
Robert Davie	2
Richard Futtner	1
Christopher Godding	1
Moses Colegill	3
John Fryer	2
James Kitch	3
Edmund Stevens	1
Anthony Kitch	3
Edmund Duckett	1
Widow White	1
Edward Trippick	3
William Hellier	1
Richard Carter	1
William Launder	1
Richard Hopkins	1
Elmor Annedowne	1
hearths	56

Increased 11

Hearths not chargeable

John Penny	1
Thomas Browning	1
Widow Rolfe	1
Daniel Jumper	1
John Shambler	1
Henry Peeke	1
hearths	6

Fol. 27r(ii)

122. BURE

Hearths chargeable

Mister William Goldyer	8
William Barrowe	3
Martin Pack	2
Richard Emberly	2
Widow Blake	3
Thomas Sharpe	2
Humphrey Welsteed	1
Nicholas Cox	2
William Trill	3
Stephen Pack	1
Richard Trill	1
John Sharpe	1
John Broadhead	1
Edward Parnell	1
Henry Preston	3
John Reeks	1
Henry Peeke	1
Widow Yeats	1
John Coppedeake junior	1
John Wise[1]	2
John Coppedeake	1
Robert Teever	1
Widow Boare	1
Widow Peeke	1
Widow Baker	2
John Boare	2
William Warren	2
John Cox	1
Widow Kerby	3
John Burden	2
Thomas Burgame	1
Richard Forder	1
Richard Creed	1
John Lester	1
John Greenewood	1
Richard Litchfeild	1

112. BURE—*cont'd.*

Widow Sambrough	1
William Warren	1
hearths	66

Decreased 4

Hearths not chargeable

Richard Pullen	1
Bartholomew Bryant	1
Widow Pullen	1
Richard Morris	1
John King	1
Thomas Clerke	1
William Geale	1
Widow Bore	1
Widow Hinnon	1
Stephen Henning	1
Dorothy Boare	1
William Warren	1
Thomas Redford	1
John Blake	1
William Reeks	1
Thomas Hellier	1
Ann Barnes	1
John Hellier	1
Widow Leonard	1
Robert Lecar	1
William Wise	1
Widow Peeke	1
Toby Barton	1
Richard Leonard	1
Widow Hiscoke	1
Henry Taylor	1
Widow Warren	1
Margaret Goodyer	1
William Pilgrim	1

Fol. 27v(i)

Widow Reekes	1
William Chestle	1
hearths	31

1. *Originally* White

123. STREET[1]

Hearths chargeable

John Blake	4
John Pilgrim	2
Henry Baker	3
Henry Spencer	3
Widow Newen	1
Richard Puntice	1
Thomas Hiscock	1
William White	2
William Dale	1
Thomas Puntice	1
William Marshall	4
Henry Thorne	1
John Hancock	1
William Hancock	3
Simon Welsteed	2
William Lavender	1
Edward Elliott	1
Widow Gallopp	1
Walter Kitch	2
hearths	35

Increased 6

Hearths not chargeable

John Saunders	1
William Forder	1
Joseph Forder	1
William Creed	1
Widow Jones	1
Widow Puntice	1
Anthony Yeats	1
Widow Poole	1
Thomas Bissopp	1
William Bryant	1
Thomas Mintron	1
John Mann	1
Elizabeth Standard	1
hearths	13

1. Streete

124. HINTON

Hearths chargeable

John Hildesly esquire	13
Widow Hastings	6
Edward Drayton	1
John Menshew	1
Edmund Moore	1
Widow Holloway	2
Thomas Burgan	1

William Launder	1
William Spelt	1
Thomas Lane	1
John Wiseman	2
James Ivemay	2
John Keny	2
William Warwick	1
Moses Pack	2
William Etheridg	4
William Lock	1
Widow Rogers	1
Richard Rogers	2
William Rogers	1
Matthew Trill	3

Fol. 27v(ii)

Robert Tucker	2
Richard Wakeford	1
John Rooke	2
William Pullen	1
hearths	55

Hearths not chargeable

Catherine Smith	1
Edith Rookely	1
Joan Reeks	1
Avis Trill	1
John Lowe	1
Elizabeth Page	1
Richard Pullen	1
hearths	7

125. SOPLEY

Hearths chargeable

John Deane and Richard Deane	5
John Wagg	2
Richard Elliott junior	2
Nicholas Norris senior	1
Richard Elliott senior	1
Leonard Cox	1
Margaret Jeffery	2
Richard Frampton	2
George Jeffery	2
Mary Lane	2
Thomas Flewell	1
Widow White	4
William Mowle	1
Widow Windover	2
Mister Cush	5
Nicholas Norris junior	3
Robert Lucas	1
Thomas Gross	1
Thomas Trill	3
Eleanor Cornes	2
Martin Sibbott	2
William Norris	1
William Jeffery	1
John Lowell	1
Thomas Norris	1[a]
Henry Saunders	1
hearths	50

Increased 3

Hearths not chargeable

Henry Younges	1
William Potter	1
Anthony Saunders	1
Stephen Emberley	1
Dorothy Bidlecomb	1
John Fullford	1
hearths	6

(a) half a year

126. WALHAMPTON AND SHARPRICKS[1]

Hearths chargeable

John Nash	5
Thomas Dance	1
Robert Ivemay	5
Thomas Smith	2
John Meden	1
John Troth	1
Mister Bartholomew Buckly	1
John Collins	2

Fol. 28r(i)

John Jurdan	4
Richard Jones	2
Sir Henry Worsley	1
William Gookey	4
William Haynes	3
William Jordan	1

126. WALHAMPTON AND SHARPRICKS—*cont'd.*

John Wavell	1
William Scott	3
Edward Fisher	3
Edward Hall	1
Mister Luke's tenement	4
hearths	49

Hearths not chargeable

John Hameds	2
John Dominicke	2
Ann Rickett widow	1
Richard James	1
Widow White	1
Widow Hart	1
Margaret Brookes	1
John Welsteed	1
John Hedford	1
William Bradshaw	2
Widow Cooke	1
John Dale	1
Robert Feltham	2
hearths	17

1. Walhamton & Sharpricks

127. SWAY

Hearths chargeable

Mister John Wilson	7
William Penny	8
Mister Richard Coleman	4
Stephen Sumersett	3
Ogden Eames	1
John Parsons	1
Evan Kittyer	3
Widow Drapp	1
John Richards	3
Bartholomew Roades	2
Simon Suffeild	2
Widow Castle	1
Widow Harding	4
Thomas Buckly	1
Nicholas Veale	2
William Buttler	1
Ralph Carpenter	1
Philip Parnell	1
James Grubb	1
Thomas Walle	1
James Parnell	1
William Parnell	1
hearths	50

Increased 2

Hearths not chargeable

Richard Moore	1
Roger King	1
William Gregory	1

Fol. 28r(ii)

William Durrant	1
William Gostone	1
Widow Elcombe	1
William Parnell junior	1
Robert Hellier	1
Widow Streete	1
John Elinge	1
hearths	10

128. ASHLEY

Hearths not chargeable

Stephen Corbin	3
John Smith	1
Mistress Elizabeth Stevens	2
Richard Busey	6
Elizabeth Reeks	1
William Imber	1
Richard Rogers	2
Widow Fry	1
Widow Lane	1
John Godsgrace	1
Mary Francklen	1
Nicholas Hookey	1
Mistress Abarrowe	8
William Corbin	8
William Mackerell	4
William Moyle	1
Richard Coward	2
David Hennen	1
Thomas Parry	1
William Edwards	5
Richard Whitway	1

William Renn	1
Thomas Stevens	1
Henry Warder	2
James Parsons	2
John Smith	1
John Edwards	3
William Parsons	4
Joan Parsons widow	1
Ralph Warwick	1
Ann Rogers	1
John Newman	1
Thomas Parr	1
John Parsons	2
Widow Blake	3
William Durland	1
Richard Lane	4
Richard Burt	3
Widow Martin	1
William Busey	2
William Reeks	2
William Meservice	3
Henry Arnell	1
William Hillier	1
George Taylor	1
Toby Newen	1
John Bath	3
John Foot	1
Matthew Heeles	1
Elizabeth New	1
Widow Stevens	1
hearths	108

Increased 12

Fol. 28v(i)

Hearths not chargeable

Widow Gubber	1
William Peeke	1
Richard Poore	1
Thomas Hall	1
Mary Pittman	1
John Bukle	1
William Peeke	1
Widow Jeffery	1
Margery White	1
Peter Dickery	1
Matthew Younges	1
Roger Barrow	1
Nicholas Penny	1
Thomas Bowne	1
Henry Newman	1
Thomas Halls	1
Widow Lyne	1
Robert Edwards	1
William Salt	1
Thomas Trill	1
Widow Parsons	1
Roger Downer	1
Martin Burgon	1
Widow Warwick	1
Widow Spelke	2
hearths	26

129. HORDLE

Hearths chargeable

Mister David Warrell	6
Humphrey Davy	2
Simon Fery	1
James Parsons and Ann Edwards	2
Susan Welsted	1
Roger Davis	1
Richard Budden	1
Ann Arnum	3
John Burry	3
John Smith	2
Widow Bengar	1
John Bath	3
hearths	26

Hearths not chargeable

William Becke	1
Robert Wheeler	1
Thomas Beck	1
Edward Burton	1
hearths	4

130. CHEWTON

Hearths chargeable

William Chamberlaine esquire	4
Robert Branford	1
Thomas Pettman	1

130. CHEWTON—*cont'd.*

Fol. 28v(ii)

Widow Tarver	2
James Pittman	1
Thomas King	1
William Budden	2
William Brice	2
Stephen Corbin	1
James King	1
William Crowcher	1
Roger King	1
Roger Meservice	1
Laurence Barnes	2
Robert Jenkins	5
Edward Goldwyre	3
Ann Stevens	3
Stephen Perry	1
John Dewy	1
John Stevens	1
Thomas Lane	2
Elizabeth Palmeter	1
William Spelt	1
William Stevens	1
Michael Avery	1
Widow Garrett	1
Susan Stevens	1
Thomas Hopgood	1
hearths	47

Increased 6

Hearths not chargeable

Matthew Holloway	1
Henry Fullford	1
Leonard Buckle	1
John Baker	1
James Gelredge	1
Richard Frampton	1
Bexally Ganny	1
Henry Wise	1
James Wheeler	1
John Newen	1
James Burnard	1
Widow Stevens	1
Thomas Bond	1
William Samber	1
John Parr	1
Widow Phelps	1
Thomas Hendey	1
John Clerke	1
Roger Hendy	1
Widow Mowland	1
hearths	20

131. IFORD[1]

Hearths chargeable

Richard Warne	8
Henry Ford	5
Thomas Tarrant	9
Edward Curle	3
Thomas Holloway	2
Thomas Hicks	4

Fol. 29r(i)

William Whitway	4
William Cleeves	1
Richard White	3
Henry Barry	2
Widow Kitch	2
John Hippitt	1
Edward Burgan	1
Richard Edwards	1
William Curle	1
John Pitt	1
Edward Cranborne	1
Arthur Harmwood	1
William Harmwood	5
George Scott	1
William Gregory	1
Silvester Tapp	1
Edward Therle	1
William Rann	1
hearths	60

Increased 5

Hearths not chargeable

Henry Bugger	1
Widow Finch	1
Widow Head	1
hearths	3

1. Efford

132. KEYHAVEN

Hearths chargeable

Thomas Penny	1
Thomas Trill senior	3
John Scott	3
William Penny	3
William Darling	1
Charity Kitch widow	2
Joan Tivito	1
John Fox	1
Ann Frost	1
William Curle	3
Richard Houchins	3
Robert Wavell	2
John Wavell	3
George Scott	2
Thomas Tivito	3
William Fox	1
James Rolfe	1
hearths	34

Increased 2

Hearths not chargeable

William Thernell	1
Henry Gookey	1
Henry Michell	1
Hannibal Penicoate	1
hearths	4

133. MILFORD[1]

Hearths chargeable

Christopher Ayrey clerk	5
Mister Nicholas Howard	4
John Howard	2
William Francke	2
Henry Rowden	1
Thomas Thomas	1

Fol. 29r(ii)

Josias Norden	1
Nicholas Poyle	1
John Scott	1
Richard Grillingham	1
Anthony Langhard	1
John Scott	1
Richard Gleed	1
Daniel Hobbs	1
William Curle	1
Maurice Gates	1
William Cotten	1
Henry Vincent	2
Robert Wavell	1
Rickman Moore	3
Henry Vinecourte	1
John Pitt	2
Rachel Fursby	3
Henry Gee	2
Thomas Wade senior	3
Theophilus Ayres	3
Nicholas Rickman	1
John Cleeves	1
John Furner	1
James Rickman	2
George Getheredg	3
Anthony Langard	1
Thomas Wade	1
hearths	57

Increased 3

Hearths not chargeable

Joan Warner	1
William Moore	1
Joyce Coles	1
Richard Perce	1
Sedwell Pyne	1
hearths	5

1. Milforde

134. ARNEWOOD

Hearths chargeable

James Arnewood	4
John Mowland	1
Henry Kittyer	4
James Elliott	1
John Dibsdale	3
William Collins	1
William Long	1
William Stent	2
William Kittyer	3
Christopher Brixey	2
Edward Elliott	1

134. ARNEWOOD—*cont'd.*

Thomas Buttler	1
Humphrey Spratt	1
John Palmer	1
John Auger	1
Widow Kittyer	2
William Mansbridge	1
George Kittyer	2
Thomas Moores	1
Richard Forder	1
William Slatford	1
William Slatford	1

Fol. 29v(i)

Roger Dible	1
Barnard Tilly	1
Susan Stevens widow	1
Roland Major	1
Walter Arnell	1
Robert Wheeler	1
Bartholomew Osgood	1
John Wavell	1
John Lush	1
Widow Chubb	1
hearths	46

Increased 8

Hearths not chargeable

John Hooper	1
John Parner	1
John Knell	1
Mark Wiseman	1
Robert Woads	1
Edward Tredgoll	1
Widow Shinell	1
John Veale	1
hearths	8

135. CHRISTCHURCH BOROUGH[1]

Hearths chargeable

Mister Henry Rogers	8
John Spencer	8
Thomas Stevens	3
Nicholas Emberly	1
Ambrose Herne	3
John Detty	1
Elizabeth Winsey	2
Austin Dunning	1
Elizabeth Gange	2
Frances Tewksbery	1
Thomas Newen	7
Thomas Stevens	4
John Parsons	2
William Garrett	1
Thomas Kerby	1
Richard Pawson	4
Henry Hopkins	2
Nicholas Slade	3
Walter Forde	4
John Markett	1
James Dewey	9
Thomas Crew	2
Henry Mantle	1
William Pollington	3
John Holloway	1
William Earle	2
Knappen Mills	2
Richard Carter	1
Widow Dash	1
Thomas Chappell	1
John Byles	1
William Deane	1
James Doegood	2
Robert Boorne	5
Widow Heyly	1
John Foquett	2
Richard Coles	2

Fol. 29v(ii)

Richard Collgill	4
Widow Stoakes	4
John Brenton	4
John Merriott	2
Widow Ager	1
John Ager	1
Mistress Grandum	6
Mistress Divis	2
James Westbery	8
William Andrews	3
John Summers	1
John Kitch	1
John Earle	4

John Bemister	3
Jesse Standard	3
William Foot	2
Henry Pack	4
Martin Rolfe	3
George Hellier	4
Thomas Doegood	2
Thomas Hunt	1
Christopher Bullock	1
Henry Butten	2
Christopher Boorenn	2
John Lester	1
John Welchman	6
William Beeston	2
James Hoyle	2
Andrew Fabin	2
John Earley	3
John Gosgill	3
Henry Richman	2
Edward Broadhead	2
John Broadhead	1
Thomas Boare	1
William Bounds	2
Elizabeth Jenkins	1
Nicholas Dale	4
Anthony Carter	2
Widow Carter	1
Humphrey Richards	1
Nicholas Gale	1
Walter Cuttler	2
Christopher Fabin	5
Widow Stoakes	3
Bartholomew Bidlecombe	1
Michael Siferwest	1
Richard Coles	2
William Pittman	2
Thomas Hugman	1
John Carpenter	1
John Spranklen	1
Henry Warren	1
Eleanor Williams	1
Henry Dunning	4
Widow Cox	4
Widow Colgill	3
hearths	246

Increased 38

Hearths not chargeable

Elizabeth Goldyer	1
Widow Price	1
Widow Walden	2
Ann Ney	2

Fol. 30r(i)

William Dewy	2
John Brice	2
John Rookely	1
Ann Chubb	1
Anthony Saunders	1
Widow Kitch	2
Richard Hunt	1
Robert Hodges	1
Giles Forder	1
Widow Jermayne	1
Widow Blake	1
Samuel Carter	1
Stephen Kember	1
Thomas Forder	1
Widow Rabbetts	1
Widow Walden	1
Widow Marrimer	1
Widow Flory	1
Thomas Price	1
Widow Jones	1
Widow Spragg	1
Ellis Peeke	1
Thomas Blach	1
Widow Bullock	1
Richard Scott	1
William Corbin	1
Sidrach Long	1
Widow Andrews	1
Philip Long	1
Martin Blach	1
Margaret Baker	1
John Carter	1
Edward Byles	1
Widow Virge	1
Thomas Rookely	1
Martin Jurden	1

135. CHRISTCHURCH BOROUGH—*cont'd.*

Widow Inwood	1
Widow Newsham	1
Robert Ellis	1
Athey Price	1
George Hodges	1
John Corbin	1
Elizabeth Keene	1
Widow Moores	1
William Hodges	1
Widow Purcas	1
Henry Goodyer	1
Robert Elis senior	1
John Gallopp	1
Walter Pittman	1
Widow Smith	1
Widow Collins	1
Isaac Baily	2
Richard Inwood	2
Widow Dixon	2
Widow Trew	2
William Collins	1
John Blach	1
Jane Newen	2
Robert Durneford	1
Richard Jenkins	2
Bridget Whitman	1
Widow Baily	1
William Peeke	2
William Trigoll	1
Henry Spencer	2
Robert Bartholomew	1
Joan Trigoll	1
John Jurden	1
John Price	1
hearths	87

1. Christchurch Borrough

The number of hearths chargeable within the hundred and borough of Christchurch	1272
Not chargeable	349

Fol. 30r(ii)

REDBRIDGE HUNDRED

136. COLBURY[1]

Hearths chargeable

Sir John Mill	18
Mister George Strode	6
Mistress Caplen	5
John Pooke	3
Simon Olis	1
Francis Bidlecomb	1
Richard Masey	1
Robert Kent	1
Robert Baker	1
Widow Scott	1
John Bolton	1
William Mewsellwheat	1
Richard Gregory	3
hearths	46

Increased 2

Hearths not chargeable

John Scott	1
John Hilla	2
hearths	3

1. Colebury

137. DURLEY

Hearths chargeable

Mister John Barnard	8
Thomas Kent	5
Widow Rutter	4
John Turnham	3
Henry Daniell	1
Stephen Mansbridg	1
hearths	22

138. WADE AND OWER

Hearths chargeable

Mister Betts	6
Mister Sanley	7
Mister Young	6
Thomas Hooper	4
John Blake	3
Thomas Ballard	1
Charles Frowde	1
Thomas Silver	1

John Cooke 3
Thomas Hooper 1
Robert Day 1
John Smith 1
William Light 1
Robert Leighborne 2
Stephen Mansbridge 2
hearths 40

Decreased 3

Hearths not chargeable

John Wake 1
Robert Gaundy 1
hearths 2

139. STREET[1]

Hearths chargeable

Edward Newman 4
Kent 3
William Bidle 2
John Beestone 1
James Puller 1

Fol. 30v(i)

Michael Williams 3
Nicholas Clerke 1
Simon Menshew 3
hearths 18

Increased 3

Hearths not chargeable

John Brooker 1
John Sherrior 1
Thomas Weyman 1
John Daunce 1
Widow Hobby 1
Richard Langford 1
Robert Clayden 1
Widow Springe 1
Mary Penny 1
hearths 9

1. Streete

140. BALDOXFEE[1]

Hearths chargeable

John Lovell 4
Robert Skinner 3
Brian Waldron 3
John Thextone 2
hearths 12

Decreased 1

1. Baldox Fee

141. RUMBRIDGE

Hearths chargeable

Henry Paynter 1
William Gray 2
Thomas Harvest 4
Widow Gay 4
Henry Goast 1
Widow Painter 3
Michael Dance 1
Elias Spicer 2
Robert Jones 1
Richard Iver 3
John Kent 1
Widow Turneham 2
Humphrey Thomas 1
John Palmer 1
Elias Rolfe 1
hearths 28

Hearths not chargeable

Henry Nayle 1
William Conings 1
John Salt 1
Robert Rolfe 1
Robert Pricksmall 1
Geoffrey Allingham 1
Richard Lovell 1
hearths 7

142. LANGLEY

Hearths chargeable

Thomas Chevers 3
James Parker 2
John Rider 1
Thomas Lamboll 2

Fol. 30v(ii)

John Nayler 2
John Longland 1
John Riggs 1
Widow Rolfe 1

142. LANGLEY—*cont'd.*

Mister Edward Stroade	1
Thomas Snuggs	1
Richard Churcher	3
hearths	18

Decreased 3

Hearths not chargeable

John Dumper	1
Henry Lyant	1
Widow Lyant	1
Thomas Luter	1
Richard Richman	1
Thomas Longland	1
Edward Annedowne	1
John Boyes	1
Thomas Boyes	1
hearths	9

143. MARCHWOOD

Hearths chargeable

Felix Lovell	5
Richard Churcher	6
Robert Benister	3
Mistress Masey	1
John Abbott	1
Richard Gregory	2
hearths	18

Increased 1

Hearths not chargeable

James Phelipps	1
John Hyde	1
Robert Laurence	1
John Henbeast	1
hearths	4

144. BISTERN AND BARTLEY[1]

Hearths chargeable

Henry Fufford	7
Widow Willis	2
John Laurence	1
Widow Dale	2
Richard Storme	2
John Prixmell	1
Richard Cernett	1
Henry Silver	1
John Smith	1
Richard Russell	2
Richard Light	3
Widow Storme	1
William Lane	1
Austin Pransnell	1
Philip Page	2
Thomas Hewett	1
William Leighborne	2
hearths	31

Increased 1

1. Barkely & Bisthurne

Fol. 31r(i)

145. TESTWOOD

Hearths chargeable

Philip Leigh esquire	15
Thomas Bowlton	2
Henry Mansbridg	5
John Hardman	1
Robert Mansbridge	1
John Day	2
John Smith	2
Michael Barthorne	1
John Cotten	1
Thomas Crichill	1
Laurence Braccar	1
Widow Hill	2
Walter Hamon	2
Robert Coxhead	3
Thomas Tarrant	1
William Bennice	3
Philip Leigh esquire	2
Widow Hill	1
Robert Coxhead	2
Mark Winsor	1
hearths	49

Increased 3

Hearths not chargeable

John Burton	1
John Mansbridg	1
Simon Harding	1
Henry Hoare	1
William Covy	1
Widow Hooper	2

Robert Silver	1
Widow Penny	1
Peter Bales	1
Richard Hardman senior	1
hearths	11

146. LOPPERWOOD[1]

Hearths chargeable

Richard Hardman senior	1
William Peckham	1
Widow Moreneing	1
Richard Hardman junior	1
Edmund Russell	1[(a)]
William Buckett	1
Widow Yeatman	2
William Clappshaw	2
Henry Menshaw	1
Thomas Leighborne	1
hearths	12

Increased 1

Hearths not chargeable

Thomas Symes	1
hearths	1

(a) half a year
1. Hopperwood

147. TATCHBURY[1]

Hearths chargeable

John Iremonger	7
Robert Kite	1
John Rapley	1
Thomas Leighborne	1
hearths	10

1. Tachbury

Fol. 31r(ii)

148. ELING[1]

Hearths chargeable

John Flight	5
Widow Combs	5
Thomas Arnold	1
Thomas Stride	1
Richard Strong	2
John Kent	3
Thomas Warwick	1
Ford Roates	1
Philip Shoale	3
John Cradock	3
Richard Harvy	2
Michael Powell	2
Widow Jones	1
James Ford	1
Robert Hooker	2
John Forde	3
Robert Hill	1
Richard Winckworth	2
James Phelps	3
Mister Clements	7
John Powell	1
Henry Fussar	2
Thomas Naylor	3
Edward Belben	1
Anthony Clapshaw	6
Widow Rositer	1
Richard Storme	1
John Storme	2
Widow Russell	2
John White	2
Thomas Simpson	2
Arthur Wiseman	1
William Oldinge	1
Edward Chapman	1
John Raply	1
William Harris	1
Thomas Harris	1
Thomas Batchelor	1
Thomas Abbott	1
Matthew Cradock	2
John Worsham	2
Thomas Rolfe	2
William Hatcher	1
John Gray	1
John Harris	2
John Arminer	1
John Houchins	1
William Carter	1
Thomas Newtor	1
Widow Summers	2

148. ELING—*cont'd.*

John Powell	1
Thomas Greene	2
Widow Dossell	1
William Evanke	1
Catherine Warwick	1
Matthew Horde	1
Richard Jones	2
William Rogers	2
Martin Fulford	1
Robert Olding	1
William Harris	1
Robert Combest	1
George Brice	1
Abraham Olding	3
John Abram	1
William Fry	11
Robert Over	1
Thomas Spencer	1
Richard Oliver	2
William Flight	3
Mister Urry	1
Timothy Clentch	1
Edward Amy	1

Fol. 31v(i)

Francis Davis	1
Henry Henbest	1
hearths	140

Increased 10

Hearths not chargeable

Robert Humphry	1
Walter Watts	1
Elizabeth Bible	1
Widow Wolfe	1
Seth Merrett	1
Richard Whorly	1
Robert Whorly	1
William Stride	1
Richard Dibill	1
Edward Hoorley	1
Stephen Wolfe	1
hearths	11

1. Elinge

149. STONE

Hearths chargeable

Francis Earleman	6
John Weight	1
John Collis	2
John King	2
Thomas Randoll	1
William Randoll	1
Widow Rickett	1
hearths	14

Hearths not chargeable

George Mann	1
Ann Zoffe	1
hearths	2

The number of hearths chargeable within the hundred of Redbridge is 454

Not chargeable 58

WESTOVER LIBERTY

150. MUSCLIFFE

Hearths chargeable

William Hookey	3
Widow Warne	2
John Edwards	4
Robert Edwards	2
Richard Hascoll	3
Widow Lyne	3
Widow Worland	1
Mister Wilson	1
James Hawkins	3
Widow Moores	2
Richard Hopkins	1
John Corbin	1
Edward Elliott	2
John Harwood	3
Hugh Slidle	1
William Corbin	1
Thomas Wine	1
hearths	34

Increased 4

Hearths not chargeable

Widow Moores	1

Henry Moore's children	1
Widow Gibbons	1
Peter Coleman	1
Henry Layding	1
Margaret Bugby	1
Thomas Collins	1
Richard Paine	1

Fol. 31v(ii)

Margaret Read	1
Widow Harding	1
William Lyne	1
John Willmott	1
hearths	12

151. LONGHAM

Hearths chargeable

William Wilkins	4
Mister Thomas Cole	2
John Elcombe	2
Robert Bishopp	1
William Stagg	2
Widow Elliott	2
Mister Peate	4
Arthur Cole	4
Samuel Annstie	3
Widow Bramble	2
Widow Biddlecombe	2
Thomas Noyes	2
John Warwick	1
Mister Thomas Lyne	3(a)
William Pearce	1(a)
Richard Macham	1
Robert Bishopp	1
Thomas Cole	1
Elizabeth Spencer	1
Mister Arthur Cole	1
Ursula Bidlecomb	1
Thomas Noyes	1
hearths	42

Increased 9

Hearths not chargeable

Edward Thorne	1
Ralph Forde	1
Thomas Hardly	1
Widow Wilkins	1
hearths	4

(a) hearths of half a year standing

152. MUCCLESHELL[1]

Hearths chargeable

George Carew	7
Michael Parke	2
Henry Bond	2
Widow Edwards	4
John Bond	2
Richard Reeks	2
Nathaniel Elmes	3
Robert Holloway	2
George Rolfe	1
Henry Hookey	1
Francis Dale	2
John Sleate	2
hearths	30

Increased 13

Hearths not chargeable

Richard Edwards	1
William Crowcher	1
Laurence Hall	1
Elizabeth Tarrant	1
William Vye	1
Richard Seimore	1
Thomas Corbin	1
Christopher Parsons	1

Fol. 32r(i)

William Seimore	1
William Pottle	1
Christopher Parsons	1
John Ricketts	1
Henry Merrett	1
Methuselah Harvy	1
Richard Sleate	1
hearths	16

1. Musleshell

153. THROOP[1]

Hearths chargeable

Sir Henry Hastings	4
Robert Reeks	2
Thomas Harvy	1

153. THROOP—*cont'd.*

Widow Paskett	1
Widow Richardsons	3
John Dale	3
Susan Stevens	2
Thomas Bound	2
John Deane	2
Richard Hookey	3
William Edwards	1
Thomas Bond	1
Richard Man	1
Widow Reekes	3
Henry Trim	5
Henry Emberly	2
Christopher Parsons	2
Nicholas Hookey	2
Widow Bond	1
hearths	41

Increased 3

Hearths not chargeable

John Bidlecombe	1
John Crowcher	1
Mary Troake	1
Mary Sleate	1
hearths	4

1. Throope

154. HOLDENHURST[1]

Hearths chargeable

Widow Cerly	1
Thomas Harvie	2
Mister Richard Deane	3
Henry Deane	2
Simon Deane	3
Henry Reekes	3
Richard Deane	1
William Kinge	2
Robert Reekes	1
Widow Deane	1
Widow Gard	1
Widow Holloway	1
hearths	21

Increased 3

Hearths not chargeable

Annis Hawkins	1
Widow Collins	1
Widow Hetchells	1
Widow Lock	1
Widow Paskett	1
Henry Blake	1
Thomas Barber	2

Fol. 32r(ii)

Edward Gookey	1
Nicholas Stroake	1
John Mann	1
Richard Moores	1
Joseph Troake	1
hearths	13

1. Holnehurst

155. IVER[1]

Hearths chargeable

John Richardson	3
Michael Plowman	3
James Peeke	2
Richard Mantle	1
John Hiscock	1
Thomas Kember	2
James Mantle	1
Richard Whittington	2
Richard Emberly	2
John Carpenter	1
Widow Carpenter	1
Stephen Reeks	1
Simon Peeke	3
Henry Mantle	3
Henry Peeke	1
hearths	27

Hearths not chargeable

William Mantle	1
John Fry	1
Anthony Gookey	1
William Gibbs	1
William Pawsons	1
William Mackerell	1
William Kinge	1
Edward Paskett	1
hearths	8

1. Ivar

156. TUCKTON

Hearths chargeable

Richard Emberly	1
William Reeks	3
John Mantle	1
Widow Peeke	1
William Watkins	5
Ambrose Plowman	2
Edward Odber	4
Henry Hopkins	1
Stephen Holloway	2
Stephen Carter	1
Alice Kember	1
Robert Reekes	2
Widow Hake	1
Stephen Pack	3
Richard Mann	1
Stephen Pack	1
hearths	30

Hearths not chargeable

Henry Kember	1
Henry Kember	1
Widow Somersett	1
Widow Newen	1

Fol. 32v(i)

Roger Sibley	1
Richard Cotten	1
Richard Kember	1
William Carter	1
hearths	8

157. NORTH ASHLEY[1]

Hearths chargeable

Richard Curtis	13
Mister William Slann	7
George Kerly Senior	3
Matthew Greene	2
Joan Andrews widow	3
John Warne	2
William Guy	1
Widow Wareham	1
Peter Kerley	1
John Corbin	2
Elizabeth Edwards widow	2
Matthew Pinhorne	1
William Chatter	2
Henry Wing	1
Joan Mills widow	1
John Bull	1
George Newport	1
Francis Wiseman	1
Joan Warne widow	1
Andrew Whitaker	1
Christopher Kinge	3
Henry Kinge senior	2
Henry Kinge junior	3
William Forde	1
Phineas Melledge	1
Arthur Blanchard	2
Henry Browne	1
Simon Wareham	1
George Kerly junior	1
Thomas Guy	1
Paul Wareham	1
William Slann	1
Joan Wiseman widow	1
Oliver White	3
hearths	69

Increased 11

Hearths not chargeable

Edward Knowles	1
Jasper Mowland	1
John Sandy	1
William Perkins	1
Robert Mills	1
Ann Lawes widow	2
John Foreman	1
hearths	8

1. North Ashly

The number of hearths chargeable within the liberty of Westover is	294
Not chargeable	73

Fol. 32v(ii)

158. DIBDEN LIBERTY

Hearths chargeable

William Cooper	1
Robert Jones	2

158. DIBDEN LIBERTY—*cont'd.*

Edward Riggett	2
Andrew Small	3
Thomas Stride	2
Nicholas Corpish	1
Thomas Willts	1
Farmer Gauntlett	6
Mister Joseph Mathews	3
William Riggett	8
John Yeatman	1
William Cowdry	1
Andrew Cooper	2
Edward Hiller	1
Elizabeth Cornish	1
Giles Colechester	2
William Grubbie	1
Joseph Tarver	2
George Caucell	1
John Willts	1
Richard Suffeild	3
Thomas Petty	5
Rebecca Colchester	2
Mister Petty	4
Robert Arminer	1
Thomas Martin	1
Robert Beckett	3
Henry Etheridg	1
Simon Wheeler	1
John Lewes	4
Richard Abraham	3
Mary Yeatman	1
Richard King	2
Edward Hooper	3
John Ravell	3
Barbara Covey	1
William Davis	1
Thomas Ragett	3
John Hebert	2
Anthony Binsted	1
Thomas Upjohn[1]	1
Simon Rookley	2
Richard Gillowe	1
Anthony Bryant	1
George Hare	1
Nicholas Cooper	2
William Willts	1
Elizabeth Wheeler	1
James Cosh	1
Thomas Lindsey	1
Richard Evans	1
Christopher Wheeler	1
Thomas Upjohn[1]	1
hearths	102

Increased 1

Hearths not chargeable

John Lewes	1
Thomas Peaze	1
Thomas Peaze junior	1
Robert Wheeler	1
Jasper Lewes	1
Richard Dible	1
Thomas Willts junior	1
Widow Parsons	1

Fol. 33r(i)

Thomas Payne	1
Thomas Martin junior	2
George Wedmer	1
Peter Norwood	1
Nicholas Bemon	1
John Wheeler	1
John Wheeler junior	1
William Treherne	1
Richard Treherne	1
hearths	18

1. *Written as* Ugjohn, *but definitely* Upjohn

159. BREAMORE LIBERTY

Hearths chargeable

Robert Lord Brookes	19
Mister Crabb	6
Mister John Gray	6
John Warwick	3
Thomas Richards	1
Valentine Edsall	1
Elizabeth White	2
William Fry	2
Catherine Poore	4
Arthur Poore	5
Margaret Curtis	3
Ann Rooke	3
John Newman	1

John Trusler	2
Henry Mowland	2
Henry Harris	1
William Frith	2
Henry Curtis	2
Joyce Rooke	2
Mary Harris	2
William Mowland	3
Richard Browne	3
Henry Browne	3
John Frost	2
Henry Dove	2
William Dove	1
Henry Thomas	2
Edward Triphook	3
John Mowland	1
Alice White widow	2
Rebecca Curtis	1
Henry Ally	1
Henry Rooke	1
William Moore senior	2
Matthew Holloway	1
Mister William Crabb	3
John Chubb	1
Edward Precy	3
William Broadford	3
Elizabeth Gray	2
John Fyfoot	2
William Broadford	3
James Warwick	1
William Line	2
Henry Johnson	3
William Holloway	1
Richard Holloway	3

Fol. 33r(ii)

William Moore junior	1
William Frost	2
Roger Burch	1
Edward Mowland	1
William Absolon	1
Christopher Chubb	1
Arthur Goddard	2
Henry Fulford	1
William Roe	1
Widow Randoll	1
Thomas Lane	3
hearths	139

Increased 9

Hearths not chargeable

John Pragnell	1
Henry Pragnell	1
William Parker	1
Ralph Churtis	1
Cicely Thomas	2
Ann Chubb	2
Ambrose Bampton	1
Henry White	1
Thomas Rooke	1
John New	1
John Holloway	2
The almshouse	2
hearths	16

160. LYMINGTON BOROUGH[1]

Hearths chargeable

Mister Thomas Urry	8
William Durling	1
The Sign of the Crown	6
Josias Norden	6
John Lampert	5
William Wilkins	2
Mistress Burrad	8
John Cramborne	1
John Dobbins	2
John Edwards	3
John Asshly	2
Bartholomew Bulkely	7
Thomas Samber	5
Lewe[2] Newman	3
Widow Rose	3
Geoffrey Gray	2
Widow Herbert	3
Edward Thorne	3
Mistress Joardame	2
Francis Merrett	2
Michael Quint	2
Thomas Burford junior	1
Henry Williams	2
Richard Kinge	3
Henry Dod	5

160. LYMINGTON BOROUGH —*cont'd.*

Edward Stacy	3
John Nicholls	4

Fol. 33v(i)

William Bradshaw	3
Thomas Burford	3
John Beare	2
Robert Huchens	3
Bethlem Lacy	2
Bartholomew Warne	1
John Evans	1
John Thirston	3
Edward Carpenter	1
Thomas Crew	2
Thomas Gleven	8
Thomas Harold	2
Thomas Bellman	1
Henry Wall	3
Henry Lyne	4
Mister Francis Guidott	8
John Uphill	1
Thomas Vinren	3
Dorothy Mutcher	4
Robert Edwards	1
Bartholomew[3] Harmwood	4
Humphrey Bewfeild	4
Robert Meux	2
Daniel Edwards	4
John Kinge	2
Thomas Coombers	5
Edward Jackett	3
Henry Kerby	4
William White	2
John Deere	2
Thomas Tompkins	7
William Tellier	3
Richard Barnaby	2
Thomas Eeds	2
Robert Forder	1
John Harmwood	3
Joan Dore	5
Richard White	3
Edmund Rowland	2
Walter Penton	3
Thomas Samber	2
hearths	215

Increased 15

Hearths not chargeable

Mark Hurst	1
Stephen Hurst	1
Widow Cooper	1
Widow Bidges	2
Thomas Parks	1
Thomas Burnett	2
William Swettman	1
Simon Badcock	1
Thomas Day	1
Peter Burnett	1
John Thorne	2
John Hills	2
Joan Russell	1
Michael Chrichman	2
Thomas Staple	1
William Hawkins	1
George Durlon	1
Mary Haynes	2
Richard Garrett	1
George Shepherd	1
John Jervis	1
John Hoskins	1
Mary Easton	1
Merrell Oliver	1

Fol. 33v(ii)

William Badcock	1
Andrew Hurst	1
Widow Burnett	2
hearths	34

1. Lymington Borough
2. *Probably* Lewis
3. *Forename abbreviated as* Brath

161. OLD LYMINGTON[1]

Hearths chargeable

John Butten esquire	19
Philip Dore	9
Woodsed Farm	5
John Laurence	4
Richard Parsons	3

William Edwards	2
Widow Scott	2
John Newell	2
George Burrad	5
George Woort	2
John Longe	2
John Shepherd senior	1
John Hawkins	2
Thomas Elliott	3
Widow Studley	3
John Studley	1
Thomas Wansey	5[(a)]
Giles Whing	3
James Studley	2
William Shepherd	2
Mister Warner	2
Ellis Holloway	3
Gregory Mosell	4
John Woort	2
John Woorte	4
Thomas Deckland	1
Ann Chidle	1
John Blake	2
John Hills	2
John Smith	2
hearths	103

Hearths not chargeable

Widow Oliver	1
Thomas Cooper	2
Widow Brett	1
John Oliver	1
Widow Stanly	1
Widow White	1
John Dorland	1
Richard Uphill	1
Andrew Lockyer	1
Thomas Combs	2
Widow Shepherd	1
John Tyller	1
Peter Harberden	1
John Ellen	1
John Johnson	1
Christopher Brixey	2
Edward Burbridg	1
John Badcock	1
Edward Combs	1
John Colestock	1
John Warner	3
Fol. 34r(i)	
Mister Guidatt	1
John Lamport	1
hearths	28

The number of hearths chargeable within the several liberties of Dibden[2], Breamore[3] and Lymington[4] is 556

Not chargeable 96

(a) standing a quarter of a year
1. Old Limington
2. Dibdenn
3. Breamer
4. Limmington

162. BEAULIEU LIBERTY[1]

Hearths chargeable

William Byles	2
Edward Stowell	4
Charles Abbott	3
Edmund Pescod	3
William Hunt	4
Elizabeth Rolfe	2
Nicholas Baily	5
Andrew Lyne	2
John Fitcher	2
Henry Complin	2
John Kerby	8
Margaret Godfrey	1
Alice Dowe	6
Edward Frost	1
Richard Smith	3
Richard Rolfe	4
William Haksford	1
Thomas Smith	1
Ruth Rolfe	4
William Harford	1
Thomas Smith	1
Ann Gregory	2
John Bidlecombe	4
Henry Pescod	5

162. BEAULIEU LIBERTY
—cont'd.

John Bartlett	2
Widow Archer	6
Richard Lambert	4
Thomas Lovell	2
Stephen Smith	3
Ruth Rolfe	1
George Cole	4
Edward Lyne	8
Thomas Welch	2
John Welch	2
William Greene	2
Richard Drover	1
Thomas Batley	14
William Dowe	8
Edward Martin	1
Margaret Warner	4
George Bragge	3
John White	2
Nicholas Houchins	1
John Barram	3
Widow Elliott	2
Nicholas Welch	2
Marian Garrett	2
hearths	150

Fol. 34r(ii)

Hearths not chargeable

John Philipps	1
John Carpenter	1
John Rabetts	1
Widow Drover	1
Widow Rawlins	1
Richard Right	1
Goodwife Glaspoole	1
Edward Rawlins	1
Widow Hills	1
John Day	1
Peter Royall	1
John Phipps	1
Edward Rawlins	1
Goodman Rowe	1
Andrew Strugnell	1
Widow Bramble	1
Michael Mills	1
Robert Jones	1
Henry Godfry	1
Ephraim Kent	1
Leonard Page	1
Widow Woods	1
John Pettis	1
Robert Philipp	1
Henry Drover	1
Widow Rookely	1
John Perrum	1
Goodman Wassell	1
Goodman Hemmings	1
Widow Rawlins	1
Goodman Dover	1
William Purdue	1
Edward Lynne	1
John Iremonger	1
Edmund Woodlyne	1
Humphrey Ireland	1
Goodman Dore	1
Daniel Poste	1
Goodman Chack	1
Reynold Waterman	1
Goodwife Merriweather	1
hearths	41

The number of hearths chargeable within the whole division of the New Forest[2] is	5286
Not chargeable	1263

1. Bewly Liberty
2. New Forrest

Fol. 35r(i)

ALTON DIVISION

ALTON HUNDRED

163. ALTON WESTBROOK[1]

Hearths chargeable

Richard Holland	14
Roger Harrison	13
John Buttler	2
Richard Viccary	2
Widow and Robert Braman	5
Roger Parkhurst	4

John Hockly	4
Andrew Pile	3
Nicholas Kemp	3
Anthony Compton	3
George Hunt	3
Thomas Pinck	4
Thomas Mathew	3
George Dowe	1
William Bone	1
George Sweetapple	2
Thomas Eastman	3
Richard Carpenter	3
John Betsworth	3
John Goodyer	5
John Carter	1
Ralph Bushell	2
Robert Smith	3
Robert Cranstone	6
Edward Albrey	6
Moses Neeve	7
William Wake	4
Joseph Stevens	5
Richard Stent	3
Henry Harding	4
Robert Lamport	4
Laurence Odison	3
John Gill	3
William Turner	2
Thomas Nichollson	3
Andrew Ayres	3
Laurence Geale	7
Nicholas Gates	2
Thomas Mathew	4
Thomas Andrews	2
Benjamin Neeve	3
John Eastmeane	3
Richard Smith	2
William Phey	2
George May	3
Humphrey Hedrington	2
Laurence Stevens	1
John Gregory	4
William Normanton	5
James Mathew	1
Simon and William Puckeridge	2
Thomas Puckeridg	5
Edward Rainger	1
John Stanly	2
Thomas Stead	2
Widow Tindall	2
Widow Wells	4
George Froude	3
Richard Buttler	1

Fol. 35r(ii)

William Normanton junior	2
Philip Hobbs	1
Andrew Andrewes	2
Richard Feilder	2
William Hamone	2
Simon Walker	1
Roger Turner	2
hearths	217

Hearths not chargeable

William Rivett	2
John Feilder senior	2
John Feilder junior	2
William Browne	2
Richard Sparsment	2
William Dudney	2
John Neller	1
Edward Albery	1
John Marshall	2
George Mersh	2
Laurence Stevens	1
Christopher Vallor	2
Thomas Liminge	2
Laurence Robinson	1
John Cooper senior	1
John Cooper junior	1
John Cooper	1
Widow Peckett	1
Peter Baily	1
Widow Liminge	1
Simon Knight	1
Nicholas Warner	2
Widow Palmer	2
Ann Palmer	1
Edward Andrews	2
Anthony Jones	1

163. ALTON WESTBROOK *—cont'd.*

Tristram Tylly	2
Thomas Neeve	2
Widow Baker	1
Widow Warner	1
Simon Warner	1
Nicholas Burrowe	1
Richard Budd	2
Robert Allen	1
Edward Berry	2
William Constance	2
John Stevens	2
Henry Bristowe	2
William Weeller	2
John Andrews	2
Mark Frost	1
William Baker	2
Widow Gates	2
Thomas Cooper	1
William Smith	1
John Barrett	2
William Morrell	1
William Baker	2
John Harris	2
Joan Hockly	1
Martha Carter	1

Fol. 35v(i)

Sarah Hunt	2
Thomas Betsworth	2
Moses Gardner	2
Richard Smith	1
John West	2
Henry Baily	2
hearths	89

1. Alton Westbrooke

164. ALTON EASTBROOK[1]

Hearths chargeable

Mister Daniel Buttler	6
William Gates senior	4
Matthew Hawkins	8
Francis Lamport	5
Laurence Lamport	3
Jonathan Slye	7
William Gates junior	4
Laurence Eastman	4
Michael Mills	4
Mordecai Hall	1
George Allom	1
Daniel Netter senior	1
Daniel Netter junior	2
John Searle	1
Richard Searle	2
Henry Wheler	2
William Normanton	3
Nicholas Knight	1
Richard Searle senior	4
Desire Smith	2
William Upton	2
Thomas Skinner	1
John Newell	2
Thomas Westbrooke	2
Richard Habben junior	3
Richard Habben senior	3
Edward Heather	3
John Feilder	1
John Dearing	3
Nicholas Allon	2
John Mortimer	1
Thomas Tuckes	3
Thomas Mersh	2
Robert Gunning	1
Thomas Wedge	1
Mister Henry Mathew	3
Andrew Eyers	2
William Barzill	3
Widow Wake	1
Thomas Bristowe	1
Richard Palmer	2
Thomas Collins	1
Peter Baily	1
Elizabeth Kinge	2
Richard Hamone	3
Thomas Mills	1
Zacharias Clerke	1
Stephen James	1
John Joye	2
Thomas Trye	1
William Bond	2
John Moore	2

Fol. 35v(ii)

Richard Sley	2
William Ballett	1
William Page	1
William Sharpe	2
George Page	1
hearths	131

Hearths not chargeable

Ann Blanchard	1
John Collins	1
William Bazill	1
Thomas Symes	1
Nicholas Frost	1
John Feilder senior	1
John Feilder junior	1
Francis Sparks	1
John Porter	2
Thomas Breagly	1
Mary Hamond	2
Richard Browne	1
John Nichollson	1
Widow Gibson	1
Edward Eggby	1
Thomas Sparks	1
John Bushell	1
Thomas Boyes	1
Joan Curle	2
Edward Feilder	1
John Deane senior	1
John Deane junior	1
John Perry	1
Thomas Bassill	1
Thomas Bullock	2
John Eames	1
John Spurrier	1
John Carke	1
Charles Curteme	1
Henry Arnold	1
Samuel Webb	1
Gabriel Burrow	1
Widow Slide	2
John Hunt	1
William Conne	1
William Warterne	1
Charles Newbolt	1
Benjamin Hall	2
William Barrett	1
Widow Winner	1
Edward Bromley	1
John Cornelius	1
Henry Hamon	1
hearths	49

1. Alton Eastbrooke

165. ANSTEY[1]

Hearths chargeable

William Lipscombe	3
William King	1
Mister Brooks' school	4
Robert Viccary	1
Henry Crockford	1
Edward King	1
hearths	11

Fol. 36r(i)

Hearths not chargeable

Widow Rowte	1
John Manninge	1
Widow Kinge	2
Peter Hall	1
John Tredge	1
Richard Edsby	1
Crews Pooke	1
Widow Hobbs	1
hearths	9

1. Anstee

166. THEDDEN[1]

Hearths chargeable

Mister John Hunt	4
Lewis Goodyer	7
Barnard Knight	5
Mistress Buckly	1
Richard Jefferys	1
hearths	18

Hearths not chargeable

Richard Sparks	1
Richard Cowdry	1
hearths	2

1. Thidden

167. WILLHALL[1]

Hearths chargeable

John Knight	4
hearths	4

1. Winhall

168. BINSTED POPHAM

Hearths chargeable

Carew Reynolds esquire	10
John Frost	2
Henry Wheeler	3
Nicholas Hunt	3
Nicholas Hunt	1
Widow Stent	5
John Sandall	3
Mister Smith	3
John Morgan	3
Thomas Hunt	7
Peter Burningham	1
Joseph Stent	2
Richard Mathew	1
Henry Mathew	1
George Merchant	2
George Cooke	2
John Person	1
Henry Over	1
William Quaite	2
Thomas Porter	1
Mister Edmund Hooke for the Great Lodge	10
For Goose Green Lodge	5
hearths	68

Hearths not chargeable

Widow Wheeler	1
Robert Swayne	2
Richard Quallett	1
Robert Pallington	1
Robert Hunt	1
Henry Nicklin	2
Chloe Kinge	2
The almshouse	2
Widow Hunt	2
[ ] Baker	1
[ ]	2
[ ]	1

Fol. 36r(ii)

Thomas Hunt	1
George Pollard	1
Robert Cooper	1
Thomas Smith	1
Widow Budds	3
hearths	35

169. CHILTLEY[1]

Hearths chargeable

Thomas Albery	8
George Gasse	7
John Greene	3
John Hammon	4
Widow Collger	5
Nicholas Porter	2
John Neale	3
William Legge	1
Thomas Dudman	1
Henry Glasier	3
John Avery	1
Thomas Bridger	1
John Luff	1
John Purdue	3
Mister Palmer's house	2[(a)]
hearths	45

Hearths not chargeable

William Pummell	1
Thomas Harwood	1
John Fullcocke	1
Richard Marshall	1
Robert Wartridge	1
Robert Bowles	1
hearths	6

(a) void
1. Chiltlee

170. BRAMSHOTT

Hearths chargeable

John Hook esquire	15
Mistress Margaret Hooke	7
Mister Woolmay	7
Mister Nicholas Wither	5
William Tribb	3
William Pack	4

John Buttler	3
Richard Hewes	3
Thomas Boxall	2
William Purdue	1
Richard Stent	1
Edward Newman	1
Robert White	2
John Bicknell	2
Thomas Lock	2
William Bone	1
Widow Hall	1
Francis Marshall	1
Roger Heather	2
Mister Yalden's house	1[a]
hearths	64

Hearths not chargeable

Edmund Fullick	1
Benjamin Chase	1
Widow Jessapp	2
Widow Glasier	2
Thomas Hansome	1
William Right	2
hearths	9

(a) void

Fol. 36v(i)

171. LUDSHOTT

Hearths chargeable

Andrew Wall esquire	11
Henry Cleere	3
John Benfold	3
Richard Bristowe	2
John Bristowe	6
William Randoll	1
Raphael Vallor	1
Thomas Turke	1
Charles Osborne	1
Henry Hounsome	2
Richard Tribb	2
Nicholas Snelling	3
Nicholas Bunch	1
Widow Streater	6
William Tribb	2
hearths	45

Hearths not chargeable

Widow Clerke	1
Widow White	1
Richard White	1
John Booker	1
John Hounsome	1
John Lampart	1
Robert Bagen	1
John Smith	1
Anthony Tribb	1
Goodman Larby	1
Daniel Avery	1
William Honney	1
hearths	12

172. BROXHEAD

Hearths chargeable

Mister Moory Fauteleroy	10
William Lee	3
John Kellzill	4
Thomas Ayley	1
Francis Locksum	2
Francis Greensell	1
William Channell	1
John Hebb	3
John Albery	2
Edward Newman	1
Richard Corfe	2
hearths	30

Hearths not chargeable

Laurence Childs	2
William Stillman	1
Thomas Viccary	1
John Nichollson	1
Thomas Albery	1
Henry Farly	1
hearths	7

173. WEST WORLDHAM[1]

Hearths chargeable

Sir Nicholas Steward baronet	11
Thomas Stent	9
William Dunce	3

173. WEST WORLDHAM—*cont'd.*

Richard Dunce	1
Richard Woodman	2
Thomas Nash	3
hearths	29

Fol. 36v(ii)

Hearths not chargeable

Nicholas Knight	1
Robert Deacon	2
Robert Viccary	1
hearths	4

1. Westwordleham

174. ROTHERFIELD[1]

Hearths chargeable

Sir Humphrey Bennett knight	23
Ballams Farm	2
Richard Pollinge	2
Stephen Ramsdeane	6
Gilbert Wilkins	3
hearths	36

1. Rotherfeild

175. OAKHANGER[1]

Hearths chargeable

Mister William Christmas	6
Robert Hudson	6
Robert Beadle	3
Robert Boxall	4
William Huntingford	2
John Missingham	4
Thomas Lynne	2
William Porter	8
Mister Christmas	4
William Heath	4
Henry Newlinge	2
Henry Newling	2
George Kempe	3
Richard Grace	1
John Newling	1
Widow Seimor	2
hearths	54

Hearths not chargeable

Widow Tull	1
Widow Feltham	1
John Wheatland	1
Richard Alexander	1
hearths	4

1. Okehanger

176. GREATHAM

Hearths chargeable

Richard Love esquire	10
Mister John Love	4
John Chase	5
Isaac Hellier	2
Widow Hellier	2
Nicholas Scriven	5
Mistress Holloway widow	3
William Holloway	3(a)
Richard Mills	3
William Gamon	2
William Chase	2
Richard Newling	2
Thomas Figge	1
William Greene	1
William Bettsworth	1
Robert Eldridg	1
Henry Hounsome	1
Widow Hellier	1
hearths	50

Fol. 37r(i)

Hearths not chargeable

Richard Holle	1
Richard Hill	1
Widow Collier	1
Widow Greene	1
Widow Chase	1
Richard Smith	1
Widow Skinner	2
George Newlin	1
Peter Bensted	1
Widow Bridger	1
John Newlin	1
hearths	12

(a) 1 pulled down

177. FROYLE[1]

Hearths chargeable

John Fines esquire	21
Thomas Lamboll	8
Nicholas Whalle	2
William Newman	7
John Newman	3
Richard Whitehall	3
Robert Rowte	1
William Towers	2
James Major	2
Richard Hodges	2
John Smith	1
Nicholas Eedes	2
John Gates	2
Thomas Poett	1
Francis Eedes	1
Darby Warner	1
Henry Wake	2
Thomas Eedes	3
Barnard Burningham	6
James Hunt	1
Thomas Newman	5
Edward Morris	1[(a)]
Richard Trusler	1
Richard Chaundler	3
William Norman	5
Henry Warner	3
George Hawkins	2
John Stileman	3
Widow Newman	3
Thomas Bristowe	2
George Pecke	2
Robert Winslott	3
John Gillett	3
Robert Sentwell	2
Thomas Eedes	3
Thomas Warner	3
William Stacy	2[(a)]
Thomas Palmer	1
Thomas Blanchard	3
George Mathew	3
James Cooper	1
Mister Farrer	5
hearths	130

Hearths not chargeable

George Baldchild	1
Widow Wilkinson	1
Robert Terry	1
Richard Rowse	1
Henry Major	1
Andrew Earle	1
John Earle	1
John Vinson	1
Richard Tribb	1

Fol. 37r(ii)

Francis Silvester	1
Widow Labourer	1
William Forder	1
Widow Slaughter	1
Richard Knight	1
hearths	4

(a) 1 overcharged

1. Froile

178. HOLYBOURNE

Hearths chargeable

Thomas Christmas	5
John Trimer	5
Elizabeth Neave widow	3
Andrew Baldwin	4
John Heyman	2
Richard Trimer	1
Edmund Trimer	2
Joan Baldwin	2
Thomas Russell	3
John Hunt	2
Richard Andrews	3
Ann Hooker	2
Mister Yeats	2[(a)]
Edmund Trimer	3
John Croniston	3
Richard Jefferyes	3
William Smith	3
William Dawes	3
Richard Pratt	3
John Beckner	1
Elizabeth Watts	1
Ann Spurrier	1
Alice Lock widow	1

178. HOLYBOURNE—*cont'd.*

James Wilkinson	1
William Baldwin	3
Nathaniel Mathew	2
Thomas Grover	1
Thomas Dennis	3
Edward Langford	3
hearths	71

Hearths not chargeable

John Stacy	1
Ferdinand Porter	1
Henry Young	1
John Mapp	2
John Morely	1
John Cooke	1
Robert Willer	1
Richard Chaundler	1
Richard Wells	1
Richard Hill	1
Widow Carpenter	1
John Upton	1
George Dudman	1
hearths	14

(a) 1 more built

179. WESTCOTT[1]

Hearths chargeable

Henry Smith	4
John Miller	3
Widow Stent	3
Barnard Lee	2
Robert Trimer	2
John Bayly	2
Widow Eames	1
William Shore	1
hearths	18

Hearths not chargeable

William Hole	1
hearths	1

1. West Court

Fol. 37v(i)

180. WYCK[1]

Hearths chargeable

Mister Handman	6
Clement Boyes	2
Richard Milles	1
William Piper	1
Charles Cheyney	4
Thomas Clerke	4
hearths	18

Hearths not chargeable

William Cawte	1
hearths	1

1. Weeke

181. BINSTED REGIS

Hearths chargeable

Mistress Norton	11
Mister Samuel Woodford	6
Robert Careless	4
John Purdue	3
Widow Smith	2
Richard Underwood	1
Robert Beard	1
Thomas Rivers	3
Widow Forder	1
John Mew	1
William Morgan	3
William Wheeler	2
Thomas White	1
Thomas Missingham	1
Barnard Burningham	4
hearths	45

Hearths not chargeable

John Newell	1
Richard Rivers	1
Ellen Mannell	1
Widow Frost	1
Widow Dudman	1
Thomas Frost	1
Widow Rivers	1
Widow Purdue	2
Richard Hewes	1
John New	1
Richard Underwood	1
hearths	12

182. ISINGTON[1]

Hearths chargeable

Nicholas Wheeler	9
John Wheeler	3
Robert Newman	2
Henry Buckham	1
Jerome Viccary	1
Edward Money	3
John Lock senior	3
Ralph Andrews	1
James Hunt	3
Robert Viccary	3
Widow Hawkins	2
Richard Capplin	3
Richard Cooper	3
Philip Lamboll	3
George Chaundler	3
John Hawkins	1
Francis Knight	1
Thomas Mitchell	2
John Jackson	1
John Over	2

Fol. 37v(ii)

William Sandale	2
James Viccary	2
Francis Thackham	1
John Hawkins	1
Edward Turvill	1
Richard Cooper	2
John Bunch	1
John Lock junior	1
George Frost	1
Christopher Frost	1
Thomas Cawte	2
Peter Butt	1
William Brathwaite	3
hearths	69

Hearths not chargeable

Philip Butt	1
Henry Bagin	1
William Soane	1
John Lassam	1
William Whitehall	1
Ursula Browne widow	1
Mary Bettsworth	1
Richard Hunt	1
Widow Baily	1
Joseph Feilder	1
Richard Caplin	1
John Budd	1
Elizabeth Cosens widow	1
Robert Trusler	1
Anthony Coles	1
Nathaniel Mersh	1
William Coombs	1
hearths	17

1. Issington

183. SOUTH HAY[1]

Hearths chargeable

George Wakeford	6
More for Inmans	2
More for Blackmore	1
More for Ridgers	1
John Chapman	2
For Kingsholt Hill	2
Bridger Philip[2]	3
Richard Smith	4
Henry Bicknell	2
Reuben James	1
Mister Henry Christmas	8
John Hunt	2
Robert Stilloway	3
Mister James Heighes	16
William Deacon	1
Richard Morris	1
William Cosens	3
Jerome Christmas	7
William Greene	2
Robert Bensteed	2
William Marshall	5
Thomas Heather	3
John Newell	1
hearths	78

Hearths not chargeable

Richard Pescodd	1
Widow Money	1
Henry Forder	1

183. SOUTH HAY—*cont'd.*

John Mory	1
Richard Roe	1
George Appleton	1

Fol. 38r(i)

Widow Edwards	1
Richard Forder	1
hearths	8

1. Southaye
2. *Probably* Philip Bridger

184. EAST WORLDHAM[1]

Hearths chargeable

Mister Henry Mosse	3
Mister William Christmas	3
Mister John Tille	5
William Heather	3
Samuel Box	2
William Gregory	3
John Freeland	1
Edward Heighes	1
Nicholas Dunn	1
Thomas Bone	1
Thomas Chase	2
Thomas Moorey	6
hearths	31

Hearths not chargeable

Zacharias Dance	1
John Davie	1
Peter Goble	1
Thomas Lambolle	1
Nicholas Woods	1
Mary Heighs	2
James Hunsome	1
Richard Porter	1
Thomas Pamplin	1
Elizeas Shelly's house down	2
hearths	12

1. East Worldeham

185. DOCKENFIELD[1]

Hearths chargeable

Mister Knight	5
Mister Christmas	4
Richard Cooper	6
William Cleere	6
James Knight	3
Roger Marshall	1[(a)]
Edward Spicer	1
Richard Mills	1
Richard Lunn	1
John Page	1[(b)]
Robert Boxall	1
hearths	30

Hearths not chargeable

Edward Budd	1
Richard Jeffery	1
Robert Harding	2
Widow Marshall	1
Robert Marshall	1
hearths	6

(a) 1 down
(b) 1 overcharged
1. Dockensfeild

186. HOLTHAM AND HERDS[1]

Hearths chargeable

John Gibman	5
hearths	5

1. Hotham & Herds

Fol. 38r(ii)

187. NEATHAM

Hearths chargeable

Richard Jefferyes	3
Robert Pratt	3
John Inwood	12
William Lock	3
Robert Legat	2
John Edzer	2
Edward Jeffery	1
Richard Stillaway	1
Henry Christmas	1
hearths	28

Hearths not chargeable

Nicholas Stent	1
Widow Spurrier	1
hearths	2

188. WHEATLEY[1]

Hearths chargeable

Richard Knight	7
William Kitchiner	4
Thomas Rivers	3
Widow Heighs	3
John Stent	3
Robert Skinner	1
John Roe	3
hearths	24

Hearths not chargeable

George Restler	1
John Nicklin	1
Nicholas Brewer	2
Robert Priseman	1
hearths	5

1. Wheatly

189. KINGSLEY

Hearths chargeable

William Huntingford	1
Raphael Vallor	1
Richard Hill	1
William Baker	1
Henry Venn	5
John Chitty	3
William Valler	6
Edward Mills	3
John Michell	3
John Reede	3
James Bridger	3
Benjamin Mathew	1
Richard Reynolds	3
Widow Harding	2
John Hewes	3
Widow Reede	6(a)
Ambrose Dallman	3
Francis Fletcher	2
William Petoe	4
Richard Guy	1
Richard Smith	2
Edward Hooker	1

Fol. 38v(i)

Nicholas Kelsey	2
William Deacon	1
William Bicknell	3
Henry Trigg	1
Benjamin Smith	3(b)
Edmund Cleere	4
John Bicknell	3
John Huntingford	3
John Paice	2
Widow Appsley	1
John Page	3
Richard Lunn	1
Thomas Page	1
John Verndell	2
Richard Blackhouse	2
William Prowtinge	5
John Mathew	2
Richard Hoare	1
Robert Maybancke	1
George Kempe	1
John Childs	1
Mister Henry Heighs	6
Richard Luttman	3
John Roade	1
Thomas Kelsey	1(b)
James Knight	1
Widow Mathew	2
hearths	115

Hearths not chargeable

William Peckett	1
Elizabeth Peckett	1
Widow Cover	1
Widow Reede	2
John Harding	1
Thomas Hammon	1
Robert Tull	1
Joan Barden	1
Nicholas Greenetree	1
Nicholas Freeborne	1
Widow Harding	1
John Whitland	1
William Winter	1
Peter Dunce	1
Widow Dunce	1
Robert Lockyer	1
James Gray	1
Jennifer Collins	1

189. KINGSLEY—*cont'd.*

Thomas Turvell	1
Thomas Hansome senior	1
Hugh Robinson	1
Widow Hamon	1
Widow Wheeler	1
Richard Trigg	1
John Okeshott	1
George Kelsey	1
John Kelsey	1
Thomas Newlin and Mary Palmer	2
Ryefeilds the house down	1
hearths	31

(a) 5 taken down
(b) 1 overcharged

Fol. 38v(ii)

190. HARTLEY MAUDITT[1]

Hearths chargeable

Sir Nicholas Steward baronet	15[(a)]
Mister Pargiter	5
Mister Pargiter	1
Edward Wheeler	4
Christopher Mathew	1
John Mathew	3
Thomas Philipps	3
Thomas Newlin	3
John Westbrooke	1
Christopher Lockyer	1
George Heath	2
Peter Fey	1
William Edwards	1
Richard Westbrooke	2
hearths	43

Hearths not chargeable

Robert Lyde	1
Richard Coles	1
Widow [ ] icas[2]	1
Widow Cornwall	1
Widow Porter	1
Widow Mills	1
Richard Skilton	2
Richard Porter	1
John Edwards	1
hearths	10

(a) 1 overcharged
1. Hartly Mauditt
2. *Initial letter of surname altered and unclear*

191. CHAWTON

Hearths chargeable

Richard Knight esquire	21
Thomas Pryer junior	6
Thomas Moory	4
William Dawes	3
John Alderslade	4
William Mulford	5
Robert Knight	4
John Knight	5
Roland Prowting	4
Richard Knight	1
John Page	6
Thomas Cornwall	2[(a)]
Honor Richards widow	2
William Pratt	3
Richard Knight	1
Widow Newell	1
Richard Harris	1
William Fisher	6
Thomas Morley	3
Robert Young	1
William Budd	3
hearths	86

Fol. 39r(i)

Hearths not chargeable

Richard Goodchild	1
Charles Eames	1
Almshouse	3
Thomas Coleman	2
Thomas Harrison	1
John May	1
William Mathews	1
Thomas Knight	1
John Prior	1
William Morey	1

Thomas Pryor senior	1
hearths	14

(a) 1 taken down

The number of hearths chargeable in the hundred of Alton is	1592
Not chargeable	37

BISHOPS SUTTON HUNDRED[1]

192. NEW ALRESFORD

Hearths chargeable

William Bradley	3
John Cooke	3
Mistress Joan Worlidg	6
William Hodson	4
Richard Shackleford	4
John Nevill	3
Widow Freeland	3
Thomas Street	4
Thomas Drewe	6
Jacob Russell	2
William Smith	4
Thomas Busey	1
Thomas Astlett senior	3
Justinian Astlett	2
William Butcher	2(a)
Nicholas Scriven	3
Nathaniel Bradley	5
John Bradley	3
Richard Hockly	4(a)
William Johnson	2(a)
Thomas Bulbeck	1
Henry Worlidge	3
William Sweetapple	3
Jasper Cottman	2
Richard Goffe	1
William Westerton	2(a)
Thomas Edwards	2
William Goldsmith	1
John Mannery	3
John Shale	1
John Newman	2
Charles Lipscombe	3
Widow Costin	2
John Nevill	2
Edward Newland	1
John Veake	1
William White	3
Samuel Westerton	2
Richard Restall	2
Henry Andrews	7(b)
William Wickham	1
Francis Howell	1
John Shackleford	1

Fol. 39r(ii)

Thomas Mersham	3(a)
John Andrews	2
Ellen Grigg widow	2
Gervase Abbin	10(b)
Christopher Bradley	3
Edward Jacques	2
Christopher Launder	2
Edmund Welch	5
William Hollis	2
Edward Small	2
John Astlett junior	2
Widow Godfrey	1
Arthur Mersham junior	1
Thomas Hobbs	2
Thomas Humphryes	2
Henry Budd	2
John Restall	1
John Figgins	1
John Younge	1
Robert Barnard	8(a)
John Withers	3
Arthur Mersham senior	2
Thomas Standen	6
Mistress Burgis	2
Richard Reeves	3
Edward Grossmith	2
John Grossmith	2
Edward Springe	3
William Evens	1
John Cooper	2
Lucy Welch	4
Andrew Grossmith	2
John Streape	1
Mister Markwicke	6
William Wade	3

192. NEW ALRESFORD—*cont'd.*

Thomas Clerke 3
Thomas Smith 3
Jacob Astlett 2
Thomas Todd 2
Thomas Goffe 1
William Atkinson 2
Widow Tomkins 1
Thomas Clerke junior 2
William Twine 2
Benjamin Warren 1
James Norton 6
Timothy Smith 1
Edward Cooper 2
Mister Waltensis 5
Edward Weekes 3
Richard Johnson 2
Widow Wade 2
John Aslett 3
hearths 253

Hearths not chargeable

William Edwards 1
Nicholas Jackman 1
Robert Budd 1
Laurence Barling 1
Widow Poole 1
Christopher Smith 1
Mary Baslett 1
Nicholas Garrett 1
George Harris 1
Widow Dent 1
Widow Richards 1

Fol. 39v(i)

John Page 1
Widow Frost 1
Widow Stacy 1
John Simpson 1
Daniel Vecke 1
Thomas Leeman 1
Margaret Baslett 1
Robert Wash 1
George Poole 1
Ann Feilder 1
Widow Faithfull 1
James Frost 1
Ralph Gunter 1
Widow Todd 1
Widow Hobbs 1
Dorothy Yarrington 2
Ann Cooper 2
Thomas Hobbs 1
Widow Trininge 2
Robert Worsham 2
Widow Evens 2
Goodwife Chackford 1
William Edwards 1
John Hockley 1
Robert Leather 1
hearths 41

(a) 1 down
(b) 1 overcharged
1. Sutton Hundred

193. ROPLEY

Hearths chargeable

Mister William Vennables 9
John Mahew 3[a]
Robert Budd 4
Thomas Budd 1
Thomas Mahew 2
John Taylor 1
Thomas Weene 1
Thomas Andrews 1
John Gilbert 1
Humphrey Andrews 1
John Gibson 1
William Weekes 1
James Blanchard 2
Henry Blanchard 1
James Budd 3
Richard Weene 1
Widow Andrew 2
Giles Mills 2
John Budd 2
William Godwin 1
John Lake 2
Widow Hellier 1
John Lipscombe 1
William Applegarth 2
Thomas Oliver 3

Robert Wrestler	1
John Hackman	3
Robert Weene	2
Thomas Lipscombe	2
Mister John Cole	12
John Lowman vicar	3
William Collins	2
Thomas Taylor	2
Andrew Merriott	4
John Twitt	1
Richard Harwood	1
John Long senior	3

Fol. 39v(ii)

John Rowland	1
William Veare	3
Christopher Perdock	1
Robert Yalden junior	5
Henry Gilbert	4
James Warthington	3
Richard Harwood	2
John Okely	2
William Andrew	1
Christopher Hyde	1
William Worthington	1
John Gilbert	1
Nicholas Greenewood	2
John Barnard	6
John Bull	3
John Andrews	3
Thomas Ferrett	2
John Winter	2
John Worthington	2
John Mahew	2
Robert Yalden senior	3
John Gilbert	3
James Andrew	1
John Bargent	1
Richard Godwin	1
Michael Blanchard	1
Jasper Smith	1
Robert Sherrier	1
William White	1
William Andrews	3
hearths	148

Hearths not chargeable

Edward Cadrey	1
Thomas Cadrey	1
William Ham	1
Richard Budd	1
James Worthington	2
William Wheatly	1
Christopher Baker	1
John White	1
John Page	1
John Weene	1
Widow Gilbert	1
Thomas Cooper	1
Simon Poore	2
Thomas Harris	1
Widow Baker	1
Thomas Cooper	1
John Smith	1
Thomas Pare	1
Peter Privett	1
Widow Vandell	1
Peter Arnold	1
Henry Steele	1
Henry Ball	1
John West	1
John Cave	1
Thomas Oliver	1
Widow Oliver	1
John Kinchin	1
John Palmer	1
Robert Buckhurst	1
Widow Lumford	1
Widow Money	1
Richard Rabnett	1

Fol. 40r(i)

John Oliver	1
John Pincke	1
Peter Edney	1
Richard Privett	1
Widow Labrane	1
Robert Gammon	1
Widow Darby	1
Henry Heath	1
Widow Heath	1

193. ROPLEY—*cont'd.*

John Hackman	1
Robert Baker	1
hearths	46

(a) 1 down

194. HEADLEY

Hearths chargeable

Mister Albery Tompson	6
Widow Martin	3
John Stillwell	4
Richard Boxall	1
John Martin	3
John Baker	4
Henry Mathew and John Mills	4
Roger Barden	3
William Norris	3
William Albery	2[(a)]
William Moorer	3
Nicholas Morten	3
John Vallor senior	5
Nicholas Swanne	5
William Gill	3
Thomas Heath	1
John Crich	4
Robert Vallor	4
John Vallor junior	1
Henry Vallor	4
Henry Lock	1
John Gates	1
Abraham Gill	3
Henry Baker	2
Widow Fish	3
William Bettsworth	3
John Huntingford	1
John Bucknell	1
John Baker	3
Richard Lee	3[(b)]
John Randoll	2
Nicholas Baker	1
Nicholas Baker	1
Nicholas Jennings	3
Abraham Harding junior	3[(a)]
Widow Caplen	2
John Frost	1
William Baker	1
John Hounsome	4
Robert Hardinge	3
Thomas Mathew	1
William Channell	3
George Page and Williamson	4
William Brooter	3
Robert Varndell	3
Abraham Harding senior	3

Fol. 40r(ii)

John Bellinghurst	1
John Moorer	1
John House	1
Widow Valor	1[(c)]
hearths	129

Hearths not chargeable

William Larbee	1
Thomas Mill	1
Widow Hunsom	1
John Robinson	1
John Newman	1
Edward Robinson	1
George Dutten	1
Widow Robinson	1
Thomas Banister	1
John Holt	1
Thomas Baker	1
Robert Figg	1
Peter Hunt	3
John Moorer	1
Richard Shrubb	1
Edmund Shrubb	1
Anthony Shrubb	1
William Shrubb	1
Widow Perryne	1
Peter Combes	1
Abraham Farr	1
Daniel Norris	1
Thomas Kitch	1
Joan Hunt	1
Thomas Page	1
Edward Turner	1

Isaac Smither	1
Old Giles	1
Christopher Baker	1
John Denier	1
William Fuller	1
Robert Albery	1
William Smither	1
Nicholas Hedger	1
John Mahew	1
John Grice	1
Christopher King	2
Roger Barden	1
Henry Lock	1
North Farm	2
hearths	44

(a) 1 down
(b) 1 taken down
(c) 1 overcharged

195. BISHOPS SUTTON[1]

Hearths chargeable

Mistress Barbara Venables	4
Richard Seward	2
William Frost	1
John Cager	2
Deborah Waight	4
William Bricknell	1
Robert Fry	1
Roger Crockford	3
John Hewlett	1
Robert Mingham	2

Fol. 40v(i)

Nicholas Bull	3
Robert Bagen	2
Thomas Fidden	2
John Gilbert	1
John Bull	5
William Hobbs senior	1
John Bull	2
Roger Pincke	1
Jasper Smith	1
Robert Bassett	1
William Hobbs junior	1
Thomas Seward	4
hearths	45

Hearths not chargeable

John Suckett	1
John Smith	1
John Crockford	1
Thomas Aldridge	1
Thomas Sherrier	1
Richard Mills	1
George Kittlewell	1
Richard Gregory	1
William Privett	1
Widow Stevens	1
Edward Tribb	1
Roger Combs	1
Ann Fry	1
Widow Bright	1
John Wickham	1
John Blake	1
William Barkham	1
Henry Newman	1
hearths	18

1. Sutton

196. WEST TISTED

Hearths chargeable

Sir Benjamin Titchborne	4
Mister James Love	4
Mister Thomas Coward	4
Mister Richard Lacye	5
Thomas Hall	6
Peter Pincke	4
John Whittier	4(a)
Henry Knight	1
Moses Ratclife	1
John Winter	1
Henry Smith	1
Thomas Whittier	1
William Fry	1
John Brewer	1
Laurence Cooper	1
Richard Chase	1
Andrew Whittier	3
hearths	43

Hearths not chargeable

Widow Baker	1
Thomas Baker	1

196. WEST TISTED—*cont'd.*

Fol. 40v(ii)

Thomas Privett	1
Widow Cornish	1
Oliver Attwood	1
William Westbrooke	1
John Brewster	1
William Colleer	1
John Bicknell	1
Thomas Brewer	1
hearths	10

(a) 1 down

Hearths not chargeable

Henry Hasted	1
Charles Shackleford	1
James Crockford	1
Nicholas Nicholson	1
Peter Edney	1
Widow Baily	1
Widow Hellier	1
hearths	7

197. BIGHTON

Hearths chargeable

William Parker	2
Mistress Burgis	6
Mary Fann widow	3
William Evans	2
William Garrett	1
John French	3
Ann Parker widow	1
Daniel Hasted	1
Amy Edney widow	2
Michael Carpenter	2
John West	2
John Gregory	1
William Passingham	3
John Evans	2
John Cradock	2
Stephen Blunden	3
Widow Wellman	1
James Penfold	1
Peter Evans	3
John Okely	1
John Smith	2
Mary Privett widow	1
Nicholas Parker	2
Robert Evans	1
Nicholas Parker	5
Humphrey Hyde	1
Edward Evans	2
Nicholas Parker	3
Richard Gregory	1
hearths	60

198. BRAMDEAN[1]

Hearths chargeable

Mister Charles Browning	15
Stephen Greene	8
Peter Greene	6

Fol. 41r(i)

John Smith	5
John Camish	3
Ezekiel Bagin	3
Nicholas Turner	3
Thomas Cobb	2
William Edwards	2
George Aldridge	2
Joseph Pargett	2
John Rooke	3
hearths	54

Hearths not chargeable

Joseph Weekes	1
Widow Moulton	1
Widow Carter	1
Thomas Turner	2
Richard Rooke	1
Widow Cooke	1
Henry Gill	1
Goodwife Skilton	2
Widow Budd	1
Thomas Purse	2
William Downes	1
William Veare	1
Robert Poole	2
hearths	17

1. Bramdeane

The number of hearths chargeable within the hundred of Bishops Sutton is	732
Not chargeable	183

SELBORNE HUNDRED[1]

199. EMPSHOTT

Hearths chargeable

Mister George Tuckey	7
Mistress Mary Chase	9
Mister Thomas Mathew	7
Richard Chase	5
Edward Greene	4
Richard Farleigh	6
Richard Foster	2
Robert Croswell	3
John Compton	2
William Eames junior	2
John Cole	2
Mary Turner widow	2
John Chapman	2
James Fish	3
Elizabeth Mill widow	1
Robert Turner	1
Robert Palmer	3
Thomas Palmer	1
Mister George Tuckey	3
William Heath	2
hearths	67

Hearths not chargeable

Widow Cox	1
John Beagly	1
hearths	2

1. Selbourne Hundred

200. HAWKLEY[1]

Hearths chargeable

Mister Philip Pococke	6[(a)]
[ ]irker	6
[ ] Austin	4
[ ] Peacock	3
[ ] Cooper senior	4
[ ] Carter junior	1

Fol. 41r(ii)

Thomas Gammon senior	3
Thomas Newlin	1
Christopher Cowdrey	2
Daniel Gammon	4
Philip Pocock	3
Lionel Newham	1[(b)]
Zacharias Gammon	1[(b)]
Nathaniel Oliver	1
Richard Lillywhite	1
John Cooper junior	2
John Trigg	3
Daniel Gammon	3
Thomas Tunworth	1
Thomas North	3
John Newlin	3
John Austin	3
Thomas Gammon junior	1
Henry Miner	1
Thomas Austin	2
William Carter senior	1
Arthur Figg	1
hearths	65

Hearths not chargeable

Nicholas Hockly	1
Widow Dudman	1
William Tilbrow	1
John Legge	1
Guy Fellowes	1
Thomas Linshott	1
John Edghill senior	1
John Edghill junior	1
John Small	1
William Rives	1
Thomas Hill	1
Robert Carter	2
Widow Farly	2
hearths	15

(a) 1 overcharged
(b) 1 taken down
1. Hawkely

201. EAST TISTED

Hearths chargeable

Mister Todd	8
Francis Lowe	3
William Mathew	3
Mister Clancye	3
Philip Coles	2(a)
Thomas Preston	1
Thomas Straddick	1
Stephen Aldred	1
Edward Larby	1
John Richards	2
Robert Carter	2
John Pitter	2
Thomas Gillmer	1
Thomas Silvester	1
John Hyde	2
The lodge	2
John Earle	10
James Larby	2
hearths	47

Hearths not chargeable

John Lynne	2
Henry Dennis	1
Lewis Davis	1
Robert Broadfeild	1
Thomas Borden	1
John Baker	1
Henry Lynne	1
Widow Larby	2
hearths	10

(a) 1 taken down

Fol. 41v(i)

202. NEWTON VALENCE

Hearths chargeable

[ ] Champion	10
[ ] Henwood	4
Richard Glyde	6
Robert Turner	7
John Henwood	3
William Bensteed	3
Daniel Carter	1
Richard Budd	2
Nicholas Sexton	1
John Knight	4
Nicholas Weene	3
Michael Blanchard	1
Christopher French	2
Richard Brewer	1
Daniel Pitter	2
Simon Windebancke	1
John Andrews	1
Robert Bennett	1
William Bennett	2
William Windebancke	1
hearths	56

Hearths not chargeable

George Pincke	1
William Newlin	1
Christopher Hill	1
Widow Kill	1
Widow Reading	1
John Netherleft	1
Widow Carter	1
Thomas Dudman	1
hearths	8

203. NOAR[1]

Hearths chargeable

Mister Robert Farr	4
Mister King	3
Philip Pacock	3
Robert Lukin	4
Robert Harding	1
Stephen Struddick	1
Edward Pack	1
Christopher Porter	1
Richard Tevell	2(a)
hearths	20

Hearths not chargeable

William Porter	1
William Money	1
Widow Nuttingham	1
hearths	3

1. Ower alias Noare

204. NORTON

Hearths chargeable

Peter Burningham	6

Thomas Richards	3
John Daman	1
hearths	10

205. SELBORNE

Hearths chargeable

William Kirver	5[(a)]
Thomas Mathew	2
John Worsham	3

Fol. 41v(ii)

William Lillywhite	1
Thomas Phelpes	1
William Heath	3
Thomas Baker	2
John Turner	3
John Turner	2
Widow Baker	1
Widow Graffett	2
William Skilton	1
Robert Heath	1
Laurence Willis	1
Peter Wells	3
Michael Silvester	2
Samuel Okey	2
William Freebone	2
Henry Wake	2
Philip Laurence	3
James Purse	1
Richard Hayle	2
Mister Longworth	5
Mister Longworth	8
Widow Baker	4
Thomas Albery	9
William Aslett	1
Thomas Richards	2
John Baker	1
James Hack	3
Widow Mathew	2
Widow Mathew	1
Christopher Pincke	1
William Cooper	1
Widow Baker	2
hearths	84

Hearths not chargeable

Widow Cooper	1
Widow Hayle	1
Thomas Struddick	1
Widow Lasham	1
Philip Baker	1
William Ruben	1
Richard Scutt	1
John Heath	1
William Beacher	2
William Chase	1
Nicholas Skilton	1
John Coleman	2
John Carpenter	2
Richard Skilton	1
Mary Darling	1
Edward Lavington	1
hearths	19

(a) 1 down

206. FARRINGDON[1]

Hearths chargeable

Mister Edward Caige	5
Mister Peter Beale	8
Mister Jethro Beale	4
John Knight	7
William Knight	3
John Tribb	1
John Clare	3
Robert Sparrow	5
John Fry	2
Nicholas Knight	2
William Knight	3
Thomas Wake	3
Mister Charles Morrow	3
John Knight	5

Fol. 42r(i)

Laurence Gourde	1
John Hamm	2
Daniel Knight	2[(a)]
Widow Neale	2
Widow Rabinett	2
Simon Windebanck	1
Philip Pitts	1
Stephen Shrubb	2
Richard Godwin	3
John Larby	2

206. FARRINGDON—*cont'd.*

Laurence Gourde senior	2
Robert Carter	1
John Applegarth	4
Richard Larby	2
William Knight	6
Nicholas Harrison	2
Moses Kill	1
Nicholas Harding	3
John Battaille	1[b]
William Carter	2
William Lower	1
Robert Carter	3
Widow Wake	4
Peter Neale	1
hearths	104

Hearths not chargeable

Widow Suckett	1
Robert Carrick	1
George Knight	1
Richard Joye	1
Francis Starkey	1
William Rabnett	1
Widow Lucy	1
Widow Faithfull	1
Edward Carrick	1
John Faithfull	1
hearths	10

(a) 1 taken down
(b) 1 overcharged
1. Farrington

207. TEMPLE

Hearths chargeable

Widow Preston	2
William Cosens	5
Edward Wilkinson	2
Widow Philipp	3
Thomas Philipp	2
Thomas Preston	2
Thomas Philipp	1
Thomas Preston	1
John Bristow	8
John Bristow	1
John Hammon	3
Laurence Willis	1
William Fawchin	2
Robert Carter	1
John Baker	1
Richard Peckett	1
Isaac Upsdell	2
hearths	38

Fol. 42r(ii)

Hearths not chargeable

Edward Carpenter	1
hearths	1

The number of hearths chargeable in the hundred of Selborne is	492
Whereof for half a year	2
Not chargeable	68

FINCHDEAN HUNDRED[1]

208. PETERSFIELD[2]

Hearths chargeable

Sir John Norton	14
Arthur Bold esquire	12
Mister Osmond Bilson	4
Mister John James	5
Mister John Heather	5
Mister Walwin	4
John Durrant	5
Robert Parker	6
Thomas Walker	4
Nicholas Hastheed	6
Mister Arthur Tawke	8
Thomas Jaques	16
Edward Rooke	4
Mister Francis Worlidge	6
Mister Thomas Holt	8
Mistress Ann Worlidge	3
Mister John Rose	6
Mistress Cole	6
Mister Mathews	5
Mister Palmer	9
Henry Mills	6
Mistress Meadkirke	4
Mistress Roberts	5

Mister William Knight	3
Thomas Westbrooke senior	8
Francis Gearing	2
Thomas Page	2
William Budd junior	2
William Heather	4
William Houndsome	2
Giles Hall	3
Richard Collier	2
Blewett Long	2
Christmas Hunt senior	2
William Standford	2
Richard Godwin	3
John Winter	3
William Budd senior	1[(a)]
Henry Clayton	7
John Holt	6
Richard Woollgar	3
William Dennier	3
Nicholas Hall	1
Christmas Hunt junior	3
William Chaundler	2
Richard Hoggsflesh	3
Ezekiel Rattcliffe	1
James Pace	4
Fol. 42v(i)	
Goodwife Willmott	1
Anthony Reading	2
John Westbrooke	2
Robert Palmer	2
William Colebrooke	1
John Addams	2
Thomas Rattcliffe	2
John Girdler	2
William Wooldridg	4
Robert Street	5
John Eames senior	8
Widow Chapman	4
Nicholas Allen	3
Bartholomew Heath	1
John Gilbert	6[(b)]
Mistress Legg	2
Edward Patrick	3
Mister William Markwick	3
John Ameres	3
Mistress Pey junior	4
William Newell junior	2
Mister Thomas Vallor	6
John Jones	5
John Hall	2
John Widmore	3
Anthony Peckham	2
William Basten	1
Ann Gilbert	1
Richard Rookes	2
Mister Owen	3
John Simons	5
James Davies	5
Ezekiel Gardner	1
John Richman	1
John Young senior	3
Thomas Stoner	1
William Stoner	1
Henry Birch	1
John Pescodd	1
Joseph Pescod	3
William Simons junior	2
Edward Perriour	2
Mary Hall	1
Jerome Collier	5
William Hunt	2
William Simons	3
Catherine Rogers	2
Richard Walker	2
John Rives	4
Abraham Knight senior	2
William Richards	5
John Barnard junior	2
Arthur Golding junior	1
William Polling	2
Thomas Silvester	2
Richard Gardner	2
John Bennett	2
John Younge junior	2
William Winter	2
William Dallner	2
Abraham Knight junior	2
Daniel Chase	3

208. PETERSFIELD—*cont'd.*

Fol. 42v(ii)

George Mundey	1
John Bridger	1
Nicholas Knight	1
George Vaughan	2
Richard Hewett	3
William Rooke	2
Nicholas Knight	2
Randal Eames	2
Giles Sticker	4
Robert Rowte	3
Richard Eames	2
Thomas Soone	4[a]
Richard Mumford	3
Thomas Westbrooke	2
John Grinsteed	1
Charles Bissill	2[c]
Thomas Baker	2
Henry Slefeild	3
Thomas Rowte	4
John Baker	2
Widow Goodwin	1
Thomas Goodwin	2
Timothy Goodwin	1
Peter Heather	2
Thomas Long	3
John Barnard senior	3
John Perynn	1
Robert Roberts	2
John Forder	1
William Willmott	2
John Feilder	3
John Gammon	3
Mistress Pey senior	4
Thomas Ameres	2
Widow Sedwick	2
William Gamon	5
William Holdropp	1
Mister Biggs	4
John Pooke	5
George Goldringe	1
Mister Ew[3] Rooke	3
Edward Games	3
William Peryer	1
John Page	1
Simon Flood	3
Thomas Brewer	2
John Eames junior	2
Thomas Naynow	2
Widow Spershott	1
Frederick Guphill	2
John Barram	1
Thomas Browne	2
John Thomas	3
Widow Michell	3
William Naynow	3
hearths	512

Fol. 43r(i)

Hearths not chargeable

Widow Rook	1
Henry Forde	2
Thomas Bucklin	1
Edward Harris	1
Robert Standford	1
John Dallemore	2
Widow Chawline	1
Tristram Burroughes	2
Widow Cooper	1
William Forde	1
Edward Humphry	1
Guy Rolfe	1
John Hunt	2
John Godwin	1
Robert Vallor	2
William Collier	2
John Ruffin	2
John Bridgier	2
Widow Burgis	1
Mary Salter	2
Widow Axeby	1
John Glasier	1
Widow Goble	2
John Bernard	1
Widow Silvester	1
Henry Reynolds	1
William Heather	1
John Legg	2
John Parker	2
Peter Dyer	1
Frederick Gupphill	1

John Compton	1
William Ansell	1
Widow Rooker	1
Roger Colepis	1
William Palmer	2
John Triggs	2
Richard Stocker senior	1
Elizabeth Hall	1
Widow Triggs	1
Robert Legg	1
Joan Browne	1
John Forde	1
William Deane	1
Alexander Weller	1
Widow Owen	1
Roger Fletcher	1
Richard Stocker	1
Arthur Golding senior	1
Widow Story	2
Edward Trigg	1
Widow Fry	1
John Richman	1
John Emery	1
Matthew Goble	2
Richard Booker	2
hearths	73

(a) 1 overcharged
(b) 1 taken down
(c) 1 down
1. Finchdeane Hundred
2. Petersfeild
3. *Possibly short for* Ewen

209. SHEET[1]

Hearths chargeable

William Brewer	7
Richard Sprince	4
William Tipper	5
Richard Baker	2
Peter Younge	3
Widow Sommers	1

Fol. 43r(ii)

Joan Brooman	7
Jerome Beale	2
Nicholas Bennett	3
John Lock	3
Roger Browne	1
John Pescodd	2
John Reading	3
Laurence Penn	3
Widow Bettsworth	3
John Knight	3
John Inwood	1
Widow Wright	2
Nicholas Stoneham	1
John Waker	2
Thomas Twine	1
Mister Robert Bartlett	4
hearths	63

Hearths not chargeable

Nathaniel Whites	1
David Rickman	1
John Tallman	1
Thomas Willcott	1
Richard Mould	1
Francis Sharp	1
Joan Elsteed	1
Edward Holloway	1
Widow Holloway	1
Robert Bettsworth	1
Richard Jenman	2
Nicholas Inwood	2
hearths	14

1. Sheete

210. NURSTED

Hearths chargeable

Mister Peacock	10
William Ratcliff	10
Mark Ameers	3
John Read	1
William Eedes	3
John Collins	1
Arthur Colebrooke	3
William Reading	3
hearths	34

Hearths not chargeable

William Fry	2
hearths	2

211. WESTON

Hearths chargeable

Leonard Bilson esquire	17
Thomas Kent senior	4
Thomas Kent junior	1
Francis Randoll	3
James Terry	2
John Ayling	2
Henry Smith	3
Mister Bettsworth	9
Richard Newton	3
John Ayling	3
William Shallett	2
Laurence Bernard	1
Robert Tribb	1
Richard Pitt	1
Jacob Vooke	4

Fol. 43v(i)

Francis Miller	3
William Cox	1
John Davis	1
hearths	61

Hearths not chargeable

John Freeland	1
Northam Wise	1
hearths	2

212. BURITON

Hearths chargeable

Richard Cooper esquire	5
Doctor Barker	9
Mistress Hanbury	14
Mister Bettsworth	8
Richard Ransteed	2
John Searle	3
Ralph Tribb	1
Richard Searle senior	1
Henry Mundey	1
Anthony Pligder	1
Timothy Reading	4
Philip Shoulders	2
Richard Searle junior	5
Richard Searle junior	2
William Page	4
William Searle	4
Randal Searle	1
William Parker senior	2
Richard Bridger	1
John Reading	1
Thomas Mathews	2
Richard Ransteed	1
John Marman	1
Robert Winckworth	1
William Parker junior	2
hearths	78

Hearths not chargeable

Alexander Parker	2
Richard Plidger	1
Widow Jennings	2
Goodman Vallor	1
Widow Taylor	1
Richard Stevens	1
Widow Brooman	1
Widow Druatt	1
Thomas Patrick	1
Thomas Wise	1
Goodman Bucketts	2
Gregory Sherryer	1
John Wyatt	1
William Taylor	2
Thomas Poate	1
John Powell	1
Anthony Foster	2
Widow Bridger	1
Anthony Milles	1
Richard Chantrell	1
Widow Patrick	2
Widow Whitcombe	1
hearths	28

Fol. 43v(ii)

213. IDSWORTH[1]

Hearths chargeable

Sir Robert Bannister	20
Thomas Vallor	5
Edward Hebberden	6
Nicholas Bayes	2
Edward Renwood	1
Richard Mersh	1
Richard Grainger	1

Thomas Andrews	3
William Smith senior	1
George Stent	1
Arthur Pullinger	4
Edward Young	1
Edward Younge	2
Robert Harrison	1
John Millard	2
John Valler	1
Robert Staingemore	1
Richard Warne	2
George Nichollson	2
Richard Rogers	2
Nicholas Grover	1
Richard Gilbert	3
William Westover	2
William Smith junior	2
John Jennings	1
Thomas Mills	3
hearths	71

Hearths not chargeable

Widow Renwood	1
John Turner	1
Thomas Flood	2
Robert Barnard	1
John Forder	1
Richard Moorey	1
William Smith	5(a)
hearths	12

(a) burnt down
1. Edsworth

214. CHALTON

Hearths chargeable

Doctor Gillingham	7
John Attweek	4
Richard Bedford	4
Arthur Lodger	3
David Mingham	2
Thomas Truddle	2
John Fleet	2
William Smith	2
Thomas Standford senior	1
John Tullatt	2
Thomas Hedger	1
Thomas Horne	1
Thomas Standford junior	1
Philip Sherrier	1
Agnes Harrison	1
William Weekes	1
Richard Pay	1
John Biding	1
John Stripe	1
Robert Biding	1
hearths	39

Fol. 44r(i)

Hearths not chargeable

Robert Porter	1
Robert Painter	1
Widow Weekes	1
Widow Kates	1
Roger Fry	1
Edward Spittsberg	1
Thomas Truddle	2(a)
hearths	8

(a) 1 overcharged

215. CLANFIELD[1]

Hearths chargeable

Mister William Fossbrooke	6
Daniel Weight	7
John Randoll	5
Thomas Boghurst	3
Henry Boghurst	2
Thomas Hastler	2
John Pawfoot	4
Richard Dallirose	3
James Batt	2
Richard Freeland	6
John Hastler	1
Thomas Garrett	1
Anthony Cooper	3
William Braman	1
Thomas Eames	2
Richard Bridger	3
Richard Knight	1
Roger Prior	1
Ebden Mersham	2

215. CLANFIELD—*cont'd.*

Widow Kinge 1[(a)]
Widow Compton 1
John Martin 2
hearths 59

Hearths not chargeable

Widow Braman 1
hearths 1

(a) 1 overcharged
1. Clanfeild

216. CATHERINGTON

Hearths chargeable

Christopher Cosier vicar 4
Thomas Ayleward 3
Richard Quallett 5
Clement Michiner 2
Thomas Baily 2
Thomas Hoare 2
Richard Michiner 1
Thomas Baily 1
Richard Aldred 3
William Knowlton 1
Thomas Collins 1
Thomas Hoare 1
Edward Hoare 1
John Kench 3
Robert Brett 4
Widow Lowder 3
Nicholas Bensteed 2
John Blunt 4
Ralph Phinn 3
Richard Page 1
William Barnet 3
Widow Padwicke 1

Fol. 44r(ii)

Richard Biggs 2
William Gutter 1
William Biding 3
Clement Dorrell 4
Nicholas Richards 5
John Bassett 3
Henry Guy 1
Hugh Davis 3
James Neave 6
Nicholas Padwick 1
John Collins 2
William Poate 1
John Guy 2
George Hattrell 2
William Burtt 1
hearths 88

Hearths not chargeable

Widow Snowe 1
Widow Haynes 1
Widow Freeborne 1
Widow Bird 1
Widow Rampton 1
John Appleford 1
Thomas Tee 1
Laurence Plidger 1
Widow Padwick 1
John Feeke 1
Edward Crockford 1
Eleanor Harte 1
Widow Carter 1
Edward Hoare 1
William Hedgcock 1
Edward Carter 1
Widow Kent 1
Nicholas Padwick 1
hearths 18

217. HINTON DAUBNEY

Hearths chargeable

Laurence Hyde esquire 17
Mistress Englefeild 14
Richard Poate 5
William Pescodd 4
William Stiggins 5
Thomas Millesh 1
Theophilus Dotterell 2
Widow Abnett 1
John Barnard 6
Edward Barnard 4
Thomas Pratt 2
William Barnard 3
Widow Ismonger 1
Theophilus Dotterell 3

John Barnard	1
John Sparks	1
Robert Goddard	1
Giles Freeborne	1
John Steele	2
Thomas North	1
John Eames	4
George Harbour	3

Fol. 44v(i)

William Peate	1
Edward Ayleward	2
Richard Swann	1
William Newman	1
Edward Marcham	1
Thomas Collins	3
John Eyles	4
Robert Hellyer	5
Widow Long	1
William Martin	3
hearths	104

Hearths not chargeable

Widow Long	1
Richard Gregory	1
Widow Smith	1
Roger Padwick	1
Widow Binsteed	1
Ellen Pratt	2
hearths	7

218. BLENDWORTH

Hearths chargeable

John Biding	5
Francis Foster	4
John Appleford	4
Widow Wingham	1
Edward Higgin	2
John Flower	1
Richard Seward	1
Widow Foster	3
Joseph Croswelier	1
Richard Appleford	3
George Foster	2
Regland Eyres	3
Thomas Steele	1
Robert Lane	1
Widow Stalter	1
John Carpenter	4
William Weekes	1
Mister Francis Arrundell	5
John Nicholas	1
Richard Longe	2
Mister Toby Shaw	4
Henry Heycroft	6
Widow Dorrill	3
John Adderly	3
Widow Carpenter	3
John King	3
Widow Pocock	2
John Bulbecke	1
John Lockyer	2
John Pledger	1
Thomas Harte	1
John Coote	2
John Weekes	1
Robert Moory	1
Thomas Bulbeck	1
William Bydinge	1
hearths	81

Fol. 44v(ii)

Hearths not chargeable

Stephen Newland	1
Henry Newland	1
William Farly	1
Thomas Heather	1
Thomas Cooke	1
Widow Kyte	1
Francis Foster	2
Richard Biding	2
John Biding	2
hearths	12

The number of hearths chargeable in the hundred of Finchdean[1] is	1190
Whereof for half a year	4
Not chargeable	175

1. Finchdeane

EAST MEON HUNDRED[1]

219. EAST MEON[2]

Hearths chargeable

George Belt	1
William Randoll	8
Simon Keete	2
Robert Randoll	6
Roger Smith	1
John Earewaker	1
Anthony Marshall	1
John Collins	1
Thomas Randoll	6
John Clever	3
Thomas Pinck	1
Mister Carthright	4
William Parvin	8
Anthony Terryll	7
John Durrant	2
John Poate	4
Thomas Cropp	3
Richard Dallarose	5
Mister Richard Downes	5
Robert Suckett	4
Anthony Barlow	2
William Garrett	4
John Chaundler	4
Widow Terrill	4
Thomas Chase	1
John Goddwin	1
John Marriner	2
Hugh Jerman	4
Courteous Ramson	2
Anthony Jerman	1
William Harwood	2
John Hammond	2
hearths	102

Hearths not chargeable

Widow Carpenter	1
William Beckinsall	1
Henry Ladd	1
Peter Screven	1
Edward Clever	2
Peter Langridge	1

Fol. 45r(i)

Richard Cole	1
Widow Prowting	1
Widow Kempe	1
Richard Earwaker	1
Nicholas Long	1
Anthony Long	1
Walter Garrett	1
Widow Pincke	1
Widow Strowder	2
Widow Feilder	2
Widow Musgrave	1
John Brewton	1
John Dyer	1
Thomas Richards	1
Thomas Suckett	1
John Wells	1
Robert Taylor	1
William Hillier	2
Widow Fry	1
John Morris	1
Anthony Earwaker	1
hearths	31

1. Eastmeon Hundred
2. Eastmeon

220. OXENBOURNE

Hearths chargeable

Thomas Pooke	4
Widow Aburrowe	3
John Pooke	2
Andrew Humphrys	1
Richard Ayleward	2
William Baker	3
John Luff	3
John Hebb	2
Nicholas Hebb	2
Nicholas Pincke	1
Anthony Long	3
Anthony Brewton	1
Michael Jay	2
William Prickler	2
Richard Knight	1
Widow Ayleward	1
Thomas Booker	9

Mister Charles Bramly	4
Anthony Bulbeck	4
Nicholas Bulbeck	2
hearths	52

Hearths not chargeable

Thomas Page	1
Ann Smith	1
hearths	2

221. LANGRISH

Hearths chargeable

Mister Nathaniel Long	7
William Baker	3
Thomas Reddway	3
Mister Titchbourne	1
Anthony Langrish	3

Fol. 45r(ii)

Widow Earwaker	2
Anthony Suggett	1
Richard Parsons	2
John Pitt	1
Widow Knight	1
Thomas Aldridg	3
Widow Longrish	2
Robert Dumper	1
Richard Hersey	1(a)
William Hall	1
William Box	1(a)
hearths	33

Hearths not chargeable

Nicholas Dumper	1
Nicholas Beane	1
Robert Dumper	1
John Beane	1
William Hall	1
John Corps	1
John Mee	1
Edward Corps	1
Widow White	2
John Gale	1
John Pitt	3(b)
hearths	14

(a) 1 down
(b) burnt down

222. RAMSDEAN[1]

Hearths chargeable

Mister William Carthridge	6
Thomas Collier	4
John Tribb	4
George Collins	2
George Collins	2
William Silvester	3
Richard Maudlin	6
William Steele	4
Peter Maidlow	2
Ann Maidlow	3
Ann Silvester widow	3
William Baker	3(a)
Richard Austin	3
Thomas Hill	3
John Burrell	4
Mister Downes	4
William Luffe	5
John Boyes	1
Nicholas Langrish	2
hearths	64

Hearths not chargeable

Nicholas Pinck	1
John Vinden	1
John Collins	1
Widow Trimer	1
Nicholas Bone	2
Thomas Greene	1

Fol. 45v(ii)

Christopher Lloyde	1
John Verndell	2
Edward Silvester	1(b)
John Vinden	1
hearths	12

(a) 1 down
(b) burnt down
1. Ramsdeane

223. FROXFIELD[1]

Hearths chargeable

Mister John Haspoole	5
John Browinge	3
John Hellier	2
Edward Longrish	5

223. FROXFIELD—*cont'd.*

Nicholas Heberden	4
Ralph Tribb	3
Hugh Silvester	3
Roger Silvester	2
Richard Baker	3
John Hersey	3
John Vinden	3
William Gamlin	2
Guy Wheeler	4
William Rooke	5
Thomas Tocock	7
William Marriner	5
Charles Glyde	6
Richard Heath	3
John Baker	2
Joshua Empknapp	3
John Silvester	2
Richard Hellier	3
John Aldred	3
John Oades	7
Richard Baker	1
Henry Dowling	4
Joseph Okely	3
John Terry	3
John Knight	3
John White	3
Richard Triggs	3
Zacharias Vidler	3
John Mathew	2
Joan Spencer	3
John Gudge	2
John Baker	6
John Marshall	3
Francis Norris	3
John King	3
Robert Poate	2
John Bone	2
Thomas Knight	3
Philip Knight	3
John Newland	1
Henry Foster	1
Edward Hellier	3
Widow Porter	3
hearths	151

Fol. 45v(ii)

Hearths not chargeable

John Baily	1
Richard Eaton	1
John May	1
William Rew	2
Humphrey Kinge	2
Henry Eaton	1
Widow Heale	2
Robert Hellier	1
Widow Gudge	2
Edward Hellier	1
John Bridger	2
Richard Harber	1
Anthony Kerby	1
Goodman Dumper	1
Thomas Parker	2
William White	1
Goodman Nosse	1
Henry Foster	1
John Oliver	1
Jane Pincke	1
Goodman Amorosse	1
Solomon Smith	1
Thomas Hasteed	1
hearths	34

1. Froxfeild

224. COMBE

Hearths chargeable

Nicholas Pinck	3
Richard Jerman	3
Richard Heather	2
John Silvester	3
Jesse Silvester	3
Richard Silvester	4
Thomas Mersh	1
John Bulbeck	3
John Breda	3
hearths	25

Hearths not chargeable

Richard Constance	1
hearths	1

225. RIPLINGTON

Hearths chargeable

Francis Dickens esquire	10
Robert Pinck	3
William Silvester	4
Richard Clerke	2
Mister Palmer's house	2(a)
hearths	21

Fol. 46r(i)

Hearths not chargeable

John Byon	1
George Page	1
Widow Tyler	2
Widow Brexton	2
Richard Page	2
Thomas Guy	1
Anthony Kirber	1
hearths	10

(a) void

226. AMBERSHAM

Hearths chargeable

Francis Lord Viscount Mountague	6
John Colebrooke	10
Edward Legatt	2
Mister Anthony Younge	14
Christopher Sowter	4
Richard Ayling	1
Anthony Coprene	7
Richard Drew	4
Thomas Long	1
William Woods	1
Edward Warde	1
John Ayling	2
Francis Blackwell	4
John Jones	6
John Wakeford	6
Ann Kerver widow	3
Nicholas Gray	10
John Yalden	7
John Bettsworth	4
Richard Cooper	3
Robert Poore	6
Robert Sopp	3(a)
hearths	105

Hearths not chargeable

William Shotter	1
William Souter	1
David Wakeford	1
Richard Moone	1
John Tresler	1
Almshouse	3
hearths	8

(a) void

227. STEEP[1]

Hearths chargeable

Mister William Harling	7
William Colebrooke	6
Roger Ayleward	5
Roger Geale	5
Mistress Clements widow	4
William Tribb	3
Richard Baker	6
William Woolgar	9
John Eames	5

Fol. 46r(ii)

John Hasteed	3
Thomas Eames	6
Gregory Tanner	3
William Cowdry	3
William Bettsworth	1
Robert Milles	4
Thomas Collier	3
John Westbrooke	5
Anthony Heather	3
Richard Figge	3
Thomas Woolger	4
Henry Newland	2
John Hooker	3
John Pooke	4
John Webb	1(a)
Mister Peacock	3
Edward Jennings	1
John Creswell	4
Samuel Briday	4

227. STEEP—*cont'd.*

Henry Rolfe	1
John Restall	2
Richard Restall	1
John Minchin	1
Richard Luttman	1
Widow Osbourne	1
John Pincke	2
Edward Aldred	5
Andrew Woods	1
William Sewarde	1
Peter Compton	1
Francis Russell	1
William Mundey	1
John Booker	1
Francis Russell junior	3
Widow Roake	1
John Rolfe	2
Robert Hills	3
William Hall	1
Dorothy Petty	1
Francis Roake	1
Zacchaeus Gardner	3
Oliver Russell	3
hearths	148

Hearths not chargeable

Richard Quallett	1
John Wade	1
Richard Welch	1
Widow Nexon	1
Thomas Hill	2
Roger Barfoote	1
John Moreton	1
Joan Cooke	1
Anthony Parr	1
Joseph Moorey	2
Widow Bridger	1

Fol. 46v(i)

Edmund Snugg	2
John Vallor	1
John Parsons	2
Ralph Jennings	2
Nicholas Fry	1
Seth Heather	1
Widow Booker	1
Widow Johnson	1
Thomas Grinsted	1
Widow Writh	1
Richard Baker	1
Widow Collier	1
William Stiggins	2
hearths	30

(a) 1 overcharged
1. Steepe

228. BORDEAN[1]

Hearths chargeable

Sir William Lewis baronet	13
Richard Corps	11
Nicholas Andrews	4
Thomas Upsdale	4
John Westbrooke	4
Richard Lock	2
John Foster	3
Richard Compton	3
William Goodyer	2
John Mundey	2
Anthony Hockley	1
John Knight	1
hearths	50

Hearths not chargeable

John Corps	1
hearths	1

The number of hearths chargeable in the hundred of East Meon[2] is	751
Not chargeable	137
The number of hearths chargeable within the whole division of Alton is	4756
Not chargeable	933

1. Borden
2. Eastmeone

Fol. 47r(i)

FAWLEY DIVISION

229. THE CITY OF WINCHESTER[1]

Hearths chargeable

Sir Robert Mason	16[(a)]
Stephen Searle	8
Thomas Jeffery	2
Thomas Carpenter	2
Andrew Elmes	1
Richard Cobb	2
William Gifford	1
William Buttler	6
Mister Goddard	12
Thomas Foster	2
Philip Trimnell	6
Mister Richard Ayleward	1
Jerome Addams	3
John Whiteland	2
Robert Coleman	2
Ralph Browne	2
Edward Richardson	6
Lancelot Kerby	4
Henry Browne	3
John Austen	2
Thomas George	2
Nicholas Waterman	2
John Hayling	4
Thomas Milles	2
James Sparkman	2
Richard Colley	4
William Clerke	4
Stephen King	1
Patience Wiltshire	3
Richard Pildrim	6
Mister Complin junior	1
Thomas Vinn	2
Thomas Gosling	5[(b)]
John Buttler	2[(b)]
Widow Tarleton	2
Mister Benjamin Clerk	6
Widow Johnson	3
Richard North	3
Mister John Birch	8
Jerome North	3[(b)]
John Allen	2
William Barfoott	2[(b)]
Leonard Barfoott	2
William Stevens	4
Edward Napp	2
William Blissett	2
Samuel Bushell	4
Richard Bidinge	2
Richard Vander	2
John Hayward	3
Richard Mumford senior	5
Mister William Cradock	3
Richard Waldron	3
Mister Nicholas Purdue	8
Richard Laurence	2
Mister Richard Edwards	15
Edward Napp	1
Richard Lawrence	2
Giles Martyne	1
Thomas Newman	4
John Vinn	3
Richard Osmond	3
Philip Taylor	4
Nicholas Taylor	3
Jonathan Mann	3
John Buttler	2

Fol. 47r(ii)

William Waldron	2
Jenkins Davies	3
Thomas Banes	10
Nicholas Lampard	3
John Taylor	1
Thomas Chapman	2
Robert Reyley	1
Thomas Willmott	4
Patrick Farrell	3
Widow Cross	7
Widow Mersh	1
Widow Mersh	1
Widow Moggeridg	5
Widow Lamphier	3
Mister Richard Golledg	23

229. THE CITY OF WINCHESTER—*cont'd.*

Richard Pildrin	1
Mister John Mundey	3
Mister Francis Smith	10
Mister John Cleere	3
Mister Ferdinand Bye	7
Alexander Woodson	6
John Mersh	2
Charles Hack	7
Widow Dawkins	2
Edward Fidden	2
Robert Abram	2
John Harris	3
Peter Fussell	4
Christopher Speeringe	2
John Pope	2(c)
Mister William Hancock	13
Mister Ellis Mew	4
William Vinn	2
Widow Allen	6
Nicholas Ashton	6
William Uvedale esquire	10
Alexander Oram	3
Thomas Langford	2(b)
Nathaniel Goddin	4
John Bowes	2
John Nuttier	2
Edmund Clerke esquire	13
John Isron	2
William Homard	2
Stephen Tyler	1
Robert Philipps	2
Henry Dixon	3
Richard Beare	5
Widow Powell[2]	2
John Heyward	4
Mister Middleton	2
William Lane[2]	2
Mister Roger Coram	4
Mister John Cleere	7
John Sutton[2]	2
George Tarleton	2
Thomas Greene	3
John Dalby	3
Richard Davis[2]	2
Edward Appleford esquire	7
Doctor Nicholas Stanley	15
Mistress Grew[2]	3
Widow Bates	3
Rebecca Parrey[2]	5(d)
Nicholas Bates	1
Mistress Febert	2
Matthew Tompson	4
Christopher Kemon	4
Nicholas Mersh senior	4
John Plentice	3
Giles Northgate	3
Widow Hodson	3

Fol. 47v(i)

John Alison	2
Michael Pildrim	5
Robert Clerke	1
Peter Barrett	4
John Major	3
William Oram	3
Laurence Lampard	6
Mister Richard Stansby	6
Guy Badcock	4
Doctor Arthur Taylor	8
Henry Willis	3
Benjamin Swaine	2
John Skeele	2(a)
Mistress Ann Neale	6
Mister John Colson	6
Robert Pescod esquire	8
Mistress Guderidg	2
William Clement	2
Robert Finckley	5
Thomas Webb	3
Joseph Bellbin	8
Mister Edward Fyfeild	7
John Jerome[3]	1
Michael Fitchett	2
Nathaniel Combs	1
John Richardson	2
John Scrutton	2

Widow Gale 3
Thomas Buttler 2
Mistress Hussey 4
Thomas Oades 2
Widow Cosh 3
William Lardner 11
Anthony Yeoman 2
Thomas Cradock 6
Henry Browne 2
George Buttler 2
Mister Edward Harfeild 5
Thomas Tarleton 7
Mister William Smith 7[e]
Widow Buttler 2
Henry Sessoe 6
Widow Weight 7
Henry Badger 4
Shadrack Lyne 8
Thomas Cropp 6
Mister Thomas Coward 7
Widow Newbolt 6
Mister William Harwood 4
William Webb 4
Robert Steele 2
John Tipper 3
John Fletcher 3
Mister Godson Penton 6
John Lampard 3
John Helliar 1
Richard Edwards senior 4
Humphrey Bowry 3
William Barton 2
Mister Barnard Love 7
Robert Philipps 2
Joseph Horrell 4
John Badger senior 5
Thomas Lambert 3
Mister Richard Harris 9
Mister Thomas Grantham 5
Philip Rudsby 5
Mister Thomas Wavell 5
Mister Philip Jones 8
John Tombs 2
Mister Richard Tipper 4
Mister John Emery 12
Widow Tutt 4
Mister Thomas Muspratt 6
Richard Taylor 4

Fol. 47v(ii)

James Barfoott 4
Mister Richard Dennett 9
Mister Edmund Budd 2
Mister John Mew 6
Lancelot Barrows 5
Richard Speering 2
William Bates 4
Thomas Wall esquire 8
Robert Michell 2
Thomas Colson 2
Mister Martyn 3
John Badger junior 4
William Ireland 1
Mister Forde 9
Henry Kelsey esquire 8
Mister Yalden 8
Mister Yalden 3
Mister William Taylor mayor 4
Thomas Vincent 2
Humphrey Bishopp 2
Henry Goodman 5
Mister John Harfell 6
Mister John Mundey 4
Mister Godson 3
Mister John Purdue 1
Mister John Warner 15
Thomas Henly 3
Henry Hewes 2
Mister Edward Traffells 4
Mister James Guy 4
Mister Thomas Pestle 5
John Gilbert 1
Josias Biles 3
John Wiltshire 2
Humphrey Vander 4
Mister Peter Symons 6
Benjamin Smith 6

229. THE CITY OF WINCHESTER—*cont'd.*

Richard Nose	2
Richard Allen	6
Widow Taylor	6
Roger Lane	4[(b)]
Henry Daubney	4
Mister Stephen Welsted	5
Laurence Plant	1
Mister Thomas Coward	7[(f)]
Richard Knight	2
Roger Harman	2
Widow Moss	2
James Sparkman	2[(f)]
John Goater	2
Widow Michell	2
Widow Joyner	1
John George	2
Laurence Broadway	1
John Alison senior	3
William Harfell	1
Richard Ransteed	3[(f)]
Thomas Rudley	1
Stephen Bishopp	2
John Comfort	2
John Gauntlett	2
Peter Tarleton	1
Richard Speering	3
Mister Wiltshire	4[(f)]
John Gifford	2
Robert Abbott	1
Edward Crabb	2
Ambrose Harfell	1
Mister Powlett	3[(f)]
James Fitt	1

Fol. 48r(i)

George Poole	2
Widow Baker	2
William Upton	1
Mister Roger Coram	8[(f)]
Arthur Mathewes	3[(f)]
John Prince	1
Widow Clerk	1
Thomas Baily	2
William Prince	1
John Jaques	3
Widow Tompson	3
William Lake	2
William Newbolt	1
William Burgis	3[(f)]
William Pirkins	3[(f)]
William Mansack	2
Mister West	5[(f)]
Doctor Taylor	4[(f)]
Roger Jaques	2
Widow Trussell	1
Mister Philipps	2
Richard Lane	4[(f)]
Richard Tipper	2[(f)]
John Webb	1
James North	1
Richard Younge	1
John Badger junior	1
Doctor Burte	8[(f)]
Mister Yalden	3[(f)]
William Barrett	4
Widow Taylor	2
Thomas Todd	3
James Lockett	2
Lavington[4]	1
Widow Smith[2]	1
hearths	1191

Hearths not chargeable

Stephen Whitley	1
Thomas Addams	1
Richard Waldron	1
Widow Hussey	1
Thomas Addams	2
Timothy Knight	1
Giles Uphill	1
Widow Miller	2
Widow George	2
Widow Gifford	2
Widow Read	2
Widow Cradock	1
William George	1
John Newbolt	1
Anthony Davis	2
Nicholas Farr	1
John Wilson	1

Edward Addams	1
John Day	2
Widow Ely	2
William Hincks	1
John Skirvill	2
William Clerk	2
Adam Vander	1
Henry Walker	1
Richard Cawte	1
Michael Buttler	1
Predix Bethwine	1
Widow White	1
Jerome Overton	1
Widow Randoll	1
Henry Clerke	1
Peter Pearce	1
Edward Fishwick	1
Bartholomew Webb	1
James Costin	2

Fol. 48r(ii)

Widow Vinn	1
Widow Goodale	1
James Pearce	1
James Kinge	1
William Symes	1
Guy Jeffery	2
Mistress Button	2
Thomas Stone	2
Widow Skeele	1
William Rumsey	1
Matthew Rainger	2
John Tyler	2
Nathaniel Eacon	1
Widow Godson	1
Robert Bowes	2
James Parker	1
Thomas Wilkins	1
William Evins	1
Francis Abram	1
John Winall	2
George Williams	2
Widow Jerome	1
Widow Beard	1
Richard Mann	1
Richard Leversuch	2
Richard Lawrence	2
Ann Searlle	2
William Vander	1
Widow West	1
Widow Tarleton	1
Widow Silvester	2
John Pitt	1
Mister Lambe	1
James Luke	1
Richard Atkins	1
John Stacie	1
Walter Harfell	1
William Swaine	1
John Browne	2
Edward Knight	1
Richard Knight	1
William Wattson	1
Thomas Brantham	1
Widow Michell	1
William Gibbons	1
Richard Vander	1
Widow Cosens	2
Widow Shepherd	2
Widow Swaine	1
Widow Felton	1
Widow Sheare	1
Widow Vaugham	2
Nicholas Jennings	1
Richard Elmes	1
William Stronge	2
Widow Foy	1
Henry Eltott	2
Widow Bages	2
William Reed	2
Widow Philipps	2
William Barnard	2
James Eltott	1
Widow Nicholls	1
Widow Speering	1
George Cornish	1
Widow Barnard	1
Widow Newman	1
John Lawrence	1
Robert Cradock	1
Laurence Bignall	1

229. THE CITY OF WINCHESTER—*cont'd.*

Richard Pirke	1
hearths	140

Decreased 19

(a) 2 overcharged
(b) 1 overcharged[2]
(c) 4 overcharged[2]
(d) 2 pulled down
(e) 2 decreased
(f) void[2]

1. The Citty of Winchester
2. *Added later*
3. Jeroms
4. *Possibly originally* Lemington *changed to* Lavington

Fol. 48v(i)

FAWLEY HUNDRED

230. OVINGTON

Hearths chargeable

Mister Matthew Stock	4
Mister Yalden	4[(a)]
Nicholas Barling	1
Nicholas Hooker	1
John Oliver	1
William Bushell	1
Samuel Dunch	1
Widow Browne	1
Mister Thomas Charker	3
Widow Addams	1
Thomas Cooke	1
John Eedes	1
Thomas Mathew	1
Widow Goddard	1
Henry Garrett	1
Widow Browne	3
John Rabnett	1
Mister William Cleverly	3
Thomas Cloade	5
hearths	35

Hearths not chargeable

Widow Cook	1
John Hannington	1
Widow Garrett	1
Thomas Hooker	1
Thomas Garrett junior	1
John Fawkner	1
John Addams	1
Thomas Garrett senior	1
John Foye	1
Roger Middleton	1
Thomas Wickham	1
Thomas Morley	1
hearths	12

(a) 1 pulled down

231. EASTON

Hearths chargeable

Thomas Harding	9
Robert Forder	5
Mister Gilbert Colles	9
William Philipps	3
John Harwood	2
Theophilus Cole	3
Thomas Fay	1
Thomas Launston	3
Mister Brian Holloway	3
John Comes[1]	1
William Collier	2
Henry Demick	1
Thomas Earle	2
John Eedes	1
Thomas Broadway	2
Thomas Dowse	1
Thomas Woods	1
John Streep	1
John Kidgell	1
John Mathew	1
Henry Twinny	1
William Philipp	1
John Webb	1
Ralph Baker	2
William Lane	1
Widow Eedes	1
William Dally	2
Thomas Cooke	2

Fol. 48v(ii)

Thomas Whale	2
Thomas Eedes	1
Richard Forde	1
Anthony Addams	1

William Lock	1
Simon Bushell	1
Robert Jacobs	1
Widow Coles	1
Widow Burbanck	1
hearths	73

Hearths not chargeable

Thomas White	1
Nathaniel Eatton	2
Widow Morrant	1
Nicholas Colles	1
Thomas Clerke	1
hearths	6

1. es *added later*

232. WINNALL[1]

Richard Kinge	4
Richard Arnold	5
John Arnold	5
John Wake	1
hearths	15

Hearths not chargeable

Widow Shepherd	1
Widow Cox	1
John Earle	2
Richard Goddard	1
Jerome North	1
hearths	6

1. Winhall

233. CHILCOMB[1]

Hearths chargeable

Mister John Hager	4
Edward Hooker	5
George Weels	3
Henry Crosswell	5
John Harfell	3
John Foster	3
William Seedes	3
hearths	29

1. Chilcombe

234. MORESTEAD

Hearths chargeable

Mister Henry Cropp	2
Thomas Hooker	3
John Reade	3
Richard Hooker	3
hearths	11

Hearths not chargeable

John Hooker	1
Thomas Heath	1
Robert Glaspoole	2
hearths	4

Fol. 49r(i)

235. NORTH TWYFORD

Hearths chargeable

Mister John Jackson	4
Mister Newbery	4
Roger Hockley	2
John Earle	5
Ralph Wooll	3
Widow Browning	3
John Cole	3
William Smith	3
Ralph Hyde	1
Richard Goldsmith	1
Richard Wooll	2
hearths	31

Hearths not chargeable

Richard Fay	2
Edward Cowdry	1
William Trublefeild	1
John Hatchett	1
John Lawrence	1
Widow Middleton	1
Widow Wooll	1
Widow Wisdome	1
Widow Dibden	2
Richard Baker	1
William Franklin	1
hearths	13

236. SOUTH TWYFORD

Hearths chargeable

Charles Wells esquire	14
Mister Henry Mildmay	9
Mister Dare	6
John Lavington	6
Robert Beare	5

236. SOUTH TWYFORD—*cont'd.*

Richard Wooll	4
Thomas Hadly	4
Widow Charker	4
William Glaspoole	2
Thomas Wingham	2
Samuel Hewson	1
John Cole	3
Widow Dummer	4
George Smith	2
George Seager	3
John Welch	3
Widow Seager	1
John Younge	2
Andrew Weight	2
Widow Smith	1
Widow Bidle	1
Richard Hawtutt	1
John Broadway	1
Richard Mariner	1
Thomas Cosens	1
Christopher Rutter	2
William Gifford	3
Ralph Beane	1
Robert Harfell	1
Thomas Stevens	2
John Cloade	1
William Inwood	2
Widow Vinn	1[a]
Walter Moore	1
Robert Godwin	1
John Frith	1
Widow Newman	2
hearths	101

Hearths not chargeable

John Todd	1
John Dibden	2
Richard Cole	1
Widow Harfell	1
Susan Rogers	1

Fol. 49r(ii)

John Harfell	1
Robert Godwin	1
Thomas Singleton	1
Thomas Purse	1
Michael Weight	1
John Hawtutt	2
William Gifford	1
Widow Newman	2
hearths	16

(a) 1 overcharged

237. OWSLEBURY[1]

Hearths chargeable

Edward Trussell esquire	12
John Cooke	5
Mistress Arundell	13
Henry Harwood	3
Thomas Cawte	1
William Smith	3
John Chandler	3
Francis Cawte	5
Thomas Twinham	3
Nicholas Strong	2
Richard Hoare	2
Matthew Mariner	1
Robert Edwards	1
Thomas Edwards	3
Edward Sone	3
William Chandler	3
Robert Champe	1
Edward Boyes	3
Thomas Soane	5
Richard Symes	2
John Bone	1
Thomas Cawte	2
Mister Henry Mildmay	8
William Stubbington	3
Edward Collins	2
John Newlin	3
John Dennett	3
Richard Yeomans	1
Richard Colebrooke	1
Henry Carpenter	1
John Wooll	1
James Tewes	3
Nicholas May	2
Thomas Hasler	2
John Calloway	2
William Bassett	2
Thomas Hinks	3

William Futcher	3
William Burte	1
John Bignold	1
John Mathew	1
John Sifte	1
Daniel Charker	1
John Heywood	1
Thomas Hunt	2
hearths	125

Hearths not chargeable

Henry Hoare	1
Henry Chamberlaine	1
Richard Bufford	1
Widow Cox	1
John Glaspoole	1
Robert Budd	1
Austin Annell	1
Widow Cowdrey	1
Thomas Langford	1
William Baverstock	1
Widow Boyes	1
John Earle	1
Richard Morre	1

Fol. 49v(i)

William Heath	1
William Eacon	1
William Clerke	1
Peter Parker	1
Austin Mersham	1
Edward Dipper	1
John Bignoll	1
Henry Forder	1
John Cosens	1
John Heath	1
Henry Hockley	1
hearths	24

1. Owsleburey

238. AVINGTON

Hearths chargeable

Edmund Clerke esquire	13
John Vinon esquire	5
Henry Complin clerk	4
Thomas Cook senior	1
Thomas Cook junior	1
Richard Cooke	1
Richard Weeks	1
Robert Newell	1
Thomas Newman	1
William Collier	1
John Brooks	1
Steward Elton	1
William Moulton	1
Samuel Heyward	1
hearths	33

Hearths not chargeable

Cuthbert Akins	1
Edward Hooper	1
Widow Titheridge	1
Widow Hannington	1
William Hooker	1
hearths	5

239. MARTYR WORTHY[1]

Hearths chargeable

William Payne rector	5
Thomas Broadway	4
William Budd	3
Edward Lacie	3
Thomas Hellier	1
Robert Duke	1
hearths	17

Hearths not chargeable

John Powell	2
William Kinchen	1
hearths	3

1. Martir Worthy

240. BISHOPSTOKE[1]

Hearths chargeable

Mister Hurd	9
Doctor Hyde	7
Thomas Smith	3
Thomas Colson	3
George Colson	1
John Benham	3
Thomas Badgley	1
Robert Harding	3
Richard Rider	1
Widow Smith	1

240. BISHOPSTOKE—*cont'd.*

Thomas Smith	1
William Colebrooke	3
Richard Barber	3
James Tee	3
Thomas Showler	3
Henry Smith	6

Fol. 49v(ii)

Widow Harfell	2
William Glaspoole	3
Benjamin Colley	5
Richard Stubbington	2
Thomas Barfoott	2
Abram	2
John Glaspoole	3
John Booker	2
Widow Butcher	3
William Fisher	5
William Stock	2
John Woodman	3
Widow Heyward	9
Edward Philipps	2
John Futcher	3
John Cosens	3
Edward Heath	1
Widow Symes	3
Widow Stubbington	4
Richard Glaspoole	3
Robert Barber	2
Richard Hinks	3
William Porter	2
Christopher Earle	3
Henry Stubington	4
William Holt	3
Nicholas Potter	2
Widow Cosens	3
Widow Heyward	3
Mister William Young	6
Stephen Dummer senior	4
Stephen Dummer junior	4
William Heyward	1
William Graunt	3
William Newman	1
Richard Booker	1
William Case	1
John Warner	5
William Boyes	2
hearths	166

Hearths not chargeable

Richard Booker	1
Robert Glaspoole	1
Anthony Heyward	1
John Smith	1
Philip Studd	1
John Pincke	1
Widow Pledger	1
Thomas Hasted	1
Richard Wattkins	2
George Smith	1
Robert Jerman	1
James Tee	1
Roger Churcher	1
Middleton	1
Dorothy Cannings	1
Widow Smith	1
hearths	17

1. Bishopp Stoke

241. HINTON AMPNER[1]

Hearths chargeable

Hugh Stewkly baronet	20
Francis Godwin rector	8
Robert Turner	4
John Pryer	3
Robert Bone	3
John Cannings	1
Nicholas Foster	4
Thomas Rawlins	1
Nicholas Barnard	3
Peter Lacie	3

Fol. 50r(i)

Peter Godwin	3
Widow Lacie	6
John Godwin	5
Peter Clerke	1
Thomas Horner	3
Thomas Truddle	3
Henry White	4

Widow White	5
Thomas Cannings	5
John Tanner	3
Richard Mitchell	4
John Browne	1
Richard Page	2
hearths	95

Hearths not chargeable

Christopher Heath	2
John Cooper	2
Peter Harwood	2
John Bone	2
Michael Bone	1
Richard Bates	1
Hercules Moore	1
Widow Wilkins	1
Widow Hammond	1
hearths	13

1. Hinton Amner

242. KILMISTON[1]

Hearths chargeable

Mister William Lacie junior	11
Nicholas Arnold	2
Mister William Fisher	7
Thomas Hasler	3
Joseph Silvester	4
Barwick Andrewes	3
William Bone	5
Samuel Foster	6
John Oven	1
Thomas Batt	3[(a)]
John Dewy	1
John Mersh senior	2
John Hellyer	1
William Jennings	1
John Mersh junior	1
Richard Bone	1
John Bone	1
Nicholas Parker	2
Hugh Andrews	1
hearths	56

Hearths not chargeable

Stephen Holt	1
Widow Pinck	1
Edward Pennycott	1
Richard Austen	1
Peter Austen	2
Robert Browne	1
Widow Quallett	1
John Oven	1
hearths	9

(a) 1 overcharged

1. Killminston

243. BEAUWORTH[1]

Hearths chargeable

John Bassett senior	7
Richard Bassett junior	2
Nicholas Hebb	8
William Godwin	2
John Cowdrey	1
William Bullbeck	2
John Fisher	3
Thomas Beckensell	2
hearths	27

Fol. 50r(ii)

Hearths not chargeable

John Cole	1
Nicholas Cole	1
Richard Hammond	1
Thomas Rathwell	2
Edward Weekes	1
John Horwood	1
hearths	7

1. Beaworth

244. CHERITON[1]

Hearths chargeable

Henry Titchborne baronet	26
Mister John Gardner	4
Thomas Cloade	8
William Bullpitt	4
Richard Sherfeild	3
John Holloway	3
Matthew Mariner	2
William Moore	3

244. CHERITON—*cont'd.*

Name	Hearths
Rigmell[2] Weeks	1
William Bone	1
Thomas Tutt	3
Widow Trod	2
John Garrett	2
John Newland	4
Peter Newland	6
Widow Hobbs	5
Christopher Hobbs	3
Widow Newland	2
John Pratt	3
Newby	1
John Read	3
John Colson	1
Robert Bewstock	1
Mister Hugh Haswell	10
Mister John Williams	2
Henry Cosens	5
William Cleverly	3
Widow Harding	3
Widow Hobbs	3
Richard Smith	2
Richard Drinkwine	2
Richard Andrews	3
Nicholas Bastard	2
Thomas Hatchett	1
Richard Weeks	2
Ann Russell widow	1
John Quallett	2
John Lane	2
Richard Quallett	1
John Whitehorne	1
Widow Ruffold	1
Richard Croswell	2
Robert Edwards	2
John Cosens	4
Ann Oliver	1
Widow Bastard	2
Edward North	1
William Smith	1
William Blatch	2
Stephen Child	1
John Smith	1
Mark Barcombe	2
William Rathwell	5
Richard Love	2
Henry Godwin	1
John Carpenter	1
hearths	165

Fol. 50v(i)

Hearths not chargeable

Name	Hearths
William Harfell	1
Widow Newby	2
William Andrewes	1
John Garrett	1
John Collier	2
Peter Sandford	1
Andrew Jerman	1
Heritage Harford	2
Thomas Hobbs	2
Henry Quallett	2
Richard Parker	1
Andrew Wickham	1
William Quallett	1
John Quallett	2
James Daywell	1
Widow Blake	1
Roger Limington	1
Thomas Gugge	1
Richard Gooden	2
John Richards	1
Tomaz[3] Batchelor	2
John Page	1
Thomas Harding	1
Ann Smith	1
Francis Heyward	1
Robert Baverstock	1
John Hall	2
Thomas Browne	1
John Sherrier	1
Ann Bagent	2
Ann Quallet widow	2
Widow Knight	1
Richard Barton	1
Elizabeth Minkes widow	1
Widow Parker	1
Widow Stockwell	1
Widow Harriss	1
Widow Bushell	2

Widow James 1
John Willis 1
hearths 53

1. Cherriton
2. *Originally* Rignell
3. *Possibly* Thomasin

245. EXTON

Hearths chargeable

John Younge esquire 9
Henry Crowcher esquire 5
Nicholas Pratt 2
Widow Baker 3
Robert Newton 3
Robert Winter 3
Philip Mathew 6
Edward Shallett 3
Robert Ayles 7
William Rutter 3
Thomas Wyate 4
Jerome Giles 3
Thomas Arthur 1
John Horner 3
Widow Stokes 9
Nicholas Baker 1
William North 3
The parsonage 5
Mister Blunt 1
William Gray 2
Philip Allingham 3
hearths 79

Hearths not chargeable

John Slinger 1
Ambrose Gray 1
Matthew Gibbons 1
John Wyat 1
John Shakeblade 1
John Pennyatt 1

Fol. 50v(ii)

George Leigatt 1
Robert Baker 1
William Pincke 1
Henry Steele 1
Robert Edwards 1
John Titcombe 1
hearths 12

246. WEST MEON[1]

Hearths chargeable

Mister Abraham Allen 9
Widow Benham 6
Edmund Pryer 5
Nicholas Earwaker 4
Widow Earwaker 4
Thomas Pocock 3
Thomas Winter 3
Thomas Taylor 3
Thomas White 5
John Shaffte 3
Widow Froggett 3
Widow Froggett 1
Thomas Poole 4
William Mathew 3
William Bradley 4
Mister Bates 2
Widow Edwards 2
Edmund Froggett junior 1
Thomas Andrewes 4
Nathaniel Mills 3
Thomas Searle 4
Henry Knowler 2
John Pullinger 4
Catherine Scott 3
John Knight 2[a]
Richard Cornish 1
John Lane 3
Robert Harmsworth 3
John Hills 1
Widow Earwaker 1
James Earwaker 1
James Pullington 2
Thomas Hammon 1
Widow Dowling 2
Thomas Bassett 1
Nicholas Rilley 1
Nathaniel Mills 1
Henry Winter 3
Thomas Cornish 2
hearths 110

246. WEST MEON—*cont'd.*

Hearths not chargeable

John Hall	1
William Appleford	1
John Strugnell	1
William Barton	1
Richard Garrett	1
Francis Earwaker	1
William Shoriêr	2
Thomas Mills	1
Henry Dowse	1
Ann Pickett	1
John Winter	1
Henry Glover	1
Elizabeth Pollington	1
Widow Moth	1
John Allen	1
John Voller	1
Robert Slade	1
Stephen Mitchell	1
Richard Hayter	1
Edward Lock	1
Widow Froggett	1
Edward Bridger	1
hearths	24

(a) 2 overcharged
1. Westmeane

Fol. 51r(i)

247. PRIVETT

Hearths chargeable

John Aldred	3
Richard Earwaker	1
John Knight	3
John Austen	3
Robert Pullinger	4
Richard Terrill	1
John Chitty	1
Thomas Cropp	3
Nicholas Heberden	5
John Rooke	3
Thomas Newlin	3
William Hasteed	1
John Bekensell	1
William Parker	1
Richard Foster	3
Basil Bricknell	2
Henry Nash	1
Thomas Pocock	5
Widow White	3
Daniel Andrewes	1
Widow Finch	4
Peter Boyes	3
Henry Shotter	3
Thomas Rooke	1
John Pullinger	2
William Boyes	4
Peter Boyes	3
Solomon Triggs	1
William Gillmore	1
hearths	70

Hearths not chargeable

William Godfrey	2
Andrew Jacobb	2
Thomas Woolfe	1
Widow Foster	1
Richard Turner	1
John Batten	1
Susan Hasteed	1
John Jacobb	1
John	1
The Church House	3
hearths	14

248. OLD ALRESFORD

Hearths chargeable

Richard Norton esquire	8
Mister Henry Perrin	8
Doctor George Beamont	8
William Bullpitt	9
Henry Whicher	3
Arthur Lipscombe	6
Anthony Scriven	3
Richard Bassett	2
John Egger	2
Thomas Hockley	3
John Goffe	1
Ann Hockley widow	1
Edward Enges	1
Walter Barnes	2

Thomas Pryer	1
Widow Pryer	1
Richard Hockley	2
Michael Rivers	1
Richard Newell	2
Woolston Harris	5
Thomas Edwards	3
Thomas Smith	1
William Oaty	2
William Frost	1
hearths	76

Fol. 51r(ii)

Hearths not chargeable

John Page	1
Widow Hockley	2
Joan Frost	1
John Titheridg	1
Thomas Weeks	1
Widow Strowde	1
Widow Baker	1
Widow Cosens	1
Widow Pryer	1
Widow Charleford	1
John Wisdome	1
John Wade	1
hearths	13

249. MEDSTEAD[1]

Hearths chargeable

John Eames	9
Michael Harris	1
John Spencer	2
John Fidden	1
Widow Budd	2
John Budd	2
James Budd	2
Thomas Budd	1
William Barnard	4
William Cames	1
John Hickes	3
Richard Pryer	1
Richard Wake	3
John Bone	2
Widow Budd	1
John Bulbeck	3
Henry Pryer	2
Thomas Hockley	2
Robert Budd	3
William Pryer senior	1
William Pryer junior	1
Guy Pryer	3
John Battell	1
Henry Cager	3
Nicholas Hall	2
Thomas Trusler	1
Mister Richard Lane	4
Thomas Cager	3
James Merriott	3
Richard Boyes	1
Henry Baily	1
John Pryer	1
Mister John Carter	1
Francis Salter	1
hearths	72

Hearths not chargeable

Thomas Walker	1
Thomas Rice	1
Widow Hood	1
William Okely	1
William Merriott	1
Richard Budd	1
John Skinner	1
Widow Carter	1
Widow Chandler	1
William Boyes	1
Ann Tidwell	1
John Betsworth	1
William Page	1
Andrew Parker	1
Richard Okely	1
Widow Cannes[2]	1
Peter Dare	1
Richard Mowle	1
Robert Twinner	1
John Frostbery	1
Widow Harding	1
John Okely	1
Henry Clerke	1
Robert Skinner	1

249. MEDSTEAD—*cont'd.*

Widow Twiner	1[3]
hearths	25

1. Medsteed
2. *Other sources suggest that this name is* Camies
3. *Entry added in a different hand*

Fol. 51v(i)

250. WIELD[1]

Hearths chargeable

Sir Richard Lacie	8
Henry Wallop esquire	12
Robert Gunner	4
John Cooper	4
Thomas Newman	3
John Hockley	2
Robert Budd	1
John Hunt	3
Widow Merriott	1
John Michell	2
Richard Parker	3
Henry Cager	2
John Finden	2
Susan Hunt widow	3
Peter Hickman	1
William Lancaster	1
hearths	52

Hearths not chargeable

Richard Knight senior	2
Edward Heyborne	2
Richard Knight	1
Widow Morley	1
Thomas Butten	1
Daniel Butten	1
Thomas Hopkins	1
Joan Welch	1
William Lee	1
Richard Hill	2
William Hopkins	2
Robert Leonard	1
William Wotte	1
Widow Hunt	1
hearths	18

1. Weeild

251. HODDINGTON

Hearths chargeable

Jane Mathew widow	7
Mister Geoffrey Berk	4
Thomas Mathew	2
William Mathew	2
James Lee	4
William Pitter	1
Jane Mathew	2
Henry Silvester	1
Stephen Porter	1
hearths	24

Hearths not chargeable

George Lee	2
Thomas Mathewes senior	1
hearths	3

The number of hearths chargeable within this hundred of Fawley[1] is	1462
Not chargeable	298

1. Farley

BUDDLESGATE HUNDRED[1]

252. HURSLEY

Hearths chargeable

Mistress Dorothy Cromwell	28[(a)]
Mistress Younge	10
Mister Anthony Yalden	7
Widow Dowling	3
Mister Thomas Lloyd	3
Thomas Trodd	3
Thomas Symes	3
John Morley	1
William Weight	4
William Purdue	3
William Symes	2
William Glaspoole	5
Giles Kent	3
John Hickman	3
William Pickering	2
John Dowling	3

Fol. 51v(ii)

James Morley	4
Widow Watts	1
Thomas Turner	1
Philip Rider	1
Richard Morley	3
John Morley	3
Edmund Symes	1
Ambrose Purser	6
William Kewen[2]	2
Richard Symes	3
Henry Browne	3
Widow Spencer	4
William Love	6
William Russell	1
Thomas Hickman	1
Widow Light	1
Widow Renn	1
Henry Day	1
George Whitehead	1
John Herring	1
Jacob Rider	3
Thomas Michell	2
Edward Dubber	1
Thomas Feilder	7
Robert Cooke	3
Mister Robert Maunder	3
Michael Hickman	4
Thomas Trodd	3
William Launston	6
William Hewes	5
William Glaspoole	5
Richard Hickman	8
Thomas Feilder	5
Edmund Dowling	3
Richard Pucknell	2
Thomas Lowmer	3
John Leawood	1
Thomas Hickman	3
Thomas Symes	3
Alexander Churcher	3
William Launston	3
William Wickham	3
William Longland	2
Thomas Browning	1
John Michell	1
Widow Colson	1
John Pucknell	2
Widow Symes	2
Widow Symes	1
Richard Wilkins	1
Joan Pucknell	1
Robert Forder senior	3
William Allen	3
Thomas Wilkins	2
Widow Symes	3
Ralph Purser	6
Widow Symes	2
Roger Lane	4
Peter Bufford	3
John Lowmer	3
John Gradge	3
Robert Forder	3
Mister Musgrave	6
Richard Wool	2
Edward Foster	2
John Wingham	3
William Kent	2
Thomas Light	2
Widow Kent	1
hearths	271

Fol. 52r(i)

Hearths not chargeable

John Hickman	2
Thomas Wheable	1
Widow Weight	1
Richard Kent	1
Thomas Freind	1
William Wilkins	1
John Gibbons	1
Edward Bull	1
Edward Trodd	1
Alice Symes widow	1
Andrew Hasleby	1
Mary Symes widow	1
Robert Colly	1
Widow Godwin	1
Widow Bartlidge	1
William Tuggey	1
William Woods	1
William Morrant senior	1

252. HURSLEY—*cont'd.*

William Morrant junior	1
Henry Morrant	1
Stephen Barnaby	1
Christopher Gally	1
Widow Rewell	1
John Elcock	1
Thomas Woods	1
William Toote	1
Richard Trewlove	1
Widow Budd	1
William Watts	1
Thomas Light	1
Giles Trewlove	1
Richard Kemish[3]	1
Samuel Russell	1
John Snow	2
John Kinge	1
Geoffrey Palmer	1
Thomas Hinton	1
John Kemish[3]	1
Henry Spencer	1
John Symes	1
John Bould	1
John Petty	1
John Shepheard	1
Walter Gruncell	1
William Shepherd	1
George Parcher	1
Richard Cannott	1
James Fyfeild	1
Widow Fryer	1
Widow Crowch	1
Widow Kent	1
James Lock	1
William Feilder	1
Robert Morley	2
Widow Vaugham	1
Widow Smith	2
Robert Smith	2
Robert Reves	1
John Wooll	1
Widow Mathew	1
John Barling	1
William Stevens	1
Widow Browne	1
Richard Browninge	2
William Blake	1
Mark Morrant	1
John Dare	1
Nicholas Elderfeild	2
John Whale	1
Richard Wheable	1
Richard Weight	1
Andrew Woods	1
Richard Lowmer	1
Edward Foster	1
hearths	81

(a) 1 overcharged
1. Budlesgate
2. *Altered from* Kewen
3. *Text has additional minim.* Kemish *confirmed from other sources*

Fol. 52r(ii)

253. SPARKFORD[1]

Hearths chargeable

The Hospital of St. Cross	50
Andrew Bensteed	3
William Wade	3
Thomas Stevens	2
Henry Sley	3[(a)]
John Bye	2
William Hammon	1
William Colley	2
hearths	66

Hearths not chargeable

Richard Bye	1
Robert Hurst	2
Michael Heath	1
Moses Annely	1
Widow Cimber	1
Daniel Webb	1
Robert Hurst	2
hearths	9

(a) 1 overcharged
1. Sparkeford

254. COMPTON

Hearths chargeable

Henry Worsley baronet	8

Mister James Morecroft	7
Mister Taylor	11
Richard Wade	3
Thomas Charker	3
Thomas Carman	3
Richard Goldfinch	4
William Godwin	3
Sibyl Martyne	3
George Hyde	2
William Meares	2
Jerome Newbolt	2
John Calloway	1
William Harfeild	1
Catherine Symes	2
Peter Beane	1
William Greene	1
hearths	56

Hearths not chargeable

Thomas Overton	1
Richard Jolley	1
Charles Crowch	1
Widow Hart	1
John Elcock	1
Stephen Rawlings	1
Alice Elcock	1
William Cewell	1
Thomas Martyne	1
Annell	1
Colson	1
hearths	11

255. OTTERBOURNE

Hearths chargeable

Mister William Downes	3
John Fyfeild	3
Catherine Purser	2
Mister John Beale	9
John Whithead	2
Richard Noyes	4
Francis White	5

Fol. 52v(i)

Edward Cox	1
John Leach	2
John Thomas	4
Robert Mills	1
James Cox	1
William Baily	1
John Lovey	2
Frances Yeomans	1
John Williams	2
Philip Harvy	2
William Wallis	2
hearths	47

Hearths not chargeable

Thomas Martyn	1
Thomas Smith	1
Jerome Penny	1
Widow Hendly	1
Matthew Ivy	1
Francis Batchelor	1
George Hellier	1
Stephen Greene	1
William Greene	1
Widow Hunt	1
William Williams	1
Richard Speere	1
Thomas Wilson	1
William Wilson	1
William Willis	1
Widow Wilson	1
Widow Little	1
John Wareham	1
William Bachell	1
Robert Dash his house pulled down	4
hearths	23

256. MICHELMERSH[1]

Hearths chargeable

Francis Goffton esquire	7
Widow Brice	1
John Herring	3
George Ralph	1
John Iremonger	1
John Ventham	1
Widow Palmer	2
William Palmer	1
John Kelsey	1
Robert Shone	1

256. MICHELMERSH—*cont'd.*

Henry Cole	5
Widow Edwards	1
Richard Twiner	2
Richard Cable	3
Richard Peare	2
Philip Ralph	3
John Ventham	1
Richard Baily	1
John Stude	3
John Wellenough	1
William Damon	1
Mister Manningham	6
Richard Hunt	12
Richard Wheable	4
Richard Wheable	2
George Wilson	1
Thomas Reves	1
Valentine Reves	2
Widow Reves	3
John Archer	2
Thomas Penton	5
Ananias Palmer	1
Widow Richards	3
Robert Wheable	3

Fol. 52v(ii)

Edmund Davies	4
Peter Ventham	1
Gregory Hunt	1
Edward Goater	1
Thomas Rogers	1
Thomas Osgood	1
Giles Browne	1
John Browne	2
Richard Wilkins	3
Lionel Reves	2
John Pearce	2
John Pearce	2
Widow Rogers	1
John Pitter	2
Thomas Browne	1
Henry Fennell	2
Thomas Henley	6
Walter Coleman	1
Robert Coleman	1
Richard Tompson	1
Joseph Baker	1
William Churcher	3
Widow Salt	1
Thomas Jeffery	3
Dorothy Churcher	1
Robert Churcher senior	3
Robert Churcher junior	4
John Jeffery	1
Mister William Prater	4
Doctor Greene	3
George Elcock	1
Widow Whalle	3
John Bold	1
Richard Mundey	1
William Churcher	1
Widow Churcher	4
James Morley	1
Andrew Alford	1[a]
John Symes	3
Thomas Cropp	1
John Churcher	1
Argent Blunden	1
Tarrant	3[b]
William Carter	2
hearths	171

Hearths not chargeable

Richard Ventham	1
Nicholas Ventham	1
Widow Trusler	1
William Cook	1
Widow Figgens	1
Richard Kemish[2]	1
Laurence Snooke	1
Nicholas Wilkins	1
Ann Dawe	1
Widow Voakes	1
Peter Nuttgrave	1
John Wilkins	2
Widow Branich	1
Richard Yeames	1
Elizabeth Churcher	1
John Rogers	1
John Fennell senior	1
John Fennell junior	1

Widow Pearce	1
John Lacie	1
James Lynne	1
John Pearce	1
Widow Pearce	1
Walter Emery	1

Fol. 53r(i)

William Berindge	1
Widow Berindge	1
William Gunson	1
Susan Philipps	1
Widow Browne	1
Thomas Shepherd	1
Goody Mowle	1
Thomas Coleman	1
Widow Kent	1
hearths	34

(a) 1 overcharged
(b) overcharged 2
1. Mitchellmersh
2. *Text has one fewer minim.* Kemish *confirmed from other sources*

257. MILLBROOK[1]

Hearths chargeable

Mister Buttler	5
William Pildrim	2
Edward Newman	2
Mister Legey	9
David Buckett	2
John Goble	2
William Coleman	1
Widow Churcher	3
Michael White	6
Widow Hawkins	1
Widow Mayleigh	4
Ralph Blymston	1
Robert Dunn	2
George Marys	5
Widow Carter	6[(a)]
Nicholas Kente	3
Widow Gilbert	2
Thomas Bower	1
Mister Masey	4
Thomas Hatcher	3
Widow Williamson	3
John Martyn	1
Henry Brite	1
John Waterman	1
Mister John Strowde	6
William Dewman	4
William Pye	3
William Horne	5
Nicholas Horne	2
Thomas Goater	1
Mister Nevey	6
Widow Mason	2
Stephen Moody	2
Nicholas Goater	1
William Hooker	1
Widow Arminer	1
John Hoare	1
John Pye	1
William Bower	1
William Mason	1
Robert Osmond	1
Widow Waterman	4
Richard Hawkes	1
Edward Jones	2
Hugh Waterman	1
William Gawdy	1
hearths	118

Hearths not chargeable

Robert Watridge	1
Moses Marshall	1
Thomas Barton	2
John Farr	1
Thomas Knott	1
Edward Flexon	1
Francis Barrington	1
Peter Fawken	1
James Lamboll	1
James Lamboll	1
Thomas Hockey	1

Fol. 53r(ii)

Thomas Goddard	1
Widow Hills	1
Richard Mansbridge	2
Widow Mansbridge	1
Cornelius Godwin	1
Nicholas Castle	2

257. MILLBROOK—*cont'd.*

William Parrett	1
John Cropp his house down	2
hearths	23

(a) 6 overcharged
1. Milbrooke

258. NURSLING[1]

Hearths chargeable

Richard Hills	3
Robert Kelsey	2
William Arminer	3
The parsonage house	5
James Gander	3
Thomas Arnold	1
William Ayling	1
Thomas Craghill	1
Henry Whicher	2
Widow Stride	1
Thomas Dunne	3
John Mansbridge	15
John White	1
Thomas Knowles esquire	24
Mister Thomas Wright	4
Thomas Penton	1
Richard Hemist	2
Bridget Reves widow	2
Henry Waterman	2(a)
John Doe	2
Ralph Blymston	1
John Cleverly	4
Robert Wateridge	1(a)
John White	2
Richard Lee	3
Thomas Hartley	3
Mister Colson	8
Richard Forder	1
John Carter	1
Edward Beard	2
Cropp	1
Thomas Longland	1
George Aylee	1
John Smith	2
hearths	110

Hearths not chargeable

Harman Lee	1
Widow Burgis	1
William Merser	2
William Annell	2
William Davie	1
Richard Pitters	1
Richard Rymes	1
William Kent	1
Widow Longland	1
Robert Hewett	1
Richard Mercer	1
Robert Gaudy	1
hearths	14

(a) overcharged 1
1. Nuttshellinge

Fol. 53v(i)

259. BRANSBURY[1]

Hearths chargeable

Mister John Rives	9
John Allen	3
William Herring	2
Thomas Parr	1
William Stubbs	3
Austin Wiggens	1
hearths	19

Hearths not chargeable

Widow Vidler	1
hearths	1

1. Brandsbury

260. CHILBOLTON

Hearths chargeable

Henry Talmage	9
Mister Charles Appleford	10
John Huchins	1
Widow Parr	1
Richard Lewis	2
Widow Talmage	2 }(a)
Thomas Talmage	2 }
Anthony Mansbridge	1
Thomas Whitehead	3(a)
Richard Mansbridge	1
Thomas Hewes	3
Widow Purdue	2

Widow Shepherd	1
Widow Beamon	2
William Jeffery	2
John Lewis	1
Walter Sutton	3
John Batt senior	1
Robert Reves	2
Widow Abbott	2
Thomas Reves	1
Thomas Parr	2
Widow Wickham	2
John Barnaby	1
John Batt junior	1
hearths	57

Hearths not chargeable

Widow Stevens	1
John Barnaby	1
Widow Edwards	1
Anthony Houchin	1
Richard Rivers	1
John Beamon	1
Henry Kempe	1
Widow Bungy	1
Stephen Hewes	1
John Edwards	1
Widow Batt	1
Robert Barnaby	1
Widow Kempe	1
hearths	13

(a) 1 overcharged

261. STOKE CHARITY

Hearths chargeable

The Lady Phelipps	15
Mister Richard Good	5
Robert Pincke	3
Thomas Sumersett	1
Oliver Lock	2
Nicholas Burron	4
Thomas Cropp	1
Jane Tolefrey widow	1

Fol. 53v(ii)

Widow Cole	2
Richard Davie	1
William Churcher	1
hearths	36

Hearths not chargeable

Catherine Woodison	1

262. WEEKE

Hearths chargeable

Thomas Godwin	4
Thomas Harfell	1
Henry Wade	2
William Brice	3
Jonas Page	2
Robert Wickham	1
Christopher Harfell	1
hearths	14

263. WONSTON

Hearths chargeable

Mister Barnard Love	10
Nicholas Silver	4
John Faithfull	3
Widow Cropp	3
Widow Graunt	3
Thomas Tolefrey	2
John Winckworth	4
Francis Spencer	2
Richard Twine	1
Widow Twine	1
John Twine	1
Richard Beech	1
Richard Hedach	2
Thomas Harwood	1
Leonard Graunt	1
Nicholas Wake	1
Thomas Weekham	2
Widow Shonke	1
Alexander Graunt	1
hearths	44

Hearths not chargeable

Richard Twine	1
William Hatchett	1
Peter Justice	1
John Frost	1
John Baily	1

263. WONSTON—*cont'd.*

Thomas Weight 1
Widow Hawkins 1
Widow Russell 1
Richard Hawkins 2
John Taylor 1
Widow Freemantle 1
William Strong 1
Robert Reynolds 2
Widow[1] Chubb 1
hearths 17

1. *Added in a different hand*

264. LITTLETON

Hearths chargeable

John Complin 7
Richard Morley 3
Mister Alexander Henly 2
Edmund Sharpe 3
Richard Bellinger senior 1
Richard Bellinger junior 1
Richard Morley more 1
hearths 18

Fol. 54r(i)

Hearths not chargeable

William Twine 1
John Collis 1
hearths 2

265. SPARSHOLT

Hearths chargeable

Mistress Dawley 12
Edward Lane vicar 4
Thomas Wade 2
Mark Newbolt 2
Widow Buxey 3
John Browninge 1
John Blake 2
Widow Blake 3
William Browninge 2
Thomas Blake 2
Widow Lock 2
Anthony Blake 2
William Kinnell 2
Thomas Blake 1
Richard Moore 1
Richard Gifford 1
Anthony Blake 1
Widow Mislebrooke 1
William Lock 1
Edward Symes 1
Richard Blake 1
hearths 47

Hearths not chargeable

John Moore 1
Christopher Sayte 1
Widow Sayte 1
Thomas Arthur 1
Leonard Winckworth 1
Richard Mislebrooke 1
Richard Morris 1
Widow Brite 1
John Wiltshire 1
Robert Moore 1
William Stace 1
Samuel Browning 1
John Wassell 1
Solomon Collis 1
Widow Cook 2
Susan Churcher 1
Widow Symes 1
William Tompson 2
William Hoobbs 1
Doctor Gulstone's house down 3
Widow Godwin 1
hearths 25

266. HOUGHTON

Hearths chargeable

Mister Sessions 8
Widow Walker 2
Mister Nicholas 3
Edward Webb 1
William Lynne 2
Nicholas Webb 1
John Hawtutt 1
Thomas Leach 1

Henry Bedford	1
Widow Browne	1
Robert Holmbs	2[(a)]
John Hipper	1
William Purdue	1
Widow Kent	1

Fol. 54r(ii)

Widow Pittleworth	1
Richard Barfoott	2
Widow Purdue	1[(b)]
John Mersh	1
Mister Smith	2
Widow Browne	1
James Burbanck	2
Andrew Wheable	2
John Complin	3
Thomas Whittman	1
William Henchin	1
Richard Mason	1
George Frost	1
Walter Sutton	1
Richard Hawtutt	3
William Hooker	2
Widow Mafey	1
Widow Shepherd	1
Richard Hawtutt	1
hearths	54

Hearths not chargeable

Richard Collier	1
Roger Webb	1
John Willis	1
Richard Roe	1
Stephen Stowe	1
Roger Roe	1
Daniel Roe	1
John Olding	1
William Harfeild	1
Andrew Mew	1
Ann Russen	1
Widow Mew	1
Widow Mafey	1
Widow White	1
hearths	14

(a) 2 overcharged
(b) 1 overcharged

267. CRAWLEY

Hearths chargeable

Francis Morgan	16
Doctor Dorrell	6
Rookely Farm	11
William Browninge	2
Robert Baker junior	1
Widow Browning	3
Richard Loveing	2
James Weight	1
William Godwin	5
Henry Allen	1
John Tolefrey	1
William Harris	1
Robert Baker junior	2
George Penton	1
Richard Beech	2
Sibyl Page	2
Ambrose Beech	2
Robert Pitter	3
William Page	1
William Broadway	2
Mister John Turner	2
James Morgan	5
Edward Butterly	2
Widow Pitter	1
Henry Symes	3
hearths	78

Fol. 54v(i)

Hearths not chargeable

William Poole	1
Margaret Shepherd	1
Ambrose Henchen	1
Margery Pitter	1
Thomas Allen	1
Richard Franklin	1
Widow Willkins	1
Widow Gregory	1
Widow Weight	1
William Butterly	2
hearths	11

268. HUNTON

Hearths chargeable

John Calloway	3
William Spencer	3

268. HUNTON—*cont'd.*

Luke Sutton	5
William Archer	5
Thomas Bullpitt	2
Thomas Goddard	3
William Jeffery	2
John Jeffery	3
Thomas Jeffery	2
Widow Bull	3
Richard Bull	3
hearths	34

Hearths not chargeable

Henry Baker	1
Oliver Parr	1
William Goddard	2
hearths	4

The number of hearths chargeable within this hundred of Buddlesgate is	1240
Not chargeable	283

MANSBRIDGE HUNDRED

269. NORTH STONEHAM

Hearths chargeable

The Lady Flemming	22
Mister John Howell	8
Mister John Howell junior	9
William Garrman	6
Thomas Morley	5
John Holt	3
John Lawrence	3
Widow Ratte	1
Henry Cable	1
Dorothy West	2
Henry Hammon	2
Thomas Wallis	3
Walter Barrow	3
Francis Burrell	2
William Orpwood	4(a)
Jerome Bachell	1
John Thornegate	1
Edward Bauldrey	3
Francis Ratte	2
William Lambert	2
Thomas Dummer	6
Giles Garmatt	3
Joan Faye	3
Edward Budden	3

Fol. 54v(ii)

Richard Hawkes	2
Catherine Mersh	3
George Gosling	2
Richard Meeres	2
William Hill	2
Thomas Spencer	2
John Cropp	2
Henry Hobbs	3
Henry Hawkesworth	3
Thomas Weston	1
Edward Dummer	2
Peter Colson	7
David Weston	4
John North	1
Henry May	2
John Burrell	6
John Woodhill	1
Richard Weston	2
Christian Bauldry	3
Mary Bodycoate	1
hearths	149

Hearths not chargeable

Jenkins	2
William Bill	1
John Newell	1
Richard Parr	1
John Smith	1
Henry Deane	1
Thomas White	1
Nicholas Clement	1
Ann West	1
John West	1
Henry Wheeler	1
Nicholas Wheeler	1
Roger Kelsey	1
John Stubbs	1
Leonard Veare	1
Richard Bauldry	1
William Smith	1

James Holt	1
Widow White	1
Henry Day	1
Thomas Kelsey	1
hearths	22

(a) 1 overcharged

270. NORTH BADDESLEY[1]

Hearths chargeable

Samuel Dunce esquire	22
Simon Thomas	5
Martin Tolefrey	1
John Canning	2
John Tolefrey	1
Peter Purser	2
James Littlefeild	1
John Champion	2
Ambrose Cossett	2
John Roberts	2
John Cossett	1
Abraham Jackman	1
Richard Underwood	2
Elizabeth Light	1
Henry Hickman	1
Thomas Cumpton	2
Thomas Symes	2
Simon Tredgold	2

Fol. 55r(i)

John Rider senior	1
William Toote	1
William Bodycoate	1
William Greene	3
William Blunden	3
Ambrose Michell	3
John Underwood	2
Widow Burkett	4
John Goffe	3
John Glasby	1
Thomas Light	2
William Burkett	1
Thomas Newhoock	3
Thomas Cleve	1
Mister Cole	3
John Rider junior	3
Widow Mansbridge	1
Richard Barrow	2
John Hoare	3
William Dowman	1
George Whitehall	1
Richard Lee	1
hearths	95

Hearths not chargeable

Christian Mitchell	1
Mary Glasby	1
John Michell	1
Widow Reves	1
Robert Light	1
William Browmand	1
Widow Deane	1
Thomas Foster	1
Widow Michell	1
Widow Kerby	1
Andrew Foster	1
John Jerman	1
William Palmer	1
Anthony Chareford	1
Widow Fryer	1
hearths	15

1. North Badsley

271. HILL AND SIDFORD

Hearths chargeable

Mister Edmund Exton	11
John Dorneford	7
Mister Joseph Lemmett	2
William Hooker	5
William Evans	7
John Greenewood	4
Andrew Duke	5
Richard Blundy	2
Windsor	3
William Goater	1
Benjamin Allin	1
Richard Symes	2
Richard Nosse	1
Andrew Jones	1
John Allen	1
Walter Archer	3
George Penton	1
William Wheeler	2

271. HILL AND SIDFORD —*cont'd.*

Thomas Goater	3
Thomas Gissige	3
Richard Deane	1
Robert Prowting	1
John Gardner	1
Richard Hill	1
Widow Browning	1
John Prowting	2
Widow Osmond	1
Richard Jenvey	2
Richard Newman	1
Thomas Starke	3
hearths	79

Fol. 55r(ii)

Hearths not chargeable

Thomas Mason	1
John Woods	1
William Hunt	1
Widow Russen	1
Edward Fuller	2
Nicholas Deane	1
hearths	7

272. CHILWORTH

Hearths chargeable

Sir Edward Hooper	12
John Michell	2
John Hoare	2
John Lock	1
Thomas Churcher	1
John Lawrence	1
William Smith	1
John Marshall	1
Robert Hillston	1
Widow Cannings	1
Henry Philipps	1
Thomas Misling	1
John Mathew	1
John Langdew	1
Widow Rogers	1
hearths	28

Hearths not chargeable

Widow Mathewes	1
Widow Benham	1
hearths	2

273. BOYATT[1]

Hearths chargeable

Mister Thomas Dummer	6
Mistress Knowles	4
John Mathew	5
James Linckhorne	3
Alexander Churcher	2
John Lane	2
Thomas Nutcher	2
Richard Parry	2
Thomas Moore	1
Alexander Lambert	1
Andrew Woods	1
Henry Spegg	1
Widow Anger	1
Benjamin Wheeler	2
hearths	33

Hearths not chargeable

Henry Williams	1
Robert Barnes	1
Widow Newman	1
William Wareham	1
hearths	4

1. Boyat

274. BARTON PEVEREL[1]

Hearths chargeable

Mister Edmund Knowles	4
Richard Baily	1
George Wooldridge	3
Richard Cooper	1
hearths	9

Hearths not chargeable

William Jackson	1
hearths	1

1. Barton Peverell

Fol. 55v(i)

275. EASTLEIGH[1]

Hearths chargeable

John Worley 6
William Holt 3
hearths 9

1. Eastley

276. HAMBLE

Hearths chargeable

Mister John Coleman 5
Mister Jerome Willson 3
John Clerke 1
William Mullins 2
Henry Clerke 1
Matthew Clerke 1
Robert Wheeler 3
Widow Davis 2
Nicholas Channell 1
John Wheeler 1
Richard Mew senior 2
William Baker 1
Philip Battell 2
Widow Wheeler 3
James Carter 3
Stephen Bond junior 2
Richard Mew 2
John Lerrick 2
Nicholas Wheeler 1
John Delamore senior 2
Robert Prestford 1
Henry Chamberlaine 1
hearths 42

Hearths not chargeable

John Mumford 1
Widow Fry 1
Widow Hillocke 1
Henry Gauntlett 2
Richard Jacobb 1
Thomas Orchard 1
Edward Smith 2
John Cowdrey 1
John Delamoore junior 2
Thomas Cosens 1
John Chestle 1
Gregory Cosens 2
Richard Spersholt senior 1
William Spersholt senior 1
Elizabeth Horner 2
William Spersholt junior 1
Widow Spersholt 1
Nicholas Redhouse 1
John Alton 2
Widow Everett 1
Joseph Delamoore 2
hearths 28

277. SHOLING[1]

Hearths chargeable

John Heath 1
Edward Heath 1
Samuel Willis 3
Dennis Dawes 1
Widow Wharton 1
Thomas Cooper 2
Richard Coleman 2
Stephen Beale 1
hearths 12

Fol. 55v(ii)

Hearths not chargeable

John Cooker 2
John Williams 1
William Reves 1
Thomas Burgis 2
Widow Hussey 1
John Carser 1
John Lane 1
John Ring 1
Widow Powell 1
Edward Ring 1
Widow Phillipps 1
John Heath 1
Andrew Bowman 1
hearths 15

1. Sholinge

278. WOOLSTON[1]

Hearths chargeable

Mister Henry Smith	7
Mister William Higgens	4
hearths	11

1. Woollson

279. SHAMBLEHURST

Hearths chargeable

Ralph Page	5
Richard Chaplin	2
Richard Bone	4
Chamberlaine	3
Henry Major	3
John Good	1
William Mathew	2
John Lacie	2
Thomas Hewes	2
Robert Boyes	1
Ann Prince	2
Stephen Peskins	1
Richard Channell	1
Edmund Dummer	3
John Spegg	1
Thomas Aborne	2
John May	1
John Good	2
hearths	38

Hearths not chargeable

Richard Goater	1
Philip Taylor	1
Jasper Caplin	1
Richard Judd	1
William Asher	1
John Veare	1
Leonard Bell	1
Nicholas Dossett	1
John Loveing	1
John Dyer	1
William Goodby	1
Francis Smith	1
Richard Hall	1
Thomas Hammon	1
Richard Gosling	1
John Harfell	1
Andrew Veare	1
Widow Cooper	1
Widow Loveing	1
Widow Dadd	1
Widow Caplin	1
Widow Beale	1
Widow Loveing	1

Fol. 56r(i)

William Veare	1
Thomas Veare	1
Richard Veare	1
hearths	26

280. ALLINGTON

Hearths chargeable

Henry Bromfeild esquire	10
Edward Goater	3
Robert Hunton	6
College Farm	3
John Gille	1
Richard Goater	3
Nicholas Westcombe	3
Widow West	3
Thomas Goodale	1
Richard Goater	3
Richard Rider	2
Richard Cleere	3
Thomas Burgis	3
Henry Hinks	3
William Beatridge	2
Widow Neale	5
Walter Saunders	2
James Baily	2
Henry Sharpe	1
David Harwood	1
hearths	60

Hearths not chargeable

Andrew Banes	1
Richard Hinks	1
John Wright	1
Widow Gosling	2
Widow Ely	1
William Dyer	1
Richard Hellier	1

John Fuller	1
Henry Harrison	1
Hugh Philipps	1
David Heyward	1
Widow Bennett	1
William Hoare	1
Chidick Wheatley	1
John Blackgrave	1
John Gille	1
hearths	17

281. NETLEY[1]

Hearths chargeable

The Duchess of Somerset[2]	50
The lodge	4
Thomas Adderly	5
John Hoare	1[(a)]
Thomas Maydman	1
Samuel Launder	1
Richard Wright	3
Nicholas Hoare	1
John Cosens	3
William Pollard	1[(a)]
Widow Cosens	2
Esther Mansfeild	2
John Blake	1
Robert Browne	1
Francis Cartwrite	2
Samuel Willis	1
hearths	79

Fol. 56r(ii)

Hearths not chargeable

John Minchin	1
Widow Anthrom	1
Robert Hicks	1
John Hammon	1
Benjamin Freewater	1
Thomas Combs	1
Thomas Philipps	1
Widow Cosens	1
hearths	8

(a) 1 overcharged
1. Nettley
2. Somersett

282. HOUND AND SATCHELL[1]

Hearths chargeable

William Cleverly	1
Laurence Chamberlaine	4
William Reade	5
Thomas Meeres	2
Nicholas Allen	1
Thomas Lovell	1
George Westcombe	1
Edward Austen	2
Edward Fisher	1[(a)]
Humphrey Jeffery	1
Robert Martyn	2
hearths	21

Hearths not chargeable

Widow Spersholt	1
Robert Blake	1
Widow Searle	1
Richard Peace	1
William Banner	1
Thomas Ayling	1
John Clarington	1
Widow Jeffery	1
Widow Newbery	1
William Jeffery	1
hearths	10

(a) 1 overcharged
1. Hound & Sachell

283. BOTLEY

Hearths chargeable

Mister Austen	2
Thomas White	5
Mister Henry Pedley	5
Thomas Spersholt	3
Elizabeth Moulton	3
Thomas Ballard	2
John Moulton	2
Thomas Smith	1
Susan Moulton	3
William Fidler	1
John Cosens	1
William Cosens	2
Robert Boyes	6
William Barrow	1

283. BOTLEY—*cont'd.*

Thomas Parker	1
John Overton	1
Stephen Collis	4
Thomas Emery	1
William Carless	1
Mister Marshall	2[(a)]
John Lynne	3
Richard Spegge	2
John Potter	2
George Fowler	3
John West	1
Hugh Reeves	2
James Colgell[1]	5

Fol. 56v(i)

Thomas Dash	1
John Fitchett	3
John Hockley	4
Richard Strong	4
William Lambe	4
John Cull	2
Charles Bone	2
Joseph Baily	1
Stephen Bonford	1
Francis Harman	1
hearths	88

Hearths not chargeable

John Carter	1
Richard Wiltshire	1
Peter Pope	1
John Wassell	1
John Wise	1
Jerome Wattkins	1
Samuel Wilkins	2
Widow Benham	1
George Sparkman	2
Andrew Hunton	2
Richard King	2
Stephen Warner	2
Andrew Sparkman senior	2
Henry Graunt	2
Edward Kinge	2
Widow Burgis	1
Sarah Mowdy	1
Widow Forder	2
Edward Wassell	1
Robert Owten	1
Edward Marks	2
John Potter	1
Stephen Sparkman	2
Francis Harman	2
Thomas Dabb	2
John Perkins	1
William Terry	1
Richard Parker	1
Robert Baker	1
Widow Addams	1
John Emery	1
Ralph Carter	1
Widow Carter	1
Thomas Collis	1
Thomas Palmer	1
Widow Newman	1
Thomas Rawlins	1
hearths	50

(a) 1 overcharged
1. *Altered from* Codgell

The number of hearths within this hundred of Mansbridge is	752
Hearths not chargeable	205

BOUNTISBOROUGH HUNDRED[1]

284. ITCHEN ABBAS[2]

Hearths chargeable

Thomas James	7
Mister Kercher	3
Widow Burley	4
Richard Cosens	3
Christopher Cooke	1
Thomas Skeele	1
Richard Bignold	1
William Earle	3
Thomas Dowling	3
Richard Bignold	2

Fol. 56v(ii)

John Bilston	1
Francis Rolph	2

William Ware	1
Thomas Cook	2
John Newland	3
Richard Hyatt	1[(a)]
hearths	39

Hearths not chargeable

Richard Webb	2
Brian Martyn	2
Mary Jennings	1
Richard Andrews	1
John Skeele	1
John Cager	1
John Moorey	1
hearths	9

(a) 1 overcharged
1. Bownesborouge
2. Itchin Abbotts

285. SWARRATON[1]

Hearths chargeable

Mister Francklin	2
Susan Gugge widow	3
William White	2
Widow Lynne	1
Widow Gibbons	1
John Vinden	1
Simon Smith	3
Hugh Hall	1
John Steele	7
Thomas Merriott	3
William Smith	1
John Hampton	1
Widow Newman	1
Thomas Dredge	1
John Budd	1
John Merriott	1
Simon Raines	1
Henry Rookeford	1
hearths	32

Hearths not chargeable

Anthony Vipant	1
Henry Bull	1
Henry Wise	1
Widow Biggs	1
Thomas Forder	1
Nicholas Bolton	1
Widow Dredge	1
Widow Legatte	1
John Steele	1
Widow Biggs	1
John Philipps	1
Richard Cannings	1
Edmund Talmage's house down	1
hearths	13

1. Swarroton

286. ITCHEN STOKE[1]

Hearths chargeable

The Lady Powlett	6
Henry Bulbeck	5
Thomas Symes	5
Humphrey Merriott	2
William Webb	7
William Rives	5

Fol. 57r(i)

John Feilder	6
Thomas Cloade	2
William Rives	3
Richard Bruckleton	3
Robert Kinge	1
Richard Feilder	1
Richard Nevell	1
Richard Badgesly	3
John Baker	1
Christopher Cooke	2
John Collier	1
William Carpenter & John Thorne	3
John Gille	1
Widow Smith	2
William Budd	3
Richard Bacon	1
Richard Nevell senior	1
Mister Premlish	3
hearths	67

Hearths not chargeable

Thomas Baye	1
Robert Franklyn	1

286. ITCHEN STOKE—*cont'd.*

Widow Salter 1
Widow Penton 1
Richard Hickman 1
The Marquis of Winchester[2] part of his house down 13
hearths 18

1. Itchin Stoke
2. The Marquis of Winton

The number of hearths chargeable within this hundred of Bountisborough is 138
Not chargeable 41

MAINSBOROUGH HUNDRED

287. BROWN CANDOVER[1]

Hearths chargeable

Roger Coram esquire 11
Mister Alexander Grigson 6
Woolston Harris 4
James Scriven 4
Ralph Smith 5
Maurice Cooke 4
William Hickox 3
Robert Dyer 2
Richard Bowman 1
Thomas Webb 1
Edward Pickernell 1
John Sowne 1
Samuel Spencer 1
Philip Wheatland 1
Thomas Smith 2
John Brownell 1
Richard Parrick 2
Thomas Smith 1
hearths 51

1. Browne Candever

Fol. 57r(ii)

288. CHILTON CANDOVER[1]

Hearths chargeable

Sir Henry Worsley baronet 8
Mister Grigson 3
Stephen Crockford 2
William Cooper 2
hearths 15

1. Chilton Candever

289. WOODMANCOTT

Hearths chargeable

Mister John Hunt 4
Austin Kinchin 6
Thomas Knight 1
Richard Kinchin 1
Thomas Graunt 1
Thomas Rymes 1
hearths 14

Hearths not chargeable

Edward Plumer 1
John Carpenter 2
hearths 2

The number of hearths chargeable within the hundred of Mainsborough is 80
Not chargeable 2

290. THE SOKE LIBERTY EAST PART[1]

Hearths chargeable

Thomas Gregory 3(a)
Barnard Smith esquire 18
Mister William Coward 12
Mister George Hyde 8
Widow Richards 3
William Moulton 4
Widow Cropp 5
Roland Kinchin 4
Richard Seward 4
Thomas Barnard 5
James Belton[2] 3
Stephen Vanner 2
Andrew Bernard 2
William Primlish 3
Robert Bowles 2
Benjamin Dennis 2
Thomas Woads 2

Robert Harfeild	2
Michael Seeds	2
Widow Tidall	1
John Fey	2
Ralph Gille	2
Richard Pitters	3[a]
John Pittvall	3
William Broadway	4
Nathanial Robertts	3
Henry Tanner	6
William Belbin	5
Thomas Stubbington	2
Henry Grossmith	2
William Lucas	2
Samuel Roberts	3

Fol. 57v(i)

Hugh Feldew	3
Tristram Skeate	3
Robert Herd	5
Timothy Denham	3
Henry Earle	3
John Broadway	3
Mister Richard Brexton	4
William Ralph senior	2
William Ralph junior	2
Widow Allen	2
Widow Treddle	2
Mister Wright	3
Stevens	2[b]
Widow Wright	1
Mister Richard Brexton	5[b]
Thomas Hyde	6
Mister Richard Bexton	4[b]
Widow Burrett	2[b]
Robert Head	4[b]
Mister Smith	2[b]
Thomas Newton	3
Mister Rowtt	2[b]
Widow Elliott	5[b]
Hugh Feldew	5[b]
Mister Richard Brexton	5[b]
Henry Wright	3
Mary Richards	3
William Cooper	3
hearths	214

Hearths not chargeable

Robert Parker	1
Lawrence	2
Widow Sherrwood	1
William Wilkins	2
William Bachell	1
Widow Edes	1
Walter Johnson	2
Robert Harfell	1
Widow Poore	1
Peter Rymes	1
Jerome Wescombe	2
Edward Hall	1
William Clerk	2
William Benham	1
Widow Barnard	1
John Barnard	2
Savery	1
Widow Harding	1
Andrew Barnard	2
Widow Kinge	1
William Cooper	2
William Curtice	1
Richard Burgis	1
Thomas Bilstone	1
Thomas Stronge	2
William Earle	2
Thomas Wiltshire	1
Christopher Hodges	1
Richard Savin	2
Stephen Bye	1
Richard Ralph	1
Widow Feilder	1
Widow Reynolds	1

Fol. 57v(ii)

Widow Forde	1
James Barton	1
Richard[3] Mansbridge	1
Widow Trewman	1
Daniel Towch	1
Leonard Carter	1
George Eambs	1
George Bowles	2
Robert Hartley	1
William Cole	1

290. THE SOKE LIBERTY EAST PART—*cont'd.*

Thomas Forde	2
Austin Cooper	2
Widow Newman	1
Widow Curtice	2
Widow Colson	1
George Glaspoole	1
Alexander Knight	2
James Brownting	1
Widow Duke	1
Emblem Bonnett	1
Robert Parker	1
Ellen Coleman	1
Ann Elton	1
Walter Gaston	1
Isaac Pennington	1
Philip Barnard	1
hearths	76

(a) 1 overcharged
(b) void
1. The Soak Liberty East Parte
2. *Altered from* Elton
3. *Altered from* Widow

291. MILLAND

Hearths chargeable

Edward Hooker	4
William Mills	3
John Badcock	3
Edward Browne	4
John Stronge	2
Mister John Browne	4
Widow Beacham	5
Henry Badcock	4
Anthony Grafton	3
Widow Smith	2
George Cooper	2
William Combs	2
Robert Cripps	4
Mister Francis Lowman	4
Richard Addams	2
Philip Barnard	1
Widow Cropp	2(a)
William Craghill	6
Richard Clerke	1
Widow Perce	2
John Gover	2
Mister Harris	6(b)
Mister Dummer	2(b)
Thomas Cripps	2(b)
John Turner	1
John Turner junior	1
Mister Clerk	2(b)
Thomas Smith	2
hearths	78

Fol. 58r(i)

Hearths not chargeable

Widow Towch	2
John Foater	1
Thomas Lipscombe	1
Richard Griffin	2
William Herriott	1
Thomas Burgis	1
Thomas Spencer	2
Widow Westcombe	2
Widow Mansbridge	2
William Earle	2
Roger Oades	1
Widow Verrell	1
John Barnard	1
Charles Penicott	1
Daniel Dart	1
Franklin	1
Widow Shepherd	1
Anthony Grafton	1
Roger Oades	1
Robert Sherrick	1
hearths	26

(a) 1 overcharged
(b) void

292. WEST PART[1]

Hearths chargeable

The Palace of Wolvesey[2]	23
The College	55
Brian Hunt	5
Mistress Elizabeth Petty	15
Mister John Silver	8

Thomas Burgis 6
William Witherd 7
Widow Fryer 2
Widow Burgis 2
Widow Tongs 2
William Deane 5
Richard Mundey 5
Widow Fryer 3[(a)]
Mister John Frampton 8
Abraham Skinner 4
Mister John Clerke 6
Samuel Kent 5
Abraham Stratford 1
Joan Holloway 7
Widow Burrett 4
Widow Burgis 4
Mister William Whitehead 5
John Eacon 2
Arthur Biggwood 5
William Complin 5
William Colson 6
Richard Webb 2
Laurence Hyde esquire 14
Richard Mowdy 5
John Silver 2
John Donsey 3
Henry Bye 1
Richard Frost 7
Mister Christopher Meggs 7
Edward Addams 6
John Skinner 2
Robert Weckham 2
Mister Richard Frampton 5
Mistress Cobb widow 11
James Petre 6
Mistress Tookey 6
William Procter 4
Thomas Davis 7
Richard Tufton 3
William Dancaster 4
Robert Austen 2
Mistress Barlow widow 5
Anthony Wiseman 3

Fol. 58r(ii)

Robert Heyward 7
John Blissett 1
Dorothy Winter 5
Martin Cole 1
John Grunsell 2
Richard Seward 5
Widow Johnson 4
Thomas Slatford 2
Anthony Woodson 4
William Cuffley 1
Robert Cole 4
John Pudsey 4
Robert Corfe 2
Richard Corfe 2
Francis Pew 3
Thomas Fidler 2
Barnard Bowles 4
Mistress Hunter 4
Samuel Harris 2
John Baldwin 2
William Stevens 1
John Waterman 3
Robert Pope 2
Widow Wimbolt 2[(b)]
John Pocock 4
James Forder 3
Thomas Colley 4
Essex Pawlett esquire 17
Widow Davis 2
Widow Dagger 1
John Kernett 3
Walter Mersham 2
Richard Sershall 1
Widow Hurst 4
Andrew Vanderslatt 2
Mister Deane's House 14
Doctor Joseph Gulstons 10
Mister Taylor 5
Doctor Gumble 9
Doctor Burte 8
Mister Hugh Haswell 7[(c)]
Doctor Wafferer 13
Doctor Bradshaw 13
Doctor Clerke 6

292. WEST PART—*cont'd.*

Doctor Beeston	8
Henry Foyle esquire	6
Doctor Hawkins	13
Doctor Darrell	3
Doctor Hyde	11
Peter Route	6
Edward Write	2
Mister Silver's school	1
Laurence Broadway	1
Mister Richard Osgood	9(d)
William Deane	5
Thomas White	3
John Holdway	2
William Johnson	2[3]
Richard Mowdy	4(d)
Robert Wickham	2
Earle	1
Mister John Woodman 3 tenements	8
William Hancock	6(d)
Anthony Yeoman's tenements	3
Abraham Stratford	1
Thomas Symons	2
hearths	600

Fol. 58v(i)

Hearths not chargeable

Widow Smith	1
Widow Viller	1
James Robertson	1
Joseph Pledger	1
Widow Abbotts	1
Daniel Webb	1
John Broadway	1
Widow Heart	1
John Collis	1
Richard Blake	1
William Bulbeck	1
Widow Garrett	1
Widow Andrews	1
Widow Barlow	1
Richard Stevens	1
George Graunt	1
Stephen Pitt	1
Widow Hoggis	1
Thomas Mathew	1
Widow Burgis	1
William Bulpitt	1
Richard Harris	1
Richard Blake	1
William Tytheridg	1
Widow Davis	1
hearths	25

The number of hearths chargeable within the Liberty of the Soke is	892
Not chargeable	127
Hearths overcharged	12
The number of hearths chargeable for this whole division of Fawley[4] is	5755
Hearths not chargeable	1096

(a) 2 down
(b) 1 overcharged
(c) pulled 2 down
(d) void
1. West Parte
2. Wolfsey
3. voy *deleted*
4. Faweley

Fol. 59r(i)

KINGSCLERE DIVISION[1]

OVERTON HUNDRED

293. NORTH WALTHAM

Hearths chargeable

Mister George Yeate	6
Mister Gilbert Wither	5
John Pincke	4
Richard Brickleton	3
John Corbett	2
John Clapshooe	2
James Lambole[2]	4
Elizabeth Biggs	3
Richard Booker	3
Ursula Begge	2
Gilbert Cobb	1
Joan Pincke	2

John Twine	1
Alice Russell	1
Richard Penton	1
Peter Biggs	1
James Gudge	1
Thomas Gudge	1
Edward Benham	1
Richard Neale	1
hearths	45

Hearths not chargeable

Francis Warde	3
Edward Willmott	1
Wellinough Wake	1
John Silver	1
Sarah Biggs	2
John Wilmott	1
Robert Philipps	1
Thomas Kew	1
hearths	12

1. Kingscleere Divicion
2. o *inserted*

294. SOUTHINGTON[1]

Hearths chargeable

Mister Henry Holdipp	8
Mister Ayliff	2
John Hacker	5
Thomas Taplin	6
Thomas Knaper	1
Mister Francis Jackson	6
John Longland	2
Noah Perfect	1
Samuel Bannings	1
Peter Dereman	1
William Wilkins	2
Henry Nash	4
James Crooke	1
Richard Branch	2
Stephen Milles	3
Francis Fry	1
Thomas Whichelow	1
James Egerton	1
Edward Boxum	1
James Appleton	1
John Wigmoore	1
George Hellier	1
Richard Hewes	1
John Roker	1
hearths	54

Fol. 59r(ii)

Hearths not chargeable

Richard Hack	1
John Allwright	1
John Parker	1
Widow Hewes	1
Thomas Shingle	1
Thomas Henslow	1
Thomas Reade	1
Anthony Abbott	1
Widow Phillipps	1
Richard Cooper	1
Richard Farr	1
Widow Browne	1
Richard Goodalle	1
Thomas Allwright	1
John Dennett	1
James Apeton	1
John Reamen	1
hearths	17

1. Southampton

295. ASHE[1]

Hearths chargeable

William Lord Sandys	7
Sir John Trott baronet	9
Mister Eggcombe	6
Mister Holdipp	5
Mister Soper	2
John Hasse	4
Richard Bensteed	4
Edward Arthur	1
hearths	38

1. Ash

296. LAVERSTOKE[1]

Hearths chargeable

Sir John Trott baronet	17
Sir John Trott	2
Mister Edward Wall	4
William Francis	1
Francis Wilkins	1
John Launston	1

296. LAVERSTOKE—*cont'd.*

William Maphew	1
John Stanbrooke	1
Thomas Acres	1
William Jones	1
hearths	30

Hearths not chargeable

Francis Wilkins	1
Deborah Blunden	1
hearths	2

1. Laverstocke

297. QUIDHAMPTON

Hearths chargeable

Mister Christopher Bennett	8
John Widmoore	2
Thomas Ashley	1
Edward Ackers	1
hearths	12

Fol. 59v(i)

298. TADLEY

Hearths chargeable

Samuel Wheate	2
Jasper Jest	5
William Bay	3
John Curtis	4
John Appleton	2
Robert Pryers	1
John Hedges	11
Thomas Appleton	6
Richard Martin	5
Revell Martin	1
Barnard Simpson	1
Thomas Fawkner	1
Thomas Younge	3
Widow Parker	2
Thomas Garner	3
Robert Mariner	3
George Freemantle	1
Edward Taylor	2
Richard Stiff	2
Richard Carter	2
Widow Hellier	2
Edward Rumpton	1
Robert Bentley	1
William Harrell	1
William Portsmouth	2
Henry Kimber	2
Revell Martin	3
hearths	72

Hearths not chargeable

Thomas Kimber	1
Thomas Deane	1
Walter Slaw	1
Robert Alder	1
Philip Sandham	1
Richard Solsby	1
Widow Bettisworth	1
William Chappell	1
John Tarman	1
Nicholas Mywater	1
Robert Uphen	1
Thomas West	1
Richard West	1
Edward Manger	1
Nicholas Friven	1
John Duffen	1
Thomas Hellier	1
Richard Hood	1
Thomas Cole	1
William Jennings	1
Robert Hunt	1
Widow Sexton	1
Edward Cuggley	1
Richard Benham	1
Widow Mathew	1
Widow Medever	1
Luke Francis	1
Thomas Pocock	1
Thomas West	1
Thomas Southen	1
William Appleton	1
Richard Godwin	1
John Cripps	1
Wiliam Bowleworth	1
John Mason	1
Widow Jelsen	1
John Howland	1
Robert Howers	1

Richard Hack	1
Thomas Buttler	1

Fol. 59v(ii)

Thomas Towne	1
John Waterman	1
Thomas South	1
hearths	43

299. OVERTON BOROUGH[1]

Hearths chargeable

Mister Holdipp	6
Mister Thomas Mahew	5
Mister Ayliff	5
Mister Hunt	3
Andrew Sweetapple	2[a]
George Hawkins	2
John Purdue	7
Widow Woodison	2
Widow Woodward	2
Francis Carter	2
John Nash	1
Widow Coker	2
Thomas Beare	4
Samuel Gugge	2
Clement Kimber	1
John Hall	1
John Chapman	3[b]
Thomas Gilbert	1
Richard Longland	1
William Steele	1
Thomas Leather	2
Richard Browne	1
Richard Lovell	1
John Wyatt	1
William Chapman	1
Widow Wyatt	2
Anthony Abbott	2
Matthew Isley	2
Thomas Lovell	1
Richard Watridge	4
Widow Mundey	3
Widow Baily	2
Robert Fuller	2
John Haniton	2
Edward Mislebrooke junior	2
Thomas Wyat	1
Richard Goodale	1
John Bye senior	1
George Humber	1
Francis Reade	1
William Palmer	1
James Neale	1
John Gibbs	1
John Hunt	1
Thomas Knaper	3
John Wild	2
John Younge	1
Peter Cobb	1
William Cooper	1
John Kent	2
Stephen Lovell	1
Edward Ackers	1
Nicholas Harwood	5
John Watridge	1
Widow Cooper	1
Valentine Kimber	1
Richard Lacy	1
hearths	112

Fol. 60r(i)

Hearths not chargeable

William Mislebrooke	1
William Hubbert	1
Widow Wild	1
Richard Bennings	1
Noah Goldatt	1
Mary Rumey	1
Widow Smith	1
Thomas Lawes	1
Widow Casey	1
Widow Slugnells	2
James Mason	1
Widow Mason	1
William Renney	1
William Mislebrooke	1
Clement Coker	1
Jane Appleton	1
Widow Bennett	1
John Wheeler	1
John Stolle	1
Widow Carter	1

299. OVERTON BOROUGH —*cont'd.*

Widow Goldatt	1
Thomas Cleafly	1
Richard Blake	1
Robert Mislebrooke	1
Widow Joy	1
Thomas White	1
John Lee	1
Widow Crooke	1
Stephen Verse	1
Thomas Philpps	1
John Elderfeild	1
Christopher Cleafly	1
Browman Mislebrook	1
John Jay	1
Widow Mathew	1
Thomas Abbott	1
Widow Cheney	1
William Mardell	1
Mary May	1
Anthony Primer	1
Francis Hawkins	1
John Stickings	1
Henry Waite	1
William Wells	1
Thomas Mayhew	1
Robert Wells	1
Thomas Moore	1
John Kimber	1
John Stone	1
John Lake	1
Widow Cliford	1
Widow Reade	1
John Pyle	1
Widow Leather	1
George Appleton	1
John Carter	1
Widow Westwood	1
Widow Cooper	1
Mister Pile	2
hearths	59

(a) 1 decreased
(b) — decreased
1. Overton Bourough

Fol. 60r(ii)

300. BRADLEY

Hearths chargeable

Mister Joyley	6
Mister Lording	6
Mister Shottbolt	4
John Basteed	3
Annis Rowte	1
Mister John Taylor	1
John Addams	1
John West	1
John Clerke	2
Widow Parker	1
Henry Bridges	1
John Hall	1
hearths	28

Hearths not chargeable

Aringall Baily	1
Thomas Goderfeild	1
Roger Goderfeild	1
Ann Frowde	1
hearths	4

301. DEANE

Hearths chargeable

Mister George Wither	1
Mister John Harwood	9
Mister Andrew Holdipp	5
Widow Errett	2
William Small	2
Francis Ayliffe	2
Thomas Rabbetts	1
Gilbert Clapshooe	1
Henry Craught	1
John Hall	1
Widow Rickman	1
hearths	26

Hearths not chargeable

Andrew Hall	1
John Mathew	1
George Small	1
John House	1
John Goddard	1
Widow Stone	1
Hugh Younge	1

Richard Mills	1
Widow Crafte	1
Widow Haske	1
Widow Gentom junior	1
Widow Gentom	1
John Roberts	1
hearths	13

Fol. 60v(i)

302. POLHAMPTON[1]

Hearths chargeable

Edward Covey	8
John Soper	3
Thomas Bridges	3
William Elderfeild	2
Robert Ackers	1
Stephen Lovell	1
Robert Murrell	2
Francis Norris	1
Robert Cooper	1
hearths	20

1. Pollington

The number of hearths chargeable in the hundred of Overton is	437
Not chargeable	150

KINGSCLERE[1] HUNDRED

303. SANDFORD[2]

Hearths chargeable

Richard Holdway	3
William French	4
William French	3
Anthony Haniton	3
Richard Wigmore	3
James Frowde	3
William Hunt	3
Thomas Hunt	3
William Webb	3
Thomas Smith	2
Richard Willmott	1
Widow Weight	1
Widow Hunt	1
Walter Dicker	2
William Romboll	2
Peter Knight	3
Thomas Purdue	1
Widow Arnold	2
Stephen Benham	2
Benjamin Crooke	2
Stephen Dyer	1
hearths	50

Hearths not chargeable

John Godderd	2
John Champ	1
Widow Strowde	1
Widow Wheatland	1
Widow Weight	1
Edward Haniton	1
Peter Smith	1
hearths	8

1. Kingscleere
2. Standford

304. EWHURST

Hearths chargeable

Mister Richard Ayliffe	2
Mister John Ayliffe	8
Margaret Spencer	2

Fol. 60v(ii)

Thomas Smith	1
Richard Harman	1
hearths	14

Hearths not chargeable

Widow Parr	2
Widow Spencer	1
hearths	3

305. WOLVERTON[1]

Hearths chargeable

Laurence Platt	4
Mister Sutton	6
Widow Harding	1
John Poore	1
Henry May	1
John Warde	1
Widow Hawkins	1
Richard Tanner	2
Thomas Smith	1
Walter Dicker	2

305. WOLVERTON—*cont'd.*

Widow Buttler	2[a]
Walter Dicker	3
John Spencer	4
Widow Silvester	3
John Simons	1
James Waterman	1
Thomas White	3
hearths	37

Hearths not chargeable

Roger Wise	1
John Hilken	1
Richard Haniton	1
Thomas May	1
William May	1
hearths	5

(a) 1 decreased
1. Woollverton

306. HANNINGTON LANCES[1]

Hearths chargeable

Richard Fletcher	4
John Fletcher	1
Richard Buny	1
Robert Purchill	6
John Dowrey	1
hearths	13

Hearths not chargeable

Edward Lamboll	1
Maurice Wareham	1
James Rapkin	1
Robert Taylor	1
Stephen Weyler	1
Paul Tanner	1
hearths	6

1. Hanington

Fol. 61r(i)

307. NORTH OAKLEY[1]

Hearths chargeable

Thomas Sexton	6
Richard Soper	9
John Hall	1
Richard Wareham	1
Peter Whicher	2
John Newman	2
hearths	21

Hearths not chargeable

Christopher Stiles	1
John Smith	1
hearths	2

1. North Oakely

308. EARLSTONE[1]

Hearths chargeable

Mister Cornwallis	8
Widow Verundell	4
William Strowde	3
John Chafer	6
William Bossell	2
William Pratt	2
Mister Pratt	1
Alexander Mundey	1
George Mason	1
William Belton	1
Francis Wheeler	5
hearths	34

Hearths not chargeable

Edward Smith	1
Robert Smith	1
John Sandell	2
Winifred Wither	1
hearths	5

1. Earlestone

309. GUILDABLE[1]

Hearths chargeable

Nathaniel Rashley	11
James Knight	9[a]
Thomas Carring	2
Henry Chambers	2
Walter Buttler	2
William Rogers	11
hearths	37

Hearths not chargeable

Widow Mathew	1
John Appleton	1
Henry Mathew	1

Moses Appleton	1
hearths	4

(a) 1 decreased
1. Gildable

310. LITCHFIELD[1]

Hearths chargeable

Michael Smith	3
John Mansell	1
William Parker	1
Thomas Palmer	2
John Stevens	1
Thomas Fisher	1
Nicholas James	2
Edward Vause	2
William Jacobb	3
William Crooke	1
Thomas Waldron	1
hearths	18

Fol. 61r(ii)

Hearths not chargeable

John Crooke	1
Elizabeth Crooke widow	1
Bridget Stiles widow	1
John Bullpitt	1
hearths	4

1. Litchfeild

311. SYDMONTON[1]

Hearths chargeable

Sir Thomas Ogle	22
Jonas Martyn	2
John Franklin	2
George Burnett	1
Thomas Miller	1
John Trimmer	1
Thomas Bridle	1
Richard Browne	1
William Martyne	1
Thomas Edmons	5
John Burnett	4
Philip Small	3
Widow Knight	2
John Gallimoore	2
Richard Terme	3
Richard Kent	1
Richard Winckworth	2
James Clapshowe	2
Richard Hyne	1
William Francis	2
John Bassett	2
John South	1
hearths	62

Hearths not chargeable

Ambrose Box	2
John Stride	1
Edward Hall	1
Edward Bassett	1
William Bassett	1
hearths	6

1. Sidmonton

312. EDMONDSTRIP LANCES[1]

Hearths chargeable

John Blundell	5
Robert Knight	2
William Knight	1
Francis Fryer	3
Richard Rymes	3
Hugh Smith	3
Widow Bartholomew	2
hearths	19

1. Edmundsthorp Lawnces

313. EDMONDSTRIP BENHAM[1]

Hearths chargeable

Mister Colson	6
Mistress Waldropp	4
Richard Knight	2
Peter Ayliffe	6
Richard Holding	2
John Fletcher	1
hearths	21

Hearths not chargeable

William Smith	2
hearths	2

1. Edmundsthorp Benham

314. CLEREWOODCOTT[1]

Hearths chargeable

Robert Blake	6
Thomas Sexton	3

314. CLEREWOODCOTT —*cont'd.*

James Knight 2

hearths 11

1. Cleare Woodcott

Fol. 61v(i)

315. FROBURY[1]

Hearths chargeable

John Vertue 2
Mister Chamberlaine 7
Nathaniel Kent 4
Walter Dicker 5
Thomas Chambers 3
Henry Harding 2[(a)]
James Limming 2
William Sparkman 2
Widow Herne 3
William Rogers 1
Edward Parry 2

hearths 33

Hearths not chargeable

Thomas Greene 1
John Cooper 1
John Cherry 1
Widow Goddard 1
John Appleton 1

hearths 5

(a) 1 decreased
1. Frobery

316. PARSONAGE TITHING[1]

Hearths chargeable

Nicholas Dorrell esquire 8
Mister Edward Webb 9
Mister James Chamberlaine 7
Walter Wigmore 3
Thomas Lane 2
Edward Lawrence 2
William Benham 1
Widow Badcock 2
Thomas Badsley 2
Nicholas Woodward 2
William Ellis 2
Walter Allen 2
John Rose 2
William Woodward 2
Oliver Cooke 5
Adam Pollington 2
Peter Batchelor 3
Ambrose Frost 3
Richard Wigmore 5
Nicholas Knight 2
Thomas Willkins 3
Mister Robert Savage 5
Stephen Warwick 1
William Duckett 4
William Badcock 6
Hugh Hunt 5
John Hacker 2
Francis Weight 1
Richard Burtt 3
John Batchelor 1
John Laremoore 1
James Lane 1
Robert Herne 2
Robert Lane 1
Minever Blundey 2
Nicholas Hunt 2
Reuben Hopton 2
John Wimboll 1
James Holdipp 1

hearths 112

Hearths not chargeable

William Stiffe 2
Robert Hyem 2
Robert Osman 2
Geoffrey Gibbons 1
William Nash 1
Richard Warner 1
John Willkins 1
William Withers 1
Thomas Harwood 1

Fol. 61v(ii)

Robert Steele 1
Richard Hood 1
James Holdipp 2
Widow Faithefull 1

Richard Mesey	1
Edward Legatte	1
John Wimbolt	1
Robert Sexton	1
William Weare	1
Edward Limery	1
William Benham	1
Richard Neale	1
Stephen Dyer	1
James Slothfull	1
William Foyle	1
James Hellier	1
Thomas Heward	1
Henry Sexton	1
Widow Sexton	1
John Stone	1
Thomas Simpson	1
Thomas Taylor	1
James May	1
Widow Mathew	1
Widow Tappe	1
Widow Wheatland	1
Thomas May	1
Michael May	1
Widow Newman	1
Widow Mills	1
Widow Symes	1
hearths	45

1. Parsonage Tithinge

317. LORDSHIP TITHING[1]

Hearths chargeable

Esquire Fawkner	15
Thomas Saunders	3
Joseph Osmon	2
Roger Exell	1
James Holdipp	2
John Hickins	2
Daniel Ward	2
William Paine	1
Richard Primer	1
William Pearce	4
John Dicher	3
John Summer	2
James Knight	4
John Knight	2
Bernard Gold	4
William Young	2
Mister Elton	8
Mister Bourne	4
John White	4
William Gold	3
Thomas Nevell	2
Richard Jones	6
Franics Kidler	2
John Mills	1
Joseph Wigmore	6
Giles Spicer	2
Thomas Godson	5
Mister John Marks	9
Richard Wheeler	3
Nicholas Dorrell esquire	3
Edward Prior	6
Edward Woollman	5
Henry Spencer	3
John Stringer	3
Thomas House	2
John Widmore	5
James Parr	1
William Hunt	1
John Gallimore	7
Thomas Osman junior	2
Thomas House	1
Simon Basford	1
William Hoggard	1
Richard Bachelor	2

Fol. 62r(i)

John Stacie	1
Walter Golding	1
William Stacie	2
Richard Weight	1
Richard Weight	2
William Hunt	2
John Humphry	1
William Stiffe	1
John Heward	1
Peter Buttler	1
William Knight	1
Mister John Orpwood	4
Hugh Smith	1

317. LORDSHIP TITHING *—cont'd.*

Nicholas Knight	1
John Loope	2
John Fawkner	1
Widow Knight	1
Nicholas Battlemore	4
Richard Frowde	5
William Stacie	2
Edward Stares	1
George Frowde	2
Widow Spencer	2
John Sprackborne	1
James West	3
John Roberts	1
William Batchelor	5
Mister John Attfeild	10
Henry Cox	1
John Roberts	1
John Smith	1
Robert Knight	1
Thomas Bramley	3
Thomas Fostbery	1
Nicholas Batchelor	5
Richard Hawkins	3
Philip Martin	2
William Linney	1
Richard Fry	1
Nicholas Baily	1
Peter Knight	2
Richard Waterman	1
Philip Waterman	1
Peter Fawkner	2
James Frowde	2
John Hunt	6
William Stiff	1
Widow Bensone	1
Richard Cox	1
John Humphrys	1
Richard Taylor	2
Peter Lynne	1
Christopher Joyce	2
Daniel Isley	1
John Bird	2
Thomas Dicker	3
Widow Hunt	2
John Smith	4
John Weight	1
Richard Deane	1
Hugh Hunt	3
James Knight	2
Peter Stares	1
Richard Johnsonn	4
James Knight	3
Widow Stacy	1
Thomas Sexton	2
hearths	282

Fol. 62r(ii)

Hearths not chargeable

John Holdipp	1
John Holdipp junior	1
James Symes	1
Thomas Weeks	1
Widow Neale	2
Thomas Millett	1
Joseph Reade	1
Widow Worten	1
John Smith	1
Richard Prince	1
Widow Appleton	1
Widow Frampton	1
Widow Dewman	1
Leonard Flatt	1
Nicholas Holdipp	3
John Mosell	1
Widow Rowland	1
John Osmon senior	1
George Goodne	1
John Cooper	1
John Lacey	1
Richard Morris	1
William Stride	1
James Exell	1
Widow Eales	1
James Lovelock	1
Robert Feilder	1
John Beard	1
Widow Fox	1
Roger Webb	1
William Smith	1
Humphrey Mills	1

Thomas Farmer	1
Richard Batchelor	1
Thomas Appleton	1
Thomas Palmer	1
William Lamport	1
John Appleton	1
Widow Batchelor	1
Abbott Webb	1
John White	1
John Younge	1
Walter Luscock	1
William Smith	1
William Wheeler	1
Thomas Lamport	1
Gilbert Lopham	1
Richard White	1
James Benham	1
William Blye	1
Peter Benham	1
Nicholas Hunt	1
Nicholas Smith	1
Richard Whelpe	1
Giles Wilkins	1
Thomas Batchelor	1
John Cowdrey	1
James Eales	1
Michael Longe	1
John Humphry	1
John Joyce	1
Thomas Smith	1
Widow Ware	1
Giles Batchelor	1
Stephen Joylter	1
Widow Garner	1
John Smith	1
Widow Barnes	1
Widow Beate	1
Widow Winslett	1
Joan Tanner	2
Henry Webb	1
Richard Mills	1
John Godwin	1
Christopher Webb	1

Fol. 62v(i)

Widow Smith	1
Thomas Smith	1
Elizabeth Vate	1
Andrew Pricksmall	1
Daniel Hunt	1
John Mathew	1
James Budd	1
Thomas Smith	1
Widow Longe	1
Francis May	1
John Fox	1
hearths	90

The number of hearths chargeable in the hundred of Kingsclere[2] is 761

Not chargeable 205

1. Lordshipp Tithinge
2. Kingscleere

CHUTELEY HUNDRED

318. MONK SHERBORNE[1]

Hearths chargeable

Mister John Dobson	4
William Deane	6
Thomas Hooker	4
Thomas Beale	3
Francis Reanes	1
Ambrose Towne	1
John Drewett	1
John Hooker	3
Richard Hankin	5
Ambrose Hankin	3
Widow Kent	1
Philip Codrey	3
John Smith	3
Widow Coparthrite	2
Nicholas Hooker	4
Robert Wattmore	7
Robert Coparthrite	3
Thomas Cordrey	3
James Greene	1
Edward Sherwood	1
Widow Cordery	4
John Hall	2
Richard Sutton	2

318. MONK SHERBORNE—*cont'd.*

John Parker	3
Widow Reade	1
Ambrose South	1
hearths	72

Hearths not chargeable

John Rampton	2
Edward Rampton	1
John Tolefrey	1
Richard James	1
John Vaukes	1
Mary Vauks	2
Richard Cropp	2
Ambrose Vaukes	1
John Towne	1
Widow Hasker	1
William Usher	1
Thomas Yeomans	1
William Mills	1
Widow Watts	2
Widow Whiting	1
William Wild	1
John Hawkins	1
William Bye	1
William Mason	1
Widow Pocock	1
Mary Hunt	1
John Gudge	1

Fol. 62v(ii)

Widow Mason	1
John Goffe	1
Widow Joyce	1
Widow Spencer	1
Widow Vakes	1
Thomas Hawkins	1
Walter Hall	1
hearths	34

1. West Sherborne

319. HANNINGTON

Hearths chargeable

Mister Thomas Webb	6
Roland Drewett	4
Thomas Winckworth	2
John Bunney	1
John White	1
William Gudge	1
William Waterman	5
Robert Bedford	1
John Dicker	2
John Dicker	2
Richard Smith	1
Richard Wearham	1
William Garrett	1
Henry Barnes	3
John Henwood	1
Richard Dicker	5
Widow Appleton	1
hearths	35

Hearths not chargeable

Francis Britewell	1
John Drewett	1
Robert Crofte	1
John Borde	1
Widow Pearce	1
hearths	5

320. CHURCH OAKLEY[1]

Hearths chargeable

Mister Wither	8
John Baily	4
The Place House at Malshanger the Lady Kingsmell[2]	10
Mister Clerk's farm Paul etc. / Christopher Parry	5
Nicholas Winckworth	4
Valentine Parry	3
Mister John Harwood	4
Richard Whale	1[(a)]
Robert Smith	1
Robert Dovey	1
John Ederidg	1
Edward Wigg	2
Mister Wither	3
Mister Veare[3]	5
hearths	52

Hearths not chargeable

Edmund Stone	1

Richard Walter	1
William Browman	1
William Stone	1
Widow Whale	1
John Eales	1
Ralph Channell	1

Fol. 63r(i)

Richard Goodale	1
Widow Head	1
Thomas Woodrey	1
Widow Cuminge	1
Margaret Bennett	1
Widow[4] Woodison	1
hearths	13

(a) 1 decreased
1. Church Okely
2. the Lady Kingsmell *added later.*
3. *Altered from* Yeare
4. *Altered from* William

321. WORTING[1]

Hearths chargeable

Mister White vicar	10
John May	6
John Smith	10
John Small	1
William Parry	2
Widow Justice	1
John Barge	1
Oswald Huse	1
hearths	32

Hearths not chargeable

Philip Page	1
hearths	1

1. Wortinge

322. WOOTTON ST. LAWRENCE[1]

Hearths chargeable

William Wither esquire	16
Sir Robert Howard knight	10
Thomas Hall	2
Nicholas Winckworth	3
Widow Prince	1
William Golding	3
Roger Gallant	1
Robert Wither	5
William Grantham	3
John Mersom	1
Robert Garrett	2
Charles Buttler	2
Vicarage	6
John Palmer	1
John Ederidg	1
Edward Penton	2
Henry Bevis	2
Thomas Winckworth	1
Widow Painter	1
William Carter	3
George Hall	2
Widow Spencer	1
Richard Standbridg	3
Widow Miller	2
Mistress Mary Ayliff	11
Thomas Simpson	4
Widow Pearce	2
Henry Page	3
Henry Wyatt	1
John Watridge	2
Edward Wigge	2
John Primer	1
Widow Alee	1
Thomas Browne	1
Widow Browne	1
Widow Hall	1
hearths	104

Hearths not chargeable

Anthony Watridg	1
William Small	1
Richard Sutton	1
Widow Golding	1
John Wyatt	1
Widow Conditt	1
Roger Goddard	1
John Ederidg	1

322. WOOTTON ST. LAWRENCE—*cont'd.*

Thomas Fawkner	1
William Lewcy	1

Fol. 63r(ii)

Maurice Horbett	1
William Hoare	1
Edmund Perton	1
Luke Hack	1
Thomas Freemantle	1
John Paine	1
Widow Miller	1
John Hoare	1
Widow Hoare	1
Widow Browne	1
Thomas Lacie	2
James Burgis	1
William Hunt	1
Thomas Bye	1
Thomas Longe	1
Robert Browne	1
Widow Wateridge	1
Laurence Watts	1
hearths	29

The number of hearths chargeable in the hundred of Chuteley[2] is	293
Not chargeable	82

1. Wooten St. Lawrence
2. Chutely

PASTROW[1] HUNDRED

323. TANGLEY

Hearths chargeable

Dorothy Waterman	3
John Whicher	2
John Wisdome	2
Richard Wisdome	1
Henry Bowther	1
Christopher Messor	1
William Maulter	3
John Cooper	1
Thomas Waterman	3
John Bruce	1
Thomas Willis	1
Henry Merser	1
Thomas Drewley	1
William Piller	1
Widow Sparkman	1
John Merser	3
Richard Paine	1
John Hay	2
Hugh Waterman	5
Christopher Jeffery	3
William Messor	2
John Hayes senior	1
John Merser	2
Stephen Sparkman	2
William Kinge	1
hearths	45

Hearths not chargeable

John Cooper	1
Elizabeth Kitch	1
Henry Petty	1
Thomas Beale	1
John Shoule	1
Peter Merser	1
Thomas Mills	1
John Cole	1
William Nash	1
Thomas Holdway	1
Widow Merser	1
Widow Cooper	1
hearths	12

1. Pastrowe

Fol. 63v(i)

324. VERNHAM DEAN[1]

Hearths chargeable

Robert Joyce esquire	13
John Lock	4
Widow Herriott	2
William Kent	4
Richard Shelwood	2
Robert Sutton	2
Thomas Watridge	2
Anthony Heys	1
George Goddard	2
Widow Newman	2

William Elton	1
John Risord	1
William Fellowe	2
Robert North	3
John Nayder	2
John Blake	2
Widow Talmage	2
William Chaundler	3
Hugh Hilliard	3
William Hogges	3
John Rumboll	2
Thomas Randoll	2
John Barnard	4
Andrew Laundres	1
Thomas Holdway	1
Thomas Pearce	2
Thomas Limelooke	2
John Fellowe	1
Thomas Strowde	1
William Bunney	1
James Figgins	1
John North	2
Richard Mason	5
Christopher Wooderidg	3
William Flower	1
William Flower junior	2
Thomas Watts	2
Widow White	1
William Rigors	1
Edward Figgens	1
William Harris	1
Thomas Kinge	4
hearths	97

Hearths not chargeable

John Oates	1
George Smith	1
Edward Smerehead	1
Robert Smith	1
John Longman	1
Thomas Webb	1
Thomas Heath	1
Widow Heath	1
William Webb	1
Edward Branny	1
William Wigmore	1
John Page	1
Richard Goslinge	1
Richard Bender	1
Widow Tolefrey	1
James Diaper	1
William Pearce	1
Thomas Symes	1
Edward Adams	1
Widow Mertham	1
Widow Sloper	1
Thomas Gosling	1
William Blaner	1
John Dowling	1
William Dente	1
William Slowe	1
Henry Spencer	1
William Tanner	1

Fol. 63v(ii)

Robert Hopkins	1
Widow Palmer	1
Widow Smith	2
John Blunden	1
Richard Oates	1
John Blanner	1
Richard Kent	1
hearths	38

1. Fernhams Deane

325. LINKENHOLT[1]

Hearths chargeable

Ann Hopkins	4
Richard Brownejohn	3
Robert Sellen	2
Richard Hellier	1
William Elton	3
John White	1
Sir Thomas Badd	3
Thomas Bennett	1
Richard Cole	1
William Gaines	1
hearths	20

Hearths not chargeable

Dorothy Mackerill	1
Dorothy Beare	1
hearths	2

1. Linckenholte

326. COMBE[1]

Hearths chargeable

Mister Gilbert Wither	9
Robert Flower	3
Robert Parker	2
Widow Blunt	3
Samuel Smith	2
Francis Blake	2
Ann Parker	1
Widow Feilder	1
Robert Rumboll	1
The vicarage	5
Elizabeth Parker	2
Widow Holdway	1
Robert Rumboll senior	1
Widow Kemp	1
Robert Kemp	1
Robert Blake	2
Robert Kemp senior	1
hearths	38

Hearths not chargeable

Widow Bullpitt	1
John Robertson	1
Robert Lambert	1
Henry Hill	1
Anthony Rumboll	1
hearths	5

1. Coombe

327. CRUX EASTON[1]

Hearths chargeable

Mister Henry Welsted	5
William Elton	6
Gilbert Biggs	3
— hearths	14

Fol. 64r(i)

Hearths not chargeable

Mary Dancaster	1
Margaret Tittcombe	1
Joan Knight	1
James Dancaster	2
George Upton	1
hearths	6

1. Crooks Easton

328. BRICKLETON

Hearths chargeable

Richard Harwood	4
William Fowler	3
William Hellier	4
Mister Gold	6
William Wilkins	2
Thomas North	2
hearths	21

Hearths not chargeable

Simon Horne	1
hearths	1

329. WOODCOTT

Hearths chargeable

John Heyes	10
William Winckworth	2
William Vincent	6
John Mackerill	2
John Stiles	1
hearths	21

330. FACCOMBE[1]

Hearths chargeable

Mister Thomas Blake	20
Mister Tabor	8[(a)]
Mistress Margaret Reade	4
Thomas Bullpitt	3
John Talmage	3
Peter Talmage	5
John Selfe	1
John Bullpitt	2
Thomas Bullpitt	1
Edward Shereman	1
Thomas Rumboll	1
John Miles	1
Robert Browne	1
John Willis junior	2
John Watts	1
John Lipscombe	3
Edward Harwood	1
Henry Carter	1
Peter Cooper	1
Robert Luke	1[(a)]

John Willis	1
Widow Benham	1
hearths	63

Hearths not chargeable

Richard Parker	1
Widow Herring	2
Matthew Shereman	2
Joseph Gridge	1
Christopher Pearce	1
Widow Cannon	1
John Smith	1
John Apers	1
John Sheereman	1
hearths	11

(a) 1 decreased
1. Fackcoombe

Fol. 64r(ii)

331. HURSTBOURNE TARRANT[1]

Hearths chargeable

Mister Christopher Tisteed	5
Charles Pointlett esquire	5
Mister William Shesey	6
Jude Hellier	3
William Hearne	1
Jasper Mundey	1
Mister Thomas Dowse	2
Peter Selfe	1
Thomas Widley	2
Widow Waterman	2
Robert Hall	2
Thomas Stock	3
George Browne	2
William Mills	2
Robert Ivory	1
William Elton	1
Zacharias Hellier	3
John Beawmont	4
Mister Edward Mills	1
John Holdway	1
Thomas Bullpitt	2
Widow Wither	2
Robert Wither	1
John Childs	2
Mister Russell	2
John Wooderidge	1
Robert Bunney	5
William Poore	2
Mister John Kingsmill	3
Edward Osborne	3
John Shellwood	3
Mister John Osborne	4
Barnard Addoms	1
John Purchill	1
Francis North	3
John Hammon	2
John Iremonger	2
Thomas Diaper	2
John Wyatt	1
John Longman	2
John Wall	1
William Watts	2
Thomas Mundey	3
Zacharias Hellier	1
William Hopgood	2
Edward Yeareley	2
hearths	103

Hearths not chargeable

Andrew Purdue	1
William Palmer	1
John Cannings	1
Stephen Harding	1
Thomas Cleately	1
William Bullpitt	1
John Davis	1
Thomas Davis	1
Thomas Cannings	1
William Kent	1
Widow Badgsley	1
Richard Feilder	1
Peter Whale	1
Richard Coleman	1
Widow Watts	1
Widow Wither	1
Widow Wearing	1
John Willis	1
Alice Cole	1
John Portsmouth	1

331. HURSTBOURNE TARRANT —*cont'd.*

Joseph Portsmouth	1
Widow Lock	1
Andrew Holdway	1
John Alexander	1

Fol. 64v(i)

Thomas Coleman	1
Richard Waterman	1
William Rumboll	1
Widow Bullpitt	1
Widow Brexton	1
Widow Bunney	1
Widow Mason	1
Timothy Bunney	1
James Hart	1
John Mundey	1
Whitehorne	1
hearths	35

1. Hursbourne Tarrant

The number of hearths chargeable in the hundred of Pastrow	422
Not chargeable	113

EVINGAR HUNDRED[1]

332. EAST WOODHAY[2]

Hearths chargeable

Edward Goddard esquire	15
Doctor William Luce	8
Mister William Goddard	8
Mister Thomas Seymore	7
Mister Thomas Kemp	9
Philip Harris	4
John Parker	6
Widow Pallter	1
Widow Peareman	1
John Mundey	1
William Wither	1
Widow Mills	3
Richard Osgood	1
Henry Parris	1
Richard Withers	1
John Osgood	3
Robert Buttler	1
Widow Hellier	1
John Ansell	1
Geoffrey Winter	2
John Mundey	1
William Sutton	2
Widow Andrewes	2
Robert Parker	1
Robert Atherin	1
James Braxlow	5
William Penton	2
Widow Pyle	4
William Buttler	1
William Bellord	1
William Goringe	2
Edward Drewsand	1
Edward Barbone	2
William Betham	3
William Doare	2
John Stile	2
Thomas Edmunds	1
Widow Bullpitt	1
Andrew Mundey	1
John Walsdeane	2
Henry Crooker	2
William Greene	1
Richard Bunny	1
Thomas Lamborne	2
William Sutton	1
Thomas Pearce	2
Widow Dismore	5
William Glass	3
James[3] Cooke	1
Edward Fatthorne	1
Widow Hall	1
Widow Sherton	1
Philip Villers	3
John Bishopp	1
Thomas Heards	4

Fol. 64v(ii)

Thomas Knight	2
Widow Kibelitte	1
Thomas Barnes	1

Richard Wild	2
William Alexander	2
Widow Bristowe	4
Thomas Henley	1
Widow Fillis	3
John Smart	2
Humphrey Bristowe	1
William Rumey	3
William Broomes	1
Richard Kipson	2
Thomas Watts	1
Richard Wheeles	1
Henry Bye	2
Widow Betham	3
John Cleasey	1
Peter Browne	1
William Mundey	1
Thomas Bearebone	4
James Knight	3
Simon Pike	3
William Hall	5
Maurice Barnard	5
William Blaystone	2
hearths	199

Hearths not chargeable

John Curring	1
Richard Lamborne	1
Widow Sandys	1
James Hasker	1
John Goodale	1
William Edwards	1
Widow Knight	1
John Younge	1
Thomas Cox	1
John Kemp	1
Christopher Parker	1
Widow Bythard	1
John Dod	1
Widow Primer	1
William Dines	1
Richard Hall	1
Robert Pearce	1
John Woods	1
Francis Moore	1
Widow Watts	1
Henry Hollard	1
John Haymes	1
Barnard Bristow	1
Joseph Jaye	2
Widow Younger	1
Stephen Knight	1
Robert Hall	1
Widow Younge	1
William Mundey	1
Richard Moncke	1
Henry Barlow	1
Maurice Mantle	1
John Feild	1
Widow Pinfeild	1
Thomas Browne	1
Widow Tanner	1
John Atterine	1
Edward Holdinge	1
Thomas Rookes	1
Walter Hasman	1
John Smith	1
Thomas Brooke	1
Thomas Benham	1
Widow Harding	1
Thomas Browne	1
James Knight	1
William Brookely	1

Fol. 65r(i)

Edward Barkwood	1
Francis Atkins	1
Richard Palmer	1
Thomas Greene	1
Edward Taylor	1
William Moth	1
John Hull	1
John Aley	1
Widow Morrell	1
Robert Eastman	1
George Eastgate	1
Alice Flower	1
Widow Norrice	1
John Mills	1
Christopher Halle	1
Widow White	1
William Hall	1
William Pitt	1
Richard Heart	1

332. EAST WOODHAY—*cont'd.*

Robert Lawrence	1
William Martine	1
Richard Brownsden	1
Robert Basing	1
William Currant	1
John Rumboll	1
Samuel Hinton	1
Edward Setter	1
Philip Smith	1
William Martin	1
John Hellier	1
John Martine	1
Widow Alee	1
Francis Lower	1
John Goldocke	1
Stephen Browne	1
John Pincer	1
Francis Watts	1
Samuel Misson	1
William Lake	1
Widow Dare	1
Thomas Smith	1
Widow Barnes	1
Widow Fines	1
Edward Smith	1
Walter White	1
William Horne	2
William Browne	1
John Frowde	1
John Coxard	1
John Brackley	1
John Brunsden	1
John Rimes	1
John White	1
David Wimbolt	1
William Warren	1
Thomas Collett	1
Widow Beawmont	1
Hugh Weight	1
Richard Beard	1
William Bristow	1
Widow Tooker	1
John Kinge	1
William Faithfull	1
Adam Limlock	1
John Bristow	1
Dorothy Andross	1
Edward Smith	1
Richard Clerke	1
Thomas Clutthook	1
John Fisher	1
Richard Cole	1
Maurice Hill	1
Venis Richmond	1
Peter Glaustafe	1
Widow Haynewell	1
John Brooker	1
David Goodlock	1
Widow Kidgar	1
Adam Smartt	1
John Cooper	1

Fol. 65r(ii)

Widow Smith	1
Robert Herring	1
James Buller	1
James Nuttkins	1
Thomas Goddard	1
hearths	134

1. Evinger
2. East Woodhey
3. *Added later*

333. BURGHCLERE[1]

Hearths chargeable

Mister John Lawde	11
Mistress Brownejohn	12
John Waden	4
William Waterman	6
George Attron	2
Andrew Peade	2
Francis Hawkins	4
Widow Martin	2
Richard White	4
James Sibbers	2
Widow Hawkins	2
James Wither	4
John Earley	3
Nicholas Rumboll	1
John Cooper	2
Mister James Gardner	4
John Knight	2

Edward Joyte	1
Thomas Joyte	1
Widow Arnold	5
Richard Wheeler	2
Widow Wimbolt	4
John Fellow	2
John Peades	1
John Wheeler	4
Robert Hellier	3
William Pearce	2
Mister William Gowen	4
Widow Pippin	3
Widow Steptow	1
James Pocock	2
James Pilkin	2
John Harding	3
Thomas White	5
John Winckworth	3
William Cooke	7
William Appleford	3
Richard White	1
Widow Annell	5
William Symes	1
Edward Cooper	1
William Cooper	1
Andrew Hall	3
Widow Silrey	3
Henry Hayes	2
Francis Philpott	1
Robert Stoner	1
Edward Pittman	1
Peter White	2
Widow Griffin	2
Widow Stoner	1
Edward Maskell	1
William Hearne	1
William Smith	1
Robert Beale	1
William Holdway	2
Thomas Wimbolt	1
John Bargin	1
hearths	158

Fol. 65v(i)

Hearths not chargeable

Widow Buttler	1
John Stiles	1
Christopher James	1
Widow Withers	1
Bagin	2
Thomas Russell	1
William Golding	1
George Lewden	1
Simon Stepto	1
Daniel Currant	1
William Smart	1
William Smith	1
Ralph Dullard	1
Widow Palmer	1
William Wild	1
Richard Oldman	1
Widow White	1
Nicholas Buttler	1
Henry Hunt	1
Sarah Turton	1
Christopher Champ	1
George Lewden	1
Widow Martin	1
hearths	24

1. Borowcleere

334. HIGHCLERE

Hearths chargeable

Richard Lacie esquire	24
Christopher Massey rector	4
John Knight	1
Thomas Knight	1
Arthur Holdway	2
Thomas Dill	2
John Wimbolt	1
William Neale	2
John Bernard	1
Mary Waterman	2
Edward Alford	3
John Hickley	1
John Freeborne	3
Widow White	1
John May	2
Nicholas Steptoe	1
William Lampe	1
John Robson	1
John Robson	2

334. HIGHCLERE—*cont'd.*

Edward Cooper	1
Andrew Beavis	5
James Cleanes	2
Henry Pryor	1
James Knight	1
John Weary	1
William Holdway	1
Walter Hellier	2
Moses Bond	3
John Chandler	3
John Hornell	3
Richard Aley	1
Anthony Hellier	1
Michael Hockley	2
James Sawyer	2
Robert Bristow	1
John Deane	1
Richard Hopgood	2
Peter Tellew	2
Thomas Allen	1
Maurice Longe	2
William Fetter	4
William Neale	2
Peter Neale	2
Philip Cummin[1]	3
Edward Elton	2
John Taylor	2
John Tull	2

Fol. 65v(ii)

William Basten	2
John Basten	3
John Walter	2
hearths	117

Hearths not chargeable

Widow Freeborne	2
James Crook	1
John Crooke	1
Arthur Wimbolt	1
William Waterman	2
William Cooper	1
Thomas Allen	1
John Browne	1
Nicholas Walter	2
John Shywell	1
John Sayer	2
John Tull	2
Widow Bernard	1
James Newman	1
Jane Bernard	1
William Page	1
Richard Tufton	2
Christopher Philpot	2
William Limbers	1
John Ryves	1
Daniel Browne	1
Nicholas Palmer	1
John Winter	1
William Winter	1
John Richards	1
William Alee	1
Richard Palmer	1
Widow Stoner	1
Widow Legg	1
Ann Holdway	1
Christopher Lane	1
Widow Withers	1
Simon Withers	1
hearths	41

1. *Probably* Cummin *but written* Cumnin

335. NEWTOWN[1]

Hearths chargeable

John Biss clerk	3
Thomas Lording	3
Thomas Godwin	2
Edward Barttlet	3
John Sley	2
John Hall	3
Richard Winch	5
Roger White	2
Christopher Smith	2
Thomas Bruth	3
Robert Persons	2
William Chapman	4
Daniel Feller	3
Joseph Fuller	2
Richard Andrews	1
Thomas Persons	1
Widow Harding	1

John Gowen	1
Thomas Withers	1
Adam Stoner	1
John Stoner	1
Richard Charlock	1
Christopher James	2
Edward Hall	1
hearths	50

Fol. 66r(i)

Hearths not chargeable

Christopher Richardson	1
Joan Martyn	1
John Pricksmall	1
Richard Rogers	1
Philip Worth	1
Richard Prince	1
Robert Stove	1
Joan Young	1
Richard Martyne	1
Widow Voller	1
Joan Bartolomew	1
Alice Palmer	1
John Young	1
Arthur Webb	1
Joan Stone	1
Thomas Clabor	1
William Chestle	1
William Chestle junior	1
Robert Shewell	1
John Thridge	1
Richard Stubbs	1
Francis Stone	1
John Stone	1
Stephen Reade	1
William Whiteeare	1
Margaret Staplle	1
Samson Saige	1
William Trench	1
Daniel White	1
Henry Reade	1
Robert Basor	1
John Palmer	1
James Gollinge	1
Paul Frost	1
Margaret Weston	1
Thomas Rumbolt	1
Thomas Gessett	1
Thomas Wyman	1
Widow Drew	1
John Stronge	1
hearths	40

1. Newtowne

336. BAUGHURST[1]

Hearths chargeable

Mister Musgrave	3
Richard Dicker	4
Richard Baghurst	3
Robert Dicker	3
Thomas Smith	2
Richard Dicker	1
Richard Greene	1
Robert Greene	2
Richard Stiff	1
Widow Avery	3
Richard Potter	2
James Greene	1
Widow Gast	2
Widow Mersh	2
John Friben	1
John Young	2
Richard Dicker	1
Edward Harmsworth	3
Joan Spencer	4
John Payse	3
John Greene	2
Thomas Deane	1
hearths	50

Hearths not chargeable

James May	1
Matthew Serwood	1
Thomas Kent	1
Bartholomew Valenter	1
John Dicker	1
John Godmeane	1
William Dicker	1
Robert Dicker	1
Richard Littleworth	1
Thomas Allen	1
hearths	10

1. Baghurst

Fol. 66r(ii)

337. ASHMANSWORTH

Hearths chargeable

Doctor William Lucey	2
Edward Elton	2
Edward for the farm	2
Nicholas Sayer	1
John Griffen	1
Edward Talmage	2
Richard Barlow	4
William Greene	1
Robert Harding	2
William Neale	1
William Cole	2
Ruth Holdway	2
Elizabeth Holdway	2
John Hawkins	2
Edward Talmage	1
John Presse	2
Robert Lake	2
Silvester Stevens	1
William Carter	2
John Potter	1
hearths	35

Hearths not chargeable

William Bullpitt	1
Thomas Holdway	1
William Holdway	1
William Drewly	1
Alice Dereman	1
Robert Harding	1
Henry Cole	1
Walter Jervice	1
John Holdway	1
Widow Cole	1
hearths	10

338. ECCHINSWELL[1]

Hearths chargeable

Richard Wheatland	4
Maurice Mosdell	1
Edward Pricksmall	3
John White	1
George Glover	3
William Goddard	2
John Burneface	1
Henry Oneey	1
John Walter	2
John Fletcher	3
Robert Allen	2
Nicholas Walter	2
Nicholas Winckworth	5
John Hawkins	1
Richard Winckworth	3
Widow Dancaster	1
John Rumboll	1
John Winckworth	1
Thomas Walter	1
Nicholas Placye	1
William Benham	3
William Walter	2
Henry Fowell	2
John Penton	1
Mister Dove	3
Nicholas Tanner	1
Peter Fosberry	1
Thomas Henwood	2
Matthew Dyer	6
Edmund Goddard	5
Richard Kent	2
Richard Beare	1
Anthony May	1
Robert Buxey	1
George Painter	1
Richard Wheatland	4
hearths	75

Fol. 66v(i)

Hearths not chargeable

Nicholas Saunders	1
Thomas Mosdell	1
William Imperell	1
John Mosdell	1
Thomas Smith	1
Mary Smith	1
John Herriott	1
Thomas May	1
Richard Baily	1
George Forde	1
Charles Whitaker	1
Richard Battlemore	1

Thomas Sparkfeild	1
Richard Palmer	1
John Palmer	1
Andrew Palmer	1
John Lawes	1
Paul Primer	1
Widow Waldropp	1
Peter Waldropp	1
William Winckworth	1
George Poynter	1
Michael Barnard	1
William Turfeild	1
Peter Parker	1
Widow Sparkfeild	1
Thomas Smith	1
hearths	27

1. Itchinswell

339. WHITCHURCH BOROUGH[1]

Hearths chargeable

Thomas Brooks esquire	10
William Poyntter	6
William Dinner	1
William Benham	3
Edward Pearce	5
Richard Holloway	3
Joseph Randoll	1
Widow Parry	1
Nicholas Squire	2
William Neale	1
Peter Newman	1
Thomas Cooper	1
Peter Osmand	1
Robert Buxey	1
Richard Skeate	2
John Doswell	3
John Fisher	2
James Webb	10
Andrew Tanner	1
Thomas Wheatland	5
Edward Martin	2
John Keene	2
Nicholas Collis	2
Mary Long	3
Alice Harper	2
Edward Weight	1
Thomas Battell	1
Thomas Allen	3
Matthew Millett	2
Thomas Parry	2
John Smith	1
John Chickock	1
James Osmond	1
Christopher Hardwell	1
John Batchelor	1
John Browne	1
Edward Farmer	1
Widow Braxtone	2
William Poore	1
Dennis Long	8
Thomas Long	1

Fol. 66v(ii)

Widow West	4
Widow Feltham	1
Roger Winter	1
Rumboll Cullens	2
Nicholas Kent	1
Stephen Hall	2
Widow Wigmore	2
John Drewham	1
William Dover	1
William Wheeler	1
Ambrose Cally	1
John Buller	1
Edward Pearce	2
John Francis	3
Richard Weston	3
John Rickers	3
Richard Feltham	1
William Benham	3
William Benham	1
Widow Benham	1
Thomas Neave	3
Widow King	1
John Paringe	1
Edward Suckley	1
John Cox	2
William Huchins	3
hearths	145

339. WHITCHURCH BOROUGH *—cont'd.*

Hearths not chargeable

Widow Barker	1
Widow Barrett	1
Richard Cawte	1
William Hall	1
Nicholas Barrett	1
Richard Cawte	1
Samuel Buller	1
Widow Stacy	1
John Randoll	1
Richard Wilkins	1
Thomas Tarrant	1
Thomas Whale	1
Joseph Haslett	1
Samuel Lane	1
Mary Broadfeild	1
Nicholas Hall	1
William Carrett	1
Mary Carrett	1
William Newman	1
William Whiting	1
William Taylor	1
John Sutton	1
John Poynter	1
Thomas Deane	1
Thomas Eaton	1
Richard Rewell	1
John Gray	1
William Newman	1
Widow Garrett	1
Widow Walter	1
Jasper Hill	1
James Hill	1
Edward Billett	1
John Huchins	1
James Squire	1
William Knight	1
William Parker	1
John Stanton	1
William George	1
John Biffin	1
hearths	40

1. Whitchurch Burrowe

Fol. 67r(i)

340. WHITCHURCH TITHING[1]

Hearths chargeable

Mister Richard Ayliff	4
Richard Smith	1
Thomas Foster	1
Anthony Brampston	3
William Cooper	2
Mister Michael Scrimpton	8
John Cropp	1
James Pearce	2
Richard Forde	3
William Easton	1
John Compton	3
James Buttler	2
Richard Lardner	4
George Penton	2
Robert Parker	2
Thomas Austen	1
Edward Suckley	1
John Pearce	2
John Yeare	1
Robert Rumboll	1
Robert Cooper	1
John Canlassheere[2]	1
hearths	47

Hearths not chargeable

John Seale	1
James Philipps	1
Ann Greene	1
Robert Barker	1
William George	1
William Russen	1
John Dampner	1
Ann Williams	1
Nicholas Hall	1
William Bright	1
hearths	10

1. Whitchurch Tithinge
2. Canlassheere *added later*

341. WHITCHURCH PARSONAGE

Hearths chargeable

Thomas Brooks esquire	10

Jasper Benyeare	4
Edward Drewly	1
Robert Waterman	1
John Cooper	1
William Clerke	1
Thomas Waterman	1
hearths	19

Hearths not chargeable

John Sutton	1
Robert Smith	1
John Cantage	1
hearths	3

342. BOURNE PARSONAGE

Hearths chargeable

Mister Richard Beckley	6
Thomas Beckley	1
John Rumsey	3
Richard Cooke	1
Mister Claybrooke	2
Widow Parker	3
Richard Salmon	1
Robert Wisdome	1
Widow Morrell	2
Thomas More	2
Robert Carter	2
Mister Tarman	2
Robert Thorngate	4
Robert Wild	2
Thomas Philpott	1
Widow Hodges	1

Fol. 67r(ii)

William Moore	3
George Persons	3
Rigell Poore	4
Robert Sutton	2
John Nicholas	3
William Waterman	1
hearths	50

Hearths not chargeable

Robert Lock	1
Mary Waltham	1
Widow Moore	1
John Colley	1
Thomas Tapner	1
Ann Hedges	1
John Lawes	1
John Goodale	1
William Seale	1
Edmund Gilmons	1
Widow Rumsey	1
Widow Bawd	1
Widow Knight	1
Widow Gadge	2
Widow Story	1
Thomas Silvester	1
Thomas Marks	1
Benjamin Taplin	1
William Mills	1
Widow Beale	1
Robert Dowland	1
John Dowland	1
hearths	24

343. HURSTBOURNE PRIORS

Hearths chargeable

Henry Wallopp esquire	26
Walter Knight	4
Robert Waterman	1
Thomas Nicolls	2
Edmund Heath	3
John Marriner	1
Benjamin Smith	1
William Smith	1[a]
Ruth Buttler	1
Austin Stone	1
John Ryves	1
John Booker	1
Thomas Cox	2
Joan Hack	2
Edmund Symes	1
John Collens	3
Robert Fhisher	2
Ruth Greene	3
Widow Fishe	1
Robert Tompson	1
Mark Hunt	2
William Over	1
Nicholas Pricksmall	2
Maurice Jones	1
Edward Blanchard	1

343. HURSTBOURNE PRIORS *—cont'd.*

Ruth Sutton	1
Nicholas Rutter	1
John Holmes	1
hearths	68

Hearths not chargeable

Thomas Dowse	2
Henry Weston	1
Joan Carter	1
Robert Nevell	1
Thomas Disman	1
Widow Jewell	2
hearths	8

(a) 1 decreased

Fol. 67v(i)

344. CHARLCOTT[1]

Hearths chargeable

William Soper	1
Thomas Wayes	3
Andrew Webb	3
Henry Smith	1
hearths	8

Hearths not chargeable

William Collens	1
Henry Deereman	2
hearths	3

1. Charlecott

345. BRADLEY

Hearths chargeable

John Carter	7
John Band	3
Thomas Stepto	1
William Biffen	1
William Band	2
hearths	14

Hearths not chargeable

John Martin	1
William Band	1
hearths	2

346. STOKE

Hearths chargeable

Thomas Rattey	1
Matthew Rumboll	2
Edmund Rattey	1
John Holdway	1
Edward Cannon	1
Nicholas Hearne	1
Thomas Knight	2
Henry Bay	2
William Leach	1
William Parker	1
William Hawkins	1
Roger Stacy	1
John Batchelor	2
Laurence Cole	1
Richard Bunney	1
George Philpott	1
hearths	22

Hearths not chargeable

Robert Lake	1
Robert Russell	2
Roger Humphreys	1
Nicholas James	1
William Nichols	1
Joan Cooper	1
Thomas Ederwell	1
William Hampshire	1
William Hayward	1
William Philpott	1
hearths	12

347. EGBURY[1]

Hearths chargeable

Robert Oxenbridge esquire	13
Nicholas Bernard	1
Robert Seaman	1
John Joyce	1
John Bond	1
Mister Robert Sutton	4
John Godden senior	3
John Godden junior	1
Nicholas Broadway	2

Jonas Golding	2
William Felix	1
hearths	30

Fol. 67v(ii)

Hearths not chargeable

Richard Poore	1
John Badge	1
Edward Bond	1
William Blake	1
William Hall	1
hearths	5

1. Egberry

348. SWAMPTON[1]

Hearths chargeable

Robert Heyes	2
Robert Heyes junior	1
Edward Penton	1
Widow Addams	1
William Lane	1
James Gosling	3
Roger Freemantle	2
Widow Boxholt	2
William Moore	2
Widow Shingle	1
Thomas Barker	1
Mister Peter Blake	3
John Wells	1
Widow Hodges	1
William Bridges	1
Thomas Cannon	15
Edward Drewley	2
William Lee	1
Richard Barker	1
Widow Wilkins	1
Mister Herriott	2
John Landon	4
hearths	49

Hearths not chargeable

Joseph Orred	1
Joan Wimbolt	1
John Hedges	1
John Seely	1
William Merry	1
Robert Glover	1
John Silvester	1
John Savis	2
hearths	10

1. Swamton

349. BINLEY

Hearths chargeable

Mister Richard Wither	10
Henry Gynes	1
William Poore	1
James Isron	2[a]
Thomas Isron	3
Thomas Philpott	1
William Holdway	1
Widow Shearethorne	1
William Pittfall	1
William Osman	1
William Floyd	1
Robert Longman	3[b]
Richard Holdway	2
hearths	28

Hearths not chargeable

George Clavett	1
William Flood	1
Nicholas Philpott	1
Simon Stiles	1
Widow Smuggs	1
Thomas Vinsent	1
Widow Philpott	1
Widow Figges	1
hearths	8

(a) 1 decreased
(b) 2 decreased

Fol. 68r(i)

350. FREEFOLK MANOR[1]

Hearths chargeable

Sir Matthew Hollworthy knight	17
Thomas Sexton	4
Nicholas Gilbert	2
hearths	23

1. Freefolke Mannor

351. FREEFOLK PRIORS

Hearths chargeable

John Silver	2
William Rolph	4
William Webb	1
William Benham	1
Thomas Benham	1
William Benham junior	2
Widow Sutton	2
John James	1
Robert Greene	1
John Covey	1
John Lempster	4
Widow Benham	3
hearths	23

Hearths not chargeable

Andrew Cleafley	1
Peter Piper	1
Widow Sneade	1
hearths	3

352. WEEK[1]

Hearths chargeable

Joseph Leach	11
Francis Mundey	3
Robert Dowley	1
John Horne	1
Widow Kidgell	1
Alexander Woods	1
William Beale	1
William Pearcy	2
Widow Silvester	1
Clement Dorrell	1
Thomas Horne	2
hearths	25

The number of hearths chargeable in the hundred of Evingar[2] is	1235
Not chargeable	445
The number of hearths chargeable within the whole division of Kingsclere[3] is	3248
Hearths not chargeable	995

1. Weeke
2. Evinger
3. Kingscleere

Fol. 69r(i)

BASINGSTOKE DIVISION

ODIHAM HUNDRED

353. GREYWELL[1]

Hearths chargeable

Sir Thomas Higgins	22
Thomas Hockly	7
John Hockly	2
John	2
James Readinge	3
Michael Brickleton	2
William Rampton	1
Richard Beare	2
Ann Smith	1
John Readinge	2
Richard Berington	1
Richard Rampton junior	2
John Woods	2
James Fry	3
William Nash	4
Thomas Pearman	4
Richard Pearman	2
James Pearman	2
Ann Reading widow	3
Thomas Rampton	1
Richard Spire	3
Richard Lynam	4
Edmund Chitty	2
William Chitty	4
Thomas Kinge	1
John Moore	1
Richard Heare	3
James Payce	2
Thomas Baker	1
Richard Baker	1
hearths	90

Hearths not chargeable

Richard Pirce	1
Richard Rampton	1
John Box	1

James Jones	2
Hugh Holle	3
Abraham Kinchen	1
Edmund Pearman	1
hearths	10

1. Grewell

354. WINCHFIELD[1]

Hearths chargeable

Benjamin Rudyard esquire	14
Mister Seston	7
Robert Miths	3
Nicholas Searle	1
Thomas French	1
Widow Cordrey	1
Widow Mitchener	1
Edward Frost	1
Thomas Wright	1
John Cowlet	1
John Bensteed	1
John Bicknell	2
William Reade	2[(a)]
Jerome Natts	1
William French	1
William Cooper	6
Thomas Brazier	2
John Clerke	1
Widow Moore	2
Widow Bell	1
[ ] Barnard	3
[ ] Warner	[ ]
[ ] Goodby	1
[ ] Sparwell	3

Fol. 69r(ii)

Thomas Waterman	3
Widow Philps	1
Goodman Hill	1
Francis Shrimpton	1
John Oldfeild	2
Edward Hall	1
John Harte	4
John Searle	1
hearths	72

Hearths not chargeable

William Searle	1
Widow Cowles	1
Widow Fox	1
Widow Forlen	1
Widow Hendy	1
Widow Baily	1
John Parry	1
Theophilus Morgan	1
Widow Richardson	1
hearths	9

(a) 1 overcharged
1. Winchfeild

355. NORTH WARNBOROUGH[1]

Hearths chargeable

John Raynger	3
Widow Hunt	3
Widow Hole	2
William May	2
Thomas Readinge	3
Thomas Linter	2
Thomas Burle	1
James Godden	2
Henry Searle	1
Thomas Taylor	2
Henry Hardy	3
Edward Hawkins	1
Robert Hawkins	2
Ellen Searle widow	1
John Readinge	2
William Heare senior	1
William Heare junior	2
William Trigge	1
Richard Willmott	2
John Porter	1
Daniel Scott	3
Thomas Kinge	1
Ann Searle widow	2
John Gilbert	1
Thomas Ryder	3
Henry Pratt	2
John Bird	3
Mister Barneham	6
Edward Hawkins senior	1
John Hooker	2

355. NORTH WARNBOROUGH *—cont'd.*

William Lee	1
William Draper	3
Richard Harris	1
Ann Parker widow	11
Widow Kelsey	1
Thomas Walker	1
James Withers	2
Robert Waldon	2
Richard [See]	1
Thomas Thorne	5
hearths	90

Fol. 69v(i)

Hearths not chargeable

Widow Aslett	1
Edward Hoare	1
Henry [ ]	1
Christopher Girdler	1
John Hellier	1
John Hickman	1
Joan Nash	1
Nicholas Aslett	1
Lambert Kelsey	1
George Newall	1
Henry Twine	1
Widow Blith	2
John Mathew	2
Richard South	1
Widow Godfrey	2
Widow Godden	1
Stephen Richards	1
John Stroude	1
Robert Warner	1
Henry Cromham	1
John Newell	1
John Mondey	1
Widow Hellier	1
John Cooke	1
James Wheeler	1
John Reeves	1
Thomas Walker	1
Andrew Newman	1
hearths	31

1. Northwarneborowe

356. DOGMERSFIELD[1]

Hearths chargeable

Mister Anthony Bathurst	10
Mister William Godson	9
Mister Edward Goodyer	7
Mister John Hammon	4
Mister George Searle	4
William Wigley	4
John Ewins	1
William Gunner	2
Richard Blundell	3
John Browne	1
Ralph Newman	4
Richard May	1
Thomas Mabbutt	1
John Johnson	1
William Nash	4
Richard Draper	1
William Clements	1
Richard Blake	1
Thomas Mathews	2
Edward Baker	1
Richard Clements	3
Bartholomew Rivers	3
William Swann	3
Thomas Pullin	3
Thomas Wright	2
John Bradshaw	2
Josias	3
Roland Bath	1
John Kember	1
John Clements	2
Julian Smith	5
Hugh Evans	3
William Merchant	1
William Taylor	1
Alexander Cooke	2
John Tubb	1
Michael Barnard	1
William Draper senior	2
John Draper	3
James Godson	4
Thomas Searle	3

Fol. 69v(ii)

William Batchelor	3
William Draper junior	1
Thomas [F de]	2
James Merchant	1
Ambrose Gunner	1
Edward Goodyer	2
hearths	121

Hearths not chargeable

Widow Mabbancke	1
Widow Heather	1
Nicholas Harmwood	1
John Forde	1
William Wye	1
Leonard Kimber	1
John Chaundler	1
James Merchant	1
William Vittery	1
John May	1
hearths	10

1. Dogmansfeild

357. ODIHAM

Hearths chargeable

Sir	13
John Cole esquire	12
John Woolldridge esquire	11
Mister Pickeringe	7
Mistress Complin	11
Mister South	3
Mister Chidley	6
Mister Terry	12
Mister B	6
Widow Hearne	3
Mister Cadden	8
Goodwife Gilbert	1
Mistress Vaus	2
Mark Weight	4
Francis Woods	3
John Thorneton	2
Richard Hooker	5
Benjamin Smith	5
Edward Hooker	3
Robert Money	5
Mister Harris	5
Widow Waters	1
Nicholas Thorneton	3
Mister Manneringe	4
Edward May	4
Stephen Bye	3
Edward Bradbre	2
Laurence Batchelor	2
Thomas Chaundler	3
Mister Glascock	4
Mister Tutchin	4
Jonathan Mappleton	4
Richard Limington	5
Mistress Blaze	2
William Pitter	2
Widow Turkas	2
Widow Flowry	3
Robert Cooper	2
John Berry	3
John Tyler	2
William Nellier	3
Walter Chase	3
Mistress Tayste	4(a)
Anthony Weight	4
John Limynge	1
William Bourne	5
Robert Dearinge	5
Christopher Soane	6
John Shonke	6
Daniel Clements	9

Fol. 70r(i)

Thomas Hooker	8
John Clerke	3
Henry Wither	2
Mark Wither	3
William Hall	1
Richard Seelye	5
Widow Vinden	3
Richard Lunston	5
Henry Smith	2
Thomas Hawkins	2
Thomas Bushell	2
Edward Hills	2
William Greene	3
Thomas Browne	1

357. ODIHAM—*cont'd.*

Laurence Warner	1
John Woolveridg esquire	6
Mistress Craswell	2
Widow Weight	3
William Barnard	1
John Moore	1
Thomas Winhall	2
Thomas Seynall	4
George Stanton	3
William Lee	1
John Moore	1
Edward May	9
Mistress Vause	2
hearths	295

Hearths not chargeable

Anthony Thomas	1
Andrew Wigge	1
Edward Symons	2
Elizabeth Symons	1
John Wieth	1
Thomas Watts	2
Thomas Stacye	1
John Thomas	2
Widow Cartwright	2
Nathaniel Evelin	2
Thomas Hillis	2
George Warner	1
William Draper	1
Rose Hodman	1
Gilbert Hodman	1
William Wynn	1
Richard Bye	1
Thomas Bye	1
Robert Soane	1
Thomas Stirte	2
William Grigge	2
Christopher Scarbrough	2
Alexander Jones	1
William Kinchin	2
Thomas Wigge	2
John Hudston	1
Thomas Tippin	2
Edward Walker	1
Peter Knight	1
Thomas Kendrey	1
William Vice	1
William White	1
William Cawte	2
John Searle	2
William Limston	2
William Start	2
hearths	53

(a) decreased 2

Fol. 70r(ii)

358. MURRELL[1]

Hearths chargeable

John Feilder	5
Francis Searle	7
Widow Woodison	12
John Younge	5
Robert Parker	4
John Feilder esquire	15
Richard Reede	1
Barnard Bartholomew	4
John Patrick	4
John Harte	2
John Watts	4
John Bartholomew	3
hearths	64

Hearths not chargeable

George Marshall	2
Edward Ludley	1
hearths	3

1. Murrall

359. RYE

Hearths chargeable

Mister Richard Younge	9
John River	3
John Dedman	2
John Cooper	2
John Draper	2
John Brewer	3
hearths	21

360. STAPELY[1]

Hearths chargeable

Robert Earle	4
John Earle	4
Stephen Hunt	5
Robert Woods	2
Henry Goodyer	1
Michael Belton	1
hearths	17

Hearths not chargeable

Thomas Hellis	1
Robert Helton	1
hearths	2

1. Stapley

361. HILLSIDE

Hearths chargeable

Mister Walter Harwood	10
Mister Henry Moore	8
Andrew Werndell	2(a)
William Missingham	4
John Payce	4
Peter	2
Richard Sandwich	2
William Wynn	1
Thomas Jeffery	1
Thomas White	3
Abraham Trigg	2
John Barkshire	3
John Heyman	1
Nicholas Nash	3
Matthew Eyles	2
John Rivers	3
John Vicary	3
Fol. 70v(i)	
John Nash	3
Widow Nash	1
John	3
hearths	61

Hearths not chargeable

John Shrubb	1
John Rogatt	1
Nicholas Nitingall	1
Robert Willinott	1
John Eyles	1
Thomas Shrimps	1
John Cooper	1
Eales	1
Warner Smith	1
John Hollis	1
Thomas West	2
Richard Stares	1
Widow Steares	2
Richard Bolton	1
Judith Bolton	1
hearths	17

(a) 1 overcharged

362. SHERFIELD-UPON-LODDON[1]

Hearths chargeable

Sir Thamo[2] Reresby	15
Mister Feilder	5
Mister Knight	5
Mister Chasse	8
Mister Parkhurst	5
Mister Wither	4
Thomas Normond	3
John Combs	1
Edward Harrise	5
John Bull	1
Widow Watts	3
William Payse senior	3
William Payse junior	3
Christopher Maynard	3
Martha Bowden	4
Christopher Hayes	5
William Burden	4
Richard Alexander	2
John Lane	1
Robert Blackman	2
Richard Spyre	2
Alexander Dedman	1
Robert Cane	2
Alexander Parr	1
William Bye	3
John Hanniton	1
Richard Spencer	1
Mister Reade	2

362. SHERFIELD-UPON-LODDON—*cont'd.*

William Keates	3(a)
John Suscor	5
Richard Mersh	1
John Leagrave	2
John Goodchild	4
John Marshall	5
Philip Blake	2
John Britton	2
John Porter	2
hearths	121

Fol. 70v(ii)

Hearths not chargeable

William Coates	2
Stephen Dibbs	1
James Bray	1
William Hinwood	1
John Fawkner	1
William Newell	1
William Spencer	1
John Summers	1
Widow Sharpe	1
Francis Talbutt	1
Widow Puckeridg	1
John Benevell	1
Edmund Baily	1
Walter Kent	1
Matthew Clerke	1
Richard Grantham	1
Thomas Tococke	1
Robert Littleworth	1
Widow Petty	1
Richard Mersh	1
William Harwood	1
Thomas Payse	1
hearths	23

(a) decreased 2
1. Sherfeild
2. Thamo. *written over* Seamo. *Probably* Sir Tamworth Reresby

363. HARTLEY WINTNEY[1]

Hearths chargeable

Mister George Watts	12
Mister Matthew Preist	5
Thomas Patrick	4
Mister Hensen	2
William Mortimer	2
Mister Wheatley	8(a)
Richard Clerke	4
Mister Justice	19(b)
William Amlen	8(a)
Mister Roy	7
William Payne	2
James Jeblett	2
William Jeblett	4
Mister Gethins	3
Robert Exall	7
Widow Smith	4
Thomas Winter	7
William Smith	2
Robert Payse	2
William Dumersh	5
Edward Ellis	3
John Edmunds	4
Thomas Patrick	5
Widow Heath	4
William Goddard	3
John Ellis	8
Thomas Johnson	4
Thomas Powlter	5(a)
Richard Hellhouse	1
Nicholas White	3
John Exall	2
John Woodeson	7
William South	5
John Eaves	4
William Marlow	2
John Potter	2
William Payne	3(a)

Fol. 71r(i)

Israel Woodison	3
William Cartwright	4
Widow Smith	2(a)
Robert Stacy	2
John Seaser	1
Mister Howell	3
Mister Ball	3
hearths	192

Hearths not chargeable

Widow Winter	1
John Woodgate	1
Widow Moiden	2
Robert Jennings	1
Widow Goddard	1
John Amblen	2
John Woodenge	1
William Willis	1
Richard Lewis	2
William Chantrell	2
Thomas Stafferton	2
Widow Barrowes	1
Richard Barrowes	2
John Greene	2
Edmund Parker	1
Widow Foxley	2
John Barker	2
John Shackleforde	2
Thomas Newe	2
Widow Cartwright	1
Richard Wigge	1
Julian Tyler	2
George Parker	2
William Ditch	2
Nicholas Turner	1
Peter Wallis	1
George Payne	1
Edward Payne	2
Jerome Cox	1
William Amblen	2
William Fulker	1
Christopher Ruggatt	1
Widow Baily	1
Francis Cottman	1
hearths	49

(a) 1 decreased
(b) 2 decreased
1. Hartly Winkney

364. BENTWORTH

Hearths chargeable

Robert Hunt	8
George Madgwick	6
James Hockly	4
Richard Collins	2
William Wynter	1
William Kinge	5
John Henwood	6
John Wheeler	6
William Cooper	2
Thomas Madgwick	3
William Hunt	3
James Hill	1
Ann Gregory	3
Joan Gunner	1
Widow Wynter	2
John Hyde	1
Robert Hunt	1
Robert Godfrey	2
John Newman	7
Fol. 71r(ii)	
Richard Collins	2(a)
John Ham	3
Henry Addams	3
John Hewlett	1
William Bachell	2
Sarah Hunt	4
Richard Benham	5
hearths	84

Hearths not chargeable

Widow Rider	1
hearths	1

(a) decreased [ ]

365. WESTON PATRICK[1]

Hearths chargeable

Mister John Kinge	5
Michael Merriott	4
Thomas Browne	4
John Oathen	1
Widow Kerby	1
Widow Rawlins	1
John Hockley	1
Michael Hall	1
Robert Hill	1
Widow Kimber	2
Ralph Waterman	1
hearths	22

365. WESTON PATRICK—*cont'd.*

Hearths not chargeable

Thomas Chaundler	2
Richard Chaundler	1
Thomas Noyes	1
hearths	4

1. Weston Patricke

366. SHALDEN

Hearths chargeable

Thomas Crowcher	12
William Gregory	5
Mary Lipscombe	9
Margaret Lipscombe	2
Mister Richard Serjeant	4
Mister John Twyne	6
Christopher Tilbery	1
William Eagle	2
John Eames	4
Robert Lipscombe	1
Laurence Pitter	1
Thomas Michell	1
John Allen	1
Peter Gregory	2
Thomas Eames	1
Stephen Vidler	1
John Woods	1
hearths	53

Hearths not chargeable

Robert Henwood	2
Robert Eagle	1
Robert Kinchin	1
Widow Gregory	1
Richard Hall	1
Thomas Mannington	1
Robert Henwood	1
hearths	8

Fol. 71v(i)

367. LASHAM[1]

Hearths chargeable

Mister Plowden	7
Mister Laurence	3(a)
William Godfrey	2
Peter Michell	3
Christopher Cooper	4
John Page	3
William Warner	1(b)
Widow Page	2
Robert Bettser	1
John Browne	1
William Albery	1
Widow Trusler	1
Edward Gregory	1
Philip Fleete	1
John Gunner	2
Robert Merriott	1
John Trusler	1
Isaac Merriott	3
John Dowlinge	1
hearths	39

Hearths not chargeable

Thomas Turner	1
Richard Younge	1
Humphrey Pyle	1
Robert Ball	1
Robert Stacy	1
Thomas Baily	1
John Gregory	1
James Browne	1
John Bristow	1
Thomas Bristow	1
Laurence Clerke	1
John Pooke	1
Ann Davis	1
William Warner	1
hearths	14

(a) 4 decreased
(b) 1 decreased
1. Sarsham. *A tithing of this name has not been identified and a probable reading is* Lasham

368. SOUTHROPE[1]

Hearths chargeable

Mister Nathaniel Hyde	6
Thomas Kinge	12
John Winckworth	6
Henry Barnard	3(a)
William Edwards	1
John Knight	1

Anthony Hellier	1
John Mathew	1
Daniel Rowell	1
Widow Hockley	1
Widow Elcock	2
Henry Prowtinge	1
John Willmot	3
James Collier	1
Laurence Mathew	2
Widow Wallington	1
Stephen Wise	1
George Oliver	1
Stephen Goodyer	2
William Terry	3
Robert Reeve	2
Robert Rivers	1
William Eames	1
hearths	54

Fol. 71v(ii)

Hearths not chargeable

Widow Rise	1
George Hawkins	2
Thomas Lee	1
Thomas Meere	1
Thomas Elderfeild	1
John Woodman	1
Thomas Andrews	1
Bridget Hall	1
Richard Dredg	1
James Hounsham	1
George Elderfeild	1
Richard Meere	1
John Wise	1
Widow Winter	1
John Willis	1
hearths	16

(a) 1 overcharged
1. Southrop

369. ELVETHAM BERNARD[1]

Hearths chargeable

William Turner	1
George Hone	3
George Bignall	3
Widow Seland	4
Widow Browne	1
John Ruggatt	1
Matthew Ives	1[(a)]
John Colles junior	3
Anthony Browne	1
John Turner	5
William Patrick	1
John Vinden	2
Sir Robert Reynold's house	3
hearths	30

Hearths not chargeable

John Coles senior	1
Widow Limingham	2
John Anne	2
Edward Hill	1
Francis Leates	1
Robert Bagent	2
Richard Coles	1
George Street	1
Widow Turner	2
Widow Rymes	1
Simon Beasent	2
hearths	16

(a) 1 overcharged
1. Elvetham Barnett

370. ROTHERWICK[1]

Hearths chargeable

Francis Tinley esquire	13
Barnard Haniton	4
John Heather	3
Robert Noyes	6
Henry Payse	4
Richard Finley	3
John Milton	5
Joseph Hodges	2
John Wheeler	2
Widow Nash	3
Widow Hawkins	2
John Ashyngton	5
James Melton	2
Ralph Bagent	3

Fol. 72r(i)

Widow Clerke	1
John Martin	1

370. ROTHERWICK—*cont'd.*

Widow Lambolle	2
Alexander Webb	2
Henry Stone	3
Stephen Westend	2
Widow Benham	2
Harmand Watts	3
Widow Evers	1
Nicholas Palmer	2
John Smith	3
Christopher Nashe	2
Richard Ayliffe	2
Richard Reeves	1
Henry Clerke	1
John Complin	2
Thomas Roberts	1
hearths	93

Hearths not chargeable

Widow Blake	1
Thomas Beldham	1
Brian Payne	2
Margaret Foster	1
William Bartholomew	1
Henry Aslett	1
William Turner	2
Julian Aslett	1
Robert Nash	1
Dorothy Foster	2
Widow Fawkner	1
William Goodchild	1
Widow Wigge	1
Widow Evers	2
Joan Albrey	1
Henry Barnes	2
Widow Evered	1
Widow Shrimpton	2
Henry Smith	2
William Foster	2
hearths	28

1. Rotherwicke

371. ELVETHAM STURMY[1]

Hearths chargeable[2]

Edward Chatterton	17
Henry Robinson	15
Walter Osgood	3
James Downes	3
Widow Cobb	4
Mister Littlefeild	4
Mister Hollis	4
John Trigge	1
John Searle	3
Sir Robert Reynolds	20[3]
Lancelot Ellsly	3
Sir Robert Reynolds	1
Guy Greenham	5
Edward Heyman	1
John Waterman	1
Thomas Ives	3
Robert Boxall	1
Nicholas Searle	1
Widow Goodale	1
Walter Osgood	2
Anthony Over	4
Mister Deane	5
Mister Hammon	6
John Bowne	3
John Chaundler	4

Fol. 72r(ii)

Hearths not chargeable

Edmund Milland	2
Mister Deane	2
Robert Johnson	1
Bartholomew Jone	2
Nicholas Farlen	1
John Eives	1
John Payse	2
Widow Goodyer	1
Widow Small	2
Widow Heath	1
William Watts	2
Daniel Scott	1
Nicholas Watts	1
William Mathews	1
Ann Richards	2
Richard Tocock	1
Bartholomew Aslett	1
Widow Meeres	1
Widow Mathews	1
Widow Newell	1

John Kinge 1
Widow Kinge 1
Henry Middleton 1
Widow Marlow 1
Thomas Millett 2
Henry Somredge 1
Widow Hunter 1
James Juner 2
Richard Clements 2
John Browne 2
hearths 41

1. Elvetham Stermy
2. *Total number of hearths omitted*
3. *Margination illegible*

372. LISS TURNEY

Hearths chargeable

Sir John Norton baronet 14
Robert Yalden 3
Richard Randoll 5
Richard Aylinge 5
William Aylinge 6
William Horner 3
Thomas Morris 3
Robert Boxall 4
Joseph Cowdrey 7
Richard Bidinge 5
William Aldred 3
Thomas Hill 2
John Cooke 1
Richard Terry 1
Henry Tipper 4
Anthony Yeoman 1
John Summers 2
Richard Fullwick 3
Richard Showler 3
Guy Eames 2
Richard Eames 2
Nicholas Bettsworth 2
William Mills 1
Anthony [osbolt] 1
Thomas Bettsworth 2
William Rolfe 1
Widow Tipper 1
Thomas Bridger 1
Thomas Eames 2
hearths 90

Hearths not chargeable

Francis Westhook 2
Philip Okeshott 2
Thomas Philipps 2
William Broke 1

Fol. 72v(i)

Thomas Browne 1
Richard Habbin 1
Henry Martin 1
Herbert Hodson 1
Henry Ellett 1
Widow Broadbridge 1
Peter Page 2
Nicholas Downeinge 2
Widow Hickman 1
William Faye 2
Widow Hampson 1
Nicholas Hoggsflesh 1
Widow Whitley 1
hearths 24

373. LOWER BRAMSHILL[1]

Hearths chargeable

John Currant 3
Robert Deane 2
Samuel Hewett 2
hearths 7

1. Lower Bramsdell

The number of hearths chargeable within the hundred of Odiham is 1734
Not chargeable 359

HOLDSHOTT HUNDRED

374. HOLDSHOTT

Hearths chargeable

Sir Andrew Henly 10
William Cootes 3
Robert Woodhouse 4
William Hayward 1
John Wallis 3

374. HOLDSHOTT—*cont'd.*

Edward Weith	3
Henry Browne	1
William Hall	2
Robert Croswell	4
Robert Canne	3
Thomas Turner	2
Thomas Vinnerye	2
Edward Dorney	2
John Gregory	4
Mister John Mannering	1
Edward Woodhouse	2
John Richards	1
John Feilder	2
George Atwater	1
Robert Hall	1
John Woodison	1
hearths	53

Hearths not chargeable

Christopher Cowdrey	1
Edward Pickerney	1
Elizabeth Harmwood	2
Procter Turner	1
Robert Clements	2
hearths	7

375. BRAMSHILL[1]

Hearths chargeable

Sir Andrew Henly	50
Richard Turner	6
Mister John Hewett	5

Fol. 72v(ii)

William Millham	3
William Barnes	3
William Mosden	1
Henry Burgis	3
Edward Beedle	3
Richard Larmor	3
Barnard Baily	2
Daniel Trimer	1
James Parsley	1
Edward Walker	1
Robert Barrett	2
Widow Webb	1
John Doe	1
Edward Baily	2
John Laurence	1
hearths	89

Hearths not chargeable

Humphrey Barnes & Burrett	1
Humphrey Burrett	1
John May	1
Richard Greene	1
William Turner	1
Widow Trigge	1
Thomas Angfeild	1
Richard Hellier	1
Richard Cooper	1
Robert Cricher	1
Sarah Knight	1
Ann Hall	1
John Laurence	1
hearths	13

1. Bramsell

376. HECKFIELD[1]

Hearths chargeable

Mistress Craswell	12
Edward Cook esquire	11
Mister Robert Richards	4
Mister Browne	3
Mister Pecke	6
William Beedle	5
Peter Cooke	7
Mister William Beale	7
Mister Chamberlaine	2
John Harris	3
Widow Philipps	2
John Puckeridge	2
John Beedle	2
William Petter	1
John Marlow	4
Christopher Foster	2
William Woodson	1
John Beele	11
Thomas Thurbourne	1
Robert Alexander	4
Widow Ware	4
Stephen Watts	2

Richard Poulter	1
Titus Allen	1
Robert Beedle	2
John Woods	2
Thomas Wallis	2
John Woods	1
John Chricher	4
Widow Champ	1
John Marsey	2

Fol. 73r(i)

Mister Manneringe	2
Robert Withe	2
Robert Withe	2
Thomas Beedle	2
Leonard Ayres	1
Thomas Greeneway	2
Richard Portsmouth	2
James Wallis	3
Robert Clements	3
William Watts	3
Widow White	5
Christopher Gravett	1
Henry Alexander	1
Widow Hall	2
John Hetton	3
Thomas Free	1
John Martin	4
Widow Trymer	2
George Cleere	2
Thomas Vinden	2
Mister Studwick	2
Richard Guy	4
Christopher Alloway	2
Henry Tilly	1
hearths	163

Hearths not chargeable

Thomas Puckeridge	2
Widow Oades	2
Christopher Alloway	1
Thomas Barrett	1
William Turner	2
Stephen Kent	1
hearths	9

1. Heckfeild

377. HARTLEY WESPALL[1]

Hearths chargeable

William Pitt esquire	18
Summersett's house	6
Simon Goodale	2
Richard Smith	3
Thomas Athrom	3
William Withe	3
William Hellier	4
John Bristow	1
Thomas Goodchild	1
Thomas Maynard	4
John Wyatt	1
William Foster	1
Widow Bath	1
Widow Gregory	1
Robert Benham	1
John Wigge	1
The parsonage	4
Henry Sex	2
Richard Searle	2
hearths	59

Fol. 73r(ii)

Hearths not chargeable

Widow Bartlett	1
Matthew Bristow	1
George Bristow	1
William Eales	1
Barnard Bristow	1
Floyd	1
hearths	6

1. Hartley Westpell

378. EVERSLEY

Hearths chargeable

Doctor Bristoll	6
Mister Westwood	8
John Bonvell	7
John May	5
Mister Northfolk	4
Robert Marten	3
Christopher Richards	3
John Chraswell	1
John Potter	2
John Banborne	2

378. EVERSLEY—*cont'd.*

John Maymore	1
William Ridges	2
Widow Goodchild	1
Edward Bossell	1
Mister Stafferton	2
John Hine	3
Richard Miller	2
Thomas Poole	3
Thomas Chery	5
Thomas Richards	4
Widow Baily	1
Christopher Waterman	2
Thomas[1] Welch	3
William Oades	5
Richard Oades	2
Richard Hayman	3
William Appleton	1
Thomas Clements	3
John Cooper	2
Edward[2] Perry	6
Deodatus Barrow	3
Robert Watts }	4
& for May's house }	3
John Watts	3
Thomas Watts	4
William Watts	3
Widow Perry	1
Adam Chaplen	2
Thomas Bartholomew	2
Thomas May	1
Edward Potter	2
James Carpenter	1
John Oades	2
Richard Chaplen	1
William Rawton	4
Christopher Martin	3
John Aslutt	3
William Borne	3
Anthony Ayliff	3
William Millett	3
John Taylor	4
William Carpenter	4
William Alexander	3
Thomas Hills	3
Nicholas Baily	4
Thomas Poynter	3
John Alexander senior	2
Robert Carter	2
Widow May	2
John Cowdry	3
Fol. 73v(i)	
William Dymersh	6
Thomas Mills	1
John Alexander junior	3
William Pryer	4
hearths	188

Hearths not chargeable

Warren House	2
William Elsley	1
John Frye	1
William Carter	1
John Chaplen	1
James Millett	1
Margaret Cowdrey	1
John Jennings	1
Sibyl Clemes	1
William Payse	1
Joan Kember	1
Widow Everad	1
Deodatus Barrow	1
Geoffrey Millet	1
Charles Mason	2
William Ponfrey	1
William Gregory	1
Edward Baily	2
Thomas Kember	2
hearths	24

1. T *written over* W
2. Wid *expunged and* Edward *written above in a different hand*

379. MATTINGLEY

Hearths chargeable

Mister John Deane	9
Mister John Tutt	9
Brian Richards	9
Nicholas Knight	6
Richard Greene	3
John Mills	3

Anthony Craswell	4
William Goodchild	1
John Nash	3
Richard Mulford	3
John Stocker	5
Richard Mulford	3
William Dowlinge	2
Thomas Alexander	2
Christopher Alexander	3
Richard Hall	1
James Woodcock	3
Christopher Goodchild	2
Zacharias Alexander	1
William Weith	1
William Wakes	2
Widow Trimer	2
Widow Hellhouse	3
Daniel Oades	7
Anthony Mayne	3
John Mason	2
William Chaundler	3
John Woodcock	5
Henry Hogges	1
Arthur Runeger	4
Nathaniel Wilkes	3
hearths	108

Fol. 73v(ii)

Hearths not chargeable

Widow Scott	1
Widow Jones	2
Richard Morley	2
Widow Jones junior	1
Widow Hill	1
Widow Alexander	1
John Chaundler	2
Richard Russell	1
Widow Crowcher	1
Thomas Brickleton	1
John Woodcock	2
hearths	15

380. STRATFIELD TURGIS[1]

Hearths chargeable

Mistress Susan Pitts	9
Edward Searle	6
The parsonage	5
John Chase	4
Robert Clements	4
Daniel Newell	4
George Beedle	2
William Ives	2
Philip Wigge	2
Henry Stacy	1
Thomas Pether	2
Mister Meggs	1
John Searle	1
Robert Dines	1
Abraham Wheeler	1
Philip Bolton	1
Thomas Graunt	1
hearths	47

Hearths not chargeable

Widow Wheeler	1
Widow Saywell	1
hearths	2

1. Stratfeild Turgis

381. MINLEY

Hearths chargeable

Mister Carrick	9
John Lashfourd	4
hearths	13

382. HARTLEY MAUDITT[1]

Hearths chargeable

Mister William Feilder	8
John Chase	4
Thomas Parr	4
John Clerke	2
William Stone	3
Thomas Tooke	2
Widow Masters	1
Walter Masters	2
James Mulford	3
Christopher Alloway	2
hearths	31

1. Hartley Maudett. *This parish is also recorded under Alton hundred, where it would normally be expected to be found. No tithing of this name has been identified in Basingstoke hundred*

Fol. 74r(i)

383. STRATFIELD SAYE[1]

Hearths chargeable

George Pitt esquire	48
And for the mill & Powlenges	4
Doctor Dominick	6
Mister Zankey	8
Mistress Harrison	3
Mistress Horne	6
Mister Pitts	3
For Eastwood Farm	3
For Bignalls	4
John Appleton	4
George Thorpe	4
Widow Clerke	3
William Archer	4
Richard Floyde	3
Widow Canne	3
Richard Keepe	6
Richard Keepe	3
Andrew Keepe	3
William Thire	3
William Hawkins	3
Thomas Reggs	1
John Horne	4
John Clements	2
John Payse	3
John Meere	3
John Paise	3
Thomas Paise	1
John Cook	1
Hugh Ewhurst	2
Edward Marlow	2
William Hall	3
Ralph Hellier	4
Widow Russell	2
Widow Riggs	2
Francis Normand	1
John Graunt	3
Widow Hood	2
Edward Puckeridge	1
John Ewhurst	1
William Jackson	3
John Wells	2
Widow Stephens	1
William Hall	1
Hugh Thorpe	3
William Hall	1
Thomas Swayne	3
John Godwin	1
William Smith	1
George Alexander	5
hearths	181

Hearths not chargeable

John Goodwin	1
William Fuse	1
Widow Bodley	1
Richard Warde	1
Thomas Marshall	1
Widow Bignall	1
John Harris	1
Nicholas Fuse	1
Widow Jennings	1
George Cooper	1
Barnard Tugfeild	1
John Godwin	1
hearths	12

1. Stratfeildsey

Fol. 74r(ii)

384. SILCHESTER[1]

Hearths chargeable

Sir Thomas Draper	5
Mister Richard Hyde	14
Mister Whisler	5
Edward Hack	8
John Charter	3
William Studman	3
Thomas Portsmouth	2
William Martin	3
John Cleft	3
Widow Gunnell	1
John Symons	2
Randal Bye	2
Stephen Bye	1
John Stiff	1
George Stare	1
Thomas Wright	1
Robert James	2
Henry Portsmouth	1

Jasper Randoll	2
William Portsmouth	1
Robert Stare	1
Thomas Erewaker	1
Widow James	2
John Portsmouth	1
hearths	66

Hearths not chargeable

Richard Portsmouth	2
Edmund Engfeild	2
Widow Bye	2
John Fry	2
William Billemore	2
Edmund Stare	2
Ralph Fry	1
Widow Puckeridg	1
Margaret Portsmouth	1
John Paise	1
Widow Stare	2
Richard Hyde	1
Thomas Stent	1
Nicholas Shonke	1
John Kent	1
William Jackson	1
Richard Bye	1
Nicholas Frewen	1
William Bye	1
Thomas Baker	1
Richard Higgs	1
John Bye	1
Nicholas Paise	1
John Portsmouth junior	1
William Keates	1
hearths	32

1. Sillycester

385. MORTIMER

Hearths chargeable

William Wattmer	6
Thomas Gray	5
Thomas Blaunch	3
Thomas Lucey	4
John Mills	5
John Napper junior	5
Robert Mill senior	3
Robert Lane	3
William Wattmer junior	4
John Remington	3

Fol. 74v(i)

John White	5
Richard Herbert	3
John Paise	4
Thomas Legge	3
John May	3
Savage Booth	3
William Legg	2
John Jerman	6
William Carter	3
William Holland	3
John Hatt	3
James Martyn	2
William Matthews	1
Barnard Pryor	2
William Headland	4
Robert Aylward	4
Randal Wheate	2
hearths	93

Hearths not chargeable

Thomas Champ senior	1
Thomas Champ junior	1
Richard Blake	1
Thomas Clifford	1
Widow Cooper	2
John Chamberlaine	1
James Bennett	1
William Henwood	1
Walter Stacy	1
John Ensum	1
Richard Kent	2
William Beard	1
William Blaunch	1
James Bent	1
William Bent	1
Richard Pryor	2
Richard Bentley	1
Widow Carter	1
Edward Attkins	1
John Mathew	1

385. MORTIMER—*cont'd.*

John May 1
William Peacher 1
hearths 25

The number of hearths chargeable within the hundred of Holdshott is 1094
Not chargeable 152

BERMONDSPIT HUNDRED[1]

386. FARLEIGH WALLOP[2]

Hearths chargeable

Henry Wallopp esquire 17
John Hockley 4
John Taplyn 4
hearths 25

1. Bermanspitt Hundred
2. Farley Wallopp

387. NUTLEY[1]

Hearths chargeable

Thomas Dunce 5
Mister William Soper 5
William Lynne 1
John Pewsey 1

Fol. 74v(ii)

Philip Combs 1
William Addams 1
John Lawes 1
Mister Waterman's house 1
hearths 16

Hearths not chargeable

Mister William Waterman 1
Widow Blunden 1
Philip Gregory 1
George Brooman 1
hearths 4

1. Nuttley

388. DUMMER

Hearths chargeable

Mister Davis 4
Mister William Soper 7
Mistress Terry 6
James Smith 1
James Feilder 2
Richard Kent 1
Roger Browne 2
William Soper 2
Peter Soper 1
Richard Neele 1
George Ilsley 6
John Poynter 1
John Warner 1
John Shipman 3
Widow Weston 1
John Biggs 1
John Stent 2
Francis Canner 1
Philip Soper 2
Mistress Smith 2
Thomas Hosier 1
Thomas Wither 1
Robert Pryor 1
Ann Weston 1
John Hack 2
Stephen Michen 1
John Lamboll 1
Richard Penton 3
Richard Honner 1
John Sempson 1
Arthur Feilder 1
hearths 60

Hearths not chargeable

George Ilesley 1
William Harding 1
Widow Hanniton 1
James Bignoll 1
Robert Sewell 1
hearths 5

389. HERRIARD[1]

Hearths chargeable

Thomas Jarvis esquire 25
Mister William Guydott 6
The vicarage 6
William Norgrove 3

Widow Egerton	3
Richard Boyes	3
hearths	46

1. Hearriard

Widow Tadborow	1
Widow Jermye	1
Robert Fry	2
hearths	15

1. Ilsfieild

Fol. 75r(i)

390. ELLISFIELD[1]

Hearths chargeable

Mister Robert Stocker	8
Mister Cranfourd	3
Jerome Triminge	3
Michael Merriott	2
Robert Tilborrowe	2
Edward Randford	3
Barnard Smeathe	1
John Crauft	2
John Fry	1
Nicholas Merrott	1
Thomas Benham	4
John Dyer	2
Zacharias Vidler	1
William Tilborrowe senior	2
William Silver	2
Thomas Merriott	3
John Prise	1
John Russell	1
Ralph Symes	1
Oliver Tilborowe	3
William Tilborowe junior	3
John Eggerton	1
hearths	50

Hearths not chargeable

John Welsteed	1
Widow Frizer	1
John Richardson	1
Widow Murrell	1
Nicholas Kelsey	1
Widow Boswell	1
Francis Tilborowe	1
Widow Kelsey	1
Henry Perse	1
William Tilborowe	1
Widow Moore	1

391. UPTON GREY[1]

Hearths chargeable

Mister William Knight	9
Widow Hall	2
Thomas Kinge	5
Barnard Hunt	3
Ambrose Cleve	2
Richard Nash	1
Malachi Gudney	8
Thomas Edwards	2
James Silvester	1
Widow Bignall	1
William Dunce	1
William Barnard	1
Thomas Terry	1
Nicholas Cooper	1
Mister John Clefft	5
Mister Noye Webb	4
Henry Willis	3
Roger Hawkins	1
Henry Lee	2
John Terry	2

Fol. 75r(ii)

Ambrose Wilks	1
James Terry	1
John Mufford	1
Widow Bugley	1
hearths	59

Hearths not chargeable

Widow Henwood	1
Widow Dudman	1
Widow Graunt	2
Robert Othen	1
hearths	5

1. Upton Gray

392. SOUTH WARNBOROUGH[1]

Hearths chargeable

Richard Bishopp esquire	21
Doctor Mew	6
William Burch	4
Widow Burch	2
Mistress Avis Blundell	6
Mister Clase Goodard	3
Robert Hoare	6
George Bigner	4
Henry Aslett	1
Henry Cooper	2
John Aslett	1
John Barnes	2
Roger Hoare	1
Henry Peale	2
John Hibbs	1
John Hoare	1
Nicholas Combs	1
James Silvester	3
Joseph Marshall	1
Richard Meeres	1
Daniel Mathews	2
George Hawkins	1
John Hill	1
George Nash	1
Thomas Kinge	1
Peter Lillywhite	1
John Present	3
hearths	79

Hearths not chargeable

Lancelot Penbrooke	1
John Marshall	1
John Hodges	1
William Major	1
Joan Marshall	1
Robert Vicary	1
Widow Bachell	1
Widow Mathew	1
Edward Trimmer	1
Joan Bristow	1
George Mathew	1
John Sparks	1
George Sparks	1
hearths	13

1. Southwarneborrowe

Fol. 75v(i)

393. WESTON CORBETT

Hearths chargeable

Edward Rolfe	2
George Greene	2
hearths	4

394. PRESTON CANDOVER[1]

Hearths chargeable

John Oades	6
Robert Lipscomb	4[a]
Thomas Gearly	1
John Twyne	1
Walter Thorpe	2
John Mathews	2
William Wilks	1
John Bossell	1
Thomas Cannings	1
John Hall	3[b]
Edmund Pincke	1
Hugh Lowman	3
Joseph Russell	2
Hugh Cobb	1
Nicholas Burton	1
Philip Hanniton	1
John Rives	1
Henry Thorpe	1
Widow Michell	1[c]
Robert Allen	1
Mark Cradock	2
John Dory	1
John Allen	1
John Wigge	1
Richard Wigge	1
James Ryves	1
John Shereman	2
Mister John Yearly	3
William Pincke	3
James Feilder	1
John Wigge	1
John White	1
Mister William Waterman	2
Hugh Lowman	12
William Elmes	1
hearths	69

Hearths not chargeable

Widow Michell	1
Richard Warren	1
Mary Oades	1
Thomas Kerby	1
Thomas Shereman	2
Edward Elkes	1
John Barnaby	1
John Pincke	1
Ann William	1
Thomas Whale	1
William Scriven	1
Joan Michell	1
William Light	1
John French	1
Dorothy Allin	1
Thomas Wigge	1
Isaac Tilborowe	1
Widow Stanley	1
Richard Alwright	2
hearths	21

Fol. 75v(ii)

The number of hearths chargeable within the hundred of Bermondspit[2] is	408
Not chargeable	63

(a) decreased 3
(b) decreased 2
(c) decreased 1
1. Preston Candever
2. Barmanspit

CRONDALL HUNDRED

395. HAWLEY

Hearths chargeable

Mister Watts	9
Thomas Smith	4
Richard Smallpese	3
Gilbert Polson	7
John Cox	1
Brian Smith	1
Giles Hatt	3
Richard Browne	6
John Allen	3
John Harding	8
William Thayre	4
John Hooker	1
Leonard Draper	1
Widow Watts	3
Thomas Heather	2
Mary Blake	3
Robert Watts	5
Robert Tanner	3
William Kinge	2
Robert Leckford	1
Thomas Webb	5
Laurence Riggs	1
John Trigg	1
Thomas Carpenter	2
John Wheeler	2
John Denton	1
Richard Smith	6
Laurence Riggs	1
Henry Mitchener	2
Henry Hills	1
Laurence Riggs	1
Robert Snowe	2
Thomas Gardner	3(a)
Thomas Swayne	1
Widow Elfourd	3
Robert May	1
Samuel Courtness	2(a)
Robert Rowland	1
Henry Hambleton	1
John Giles	3
hearths	110

Hearths not chargeable

Widow Crichfeild	1
John Ellis	1
Robert Bargent	1
John Rogers	1
Widow Greene	1
George Parry	1
Widow Hill	1
hearths	7

(a) decreased 1

Fol. 76r(i)

396. FARNBOROUGH[1]

Hearths chargeable

The Place House	12

396. FARNBOROUGH—*cont'd.*

Robert Barrett	3
Robert Juner	3
John Finch	7
Robert Parks	3
John Chitty	3
Nicholas Jolliff	1
Andrew Finch	2
Richard Jolliff	1
Richard Wattson	2
Vincent Clifford	2
Robert Howell	2
Henry Finch	4
Richard Rogers	3
Nicholas Neale	3
Thomas Kerby	2
Henry Rogers junior	1
John Biscoe	2(a)
Henry Rogers senior	2
Mister William Ong	3
Henry Hall	2(a)
Joan Woodward	1
Mary Ellis	1
William Gunner	3
Mark Carpenter	2
William Carpenter	1
William Jewer	1
James Edmunds	2
Elleger Aslett	2(b)
Richard Aslett	3
Thomas Gunner	3
Christopher Gravett	1
Daniel Courtness	3
Widow Theare	3
hearths	89

Hearths not chargeable

Richard Goslinge	1
Robert Carter	2
Isaac Poulter	1
William Seller	1
John Cooper	1
Richard Edmunds	1
Richard Gunner	2
James Edmunds	2
William Goodener	1
Nicholas Neale	1
William Hall	2
Widow Gates	2
John Kerby	2
William Conwood	1
Widow Moore	1
Widow Harding	1
Widow Hewell	1
Ellen Soare	2
Vincent Slithurst	2
Widow Martin	2
Widow Terry	1
Francis Hoare	1
John Wye	2
William Edmunds	2
Widow Bistowe	1
Widow Binfeild	1
William Thackham	2
hearths	39

(a) 1 decreased
(b) decreased 1
1. Farneborrowe

Fol. 76r(ii)

397. YATELEY[1]

Hearths chargeable

John Ball esquire	13
George Solmes	14
Mister Solmes	2
Mister Cayse	4
Mister Edmund Price	10
Mister William Cames	6
Thomas Raye	5
Thomas Searle	6
John Bristow	2
Thomas May	3
Edward Savage	1
Widow Clerke	2
Widow Clerke	4
Thomas Inwood	3
Richard Galles	3
William May	2
John Jeffery	3
Stephen Hall	1
Thomas Turner	3
William Ayleworth	2

John Okehurst	2
Humphrey May	3
Robert Travis	2
William Dee	5
Thomas North	2
Humphrey Heale	3
Robert White	5
Widow Gorroway	2
John Michin	3
William Fry	3
James Leach	3
Widow Collier	2
Hugh Philipp	4
John Browne	1
Richard Pitt	6
Robert Travis	3
Edward Heale	3
William Hatt	5
Edward Ellis	3
Edward Heale	2
Thomas Spencer	3
Widow Poulter	6
William Marke	1
Richard Evered	2
Widow Puckeridge	3
Thomas Maynard	2
John Millard	2
Daniel Harman	5
Humphrey Millard	1
Robert Cortness	2
James Swayne	3
James Collier	2
John Sex	3
Mister John Barker	6
Gilbert Wilks	3
Mister John Ball	3
hearths	197

Hearths not chargeable

Thomas Chinps	1
William Martin	2
Joseph Petty	1
Jerome Turner	1
William Prowtinge	1
Widow Fry	2
Thomas Fry	2

Fol. 76v(i)

William Pye	1
Widow Burrowglus	1
John Neale	2
John Barnes	2
Widow Smith	1
James Juner	2
Nicholas Watts	1
William Benham	1
Thomas Alexander	1
William Okehurst	1
Widow Reading	1
Thomas Spencer	2
Brian Harmewood	1
Widow Richards	1
Thomas Barker	1
Thomas Stone	1
Richard Alexander	1
Widow Shonke	1
Widow Allin	1
Widow Hill	1
Thomas Payse	1
William May	1
Richard Smith	1
William Reade	1
Richard Alexander	1
John Taplin	2
Widow Pryer	1
Widow Warren	2
Samuel Greeneway	1
Anthony Wither	1
Robert Summer	2
Thomas Greenway	1
Thomas Maynard	1
Richard Goodchild	1
William North	1
John Alexander	1
John Moore	1
Nicholas Batchelor	1
Widow Wisdome	1
Thomas Alexander	1
Widow Sabin	1
John Worten	1
George Taylor	2
William Maynard	2

397. YATELEY—*cont'd.*

Henry Turner	2
John Worten	1
hearths	65

1. Yeately

398. CRONDALL

Hearths chargeable

Mister Samuel Blunden	6[(a)]
John Browman	15
Henry Frost	2
James Philipps	2
Richard Exall	1
Ralph Lowman	2
Edward Peck	2
John Lunn	6
Nicholas Deane	9
William Hooker	1
Henry Frost	5
John Bagent	1
Henry Grover	1
John Petter	1

Fol. 76v(ii)

William Hunt	4
Edward Baker	3
Widow Ragett	4
Robert Philipps	3
William Hoare	3
Stephen Hunt	2
Thomas Arelett	2
John Prismall	1
John Frost	1
William Mance	1
John Hobtrow	1
Thomas Lylewhite } Widow Rivers	2
Edward Baker	2
Widow Aldred	1
Robert Edsall	1
hearths	85

Hearths not chargeable

Widow[1] Long	1
Widow Fidler	1
Robert Gregory	1
William Barkshire	2
Widow Woway	1
John Appleton	1
George Marshall	1
Thomas Hoggsflesh	1
William Cooke	1
John Heather	1
Francis Hoare	1
Philip Magbin	1
Goody Evelinge	1
Robert Gary	1
John Marshall	1
Anthony Vidler	1
Widow Gillum	1
William Legg	1
Widow Michener	1
James Deane	1
hearths	21

(a) 1 decreased
1. *Probably* Wid *written over* Will

399. SWANTHROPE[1]

Hearths chargeable

John Cawte	4[(a)]
John Boxall	2
Robert Terry	8
William Burley	1
Thomas Rivers	1
William Giggs	2
William Cawte	3
Christopher Burley	2
William Baker	4
William Cox	2
John Frost	3
Stephen Aslett	1
hearths	33

(a) 1 decreased
1. Swanthropp

Fol. 77r(i)

400. DIPPENHALL[1]

Hearths chargeable

William Feilder	9
John Spradborowe	2
William Vittery	2
William Reeves	6
William Frost	1

William Stone	1
Francis Edes	1
Anthony Fernebone	2
Richard Chaundler	5
William Goodyer	1
hearths	30

Hearths not chargeable

Widow Heyes	2
John Hobtrick	1
John King	1
Thomas Hawkens	1
John Marshall	1
George Gillman	1
John Goodyer	1
William Deane	1
hearths	9

1. Dipnall

401. LONG SUTTON[1]

Hearths chargeable

Mister John Terry	9
William Burley	5
Stephen Hunt	3
Thomas Knight	6
Benjamin Hancock	5
John Stare	4
John Hawkins	2
Richard Windatt	3
Stephen Grenestone junior	3
Thomas Brice	2
Stephen Hunt	3
George Baker senior	1
George Baker junior	1
Stephen Porter	1
John Hall	1
hearths	49

1. Longe Sutton

402. WARBLINGTON

Hearths chargeable

Mister Stephen Terry	7
Nicholas Knight	3
Stephen Cranstone senior	1
Hugh Potter	1
Henry Barnes	1
William Barnes	1
William Kent	1
George Hoare	2
Stephen Cranston junior	5
William Robinson	1
Robert Terry junior	1
Robert Terry senior	6
John Hall	1
Thomas Cranstone	4
Thomas Hasker	3
Robert Terry	3
Robert Silvester	1
hearths	42

Fol. 77r(ii)

403. EWSHOTT

Hearths chargeable

Mister William Wall	13
Mister Matthew Wallbank	9
Moses Terry	7
Anthony Grover	1
George Eedes	3
Mister Richard Younge	2
John Wooldridge senior	3
John Wooldridge junior	3
William Trigg	3
Stephen Hart	3
Henry Mancey	1
Thomas	3
Richard Hart	3
Mister Humphrey Weaver	3
John Gunner	2
Thomas Hoare	2
Widow Turner	1
John Boxall	4
William Wheele	2
Philip Hoptruse	1
Thomas Elridge	1
Francis Hoare	4

403. EWSHOTT—*cont'd.*

Edward Baker	1
Henry Collins	1
Thomas Spredbrowe	2
hearths	79

404. ALDERSHOT[1]

Hearths chargeable

Francis Titchborne esquire	15
Mister Edward Goodyer	6
Thomas Boxall	6
George Burley	3
Richard Feilder	5
Thomas Dare	3
George Boxlett	3
William Wheeler	3
Thomas Smart	5
Widow Moone	1
John Reede	1
Thomas Pattfall	1
Thomas Boxlett	3
William Wheeler	3
Lambert Searle	3
Thomas Dare	3
Eustace Huntingfre[2]	2
James Draper	3
John Merser	4
Peter Watts	4
George Robinson	1
Francis Cawood	2
Richard Bagin	3
Benjamin May	2
James Meere	2
Thomas Mallard	1
William Budd	2
Robert Inwood	2
John Mathews	2
William Wheeler	1
George Wheeler	1
John Finch	3
John Newland	3
Edward Inwood	1
Widow Whittman	1

Fol. 77v(i)

Thomas Parke	3
George Stoner	1
Widow Vaughan & William Inwood	3
hearths	111

Hearths not chargeable

Widow Robinson	2
Thomas Trigg	1
Thomas Woodyer	1
William Reed	1
Joseph Allen	2
Widow Kinge	1
John Legg	2
Roger Inwood	1
Benjamin Allen	1
Richard Reed	1
John Westbrooke	1
Thomas Mills	1
George Conwood	1
John Lunn	1
Moses Terry	2
James Bradbridge	2
Moses Bagin	2
Edward Underwood	2
Widow Giles	1
hearths	26

1. Aldershott
2. *Altered from* Huntingere

405. CROOKHAM[1]

Hearths chargeable

Hercules Powlett esquire	6
Richard Terry	5
William Ditty	3
Widow Sturt	2
Widow Terry	1
Widow Rivers	1
William Barnard	1
George Walker	3
Andrew Sone	2
Francis Winchester	2
George Cooke	2
John Lunn	1

John Eyres	4
William Smither junior	4
Richard Brackley	1
Thomas Coles	3
John Pitt	2
John Trigg	3
Stephen Deeringe	3
Widow Cooper	5
George Goodyer	4
John	1
William Appleton	1
Richard Terry junior	2
William Smither senior	3
Edward Mahew	7
Mistress Warner	6
John Bignall	1
Widow Grover	2
John Searle	2
Richard Terry	2
Moses Terry	2
Richard Draper	2
Richard Caute	2

Fol. 77v(ii)

Widow Knight	2
Thomas Hills	3
Anthony Terry	2
Henry Dare	2
Edward Pike	2
Richard Davy	1
John Hoare	1
Hall	2
Widow Barnard	2
hearths	107

Hearths not chargeable

William	2
John Wyatt	1
Almshouse	3
Thomas Smith	1
Widow Gillum	1
Stephen Goodyer	1
Widow Winter	1
Widow Burgis	1
Peter Harison senior	1
John Harrison	1
Andrew Stent	1
Widow Goodyer	1
Peter Harrison	2
Francis Davy	1
Jones	1
Widow Stent	2
William Porter	3
hearths	24

1. Crookeham

406. COVE

Hearths chargeable

William Taylor	6
Richard Smith	3
John Cobbett	3
Robert Knight	3
Thomas Streate	3
Nicholas Watts	3
Robert Watts	2
John Wattson	1
John Wattson	2
Harud Rogers	2
Widow Heather	3
William Watts	2
Nicholas Goddard	3
Richard Courtnell	1
John Watts	3
Harud Rogers	2
George Gosden	4
Thomas	2
Nicholas Bristow	1
Peter Hersent	2
William Gunner	1
William Gosden	1
hearths	53

Hearths not chargeable

John Burrett	1
Widow Fulmer	3
Widow Bristowe	3
John Rogers	1
Peter Hersent	1

Fol. 78r(i)

Henry Westbrooke	2
Stephen Rawlins	1
Robert Ives	1
hearths	13

406. COVE—*cont'd.*

The number of hearths chargeable within the hundred of Crondall[1] is	1019
Not chargeable	164

1. Crondoll

407. BENTLEY LIBERTY

Hearths chargeable

Nicholas Powell esquire	12
John Ryve	12
Robert Vinden	6
William Bagin	5
John Hunt	4
Thomas Egger	3
Moses Tovery	6
Thomas Purse	10
George Rutter	4
Thomas Eyres	4
Ann Rivers	3
John Egger	4
William Hawkins	3
William Stone	3
Moses Terry	4
William Mitchenell	3
John Normond	4
William Lamboll	2
William Egger senior	1
Adam Whitehall	1
George Mounger	1
John Forder	2
William Peacock	2
William Glasbrooke	2
Christopher Greene	2
Stephen Woodman	1
William Egger junior	1
Martin Warden	1
Richard Kempe	1
Thomas Cooper	1
Thomas Wheatstone	2
Thomas Beale	1
Bartholomew Moore	1
Thomas Preston	3
William Ham	1
John Funter	2
John Brewer	1
James Goodyer	3
Robert Egger	3
William Knight	5
Widow Eyres	1
John Hault	1
William Goodyer	1
John Hawkins	4
hearths	132

Hearths not chargeable

Widow Cooper	2
Robert Bell	1
John Silvester	2

Fol. 78r(ii)

John Mattersfeild	2
Richard Trimer	1
William Boxall	1
hearths	9

MICHELDEVER HUNDRED

408. SOUTHBROOK[1]

Hearths chargeable

Mister Edward Moory	6
Mister Richard Stansby	9
William Eedes	1
Henry Earle	1
Richard Whitehead	1
James Collier	3
William Wickham	1
Robert Wise	1
Walter Bradley	2
John Harding	4
Thomas Perryn	5
Thomas Edwards	2
Stephen Wickham	4
John Whitehead	2
Daniel Ball	2
John Collier	1
George Wise	1[a]
John Edyer	1
Widow Bull	1
Robert Lock	1
John Baily	1
Goody Tutt	2

William Longe	1
Widow Moring[2]	1
Arthur Griffin	1
Brian Marriner	1
John Blundell	2
John Wells	2
Hugh French	1
hearths	64

Hearths not chargeable

John Lane	1
Edward Michell	1
John Harding	1
William Tutt	1
William Smith	1
James Eedes	1
Henry Bye	1
Widow Harfsell	1
Widow Barnard	1
Widow Elton	1
Thomas Kempe	1
Widow Fry	1
Robert Woods	1
John Inwood	1
William Greene	1
Widow Blundell	1
Andrew Rabbetts	1
Henry Pine	1

Fol. 78v(i)

Thomas Farmer	1
Widow Carpenter	1
Alice Wild	1
John Collier	1
Widow Wickham	1
Henry Mansbridge	1
Widow Cleverly	1
Widow Lane	1
Richard Hach	1
hearths	28

(a) decreased 1
1. Southbrooke
2. *The text has an additional minim*

409. WESTON

Hearths chargeable

Richard Whitehead	2
William Belton	1
Widow Bridle	2
William Spencer	3
Brian Marriner	2
Widow Pope	4
Mark Bull	1
Thomas Weight	3
John Cager	5
Richard Smith	1
hearths	24

Hearths not chargeable

William Browne	1
William Bull	1
Margaret Jeffery	1
Robert Gugge	1
John Watts	1
John Jewell	1
John Windsor	1
hearths	7

410. SLACKSTEAD[1]

Hearths chargeable

Nicholas Smith	2
Mister Badforde	2
William Hellier	2
Stephen Rogers	1
Widow Hockly	1
Widow Miller	1
Thomas Winckworth	1
hearths	10

Hearths not chargeable

Widow Harmes	2
hearths	2

1. Slacksteed

411. WEST STRATTON

Hearths chargeable

Michael Bannister	5
Richard Bull	3
John Collier	3
Widow Parr	3
Widow Perry	2
Widow Hack	2
Widow Simons	2
hearths	20

Fol. 78v(ii)

412. CRANBOURNE[1]

Hearths chargeable

Mister John Ryves	12
Timothy Waterman	3
Nicholas Silver	5
hearths	20

Hearths not chargeable

Widow Wheatland	1
Leonard Piball	1
Thomas Silver	1
Richard Martin	1
John Wake	1
John Humber	1
Thomas Lyne	1
George Waterman	1
Richard Webb	1
Richard Bowles	1
Richard Diddams	1
hearths	11

1. Cranebourne

413. NORTHBROOK[1]

Hearths chargeable

Richard Standbrooke	2
Francis Winckworth	1
John Cooper	3
Anthony Tompsone	2
Joan French	1
Joan Blundell	1
William Blunden	3
Robert Winckworth	2
hearths	15

Hearths not chargeable

William French	1
Thomas Mansbridge	1
Peter Cernett	1
John Parrock	1
Thomas Tyre	1
hearths	5

1. Northbrooke

414. EAST STRATTON

Hearths chargeable

Thomas Earl of Southampton	25
John Purchill	3
Stephen Evens	1
Nicholas Annell	2
Thomas Archer	1
John Archer	3
William Hall	2
John Hooker	2
William Feilder	1
Widow Dennett	2
Widow Woods	1
William Hussey	1
John Webb	1
Valentine Parr	3
Bartholomew Hooker	1
Peter Twyne	1

Fol. 79r(i)

Thomas Blaunchett	2
Thomas Dee	1
Thomas Silvester	1
John Mills	3
William Porter	3
John Hooker	1
William Turner	1
Ellen Skeele	2
Richard Purchill	1
Elizabeth Madgwick	1
Simon Cooper	1
John Smith	1
Richard Eedes	1
John Hellier	3
Stephen Archer	1
hearths	74

Hearths not chargeable

William Lampard	1
Widow Fawkner	1
John Kempe	1
Widow Snuggs	1
William[1] Wey	1
Edward Trewliff	1
Widow Rymes	1
Thomas Carpenter	1

Thomas Mills	1
John Hooker	2
George Poynter	1
Richard Heath	1
hearths	13

1. Will *written over* Wid

415. ABBOTS WORTHY

Hearths chargeable

Mister Edward Moorey	7
Mister John Fyfeild	2
John Webb	1
John Wayte	1
Wayte	1
Dorothy Pincke	1
William Wayte	1
William Hardinge	1
Thomas Burnett	1
Richard Wright	1
Mister Hurst	2
Cornelius Webb	7
hearths	26

416. NORTHINGTON

Hearths chargeable

Sir Robert Henley	13
Widow Collier	2
William Gosler	1
Philip Bannings	2
George Newham	1
Maurice Collier	1
John Kernett	1
Henry Sommers	2
John Kiftall	1
William Cobb	1
Richard Hall	1
William Stroude	6
Henry Buttler	1
Ralph Reeves	2[a]
John Forder	1
Widow Speering	2
William White	1
Henry Parrick	1
Richard Cannings	1
John Speeringe	2

Fol. 79r(ii)

Thomas Hinkes	1
John Harding	2
William Dyer	4
Robert Soper	5
James Scriven	2
Mister Younge	1
hearths	57

Hearths not chargeable

Christopher Pine	1
Thomas Bray	1
John Winckworth	1
William Light	1
James Biggs	1
William Combs	1
Widow Hall	1
Henry Summers	1
hearths	8

(a) 1 decreased

417. POPHAM

Hearths chargeable

Richard Hunt esquire	8
Richard Grantham	2
John Turner	2
Robert Moth	1
John Russell	1
James Biggs	1
Robert Kempe	2
Margaret Twyne	1
Thomas Marshall	1
Richard Smith	1
Richard Russell	1
Philip Blake	1
hearths	22

Hearths not chargeable

Margaret Simpson widow	1
Thomas Rabett	1
hearths	2

The number of hearths chargeable within the hundred of Micheldever is	331
Not chargeable	76

418. BASINGSTOKE TOWN[1]

Hearths chargeable

Name	Hearths
Mister William Rimes senior	6
Mister William Rimes junior	4
Edward Cleve[2]	5
Laurence Palmer	2
Silvanus Heather	4
Widow Barnard	11
John Esgatte	7
Widow Terry	6
Mister William Beck; John Cherry; Henry Stone (bracketed)	3
John Curtis	1
Eleanor Box	12
John Langester	3
Andrew Collier	3
Joseph Mansfeild	2
Henry Morrifeild	2
Mister Barnard Ryves	4
Henry Barfoot	3
Thomas Waltheridge	1
Widow Weston	2
Edward Hill	1
James Heather	2

Fol. 79v(i)

Name	Hearths
Richard Michen	2
John Kinchen	1
James Crinble	4
John Cowdrey	3
John Weston	2
John Sweetapple	1
Edward Cowdry	2
William Mathew	6
Richard Geburne	1
Richard Jayes	1
Thomas Greene	2
Mister Edmund Pittman	5
Thomas Kitchener	3[a]
Mister George Buttler	4
Widow Cherry	16
John Windover	2
Richard Smith	1
John Watts	5
Thomas Quayte	10
William Hawkens	3
Mister Hugh White	3
Alexander Kempe	3
George Hall	4
Thomas Eedes	3
Mister Richard Spittle	18
Mister John Mills	6[b]
Anthony Browne	1[c]
Thomas Marshall	1
Nicholas Dredge	1
William Elliott	3
John Standbridge	5
William Bayly	2
William Harford	4
George Browne	3
William Cowdrey	4
Nicholas Rabbetts	2
John Tharpe	4
Barnard Fletcher	2
Joseph Ashbourne	7
James Mourne	3
John Twyner	2
William Yeeles	4
George Horne	3
William Coleman	5
John Coleman	4
Richard Alexander	2
Oliver Abbott	4
John Crauft	2
Widow Buttler	2
John Trymer	4
William Greene	4
Philip Robbins	5
Thomas Coleman	3
George Prince	5
John Browne	2
Obadiah Kew	4
William Smith	6
Timothy Burden	4
Mister Richard Buttler	5
Mistress Collier widow	6
Richard Allen	4
William Allen	1

William Morrell	1
Nicholas Greene	3
Barnard Allen	3
Richard Seagrave	2
Thomas Hack	1
William Clough	2
Edward Dredge	2
John Sutton	1
William Wither	2
Stephen Remnant	4
Mister John Coleman	4
Mister George Edwards	2
Mister Barnard Wright	7
Robert Kew senior	1
Robert Kew junior	1

Fol. 79v(ii)

John Mannings	4
Mister William Blunden junior	4
William Carter	2
Christopher Broome	2
Humphrey Hunt	2
William Cater	3
Robert Blunden	2
Joseph Younge	2
John Michen	3
John Browne	4
Samuel Kitchener	4
Ralph North	3
Thomas Mackerell	3
Mister Richard Hanniton	6
Christopher Ingram	3
Jasper Upton	2
John Turner	5
Widow Rives	4
John Norris	2
Mister William Spire	3
Mister John Davis	5
Mister Mayne	5
Mister James Parkhurst	2
Samuel Michener	1
Laurence Stevens	4
Walter Barfoot	6
John Spire	2
Thomas Woodison	2
John Watts junior	1
Edward Webb	2
Mister Richard Brackly	8
Mister Thomas Denham	5
William Lambe	7
Mister Richard Woodrough	6
John Wither	2
John Warham & Widow North	6
Thomas Head	3
Daniel Towers	2
Mister Francis Moore	6
Edward Stocker	1
William Knight	3
Henry Smith	1
Richard Wattmer	2
Widow Smith	3
Richard Farly	2
Richard Pittman	1
William Spencer	4
Richard Kiftall	2
William Warner	1
John Jackson	2
James Lee	3
Thomas Kew	1
Widow Spire	2
William James	2
George Addams	1
Edward Clapshowe	2
Mister Edward Ashton	8
Richard Burnard	2
Richard Hall	3
Thomas Knight	5
Edward Mathew	2
John West	2
Thomas Hall senior	1
Nicholas Barnard	2
Mister John Barwick	3
Mister John Davis	5
William Haynes	2
George Stowte	2
George Hellier	1
Walter Frowde	2
Widow Houchins	5

418. BASINGSTOKE TOWN
—cont'd.

William Blunden senior	5[(b)]
John Randall	1
John Horne	4
Richard Cox	3

Fol. 80r(i)

Thomas Hall junior	1
John Browne	3
John Standbridg senior	3
John Wells	2
George Bunney	1
Robert Michen	1
Christopher Staple	2
Henry Ellingworth	2
Edward Deverell	2
Mister John Wade	5
William Warner & John Puckeridge	12
hearths	624

Hearths not chargeable

Richard Kew	2
Richard Fawkner	2
Henry Vincent	1
William Harris	1
Robert Davis	1
Thomas Wyatt	1
William Stocker	1
Michael Coleman	1
Ralph Lee	1
William Panford	1
William Cooke	1
John Holder	1
Robert Batt[3]	1
Fabler Matten	2
William Baff	1
Jasper Alderton	1
Edward Mourne	1
Ann Longe	1
Nicholas Foster	1
Robert Heyward	1
Richard Christmore	1
Nicholas Heather	1
Richard Gates	2
Widow Harris	1
George Browne	1
John Mogg	1
William Draper	1
Edward Woodison	1
Widow Porthmouth[4]	1
Widow Draper	1
John Frowde	1
Richard Hasker	1
William Snuggs	1
Henry Wright	1
Widow Eales	1
Widow Wells	1
George Drill	1
Dorothy Williams	1
Henry Cater	1
Peter Lamport	1
William West	1
John Sivell	1
Tristram Johns	1
John Wright	1
Philip Pirsey	1
Giles Joanes	1
Edward Fox	1
Thomas Parrick	1
Widow South	1
Richard Golden	1
Barnard Seygrave	1

Fol. 80r(ii)

Robert Hambleton	1
William Johnson junior	1
Barnard Holdborne	1
Christopher Holdborne	1
Peter Lawder	1
John Cotterell	1
William Johnson senior	1
Thomas Austen	1
Richard Addams	1
Robert Farrock	1
Thomas Browne	1
Richard Scott	1
Thomas Addams	1
Matthew Harris	1
James Turner	1
Richard Taylor	1
Henry Heather	1

Widow Taylor	1
Joseph Browne	1
Richard Langester	1
Henry Heather	1
John Walteridge	1
William Taylor	1
Henry Percy	1
Andrew Addams	1
Robert Spire	2
George Taylor	1
John Ambleton	1
John Taylor	1
Edward Michener	1
William Turner	1
Thomas Dent	1
William Hewes	1
John Stocker	1
Widow Oades	1
James Mogg	1
Richard Stocker	1
William Smith	1
Edmund Mitchener	1
John Dent	1
Postumous Wyatt	1
Edward Ives	1
Widow Petty	1
John Rabnutt	1
Thomas Turton	1
John Alder	1
Robert Purse	1
John Crawte	1
Widow Knight	2
Robert Barfoot	1
William Runger	1
Robert Greene	1
Robert Craswell	1
John Pincke	1
Moses Parr	1
Widow Craswell	1
James Searle	1
Thomas Neale	1
Widow Younge	1
Andrew Craswell	1
Giles Goodwin	1
Richard Hawkens	2
John Mortimer	1
Thomas Bramly	1
John Edwards	1
James Addams	1
Richard Addams	1
Fol. 80v(i)	
William Philipps	1
William Spencer	1
Thomas Addams	1
Richard Gearle	1
William Turner	1
John Murrell	1
Richard Ashton	1
Widow Cleve	1
John Harris[5]	1
John Spire	1
Cuthbert Walker	1
John Beale	1
Widow Thombs	2
Francis Payce	1
Benjamin Collins	1
John James	2
William Cooper	1
Thomas Eedes	1
Walter Batchelor	1
Robert Ansell	1
Joseph Griffen	1
hearths	162

(a) decreased 1
(b) 1 decreased
(c) 2 decreased
1. Basingstoke Towne
2. *Altered to* Cleve *in a different hand. Name underneath is illegible.*
3. *Altered from* Baff
4. *Altered from* Northmouth
5. *Altered from* Parris

419. HAZELEY[1]

Hearths chargeable

Abraham Hill senior	2
Nicholas Oades	1
Widow Attwater	2
John Barrett	2
William Hill	2
John Hill	2
Margery Penbrook	3
William Biggs	2

419. HAZELEY—*cont'd.*

Edward Woodison	2
Robert Webb	2
Richard Heyfor	5
George Walker	2
Abraham Hill junior	2
Thomas Drackford	3
Thomas Feilder	2
John Lamport	5
James Yates	3
Abraham Hill	2
Edward Pickernell	1
hearths	45

Hearths not chargeable

Henry Hill	2
Robert Hall	1
Ellis Legg	1
Robert Hocker	1
Leonard Gudge	1
Thomas Shackleford	1
Jerome Penvell	1
Mary Inwood	1
Francis Baker	1
John Strowde	1
Simon Waldropp	1
hearths	12

1. Hasell

The number of hearths chargeable within the liberty of Basingstoke	669
Hearths not chargeable	174

Fol. 80v(ii)

BASINGSTOKE HUNDRED EXTRA

420. MAPLEDURWELL[1]

Hearths chargeable

John Clapshow	3
Henry Smith	5
Widow Scott	2
Widow Mathewes	5
Henry Gold	1
Robert Kinge	1
John Gold	1
Christopher Fry	2
Henry Cooper	2
John Summers	4
Roger Smith	3
Robert Gold	1
Widow Millett	1
John Morlin	2
John Summers junior	1
William Ayres	1
Robert Garry[2]	2
John Justice	1
Widow Martin	1
Nicholas Gary	2
Benjamin Mathew	1
hearths	42

Hearths not chargeable

John Alexander	1
William Sumner[3]	1
John Neave	1
Richard Gold	1
Widow Naish	1
John Gold	1
Joan Sumner[3]	1
John Silver	1
William Portsmouth	1
Widow Sumer[3]	1
Thomas Summer[3]	1
Arthur Summer[3]	1
John Snellinge	1
Widow Russell	1
William Gold	1
hearths	15

1. Mapledorewell
2. *Altered from* Barry
3. Sumner *has been rendered in a variety of ways, some with marks of abbreviation over the* m, *some without. The name has in each case been left in its unextended form. It is clear from other sources that the name is* Sumner *rather than* Summer.

421. WINSLADE

Hearths chargeable

Mister Merriott	3
Mister Yarly	6

Mister Pinck	8
William Fry	5
Nicholas Bensteed	2
William Robinson	4
Mister Goldfinch	2(a)
John Parry	2
Benjamin Mathew	1
hearths	33

Fol. 81r(i)

Hearths not chargeable

Widow Tanner	1
John Blake	1
Richard Blake	1
Gilbert Dennice	1
Richard Durman	1
hearths	5

(a) 1 decreased

422. CLIDDESDEN[1]

Hearths chargeable

Mister Edward Mooreinge	7
Henry Barrett	3
Ambrose Daman	2
William Box	3
William Beck	5
William Prince	5
John Kelsey	5
Widow Caute	1
George Fletcher	3
Richard Kersley	1
Richard Legatte	1
Thomas Martin	2
Richard Hunt	1
John Stagg	1
John Belchamber	4
Henry Fry	1
Arthur Russell	2
Edward Charter	2
Humphrey Nitinghall	1
Widow Carnall	2
Thomas Tilborowe	4
hearths	56

Hearths not chargeable

Philip Russell	1
Thomas Charter	1
John Laurence	1
Widow Meeres	1
Widow Smith	1
hearths	5

1. Clidsden

423. NATELY SCURES[1]

Hearths chargeable

Christopher May	4
Mister Nuttby	3
John Pettoe	2
Mister Dunfeild	3
Henry Goodyer	2
Thomas Frost	1
Roger Gary	2
Robert Noysh	3
Philip Eames	2
William Albery	2
Widow South	7
Lambourne Searle	5
Philip Gillam	3
Daniel Scott	3
Widow Winter	1
Andrew Holt	4
Richard Kinge	4
William Hall	4
Roger Wilkins	6
hearths	61

Fol. 81r(ii)

Hearths not chargeable

Andrew Batchelor	1
Edward Cilsen	1
Nicholas Gary	2
hearths	4

1. Nattly Scuers

424. OLD BASING[1]

Hearths chargeable

Richard Baker	3
William Hasker	3
William Carter	3
Richard Hellyer	3
John Normand	7
Nicholas Barton	5

424. OLD BASING—*cont'd.*

Mister Cuffold	10
Peter Corrant	4
Robert Kempe	3
Henry Herbert	2
Thomas Fawkner	3
Richard Baily	2
James Harwood	1
John Mulford	3
Richard Payse	2
William Barber	5[(a)]
Matthew Upton	2
John Lipscombe	3
Edward Lamport	5
James Harwood	3
Richard Pittman	5
Richard Gary	2
John Ackland	1
James Lee	4
Richard Chase	4
William Lee	4
Mister Osbourne	4
John Hooker	2
Clement Inould	1
Widow Upton	2
Widow Sex	2
William Wisdome	2
Edward Woodison	3
Edward Baker	3
Henry Gilbert	3
John Follwell	5
William Allaby	4
Robert Hooker	5
Mister Wackfeild	5
William Stiles	3[(b)]
Edward Ackland	8
Clement Frost	2
Edward Wackfeild	4
Thomas Whicher	3
Richard Spire	1
John Puckeridge	3
Anthony Cooper	3
John Osbourne	4
Thomas Hattrell	4
William Luess	6
William Lusse	5
William Hooker	2
John Sharpe	1
John Lamport	4
Henry Horne	1
Thomas Hill	4
John Fidler	1
Widow Hooker	3
hearths	194

Fol. 81v(i)

Hearths not chargeable

Walter Bird	1
Alexander Moss	2
Francis Harwood	1
William Harwood	1
Alexander Grover	1
John Harwood	2
John Wakfeild	6
William Inould	2
Edward Jennings	2
Isaac Wright	1
hearths	19

(a) 1 decreased
(b) 1 pulled down
1. Basinge

425. EASTROP[1]

Hearths chargeable

William Hodges	5
William Hawkins	3
John Sharpe	2
Widow Petty	1
Thomas Scriven	1
John Denyer	3
Thomas Lamboll	2
William Morrell	1
Hackwood House	2
Andrew Addams	2
hearths	22

1. Easthropp

426. WOODGARSTON[1]

Hearths chargeable

William Carter	6[(a)]
Peter Bigges	3
Widow Gary	3
hearths	12

Hearths not chargeable

Edward Tayler	1
Richard Weekes	1
hearths	2

(a) 1 decreased
1. Woodgaston

427. STEVENTON[1]

Hearths chargeable

Sir John Lukenor	10
Mister Orpwood	3
Doctor John Harmor	9
John Brothers	4
Thomas Small	5
William Patience	2
Michael Noyse	2
Charles Coney	2
Arthur Crooke	1
Austin Ansell	1
Richard Smart	1
John Philipps	1
William White	1
hearths	42

Hearths not chargeable

James Duttman	1
Thomas Fronknell	1
Widow Dounce	1
hearths	3

1. Stevington

Fol. 81v(ii)

428. SHERBORNE ST. JOHN[1]

Hearths chargeable

Chaloner Chute esquire	43(a)
John Thorner esquire	39(b)
Mister Charles Kinge	7
Anthony Barton	6
John Dickeson	4
Widow Wild	1
Thomas Spire	1
Robert South	3
George Michell	3
George Watts	1
Richard Barnard	3
John Weekes	1
John Cooper	1
John Carter	7
William Hellier	4
Nicholas Webb	3
Matthew Symes	1
William Caplyne	1
Henry Kent	2
Francis Clanter	3
Rannell Rice	5
Richard Petty	6
William Moth	3
Ralph Gardner	3
Widow Benger	2
William Ellett	3
William Carter	2
Widow Gardner	2
Nathaniel Cleane	3
William Ware	7
Widow Millard	2
John Goodale	1
Thomas Wellings	1
Vincent Smith	1
Widow Edwine & Robert Read	2
John Kent	3
The farmhouse	3
The parsonage	6
Thomas Clapshow	1
William Permyn	5
John Moth	2
Widow Jerman	1
William Collins	3
John Kent	1
Mister William Jackman	3
Roland Cannings	2
Philip Hall	3
Robert Hall	1
Richard Moth	1
Mister Saunders	5
James Moth	1
Richard Dounce	1
Richard Benham	1
hearths	221

428. SHERBORNE ST. JOHN *—cont'd.*

Hearths not chargeable

William Taplin 1
John Hodges 1
Widow Yeats 1
John Gardner 1
Widow Goodale 1
hearths 5

(a) decreased 2
(b) decreased 3
1. Sherbourne St John

Fol. 82r(i)

429. BRAMLEY[1]

Hearths chargeable

Mister Love 5
Ralph Kent 6
John Hall 2
Samuel Wheat 1[(a)]
James Bedford 2
John Hewes 2
Edward Remington[2] 5
James Woods 7
John Moundy 2
John Tee 1
Walter Wattmore 3
James Triggall 1
William Hasker 3
Ralph Nitinghall 2
Francis White 4
William Weekes 2
Edward Payse 3
John White 3
Nicholas Eggerton 4
William Morris senior 3
Widow Hanington 1
Thomas Woods 1
Robert Hall 1
Widow Baily 1
Widow Pope 6
Widow Pryer 2
Richard Hasker 6
Edward Glover 3
Widow Hasker 4
Thomas Wheeler 2
Thomas Stiff 6
Mister Lentall 6
Edward Alexander 5
John Chambers 2
William Morris junior 2
John Wigley 1
Richard Hardinge 1
hearths 110

(a) 1 decreased
1. Bramly
2. *Text has an additional minim.* Remington *confirmed from other sources.*

430. TUNWORTH[1]

Hearths chargeable

John Hall senior 3
John Hall junior 4
Thomas Hall junior 5
John Clerke 4
Widow Bickner 4
Richard Waterman 2
Edward Glaspoole 1
Philip Parr 1
hearths 24

Fol. 82r(ii)

Hearths not chargeable

John Prowtinge 1
Widow Searle 1
Christopher Waterman 1
hearths 3

1. Tunnworth

431. NEWNHAM[1]

Hearths chargeable

Mister Richard Hooke 10
Mister Andrew Whelpdell 6
Thomas Prince 4
Eustace Barton 5
Thomas Parker 1
William Amblin 3
George Baily 1
William Smith 2
Nicholas Fidler 3
John Lamport 2

Henry Strowde 1
George Cottman 1
Robert Naish 3
John Wheeler 1
Richard Tille 3
John Vicary 8
William Trigge 1
Thomas Rolph 2
Widow Attkinson 7
Widow South 1
Robert Potter 4
James Knight 2
hearths 71

Hearths not chargeable

William Smith 1
John Upton 1
Thomas Batchelor 1
John Hooker 1
Jerome Aslett 1
Thomas Aroys 1
John Sex 1
Widow Seager 1
Widow White 1
Joan Kember 1
James Upton 2
hearths 12

1. Newneham

432. CHINEHAM[1]

Hearths chargeable

Mister William Moore 18
hearths 18

1. Chinham

Fol. 82v(i)

433. UP NATELY[1]

Hearths chargeable

Nicholas Milton 6
Thomas Poulter 2
Henry Egger 3
Thomas Hebb 3
John Found 2
Henry Kinge 3
Robert Ayres 2
William Bettsworth 1
John Pettoe 1
Thomas Weene 1
William Cooper 2
William Hooker 2
Bartholomew Poulter 1
John Plott 10
hearths 39

1. Upnately

The number of hearths chargeable within the hundred of Basingstoke Extra is 943
Not chargeable 74

The number of hearths chargeable in the division of Basingstoke is 6330
Not chargeable 981

Fol. 83r(i)

ANDOVER DIVISION

HUNDRED OF ANDOVER INFRA

ANDOVER TOWN[1]

434. ALDERMANS ROW

Hearths chargeable

John Upton 5
Mister Peter Blake 9
Mister William Barlowe 3
Mistress Elizabeth Waler 3
Tobias Beazer 1
James Piper 1
Roger Bird 4
Robert Bird 1
Richard Jellyfe senior 3
Richard Emett 2
Silas Gage 2
William Cornelius 1
William Alford 2
John Glover 2
Benjamin Tarleton 3
George Merrick 2
William Butcher 4
William Gammon 3

434. ALDERMANS ROW—*cont'd.*

Thomas Richardson	2
John Saunders	4
Elizabeth Long widow	4
Robert Long	1
Mister William Gold	1
Joseph Turner	5
Roger Bird	3
Thomas Jacques	3
William Palmer	2
John Seagrove	2
Henry Rainger	2
Reuben Wild	2
Mistress Mary Thurman	5
George Bray	4
Richard Smith	1
Mister John Burratt	6
Mister John Kingsmill	7
Robert Humphry	2
Richard Ventham	3
John Stanford	4
Alexander Cooper	3
William Golden	1
Elizabeth Bugley	2
George Paine	1
John Keate	1
Thomas Treadle	2
William James	4
Francis Gray	2
Thomas Grace	2
William Bayly	2
Robert Garrett	2
James Pearcy	1
Edward Emett	1
Robert Smith	1
Richard Wheatly	2
Thomas Hayward	3
John Borde	3
William Cooke	1
Robert Dawkins	3
Philip Barnard	5
Robert Piper	5
Richard Weight	4
Robert Moreing	1
William Barwick	7
Mister Walter Robinson	3
Mister Joseph Hincksman	7
Mister Michael Hincksman	4
Mister James Samborne	5
Thomas Whatley	6
William Sweetapple	3
John Throllopp	2
Henry Long	2
Mister William Wimbleton	4
Mister John Popinay	3
Mister Richard Blake	4
Richard Jelliffe junior	2
John Plipott	2
William Scullard	3
George Noyes	4
Widow Bylands	1

Fol. 83r(ii)

Richard Goodale	1
George West	1
Christopher Hopkins	2
William Weight senior	7
Richard Cooke	4
John Abbott	1
Philip Church	3
Richard Keele	4
Widow Gage	3
John Hatchett	3
Mistress Thurman	3
hearths	262

Hearths not chargeable

Abraham Ventham	2
George Napper	2
John Hellier	2
Mary Knight	1
Widow Drew	2
Joseph Weight	1
Alexander Cooke	2
Richard Butcher	2
Widow Pewsey	2
Widow Beazer	1
Widow Gold	2

Nicholas Blake	1
Widow Ash	1
Robert Tarleton	2
Widow Turner	1
Goody Mountayne	2
George Manfeild	2
Roland Griffin	2
William Earle	2
Robert Penton	2
William Scullard	1
Widow Eaton	1
Thomas Hayes	1
Widow Smith	1
William Fowles	1
Widow Wheatland	1
Widow Buttler	1
Widow Fleetwood	1
Thomas Halloway	1
Widow Rogers	1
John Rivers	1
John Johnson	1
Christopher Cowley	1
Jethro Clittson	1
William Spring	1
George Smith	1
Ann Clittson	1
John Brexton	2
Richard Flood	2
William Sutton	1
Thomas Guyett	2
Widow Small	2
Richard Hurst senior	1
Leonard Crosse	2
Goody Spreadborough	1
Maurice Shipton	2
John Borde	1
William Hapgood	1
John Lewis	1
William Lane	1
Elias Ellis	2
Thomas Marshall	2
Richard Stronge senior	1
William Woolly	1
Thomas Young	1
William Greene	1
Nathaniel Spittle	1
Richard Strong junior	1
John Tredgold	1

Fol. 83v(i)

Peter Ogborne	1
Gilbert Gosling	1
Widow Moreing	1
Widow Bonney	1
Widow Game	2
Widow Woods	1
Nicholas Beakly	1
William Scullard	1
George Purdue	1
John Wheatland	1
Richard Honeywell	1
Richard Smith	1
John Palmer	1
Charles Cooke	1
Widow Wilde	1
Widow Godden	1
Robert Lawrence	1
Widow Blake	1
John Blake	1
John Hix	1
John Palmer	1
Stephen Silvester	1
Peter Cleeve	1
John Wheatley	1
John Cleeve	2
William Cleeve	1
John Palmer junior	1
Widow Miller	1
Widow Cooke	1
Robert Dowley	1
Thomas Russell	1
John Chandler	1
Mary Rattue[2]	1
Richard Cimcodd	1
William Goodale	1
Thomas Knightlin	1
Thomas Downton	1
Robert Frampton	1
Robert Seyword	1
Simpson Mathewes	2
Peter Cleeve	1
Richard Read	2

434. ALDERMANS ROW—*cont'd.*

Widow Knight	1
Widow Miller	1
Leonard Sparkman	1
John Kinge	1
Thomas Miller	1
Richard Bevis	1
John Purdue	1
Widow Harfeild	1
Richard Goodale junior	1
John Scodsden	1
William Payne	1
Gilbert Payne	1
William Blake	1
Thomas Lewenton	1
Richard Godden	1
John Hunt	1
John Miller	1
Thomas Pearce	2
Robert Hopgood	2
Alexander Banks	1
William Page	2
John Tompson	1
Richard Reynolds	2
Thomas Bengley	1
Richard Norrice	1
Amy Feilder	1
Widow Chubb	1
Widow Baker	1
Thomas Hebberds	1
Margery Curtice	1
Thomas Bent	1
Edward Cooke	2
John Abbott	1
Richard Sivyer	1
Richard Hurst	1

Fol. 83v(ii)

John Prince junior	2
George Cornelias	2
Adam Cannon	1
Robert Neale	1
Robert Boney	2
Widow Wilde	1
Widow White	1
Widow James	1
Richard Pyle	1
George Payne	1
John Weyman	1
Edward Cooper	1
Richard Mundy	1
Robert Bird	1
John Tredgold	1
hearths	186

1. Andover Towne
2. *Altered from* Pattue

435. PRIORY IN ANDOVER

Hearths chargeable

John Prince	4
Benjamin Bonney	3
Thomas Feilder	5
Humphrey Paynter	5
Mister John Rachbond	18[(a)]
William Bampton	2
Abraham Weight	2
William Tanner	2
William Longrove	2
Mister Nicholas Venables	12[(b)]
& for Finckley	5
Widow Swetapple	2[(c)]
Robert Mansfeild	3
Widow Richardson	3
Mister John Morton	5
Thomas Noyes	4
Widow Morlow	3
hearths	80

Hearths not chargeable

Elizabeth Hunton	1
Adam Cannon	2
Samuel Hollis	2
John Tarleton	2
John Pittman	2
Widow Peacy	2
Robert Ash	2
Meredith Davyes	2
John Hewlett	2
Nicholas Dyaper	1
William Westen	2
Charles Tompkins	1

Widow Speering	1
John Bampton	1
Lancelot Hampshire	1
Baskfeild Ruddley	2
John Prince junior	1
John Reeves & Peter Salmon	2
John Evens	1
Robert Paynter	1
William Perry	1
Widow Bagger	1
Martin Hayward	2
Ann Noyes	1
James Hatchet	1
hearths	37

(a) 1 overreckoned
(b) 2 decreased
(c) 2 overcharged

Fol. 84r(i)

436. WINCHESTER STREET IN ANDOVER[1]

Hearths chargeable

William Oram	12
Benjamin Bradborne	2
Thomas Johnson	3
Giles Tompkins	12
John Tompkins	3
William Waler	3
Thomas Forde	11
Richard Channell	2
John Noyes wife	3
Michael Ruttley	6
Widow Cooper	4
Widow Scullard	2
Edward Waldron	1[(a)]
John Barber	2
John Overton	3
Mark Hobbs	2
Andrew Moreing	2
William Hinxman	9[(b)]
Richard Winckworth	2[(c)]
Benjamin Dyaper	1
Thomas Earle	1
Thomas Minchin	2
James Sumersett	2
William Brode	4
Robert Cox	3
Paul Short	2
Thomas Barwick junior	3
Robert Everett	4
Thomas Hogges	2
Mistress Thornebrough	7
John Knowles	1
Richard Lovegrowe	2
Edward Channell	2
Zacharias Scullard	2
Robert New	1
John Hyde	3
Edward Hunt	5
George Cornelius	1
Thomas Smith	1
Widow Bird	6
Mister Thomas Westcombe	20
Thomas Bonney	1
Martha Waller widow	3
William Loringe	2
Widow Mounteine	4
Robert Mounteine	3
John Dallymore	2
Mister Cockey	3
Maurice Shipton	2
Mister William Gold	4
William Knowles	1
John Cleeve alias Godden	6[(d)]
James Fleetwood	10[(e)]
Mister Samuel Holmes	6
John Longe	2
Widow Channell	5
Andrew New	5
William Inhance	6
William Holman	2
Widow Browne	4
Richard Baker	1
Anthony Moreing	1[(a)]
Thomas Gilmore	2
Richard Wells	2
John Smith	2
Richard Seagrove	2
William Peacey	1

436. WINCHESTER STREET IN ANDOVER—*cont'd.*

John Gage	1
John Cooke	2
William Reade	3
Anthony Tatwell	6
Sir John Trott	1
hearths	254

Hearths not chargeable

William Fleetwood	2
Thomas Barnard	2
Thomas Andrews	1
Thomas Medhurst	1
Richard Mundy	1
John Lovegrove	1
Richard Bonney	2
Michael Crouch	2
John Baverstock	1
John Goodenough	2
John Burnett	1

Fol. 84r(ii)

Michael Gardner	1
William Tanner	1
Lancelot Hampshire	1
William Tombs	1
Joseph Bath	1
William Elton	2
John Drewley	2
Francis Goodale	1
Thomas Hooper	1
George Moreing	1
Robert Bonney	1
Richard Martin	1
Widow Holdway	1
Richard Godden	1
Andrew New junior	1
John Jones	2
Widow Poole	2
John Silence	1
Thomas Pittman	1
Edward Chard	1
Thomas Leach	1
Tobias Knightlin	1
John Cortney	1
Richard Templer senior	1
Widow Bottome	1
John Barnaby	1
Richard Templar junior	1
Widow Knowles	1
Widow Jenkins	1
John Kent	1
Barnard Emett	1
Thomas Emett	1
Henry Cornelius	1
Widow Harfell	1
James Veare	1
Zacharias Scullard junior	1
George Merrick	1
Edward Leach	1
Richard Foster	1
John Gardner	1
Ralph Courtney	1
Alexander Knight	2
Ralph Channell	2
Richard Jennings	1
Widow Eaton	1
John Gearle	1
Widow Sutton	1
Richard Clerke	1
Richard Dumer	1
Edward Chard junior	1
Elizabeth House	1
Ezekiel House	1
Thomas Drew	1
John Piper	2
William Grunsell	2
Richard Mills	1
John Speering	2
Thomas Turner	1
hearths	83

(a) 1 overcharged
(b) 1 down
(c) 1 increased
(d) 6 overcharged
(e) 2 down

1. Winchester Street in Andever

437. CHARLTON[1]

Hearths chargeable

Widow Noyes	4

William Sweetapple	3
Giles Carter	2
John Hopgood senior	1
John Hopgood junior	1
John Deekes	1
Luke Pearce	1
John Mundy	2
William Legate	3
George Beare	1
William Beare	1
Joseph Beare	2
John Beare	1
William Penton	1
John Salmon	1
William Lively	3
William Mundy	3
Thomas Penton	2
John Grace	1
William Tredgold	2
Peter James	4

Fol. 84v(i)

Richard Browne	2
Christopher Francis	1
John Francis	1
Richard Dennett	1
Widow Blake	3
John Greene	3
hearths	51

Hearths not chargeable

Thomas Figgas	1
Edward Rattue senior	1
Christopher Cole	2
James Deekes[2]	1
John Brice	1
John Farre	1
Joan Sadler	1
Thomas Tredgold	1
Thomas Mundy & Richard Taphurst	2
Christopher Iremonger	1
Edward Scullard	1
John Dowlance	2
John Rattue	1
Sidrach Rattue	1
Mary Blackman	1
William Robinson	1
Thomas Rattue	1
Edward Talmage	1
Thomas Pricklowe	1
Richard Blanchard	1
Robert Flood	1
Joan Blanchard	1
Thomas Foster	1
Widow Whale	1
Henry Hiller	1
Matthew Crouch	1
Sidrach Spanell	2
John Lively senior	1
Richard Peeke senior	1
William Gale	1
Thomas Clerke	1
William Salmon	1
Widow Harte	1
Widow Watts	1
Widow Cooper	1
Widow Aldred	1
John Read	1
William White	1
Richard Deare	1
George Figgas	1
John Cooper	1
Edward Lewington	1
Widow Day	1
John Cannon	1
Thomas Wigmore	1
hearths	49

1. Charleton
2. *Altered from* Beekes

438. HATHERDEN

Hearths chargeable

Mister Robert Noyes	6
Mistress Jane Noyes	6
George Selfe	3
William Knight	1
John Neale	1
Thomas Hopgood	1
Richard Iremonger	1
hearths	19

438. HATHERDEN—*cont'd.*

Hearths not chargeable

Thomas Lewington	2
Daniel Baverstock	2
William Mundy	1
hearths	5

Fol. 84v(ii)

439. FOXCOTT

Hearths chargeable

John Sweetapple	2
William Blake	1
Peter Francis	3
Thomas Mundy	1
Laurence Brownejohn	1
Henry Jeffery	3
Widow Page	1
Mister Noyes	3
Alexander Payne	1
Stephen Mercer	3
Hugh James	2
hearths	21

Hearths not chargeable

Elizabeth Rosswell	1
John Dalby	1
Nicholas Judd	1
Widow Egg	1
Widow Haydon	1
Mary Payne	1
hearths	6

440. KINGS ENHAM

Hearths chargeable

Daniel Kingsmill[1] esquire	8
Charles Powlet esquire	6
Mister Isaac Chancy	7
Alexander Daniell	2
Richard Clerk	1
John Poore	2
William Phillpott	3
Gilbert Palmer	2
Elizabeth Blake widow	3
John Meales	3
Widow Plowman	1
Henry Holdway	1
hearths	39

Hearths not chargeable

Richard Beavice	1
Richard Tittcombe	1
John Harrice	1
Thomas Tredgold	1
John Dowce	1
John Pittman	1
John Tredgold	1
Henry Holdway	1
Thomas Swettapple	2
William Lewis	1
Thomas Golding	1
John Golding	2
Robert Feilder	1
Richard Golding	1
Robert Herne	1
William Potter	1
John Spratt	1
Robert Savadge	1
Dorothy Bayliff	1
Robert Kinge	1
Nathaniel Mundy	1
Edward Smith	1
Widow Seyward	1
Widow Seyward senior	1
Joan Chaundler	1
William Fleetwood	1
hearths	28

The number of hearths chargeable in the hundred of Andover Infra[2]	726
Hearths not chargeable	394

1. *Text has one less minim*
2. Andever Infra

Fol. 85r(i)

HUNDRED OF ANDOVER EXTRA[1]

441. FYFIELD[2]

Hearths chargeable

Mister Lawrence	5

Mister Winckworth	6
William Blake	3
Christopher Fleetwood	2
John Kent	1
Thomas Smith	1
Mistress Wattson	1
William Kenton	1
Richard Hutchins	1
John Clerke	1
William Bedord	1
John Mundy	2
Peter Guye	1
John Nuttkin	1
William Collins	1
Richard Bullock	3
Matthew Gale	1
Adam Holloway	1
Thomas Clerke	1
hearths	34

Hearths not chargeable

John Smith	1
William Fuller	1
Widow Beale	1
Widow Hedd	1
hearths	4

1. Hundred of Andever Extra
2. Fifeild

442. UPPER CLATFORD[1]

Hearths chargeable

Philip Stone	10
William Winckworth	1
Thomas Carter	1
Stephen King	1
Edward Waldron	3
Widow Gearle	1
Henry Tarrant senior	1
Henry Hewit	4
Thomas Johnson	1
William Plumpton	2
William Gale	1
William Hyde	1
William Stacy	1
John Fay	1
Devorix Batt	1
William Poore	2
Mistress Brewer	3
William Harding	2
William Oram	2
William King	1
Edward Godfrey	2
Thomas Tarrant junior	2
George Tarrant	5
Edward Feilder	1
George Noyes	2
Benjamin Tarant	2
Robert Poore	4
Robert Walter	1
Thomas Mowdey	1
Henry Tarrant junior	1
William Gale senior	1
Mister Aubery	4
Thomas Feilder	1
hearths	67

Hearths not chargeable

Robert Knight	1
Robert Page	1
Robert Sutton	1
John Warham	1
Richard Smith	1
Mary Leach	1
Thomas Bedford	1
Widow King	1
Robert Plumpton	1
Thomas Oram	2
Richard Feilder	1
Thomas King	1
Ralph Heyres	1
John Newell	1
John Hopgood	1
[Widow] Broadway	1
[William] Knight	1
[ ] Morrell	1

Fol. 85r(ii)

John White	1
Widow Togge	1
William Trewlove	1
Humphrey Sharpe	1
Robert Waldron	1
Widow Fibbs	1

442. UPPER CLATFORD—*cont'd.*

William Holmes	1
Catherine Kinge	1
Thomas Marks	1
Thomas Kent	1
Widow Toppes	1
hearths	30

1. Up Clatford

443. ABBOTTS ANN[1]

Hearths chargeable

Anthony Cooke	1
Edward Clerke	2
John Prince	1
John Rattue	1
Richard Gale	1
Doctor Hyde	10
Christopher James	8
Mister Foyle	4
Robert Coventry	1
Philip Hatchett	1
Christopher Cary	2
John Bunckly alias Pewsey	1
John Whale	1
Simon Towton	1
John Bayly	1
Widow Drew	1
Nicholas Faithfull	1
Widow Hurst	1
Widow Thomas	1
Thomas Wickham	1
Henry Coventry	1
Richard Davis	1
Thomas Dalby senior	1
Widow Morrant	3
Richard Downes	1
Robert Cole	2
Christopher Cary's other house	1
Thomas Dalby junior	2
William Towton	1
Widow Dalby	1
Peter Gale	2
hearths	57

Hearths not chargeable

Robert Hurst	1
John Horne	1
Thomas Adams	1
Widow Hurst	1
Robert Gover	1
Richard Kempe	1
Widow Carter	1
Widow Holloway	1
Widow Tapner	1
Widow Spratt	1
Widow Russell	1
Widow Towton	1
Thomas Bredmore	1
Thomas Baker senior	1
Thomas Collins	1
William Drew	1
William Sharpe	1
Thomas Baker junior	1
Widow Pewsey	1
Robert Bendale	1
Griffin Burger	1
hearths	21

1. Abbotts Anne

444. KNIGHTS ENHAM

Hearths chargeable

Mister Thomas Brathwaite	4
Mister Richard Pyle	6
Mistress Joan Blake	3
William Woodman	2
John Holdway	3
Richard Barnard	1
Edward Blake	6
James Hawkins	1
John Smith	1

Fol. 85v(i)

Richard Peace	1
Nicholas Hawkins	1
hearths	29

Hearths not chargeable

Widow Daunce	1
Widow Channell	1
John Feilder	1

Widow Pipler	1
Widow Drayton	1
William Meales	1
hearths	6

445. PENTON GRAFTON

Hearths chargeable

Mister Saunderson	5
The farm	5
Edward Wall	4
Mister Stevens	4
Thomas Grace	3
Mister Poyntter	2
Mister Goldstone	2
John Grace	1
John Noyes	1
Henry Tarrant	3
John Bunckley	1
Widow Cole	2
William Noyes	3
Mister Seyward	3
George Selfe	2
Richard Bendale	2
Widow Davis	1
Hercules Tarrant	2
George Wale	1
Thomas Wale	2
Widow Limpas	4
Samuel Tarrant	3
John Bunckly	1
John Mercer	2
Peter Gale	2
William Gale	1
Thomas Tarrant	3
Rambridge[1] Lodge	1
John Jackman	1
William Blake	1
Widow Bunckley	1
John Barnes	1
hearths	70

Hearths not chargeable

Robert Walter	1
Edward Ivye	1
Widow Kite	1
Widow Heydon	1
John Tarrant	1
Richard Wale	1
Richard Tarrant	1
Richard Whale	1
Robert Noyes	1
Samuel Tarrant	1
John Jones	1
Richard Browne	1
John Kifte	1
David Tarrant	1
John Crowch	1
John Stevens	2
Robert Noyes	1
Widow Jones	1
William Davis	1
Richard Whale junior	1
Widow Symons	1
Thomas Mundy	1
Elizabeth Miles	1
William Kifte	1
Widow Davis junior	1
Widow Spadwell	1
William Crowch	1
Francis Twine	1
hearths	29

1. Rambridg

Fol. 85v(ii)

446. PENTON MEWSEY

Hearths chargeable

The farmhouse	7
Mister Russell	5
John Hellier	3
John Moncke	3(a)
David Fray	1
William Smith	1
Thomas Lancaster	1
William Mundy	1
Jasper Mundy	1
Mister Carter	3
Robert Grace	1
John Knowles	1
John Crouch	1
Henry Knowles	1
Mister Poynter	1

446. PENTON MEWSEY—*cont'd.*

John Blake	2
John Hellier	2
John Lewis	1
John Twine	1
Henry Read	1
Stephen Osgood	1
John Grace	1
John Crowch	1
hearths	41

Hearths not chargeable

Widow Cradock	1
Widow Read	1
Thomas Crowch	1
Richard Noyes	1
Widow Beare	1
Widow Trewelove	1
Thomas Dalby	1
hearths	7

(a) 1 down

447. CHOLDERTON

Hearths chargeable

Mister Robert Read	4
Robert Hellier	1
Mistress Ann Moody	2
Bridget Browne widow[1]	1
Widow Sweetapple	3
William Sweetapple	3
Tristram Fabin	1
William Wells	1
hearths	16

Hearths not chargeable

Edward Hobbs	1
Widow Browne	1
William Drew	1
William Salter	1
Thomas Uppery	1
Bridget Wells	1
Widow Martin	1
Thomas King	1
Richard Knight	1
Thomas Ryman	1
Richard Lewis	1
Widow Chapman	1
Joan Bedford	1
John Painter	1
William Newton	1
Widow Salmies	1
Richard Noyes	1
Widow Bevis	1
Widow Bundee	1
hearths	19

1. vidua

Fol. 86r(i)

448. AMPORT

Hearths chargeable

The Lord Henry Powlett	7[a]
Mister Henry Edes	7
Thomas Long	1
Widow Andrews	2
Richard Downes	3
Widow Aubrey	1
Peter Wallis	5
Giles Jasper	1
Mary Crocker	1
Thomas Williams	2
John Skeene	1
Thomas Miller	2
John Carde	1
Widow Shanke	1
John Drake	3
William Sweetapple	2
Robert Crocker	2
Henry Plowman	1
Thomas White	1
Robert Downes	1
Richard Wallis	1
Mister John Pittman	3
hearths	49

Hearths not chargeable

Edward Jesper	1
Widow Godden	1
Richard Pascall	1
John Smith	1
John Williams	1
Widow Batt	1
William Chamber	1

Widow Dugoe	1
Luke Spratt	1
Widow Bull	1
John Chitty	1
Thomas Gibbons	1
John Chech	1
Widow Bayly	1
Robert Frowd	1
Robert Oborne	1
William Norrice	1
Widow Wallis	1
Widow Gibbins	1
Widow Day	1
hearths	20

(a) 2 down

449. THRUXTON

Hearths chargeable

Henry Rogers esquire	15
John Fulker	5
Michael Clerke	2
James Easton	3
George Downes	1
Richard Carpenter	1
Robert Berrett	1
Richard Hyde	1
Roger Hall	6
Edward Miles	1
William Ball	1
Nicholas Bath	1
John Woodward	1
John Cowdrey	1
John Downes	2
Margaret Downes	1
Barbara Franckline	1
John Cuttler	1
Mister William Chandler	1
William Beale	3
John Beale	2
Thomas Beale	2
Thomas Joyat	1
Thomas Stockley senior	1
Thomas Stockley junior	1
hearths	56

Fol. 86r(ii)

Hearths not chargeable

John Downton	1
Ursula Phillipps	1
Robert Clerke	1
William Cowdrey	1
Hugh Collins	1
Ellen Cowdrey	1
Francis Harding	1
Alice Goodale	1
hearths	8

450. APPLESHAW[1]

Hearths chargeable

George Rumbold junior	2
Thomas Meare	1
John Gale senior	2
John Ivye	2
George Faye	2
George Rumbold	1
William Rumbold	2
Nicholas Skeate	3
Lancelot Browne	1
Edmund Morrell	1
Edward Browne	1
Edward Blackmore	1
William Ward	1
Widow Isron	1
Richard Crowch	1
James Hellier	1
hearths	23

Hearths not chargeable

Thomas Powell senior	1
Thomas Powell junior	1
Widow Allen	1
William Warde	1
William Washbeard	1
John Skeate	1
Richard Crowch	2
Thomas Goyat	2
Widow Goyat	1
John Hunt	1
Edward Addams	1
Widow Crowch	1
William Elton	1

450. APPLESHAW—*cont'd.*

William Jowles	1
Thomas Rumsey	1
John Annett	1
Widow Cole	1
Ludd Biggs	1
Robert Stulby	1
Thomas Pewsey	1
William Morrell	1
Richard Morrell	1
Edward Addams	1
William Gasthall	1
John Crowch	1
Jasper Smith	1
Thomas Dummer	1
Richard Dummer	1
Edward Williams	1
Philip Allen	1
Elizabeth Heyter	1
Edward Addams junior	1
John Hyde	1
Widow Crowch	2
hearths	37

1. Appleshire

Fol. 86v(i)

451. SOUTH TIDWORTH AND SARSON[1]

Hearths chargeable

Mister Smith	21
Mister Floyde	4
John Wheeler	4
Nathaniel Cole	1
Henry Cole	2
Richard Cole	2
Thomas Head	2
Mary Cole	1
Mister Duke	9
John Crocker	2
Robert Downes senior	1
Robert Downes junior	1
John Downes	1
Widow Rawlins	2
Widow Parrick	2
William Skeat	2
Richard Appery	1
Richard Brighte	3
Mister Sherly	4
William Head	2
Roger Carde	2
Edward Dewey	1
Richard Lanckfell	1
Richard King	1
hearths	73

Hearths not chargeable

Robert Pipper	1
Robert Drake	1
John Stockley	1
Margery Batt	1
Robert Pascall	1
William Pascall	1
Richard Missa	1
Thomas Missa	1
Ann Gearle	1
Robert Lawrence	1
Henry Humber	1
hearths	11

1. Tidworth and Sarson

452. QUARLEY[1]

Hearths chargeable

John Pittman esquire	7
Mistress Joan Pittman	2
William Eatwell rector	4
Alexander Symons	2
Christopher Gale	1
Edward Pittman	1
Gilbert Pittman	2
Robert Birte	1
Ann Pinnell	1
Edward Yalden	1
Robert Mundy	1
Richard Mundy	1
Hugh Pittman	1
William Towler	1
Thomas Harris	1
William Mundy	1
hearths	28

Hearths not chargeable

Richard Pinnell	1
Joan Brunsden	1
hearths	2

1. Quarly

Fol. 86v(ii)

453. GRATELEY[1]

Hearths chargeable

Philip Baker vicar	3
Mister Legg	3
Mistress Pittman	3
Henry Spreadborough	3
John Skeate	3
William Hopkins	2
Henry Skeate	2
John Gaynes	2
William Rumbold	2
Richard Goddard	2
Widow Chapman	1
John Edwards	1
Tristram Skeate	1
Magdalen Skeate	1
Widow Goddard	1
Alice Skeate	1
John Baker	1
Richard Kent	1
hearths	33

Hearths not chargeable

John Kent	1
John Reynolds	1
Edward Norrice	1
Mary Kimber	1
Dorothy Kimber	1
Robert Payne	1
hearths	6

1. Grately

454. KIMPTON

Hearths chargeable

Mister Calloway	11
Mister Hobbs	6
William Hopkins	1
Edward Gale senior	1
Widow Goodale	1
Robert Barker	2
Edward Gale junior	1
Widow Hopkins	2
Mister Wheeler	9
John Batt	2
Widow Noyes	2
Edward Hunt	1
Christopher Fleetwood	6
Nicholas Millett	2
Thomas Grayly	1
Thomas Gale	2
John Gale	2
Widow Annetts	2
William Hopkins	1
hearths	55

Hearths not chargeable

Richard Bullpitt	1
Widow Vedinge	1
Widow Head	1
Robert Matton	1
Silas Tyball	1
Ralph Bishopp	1
Richard Banston	1
John Banston	1
William Cooper	1
Thomas Kent	1
William Shorier	1
hearths	11

Fol. 87r(i)

455. MONXTON

Hearths chargeable

Mister Edward Styles & Anthony Gossemer	10
Mister Hugh Reade	5
Richard Waldron	1
Widow Baldwin	1
Henry Skeate	1
Richard Baldwin	9
Robert Castleman	1
Richard Rawlings	2
George Baldwin	1
Richard Hurst	1
Richard Whale	1
William Jacob	1

455. MONXTON—*cont'd.*

Richard King	3
Jerome Hayes	1
Edward Noyes	3
Thomas Whale	2
John Althrage	5
Syndens Goddard	1
hearths	49

Hearths not chargeable

William Mundy	2
William Dod	1
William Redford	1
William Hyde	1
Widow Swifte	1
Widow Gardner	1
Widow Andrewes	1
Widow Heyes	1
Widow Brexton	1
Adam Baldwin	1
John Redford	1
Robert Cooke	1
Henry Waldron	2
John Goddard	1
Widow Rawlings	1
hearths	17

The number of hearths chargeable in the hundred of Andover Extra[1]	680
Not chargeable	228

1. Andever extra

THORNGATE HUNDRED[1]

456. OVER WALLOP[2]

Hearths chargeable

Mister Cole & Edward Complin	10
John Kent of Tongham[3]	3
William Burges	2
William Summer	1
John Smith	1
David Osgood	1
Richard Osgood	2
James Gearle	1
Richard Kent	4
Alexander Faithfull	2
Thomas Pile	3
Mister Bennett	2
Edward Hattett	3
Henry Pragnell	1
David Aldredge	1
John Batt	1
Edward Cooper	4
Nicholas Shepherd	1
John Purdue	3
John Palmer	2
John Kent	2
William Bayly	1
Widow Whither	1
John Asher	1
John Hyde	1
Richard Freemantle	2
Peter Purchis	1
John Holloway	4
Robert Pile	3
Widow Tombs	1
John Pile	1

Fol. 87r(ii)

Thomas Kent	2
Edward Upden	1
Mister Merriott	1
Richard Atneave	2[a]
Robert Whitcher	1
John Whitcher	2
Edward Pickernell	1
John Drake	2
Captain Pile	6
Mister Symmes	10
Alexander Drake	1
John Pile	1
Henry Asher	1
William Bundy	1
George Browne	1
John Cantlett	1
hearths	100

Hearths not chargeable

John Bundy	1
John Gearle	1
John Whitcher	1

Thomas Kent	1
Richard Ivye	1
Widow Whitcher	1
John Baily	1
Widow Harding	1
Alexander Walter	1
Widow Wallis	1
John Bundy	1
Peter Osgood	1
Richard Bilston	1
William Kinge	1
Ellen Kinge	1
Richard Parrock	1
Widow Drew	1
Widow Stronge	1
Robert Parmon	1
Widow Senex	1
Lancelot Heyward	1
Robert Nayle	1
hearths	22

(a) 1 deduct
1. Thornegate Hundred
2. Upper Wallopp
3. Thongham

457. NETHER WALLOP[1]

Hearths chargeable

The Lord Henry Powlett	11[(a)]
The Lord Henry Powlett	8
Richard Kent	5[(b)]
Mister Dowling rector	3[(a)]
Alexander Faithfull	5[(c)]
Widow Lyewood	1
John Pointer	2
Thomas Poynter	1
Christopher Batt	1
Thomas Lywood	1
James Purdue	1
Hugh Dennett	1
Hugh Lyewood	1
Simon Asher	1
John Faithfull	2
Edmund Gearle	1
Nicholas Wonson	1
William Ventham	1
Joseph Saunders	2
Widow Thomas	1
Robert Skeane	1
Robert Pressey	1
Josiah Wickham	1
Stephen Leach	6
Samuel Collins	2
David Mills	1
John Dennett senior	1
Hugh Chitty	1
William Blackman	1

Fol. 87v(i)

Richard Asher	1
Richard Lyewood	1
Richard Dennett	1
Thomas Goddard	1
William Cooper	1
John Legg	2
Mister Smith	6
Mister Richard Goore	2
Mister Robert Pile	5
Thomas Gearle	1
William Allen	1
John Chitty	1
John Kent	1
John Burrett	1
Jonathan Chitty	1
Richard Saunders	1
hearths	92

(a) 2 down
(b) 1 overcharged
(c) 1 down
1. Nether Wallopp

458. HEARTHS IN BUCKLAND[1]

Hearths chargeable

Thomas Cox	6
James Griste	1
John Jerome	2
Thomas Dennett	2
Widow Gerrat	1[(a)]
hearths	12

Hearths not chargeable

Thomas Longman	1
Matthew Austen	1

458. HEARTHS IN BUCKLAND *—cont'd.*

John Leywood 1
William Weight 1
Andrew Blatch 1
William Longman 1
John Dennett 1
Philip Towton 1
Richard Mills 1
Alexander Chitty 1
Richard Burrett 1
David Hearth senior 1
Austin Mondy 1
Robert Welloway 1
John Spencer 1
Robert Noyes 1
Richard Kent 1
John Welloway 1
Thomas Dennett 1
Richard Towton 1
Edward Garrett 1
George Chitty 1
Thomas Leywood senior 1
Richard Howard senior 1
Richard Howard junior 1
William Stone 1
George Pile 1
Thomas Leywood 1
hearths 29

(a) 1 overcharged
1. **Hearths in** Bucklands

459. MIDDLE WALLOP[1]

Hearths chargeable

Mister Sherfeild 6
Richard Westbery 6[(a)]
John Heyward 1
Richard Crawly 1
John Drake 1
Richard Hurst 2
Alexander Hurst 1
Hugh Holloway 4
Widow Head 1
Nicholas Faithfull 3[(b)]
Nicholas Hatchett 1
Alexander Faithfull 4

Fol. 87v(ii)

Nicholas Gearle 1
Mister Thomas 4
Widow Kent 1
William Hatchett 1
John Leach 1
John Batt 1
William Burges 1[(c)]
Widow Kent 1
Robert Pressey 1
Edward Complin 1
Alexander Aneave 1
John Gearle 1
John Purdue 1
hearths 47

Hearths not chargeable

John Chitty 1
Widow Heyward 1
John Holmes 1
George Hatchett 1
Philip Kent 1
John Beacham 1
Widow Perrin 1
John Marsh 1
John Atneave 1
William Atneave 1
hearths 10

(a) 1 deduct
(b) 3 overcharged
(c) 2 deduct
1. Middle Wallopp

460. SHIPTON AND SNODDINGTON[1]

Hearths chargeable

Mister Alexander Goddard 3
James Woodward 4
John Harding 4
Richard Sellwood senior 3
Thomas Gale 5
John Bower 2

Henry Nayler	2
Richard Ivy	1
William Osgood	1
John Ivy	1
Richard Gilbert junior	2
Widow Spencer	1
Thomas Kent	1
John Mathew	1
Widow Gilbert & Thomas Gilbert	3
Anthony Harding	1
Richard Sellwood junior	1
Henry Nayler	2
John Spencer	1
Peter Hobbs	1
hearths	40

Hearths not chargeable

Peter Kent	1
Arthur Bird	1
John Aldridg	1
Stephen Bamon	1
Thomas Bower	1
Widow Hobbs	1
Widow Noyes	1
Ferdinand Noyes	1
Richard Thorne	1
Roger Knight	1
Widow Wheeler	1
John Reves	1
John Gilbert	1
Thomas Bundey	1
hearths	14

1. Shipton and Snoringeton

Fol. 88r(i)

461. EAST DEAN[1]

Hearths chargeable

Henry Whithead esquire	8
Mister Richard Ashley	5
William Row	3
Alexander Thomas	1(a)
Widow Fox	3
Edward Hinchman	1(b)
Widow Grantham	1
Widow Thistlewayt	2
Widow Lambe	1
George Fox junior	2
Robert Jefford	1
Robert Bacon	1
Robert Browne	1
George Langridg	1
Mark Bethridg	2(c)
Thomas Gray	1
Edward Gray	1
James Spragg	2
Widow Snow	2(a)
Edward Spragg	4
Richard Loaght	2
John Moxom	1
Robert Terry	1
hearths	47

Hearths not chargeable

Henry Pinnock	1
Robert Mondy	1
Robert Mondy	2
Widow Earland	1
Francis Rogers	1
Widow Carter	1
Thomas Oasteler	1
Richard Canterton	1
Thomas Southwell	1
Robert Shaffling	1
John Roe	1
Robert Talmage	2
Roger Southwell	1
hearths	15

(a) 1 deduct
(b) 2 overcharged
(c) 1 overcharged
1. Easte Deane

462. LOCKERLEY

Hearths chargeable

Doctor Barlowe	12
Mister Francklyn	4
Mister Thistlethwaite	7
Mistress Hurst & Mister Clifford	4
Thomas Lane	5

462. LOCKERLEY—*cont'd.*

Mabel Bennett widow 1(a)
Mister Gifford 4
John Martin 4
Richard Wingham 2
Edward Spragge 2
Thomas Collins 2
Thomas & Richard Rose 2
William Younge 1
William Mersh 3
William Baldwyn 2(a)
George Pragnell 2
Widow Skilton 1
Nicholas Mathew 1
John Cottshall 1
Edward Daingerfeild 1
Mark Betteridge 1
Doctor Dobbs 1
John Ventham 2
Richard Rose 1
Richard Hatcher 1
John Blake 1
Thomas Mersh 1
Richard Mersh 1(b)
Thomas Hatcher 1
Nicholas Cowse 1
Mister Brace 6
Austin Russen 1
William Wheable 2
Widow Baldwin 1
hearths 82

Hearths not chargeable

William Woodford 1
William Pearce 1
Thomas Pearce senior 1
Robert Pike 1
Thomas Pike 1
Tristram Mundey 1
[ ] Brooker 1

Fol. 88r(ii)

Richard Wingham 2
Nicholas Hancock 1
William Stock 1
Nicholas Gynes senior 1
Nicholas Gynes junior 1
Widow Woodford 1
John Arthur 1
John Andrews 1
Margaret Godden 1
Stephen Arthor 1
Richard Major 1
Widow Godden 1
John Bedford 1
Ann Bedford 1
Ralph Tubb 1
Alexander Newman 1
Andrew Blake 1
Joan Lynhm 1
John Perrier 1
John Pragnell 1
Widow Cleeter 1
Widow Martyne 1
Henry Mersh 1
Elizabeth Finch 1
Nicholas Wilkins 1
hearths 33

(a) 1 overcharged
(b) 1 down

463. CADNAM

Hearths chargeable

Richard Eken 2(a)
Widow Holladay 3
John Eken 1(a)
Maurice New 1
William Burgis 1
William Burgis senior 1
Richard Waterman 2
Barnaby Marshall 1
John Gray 1
Stephen Newlands 3(a)
Robert Waterman 1
Widow Waterman 1
William Seward 1
John Greene 1
Thomas Kinge 1
hearths 21

(a) 1 down

464. WIGLEY

Hearths chargeable

Matthew Webber	3
Richard Roe	3
George Jackman	3
Richard Ireland	3
Widow Waldron	3
William Palmer	1
Edmund Waldron	1
Richard Palmer	1
John Iremonger	1
John Paynter	1
Nicholas Warrick	1
Thomas Warrick	1
Widow Denman	1
Thomas Iremonger	1
Robert Jones	1
Paul Combs	1
John White	1
John Meature	1
Richard Shepherd	1
Widow Cooper	1
hearths	30

Hearths not chargeable

John Jones	1
Richard Groane	1
Christopher Cosier	1
hearths	3

Fol. 88v(i)

465. SHERFIELD ENGLISH[1]

Hearths chargeable

Mister William Titchborne	9
Francis Warner rector	3
Robert Gifford	3
Roger Pope	3
Edward Barber	2
Joan Ventham widow	1
William Sharpe	1
John Saunders	1
William Winsor	1
George Pope	2
John Long	1
Widow Moreing	3
Arthur Pope	3
Isaac Pope	3
Widow Brice	1
John Ventham	4
Nicholas Wickham	1
Edward Baugh	1
Richard Kelsey	1
William Reves	1
John Moreing	1
Richard Harris	1
Widow Harris	1
John Skilton	1
George Brice	2
William Morrice	3
hearths	54

Hearths not chargeable

Edward Perrier	1
Robert Bell	1
Richard Roude	1
Edward Roude	1
Edward Perrier junior	1
William Ventham	1
Roger Bell	1
Widow Bell	1
John Pritchett	1
Widow Gaile	1
Widow Wisham	1
Richard Bridges	1
Arthur Littlefeild	1
Widow Roude	1
Edward Arthor	1
Thomas Grunsell	1
Widow Petty	1
Thomas Rogers	2
hearths	19

1. Sherfeild English

466. EMBLEY[1]

Hearths chargeable

Mister Francis Ashley	3
Richard Hoare	2
Christopher Vine	2
Robert Annetts	3
John Anthony	1
Richard Row	1

466. EMBLEY—*cont'd.*

Widow Slanden	1
William Winsor	1
Richard Palmer	1
Widow Browne	1
William Godden	1
Richard Thomas	1
hearths	18

Hearths not chargeable

Andrew Patinton	1
John Wheatly	2
Thomas Pollard	1
Richard Pollard	1
Arthur Sleydon	1
William Palmer	1
John Pragnell	1
Edward Anthony	1
hearths	9

1. Emley

467. PITTLEWORTH

Hearths chargeable

Mister John Kelsey	9
hearths	9

Fol. 88v(ii)

468. EAST TYTHERLEY[1]

Hearths chargeable

Mister Francis Rowle	32
George Forrest	1
Silvester Langradge	3
George Ventham	2
Alexander Whitcher	3
Richard Bonner	1
Widow Woodford	1
Alexander Linton	1
Thomas Downes	1
William Bedridge	1
George Earles	2
Edward Daingerfeild	1
Edward Daingerfeild junior	4
Christopher Dobbs	2
William Williams	2
Cuthbert Wheatland	3
William Blackford	3
Richard Bonner junior	1
George Forrest	5
Robert Ventham	1
Silvester Langradge	1
Silvester Webb	1
Nicholas Kingman	1
Elizabeth Ventham	1
hearths	74

Hearths not chargeable

John Davis	1
Widow Stent	1
John Stent	1
Walter Gootley	1
Widow Morrock	1
John Bonney	1
John Littlefeild	1
Nicholas Ventham	1
Nicholas Briant	1
Robert Cole	1
Henry Case	1
Widow Austin	1
Garrett Earles	1
John Fabine	1
hearths	14

1. Eastitherley

469. BOSSINGTON[1]

Hearths chargeable

Mister Thomas Edmunds	7
Widow Pittleworth	1
Widow Coats	2
John Maffey	2
Thomas Mersh	2
hearths	14

Hearths not chargeable

Widow Loaden	1
Charles White	1
Widow Browne	1
hearths	3

1. Bosington

470. WELLOW

Hearths chargeable

John Noyes	4
Mister Reynolds	6
Mister Byles	7
John Ashley	1
William Mikes	1
John Pragnell	2
Thomas Harris	1
Mister Aldridg	1
Thomas Coleman	1
John Aldridge	1
John Kirvil	2
Richard Hoare	1
Thomas Bennis	1
John Palmer	1
Richard Salte	1
William Pearce	1[a]
John Palmer	1
John Hellis	1
Widow Hatchett	1
hearths	35

Fol. 89r(i)

Hearths not chargeable

Widow Sanckey	1
Ralph Symes	1
John Short	1
Nicholas Noyes	1
Widow Jackman	1
Robert Beare	1
Widow Langley	1
Widow Gilbert	1
Edward Kelsey	1
William Noyes	1
hearths	10

(a) 1 overcharged

471. WEST TYTHERLEY[1]

Hearths chargeable

Henry Whithead esquire	19
William Hussey clerk	6
Robert Gifford	3
Alexander Gifford	2
Widow Hannam	1
Nathaniel Webb	1
William Ford alias Turner	1
Austin Blake	1
Thomas Hobbs	1
John Aldridge	1
Edward Roe	3
Robert Ford alias Turner	1
Widow Dowce	3
Hugh Wilkin	2
John Sponder	3
Joseph Parrick	3
Paul Leedes	1
Joan Veltum	1
Edward Damerum	4
Austin Cooper	4
Mary Dennis	1
William Best	1
Thomas Marshall	1
John Leaffe	1
Walter Thomas	3
Widow Leach	1
Widow Pragnell	1
John Pragnell	1
William Ireland	2
John Burgis	2
John Humphry	1
Widow Mersh	1
Richard Hayes	2
Thomas Tuttson	1
George Bennett	1
William Collins	2
Widow Newman	2
Mister Whithead	1
hearths	86

Hearths not chargeable

Hugh Furmage	1
William Mathew	1
William Stone	1
George Yeomans	1
John Tabbet	1
Stephen Stowe	1
Joan Bethridg	1
Widow Dowling	1
Widow Heath	1

471. WEST TYTHERLEY—*cont'd.*

Richard Carde 1
Austin Leafe 2
John Ireland 1
John Beacham 1
Elizabeth Talbot 1
Roger Noble 1
Widow Webb 1
William Newby 1
Laurence Blake 1
William Webb 1
Jane Chamingham widow 1
hearths 21

1. Westitherley

472. MOTTISFONT[1]

Hearths chargeable

William Lord Sandys 35
John Poore 3
Mister John Herring 6
Mister Richard Kent 6
Mistress Ann Cox 6(a)
William Pile 2
Roger King 4

Fol. 89r(ii)

Richard Ventham 1
Henry Peinock 4
John James 2(b)
Mistress Dorothy Canterton 4
John Mersh 2
James Bartlett 1
Doctor John Howorth 7
Richard Welling 2
John Edney 3
Richard Badden 1
Mark Crowder 2
David Briant 1
Roger Edmunds 1
John Perrier 1
Edmund Vox 1
Mister Kelsey Byles 3
Widow Edney 2(a)
John Frith 1
Thomas Bessant 1
John Woods 1
William Pile 2
James Wiltshire 2
Edward Prater 1
Henry Burton 1
The mill 1
hearths 110

Hearths not chargeable

Widow Hellier 1
John Pickernell 1
William Compton 1
John Ventham 1
Widow Edmunds 1
Henry Sharlock 1
John Harfeild 1
Reuben Cotten 1
Edward Atkines 1
Thomas Houchin 1
Thomas Poore 1
Austin Langridg 1
Richard Mason 1
Edward Ventham 1
William Atkins 1
Widow Woods 1
Silvester Betridge 1
Richard Ventham 1
Edward Woods 1
George Briant 1
William Hammon 1
Robert Wiltshire 1
Richard Crowder 1
Widow Dowce 1
Richard Pinock 1
Widow Ventham 1
Thomas Fulker 1
Edward Crowder 1
Edward Moss 1
Widow Smith 1
John Head 1
Henry Rumbold 1
Thomas Hunt 1
Widow Edmunds junior 1
Sarah Dawkins 1

Widow Pritcherd	1
Richard Sharlock	1
hearths	37

(a) 1 overcharged
(b) 1 deduct
1. Motsfont

473. BROUGHTON

Hearths chargeable

Mister Anthony Hillary	5
William Gale	5
John Mersh	3
John Abbott	1
Peter Doxell senior	3
George Savage	2
Gabriel Hack	1
Henry Thomes	1
William Doxell	1
George Savage junior	1
Henry Abbott	2
Robert Reves junior	1
William Jones	1
Huff Beedle	1
Thomas Mersh	1
Peter Doxell	1
Daniel Hayter	2
Robert Humber	1
William Pragnell	1

Fol. 89v(i)

Richard Miller	2
John Smith	4
John Thurston	2
John Pragnell	3
Joseph Benford	2
John Everidg junior	1
Edward Maphew	1
Richard Barton	4
Widow Hart	2
Widow Mersh	1
Richard Chantrell	1
Henry Turner	4
John Kelsey	2
John Holloway	14
William Leaffe	2
Nicholas Hall	2
Robert Mowdy	2
Roger Tuffing	2
Edward Reves	2
Richard Kent	1
Ambrose Cortney	2
John Reves	1
John Everidg	1
Francis Taylor	1
Mistress Flexon	3
Richard Undee	1
Edward Maphew	1
Peregrine Dawkins	1
Richard Vinson	1
John Savage	2
Robert Hawted	3
Thomas Beake	3
John Bedford	2
Richard Mersh	2
William Steele junior	1
Dorothy Mafey	1
John Clerke	1
Henry Kelsey	2[a]
Mister Rathwell	4
William Lynton	1
Richard Blatches	1
Thomas Leeds	1
John Heyter	1
Mister Barbour	1
Mister Barrow	1
John Philipps	1
The schoolhouse	5
hearths	134

Hearths not chargeable

Austin Townesend	1
Maurice Greene	1
William Townsend	1
William Hurst	1
Margaret Fish	1
John Kent	1
John Pewsey	1
Thomas Taylor	1
Widow Cooper	1
Austin Linney	1
Thomas Pecotte	1
Philip Pewsey	1
Richard Heath	1
Widow Bedford	1

473. BROUGHTON—*cont'd.*

Thomas Morgan senior	1
John Lewis	1
Widow Franklyn	1
Widow Sopp	1
Roland Fishlock	1
Thomas Morgan junior	1
Robert Undee	1
John Undee senior	1
Francis Newman	1
Leonard Newman	2
William Frowde senior	1
William Frowde junior	1
Widow Long	1
John Mundey	1
Widow Kelsey	1
John Dennis	1
Richard Bower	1
William Maphey	1
Widow Rowden	1
Richard Frowde	1
Richard Pewsey	1
Thomas Sturridg	1
Thomas Bedford	1
William Steele senior	1

Fol. 89v(ii)

Thomas Fabin	1
Widow Griste	1
William Mersh	1
Edward Dennett	1
Widow Maphew	1
Barnard Godfrey	1
Widow Fabin	1
John Cewell	1
William Hunt	1
Jerome Hunt	1
Nicholas Ventham	1
Widow Price	1
Thomas Parsons	2
Henry Maphew	2
Henry Rowden	1
Widow Taylor	1
Matthew Purdue	1
Widow Hated	1
William Burrett	1
Giles Best	1
John Smith	1
William Leaffe junior	1
Edward Lowmer	1
William Hunt	1
Jerome Hunt	1
Nicholas Ventham	1
hearths	68

The number of hearths chargeable in the hundred of Thorngate[1] 1005

Hearths not chargeable 307

(a) 1 overcharged
1. Thornegate

WHERWELL HUNDRED

474. EAST ASTON[1]

Hearths chargeable

William Farr	3
Richard Mills	1
Widow Mills	1
Thomas Cuffley	1
Thomas Silver	1
Richard Skeat	3
Robert Hardwell	1
Laurence Brownjohn	1
John Hardwell	1
Richard Sharpe	2
Edward Beele	2
Widow Lock	2
Isaac Street	2[(a)]
Edward Blake	1
Richard Morrant	1
hearths	23

Hearths not chargeable

Edward Lock	1
George Felder	1
Widow Hardyman	1
Widow Allen	1
Widow Kidgell	1
hearths	5

(a) 1 increased
1. East Ashton

475. WEST ASTON[1]

Hearths chargeable

William Hunt	4
Richard Skeate	3
John Mills	2
John Embs	1
John Morrant	1
William Barter	1
Thomas Noyes	1
Alice Buckland	2
Alice Poore	2
John Purdue	2
William Farr	1
Andrew Kent	1
Thomas Hardwell	1
hearths	22

Hearths not chargeable

Mary Farr	1
Daniel Noyes	1
John Gardner	1
Thomas Meacham	1
Ingram Holyday	1
Nicholas Collett	1
hearths	6

1. West Ashton

Fol. 90r(i)

476. MIDDLETON[1]

Hearths chargeable

Philip Isron	7
Mister Emborne	1
Mister John Marks	4
John White	2
James Beacham	1
Widow Isron	1
Adam Orchard	2
Alice Woods	1
Widow Morgan	1
Thomas Bealls	1
Widow Woods	1
Richard Talmage	1
William Mersham	1(a)
Thomas Mills	1
Robert Penton	2
John Webb	1
Widow Emery	1
William Smith	1
James Silver	1
Thomas Hardwell	2
Jonathan Waldron	1
Widow Biggs	1
Stephen Curtis	1
John Purdue	1
John Barter	4
hearths	41

Hearths not chargeable

William Lawes	1
William Martyn	1
Richard Twyne	1
Nicholas Snow	1
James Jeckhan	1
Robert Browne	1
Nicholas Greene	1
Widow Wiseman	1
John Beamon	1
William Golden	1
Adam Orchard	1
Abel Bullpit	1
hearths	12

(a) 1 down

1. Midleton

477. TUFTON

Hearths chargeable

Widow Skeate	3
Widow Winckworth	2
Stephen Wilkins	1
Thomas Hare	2
John Griffin	1
James Greene	3
Widow Waterman	3
George Beacham	3
John Skeate	1
George Browne	1
William Dix	1
The farm	2
hearths	23

Hearths not chargeable

Widow Beacham	1
John Browne	1

477. TUFTON—*cont'd.*

Richard Johnson	1
Benjamin Morrell	1
Edward Brice	1
Thomas Waterman	1
hearths	6

478. BULLINGTON

Hearths chargeable

John Silver	8
Richard Cole	1
William Wilkins	1
George Beale	1
William Kinchin	1
William Skeat	1
John Mills	1
George Cropp	2
William Tanner	1
William Rolfe senior	1
[William] B[arre]tt	1
John Harding	1
John Allen & John S[ilver]	1
William Skeate & [ ]	1
hearths	22

Fol. 90r(ii)

Hearths not chargeable

William Freeman	1
Thomas Skeate	1
Widow Rolfe	1
William Rolfe junior	1
John Humber	1
Richard Hawkins	2
Henry Batt	1
Richard Littlefeild	1
John Rolfe	1
Henry Elcock	1
John Bird	1
hearths	11

479. FORTON

Hearths chargeable

Mister Nicholas Blake	6
John Houghton	5
Mister Peter Blake	2
Mister Greene	1
Stephen Poole	2
Thomas Poore	1
John Skeate	1
Thomas Dowse	1
William Warham	1
Susan Bodicote	1
Laurence Cosens	1
Richard Gardner	2
John Rogers	1
Thomas Barnaby	2
John Parr	1
William Duke	1
hearths	29

Hearths not chargeable

John Collett	1
Widow Cannon	1
John Ball	1
Widow Fidler	1
Benjamin Portsmouth	1
John Humber	1
Henry Wheatly	1
Stephen Gardner	1
James Martyn	1
Margery Egg	1
Widow Avery	1
Thomas Foster	1
hearths	12

480. CLATFORD

Hearths chargeable

William Radford	4
William Plympton	2
Edward Withers	3
Thomas Skeate	3
Nathaniel Sutton	1
Robert Hatchett	2
Widow Spring	1
Richard Hatchett	1
Robert Poore junior	1
John Fry	1
George Whicher	2
John Hopkins	1
Robert Poore senior	1

Mister Browne 2
William Cole 2
Joan Rosbludd 1
hearths 27

Hearths not chargeable

Margaret Diaper 1
John Plympton 1
Widow Russell 1
William Plympton 1
William Bucke 1
William Hopkins 2
Widow Plympton 1
Thomas Skeate 2
Sarah Thurman 1
Widow Shath 1
Widow Poore 1
Thomas Cox 1
George Dowlan 1
Widow Hopkins 1
hearths 16

Fol. 90v(i)

481. GOODWORTH

Hearths chargeable

Robert Dowlan 4
Mister Bentall vicar 4
Benjamin Withers 2
Henry Dowling 1
John Nurse 1
Widow Tremone[1] 1
Widow Sutton 1
John Nurse 1
Mister Southwoods 4[(a)]
hearths 15

Hearths not chargeable

Roger Sutton 1
James Twine 1
Widow Strong 1
John Blanchett 1
James Fuller 1
John Baverstock 1
Widow Smith 1
William Batt 1
William Monck 1
Widow Rutter 1
John Daunce 1
Richard Hattchett 1
Mister South 2
John Hopkins 1
Thomas Fuller 1
Henry Dowlan 1
Widow Twine 1
hearths 19

(a) taken down
1. *Altered from* Tremore

482. LITTLE ANN

Hearths chargeable

Griffin Rowse 6
John Kidgell 3
Widow Fuller 3
Abraham More 1
Thomas Mowdy 2
hearths 14

Hearths not chargeable

William Noyes 1
Thomas Addams 1
William Ballard 1
Nicholas Snooks 1
Roger Sutton 1
hearths 5

483. WHERWELL

Hearths chargeable

The Lord Delawarr 28
Mister Osey 5
Robert Kelsey 1
Mister Dowling 2
The vicarage 5
The inn 5
John Dalby 1
John Drinkewine 1
Widow Herring 1
Widow Sutton 2
John Poticary 2
Robert Henbrey 1
Widow Hopkins 4
Anthony Evans 2
John Houghton 2
John Houghton more 14

483. WHERWELL—*cont'd.*

John Upton	2
James Fuller	1
William Russell	4
Richard Cram	1
Richard Skeate	5
John Hack	2
Thomas [K]idgell	1
[ ] Wither	4
[Toby] Fuller	1
John Pent[on]	1
[William] Jones	3
John Scottshall	1
[Mister] [ ]tall	3
Widow [Hammon]	1
John [Bootey]	1

Fol. 90v(ii)

The mill	2
The widow Snow	1
Cottingworth House	3
Stephen Sutton	3
Richard Rawlins	13
hearths	129

Hearths not chargeable

Robert West	1
Widow Collett	1
Widow Russell	1
Christian Bozwell	1
Widow Barter	1
Thomas Goddard	1
Richard Dowlan	1
Richard Saings	1
Thomas Holdway	1
Richard Hopkins & John Bent	2
Thomas Hopkins	1
John Saings senior	2
John Saings	1
Richard Hopgood	2
William Leach	1
Stephen Buckle	1
Widow Fisher	2
Widow Snossell & William Bamon	2
Widow Smith	2
Henry Panter	1
Widow Fleetwood	1
Widow Batt	1
Widow Dench	2
John Mills	1
Widow Evens	1
Edmund Morton	1
Widow Shaflin	1
John Evens	1
Richard Kent	1
George Mathew	1
Nicholas Kent	1
William Henbery	1
Edmund Hooper	1
Widow May	1
Thomas Maywether	2
Thomas Penton	1
George Ember	1
Richard Seale	1
William Garner	2
William & Stephen Berrett	2
Widow Skeat	2
George Fuller	2
James Leach	2
hearths	56

The number of hearths chargeable in the hundred of Wherwell is 345

Hearths not chargeable 147

BARTON STACEY HUNDRED[1]

484. HEADBOURNE WORTHY

Hearths chargeable

Robert Fishwick rector	6
Nicholas Winckworth	3
Richard Godden	5
William Lock	1
Richard White	2
Mary Bargent	1
Alice Bargent	1
Widow Page	2
John Ray	1
William Smith	1

Richard Winckworth 3
Henry Buttler 1
Robert Wake 1
Jonas Page 3
Thomas Mills 3[(a)]
Edward Fyfeild 2
Richard Winckworth 1
Widow Tolefry 1
Andrew Webb 1
hearths 39

Fol. 91r(i)

Hearths not chargeable

John Jeffery 1
Richard Wake 1
Widow Shorling 1
William Harfell 1
John Griffin 1
Widow Webb 1
John Street 1
Nicholas Tolefrey 1
hearths 8

(a) 1 decreased
1. Bartonstacy Hundred

485. PRIORS DEAN[1]

Hearths chargeable

Sir Henry Titchborne 10
John Holloway 6
Mistress Beale widow 6
John Newland 6
Thomas Compton 5
William Caught 3
Maximilian Compton 3
Widow Browman 3
Widow Grace 2
Widow Pescod 2
John Foster 1
hearths 47

Hearths not chargeable

Widow Foster 2
Widow Hamman 1
Thomas Bettsworth 1
Thomas Lillywhite 1
Widow Woodison 1
Thomas Dorey 1
Widow Rogers 2
William Dove 1
John Collins 2
William Cook 2
hearths 14

1. Priors Deane

486. COLEMORE

Hearths chargeable

Thomas Corps 3
Mister Anthony Palmer 9
Mister Pocock 6
Thomas Corps 5
William Read 4
John Weene 3
Henry Renwood 3
Jerome Hersey 2
John Hersey 1
Richard Weene 1
hearths 34

Hearths not chargeable

James Garrett 1
hearths 1

487. BARTON STACEY[1]

Hearths chargeable

Francis Romboll 10
Esquire Payne for Morgans 3
Francis Romboll 1
Widow Cox 3
Thomas Durnford 1
Robert Spencer 2
Widow Wilkin 1
John Spencer 6
John Benham 4

Fol. 91r(ii)

Widow Browne 1
John Patience 1
James Knight 2
Thomas Shaw 1
Nicholas Skeate 2
Michael Nicholas 5
John Parr 1
John Browne 1

487. BARTON STACEY—*cont'd.*

Thomas Smith	3
John Leach	2
Nicholas Elliott	3
Widow Smith	1
George Cooper	1
Thomas Dudman	1
William Humber	1
Thomas Pickering	4
John Taylor	1
Thomas Perce	3
hearths	65

Hearths not chargeable

Widow North	1
Robert Wimboll	1
John Beake	1
John Holloway	1
Widow Chittick	1
Thomas Mowle	1
William Leach	1
Richard Eelles	1
Widow Spencer	1
John Beake	1
Thomas Foster	1
Widow Hooper	1
John Wake	1
John Upsdale	1
Widow Hills	1
James Hatchett	1
Simon Elliott	1
John Browne	1
William Hack	1
Richard Martyne	1
John Lellaby	1
hearths	21

1. Bartonstacy

488. SUTTON SCOTNEY

Hearths chargeable

Richard Fyfeild	10
Mister John Lardner	14
Humphrey Heath	2
William Silver	4
Richard Eedes	6
Edward Reynolds	4
John Asher	5
Thomas Bonney	2
William Harding	2
Widow Wheatly	1
Robert Cropp	1
John Brownjohn	1
John Hedach	1
George Gaver	1[a]
John Harding	1
Richard Beech	1
Richard Long	1[a]
Richard Jeffery	1
William Bennett	1
William North	1
John Beech	1
Mister William Greene	13[a]
hearths	74

Fol. 91v(i)

Hearths not chargeable

William Constantine	1
Thomas Wells	1
Thomas Tarrant	1
John Snellor	1
Thomas Millett	1
Widow Permine	1
Henry Cole	1
Widow Coopp[1]	1
William Dufsen[2]	1
Jerome Weight	1
Widow Hall	1
hearths	11

(a) 1 increased
1. *Altered from* Cropp
2. *Altered from* Duffen

489. KINGS WORTHY

Hearths chargeable

Philip Stone	3
Christopher Harding	2
John Poole	1
Thomas Frampton	1
Richard Voakes senior	1
Richard Voakes junior	1
Simon Symonds	1
Cornelius Webb	2
John Earles senior	6

George Fremantle 2
Ralph Orpington 1
Widow Pinck 1
Nicholas Clarke 1
Catherine Frayne 1
hearths 23

Hearths not chargeable
John Hobbs 1
John Harding 1
Thomas Carver 2
William Bushell 1
Widow Poole 1
Thomas Harding 1
John Stacy 1
Nicholas Langford 1
hearths 9

490. PAMBER

Hearths chargeable
Samuel Wheate 4
Francis Benwell 5
William Omedee 8
Robert Rice 4
Edward Pattee 3
Christopher Arnold 1
Nicholas Travis 3[(a)]
John Peade 1
Richard Littlefeild 1
Thomas Watts 3[(b)]
Thomas Sawcer 2
Thomas Coughter 1
Robert Read 2
William Heythorne 2
John Lane 3
Nicholas Jennings 3
James Raynscroft 2
Humphrey Biccas 2
Thomas Gosling 3
Stephen Smith 1
James Pinck 1
hearths 55

Fol. 91v(ii)

Hearths not chargeable
Ralph Beane 1
George Englefeild 1
Simon Englefeild 1
Widow Wimbleton 1
Anthony Symson 1
John Barber 1
John Paise 1
John Knight 1
Austin Browne 1
Richard Sympson 1
Thomas Wilshire 1
John Sandam 1
Anthony Mundy 1
John Wimbleton 1
Thomas Trimmer 1
William Taplin 1
Robert Richards 1
Robert South 1
John Diblin 1
William Silver 1
Widow Taplin 1
Francis Turner 1
John Travis 1
John Cleve 1
Polixine Baker 1
James Scott 1
Thomas Trimmer 1
hearths 27

(a) 1 increased
(b) 1 overcharged

491. INHURST AND HAM

Hearths chargeable
Mister Peter Hyde 4
Edward Hullpook 2
Walter Buttler 2
John Hullpook 3
George Hunt 2
George White 2
Thomas Weight 1
John Carter 1
Richard Deane 1
John Deane senior 2
hearths 20

Hearths not chargeable
Hugh Deane 1
Widow Symons 1

491. INHURST AND HAM —*cont'd.*

John Carter senior	1
Edward Cooke	1
Henry Edwards	1
Ingram May	1
Joan Bryter	1
John Deane junior	1
Widow Lymeger	1
Widow Forde	1
Laurence Whistler	1
hearths	11

492. NEWTON STACEY[1]

Hearths chargeable

Thomas Cozens	7
Thomas Wickham	4
Widow Herring	3
Alexander Allen	3
John Wheatland	2
William Herring	1[(a)]
Richard Cannons	1
William Correll	1
Henry Skeene	1
Robert Nash	1
hearths	24

Fol. 92r(i)

Hearths not chargeable

Robert Lewis	1
Bridget Brixton	1
John Brixton	1
hearths	3

The number of hearths chargeable in the hundred of Barton Stacey[2] is	384
Hearths not chargeable	105

(a) 1 down
1. Newton Stacy
2. Barton Stacy

KINGS SOMBORNE[1] HUNDRED

493. KINGS SOMBORNE[1]

Hearths chargeable

Francis Rivett esquire	16
Edward Moreing	5
Oliver St John esquire	3
Barnard Barlow	10
William Rowde	1
Henry Thornton	1
Thomas Doleman	1
John Hall	1
Robert Thorneton	2
George Street	1
Edward Baily	1
Robert Smith	1
Richard Futcher	1
Alexander Langridge	1
John Davie	1
Richard Wheable	1
John Buxie	1
John Russell	1
Robert Primier	1
Thomas Briant	1
William Langfeild	1
Henry Davie	1
Edward Greene	3
Widow Coatch	1
James Tarrant	2
Vitall Olding	1
Thomas Upsdall	1
John Barling	2
Francis Buxie	1
Richard Snow	1
John Dumper	1
Robert Mundey	1
Edward Maphew	1
Thomas Cheeke	1
Widow Scarlett	1
John Mundey	1
John Austen	1
Thomas Poore	1
John Stubbs	1
Widow Griffin	1
John Complin	8
hearths	88

Hearths not chargeable

William Mundey	1
Widow Daunce	1
Widow North	1
Widow Brewton	1
John Cheeke	1

John Cooper	1
Widow Clin	2
John Roberts	1
Thomas Eedes senior	1
William Bold	1
John Payne	1
Thomas Hasker	1
Widow Langford	1
Richard Buxey	1
Robert Woodley	1
Henry Eedes	1
Robert Griffin	1
Susan Philipps	1
Widow Goddard	1
Richard Hellier	1
Michael Russell	1
Widow Hobbs	1
Austin Stone	1

Fol. 92r(ii)

William Davice	1
John Fidler	1
Richard Dozwell	1
Walter Grunsell	1
Widow Lovell	1
Widow Hobbs	1
Widow Legg	1
Thomas Davice	1
George Vinson	1
Timothy Cornish	1
Guy Stirte	1
William Austen	1
Edward Edwards	1
Philip Jones	1
David Nutter	1
Margery Primier	1
Thomas Nutter	1
Widow Flight	1
Widow Hawkins	1
Dorothy Buxey	1
Joan Stubb	1
Robert Holland	1
Thomas Eedes junior	1
Hugh Goddard	1
Joseph Barber	1
Catherine Humber	1
hearths	50

1. Kingsomborne

494. STOCKBRIDGE

Hearths chargeable

Nicholas Pyle	3
Richard Hall	8
Henry Clerke	6
Nicholas Windover	5
John Goddard	4
William Marsh	1
John Hall	1
Widow Mowdy	1
Giles Wallington	1
Mister Lyddiard	15
Thomas Snow	1
William Reeves	1
Henry Grossmith	1
Mister Robert Joyce	1
Henry Hall	6
Nicholas Pyle	4
John Gearle	2
Robert Smith	3
Daniel Tongs	1
Nicholas Dixon	4
hearths	69

Hearths not chargeable

William Poore	1
Humphrey Miller	1
Robert Wiggs	1
Nicholas Packs	1
Peter Hall	1
Thomas Blatch	1
William Goblin	1
Goody Farmer	1
James Castly	1
Nicholas Backen	1
Thomas Piboll	1
Richard Munges	1
Widow Franklyn	1
John Hammon	1
Henry Holland	1
Thomas Sutton	1

494. STOCKBRIDGE—*cont'd.*

Edward White	1
William Swift	1
John Tanner	1
Widow Tonges	1
Richard Hopkins	1
Thomas Bearne	1
Richard Gearne	1
Philip Townsend	1
John Frye	1
John Woodly	1
Widow Woodly	1
Robert Munges	1
Fol. 92v(i)	
Walter Bell	1
Richard White	1
William Smith	1
Widow Rainger	1
Widow Perse	1
Ann Hase	1
John Winsor	1
hearths	35

495. FARLEY CHAMBERLAYNE[1]

Hearths chargeable

Oliver St John esquire	13
Mister West	4
Widow Hockley	3
Humphrey Longland	3
Joseph Pyle	2
Nicholas Smith	1
John Pyle	3
Richard Churcher	1[(a)]
hearths	30

Hearths not chargeable

Mark Bull	1
Robert Nutcher	1
Thomas Smith	1
Robert Noyes	2
Richard Churcher junior	1
hearths	6

(a) 1 increased
1. Farly Chamberlaine

496. ASHLEY

Hearths chargeable

Mister Chalkhill	4
William Lynne	7
Ursula Lynne	1
Robert Goater senior	1[(a)]
John Goater	1
Robert Goater junior	1
John Cortney	1
hearths	16

Hearths not chargeable

Richard Godden	1
Samuel Cooke	1
Widow White	1
John Combs	1
John Lynne	1
Richard White	1
hearths	6

(a) 1 overcharged

497. LECKFORD ABBOTTS

Hearths chargeable

George Cox	5
William Poore	1
Thomas Smith	1
Richard Wickham	2
William Kerby	1
William Gale	1
Widow Goddard	1
Philip Dowling	1
William Poore	2
William Sutton	1
George Hatchett	1
William Sponder	2
William Heath	1
Richard Bampton	5
William Kirby	1
Joan Paynter	3
Richard Roberts	1
hearths	30

Hearths not chargeable

John King	1
Thomas Syms	1
hearths	[2]

Fol. 92v(ii)

498. LECKFORD ABBESS[1]

Hearths chargeable

Mister Note	4
Richard Smith	4
Widow Smith	3[(a)]
John Smith	1
Henry Baily	1
James New	1
James Mitchener	2
Edward Dowling	1
hearths	17

Hearths not chargeable

William Tolefry	1
Thomas Ventham	1
John Tredgall	1
Widow Tolefrey	1
Thomas Dolle	1
William Andrews	1
Henry Cooke	1
Widow Hooker	1
Stephen Emance	1
Joseph Orchard	1
Widow Orchard	1
Robert Tolefrey	1
Richard Davie	1
William Bunning	1
Thomas Webb	1
hearths	15

(a) 1 deduct

1. Leckford Abbeesse

499. UP SOMBORNE[1]

Hearths chargeable

Widow Sutton	9
John Hasker	2
Walter Arthur	1
Thomas Shepherd	1
John Streape	1
William Fryer	1
George Russell	1
Joan Philipps	1
William Shepherd	1
hearths	18

Hearths not chargeable

Widow Coles	1
Widow Lynne	1
Thomas Allen	2
Widow Shepherd	1
William Shepherd senior	1
William Shepherd	1
Richard Guyett	1
Richard Mundey	1
hearths	9

1. Upp Somborne

500. LITTLE SOMBORNE

Hearths chargeable

Mister Wells	5
John Carde	1
Widow Thorngate	1
George Mundey	1
Widow Mundey	2
Robert Mundey	2
John Godden	3
hearths	15

Hearths not chargeable

Richard Weight	1
William Taylor	1
Thomas Hipper	1
Widow Mundey	1
Walter Blake	1
hearths	5

Fol. 93r(i)

501. BROOK STUBHIDE AND ELDON[1]

Hearths chargeable

Mister Terry	5
William Turman	4[(a)]
Walter Sutton	6
Arthur Silver	12
Mister Thomas Kelsey	5
Edward Walter	1
hearths	33

Hearths not chargeable

Widow Heyes	1
Widow Guillett	1

501. BROOK STUBHIDE AND ELDON—*cont'd.*

Robert Rowe	1
John Dale	1
Silvester Woodstone	1
Henry Burnett	1
Thomas Rumboll	1
Richard Caute	1
Henry Beamord	1
Edward Crook	1
Widow Lovelett	1
Richard Groave	1
Widow Hewes	2
hearths	14

(a) 1 deduct
1. Brooke Stubhide & Elden

502. NORTH HOUGHTON

Hearths chargeable

William Holmbs	12
John Pittleworth	6
John Thomas	5
Daniel Crowder	1
Thomas Swift	1
Lyne Edmonds	2
hearths	27

Hearths not chargeable

William Mason	1
John Kent	1
John Hunt	1
Ralph Garey	1
Cecilia Garrett widow	1
hearths	5

503. LONGSTOCK[1]

Hearths chargeable

Mister Barrett vicar	4
Mister Richard Kent	5
Farmer Herring	4
William Francis	5
Philip Dowling	2
Widow Leach	3
Nicholas Covey	1
John Vince	1
Robert Goddard	1
Charles Grunsell	1
William Prince	3
William Hopkins	1
Gabriel Floyd	1
William Grunsell	1
Widow Godden	2
William Grunsell junior	1
John Hewes	2
Richard Michinor	1
John Lashley	1
George Franklyn	2
Fol. 93r(ii)	
John Hopkins	1
Theophilus Cole	1
Richard Evance	1
Edward Beare	1
Widow Smith	1
Roger Cole	1
James Edmunds	2(a)
John Foster	1
Oliver Goddard	4
Richard Futcher	1
Alexander Whiture	1
Richard Moulton	1
Thomas Gayger	1
hearths	59

Hearths not chargeable

Alexander Poore	1
Adam Spratt	1
William Greene	1
William Domyny	1
Widow Leach	1
William Henbrey	2
John Beare	1
Thomas Orchard	1
Gabriel Floyd	2
Michael Prince	1
John Broadway	1
Walter Walter	1
Edward Williams	1
William Himbery	1
Christopher Gale	1
Widow Spratt	1
Widow Gillam	1
Widow Dine	1
George Steele junior	1

George Steele senior	1
Thomas Steele	1
Richard Walter	2
Widow Fay	1
Richard Laurens	1
John Grunsell	1
Widow Symonds	1
William Russell	1
Richard Godwin	1
Thomas Spratt	1
John Blatch	1
Thomas Brunsden	1
William Brunsden	1
Widow Smith	2
hearths	37

(a) 1 down
1. Longstocke

504. ROMSEY INFRA

Hearths chargeable

Mister Freeman	8
Nicholas Payse	4
Richard Jolleffe	1
Edmund Younge	4
Thomas Payse	3
Alexander Gass junior	2
Moses Waldron	3
Mister John Cox	3
Avery Major	8
Nicholas Turner	8
Martin Waldron	2
Mister Hancock	4
John Drinckwell	2
Mister Marris	3
Henry Wheeler junior	1

Fol. 93v(i)

John Wharton	4
Stephen Dalidowne	2
Thomas Chalke	5
Giles Ventham	4
Mister Whale	3
John Andrewes	1
Mister Blowes	8
William Majors	3
George Saunders	2
Peter Penton	3
Henry Wheeler senior	1
Richard Whettman	2[(a)]
Mister William Mundey	7
Andrew Purdue	3
Widow Thomas	2
Thomas Philipps	2
Mister Crafts	3
Mister Cradock	5
William Baker Bresior	2
Robert Deane	2
Isaac Knight	4
Mister Kent	5
Alexander Gass senior	2
Edward Forrest	1
Edward Day	1
Henry Anthony	1
Thomas Brackley	3
Richard Saunders	2
Mister Burbanck	5
John Martyne	2
Mister Gurdin	2
Nicholas Denvie	2
John Storks	4
Mister Crane	8
Nicholas Crowch	3
Clement Warren	3[(a)]
John Hennam	3
Thomas Cuffley	3
John Hack	3
William Baker	6
Mister Thomas Warrin	4
John Mountayne	5
Thomas Garrett	1
Ralph Pope	3
John Smarrt	2
Richard Cuffe	3
hearths	201

Hearths not chargeable

Nathaniel Hacker	1
James Harris	1
Richard Stripe	1
John Nelson	1
Richard Gass	1
Francis Brooks	2

504. ROMSEY INFRA—*cont'd.*

John Cooper	1
Widow Tompson	2
William Humber	1
William Dyaper[1]	1
Widow Loder	1
Widow Strong	1
John Newman	1
Alexander Taylor	1
John Cox	1
Widow Jesman	2
Widow Morgan	1
Peter Anthony	2
Edward Broade	1
Andrew Goater	1
William Drew	1

Fol. 93v(ii)

Alexander Taylor	1
Widow Smartt	2
William Newman	2
Edward Dallydowne	1
George Gesman	2
William Palmer	2
Walter Skilton	1
John Smartt	2
Henry Wheeler	2
Adam Baldwin	2
Edward Kent	2
Edward Forrest	1
William Hopgood	2
Thomas Palmer	1
Richard Palmer	2
Thomas Mundey	2
John Nelson	2
George Forrest	1
Foster	2
Richard Pile	1
Susan Holloway	1
Widow Vaine	1
Hannah Bowne	1
Widow Ivyleafe	2
hearths	63

(a) 1 deduct
1. *Altered from* Draper

505. MIDDLEBRIDGE STREET

Hearths chargeable

William Chapman	1
George Brace	3
William Mathewes	3
John Browne	1
John Penton	3
Widow Englefeild	3
Richard Lawrence	2
Richard Gass	1
Mister Richard Majors	3
Widow Brasby	6
Thomas Godden	3
Roger Richman	3
Mister John Greene	2
Aaron Cooper	1
Mister John Greene	4
Thomas Briant	1
Thomas Alwin	4
James Holton	3
Andrew Puckridge	4
Andrew Wooll	3[(a)]
Richard Burgis	2[(b)]
Thomas Allin	1
John White	3
William Godson	4
John Heyward junior	1
Andrew Storks	3
Henry Jacobb	3
Thomas Heyward	1
Widow Forrest	2
John Emance	1
William Dasten	2
hearths	77

Hearths not chargeable

Richard Mathewes	1
Richard Balden	1
John Heyward senior	1
Widow Goater	1
Widow Feger	1
Adieno Rutter	1
Widow Duke	1
Widow Richman	2

Fol. 94r(i)

Henry Richman	1

Jane Pewton 1
Widow Ellett 1
Francis Gaidon 1
Henry Hills 1
Robert Teme 1
John Briant 1
John Vallines 1
Widow Hills 1
John Teme 1
John Chapman 1
Nicholas Bloyce 1
Ralph Drew 1
Isaac Knight 1
Henry Squibb 1
William Jones 2
Richard Cropp 1
Thomas Forrest 1
hearths 28

(a) 3 overcharged
(b) 1 deduct

506. CUPERNHAM[1]

Hearths chargeable

John Ray 7
Nicholas Miles 3
Widow Pragnell 1
John Jenvie 1
John Batchelor 1
Ambrose Grove 1
Thomas Michell 1
Thomas Falkon 1
Thomas Hunt 1
John Salt 1
Robert Hayes 1
John Knight 4
William Collis 2
Richard Pickland 1
Francis Smith 1
Dorothy Hunt 1
Henry Browne 2
Robert Browne 1
William Thomas 8
Mister Edward Powlett 6
George Rattue 1
William Jolleffe 1
Henry Appleford 1
James Ballard 2
Mister Richard Godfrey 1
John Rey 2
hearths 53

Hearths not chargeable

Widow Yeoman 1
Widow Fox 2
Widow Carter 2
Richard Pickernell 1
Nicholas Diggins 1
William Kelsey 1
Widow Beckington 1
John Mathew 1
Annis Carter 1
Thomas Fryer 1
John Stevens 1
Joseph Newman 1
Thomas Cooper 1
Alice Kent 1
Margaret Winckworth 1
William Day 1
Elizabeth Thomas 1
William Jolleff 1
Thomas Jones 1
Richard Vinne 1
Richard Kelsey 1
William Hannington 1

Fol. 94r(ii)

William Newman 1
Christian Dowdey 2
Robert Whitehead 1
Elizabeth Newland 1
hearths 30

1. Cupernaum

507. WOODBURY[1]

Hearths chargeable

Edward Withers 7
Widow Coleman 2
Robert Thomas 2
William Broadway 4
William Newman 1
John Robertson 1
Robert Hymon 3
Jonathan Sansbery 2

507. WOODBURY—*cont'd.*

Richard Godfrey	3
Edward Scragle senior	1
Edward Scragle junior	3
Thomas Durman	4
George Barfoott	1
Ralph Hunt	2
Richard Cropp	3
Daniel Harding	2
William Thomas	1
John Mortemore	1
Widow Smith	1
Widow Sidford	2
John Horskins	1
Thomas Barling	1
Widow Powell	3
John Thomas	2
John Jorden	1
hearths	54

Hearths not chargeable

William Scovell	1
Thomas Scovell	1
John Newman	1
Widow Gifford	1
Peter Anthony	1
Richard Russen	1
Widow Cuttler	1
John Bye	1
hearths	8

1. Woodberry

508. WOOLS[1]

Hearths chargeable

Broadlands	14
More Court	9
Sidmore	3
William Richmond	1
Robert Thomas	1
Richard Harrison	2
Jonathan Stansbery	2
Thomas Penton	3
John Knight	5
John Cocker	1
Thomas Dummer	2
Widow Gass	3
Widow Colle	3
John Puckeridge	2
John Baily	1
John Staingmore	1
John Weight	1
Stephen Holloway	1
John Martyn	3
Widow Martyn	2
Alexander Gass	3
hearths	63

Fol. 94v(i)

Hearths not chargeable

Abraham Kent	1
Alice Cable	1
Nicholas Gysage	1
Richard Holloway	1
John Daniell	1
Widow Adasonne	1
Powlett Dowse	1
Widow Lawd	1
John White	1
Widow Bunge	1
Widow Holloway	1
Richard Churcher	1
Thomas Cowdrey	1
Thomas Martyn	1
John Cole	1
hearths	15

1. Woolles

509. STANBRIDGE[1]

Hearths chargeable

Roger Gallopp esquire	13
Mister Jefford	1
John Woolles	3
Thomas Reves	2
Robert Thomas	1
Widow Swettman	1
Thomas Blake	1
George Gearle	1
hearths	23

Hearths not chargeable

Widow Rolph	1
Widow Jackman	1
Widow Jones	1

Widow Jones	1
Widow Rogers	1
Widow Hammon	1
hearths	6

1. Standbridge

510. SPURSHOLT[1]

Hearths chargeable

The farmhouse	8
Richard Sadler	1
hearths	9

1. Sparshott

511. MAINSTONE[1]

Hearths chargeable

Isaac Knight	5
Robert Jones	1
George Whale	1
hearths	7

Hearths not chargeable

Roger Foster	1
John Watridg	1
Thomas Warden	1
John Strong	1
hearths	4

1. Maynestone

512. TIMSBURY[1]

Hearths chargeable

John Turner	2
John Hunt	1
John Mersh	2
George Forder	2

Fol. 94v(ii)

Robert Terrer	1
James Lany	1
Richard Wilshire	1
Roger Flood	1
Richard Payse	1
Anthony Arthur	4
James Lyne	1
William Cable	1
Mister Godfrey	7
Robert Payle	1
Roger Stride	3
Edmund Burgis	2
Widow Bawdin	1
John Johnson	2
Thomas Lavington	4
Francis Lavington	1
Giles Browne	2
Andrew Sharpp	2
Widow Wilson	3
Thomas Stride	2
Richard Hunt	3
Lionel Richards	2
Thomas Hunt	3
Richard Michenor	2
hearths	58

Hearths not chargeable

John Hills	1
John Paise	1
William Hills	1
Thomas Pease	1
Richard Phillipps	1
Thomas Forder	1
John Wilton	1
Widow Rose	1
Widow Lenox	1
Richard Pease	1
hearths	10

1. Timsberry

513. CHERVILLE STREET[1]

Hearths chargeable

Mister Richard Puckridg	6[a]
John Legg	2
George Squibb	1
Thomas Churcher	2
Thomas Post	1
James Symonds	1
Thomas Saunders	2
George Hoare	1
Robert Saunders senior	2
Nicholas Andrewes	2
Stephen Rolph	4[b]
John Wise	3
William Vanderplanke	2
John Holloway senior	5

513. CHERVILLE STREET —*cont'd.*

Thomas Barly	3
Nicholas Storks	3
Christopher Hoare	3(b)
Brock Scullard	7
Isaac Knight	1
hearths	51

Hearths not chargeable

Stephen Rice	1
Widow Rice	1
Mary Cowse	1
Christopher Knight	1
Thomas Gass	1

Fol. 95r(i)

Robert Foster	1
Richard Madhead	1
William Smith	1
Thomas Browne	1
Robert Saunders junior	1
Hugh Philipps	1
John Parsons	1
Thomas Richards	1
Saunder Hanbrough	1
Saunder Martyne	2
Francis Brookes	1
Christopher Neale	1
John Swagg	1
Widow Balle	1
Geoffrey Reynolds	1
Aaron Reynolds	1
Richard Right	2
Mark Heyward	2
John Holloway	1
Henry Ventham	2
John Baxton	1
Henry Thomas	1
Widow Saunders	1
Widow Mills	2
Thomas Palmer	2
Richard Foster	1
Widow Johnson	1
Richard Cropp	1
Nicholas Valence	1
Nicholas Waldron	1
James Puckeridg	1
Thomas Churcher	1
Richard Amdrilly	1
Edmund Smith	1
Henry Jolliff	1
Christopher Hoare	1
Richard Dicker	2
John Neales	1
hearths	50

(a) 1 overcharged
(b) 2 down
1. Chernell Street

514. LEE

Hearths chargeable

Mister Richard Godfrey	16
Stephen Newlands	1
John Symons	2
William White	1
Widow Benham	1
Widow Elmes	1
Richard Newland	2
Richard Browne	3
John Iremonger	2
Robert Shawe	1
William Iremonger	3
Widow Salt	1
William Allen	1
John Chard	1
Richard Deane	2
hearths	38

Hearths not chargeable

Widow Heaman	1
Isaac Gradigge	1
Richard Hunt	1
John Chard	1
hearths	4

Fol. 95r(ii)

515. ROMSEY EXTRA

Hearths chargeable

Mister Broadway	6
Mister Stevens	1
John Waight	3
Goodman Maphey	2
Thomas Hockley	4

Simon Dickens	1
Geoffrey Symes	1
Widow Tucker	3
George Weeks	4
John Briant	1
Peter Ratte	1
John Newman	1
William Newman	1
John Englefeild	2
Richard Rice	1
Goodman Neate	2
Walter Beale	3
Francis Keepe senior	2
Francis Keepe junior	2
George Baverstock	2
Thomas Burgis	1
John Cocker	2
Widow Wisdome	1[1]
Andrew Waldron	3
Widow Vawse	1
Goodman Card	1
Thomas Lymborner	3
Mistress Hancock	2
Richard Whale	4
John Hammon	2
Mister Addams	3
James Lymborner	1
Goodman Jones	2
Thomas Terrer	2
hearths	71

Hearths not chargeable

Thomas Wickham	1
William Fox	1
Barnard Puckeridg	1
Thomas Woods	1
Edward Teane	1
Henry Englefeild	1
Henry Eaton	1
William Ivy	1
Goody Vanner	1
John Hawkins	1
John Baverstock	1
Thomas Cooper	1
Richard Palmer	1
Thomas Towleton	1
Thomas Browne	1
Widow Cheasman	1
Andrew Foster	1
Oliver Christopher	1
Robert Baverstock	1
James Hussey	1
John Long	1
Thomas Light	1
William Heasley	1
Robert Coales	1
Francis Richmond	1
Thomas Palmer	1
Widow Paise	1
John Gold	1
William Warren	1
John Browne	1
John Newman	1
William Sharpe	1
Christopher Light	1
Robert Longe	1

Fol. 95v(i)

William Bower	1
Nicholas Bonner	1
John Freeborne	1
Widow Davie	1
Thomas Greene	1
John Briant	1
Widow Symes	1
Thomas Baverstock	1
Widow Foster	1
John Bellman	1
Widow Light	1
Widow Palmer	1
Abel Browne	1
John Carde	1
Widow Daunce	1
Hayden Kervill	1
Richard Rice	1
Widow Jones	1
Alice White	1
Widow Purdue	1
Zacharias Hall	1
William Hannington	1
Philip Grayly	1
Widow Fryer	1

515. ROMSEY EXTRA—*cont'd.*

Edward Purdue	1
Nicholas Michell	1
William Illsley	1
Thomas Burgis	1
Robert Cole junior	1
Henry Cocker	1
Matthew Cole	1
Widow Spragg	1
John Medley	1
Thomas Pest	1
Tristram Edland	1
Widow Smith	1
Widow Smith	1
John Griffin	1
John Beare	1
Widow Knott	1
John Vincent	1
Joan Smith	1
John Knight	1
hearths	77

1. *Altered from* 2

516. RANVILLS[1]

Hearths chargeable

Thomas Cuffley	4
hearths	4

The number of hearths within the hundred of Kings Somborne[2] is	1111
Hearths not chargeable	479
The whole number of hearths chargeable within this division of Andover[3] is	4251
Hearths not chargeable	1660
The whole number of hearths chargeable within the 7 divisions aforesaid	37794
Hearths not chargeable in the 7 divisions	08361

1. Runvills
2. Kingsomborne
3. Andeve

TEXT OF THE HEARTH TAX ASSESSMENT FOR SOUTHAMPTON, 1662

Account of Hearths in the Several Parishes 1662

Fol. 1r

517. An account of the several hearths and stoves within the parish of Holy Rood in the town and county of the town of Southampton, taken the twentieth day of September 1662

William Stanley esquire mayor[1]	13
Robert Richbell esquire	12
Henry Hart	6
Robert Bradsell	2
Widow Prince	5
Robert Elcock	5
Widow Alford	1
James Barger	4
William Hancock	4
John Fussell	4
Peter Wale	7
William Browne	5
John Rowland	4
Mister John Tayler	7
Thomas Hill	4
Robert Stote	14
Mister William Pinhorne	8
Richard White	6
William Whitman	2
Henry Pitt alderman	10
Henry Pitt alderman in his house void	8
Mister William Smith	4
William Higgins alderman	7
James Capelin alderman	5
Henry Merefield	1
Widow Filliter	15
Francis Helliard	4
Mister Clifford	5
John Rowt in his part	4
John Fawkener	4
John Roach	2
John Prangnell	3
William Plenty	5
Widow Hills	1
John Gapes	3
Widow Carey	9
Edward Pelley	2
William Carrott	3
George St Barbe	9
Anthony Gasse	2
John Chidley	1
Thomas Johnson	2
Richard Speed	4
John Suffild	2
Thomas Jarvis	2
Mister William Cole	4
Mister Richard Cornelius in his house void	4
William Horne alderman	12
John Speering	21
William House	2
Alexander Gasse	2
Mister Edward Richards	6
John Rowt in his house void	4
Henry [fold]	[ ]

Fol. 1v

James Capelin alderman in his house void	4
Anthony Abarrow	3
William Israel	4
Thomas Farr	4
John Ford	5
Thomas Brooman	3
Doctor Philips	10
Nicholas Clement alderman in his part	4

The same Nicholas Clement in his house void formerly Mary Brewer's 8
Giles Austin 3
Mister Knapton 9
Edward Downer alderman 8
John Windover 5
Jacob Ward 6
Walter Feverell 2
William Macham 5
Thomas Cornelius alderman 8
Richard Capelin 6
William Mason 6
Erasmus Bradbey 2
Edward Layte 4
Daniel Hersent 9
John Quittance 4
Richard Walker 9
Daniel Goteour 1
John Harwood 4
Cornelius Fox 5
William Stanley alderman in his house void 11
Robert Adams 2
Mister William Bernard 5
Mister Butler 6
Doctor Warner in his two houses void 9

Alexander Gasse, Robert Addams his mark } beadles

1. mayor *superscript*

Fol. 3r

518. An account of the several hearths and stoves of the parish of St Michael in the town and county of the town of Southampton taken the twentieth day of September 1662

William Craddock 2
Robert Wharford 2
Walter Feverell 1
John Okee 6
John Lews 2
Francis Dobey 2
Robert Feverell 2
Edmund Burt 5
Nicholas Friend 3
Henry Vallet 2
John Guillum 4
Dorothy Walleston 7
Thomas Baker 2
William Milbery 3
Martha Mallard 3
Stephen Todey 4
Christopher Fleet 5
William Langley 4
Richard Foster 4
John Edmonds 2
Joseph Read 2
William Bushell 2
Thomas Heath 3
John Pitt 2
Thomas Pearse 2
Richard Jacob 3
Susan Combes 5
William Bernard 4
Dominic Barrow 3
Peter South 2
93

Fol. 3v

Stephen Griffin 2
Mister Adam Cardonnell 4
Robert Cannings 2
Christopher Smith 2
Henry Weekam 2
William Brackstone 7
William Hookey 3
Henry Grey 4
John Crawley 4
James Duffild 2
David Widdall 4
William Nicholas 4
John Gilbert 4
Richard Tyler 3
Thomas Osland 2

John Milbery	3
Thomas Hu[ ]	2
John Baker	3
James Lambe	2
James Wheeler	5
George Webb	3
James Clungeon alderman	8
John Penton	2
Austin Bonfild	1
James Parker	3
Thomas Janverin	4
John Adlington	4
Richard Du Heaumes	6
Francis Weeks	3
Nathaniel Browne	4
Richard Parsons	2
Aaron Guillum	3
Widow Janverin	4
James Paige	3
William Whislad	4
Robert Atherley	4
Widow Devenish	8
Rawleigh Hull	5
Francis Say	6
William Walleston	6
William Hunt	7
Christopher Copleston	4
John Dubber	2
Joan Daniel	3

Fol. 4r

Widow Russell	4
Edward Milbery	5
Thomas Foster	1
Thomas Wallis the elder	2
Thomas Wallis the younger	1
Bugle Hall void	14
Mister Ralph Knapton void	2
William Feverell void	8
Widow Burges void	7
John Beele	2
James Duffild void	2

John Pitt
Nicholas Grante } beadles

fol. 5r

519. An account of the several hearths and stoves within the parish of St John in the town and county of the town of Southampton taken the twentieth day of September 1662

Thomas Zaines	3
Arthur Atherley	4
John Fletcher	3
Widow De La Motte	4
Thomas Fletcher	2
Bartholomew Elmes	1
Nicholas Foster	3
Oliver Ford	6
Richard Gardner	2
Nicholas Grant	8
Widow Knowler	5
John Rawlings	1
John Pearse	1
William Rawlings	1
Thomas Pave	4
Thomas Powell	
Joseph De La Motte alderman	9
Nicholas Moodey	2
William Newman	7
John Benger	2
Thomas Zaines void	2

John Pitt
Nicholas Grante } beadles

Fol. 7r

520. An account of the several hearths and stoves within the parish of St Lawrence[1] in the town and county of the town of Southampton taken the twentieth day of September 1662

Mister Arthur Bracebridge	7
Richard Hunt	7
Thomas Taylor	6

Robert Poole	2
George Targett	2
John Thornberry	5
Daniel Lelaunder	2
Robert Wroth	9
Widow Flood	2
Henry Embree	6
Richard Blashford	7
Peter Clungeon	9
Roger Culliford	3
Walter Rowt	7
William Byles	3
Samuel Downes	4
Nathaniel Blanchard	4
William Blake	5
Peter Anthony	2
Thomas Chamberlin	2
William Knapton	10
Esau Cushen	2
Stephen Finckley	2
John Cropp	7
Mister George Stanley	12
Doctor Elleston	9
Edward Palmer	3
John Zaines	3
Edward Exton alderman	9
Thomas Hawker	11
Mistress Pryaulx	7
John Thackham	5
Mister Richard Cornelius	6
James Mudge	2
Richard Heath	2
Widow Renouf	5
Nicholas Staples	1
Bartholomew Kempster	3
William Bower	1
Mister William Oviatt	8
	202

Esau Cushin
William Blac[h]e } beadles

1. St Laurence

Fol. 9r

521. An account of the several hearths and stoves within the parish of All Saints within the Bar[1] in the town and county of the town of Southampton taken the twentieth day of September 1662

John Mandfild	3
Richard Bernard	3
John St Barb	4
Thomas Trodd	3
Thomas Hawkens	4
Goody Hayward	2
John Steptoe	4
Edward Lyddell	3
Widow Samms	3
John Vovert	4
Mister Charlett	12
Edward Hooper	10
William Fleet junior	6
Joseph Flower	5
John Wheat	5
John Fox	2
Thomas Duey	1
William Jolliff	4
Mister Arthur Foocks	11
Mistress Jane Clungeon	9
Robert Neale	4
Andrew Brooman	2
Ursula Man	1
Mister William Knight	9
Mistress Pedley	4
Mister Nathaniel Robinson	5
Kingston Fryar the elder	10[2]
Christopher Bell	4
William Fleet the elder	6
Samuel Dyar	3
George Heady	2
Grafton Jackson	4
Henry Miller	6
Mister Needle and William Blancket	8
William Palmer	3
Thomas Fryar	2
Richard Luke	10
William Purbeck	3
Daniel Grantum	3

Henry Meller	}	beadles
Robert Neale		

1. All Sts within the Barr
2. *Altered from* 9

Fol. 11r

522. An account of the several hearths and stoves within the parish of All Saints without the Bar[1] in the town and county of the town of Southampton taken the twentieth day of September 1662

William Mandfild	3
William Hapgood	5
Joseph Jones	3
John Parsons	4
Richard Oldman	1
Elias Antrum	6
Thomas Heath	8
George Prince	4
Stephen Langford	4
Nathaniel Provoe	5
Roger Langley	12
Roger Younge	1
George Head	2
George Embree	7
Kingston Fryer junior	4
Roger Walker void	10
Edward Flower	4
William Lyne	4
Edward Searle	3
Sarai Downes	5
John Lee	4
Thomas Bernard	5
John Elmes	3
James Andrews	4
John Barton	2
Peter Morrell	2[2]
Nicholas Woods	3
Richard Tunton	4
Robert Bernard	3
Roger Curtys	3
Thomas Moodey	5
Thomas Pitt	4
George Prince	beadle

1. All Saints without the Barr
2. *Altered from* 1

Fol. 13r

523a. An account [of the several hearths] and stoves within [the parish of St] Mary in the town [and county of] the town of Southamp[ton and within] the ward of Portswood [in the town and] county of the town of Southampton afor[esaid] taken the twentieth day of September 1662

John Heath	2
Mister Gaywood	9
Edward Thorne	7
Thomas Heath	1
Michael Paige	2
William Fryer	2
Lionel Jurd	2
Robert Browne	3
John Elesley	1
Mister Rowt	6
Robert Kipping	3
Edward Knowler	6
John Smith	1
William Baker	6
Paul Munday	2
William Ryder	2
John Pressey	2
Thomas Pointdexter	2
Robert Lamboll	2
Francis Lamboll	3
John Paige	2
George Heath	2
John Meires	2
Henry Combes	1
Jenken Huse	6
John Twinney	2
John Fawscett	4
William Best	4
Nathaniel Knight	2
John Palmer	2
William Flowerdue	4
John Tomkins	3
John Pressy his mark	beadle

Fol. 13v

523b. [Ward] of Portswood

[s] Wall	2
[ ] Thomas	2
Henry Heath	2
Richard Symes	6
John Bulbeck	3
William Buckett	1
William Head	1
James Burt	1
Elizabeth Augar	1
Elizabeth Payne	1
John Wiseman	2
William Culverden	2
Thomas Bridges	1
John Knight gentleman at St Dyonis	13

William Webb his mark tithingman

TEXT OF THE HEARTH TAX ASSESSMENT FOR SOUTHAMPTON, 1670

Fol. 6r

A duplicate of all [ ] cha[rgeable] to pay [within the town] and county of Southampton [ ] day of June in the [two and] twentieth year of the reign [of our] Sovereign Lord [King Charles] over England etc [ ]

524. IN THE PARISH OF ST MARYS[1]

John Tompkins	2
Robert Skinner	2
Obadiah Manners	2
Daniel Grantham	2
John Bascomb	[1]
Richard Bundy	[1]
John Buckett	[ ]
John Mannings	[ ]
Henry Fullford	2
Robert Lamb[o]ll	[ ]
Francis [Emlen]	[ ]
John Page	[ ]
John Meeres	[ ]
John Combes	[ ]
Richard Provitt	[ ]
Jenkin Hewes	[ ]
Richard Kippen	[ ]
Edward Thorne	[ ]
Mister Gaywood	[ ]
Edward Knowler	[ ]
John Edmonds	[ ]
Widow Pinnell	[ ]
Edward Archer	[ ]
Thomas Bone	[ ]
John Elzly	[ ]
Thomas L[o]	[ ]
Robert [ ]	[ ]
William F[ ]	[ ]
William [Bage]	[ ]
Thomas Bradshaw	[ ]
James Bushell	[4]
George Heath	2
Daniel Lamboll	2
Henry Horne	1
Henry Giles	2
Thomas Hawkins	2

William Harding		2
Widow Fossett		[4]
Paul Mundy		2
Edward Mannings		2
John Senior		1
Widow Baker		6
John Twinney		2
Robert Frowd's widow		1
		122

1. In pish of St Marys

525. IN PORTSWOOD LIBERTY

Mark Bettridge		7
Widow Symes		6
Nicholas Butt		3
Widow Buckett		1
William Webb		1
Thomas Daniell		3
Richard Syms		2
John Fossett		6
		29

526. IN ALL SAINTS WARD WITHOUT THE BAR[1]

Thomas Dewey		9
William Yeomans		2
Edward Evered		2
William Mansfield		3
Widow Carter		5
Mister Bower		4
Thomas Bernard		5
Doctor Clutterbuck new built	2	
Joseph Jones		2
John Parsons		5
Peter Morrell		3
Mistress Hopgood		2
James Booker		2
Mister St Barbe	2	(a)
Richard Oldman		2
Ellis Antram		6
Roger Curtis		8
Mistress Prince		3
John Hore		4
Fashion	2	(a)
John Parsons	4	(a)
Thomas Heath		11
Christopher Wells		2

Alexander Gole		1
George Head		2
George Embree		7
Kingston Fryer junior		4
Edward Flower		3
William Lyne		4
Edward Searle		3
John Lee		4
Fol. 5r		
Widow Downes		5
Thomas Pitt	5	(a)
Johm Ellmes		3
John Fox		4
Widow Barton		4
John Elmes		4
Thomas Moody		6
Thomas Pitt	5	0(a)
Robert Bernard		4
Richard Taunton		4
Widow Booker		2
John Jeoffrey		2
Thomas Kiftell		4
Thomas Rowse		3
James Hagger		2
James Fawkner		2
Hugh Blake		2
Mister Henry Pitt		5
Peter Lisle		2
		186

(a) void
1. In All Sts Warde without ye Barr

527. IN ALL SAINTS WARD WITHIN THE BAR[1]

Widow Mann		4
Mister Chapline	1	(a)
Mistress Knight		9
Mister Peter Guillum		9
Mister Kingston Fryer alderman		10
Widow Bell		2
Thomas Henstridge		6
Edward Tull		3
John Zaines junior		4
Henry Miller		6
William Palmer		5
Thomas Watterman		2
Edward Flower	1	(a)
Isaac Barton		2

Thomas Hawkins		4
Richard Light		2
Major Young		[7][2]
Mister John Stepto		[1][2]
William Ludwell		[2][2]
Widow Watts		1
Mister Vovert		3
Mister Thomas Charlett		12
Mister Edward Hooper		10
Richard Ring		3
Mister Robinson		4
William Blanchard		5
Richard Chaplin		2
Walter Dyett		1
William Jolliffe		3
John Chidley		3
Mister Arthur Fowke		11
Widow Jane Clungeon		7
William Blake	2	(a)
Edward Tull	2	(a)
George Heady		2
John Plowman		3
Nicholas Hayward		4
Thomas Barter		4
William Fleete		5
William Palmer		2
Andrew Brooman		3
Mister Stephens		2
John Bidlecome		2
Thomas Pryer		2
Joseph Tibby		2
Stephen Finkley		4
Thomas Fox		2
Widow Duke		2
Hugh Ockleford		2
Isaac Barton		2
John Mansfield		2
Widow Staples		10
Robert Le Page		3
Henry Mullins		2
Stephen Sibly		4
Nicholas Hayward		4
Widow Braxton		4
		224 223 ex'

(a) void
1. In All Sts warde within the Barr
2. *Part of skin missing*

528. IN ST LAWRENCE WARD[1]

John Batchilor		5
William Turner		4
Samuel Downes		4
Captain Goddard	3	(a)
Mister Walter Rought		8
Doctor Thomas Pittis		9
Mistress Clungeon	7	(a)
Anthony Jenkins		6
Thomas Chamberlin		2
Widow Flood		2
Robert W[r]oth		9
Thomas Tayler		5
John Thorneburgh		5
[George] Targett		6
Thomas Tayler	4	(a)
Richard Hunt		5
Anthony Gasse		7
Arthur Bracebridge gentleman		7
Fol. 4r		
William Pocock		9
Bartholomew Kempster		3
Cornelius Macham		2
Wormstall	2	(a)
John Brooman		2
Richard Heath		2
Henry Norborne		6
James Crosse		7
John Rowte		7
Thomas Hawker		11
Richard Blachford		9
Edward Palmer		3
Mister de Cardonnell		9
Mister Andrews		12
Mister John Cropp		7
Mistress Tayler		2
Mister Higgens	4	(a)
Doctor Speed		10
William Combs		3
Mister Alexander	2	(a)
Widow Lyne		4
Mistress Turner		3
Richard Brooman		3
Thomas Blackmore		2
Benjamin West		2

Widow Wiseman		2	
William Head		1	
Edward Palmer		3	
Edward Sculler		1	
John Zaines		3	
Mister Biles	3	(a)	
Henry Wale		3	
John Brooman		1	
James Mudye		2	
	25	243	218
	3 [provein]		

(a) void
1. In St Larwence Warde

529. IN HOLY ROOD WARD[1]

Mister Winter		12
Mister Speereing		20
Henry Aterrifield		2
William House		3
John Ockleford	1[2]	2
Mister Stokes		2
Andrew Hewlett		2
Captain Horne		9
William Bowne		4
Alexander Gasle	1[2]	7
Mister Clifford	5	(a)
Anthony Abarrow		3
Thomas Farr		4
Widow Filliter		2
William Whittman		2
Edward Johnson		2
Richard Bodycoate	1[2]	2
Mister Cole		6
Doctor Phillipps		10
Mister Loving	1[2]	10
Mister Goddard	3	(a)
Mister Downer		8
John Windover		4
Jacob Ward	1[2]	6
Widow Austin		2
Mister John Straingwich	10	(a)
George Veale		3
Widow Varneham		2
Thomas Jarvise		2
Edward Lakes		2
Mister Fawkner	1[2]	10

William Macham		6
Thomas Cornelius gentleman		8
Richard Capelin	1[2]	6
William Pryors		2
Philip Gilliom		1
William Cooke		1
Widow Mason		6
Erasmus Bradby		2
Robert Richbell esquire mayor	1[2]	9
Richard Speed		5
Doctor Clutterbuck	1[2]	9
Mistress Carey		9
Mistress Kernes		8
Mistress Blake	1[2]	8
Francis Helliard		3
Abraham Brewer		1
Daniel Gotier		1
John Luffe		4
Widow Ireland		1
Cornelius Fox		2
Mister William Stanley	1[2]	12
Gilbert Clement		1
Mister Dodd		2
William Garrett		2

Fol. 3r

Widow Baker		2
John Fussell		2
Mister St Barbe	1[2]	5
George Powell		5
Richard Jarvice		3
George Freeman	1[2]	14
Mister Pinhorne		8
Thomas Goter		5
Richard White	1[2]	9
Mister Buttler		6
Richard Godfrey	1[2]	11
Richard Horne		4
George Prince		4
Mister William Smith		3
Mister Higgens	1[2]	8
William Langly		1
Daniel LeLandre		12
William Purbeck		4
Jane Burgis		1
Mister Tayler	1[2]	4

Christopher Smith		5	
Robert Poole		2	
Mister William Smith		3	
Mister Smith for Thomas Taylers		4	
Robert Ellcocke	1[2]	5	
Daniel Veale		4	
Henry Pittfield		2	
John Bignoll		2	
Arthur Lakes	2	(a)	
William Rowland	3	(a)	
Thomas Hills		5	
Robert Hewlett		2	
John Thackham	1[2]	3	
George Speed		2	
Peter Provo		2	
Mister Henry Pitt		9	
Daniel Hersent	1[2]	14	
Peter Whale		7	
George Powell		3	
William Gassett		2	
	23	456	437

(a) void
1. In Holy Roode Warde
2. *Added in a different hand*

530. IN ST MICHAELS AND ST JOHNS WARD[1]

John Church	2
Thomas Langford	2
Widow Oakey	6
Anthony Hewett alias Sidford	1
Thomas Foy	2
Thomas Baker	2
John Millbery	4
John Guillum	5
Widow Sharfe	2
Mister Higgens	4
Edward Clement	4
Christopher Fleet	4
William Browne	2
Thomas Peirce	2
Abraham Ayres	2
Arthur Lakes	4
Widow Combes	7
John Winter	4
Widow Fashion	4
Francis Say	2

Robert Addams	8
Henry Weekham	2
Edward Bachiler	4
William Brackstone	6
John Day	5
William Widdell	4
Thomas Dickenson	6
Arthur Atherly	2
Henry White	2
William Nicholas	4
Thomas Stonehall	4
William Pasmore	4
James Parker	2
Mister David Widdall	4
Richard Tyler	3
Mister Lea	2
Widow Peake	3
Andrew Curtis	2
Thomas Gally	2
James Wheeler	5
William Styles	2
Captain Clungeon	8
Thomas Janverine	3
William Tompkins	4
William Whisladd	2
Hugh Symmonds	4
James Addlington	4
Henry Peach	4
Richard Du Haumes	5
Samuel Critchman	2
James Knowler	2
Widow Janverine	2
James Page	5
Fol. 2r	
Oliver Foord	8
Mistress Wormestall	7
William Wallistone	6
Doctor Carterett	7
Mistress Wallistone	7
Henry Vallett	2
Richard Owder	5
Michael Friend	2
Christopher Coppleston	3
Thomas Rolfe	2
Mister Groce	2

Robert Lee	2
Henry Bellfry	2
Thomas Wallis	3
Mister Millberry	5
Mistress Russen	4
William Daniell	4
Robert Warford	2
Robert Harte	2
Thomas Hedges	3
Richard Foster	2
Mary Zaines widow	3
Widow Whisladd	4
John Fletcher	5
John Peirce	4
Thomas West	2
John Harwood	4
Widow Newman	6
Captain LeMotte	10
Nathaniel Provo	5
John Baillehache	3
William Vosse	4
Thomas Powell	3
John Rawlings	4
John Stepto for Bull Hall	13
Richard Cooper	5
Anthony Heuatt	1
Nicholas Graunt	11
John Spencer	5
Henry Bedford	2
Francis Dobey	7
Thomas Swyer	2
William Millberry	4
Charles Man	2
Robert Cannings	2
Dominic Barrow	3
Thomas Hewett	2
Nicholas Moody	2
Richard Shutt	1
Benjamin Pittfeild	2
William Peach	2
Robert Ratcliffe	2
Widow Browne	4
John Cottman	1
Walter Feverell	3
Joseph Reade	3

Giles Say	5
George Luke	4
	1599 possessed
	72 void
	1671 total

Southampton the 8 August 1671

Robert Richbell	mayor
William Stanley	Justices of the Peace for the town and county of
James Clungeon	Southampton

1. In St Michaells & St Johns Warde

531. The persons undernamed are discharged by legal certificate

Widow Pyatt
William Whale
Elias Blake
Robert Hutchins
Andrew Browne
Richard Sparkes
Thomas Gutheridge
Thomas Cole
James Flower
John Butcher
William Pearce
Widow Combes
Thomas Balding
Widow Dyer
Goodman Cully
Robert Arwood
Widow Jarvice
Giles Kember
Joseph Reeks
Widow Buckling
Evis Carter
Nathaniel King
John Seale
William Palmer

Fol. 1r

James Burrell
Widow Pitt
Robert King
John Hooper
William Strange
Stephen Goter
Robert Howard
Thomas Buttler
Jacob Barger
Widow Williams
Walter Plowman
William Cleft
William Chester
Thomas Allen
Thomas Chappell
Widow Michell
Sarah Barton
Goodman Parker
Widow Seale
Widow Geesidge
Thomas Palmer
Alexander Ockleford
Leonard Beele
William Bowles
William Ryder
Catherine Edwards
Henry Horne
Thomas Lee
Thomas Mundy
Robert Foord
Thomas Romey
Francis Lavender
Richard Bundy

These are humbly to certify that the book containing all the names and number as above written in this roll was delivered to me about the twentieth of May last and not before and that this roll was ingrossed within six days after the delivery of the said book and that since that time there hath been no Sessions held for the town and county of Southampton and farther that the above mentioned was signed only as followeth *vizt* viewed per T Carter Collector not by any constable or tithingman as by the Act of 16 Charles Second concerning the collecting of the duty by hearth money is required

Southampton 8 August 1671

W Pocock Clerk of the Peace for the town and county of Southampton

APPENDIX 1

HEARTH TAX DOCUMENTS FOR HAMPSHIRE

The following list of documents comprises all the surviving detailed hearth tax documents for Hampshire which include lists of names. Each description is preceded by the appropriate reference.

All the assessments for the county include the Isle of Wight, but not the town of Southampton for which a separate assessment was made. These separate assessments have not always survived. The returns similiarly include the Isle of Wight, but not Southampton. The exemption certificates relate to the whole county including Southampton and the Isle of Wight.

SRO SC14/2/32b **Assessment, 1662 (Southampton).**
Reproduced in this volume. A description is given in the introduction.

PRO E179/375/32 **Assessment, Lady Day 1664 (county).**
97 (originally 130) parchment membranes written on both sides in single column arrangement. Arranged, by C. A. F. Meekings, in original order in eight sections by divisions. Membranes for each division sewn together at head. Condition and legibility variable. The document is damaged in places, particularly at the feet of the membranes. Very little survives for the Andover and Portsdown divisions, and the Basingstoke, Winchester with Fawley and New Forest divisions are incomplete. Within the divisions, the assessment is divided into hundreds and liberties, and then into parishes and tithings. For each place it gives personal names and against each the number of hearths and amount payable, or the number of hearths not chargeable. This arrangement is typical of all the assessments, although the amount of tax payable is not always included.

PRO E179/176/564 **Returns, Lady Day 1664 (county).**
127 paper items, guarded and filed. Originally most of the returns were kept in disorder in a leather bag. They have been arranged, by C. A. F. Meekings, in the order of the 1664 assessment and numbered with a stamp. There is a list at the front of the file with item numbers. Condition and legibility good; incomplete. The manuscript returns were made by the constables and tithingmen. Generally, for each place, they list personal names, numbers of hearths and amounts paid. They

also give details of those who have not paid the tax and why distress could not be made.

PRO E179/176/565 **Assessment, year and a half ending Michaelmas 1665 (county).**
Reproduced in this volume. A description is given in the introduction.

PRO E179/247/29 **Assessment, year and a half ending Michaelmas 1670 (Southampton).**
Reproduced in this volume. A description is given in the introduction.

PRO E179/176/569 **Assessment, year and a half ending Lady Day 1673 (county).**
127 parchment membranes sewn together at head. Written on both sides in single column arrangement. Condition and legibility variable and very poor in places. The feet of some membranes are missing and some membranes are completely missing having been torn out. The assessment is therefore incomplete. For each place gives names and numbers under the headings hearths chargeable and persons discharged by certificate. Also gives names of collectors, and tithingmen or constables for each place.

PRO E179/247/30 **Assessment, year ending Lady Day 1674 (county).**
188 parchment membranes sewn together at head. Written on both sides in single column arrangement. Condition and legibility variable, but generally good; a few membranes are badly damaged. Almost complete. For each place gives names and numbers of hearths chargeable and details of those persons discharged by certificate; the second section is sometimes omitted.

PRO E179/176/568 **Certificates of Exemption, 1670-1671 (county).**
338 paper items, guarded and filed in two files (1-192, 192-338). Originally kept in a cloth bag. Roughly arranged by division, but somewhat muddled. Numbered with a stamp. Condition and legibility good; probably incomplete.

Some certificates are wholly manuscript, others are on printed forms. The certificates were usually made by the incumbent, churchwardens and overseers of a parish and certified by two Justices of the Peace (all named). For each parish they give the names of those exempt from paying the tax and sometimes the numbers of hearths. With large parishes the different tithings are sometimes distinguished.

PRO E179/330/1 **Certificates of Exemption, Michaelmas 1670 and Lady Day 1673 (county).**
274 loose, flattened paper items. Roughly arranged by division, but rather muddled. Numbered. Condition and legibility mostly good; some are in poor condition. No certificates for the Isle of Wight found; incomplete. Most of the certificates are on printed forms. Similar in form to those above.

PRO E179/176/570 **Certificates of Exemption, 1673-1674 (county).**
185 loose, folded paper items in one bundle. Originally kept in a cloth bag. Roughly arranged by division, but muddled. Numbered with a stamp. Condition and legibility mostly good. Probably incomplete. All the certificates are on printed forms. Similar in form to those described above.

APPENDIX 2
FORENAMES USED IN THE TEXT OF THE COUNTY ASSESSMENT WITH THEIR ORIGINAL SPELLINGS

The following is an alphabetical list of forenames used in the text where the spelling in the original document is different or the name is abbreviated. Some very common names only appear in an abbreviated form in the original (for example, Rich for Richard). With other names an abbreviated form and the full name are used interchangeably (for example, Steph and Stephen). In some cases, two spellings of a name seem to be used indiscriminately (for example, Laurence and Lawrence which also appear abbreviated to Lau and Law). Other names appear with a variety of spellings (for example, Regnold, Reygnold and Reynold) or in a form we would consider obsolete (for example, Jenever for Jennifer). *The Oxford Dictionary of English Christian Names,* E. G. Withycombe (Oxford, 1977) has been used as a guide for the modern forms used in the text.

The list is based on the 1665 Hearth Tax assessment for the county. In the 1662 Southampton assessment no abbreviated forms are used and the names have been given in their modern form in the text. The 1670 Southampton assessment is similar to the county assessment.

This list is not a comprehensive list of all the forenames in the documents.

Form of forename used in the text	*Original spelling*	*Comments*
Abraham	Abraham, Abram	Usually latter
Alexander	Alex	
Ambrose	Amb, Ambrose, Ambross	Usually first two
Andrew	An, And, Andr, Andrew	Usually second and fourth
Ann	Ann, Anne	
Anthony	Anth	
Austin	Austen, Austin	
Barnard	Bar, Barn, Barnard	Usually first and last
Bartholomew	Barth	
Basil	Bazill	
Benjamin	Ben	
Brian	Brian, Briant, Bryant	
Bridget	Bridget, Bridgett, Bridgitt	
Catherine	Kath, Katherine	Usually latter
Chloe	Cloiee	
Christopher	Christ	
Cicely	Sisely	
Clement	Clem	

Cuthbert	Cutbert, Cuttbert	
Daniel	Dan, Daniell	
Edmund	Edm, Edmund	
Edward	Edw	
Eleanor	Elinor, Ellinour, Elionour	
Elizabeth	Eliz	
Ellen	Ellen, Ellene	
Ellis	Elis, Ellis	
Esther	Hester	
Ezekiel	Ezekiell	
Ferdinand	Ferdinand, Ferdinando	
Francis	Fran, Franc, Francis	Usually first or last
Gabriel	Gabriel, Gabriell	
Geoffrey	Jeffery	
George	Geo, George	
German	Jerman	
Gervase	Jervas, Jervis	
Gilbert	Gilb, Gilbert	
Griffin	Griffen/Griffin	
Hannibal	Hannaball	
Henry	Harry, Hen, Henry	Second almost always used
Honor	Honour	
Humphrey	Hump, Humph	Usually former
Isaac	Isaack	
Jasper	Jesp(er)	
Jenkin	Jenken, Jenkin, Jenkins	
Jennifer	Jenever	
Jerome	Jerom	
Jesse	Jesse, Jessy	
Joan	Joane	
John	Jo, John	
Joseph	Jos, Josep, Joseph	Almost always last
Lancelot	Laun, Launcelott	
Laurence	Lau, Law, Laurence, Lawrence	
Leonard	Leo, Leon, Leonard	
Lewis	Lewes, Lewis	
Lionel	Lionell, Lyonell	
Malachi	Malachai	
Margaret	Marg, Margaret, Margarett	Usually last; rarely first
Mark	Mark, Marke	

Martin	Martin, Martine, Martyne	
Matthew	Math, Mathew	
Maurice	Maurice, Morris	
Methuselah	Mathusalah	
Michael	Mich	
Mordecai	Mordecay	
Nathaniel	Nath	
Nicholas	Nich, Nicholas	Almost always former
Ogden	Odgden, Ogden	
Parnel	Parnell	Contraction of Petronella
Paul	Paule	
Petronella	Petronell	See also Parnel
Philip	Philipp, Phill	Almost always former
Postumus	Posthumus	
Rachael	Rachell	
Ralph	Ralfe, Ralph	Usually latter
Randal	Randoll	
Raphael	Raphaell	
Reuben	Ruben	
Reynold	Regnold, Reygnold, Reynold	
Richard	Rich	
Robert	Rob	
Roland	Rolen, Rowland	
Samson	Sampson	
Samuel	Sam	
Sibyl	Sibbella, Sybil	
Solomon	Soloman	
Stephen	Steph, Stephen	
Susannah	Susanna	
Swithun	Swithin	
Theodore	Theodor	
Thomas	Tho	
Timothy	Thim, Thy, Thym, Tim, Timothy	
Tristram	Tristram, Trustram	
Ursula	Ursella, Ursula	
Walter	Walt, Walter	
William	Wm, Will	Usually first
Zacchaeus	Zacheus	
Zacharias	Zach	

APPENDIX 3

UNUSUAL FORENAMES

Unusual or uncommon forenames are given below in alphabetical order with the number of the place under which they occur in the text.

Name	*Place*	*Comments*
Abbott	317	
Adieno	505	
Albin	89	Same as Alban?
Ananias	256	
Argent	256	
Aringall	300	
Athey	135	
Avery	504	
Barwick	242	
Barzillay	37	
Baskfeild	435	
Batten	98	
Bethlem	160	
Bexally	130	
Blewett	208	
Boyer	38	
Brock	513	
Browman	299	
Carew	168	
Chideock	37	
Chidick	280	
Clase	392	
Cosine	93	Cosmo copied wrongly?
Courteous	219	
Crews	165	
Darby	177	
Deodatus	378	
Desire	164	
Devorix	442	
Drew	94	
Ebden	215	
Elizeas	184	
Elleger	396	
Elmor	121	
Elton	96	
Emblem	290	
Esardes	1	
Essex	292	

Name	*Place*	*Comments*
Evis	531	
Fabler	418	
Farden	86	
Ford	148	
Foule	103	
Garrett	1, 468	
Godson	229	
Gowen	100	
Harman	258	
Harmand	370	
Harud	406	
Hayden	515	
Heritage	244	
Holden	100	
Huff	473	
Ingram	475, 491	
Kemberlin	85	
Knappen	135	
Lambourne	423	
Lifften	1	
Ludd	450	
Lukenour	89	
Lyne	502	
Merrell	160	A form of Muriel
Minever	316	
Moory	172	
Nartham	211	
Noye	391	
Ogle	36	
Origen	100	
Pernasses	118	
Pittman	120	
Polixine	490	
Powlett	508	
Predix	229	
Procter	374	
Quinbanner	38	
Rannell	428	
Rawleigh	518	
Regland	218	
Revell	298	
Rickman	133	
Rigell	342	
Rigmell	244	Altered from Riginell?
Sarai	522	

Name	*Place*	*Comments*
Saunder	513(2)	
Savage	385	
Sedwell	133	
Sidrach	1, 135, 437	Spelt Sidrach/Sydrack
Silvanus	418	
Spinola	83	
Syndens	455	
Tomaz	244	Thomasina?
Venis	332	
Vitall	287, 493	
Warner	361	
Wellinough	293	
Woolston	248	

SELECT BIBLIOGRAPHY

General:

Alldridge, Nick (ed), *The Hearth Tax: Problems and Possibilities*, Papers submitted to the Conference of Teachers in Regional and Local History in Tertiary Education held at the Institute of Historical Research, London, in March 1983 (School of Humanities and Community Education, Humberside College of Higher Education, for the Conference of Teachers in Regional and Local History in Tertiary Education (CORAL), 1983)

Beckett, J. V. and Barley, M. W., Introduction, *Nottinghamshire Hearth Tax, 1664-1674* (Thoroton Society Record Series, Vol. XXXVII, 1988)

Chandaman, C. D., *The English Public Revenue, 1660-1688* (Oxford, 1975)

Edwards, D. G., Introduction, *Derbyshire Hearth Tax Assessments, 1662-1770*, VII (1982)

Emmison, F. G. and Gray, I., *County Records* (Historical Association, 1973). Contains list of extant returns in local record offices

Gibson, J. S. W., *The Hearth Tax, Other Later Stuart Tax Lists and the Association Oath Rolls* (Federation of Family History Societies, 1985)

Howell, Roger, "Hearth Tax Returns" (*Short Guides to Records*, 7, reprinted from *History*, vol. 49, 1964)

Kennedy, W., *English Taxation, 1640-1799* (1913)

Marshall, L. M., "The Levying of the Hearth Tax, 1662-1688" (*English Historical Review*, vol. 51, 1936)

Meekings, C. A. F., Introduction, *The Hearth Tax, 1662-1689*, Exhibition of Records (Public Record Office, 1962)

Meekings, C. A. F., Introduction, *Dorset Hearth Tax Assessments, 1662-1664* (Dorchester, 1951)

Meekings, C. A. F., Introduction, *Surrey Hearth Tax, 1664* (Surrey Record Society, XVII, nos 41-42, 1940)

Patten, John, "The Hearth Taxes, 1662-1689" (*Local Population Studies*, No. 7, Autumn 1971)

Pearl, Susan, "Parish Sources, Part 1, Hearth Tax: the census of the 17th century", (*Family Tree Magazine*, Vol. 7, No. 5, March 1991)

Russell, P. D. D., Introduction, *The Hearth Tax Returns for the Isle of Wight, 1664 to 1674* (Isle of Wight Record Series, Volume 1, Isle of Wight County Record Office, 1981)

Styles, Philip, "Introduction to the Warwickshire Hearth Tax Records", *Warwick County Records Hearth Tax Returns Volume I*, Walker, Margaret (ed) (Warwickshire County Council, 1957)

Thirsk, Joan and Cooper, J. P. (eds), *17th Century Economic Documents* (Oxford, 1972)

Tomlinson, Howard, "Financial and Administrative Developments in England, 1660-1688", *The Restored Monarchy, 1660-1688*, Jones, J. R. (ed) (1979)

West, J. *Village Records* (2nd edition, Chichester, 1982). Contains a list of hearth tax documents which have appeared in print up to and including 1981.

Hampshire:

Barstow, H. G., *The Hearth Tax Returns of 1665* (Eastleigh and District Local History Society, Special Paper No. 7, 1986)[1]

Christie, Peter, "An Analysis of the 1674 Hearth Tax Returns for Portsmouth", *Portsmouth Geographical Essays*, Volume II (Portsmouth Polytechnic, 1976)[2]

Economic Development in South-East Hampshire—The Evidence of the Hearth Tax (anonymous and undated typescript—HRO Hampshire pamphlets 3)

James, Thomas Beaumont, *A Handbook of Demographic, Quantitative and Nominal Records for the History of Southampton, 1450 to 1850* (Southampton 1975)

James, T. B., *Southampton Sources, 1086-1900* (Southampton Records Series, Vol. XXVI, 1983)

Michelmersh entry in Dorset hearth tax returns, 1663 (HRO Photocopy 69)

Meirion-Jones, Gwyn I., "The Use of Hearth Tax Returns and Vernacular Architecture in Settlement Studies with Examples from North-East Hampshire" (*Transactions* of the Institute of British Geographers, July 1971)

Reger, A. J. C., "Fareham and the Hearth Tax Returns" (*Fareham Past and Present*, Volume 1, Book VIII, Autumn 1968)[1]

Rosen, Adrienne B., *Economic and Social Aspects of the History of Winchester, 1520-1670* (Oxford University, Ph.D thesis, 1975)

Taylor, John Robert, *Population, Disease and Family Structure in Early Modern Hampshire, with special reference to the towns* (Southampton University, Ph.D thesis, 1980)

Watts, D. G. and Williams, C. L. Sinclair, *The Hearth Tax Returns for the Hundred of Titchfield, 1664-1665* (Titchfield History Society, 1985)[1]

Winchester hearth tax documents, 1664-1674. Photocopies, with transcripts, of documents held by the Public Record Office (HRO)

Yates, E. M., "Into the 18th Century" (*The Selborne Association Newsletter*, No. 22, June 1985)[1]

Footnotes:

1. Includes transcript of 1665 hearth tax assessment for area concerned
2. Includes transcript of 1674 hearth tax assessment and of paupers from 1665 hearth tax assessment for Portsmouth.

INDEX OF PERSONAL NAMES

In order to make this index manageable, surnames which seem likely to be variants of a single form have been grouped together under the most common spelling found (or the most modern spelling where the choice is equal) with cross-references where appropriate. Variant spellings are placed in brackets in alphabetical order after the chosen form. Titles, with the exception of baronet, Sir and Lord, have been omitted unless no forename is given. Illegible and omitted forenames and titles are denoted by —. All references are to section numbers.

[A]line
— 1
Abarrow (Abarrowe, Aburrowe)
Anthony 517, 529; Mistress 128; Thomas 72; Widow 220
Abbin (*see also* Habben)
Gervase 192
Abbott (Abbotts)
Anthony 294, 299; Charles 162; Henry 473; John 143, 434(2), 473; Oliver 418; Robert 24, 229; Thomas 148, 299; Widow 5, 100, 260, 292; William 3
Abery
John 39
Abnett
Widow 217
Aborne
Thomas 279
Abraham (Abram)
Francis 229; Henry 36; Jane 37; John 27, 148; Richard 99, 158; Robert 229; Thomas 32; Widow 36, 37
Abridge
George 51
Absolon
William 159
Ackland
Edward 424; Henry 51; John 424; Robert 51
Ackers (Acers, Acres)
Edward 297, 299; George 17; Robert 302; Thomas 296
Ackley
Richard 49
Acton
Henry 1
Adasonne
Widow 508
Adcock
William 100
Addams (Adams, Addoms)
Andrew 418, 425; Anthony 231; Barnard 331; Edward 229, 292, 324, 450(3); George 418; Henry 364; James 76, 418; Jerome 229; John 23, 50, 208, 230, 300; Laurence 29; Mister 515; Richard 25, 56, 291, 418(2); Robert 25, 72, 517(2), 530; Sidrach 1; Thomas 1, 23, 29(2), 87, 229(2), 418(2), 443, 482; Widow 29(3), 112, 230, 283, 348; William 56, 66, 387
Adderly
John 218; Thomas 281
Addes
John 1
Addington
James 25
Adey (Adye)
William 98(2)
Adlam
John 118; Widow 118
Adlington (Addlington)
James 530; John 518
Adrey
John 40

Agden
John 38; Thomas 38
Ager
John 135; Widow 135
Akins
Cuthbert 238
Albeck
John 53
Albery (Albrey)
Edward 163(2); Joan 370; John 172; Peter 1; Robert 194; Thomas 169, 172, 205; William 194, 367, 423
Albin
Henry 1
Alder
John 418; Robert 298
Alderslade
John 191
Alderton
Jasper 418
Aldred
Edward 227; John 223, 247; Richard 216; Stephen 201; Widow 398, 437; William 372
Aldridge (Aldridg)
David 456; George 198; Henry 42, 100; John 1, 43, 93(2), 460, 470, 471; Mister 470; Richard 100, 117; Robert 43, 46; Thomas 195, 221; Widow 42, 104
Alee (Aley, Ally)
Henry 159; John 332; Richard 334; Widow 322, 332; William 334
Alexander
Christopher 379; Edward 429; George 383; Henry 376; John 331, 378(2), 397, 420; Mister 528; Richard 175, 362, 397(2), 418; Robert 376; Thomas 379, 397(2); Widow 379; William 332, 378; Zacharias 379
Alford
Andrew 256; Edward 334; Widow 517; William 434
Alison
John 1, 229(2)
Allaby
William 424
Allen (Allin, Allon)
Abraham 246; Alexander 492; Barnard 418; Benjamin 271, 404; Dorothy 394; Francis 5; George 12; Henry 267; John 229, 246, 259, 271, 366, 394, 395, 478; Joseph 404; Mary 101; Nicholas 164, 208, 282; Philip 450; Richard 229, 418; Robert 163, 338, 394; Thomas 267, 334(2), 336, 339, 499, 505, 531; Titus 376; Walter 316; Widow 29, 54, 76, 229, 290, 397, 450, 474; William 81, 102, 252, 418, 457, 514
Allingham
Geoffrey 141; Philip 245
Alliston
Richard 59
Allnett
Edward 45
Allom
George 164
Alloway
Christopher 376(2), 382
Allwright (Alwright)
John 294; Richard 394; Thomas 294
Almer
John 84
Alsford
Alexander 99; John 99
Althrage
John 455
Alton
John 276
Alvin
Simon 40
Alwin
Thomas 505
Amblen (Amblin, Amlen)
John 363; William 363(2), 431

Ambleton (*see also* Hambleton)
John 418
Amdrilly
Richard 513
America
Nicholas 98(2)
Ameres (Ameers)
John 208; Mark 210; Thomas 208
Ames
John 89; Thomas 89; William 89
Amon
Robert 86
Amorosse
Goodman 223
Amy (Amey)
Edward 97, 148; Margery 102; Widow 97
Anderson
Widow 38
Andrews (Andrew, Andrewes)
Andrew 163; Barnaby 102; Barwick 242; Daniel 247; Edward 163; Henry 102, 192; Hugh 242; Humphrey 193; James 193, 522; Joan 157; John 112, 113, 163, 192, 193, 202, 462, 504; Mary 93; Mister 528; Nicholas 228, 513; Ralph 182; Richard 90, 93, 178, 244, 284, 335; Robert 93, 96; Simon 102; Thomas 163, 193, 213, 246, 368, 436; Widow 38(2), 93, 135, 193, 292, 332, 448, 455; William 80, 90, 135, 193(2), 244, 498
Andross
Dorothy 332
Andsley
Abraham 38
Aneave
Alexander 459
Angell
William 56
Anger
Widow 273
Angfeild
Thomas 375
Angood (Anngood)
Catherine 101; John 117
Anne
John 369
Annedowne
Edward 142; Elmor 121
Annell
Austin 237; Nicholas 414; Widow 333; William 258; — 254
Annely
Moses 253
Annetts (Annett)
John 450; Robert 466; Widow 454
Annstie
Samuel 151
Ansell
Alice 72; Austin 427; Edward 1, 39; John 5(2), 332; Robert 418; Widow 94; William 24, 208
Anthony
Edward 466; Henry 504; John 466; Peter 504, 507, 520
Anthram (Anthrom, Anthrum, Antram, Antrum)
Edward 17(2); Francis 7; Elias 522; Ellis 526; George 13; John 7; Laurence 38; Widow 281
Apers
John 330
Apeton
James 294
Appery
Richard 451
Appleford
Charles 260; Edward 229; Henry 506; John 4, 216, 218; Richard 1, 218; Stephen 5; Thomas 15, 17; Widow 51; William 246, 333
Applegarth
John 206; William 193
Appleton
George 183, 299; Jane 299; James 294; John 298, 309, 315,

Appleton—*cont'd.*
317, 383, 398; Moses 309; Thomas 298, 317; Widow 317, 319; William 298, 378, 405
Appsley
Widow 189
Archer
Ann 93; Edward 524; John 23, 256, 414; Mister 1; Stephen 414; Thomas 414; Walter 271; Widow 162; William 268, 383
Arelett
Thomas 398
Arland
Thomas 38
Arminer
John 148; Robert 158; Thomas 38; Widow 257; William 258
Arnell
Henry 128; Walter 134
Arnewood
James 134
Arnold
Christopher 490; Daniel 79; Henry 164; John 1, 76, 232; Nicholas 242; Peter 193; Richard 232; Thomas 24, 37, 148, 258; Widow 76, 303, 333; William 37, 79
Arnum
Ann 129
Aroys
Thomas 431
Arthur (Arthor)
Anthony 512; Edward 31, 295, 465; John 462; Laurence 60; Stephen 462; Thomas 245, 265; Walter 499; William 76
Arundell (Arrundell)
Francis 218; Mistress 1, 237
Arwood
Robert 531
Ash
Robert 435; Widow 434
Ashbourne
Joseph 418
Asher
Henry 456; John 34, 456, 488; Richard 457; Simon 457; William 279
Ashley (Asshly)
Francis 466; John 160, 470; Richard 461; Thomas 297
Ashton
Edward 418; Nicholas 229; Peter 35; Richard 418; Simon 108; Widow 51
Ashyngton
John 370
Asker
Widow 1
Aslett (Aslutt) (*see also* Haslett)
Bartholomew 371; Elleger 396; Henry 370, 392; Jerome 431; John 192, 378, 392; Julian 370; Nicholas 355; Richard 74, 396; Stephen 399; Thomas 81; Widow 355; William 205
Astlett
Jacob 192; John 192; Justinian 192, Thomas 192
Aterrifield
Henry 529
Atherin
Robert 332
Atherley (Atherly)
Arthur 519, 530; John 84; Robert 518
Atherne
Mister 17(3)
Athrom
Thomas 377
Atkins (Atkines, Attkins)
Edward 385, 472; Francis 332; James 86; Richard 1, 229; Thomas 67, 68; Widow 118; William 472
Atkinson (Attkinson)
Widow 431; William 192
Atlander
Francis 108

Atneave
John 459; Richard 456; William 459
Atterine
John 332
Attfeild
John 317
Attland
Hugh 119
Attlane
Thomas 91, William 119
Attron
George 333
Attwater (Atwater)
George 374; Widow 419
Attweek (Attweeke)
John 214; Thomas 54
Attwood
Edward 3, 46(2), 77; John 72(2), 89; Oliver 196
Aubrey (Aubery)
Henry 119; Mister 442; Richard 32; Widow 448
Auger (Augar)
Elizabeth 523b; John 134
Austin (Austen)
Andrew 68; Edmund 1; Edward 51, 282; Giles 517; James 1; John 1, 21, 80, 200, 229, 247, 493; Matthew 458; Mister 283; Peter 242; Richard 222, 242; Robert 292; Samson 29; Thomas 17, 112, 200, 340, 418; Widow 55, 468, 529; William 493; — 200
Avare
Robert 2
Avery (*see also* Havery)
Barzillay 37; Daniel 171; John 169; Michael 130; Thomas 54; Widow 336, 479
Avis
Henry 38
Awner
William 119
Axeby
Widow 208
Aycliff
Ann 1
Ayles
James 100; John 100(3); Nicholas 100; Robert 245; Stephen 100; Timothy 100; Widow 86; William 100
Ayleward (Aylward)
Edward 217; Humphrey 46; John 1(2); Richard 220, 229; Robert 385; Roger 227; Thomas 44, 216; Widow 220; William 73
Ayleworth
William 397
Ayley (Aylee)
George 258; Thomas 172
Ayliffe (Ayliff)
Anthony 378; Francis 301; John 304; Mary 322; Mister 294, 299; Peter 313; Richard 304, 340, 370; Thomas 38
Ayling (Aylinge) (*see also* Hayling)
Francis 40, 41; James 38; John 211(2), 226; Nicholas 84; Thomas 282; Richard 226, 372; Thomas 74; William 258, 372
Aylmer
Francis 41; Robert 40; William 41
Ayres (Ayers) (*see also* Heyres)
Abraham 530; Andrew 163; Leonard 376; Robert 433; Theophilus 133; Thomas 49; William 51, 420
Ayrey
Christopher 133
Aysh
Catherine 112; Widow 112
B
Mister 357
Babes
Edward 26; Peter 29
Babye
Jane 37

Bachell
Jerome 269; Widow 392; William 255, 290, 364
Backshall
Widow 84
Backton
Roger 93
Bacon (Backen)
Nicholas 494; Richard 286; Robert 461
Badcock
Guy 229; Henry 291; John 161, 291; Simon 160; Widow 316; William 1, 160, 316
Badd
Sir Thomas 48, 325
Badden
Richard 472
Badforde
Mister 410
Badge
John 347
Badger
Henry 229; John 229(3)
Badgesly (Badgley, Badgsley, Badsley)
Richard 286; Thomas 240, 316; Widow 331
Badripp
John 100; Nicholas 103; William 117, 119
Baff
William 418
Bagent (Bagen)
Ann 244; John 398; Ralph 370; Robert 177, 195, 369
Bages
Widow 229
Bagger
Widow 435
Baghurst
Richard 336
Bagin (Bagine)
Ezekiel 198; Henry 182; Joan 75; Moses 404; Richard 404; William 407; — 333
Bagley
Thomas 76
Bagshall
Arthur 40(2)
Baillehache
John 530
Baily (Bayly)
Aringall 300; Arthur 40; Barnard 375; Edmund 362; Edward 375, 378, 493; George 431; Henry 100, 163, 249, 498; Isaac 135; James 96, 280; John 1, 179, 223, 263, 320, 408, 443, 456, 508; Joseph 283; Nicholas 113, 162, 317, 378; Peter 163, 164; Richard 256, 274, 338, 424; Thomas 8, 10, 40, 106, 216 (2), 229, 367; Widow 113, 135, 182, 197, 299, 354, 363, 378, 429, 448; William 38, 81, 85, 112, 113 (2), 255, 418, 434, 456; — 40
Baker
Arthur 38; Christopher 193, 194; Daniel 1, 46; Edward 356, 398(2), 403, 424; Francis 419; George 401 (2); Henry 35, 39, 49, 89, 123, 194, 268; James 96; Jane 89; John 37, 70, 77, 130, 194(2), 201, 205, 207, 208, 223(2), 286, 453, 518; Joseph 256; Margaret 135; Matthew 1; Nicholas 194(2), 245; Peter 59, 119; Philip 205, 453; Polixine 490; Ralph 231; Richard 4, 46, 104, 209, 223(2), 227(2), 235, 353, 424, 436; Robert 83, 136, 193, 245, 267(2), 283; Thomas 46, 67, 89, 194, 196, 205, 208, 353, 384, 443(2), 518, 530; Widow 122, 163, 193, 196, 205(3), 229, 245, 248, 434, 524, 529; William 1 (2), 163(2), 189, 194, 220, 221, 222, 276, 399, 504 (2), 523a; — 1, 39, 168
Baldchild
George 177

Balden
Richard 505
Balding
Thomas 531
Baldrey *see* Bauldrey
Baldwin (Baldwyn)
Adam 455, 504; Andrew 178; George 455; Joan 178; John 292; Richard 455; Widow 455, 462; William 178, 462
Bales
Peter 145
Ball (Balle)
Daniel 408; Henry 193; John 397(2), 479; Mister 363; Richard 74; Robert 367; Widow 513; William 449
Ballard
James 506; John 38, 79; Thomas 138, 283; William 38, 482
Ballet
William 164
Bally
William 40
Balney
Mister 104
Bamister
Roger 100
Bamon
Stephen 460; William 483
Bampton
Ambrose 159; Henry 102; John 102, 435; Mary 102; Richard 497; Thomas 112; William 100, 435
Banborne
John 378
Band
Henry 1; John 345; Thomas 1; William 345(2)
Banes (Bane)
Andrew 280; Leonard 38; Thomas 229; William 524
Banks
Alexander 434
Banner
William 282
Bannings
Philip 416; Samuel 294
Bannister (Banister)
Jane 98; Michael 411; Robert 213 (Sir); Thomas 194; William 92(2)
Banston
John 454; Richard 454
Barber (Barbour)
Edward 465; John 436, 490; Joseph 493; Laurence 56; Matthew 29; Mister 473; Richard 240; Robert 240; Thomas 154; William 76, 424
Barbone (Barebone, Bearebone)
Edward 332; John 93; Thomas 332
Barcomb
George 1; Mark 244
Barden
Joan 189; Roger 194 (2)
Barfoot (Barfoote, Barfoott)
Anthony 34; Edward 35 (2); George 507; Henry 29 (2), 30, 418; James 229; John 1, 77; Leonard 229; Richard 26, 36, 266; Robert 26 (2), 418; Roger 88, 227; Thomas 240; Walter 418; Widow 26, 29; William 229
Barge
John 321
Bargent (Bargen, Bargin)
Alice 484; John 94, 193, 333; Mary 484; Robert 395
Barger
Jacob 531; James 517; Widow 96
Barges
William 86
Barker
Doctor 212; John 363, 397; Joseph 115; Richard 348; Robert 340, 454; Thomas 348, 397; Widow 339
Barkham
William 195
Barkshire
John 361; William 398

Barkwood
Edward 332
Barling
John 252, 493; Laurence 192; Nicholas 89, 230; Thomas 507; Widow 93; William 14, 16
Barlow (Barlowe)
Anthony 219; Barnard 493; Doctor 462; Henry 332; Richard 337; Widow 292 (2); William 434; —1
Barly
Thomas 513
Barnaby
John 38, 260 (2), 394, 436; Richard 160; Robert 260; Stephen 252; Thomas 479
Barnard (Bernard, Burnard)
Andrew 290(2); Benjamin 75; Edmund 46; Edward 217; Henry 368; James 130; Jane 334; John 137, 193, 208 (3), 217 (2), 290, 291, 324, 334; Laurence 211; Maurice 332; Michael 338, 356; Nicholas 88, 241, 418; Philip 290, 291, 434; Richard 50, 418, 428, 444, 521; Robert 4, 347, 192, 213, 522, 526; Thomas 1, 36, 290, 436, 522, 526; Widow 51, 229, 290, 334, 405, 408, 418; William 217, 229, 249, 357, 391, 405, 517, 518; — 354
Barneham
Mister 355
Barnes
Ann 122; Clement 81; Dorothy 113; Edward 91; Henry 319, 370, 402; Humphrey 375; John 85, 392, 397, 445; Laurence 130; Martin 118; Richard 1; Robert 88, 273; Thomas 104, 117 (2), 332; Walter 248; Widow 120, 317, 332; William 118, 375, 402; —1
Barnet
Thomas 1; William 216
Barram
John 162, 208
Barrent
Nicholas 120
Barrett
Henry 422; John 163, 419; Mister 503; Nicholas 339; Peter 229; Robert 375, 396; Thomas 376; Widow 339; William 164, 229, 478
Barrington
Francis 257; Richard 117
Barrow (Barrowe, Barrowes, Barrows)
Benjamin 96; Deodatus 378 (2); Dominic 518, 530; Francis 108 (2); James 93; John 3, 119; Lancelot 229; Mister 473; Ralph 2; Richard 1, 270, 363; Roger 128; Stephen 119; Walter 269; Widow 363; William 122, 283
Barry (Barrey, Bary)
Anthony 56; Francis 112; Henry 110, 131; John 30; Michael 104; Richard 30, 106; Roger 56; Stephen 30; Thomas 30 (2); Walter 112; Widow 30; William 29, 30, 69
Barter
Charles 108; John 14, 100, 476; Nicholas 112; Thomas 527; Widow 483; William 475
Bartholomew (Bartolomew)
Barnard 358; Edward 38; Joan 335; John 358; Richard 47; Robert 135; Thomas 378; Widow 312; William 370
Barthorne
Michael 145
Bartlett (Barttlet)
Edward 335; James 472; John 162; Robert 209; Thomas 2, 13; Widow 377
Bartlidge
Widow 252

Barton (Barten, Bartin)
Anthony 428; Eustace 431; Isaac 527 (2); James 1, 290; John 51 (2), 100, 522; Nicholas 424; Peter 19; Richard 38, 244, 473; Robert 19; Roger 51, 54; Sarah 531; Thomas 19 (2), 257; Toby 122; Widow 1, 37, 526; William 19, 229, 246
Barwick
Daniel 82; John 418; Thomas 436; William 434
Bascomb
John 524
Basford
Simon 317
Basing
Robert 332
Baslett
Margaret 192; Mary 192
Bason
Arthur 120
Basor
Robert 335
Bassett
Edward 311; John 46, 71, 216, 243, 311; Richard 93, 243, 248; Robert 195; Sarah 37, 56; Thomas 246; Widow 5; William 16, 237, 311
Bassill (Barzill, Bazill)
Thomas 164; William 164 (2)
Bastard (Basteed)
John 300; Nicholas 244; Widow 244
Basten (Bastone)
John 334; Robert 56; Widow 1(3); William 208, 334
Batchelor (Bachelor, Bachiler, Batchilor)
Andrew 423; Edward 530; Francis 255; Giles 317; Herbert 38; Henry 96; John 10, 96, 316, 339, 346, 506, 528; Laurence 357; Nicholas 317, 397; Peter 316; Richard 317 (2); Thomas 148, 317, 431; Tomaz 244; Walter 418; Widow 96, 317; William 317, 356
Bates
Jethro 40; Mister 112, 246; Nicholas 229; Richard 241; Widow 229; William 229
Bath
John 128, 129; Joseph 436; Nicholas 449; Roland 356; Widow 118, 377
Bathurst
Anthony 356
Batley
Thomas 162
Batson (Battson)
John 100; Widow 100
Batt
Andrew 56; Christopher 457; Devorix 442; George 120; Henry 478; James 215; John 260 (2), 454, 456, 459; Margery 451; Richard 56, 114; Robert 1, 418; Thomas 242; Widow 260, 448, 483; William 114, 481
Battell (Battaille)
John 1, 206, 249; Philip 276; Thomas 339
Batten (Batton)
Edward 89; John 40, 247; Mister 40; Reynold 100; William 1, 98
Batter
Samuel 100
Battlemore
Nicholas 317; Richard 338
Baugh
Edward 465
Baulch
John 1; Thomas 1
Bauldry (Baldrey, Bauldrey)
Christian 269; Edward 42, 269; Richard 269; Robert 33
Baverstock (Bawerstock)
Daniel 28, 438; George 515; John 436, 481, 515; Robert 244, 515; Thomas 515; William 237

Bawd
Widow 342
Bawdin
Widow 512
Baxton
John 513
Bay (Baye, Bayes)
Henry 346; Nicholas 213; Thomas 286; William 298
Bayliff
Dorothy 440; William 115
Bayly *see* Baily
Beacham
Andrew 1; George 477; James 476; John 76, 459, 471; Widow 291, 477
Beacher
William 205
Beachman
Richard 100
Beagly
John 199
Beake
John 487 (2); Thomas 473
Beakly
Nicholas 434
Beakon
Thomas 1
Beale (Bealls, Beele)
Edward 474; George 478; Jerome 209; Jethro 206; John 1, 255, 376, 418, 449, 518; Leonard 531; Peter 206; Richard 89; Robert 333; Stephen 277; Thomas 318, 323, 407, 449, 476; Walter 515; Widow 279, 342, 441, 485; William 89, 352, 376, 449; — 89
Beamon (Bemon)
John 260, 476; Nicholas 158; Richard 76; Widow 260
Beamord
Henry 501
Beane (Beene)
John 68, 76, 221; Nicholas 221; Peter 254; Ralph 236, 490; Robert 6; Roger 55, 62; Thomas 42, 76; Widow 4
Beard (Bierd)
Edward 258; George 37, 71; John 317; Mister 18; Richard 332; Robert 38, 181; Widow 229; William 385
Beare
Dorothy 325; Edward 503; George 437; James 5; John 160, 437, 503, 515; Joseph 437; Richard 229, 338, 353; Robert 236, 470; Thomas 299; Widow 446; William 437
Bearne
Thomas 494
Beasent (Besant, Bessant)
Simon 369; Thomas 472; William 95, 100
Beasling
Widow 113
Beaston (Beestone)
Doctor 292; John 139; Mister 18; William 135
Beate
Widow 317
Beatley
Peter 1
Beawmont (Beamont)
George 248; John 331; Widow 332
Beazer
Tobias 434; Widow 434
Beck (Becke)
Thomas 129; William 129, 418, 422
Beckensall (Beckensell, Beckinsall, Bekensell)
John 247; Richard 1; Thomas 243; William 219
Beckett
Robert 158
Beckington
Widow 506
Beckley
Richard 342; Thomas 342

Beckner
John 178
Bedbrooke
Henry 67; Nicholas 29 (2)
Bedford
Ann 462; Benjamin 47; Henry 266, 530; James 429; Joan 447; John 462, 473; Richard 214; Robert 319; Thomas 442, 473; Widow 473; William 441
Bedridge
William 468
Beech
Ambrose 267; John 488; Richard 263, 267, 488
Beedle (Beadle)
Edward 375; Elizabeth 19; George 380; Huff 473; John 376; Robert 175, 376; Thomas 376; Widow 14; William 14, 376
Begge
Ursula 293
Belbin (Belben, Bellbin)
Edward 148; James 100; Joseph 229; Peter 1; Richard 104; William 100, 290
Belchamber
John 422; Mister 40
Belden
Richard 104
Beldham
Thomas 370
Bell
Christopher 521; Isaac 1; Leonard 279; Robert 407, 465; Roger 465; Walter 494; Widow 93, 354, 465, 527
Bellfry
Henry 530
Bellinger
Richard 264 (2)
Bellinghurst
John 194
Bellman
John 515; Thomas 160
Bellord
William 332
Belom
Richard 100
Belston
Richard 84
Belt
George 219
Belton
James 290; Michael 360; William 308, 409
Bemister
Giles 117; 117 (3), 135; Peter 117; William 117
Benbery
Widow 39
Bence (Bennice)
Martin 100; Philip 100; William 98, 145
Bendale
Richard 445; Robert 443
Bender
Richard 324
Benevall
John 362
Benfold
John 171
Benford
Joseph 473
Bengar (Benger)
John 1, 519; Widow 129, 428
Bengley
Thomas 434
Benham
Edward 293; James 317; John 240, 487; Peter 317; Richard 298, 364, 428; Robert 377; Stephen 303; Thomas 32, 332, 351, 390; Widow 246, 272, 283, 330, 339, 351, 370, 514; William 1, 290, 316 (2), 338, 339 (3), 351 (2), 397
Benister
Robert 143
Benjamin
John 38

Bennett
Christopher 297; George 471; Humphrey 174 (Sir); James 385; John 2, 7, 17, 48, 208; Mabel 462; Margaret 320; Mister 456; Nicholas 209; Robert 202; Thomas 325; Widow 87, 280, 299; William 49, 51, 202, 488
Bennettland
Robert 38
Bennings
Richard 299
Bennis
Thomas 470
Benny
Richard 25
Benson (Bensone)
Nicholas 38; Widow 317
Bensteed (Benstead, Bensted, Binsted, Binsteed)
Andrew 253; Anthony 45, 59, 158; Christopher 42; Edward 20; Elizabeth 44, 56; George 42; Henry 16, 72 (2); Joan 77; John 6, 12, 23, 38, 53, 67, 354; Nicholas 216, 421; Peter 176; Richard 44, 65, 68 (3), 295; Robert 23, 183; Thomas 20, 68; Widow 12, 45 (2), 217; William 23 (2), 46, 67, 202
Benster
John 100
Bent
James 385; John 483; Thomas 434; William 385
Bentall
Mister 481
Bently
Richard 385; Robert 298; Thomas 12
Benwell
Francis 490
Benyeare
Jasper 341
Berindge
Widow 256; William 256
Berington
Richard 353
Berk
Geoffrey 251
Bernard *see* Barnard
Berrett
Robert 449; Stephen 483; William 483
Berry
Edward 163; John 357; Thomas 27
Beslant
Widow 114
Besling (Bessling)
Ralph 112; Robert 112
Best
Giles 473; William 471, 523a
Besten
Widow 1
Bestland
Henry 108
Betham
Widow 332; William 332
Bethell
Widow 29; William 29
Bether
Widow 100
Bethwine
Predix 229
Bettridge (Beatridge, Bethridg, Betridge, Betteridge)
Joan 471; Mark 461, 462, 525; Silvester 472; William 280
Betts
James 23; Mister 138; William 38
Bettser
Robert 367
Bettsworth (Betsworth, Bettisworth)
John 1, 163, 226, 249; Mary 182; Mister 211, 212; Nicholas 372; Robert 209; Thomas 163, 372, 485; Widow 209, 298; William 176, 194, 227, 433
Bevis (Beavice, Beavis)
Andrew 334; Henry 34, 322;

Richard 434, 440; Stephen 2; Thomas 100; Widow 447
Bewfeild
Humphrey 160
Bewninge
Edmund 42
Bewstock
Robert 244
Bexhill
John 80
Bexton
Richard 290
Bible
Elizabeth 148
Biccas
Humphrey 490
Bickner (Bigner)
George 392; Widow 430
Bidden
Vincent 100
Bidges
Widow 160
Biding
John 214, 218 (2); Richard 218, 229, 372; Robert 214; William 216
Bidle
Henry 100; Widow 236; William 139
Bidlecomb (Bedlecombe, Bidlecombe, Bidlecome)
Bartholomew 135; Christopher 98; Dorothy 125; Francis 136; John 52, 95, 100, 103 (2), 104, 153, 162; Richard 118, 120; Thomas 119; Ursula 151; Widow 151; William 98, 103 (2)
Biffin (Biffen)
John 1, 339; William 345
Biggs (Bigges)
Elizabeth 293; Francis 29; Gilbert 327; James 1, 416, 417; John 38, 84, 388; Joseph 1; Ludd 450; Mister 208; Nathaniel 51; Nicholas 51; Peter 293, 426; Richard 216; Robert 29; Sarah 293; Thomas 9, 29; Widow 1, 285 (2), 476; William 419
Biggwood
Arthur 292
Bignall (Bicknell, Bignold, Bignoll)
George 369; Henry 183; James 388; John 170, 189, 196, 237 (2), 354, 405, 529; Laurence 229; Richard 284 (2); Widow 383, 391; William 189; — 383
Biles *see* Byles
Bill
William 269
Billemore
William 384
Billett
Edward 339
Bilson
Leonard 211; Osmond 208
Bilston (Bilstone)
John 284; Richard 456; Thomas 290
Binckman
Mister 1
Binfeild
Widow 396
Birch *see* Burch
Bird
Arthur 460; John 1, 317, 355, 478; Robert 434 (2); Roger 434 (2); Walter 424; Widow 1, 216, 436
Biscoe
John 396
Bishopp (Bisshopp, Bissopp)
Amy 115; Ellis 38; Humphrey 229; John 1, 2, 112, 113, 332; Ralph 454; Richard 392; Robert 1, 113, 151 (2); Stephen 229; Thomas 123; Widow 113
Biskin
John 83
Bisling
Henry 1
Biss (Bisse)
John 89, 335

Bissell (Bissill)
Charles 208; Widow 1
Bistone (Bistome)
Thomas 38; Widow 117
Bistowe
Thomas 38
Bittle
George 5
Blackford (Blachford, Blashford)
Mister 109, 110; Richard 520, 528; William 468
Blackgrave
John 280
Blackhouse
Richard 189
Blackly
James 29
Blackman
Mary 437; Robert 362, William 457
Blackmore
Edward 450; Thomas 528
Blackwell
Francis 226
Blake (Blak)
Andrew 462; Anthony 265 (2); Austin 471; Bartholomew 76; Edward 444, 474; Elias 531; Elizabeth 440; Francis 326; Henry 154; Hugh 526; Joan 444; John 27, 122, 123, 138, 161, 195, 265, 281, 324, 421, 434, 446, 462; Laurence 471; Mary 395; Mistress 529; Nicholas 434, 479; Peter 98, 348, 434, 479; Philip 362, 417; Richard 1, 265, 292 (2), 299, 356, 385, 421, 434; Robert 282, 314, 326; Thomas 94, 117, 265 (2), 330, 509; Walter 500; Widow 38, 122, 128, 135, 244, 265, 370, 434, 437; William 74, 98, 252, 347, 434, 439, 441, 445, 520, 527; — 95
Blanchard
Ann 164; Arthur 100, 157; Edward 343; Henry 193; James 118, 193; Joan 437; John 40, 84, 110; Michael 193, 202; Nathaniel 520; Pittman 120; Richard 437; Thomas 100, 177; Widow 46; William 118, 527
Blanchett (Blaunchett)
John 481; Thomas 414
Blancket
William 521
Blaner (Blanner)
John 324; William 324
Blatch (Blach, Blatches)
Andrew 458; Edward 1; John 135, 503; Martin 135; Michael 99; Richard 473; Thomas 135, 494; William 244, 520
Blaunch
Thomas 385; William 385
Blaystone
William 332
Blaze
Mistress 357
Bleatham
John 89
Blissett
John 292; William 229
Blith
Widow 355
Blitch
Stephen 38
Bloss
John 100
Blowes
Mister 504
Bloyce
Nicholas 505
Bluatt
James 52
Blundell
Avis 392; Joan 413; John 312, 408; Richard 356; Widow 408
Blunden
Argent 256; Deborah 296; John 324; Nicholas 18; Robert 418; Samuel 398; Stephen 197; Widow 387; William 270, 413, 418 (2)

Blundy
Minever 316; Richard 271
Blunn
Michael 103
Blunt
Henry 112; James 1; John 216; Mister 245; Widow 326
Blye
William 317
Blymston
Ralph 257, 258
Boare (Bore)
Dorothy 122; John 122; Thomas 135; Widow 122 (2)
Bodley
Widow 383
Body
Thomas 1
Bodycoate (Bodicote, Bodycotte)
Mary 269; Richard 529; Susan 479; William 75, 270
Boghurst
Henry 215; Thomas 215
Bold
Arthur 208; John 252, 256; Michael 17; William 493
Bolter
Edward 1
Bolton (Boulton, Bowlton)
Goodman 47; Henry 117; John 136; Judith 361; Nicholas 285; Philip 56, 380; Richard 361; Robert 39; Thomas 5, 145; Widow 114
Bombye
Richard 1
Bond
Ambrose 102; Edward 89, 347; Henry 152; Humphrey 100; John 152, 347; Moses 334; Richard 100; Stephen 276; Thomas 38, 118, 130, 153; Widow 59, 153; William 24, 99, 164
Bone (Bowne)
Charles 283; Edward 37; Hannah 504; Henry 36; James 36; John 36, 223, 237, 241, 242, 249, 371; Michael 241; Nicholas 222; Richard 5, 242, 279; Robert 241; Thomas 128, 184, 524; William 75, 163, 170, 242, 244, 529
Boneham
Ann 75
Bonfild (Bonvell)
Austin 518; John 378
Bonford
Stephen 283
Bonner
John 64; Nicholas 515; Richard 468 (2); William 37
Bonnett (Bornett)
Alexander 99; Emblem 290
Bonney (Boney)
Benjamin 435; John 16, 468; Richard 436; Robert 434, 436; Thomas 436, 488; Widow 434
Bonus
Widow 114
Booker
Edward 35; James 526; John 38, 39, 171, 227, 240, 343; Richard 208, 240 (2), 293; Robert 35; Thomas 220; Widow 227, 526
Bootey
John 483
Booth
Savage 385
Borde
John 319, 434 (2)
Borden
Thomas 201
Boreman
John 23
Boshere
Robert 29
Bossell
Edward 378; John 394; William 308
Boswell (Bozwell)
Christian 1; Widow 390
Bottome
Henry 21; Widow 436

Bound (Bounds)
Edith 113; John 108; Maurice 102; Nicholas 102; Richard 114; Robert 100; Thomas 153; Widow 24; William 135
Bourne (Boorenn, Boorne, Borne)
Christopher 135; John 37; Joseph 119; Mister 317; Robert 135; William 100, 119, 357, 378
Bowden
Martha 362; Widow 104
Bower (Bowers)
Arthur 29; John 460; Mary 29; Mister 526; Richard 473; Robert 77; Thomas 257, 460; Widow 59, 100; William 38, 257, 515, 520
Bowles
Barnard 292; George 290; John 49, 229; Philip 83; Richard 412; Robert 169, 229, 290; William 33, 83 (2), 531
Bowleworth
William 298
Bowman
Andrew 277; Richard 287
Bowry
Humphrey 229
Bowther
Henry 323
Box
Ambrose 311; Eleanor 418; John 353; Samuel 184; William 221, 422
Boxall
John 399, 403; Richard 194; Robert 175, 185, 371, 372; Thomas 39, 170, 404; William 407
Boxholt
Widow 348
Boxlett
George 404; Thomas 404
Boxum
Edward 294
Boyes
Clement 180; Edward 237; Henry 51; John 30, 142, 222; Nicholas 46; Peter 29, 247 (2); Richard 68, 249, 389; Robert 279, 283; Thomas 81, 142, 164; Widow 237; William 240, 247, 249
Boyte
Nicholas 104
Braccar
Laurence 145
Brace
George 505; Mister 462
Bracebridge
Arthur 520, 528
Brackley
John 332; Richard 405, 418; Thomas 504
Brackstone
William 518, 530
Bradborne
Benjamin 436
Bradbre
Edward 357
Bradbridge
James 404
Bradby (Bradbey)
Erasmus 517, 529
Bradley
Christopher 192; Daniel 38; John 87, 99, 192; Nathaniel 192; Walter 408; William 192, 246
Bradsell
John 29; Richard 29; Robert 517
Bradshaw
Doctor 292; John 356; Thomas 524; William 126, 160
Braford
James 85
Bragge
George 162; Widow 112; William 1
Bragne
Thomas 2
Braman
Robert 163; Widow 163, 215; William 215

Bramble
Widow 151, 162
Bramly (Bramley)
Charles 220; Dorcas 103; Thomas 317, 418; William 1
Brampston
Anthony 340
Branch (Branich)
Richard 294; Widow 256
Branford
Robert 130
Branny
Edward 324
Brantham
Thomas 229
Brasby
Widow 505
Brate
Mistress 1
Brathwaite
Thomas 444; William 182
Braxlow
James 332
Braxton (Braxtone)
Widow 339, 527
Bray
George 434; James 362; John 1, 26; Thomas 416
Brazier
Thomas 354
Breagly
Thomas 164
Breda
John 224
Bredmore
Thomas 443
Bremly
John 38
Brent
George 106
Brenton
John 135
Brett
Humphrey 81; Robert 216; Widow 161
Brewcer
Richard 49
Brewer
Abraham 529; Christopher 1; John 21, 196, 359, 407; Mary 517; Mistress 442; Nicholas 188; Richard 21, 202; Thomas 1, 196, 208; Widow 31, 76; William 46 (2), 209
Brewster
John 196
Brewton
Anthony 220; John 219; Widow 493
Brexton (Brextone)
George 96; John 434; Richard 290 (3); Widow 225, 331, 455
Briant *see* Bryant
Brice
Edward 477; George 148, 465; John 135, 437; Thomas 401; Widow 256, 465; William 130, 262
Brickinden
John 10
Brickleton
Michael 353; Richard 293; Thomas 379
Bricknell
Basil 247; John 66; Lancelot 16, 17; William 195
Briday
Samuel 227
Bridger
Edward 246; James 189; John 1, 208 (2), 223; Philip 183; Richard 74 (2), 212, 215; Robert 1, 87; Thomas 169, 372; Widow 176, 212, 227
Bridges
Henry 300; Richard 465; Thomas 302, 523b; William 348
Bridle
Thomas 311; Widow 409

Bright (Brighte, Brite)
George 98; Henry 257; John 76; Richard 451; Widow 97, 195, 265; William 96, 340
Brinkhurst
Edward 1
Brissett
John 38
Bristleton
Matthew 56
Bristoll
Doctor 378
Bristow (Bristowe)
Abraham 56; Barnard 332, 377; George 377; Henry 163; Humphrey 332; Joan 392; John 171, 207 (2), 332, 367, 377, 397; Matthew 377; Nicholas 406; Richard 171; Robert 334; Thomas 47, 164, 177, 367; Widow 332, 396, 406; William 332
Britewell
Francis 319
Brittany
Roger 115
Britten (Britton)
John 362; Widow 21
Brixey
Anthony 101; Christopher 100, 134, 161; Edward 24; Richard 100, 104; Robert 24; Sarah 98; Widow 104; William 103, 118
Brixton
Bridget 492; John 492
Broadbridge (Brodbridge)
Laurence 68; Widow 372
Broade (Brode)
Edward 504; William 436
Broadfeild
Mary 339; Robert 201
Broadford
William 159 (2)
Broadhead
Edward 135; John 122, 135
Broadshaw
Ambrose 97
Broadway
John 236, 290, 292, 503; Laurence 229, 292; Mister 515; Nicholas 4, 347; Thomas 231, 239; Widow 442; William 267, 290, 507
Brokenshufe
Widow 96
Bromfeild
Henry 86, 280; John 94
Bromley
Edward 164
Brookely
William 332
Brooker
Edward 1; John 139, 332; Robert 71; Thomas 71; —462
Brookes (Brocke, Broke, Brooke, Brooks)
Francis 504, 513; John 1, 87, 238; Margaret 126; Mister 165; Robert 159 (Lord); Thomas 46, 59, 332, 339, 341; Widow 80; William 372
Brooman (Browman, Browmand)
Andrew 521, 527; George 387; Joan 209; John 398, 528 (2); Richard 528; Thomas 517; Widow 212, 485; William 40, 49, 270, 320
Broome (Broomes)
Christopher 418; William 332
Brooter
William 194
Brothers
John 427
Browne
Abel 515; Andrew 531; Anthony 1, 369, 418; Austin 490; Bridget 447; Daniel 334; Edward 291, 450; Francis 84; George 38, 331, 418 (2), 456, 477; Giles 256, 512; Henry 89, 100, 157, 159, 229 (2), 252, 374, 506; James 367; Joan

208; John 6 (2), 40, 83 (2), 100, 229, 241, 256, 291, 334, 339, 356, 367, 371, 397, 418 (3), 477, 487 (2), 505, 515; Joseph 418; Lancelot 450; Mister 89, 112, 376, 480; Mistress 95; Nathaniel 518; Peter 29, 90, 332; Ralph 229; Richard 5, 159, 164, 299, 311, 395, 437, 445, 514; Robert 38, 100, 242, 281, 322, 330, 461, 476, 506, 523a; Roger 209, 388; Stephen 332; Thomas 1, 80, 89, 100, 208, 244, 256, 322, 332 (2), 357, 365, 372, 418, 513, 515; Timothy 7; Ursula 182; Widow 37, 55, 80, 100, 112, 230 (2),252, 256, 266 (2), 294, 322 (2), 369, 436, 447, 466, 469, 487, 530; William 97, 163, 332, 409, 517, 530

Brownell
John 287

Browning (Browninge)
Charles 198; John 223, 265; Richard 252; Samuel 265; Thomas 121, 252; Widow 235, 267, 271; William 265, 267

Brownjohn (Brownejohn)
John 488; Laurence 439, 474; Mistress 333; Richard 325

Brownsden
Richard 332

Brownting
James 290

Bruce
John 323

Bruckleton
Richard 286

Brunkon
Christopher 1

Brunsden
Joan 452; John 332; Thomas 503; William 503

Bruth
Thomas 335

Bryant (Briant, Bryan)
Anthony 158; Bartholomew 122; David 472; Francis 37; George 472; John 505, 515 (2); Nicholas 468; Robert 120; Thomas 84, 120, 493, 505; William 50, 56, 123

Bryter
Joan 491

Buck (Bucke)
Widow 19; William 480

Buckett (Bucketts)
David 257; Goodman 212; John 524; Widow 40, 525; William 146, 523b

Buckham
Henry 182

Buckhurst
Robert 193

Buckland
Alice 475; Christopher 100; John 33; William 1, 100

Buckle (Bucle, Bukle)
Henry 96; John 96, 128; Leonard 130; Stephen 483

Buckler
Ralph 96; Richard 98

Bucklin (Buckling)
Thomas 208; Widow 531

Buckly (Buckley)
Bartholomew 126; Mistress 166; Thomas 94, 127

Bucknell
Andrew 84 (2); Chideock 37; John 194

Budd
Daniel 72; Edmund 229; Edward 185; Henry 192; James 193, 249, 317; John 182, 193, 249, 285; Richard 72, 163, 193, 202, 249; Robert 192, 193, 237, 249, 250; Thomas 193, 249; Widow 168, 198, 249 (2), 252; William 191, 208 (2), 239, 286, 404

Budden
Edward 269; John 100; Richard 129; Robert 100; William 130
Bufford
Peter 252; Richard 237
Bugby
Margaret 150; Richard 120
Bugger
Henry 131
Bugley
Elizabeth 434; Widow 391
Bulbeck (Bulbecke, Bullbeck)
Anthony 220; Henry 286; John 218, 224, 249, 523b; Nicholas 220; Richard 16; Thomas 1, 16, 192, 218; Widow 95; William 29 243, 292
Bulkely
Bartholomew 160; Mistress 112
Bull
Christopher 100; Edward 252; Francis 100; Henry 285; John 157, 193, 195 (2), 362; Mark 409, 495; Nicholas 195; Richard 268, 411; Thomas 100; Widow 268, 408, 448; William 409
Buller
James 332; John 339; Samuel 339
Bullock
Christopher 135; Richard 441; Thomas 164; Widow 135
Bullpitt (Bullpit)
Abel 476; John 310, 330; Richard 454; Thomas 268, 330 (2), 331; Widow 326, 331, 332; William 244, 248, 292, 331, 337
Bunch
John 182; Nicholas 171; William 100
Bunckley (Bunckly)
Edward 1; John 443, 445 (2); Widow 445
Bundy (Bundee, Bundey)
John 456 (2); Richard 524, 531; Thomas 460; Widow 447; William 456
Bunge
Widow 508
Bungy
Widow 260
Bunn
Stephen 31
Bunney (Bunny, Buny)
George 418; John 319; Richard 306, 332, 346; Robert 331; Timothy 331; Widow 331; William 324
Bunning
William 498
Burbanck
James 266; Mister 504; Widow 231
Burbridg
Edward 161
Burch (Birch)
Gilbert 39; Henry 208; John 229; Roger 159; Widow 392; William 392
Burcher
Robert 93
Burden
John 94, 122; Timothy 418; William 362
Burford
Thomas 160 (2)
Burgan (Burgame, Burgon)
Edward 131; Martin 128; Thomas 122, 124
Burger
Griffin 443
Burgis (Burges)
Ann 33; Edmund 512; Henry 375; James 322; Jane 529; John 85, 471; Mary 92; Mister 9; Mistress 192, 197; Richard 290, 505; Thomas 38, 85, 277, 280, 291, 292, 515 (2); Widow 208, 258, 283, 292 (3), 405, 518; William 229, 456, 459, 463 (2)
Burkett
Widow 270; William 270

Burle
Thomas 355
Burley
Christopher 399; George 404; John 38; Thomas 1; Widow 284; William 399, 401
Burnard *see* Bernard
Burneface
John 338
Burnell
Jerome 31; Thomas 30
Burnett
George 311; Henry 501; John 38, 311, 436; Peter 160; Thomas 160, 415; Widow 160
Burningfeild
Andrew 11
Burningham
Barnard 177, 181; Peter 168, 204; Samuel 38
Burrad
George 161; Mistress 160
Burrant
Nicholas 91
Burrell
Francis 269; Henry 81; James 531; John 8, 222, 269; Nicholas 80; Robert 22, 29; William 51
Burrett (Burratt)
Humphrey 375; John 406, 434, 457; Richard 458; Widow 290, 292; William 473; — 375
Burron
Nicholas 261
Burrow (Burroughes, Burrowe)
Gabriel 164; Nicholas 163; Tristram 208
Burrowglus
Widow 397
Burry
John 129; Thomas 1
Bursey
Giles 113; Peter 100; Robert 113
Burt (Birte, Burte, Burtt)
Anthony 100; Charles 108; Doctor 229, 292; Edmund 518; Edward 98; James 523b; John 118 (2); Richard 89, 98, 128, 316; Robert 452; Widow 118; William 108, 216, 237
Burton
Edward 129; Henry 472; John 145; Nicholas 394; Thomas 89 (2); Widow 121; William 121
Busey (Bussey)
Mary 117; Richard 128; Thomas 192; William 128
Bush
Evan 115; John 115; William 115
Bushell
Henry 38; James 524; John 164; Ralph 163; Richard 38; Samuel 229; Simon 231; Thomas 357; Widow 244; William 230, 489, 518
Butcher
John 1, 112, 531; Richard 434; Widow 240; William 81, 192, 434
Butt
Nicholas 525; Peter 182; Philip 182
Butten (Button)
Daniel 250; Henry 135; John 38, 72, 161; Mark 72; Mistress 229; Robert 1; Thomas 250; William 49, 112
Butterfeild
Ralph 1
Butterly
Edward 267; Thomas 71; William 267
Butters
Thomas 1
Buttler
Alexander 89; Charles 322; Daniel 164; Edward 56; Francis 39; George 229, 418; Henry 416, 484; James 340; John 76 (2), 163, 170, 229 (2); Michael 229; Mister 257, 517, 529; Nicholas 333; Peter 317; Richard 163, 418; Robert 332; Ruth 343; Thomas

Buttler—*cont'd.*
134, 229, 298, 531; Walter 309, 491; Widow 25, 229, 305, 333, 418, 434; William 127, 229, 332
Buxey (Buxie)
Dorothy 493; Francis 493; John 493; Richard 72, 493; Robert 338, 339; Walter 34; Widow 265
Byam
Robert 76
Bydinge
Thomas 42; William 218
Bye
Ferdinand 229; Henry 292, 332, 408; John 253, 299, 384, 507; Randal 384; Richard 253, 357, 384; Stephen 290, 357, 384; Thomas 322, 357; Widow 384; William 318, 362, 384
Byland (Bylands)
Edward 1; Widow 434
Byles (Biles)
Edward 135; John 135; Josias 229; Kelsey 472; Mister 470, 528; William 162, 520
Byon
John 225
Bythard
Widow 332
Cable
Alice 508; Henry 269; Richard 256; William 512
Cacknell
William 40
Cadden
Mister 357
Cadman
Anthony 18; Lifften 1(2)
Cadrey
Edward 193; Thomas 193
Cager
Henry 249, 250; John 195, 284, 409; Thomas 249
Caige
Edward 206
Cake
Nicholas 1
Callaway (Calloway)
James 83(2); John 237, 254, 268; Mister 454; Richard 67(2)
Cally
Ambrose 339
Cames
Widow 19, 76; William 249, 397
Camish (*see also* Kemish)
Charles 29; John 198
Canlassheare
John 340
Canne (Cane, Cannes)
Robert 362, 374; Widow 249, 383
Canner
Francis 388; Goodman 72
Cannings (Canning)
Dorothy 240; John 241, 270, 331; Richard 285, 416; Robert 518, 530; Roland 428; Thomas 241, 331, 394; Widow 272
Cannion
James 1
Cannon
Adam 434, 435; Edward 346; John 437; Richard 492; Thomas 348; Widow 330, 479
Cannott
Richard 252
Cantage
John 341
Canterton
Dorothy 472; John 25; Richard 461
Cantlett
John 456
Capelin (Caplen, Caplin, Caplyne, Capplin)
Christopher 86; James 517(2); Jasper 279; Mistress 136; Richard 182(2), 517, 529; Widow 194, 279; William 428
Capell
Jonathan 38; Widow 38
Carde (Card)
Christopher 85; George 1; Goodman 515; James 113; John

85, 448, 500, 515; Richard 471; Roger 451; Widow 113; William 117
Cardonnell (*see also* De Cardonnell)
Adam 518
Cardy
John 1
Carew
George 89(Sir), 96(Sir), 152
Carey (Cary)
Christopher 443(2); Mistress 529; Widow 517
Carisbridge (Carisbridg)
John 16(2)
Carke
John 164
Carless (Careless)
Robert 181; William 283
Carlington
Roger 6
Carman
John 76; Thomas 254
Carnall
Widow 422
Carpenter
Edward 160, 207; George 29; Henry 237; James 378; John 10, 83(2), 135, 155, 162, 205, 218, 244, 289; Mark 396; Michael 197; Peter 32; Ralph 1, 127; Richard 163, 449; Robert 4, 10; Thomas 229, 395, 414; Widow 104, 155, 178, 218, 219, 408; William 96, 286, 378, 396
Carrett (Carrott)
Mary 339; William 339, 517
Carrick
Edward 206; Mister 381; Robert 206
Carring
Thomas 309
Carrington
Widow 40
Carser
John 277
Carter
Amy 38; Annis 506; Anthony 135; Christopher 1; Daniel 202; Edward 216; Evis 531; Francis 299; Giles 437; Henry 330; James 276; Joan 343; John 37(2), 85, 86, 100, 135, 163, 249, 258, 283, 299, 345, 428, 491(2); Leonard 290; Martha 163; Mister 446; Peter 1; Ralph 96, 283; Richard 1, 121, 135, 298; Robert 24, 83, 200, 201, 206(2), 207, 342, 378, 396; Samuel 135; Stephen 156; Thomas 1(3), 2, 442; Widow 35, 46, 135, 198, 202, 216, 249, 257, 283, 299, 385, 443, 461, 506, 526; William 37, 148, 156, 200, 206, 256, 322, 337, 378, 385, 418, 424, 426, 428; — 200
Carterett
Doctor 530
Carthridge
William 222
Carthright
Mister 219
Cartwright (Cartwrite)
Francis 281; Widow 357, 363; William 363
Carver
Thomas 489
Casbert
Ralph 108; William 108, 112
Case (Cayse)
Henry 468; Mister 397; William 20, 240
Casey
Widow 299
Casten
Widow 1
Castle (Castell)
Henry 110; John 1, 27; Nicholas 257; Widow 127
Castleman
John 1; Robert 455
Castly
James 494

Caswell
Widow 38
Catchlove
John 39; Thomas 40
Cater
Henry 418; William 418
Caucell
George 158
Caute (Caught, Cawt, Cawte)
Edward 1(2); Francis 237; Gilbert 78; John 68, 399; Nicholas 19, 44, 72; Ralph 22; Richard 26, 28(2), 65, 66, 70, 229, 339(2), 405, 501; Robert 19, 29; Thomas 182, 237(2); Widow 19, 422; William 36, 180, 357, 399, 485
Cave
John 193
Caver
Stephen 1
Cawood
Francis 404
Cerly (*see also* Kerly)
Widow 154
Cernett
Peter 413; Richard 144
Certter
John 24
Cesar (*see also* Seasar)
Sir Henry 44
Cewell (*see also* Sewell)
John 473; William 254
Chack
Goodman 162
Chackford
Goodwife 192
Chacroft
Edward 74; Richard 68; Stephen 68
Chafer
John 308
Chalcroft
John 35(2)
Chalke
Thomas 504
Chalkhill
Mister 496
Chamberlaine (Chaimberlaine, Chamberlin)
Doctor 38; Henry 27, 237, 276; James 316; John 27, 385; Laurence 27(2), 282; Mister 315, 376; Thomas 1, 520, 528; Widow 17, 57; William 36, 130; — 279
Chambers (Chamber)
George 101; Henry 309; John 429; Thomas 315; William 448
Chamell
William 100
Chamingham
Jane 471
Champ (Champe)
Christopher 333; John 303; Robert 237; Thomas 385(2); Widow 376
Champin
John 1
Champion
John 270; Matthew 8; — 202
Chancy
Isaac 440
Channell
Edward 436; John 27; Nicholas 276; Ralph 320, 436; Richard 279, 436; Robert 27(2); Thomas 1; Widow 436, 444; William 172, 194
Chantrell
John 14; Richard 212, 473; William 363
Chaplen (Chaplin, Chapline)
Adam 378; John 378; Mister 527; Richard 279, 378, 527
Chapman
Andrew 51; Charles 1; Edward 1, 148; John 183, 199, 299, 505; Richard 81; Thomas 81, 229; Widow 5, 208, 447, 453; William 299, 335, 505

Chappell (Chappel)
Richard 103; Thomas 135, 531; William 298; — 100
Chard
Edward 436(2); John 514(2)
Chareford
Anthony 270
Charke
William 118
Charker
Daniel 237; Thomas 22, 230, 254; Walter 58; Widow 236
Charleford
Widow 248
Charlett
Mister 521; Thomas 527
Charlington
Widow 14
Charlock
Richard 335
Charter
Edward 422; John 384; Thomas 422
Chase (Chasse)
Benjamin 170; Daniel 208; John 91, 176, 380, 382; Mary 199; Mister 362; Richard 196, 199, 424; Thomas 1, 98, 184, 219; Walter 357; Widow 176; William 176, 205
Chason
John 1
Chatram
William 38
Chatter
John 95, 108; Widow 100; William 157
Chatterton
Edward 371
Chaundler (Chandler)
George 182; Joan 440; John 67, 219, 237, 334, 356, 371, 379, 434; Philip 100; Richard 177, 178, 365, 400; Thomas 357, 365; Widow 249; William 208, 237, 324, 379, 449
Chawline
Widow 208
Chech
John 448
Cheeke
John 493; Thomas 493
Cheeseman (Cheasman, Cheseman)
John 5; Thomas 72; Widow 5, 515
Cheffen
Thomas 100
Cheney (Cheyney)
Charles 180; Widow 299
Cherry (Chery)
John 315, 418; Thomas 378; Widow 418
Chester
William 531
Chestle
Benjamin 40; John 276; Robert 56; William 122, 335(2)
Chevers
Thomas 142
Chicke
Nicholas 74
Chickock
John 339
Chidle
Ann 161
Chidley
John 517, 527; Mister 357; Thomas 5, 70; Widow 1
Chiett
Nicholas 24
Childs (Child)
John 1, 189, 331; Laurence 172; Richard 1; Stephen 244
Chillin
Thomas 1
Chinps
Thomas 397
Chittick
Widow 487

Cleasey
John 332
Cleately
Thomas 331
Cleere
Edmund 189; George 376; Henry 171; John 229(2); Richard 1, 280; William 185
Cleeter
Widow 462
Cleeve (Cleeves, Cleve)
Ambrose 391; Edward 418; John 112, 133, 434, 436, 490; Peter 434 (2); Thomas 270; Widow 418; William 131, 434
Cleft (Clefft)
John 384, 391; William 531
Cleines
Edward 1
Clements (Clement)
Barnard 86; Daniel 357; Edward 530; Gilbert 529; John 1, 356, 383; Mister 148; Mistress 227; Nicholas 2, 269, 517(2); Richard 356, 371; Robert 374, 376, 380; Thomas 67, 378; William 229, 356
Clemes
Sibyl 378
Clentch
Timothy 148
Clerke (Clarke, Clerk)
Ann 33, 34; Benjamin 229; Doctor 292; Edmund 229, 238; Edward 443; Henry 229, 249, 276, 370, 494; James 52; John 130, 276, 292, 300, 354, 357, 382, 430, 441, 473; Laurence 367; Matthew 276, 362; Michael 449; Mister 93, 291; Nathaniel 120; Nicholas 139, 489; Peter 241; Richard 1, 19, 225, 291, 332, 363, 436, 440; Robert 229, 449; Susan 118; Thomas 122, 180, 192(2), 231, 437, 441; Widow 171, 229, 370, 383, 397(2); William 1, 229(2), 237, 290, 341; Zacharias 164
Clever
Ann 67; Edward 219; John 21, 100, 219; Mary 59; Richard 84; Thomas 21, 76, 100; Widow 1
Cleverly
Ann 22; Arthur 38; Bartholomew 21; Edward 30, 31, 49; German 21; John 19, 21, 26, 27, 69, 258; Mary 27; Nicholas 31(2); Peter 21; Reuben 35; Richard 31, 67; Thomas 26, 28, 29, 56; Widow 57, 77, 408; William 31, 56, 76, 230, 244, 282
Clewer
Edward 2, 30(2); Richard 37
Clifford
Mister 462, 517, 529; Mistress 100; Thomas 385; Vincent 396; Widow 299
Clin
Widow 493
Clittson
Ann 434; Jethro 434
Cloade
John 236; Thomas 230, 244, 286
Clough
William 418
Clungeon (Clungen)
Captain 530; James 518, 530; Jane 521, 527; Mister 33; Mistress 528; Peter 520; Thomas 1; Timothy 1
Clutterbuck
Doctor 526, 529
Clutthook
Thomas 332
Coachman
Thomas 100
Coatch
Widow 493
Coates (Coats)
Widow 469; William 362
Cobb
Christopher 100; Gilbert 293;

Cobb—*cont'd.*
Hugh 394; Mistress 292; Peter 299; Richard 229; Thomas 198; Widow 371; William 416
Cobbett
John 406
Cock
William 1
Cocker
Henry 515; John 508, 515; Widow 48
Cockey
Mister 436
Cockwell
Edward 51; Richard 40; William 40
Codrey
Philip 318
Codwin
Ralph 51
Coffin, (Cofen, Coffen)
Joseph 98; Richard 36; Thomas 100; William 36, 120
Coker
Clement 299; Widow 299
Colchester (Colechester)
Giles 158; Rebecca 158
Cole (Coales, Coles, Colle, Colles)
Alice 331; Anthony 182; Arthur 151(2); Barnard 100; Christopher 117, 437; Edward 39; George 97, 120, 162; Gilbert 231; Henry 256, 337, 451, 488; Humphrey 117; John 1, 29, 50, 93, 193, 199, 235, 236, 243, 323, 357, 369(2), 508; Joseph 100; Joyce 133; Laurence 346; Martin 292; Mary 451; Matthew 515; Mister 270, 456, 529; Mistress 76, 208; Nathaniel 451; Nicholas 231, 243; Philip 201; Richard 42, 82, 92, 112, 135(2), 190, 219, 236, 325, 332, 369, 451, 478; Robert 17(2), 68, 292, 443, 468, 515(2); Roger 503; Stephen 61; Theophilus 231, 503; Thomas 2, 19, 67, 151(2), 298, 405, 531; Widow 14, 40, 92, 117, 231, 261, 337, 445, 450, 499, 508; William 20, 22, 50, 92, 117, 290, 337, 480, 517
Coleborne
Ambrose 117
Colebrooke
Anthony 1; Arthur 210; John 36, 226; Richard 237; William 208, 227, 240
Coleman
Ellen 290; John 205, 276, 418(2); Michael 418; Peter 150; Richard 127, 277, 331; Robert 92, 229, 256; Thomas 191, 256, 331, 418, 470; Walter 93, 256; Widow 507; William 257, 418
Colepis
Andrew 29, 84; Roger 208
Colestock
John 161
Colevrden
William 92
Colgell (Colegill, Colgill, Collgill)
James 283; Moses 121; Richard 135; Widow 135
Collett
John 479; Nicholas 475; Thomas 332; Widow 483
Colley (Colly)
Benjamin 240; John 342; Richard 229; Robert 252; Thomas 292; William 253
Collger
Widow 169
Collier
Andrew 418; James 368, 397, 408; Jerome 208; John 244, 286, 408(2), 411; Maurice 416; Mistress 418; Richard 208, 266; Thomas 222, 227; Widow 176, 227, 397, 416; William 196, 208, 231, 239

Collins (Collens)
Ann 38; Barnard 85; Benjamin 418; Daniel 72; Edward 2, 237; George 222(2); Henry 6, 21, 403; Hugh 449; Jennifer 189; Jerome 37(2); John 38, 72, 126, 164, 210, 216, 219, 222, 343, 485; Richard 1, 97, 364(2); Robert 38; Samuel 457; Thomas 20, 39, 79, 100, 112, 150, 164, 216, 217, 443, 462; Walter 42, 77; Widow 1, 87, 112(3), 135, 154; William 1, 38, 78, 112, 134, 135, 193, 344, 428, 441, 471

Collis
John 87, 149, 264, 292; Nicholas 339; Solomon 265; Stephen 283; Thomas 283; William 506

Colson
George 1(2), 240; John 229, 244; Mister 258, 313; Peter 269; Richard 58; Thomas 229, 240; Widow 252, 290; William 57, 292; — 254

Combest
Robert 148

Combs (Combe, Combes, Combs, Coombs)
Edward 161; Henry 88(2), 90, 523a; John 117, 362, 496, 524; Nathaniel 229; Nicholas 392; Paul 464; Peter 194; Philip 387; Richard 90; Roger 195; Susan 518; Thomas 29, 117, 161, 281; Widow 118, 148, 530, 531; William 182, 291, 416, 528

Comes
John 231

Comfort (*see also* Cumfort)
John 229

Comley
Widow 93

Complin
Edward 456, 459; Henry 162, 238; John 264, 266, 370, 493; Mister 229; Mistress 357; William 292

Compton (*see also* Cumpton)
Alice 93; Anthony 163; John 199, 208, 340; Maximilian 485; Peter 227; Richard 103, 228; Thomas 485; Widow 29, 215; William 472

Conditt
Widow 322

Coney
Charles 427

Conings
William 141

Congden
William 38

Conmore
Francis 23

Conne
William 164

Constance
Richard 224; William 163

Constantine
William 488

Conwood
George 404; William 396

Cooke (Cook)
Alexander 356, 434; Anthony 443; Charles 434; Christopher 284, 286; Edward 376, 434, 491; George 168, 405; Henry 498; James 332; Jane 100; Joan 227; John 1, 23, 119, 138, 178, 192, 237, 355, 372, 383, 436; Maurice 287; Oliver 316; Peter 29, 376; Philip 103; Richard 29, 238, 342, 434; Robert 3, 17, 40, 42, 252, 455; Samuel 496; Thomas 1, 14, 80, 218, 230, 231, 238(2), 284; Widow 1, 14, 29, 75, 126, 198, 230, 265, 434; William 31, 256, 333, 398, 418, 434, 485, 529

Cooker
John 277

Coombers
Thomas 160

Cooper
Aaron 505; Alexander 434; Andrew 158; Ann 192; Anthony 215, 424; Austin 290, 471; Christopher 367; Edward 56, 192, 333, 334, 434, 456; George 291, 383, 487; Henry 392, 420; James 177; Joan 346; John 1, 25, 55(3), 64, 79, 89, 163(3), 192, 200, 241, 250, 315, 317, 323(2), 332, 333, 341, 359, 361, 378, 396, 413, 428, 437, 493, 504; Laurence 196; Nicholas 158, 391; Peter 330, Richard 182(2), 185, 212, 226, 274, 294, 375, 530; Robert 168, 302, 340, 357; Simon 414; Thomas 161, 163, 193(2), 277, 339, 407, 506, 515; Widow 89, 160, 205, 208, 279, 299(2), 323, 385, 405, 407, 436, 437, 464, 473; William 1, 158, 205, 288, 290(2), 299, 333, 334, 340, 354, 364, 418, 433, 454, 457; — 200
Coopp
Widow 488
Coote (Cootes)
John 67, 218; William 374
Coparthrite
Robert 318; Widow 318
Copleston (Coppleston)
Christopher 518, 530
Coppedeake
John 122(2)
Coprene
Anthony 226
Coram
Roger 229(2), 287
Corbett
John 293
Corbin
Henry 85; John 135, 150, 157; Stephen 128, 130; Thomas 152; William 128, 135, 150
Cordrey (Cordery)
Thomas 318; Widow 318, 354
Corfe
Richard 172, 292; Robert 292
Corke
Richard 40; William 25
Cornelius (Cornelias)
George 434, 436; Henry 436; John 164; Richard 517, 520; Thomas 517, 529; William 434
Cornes
Eleanor 125
Cornish
Elizabeth 158; George 229; Richard 246; Thomas 246; Timothy 493; Widow 196
Cornwall
Thomas 191; Widow 190
Cornwallis
Mister 308
Corpish
Nicholas 158
Corps
Edward 221; John 221, 223; Richard 228; Thomas 486(2)
Corrant
Peter 424
Correll
William 492
Cortney (Courtney)
Ambrose 473; Francis 95; John 436, 496; Ralph 436
Cosens (Cosins, Cozens)
Edward 50; Elizabeth 182; Gregory 276; Henry 244; John 32(2), 36, 38, 67, 237, 240, 244, 281, 283; Laurence 479; Nicholas 22, 49; Richard 22(2), 284; Thomas 10, 22, 47, 65, 85, 236, 276, 492; Widow 30, 41, 60, 104, 229, 240, 248, 281(2); William 1, 32, 67, 102, 183, 207, 283
Cosh
James 158; Margaret 104; Maurice 104; Richard 100; Widow 229
Cosier
Christopher 216, 464; Henry 97

Cossett
Ambrose 270; John 270
Costin
James 229; Widow 192
Cotten (Cotton)
John 145; Reuben 472; Richard 14, 156; William 133; — 1
Cotterell
John 418
Cottman
Charles 1; Francis 363; George 431; Jasper 192; John 530; Origen 100
Cottshall
John 462
Coughter
Thomas 490
Coules
Widow 114
Country
Jerome 1
Courtnell
Richard 406; Robert 58; Thomas 42; Widow 76
Courtness (Cortness)
Daniel 396; Robert 397; Samuel 495
Courtney *see* Cortney
Coventry
Henry 443; Robert 443
Cover
Thomas 74; Widow 189
Covey (Covy)
Barbara 158; Edward 24, 302; John 351; Nicholas 503; William 145
Coward
Anthony 1; Oliver 111; Richard 128; Simon 1; Thomas 196, 229(2); William 290
Cowdrey (Cowdry)
Christopher 200, 374; Edward 235, 418; Ellen 449; John 243, 276, 317, 378, 418, 449; Joseph 372; Margaret 378; Richard 166; Thomas 38, 95, 508; Widow 237; William 158, 227, 418, 449
Cowles
Widow 354
Cowlet
John 354
Cowley
Christopher 434; Robert 38
Cowse
Mary 513; Nicholas 462
Cox
Ann 472; Edward 255; George 497; Henry 317; James 255; Jerome 363; John 112, 122, 339, 395, 504(2); Leonard 125; Margery 102; Nicholas 112, 122; Richard 317, 418; Robert 436; Thomas 112, 332, 343, 458, 480; Widow 135, 199, 232, 237, 487; William 211, 399; — 88, 95
Coxard
John 332
Coxhead
Robert 145(2)
Coyte
William 93
Crabb
Edward 229; Mister 159; William 159
Cradock (Craddock)
John 17, 148, 197; Mark 394; Matthew 148; Mister 504; Nicholas 21; Robert 229; Thomas 229; Widow 229, 446; William 229, 518
Crafte (Crafts)
Mister 504; Widow 301
Craghill
Thomas 258; William 291
Cram
Richard 483; Thomas 112
Cramborne
John 160
Cranborne
Edward 131
Crane
Mister 504

Cranfourd
Mister 390
Cranstone (Cranston)
Robert 163; Stephen 402(2); Thomas 402
Crassman
Widow 60
Craswell (Crasswell) (*see also* Chraswell)
Andrew 418; Anthony 379; Mistress 357, 376; Robert 418; Widow 2, 418
Crauft
John 390, 418
Crawley (Crawly)
John 518; Richard 459
Crawte (Craught)
Henry 301; John 418
Creed
John 96; Richard 122; Widow 119; William 119, 123
Creswell
John 227
Crew
Thomas 135, 160
Crewis
Widow 112
Crichill
Thomas 145
Cricher (*see also* Chricher)
Robert 375
Crichfeild
Widow 395
Crickwyre
John 72
Crinble
James 418
Cripps
Edward 32(2); John 298; Richard 56; Robert 291; Thomas 291
Crisben
Mary 100
Critch (Crich)
John 194; Stephen 1
Critchman
Samuel 530
Crobie
Widow 118
Crocker
Daniel 67; John 36, 451; Mary 448; Richard 2, 36, 47; Robert 448
Crockford
Edward 216; Henry 165; James 197; John 195; Roger 195; Stephen 288
Crofte (Croft)
Robert 319; Thomas 37; Widow 37
Cromham
Henry 355
Cromwell
Dorothy 252
Croniston
John 178
Crooke (Crook)
Arthur 427; Benjamin 303; Edward 501; Elizabeth 310; James 294, 334; John 310, 334; Robert 89; Thomas 22; Widow 299; William 310
Crooker
Henry 332
Cropley
Mister 1
Cropp
George 478; Henry 234; John 257, 269, 340, 520, 528; Richard 318, 505, 507, 513; Robert 488; Thomas 219, 229, 247, 256, 261; Widow 263, 280, 291; — 258
Crosby
Thomas 1
Cross (Crosse)
James 528; Leonard 434; Richard 24, 87; Widow 229; William 87, 102
Crosswell (Croswell)
Henry 233; Richard 72, 244; Robert 199, 374; Thomas 74
Crosweller
Joseph 218

Crowch (Crouch)
Charles 254; John 445, 446(2), 450; Matthew 437; Michael 436; Nicholas 504; Richard 450(2); Thomas 446; Widow 252, 450(2); William 445
Crowcher
Barnard 118; Henry 245; James 56; John 29, 55(2), 74, 118, 153; Thomas 366; Widow 379; William 19, 55, 74, 87, 130, 152
Crowder
Daniel 502; Edward 472; Margaret 52; Mark 472; Richard 472
Cruys
Thomas 38
Cuffe
Richard 504
Cuffley
Thomas 474, 504, 516; William 85, 292
Cuffold
Mister 424
Cuggley
Edward 298
Cull
John 99, 283; Peter 99; Robert 94; William 94
Cullens
Rumboll 339
Culliford
Roger 520
Cully
Goodman 531
Culver
Widow 36
Culverden
William 523b
Cumage
Widow 104
Cumber
John 55; Widow 55
Cumell
Mary 85
Cumfort
Widow 1
Cummin (Cuminge)
Philip 334; Widow 320
Cumpton
Thomas 270
Curle
Edward 131; Joan 164; William 131, 132, 133
Currant
Daniel 333; John 373; William 332
Currell
John 100
Curring
John 332
Curteme
Charles 164
Curtis (Curtice, Curtys) (*see also* Churtis)
Andrew 530; Boatsman 38; Henry 159; John 97, 298, 418; Margaret 159; Margery 434; Peter 112; Ralph 114; Rebecca 159; Richard 110, 157; Roger 522, 526; Stephen 476; Widow 1(2), 120, 290; William 114, 290; — 110
Cush
Mister 125
Cushen (Cushin)
Esau 520(2)
Cuttler
Edward 88; John 449; Robert 55; Walter 135; Widow 507
Dabb
Thomas 283
Dadd
Widow 279
Dagger
Stephen 35; Widow 292
Dagwell
Widow 5
Daingerfeild
Edward 462, 468(2)

Dalby
John 229, 439, 483; Thomas 443(2), 446; Widow 443
Dale
Francis 152; Henry 108; John 126, 153, 501; Nicholas 135; Widow 144; William 38, 123
Dallarose (Dallirose, Dallyrose)
Richard 215, 219; Widow 1; William 40
Dallman
Ambrose 189
Dallner
William 208
Dally
William 231
Dallydowne (Dalidowne)
Edward 504; Stephen 504
Dallymore *see* Delamoore
Dam
Stephen 40
Daman (Damon)
Ambrose 422; John 204; William 256
Damerum
Edward 471
Dampner
John 340
Dancaster (*see also* Doncaster)
James 327; Mary 327; Widow 338; William 292
Daniell (Daniel)
Alexander 440; George 100; Henry 137; Joan 518; John 112, 508; Thomas 525; Widow 1; William 104, 530
Darby
Widow 193
Dare
Henry 405; John 252; Mister 236; Peter 249; Thomas 404(2); Widow 332
Darfe
Widow 119; William 119
Darling
Mary 205; William 132
Darrell
Doctor 292; Richard 116
Dart
Daniel 291; Thomas 38
Dash
Henry 72; John 38, 72; Robert 67(2), 255; Thomas 283; Widow 72, 135
Dasten
William 505
Daubney
Henry 229
Daunce (Dance)
John 139, 481; Michael 141; Richard 72; Thomas 126; Widow 444, 493, 515; Zacharias 184
Davenant
John 114(2)
Davie (Davy)
Francis 405; Henry 493; Humphrey 129; James 119; John 120, 184, 493; Richard 261, 405, 498; Robert 121; Widow 118, 515; William 103, 258
Davis (Davice, Davies, Davyes)
Ann 367; Anthony 229; Daniel 1(2); Edmund 256; Francis 148; Henry 1, 3, 59(2); Hugh 216; James 208; Jenkin 229; John 1(2), 112, 118, 211, 331, 418(2), 468; Lewis 201; Meredith 435; Mister 388; Richard 229, 443; Robert 1, 418; Roger 129; Thomas 1, 292, 331, 493; Widow 276, 292(2), 445(2); William 1, 158, 445, 493
Dawes (Dawe)
Ann 256; Dennis 277; Robert 100; Thomas 57; Valentine 57; William 178, 191
Dawkins
John 52; Peregrine 473; Robert 434; Sarah 472; Widow 229
Dawley
Mistress 265

Day (Days)
Edward 504; Ellis 1; Henry 252, 269; John 1, 145, 162, 229, 530; Robert 138; Thomas 160; Widow 437, 448; William 9, 91, 506
Daywell
James 244
Deacon (Deacone)
Boyer 38; Isaac 1; Richard 1; Robert 173; William 183, 189
Deale
John 93(2)
Deane
Andrew 29; Henry 154, 269; Hugh 491; James 398; John 1, 29, 49, 67, 120, 125, 153, 164(2), 334, 379, 491(2); Margaret 112; Mister 292, 371(2); Nicholas 271, 398; Richard 25, 125, 154(2), 271, 317, 491, 514; Robert 373, 504; Roland 92; Simon 154; Thomas 298, 336, 339; Widow 154, 270; William 39, 135, 208, 292(2), 318, 400
Deare (Deere)
John 160; Richard 437
De Cardonnell (*see also* Cardonnell)
Mister 528
Deckland
Thomas 161
Dedman
Alexander 362; John 359
Dee
Thomas 414; William 397
Deekeman
Widow 87
Deekes (Deeke, Deeks)
James 437; John 104(2), 437; William 118
Deepe
Richard 66; Widow 89
Deeringe (Dearing, Dearinge)
Henry 3; John 164; Robert 357; Stephen 405
Delamoore (Dallemore, Delamore, Dallymore)
John 208, 276(2), 436; Joseph 276
De La Motte (*see also* Lemotte)
Joseph 519; Widow 519
Delawarr
The Lord 483
Deluke
Cuthbert 92
Demick
Henry 231
Dench
Widow 483
Denham
Edward 38; Thomas 418; Timothy 290
Denman
Widow 464
Denmeade
William 4
Dennett
Edward 473; Hugh 457; John 237, 294, 457, 458; Richard 229, 437, 457; Thomas 458(2); Widow 414
Dennis (Dennice)
Benjamin 290; Gilbert 421; Henry 201; John 473; Mary 471; Thomas 178
Dent (Dente)
John 418; Thomas 418; Widow 192; William 324
Denton
John 395
Denvie
Nicholas 504
Denyer (Denier, Dennier)
John 194, 425; William 208
Dereman (Deereman)
Alice 337; Henry 344; Peter 294; Richard 87
Detty
John 135
Devenish
Widow 518
Deverell
Edward 418

Dewey (Dewy)
Edward 451; James 135; John 130, 242; Thomas 526; William 135
Dewman
Widow 317; William 257
Diaper (Dyaper)
Benjamin 436; Edward 15; James 324; John 78, 79; Margaret 480; Nicholas 435; Richard 25, 56(2), 72; Thomas 331; William 25, 504
Dibbs
Stephen 362
Dibden
James 25; John 40, 236; Thomas 37; Widow 235; William 88
Dible (Dibill)
John 93; Richard 148, 158; Robert 95; Roger 134
Diblin
John 490
Dibsdale
John 134
Dickens
Francis 225; Simon 515
Dickenson
Thomas 530
Dicker (Dicher)
John 317, 319(2), 336; Richard 319, 336(3), 513; Robert 336(2); Thomas 317; Walter 303, 305(2), 315; William 336
Dickery
Peter 128
Dickman
John 99(2)
Diddams
Richard 412
Diggins
Nicholas 506
Dill
Thomas 334
Dimock
Francis 104; William 97
Dimott (Dimote)
Ambrose 114; Anthony 113; Nicholas 112, 113(2); Thomas 117; Walter 113
Dine (Dines)
John 1; Robert 380; Widow 503; William 332
Dinner
William 339
Dipnell
Henry 29; John 29; Thomas 29(2); Widow 29
Dipper
Edward 237
Direshford
Henry 119
Disman
Thomas 343
Dismore
Widow 332
Ditch
William 363
Ditty
William 405
Divis
Mistress 135
Dix
William 477
Dixon (Dickeson, Dickson)
Edward 38; George 1; Henry 229; John 428; Nicholas 494; Thomas 25; Widow 135
Dobbins
John 160
Dobbs
Christopher 468; Doctor 462
Dobey
Francis 518, 530
Dobson
John 318
Dod (Dodd)
Henry 160; John 332; Mister 529; William 455
Doe
John 1, 258, 375; Richard 21
Doegood
James 135; Stephen 120; Thomas 135; Widow 120

Dolegarde
John 40
Doleman
John 493
Dolle
Thomas 498
Dominick (Dominicke)
Doctor 383; John 126
Domyny
William 503
Doncaster (*see also* Dancaster)
Henry 72; James 72
Done
Henry 104
Doneaway
John 1
Donsey
John 292
Dore (Doare)
David 106; Goodman 162; Joan 160; Philip 161; William 332
Dorey (Dory)
John 394; Thomas 485
Dorland
John 161
Dorneford
John 271
Dorney
Edward 374
Dorrell (Dorrill)
Clement 216, 352; Doctor 267; Nicholas 316, 317; Robert 1; Widow 218
Dorsett
John 29
Dossell
Widow 148
Dossett
Nicholas 279
Doswell (Dozwell)
John 339; Richard 493
Dotterell
Theophilus 217(2)
Dounce
Richard 428; Widow 427
Dove
Henry 115, 159; John 93; Mister 338; William 159, 485
Dover
Goodman 162; John 104; William 339
Dovey
Robert 320
Dowdey
Christian 506
Dowe
Alice 162; George 163; William 162
Dowlan (Dowland)
George 480; Henry 481; John 342; Richard 483; Robert 342, 481
Dowlance
John 437
Dowle
John 112
Dowley
Robert 352, 434
Dowling (Dowlinge)
Edmund 252; Edward 498; Henry 223, 481; John 252, 324, 367; Mister 457, 483; Philip 497, 503; Richard 40; Thomas 284; Widow 246, 252, 471; William 379
Dowman
William 270
Downer
David 24; Edward 518; Mister 529; Roger 128; Thomas 90; Widow 97
Downes
George 449; James 371; John 449, 451; Margaret 449; Mister 222; Richard 219, 443, 448; Robert 448; 451(2); Samuel 520, 528; Sarai 523b; Thomas 468; Widow 526; William 198, 255
Downinge (Downeinge)
Nicholas 24, 372

Downton
John 449; Thomas 434
Dowrey
John 306
Dowse (Dowce)
Cuthbert 29; Henry 246; John 440; Powlett 508; Thomas 231, 331, 343, 479; Widow 471, 472
Doxell
Peter 473(2); William 473
Drackford
Thomas 419
Drake
Alexander 456; John 448, 456, 459; Robert 451; Widow 89, 120
Draper
James 404; John 356, 359; Leonard 395; Richard 89, 356, 405; Robert 92; Thomas 384 (Sir); Widow 418; William 89, 355, 356(2), 357, 418
Drapp
Widow 127
Drayton
Edward 124; Widow 444
Dredge (Dredg)
Edward 418; Nicholas 418; Richard 368; Thomas 285; Widow 285
Drew (Drewe)
George 38; John 86; Ralph 505; Richard 226; Thomas 192, 436; Widow 335, 434, 443, 456; William 443, 447, 504
Drewell
Nicholas 14
Drewett (Druatt)
John 40, 318, 319; Roland 319; Widow 212
Drewham
John 339
Drewly
Edward 341, 348; John 436; Thomas 323; William 337
Drewsand
Edward 332
Drill
George 418
Drinckwell
John 504
Dring
John 115
Drinkwine (Drinkewine)
John 483; Richard 244
Driver
Robert 38; Thomas 38
Drogg
— 112 (2)
Drover
Edith 115; Henry 162; John 104; Joseph 100; Nathaniel 113; Richard 162; Widow 162
Dubber
Edward 252; John 518
Dubnell
William 5
Duckett
Edmund 121; William 316
Dudman
George 178; Henry 42; Thomas 169, 202, 487; Widow 181, 200, 391
Dudney
William 163
Duey
Thomas 521
Duffen
John 298
Duffild
James 518(2)
Dufsen
William 488
Dugoe
Widow 448
Du Haumes (Du Heaumes)
Richard 518, 530
Duke
Andrew 271; Mister 451; Robert 59, 239; Widow 290, 505, 527; William 479
Dullard
Ralph 333

Dumersh
William 363
Dummer (Dumer)
Edmund 37, 279; Edward 269; Francis 20, 36; John 40; Mister 291; Richard 436, 450; Stephen 240(2); Thomas 269, 273, 450, 508; Widow 33, 56, 236
Dumper
Goodman 223; John 142, 493; Nicholas 221; Robert 221(2); Spinola 83
Dunce
Peter 189; Richard 173; Samuel 270; Thomas 387; Widow 3, 189; William 67, 173, 391
Dunch
Samuel 230
Duncombe
William 71(2)
Dundee
William 89
Dunfeild
Mister 423
Dunman
John 119; Robert 119; Thomas 119; William 119
Dunn (Dunne)
Nicholas 184; Robert 257; Thomas 258
Dunnett
William 45
Dunning
Austin 135; Henry 135
Durland
William 128
Durling
William 160
Durlon
George 160
Durman
Richard 421; Thomas 507
Durnedall
Robert 104
Durnford (Durneford)
Robert 135; Thomas 487; — 100
Durrant (Durrent)
Benjamin 99; John 208, 219; William 127
Durrick
Thomas 37
Dutten
George 194
Duttman
James 427
Dyaper *see* Diaper
Dyatt (Dyett)
Robert 118; Walter 527
Dyde
Dorothy 67
Dyer (Dyar)
Edward 115; John 219, 279, 390; Matthew 338; Peter 208; Richard 115; Robert 287; Samuel 521; Stephen 303, 316; Widow 1, 531; William 280, 416
Dymersh
William 378
Eacon
John 292; Nathaniel 229; William 237
Eagle
Robert 366; William 366
Eales (Eelles, Eyles)
James 317; John 77, 217, 320, 361; Matthew 361; Richard 487; Widow 317, 418; William 377; — 361
Eames (Eambs)
Catherine 67; Charles 191; George 290; Guy 372; John 164, 208(2), 217, 227, 249, 366; Ogden 127; Philip 38, 423; Randal 208; Richard 37, 208, 372; Thomas 65, 215, 227, 366, 372; Widow 179; William 199, 368
Earland
Widow 461
Earle (Earles)
Andrew 177; Brian 3; Christopher 240; Garrett 468; George 75, 468; Henry 290, 408;

Earle (Earles)—*cont'd*
John 135, 177, 201, 232, 235, 237, 360, 489; Robert 360; Thomas 231; William 135, 284, 290, 291, 434, 436; —292
Earleman
Francis 149
Earlesmore
James 1
Earlsman
John 37
Early (Earley)
John 135, 333; Thomas 89, 117
Earwaker (Erewaker)
Anthony 219; Francis 246; James 246; John 219; Nicholas 246; Richard 73, 219, 247; Thomas 384; Widow 221, 246(2)
Eastgate (Esgatte)
George 332; John 418
Eastman (Eastmeane, Eastment)
John 1, 163; Laurence 164; Robert 1, 332; Thomas 163
Easton
James 449; Mary 160; William 340
Eastwood
Alexander 1; Roger 38; Thomas 38
Eaton (Eatton)
Henry 223, 515; Nathaniel 231; Richard 223; Thomas 1, 87, 339; Widow 434, 436
Eatwell
William 452
Eaves (Eives)
John 363, 371
Eburne
James 93
Ederwell
Thomas 346
Ederidg
Alice 102; John 102, 320, 322 (2)
Edghill (Eghill)
John 200 (2); Widow 52
Edland
Tristram 515
Edmunds (Edmonds, Edmons)
James 396 (2), 503; John 1, 38, 363, 518, 524; Lyne 502; Richard 396; Roger 472; Thomas 114, 311, 332, 469; Widow 472 (2); William 49, 396
Edney
Amy 197; John 472; Peter 193, 197; Widow 472
Edsall
Robert 398; Valentine 159
Edsby
Richard 165
Edwards (Edward)
Ann 129; Benjamin 93; Catherine 531; Daniel 160; Edward 493; Elizabeth 157; George 418; Henry 1, 24, 93, 491; Humphrey 47; James 38; John 46, 72, 79, 84, 93, 128, 150, 160, 190, 260, 418, 453; Nicholas 49; Richard 25, 93, 131, 152, 229 (2); Robert 128, 150, 160, 237, 244, 245; Thomas 75, 87, 192, 237, 248, 391, 408; Widow 38, 152, 183, 246, 256, 260; William 76, 102, 106, 128, 153, 161, 190, 192 (2), 198, 332, 368; — 337
Edwine
Widow 428
Edyer
John 408
Edzer
John 187
Eedes (Eades, Edes, Eeds)
Elias 35; Francis 177, 400; George 403; Henry 448; 493; James 408; John 40, 107, 230, 231; Nicholas 177; Richard 414, 488; Thomas 160; 177 (2), 231, 418 (2), 493 (2); Widow 231, 290; William 210, 408

Egerton (Eggerton)
James 294; Joan 1; John 390; Nicholas 429; Widow 389
Egg
Margery 479; Widow 439
Eggby
Edward 164
Eggcombe
Mister 295
Egger
Henry 433; John 248, 407; Robert 407; Thomas 407; Widow 86; William 407 (2)
Eken
John 463; Richard 463
Elcock (Ellcocke)
Alice 254; George 256; Henry 478; John 252, 254; Richard 100; Robert 517, 529; Widow 368
Elcombe
James 96, John 151; Richard 42; Widow 127
Elderfeild
George 368; John 299; Nicholas 252; Thomas 368; William 302
Eldridge (Eldridg, Elridge)
George 55; Joseph 97; Robert 176; Thomas 403; Widow 39
Elfes (Ealfes)
John 112; Ralph 113; Thomas 97
Elfourd
Widow 395
Elinge
John 127
Elkes
Edward 394
Elkins
Ann 90; Susan 116; Walter 97
Ellen
John 161
Elleston
Doctor 520
Ellingworth
Henry 418
Elliott (Ellett)
Edward 123, 134, 150; Henry 372; James 38, 134; John 29; Nicholas 487; Richard 104, 125 (2); Simon 487; Thomas 118, 161; Widow 100, 104, 151, 162, 290, 505; William 418, 428
Ellis (Elis)
Edward 1, 363, 397; Elias 434; John 363, 395; Leonard 40; Mary 396; Robert 135 (2); Thomas 104 (2); William 316
Elmanston
Christopher 38
Elmes (Ellmes)
Andrew 229; Bartholomew 519; John 522, 526 (2); Nathaniel 152; Philip 1(2); Richard 229; Thomas 100; Widow 514; William 394
Elsley (Elesley, Ellsly, Elzey, Elzly)
John 523a, 524; Lancelot 371; Nicholas 51; William 378
Elsteed
Joan 209
Elton
Ann 290; Edward 334, 337; Mister 317; Steward 238; Widow 408; William 324, 325, 327, 331, 436, 450
Eltott
Henry 229; James 229
Ely
Widow 229, 280
Emance
John 505; Stephen 498
Ember
George 483; John 120
Emberly
Elias 119; Henry 153; Nicholas 119, 135; Richard 122, 155, 156; Stephen 125
Emblen (Emlen)
Francis 524; John 93
Emborne
Mister 476
Embree
George 522, 526; Henry 520

Embs
John 475
Emery
George 6; John 208, 229, 283; Thomas 283; Walter 256; Widow 476; William 52
Emett
Barnard 436; Edward 434; Richard 434; Thomas 436
Empknapp
Joshua 223
Enges
Edward 248
Engfeild
Edmund 384
Englefeild
George 490; Henry 515; John 515; Mistress 217; Simon 490; Widow 505
English
—1
Ensum
John 385
Errett
Widow 301
Etheridg (Etheredg, Etheridge, Everidg)
Henry 24, 98, 103, 158; John 100, 473 (2); Widow 117; William 98, 100, 121, 124
Etherington
James 1
Evander
John 40
Evanke
William 148
Evans (Evance, Evens, Evins)
Alice 115; Anthony 483; Edward 99, 197; Hugh 356; John 160, 197, 435, 483; Peter 197; Richard 1, 158, 503; Robert 197; Stephen 414; Thomas 37, 68; Widow 192, 483; William 38, 192, 197, 229, 271
Evelin (Evelinge)
Goody 398; Nathaniel 357
Evered (Everad, Everett)
Edward 526; Richard 397; Robert 436; Widow 276, 370, 378
Evers
Widow 370 (2)
Ewbancke
Widow 40
Ewens (Ewins)
John 20, 356
Ewhurst
Hugh 383; John 383
Exall (Exell)
James 317; John 363; Richard 398; Robert 363; Roger 317
Exceter
Joan 38
Exton
Edmund 271; Edward 520
Eyres (Eyers, Eyre)
Andrew 164; John 405; Mister 76; Regland 218; Thomas 407; Widow 407
F[ ]
Thomas 356; William 524
Fabin (Fabine)
Andrew 135; Christopher 135; John 468; Thomas 473; Tristram 447; Widow 473
Faithfull (Faithefull)
Alexander 456, 457, 459; John 35 (2), 206, 263, 457; Nicholas 443, 459; Widow 192, 206, 316; William 332
Faithorn (Faythorne)
John 49; Widow 51
Falkon
Thomas 506
Fann
Mary 197
Farlen
Nicholas 371
Farly (Farleigh)
Anthony 84; Edward 3; Henry 172; John 2, 10, 43; Richard 199, 418; Widow 2, 46, 200; William 218

Farmer
Edward 339; Goody 494; Thomas 317, 408
Farr (Farre)
Abraham 194; John 257, 437; Mary 75, 475; Nicholas 229; Richard 294; Robert 203; Thomas 517, 529; William 474, 475
Farrant
John 120
Farrell
Patrick 229
Farrer
Mister 177
Farrock
Robert 418
Farthing
John 89
Fashion
Widow 530; — 526
Fassett
William 89
Fatthorne
Edward 332
Fautelroy
Moory 172
Fauvis
Widow 1
Fawchin (Fauchin)
John 42, 54; Thomas 42; Widow 42; William 207
Fawken
Peter 257
Fawker
Thomas 29
Fawkner (Fawkener)
Esquire 317; James 526; John 230, 317, 362, 517; Mister 25, 529; Peter 317; Richard 29, 418; Thomas 35, 83, 298, 322, 424; Widow 370, 414
Fawley
Widow 1
Fawscett
John 523a
Fay (Faye, Fey)
George 450; Henry 74; Joan 269; John 290, 442; Peter 190; Richard 235; Thomas 231; Widow 503; William 372
Fayth
Widow 40
Febert
Mistress 229
Fee
John 21
Feeke
John 216
Feger
Widow 505
Feild
John 1, 332; Thomas 1
Feilder (Felder)
Amy 434; Ann 192; Arthur 388; Edward 164, 442; Francis 41; George 474; James 388, 394; John 41, 65, 71, 163 (2), 164 (3), 208, 286, 358 (2), 374, 444; Joseph 182; Luke 63; Mister 362; Nicholas 25; Richard 163, 286, 331, 404, 442; Robert 317, 440; Thomas 252 (2), 419, 435, 442; Widow 29, 219, 290, 326; William 25, 57, 252, 382, 400, 414
Feldew
Hugh 290 (2)
Felix
William 347
Fellew
Daniel 335
Fellowe (Fellow, Fellowes)
Guy 200; John 324, 333; William 324
Feltham
Richard 339; Robert 126; Widow 175, 339
Felton
Widow 229

Flemming
Lady 269
Fletcher
Barnard 418; Francis 189; George 422; John 229, 306, 313, 338, 519, 530; Richard 306; Roger 208; Thomas 519; Widow 58
Flewell
Thomas 125
Flexon
Edward 257; Mistress 473
Flight
John 148; Richard 24; Widow 24, 493; William 148
Flood
Richard 40, 434; Robert 437; Roger 512; Simon 208; Thomas 213; Widow 520, 528; William 349; — 1
Flory (Florie, Flowry)
Margaret 120; Thomas 120; Widow 135, 357
Flower
Alice 332; Edward 522, 526, 527; James 531; John 218; Joseph 521; Robert 326; Roger 1; William 324 (2)
Flowerdue
William 523a
Floyd (Floyde)
Gabriel 503 (2); Godfrey 1; Mister 451; Richard 383; William 349; — 377
Flye
John 92
Foater
John 291
Follett
William 100
Follwell
John 424
Foocks
Arthur 521
Foot
John 128; William 135
Foquett
John 135
Forde (Foord, Ford)
Ambrose 101, 104; Foule 103; George 338; Henry 131, 208; James 148; John 103, 148, 208, 356, 517; Mister 229; Oliver 519, 530; Ralph 151; Richard 231, 340; Robert 104, 471, 531; Stephen 104; Thomas 120, 290, 436; Walter 135; Widow 89, 290, 491; William 157, 208, 471
Forder
Bartholomew 103; George 512; Giles 135; Henry 183, 237; James 292; John 37, 208, 213, 407, 416; Joseph 123; Richard 65, 122, 134, 183, 258; Robert 160, 231, 252 (2); Thomas 135, 285, 512; Widow 181, 283; William 123, 177
Foreman
John 157
Forlen
Widow 354
Forrest
Edward 504 (2); George 468 (2), 504; John 100; Peregrine 100; Reynold 100; Thomas 505; Widow 505
Forte
Henry 38
Fosberry (Fostbery) (*see also* Frostbery)
Peter 338; Thomas 317
Fossbrooke
William 215
Fossett
John 525; Widow 524
Foster
Amy 46; Andrew 270, 515; Anthony 46, 54, 212; Christopher 56, 376; Dorothy 370; Edward 78, 252 (2); Francis 218 (2); George 25, 218; Goodman 25; Henry 43, 223 (2);

Foster—*cont'd*
John 46, 77, 228, 233, 485, 503; Laurence 25, 87; Margaret 370; Nicholas 38, 44, 77, 241, 418, 519; Philip 43, 57; Richard 59 (2), 88, 199, 247, 436, 513, 518, 530; Robert 513; Roger 511; Samuel 242; Thomas 77, 229, 270, 340, 437, 479, 487, 518; Widow 38, 56, 68, 218, 247, 485, 515; William 43, 77, 370, 377; — 504

Found
John 433; William 1

Fowke
Arthur 527

Fowler
George 283; Mark 1; William 328

Fowles (Fowle, Foule, Fowell)
Daniel 42; Henry 338; John 49, 50; Philip 37; Samuel 97; Thomas 51 (2); Widow 40; William 434

Fowley
John 2

Fox
Cornelius 517, 529; Edward 418; George 111, 461; Henry 25; John 107, 132, 317, 521, 526; Thomas 25, 527; Widow 317, 354, 461, 506; William 132, 515

Foxley
Widow 363

Foy (Foye)
John 230; Thomas 530; Widow 229

Foyle
Henry 292; Mister 443; William 316

Framan
Francis 2

Frampton
John 292; Richard 125, 130, 292; Robert 38, 434; Stephen 102; Thomas 489; Widow 317; William 120

Francis
Christopher 437; John 339, 437; Luke 298; Peter 439; Stephen 38; Thomas 1; William 296, 311, 503

Francke
William 133

Francombe
William 53, 54

Franklyn (Francklen, Francklin, Franckline, Francklyn, Franklin)
Barbara 449; George 503; Henry 51; John 60, 79, 311; Mary 128; Mister 285, 462; Richard 267; Robert 68, 286; Simon 1; Thomas 63; Widow 473, 494; William 235; — 291

Fray
David 446

Frayne
Catherine 489

Free
Thomas 376

Freebone
William 205

Freeborne
Giles 217; John 334, 515; Nicholas 189; Simon 40; Thomas 41; Widow 120, 216, 334

Freeland (Freland)
John 41, 184, 211; Richard 215; Widow 192

Freeman (Freman)
George 529; Mister 504; Widow 1; William 478

Freemantle
George 298, 489; Richard 456; Roger 348; Thomas 322; Widow 263

Freewater
Benjamin 281

Freind (Friend)
Andrew 26; Ann 26; Henry 26; John 26, 32, 36, 57; Matthew 35; Michael 530; Nicholas 518; Richard 30; Thomas 26, 252; Widow 29, 87; William 89

Freke
Widow 100
French
Christopher 202; Edward 72; Hugh 408; Joan 413; John 197, 394; Thomas 354; Widow 72; William 303 (2), 354, 413
Frewen
Nicholas 384
Friben
John 336
Frissell
Widow 24
Frith (Fryth)
John 236, 472; Thomas 24; William 159
Friven
Nicholas 298
Frizer
George 92 (2); Widow 390
Frogbord
Widow 83
Froggett
Edmund 246; Widow 246 (3)
Frolick
Widow 87
Fronknell
Thomas 427
Frost
Ambrose 316; Ann 132; Christopher 182; Clement 424; Edward 162, 354; George 182, 266; Henry 398 (2); James 192; Joan 248; John 159, 168, 194, 263, 398, 399; Mark 163; Nicholas 164; Paul 335; Richard 292; Thomas 181, 423; Widow 181, 192; William 112, 159, 195, 248, 400
Frostbery
John 249
Froth
Henry 97
Frowde (Froude, Frowd)
Ann 300; Charles 138; Clement 12; George 163, 317; James 303, 317; John 332, 418; Richard 317, 473; Robert 448, 524; Walter 418; Widow 12, 524; William 67, 473 (2)
Fry (Frye)
Alexander 27; Ann 195; Christopher 420; Edward 80; Francis 294; George 111; Henry 422; James 353; John 155, 206, 378, 384, 390, 480, 494; Nicholas 83, 227; Ralph 384; Richard 31, 317; Robert 91, 120, 195, 390; Roger 214; Thomas 397; Walter 38; Widow 31, 54, 128, 208, 219, 276, 397, 408; William 27, 59, 148, 159, 196, 210, 397, 421; — 1
Fryer (Fryar)
Francis 312; John 121; Kingston 521, 522, 526, 527; Robert 100; Thomas 506, 521; Widow 252, 270, 292 (2), 515; William 499, 523a
Fudger
Widow 1
Fufford
Henry 144
Fullcocke
John 169
Fulker
John 449; Thomas 472; William 363
Fuller
Edward 271; George 483; James 481, 483; John 37, 280; Joseph 335; Richard 42, 77; Robert 299; Simon 37; Thomas 481; Toby 483; Widow 482; William 194, 441
Fullford (Fulford)
Ann 115; Henry 130, 159, 524; John 108, 115 (2), 125; Martin 148; Matthew 115; Nicholas 115 (2); Richard 108
Fullick (Fullwick)
Edmund 170; Richard 372

Fulmer
Widow 406
Funter
John 407
Furlonger
Robert 16
Furmage
Hugh 471
Furner
John 133; William 89 (2)
Fursby (Furzby)
John 115; Rachel 133; Widow 111
Furse
Edward 38
Fuse
Nicholas 383; William 40, 383
Fussar
Henry 148
Fussard
John 1
Fussell
John 517, 529; Peter 229
Futcher
John 240; Richard 493, 503; William 237
Futtner
Richard 121
Fyfeild
Edward 229, 484; James 252; John 255, 415; Richard 488
Fyfoot
John 159
Gadge
Widow 342
Gage
Felix 103; John 24, 436; Richard 120; Silas 434; Widow 103, 434; William 100
Gaidon
Francis 505
Gaines (Gayne, Gaynes)
John 453; William 95, 325
Gale (Gaile)
Christopher 452, 503; Edward 454 (2); John 221, 450, 454; Matthew 441; Mistress 1, 17; Nicholas 135; Peter 443, 445; Richard 443; Thomas 454, 460; Widow 229, 465; William 437, 442 (2), 445, 473, 497
Gallant
Roger 322
Galler
Bridget 51
Galles
Richard 397
Gallimore (Gallimoore)
John 311, 317
Gallopp
John 135; Roger 509; Widow 123
Gally
Christopher 252; Thomas 530
Galpin
Henry 1
Game (Games)
Edward 208; Richard 96; Widow 434
Gamlin
William 223
Gammon (Gamon)
Daniel 200 (2); John 208; Robert 193; Thomas 200 (2); William 176, 208, 434; Zacharias 200
Gander
James 258
Gange
Elizabeth 135
Ganny
Bexally 130
Gapes
John 517
Gard
Widow 154
Gardner
Ezekiel 208; Francis 1, 119; James 100, 333; John 244, 271, 428, 436, 475; Michael 436; Moses 163; Ralph 428; Richard 1, 208, 479, 519; Robert 1; Stephen 479; Thomas 395; Widow 428, 455; Zachaeus 227

Garland
George 1; Edward 49
Garmatt
Giles 269
Garner
Thomas 298; Widow 317; William 483
Garrett
Cecilia 502; Christopher 101; Edward 1 (2), 458; Elizabeth 56; Ellen 75; George 102; Henry 6, 15, 230; James 486; John 1, 52, 104, 244 (2); Marian 162; Nicholas 192; Richard 100, 160, 246; Robert 322, 434; Thomas 215, 230 (2), 504; Walter 219; Widow 98, 130, 230, 292, 339; William 113 (2), 135, 197, 219, 319, 529
Garrman
William 269
Gary (Garey, Garry)
Nicholas 420, 423; Ralph 502; Richard 424; Robert 398, 420; Roger 423; Widow 426
Gascoyne
Philip 1
Gaskin
John 96; Richard 96
Gasle
Alexander 529
Gass (Gase, Gasse)
Alexander 504 (2), 508, 517 (2); Anthony 517, 528; George 112, 169; John 19; Richard 504, 505; Stephen 1; Thomas 513; Widow 508
Gassett
William 529
Gast
Widow 336
Gasteed
Edward 86
Gasthall
William 450
Gaston
Walter 290
Gates (Gate)
Ann 104; John 177, 194; Martin 100; Maurice 133; Nicholas 163; Richard 88, 418; Robert 104; Widow 163, 396; William 164 (2)
Gatterell (Gatterill)
John 62; Richard 58; William 57, 119
Gaudy (Gaudey, Gawdy)
Edward 60; Robert 258; William 257
Gaundy
Robert 138
Gauntlett
Barnard 119; Farmer 158; George 93; Henry 276; John 229 Thomas 116
Gaver
George 488
Gay
Widow 120, 141
Gayger
Thomas 503
Gaywood
Henry 56; Mister 523a, 524
Geale
Laurence 163; Roger 227; William 122
Gearing
Francis 208
Gearle
Ann 451; Edmund 457; George 509; James 456; John 436, 456, 459, 494; Nicholas 459; Richard 418; Thomas 457; Widow 442
Gearly
Thomas 394
Gearne
Joan 115; Richard 494
Geburne
Richard 418
Gee
Henry 133

Gelredge
James 130
Gentom
Widow 301 (2)
George
John 229; Thomas 229; Widow 229; William 229, 339, 340
Gerrat
Widow 458
Gesman (*see also* Jesman)
George 504
Gessett
Thomas 335
Getheredg
George 133
Gethins
Mister 363
Gibbons (Gibbins)
Geoffrey 316; John 252; Matthew 245; Thomas 448; Widow 150, 285, 448; William 229
Gibbs
Arthur 92; Bartholomew 108; Henry 117, 120; James 120; John 97, 111, 299; Thomas 114, 120; Widow 117; William 155
Gibman
John 186
Gibson
John 193; Widow 164
Gifford
Alexander 471; John 108, 229; Mister 462; Richard 265; Robert 465, 471; Widow 104, 229, 507; William 229, 236 (2)
Giggs
William 399
Gilbert
Ann 208; Goodwife 357; Henry 193, 424; John 1, 193 (3), 195, 208, 229, 355, 460, 518; Nicholas 112, 350; Richard 213, 460; Thomas 46, 299, 460; Widow 16 (2), 193, 257, 460, 470; William 67, 114
Giles (Gilles)
Gabriel 38; Jerome 245; John 395; Old 194; Robert 1; Widow 404; William 1
Gill (Gille)
Abraham 194; Henry 198; John 49, 96, 163, 280 (2), 286; Ralph 290; Richard 29, 36; William 194
Gillett
John 177
Gillingham
Doctor 214; Widow 40
Gillman (Gilmons)
Edmund 342; George 400; John 5; Robert 17
Gillmore (Gilmore, Gillmer)
Thomas 201, 436; William 247
Gillowe
Richard 158
Gillum (Gillam, Gilliom) (*see also* Guillum)
Philip 423, 529; Widow 398, 405, 503
Girdler
Christopher 355; John 208
Gisbye
Henry 37; John 76; William 76
Gissige (Geeside, Gysage)
Nicholas 508; Thomas 271; Widow 531
Gittins
John 40; Philip 38; William 38
Glasbrooke
William 407
Glasby
John 270; Mary 270
Glascock
Mister 357
Glasier
Henry 169; John 208; Widow 170
Glaspoole (Glaspell, Glaspool)
Edward 430; George 290; Goodwife 162; Henry 32; James 79; John 46, 237, 240; Richard 240; Robert 234, 240; Widow 70;

William 1, 56, 70, 236, 240, 252 (2)
Glass
Stephen 5 (2); William 332
Glaustafe
Peter 332
Glevin (Gleven)
Thomas 104 (2), 160
Glover
Edward 429; George 338; Henry 246; John 434; Robert 348
Glyde (Gleed)
Charles 223; Richard 133, 202
Goare
Margaret 93; Richard 457
Goater (Goteour, Goter, Gotier)
Andrew 504; Daniel 517, 529; Edward 1, 256, 280; John 229, 496; Nicholas 257; Richard 279, 280 (2); Robert 40, 496 (2); Stephen 531; Thomas 257, 271, 529; Widow 505; William 271
Goble
John 257; Matthew 74, 208; Peter 184; Widow 208
Goblin
William 494
Goby
Robert 118
Goddard (Godderd, Goodard)
Alexander 460; Arthur 159; Captain 528; Clase 392; Edmund 338; Edward 332; George 324; Henry 91; Hugh 493; John 1, 38, 104, 301, 303, 455, 494; Mister 229, 529; Nicholas 406; Oliver 503; Richard 61, 95, 232, 453; Robert 217, 503; Roger 322; Syndens 455; Thomas 257, 268, 332, 457, 483; Widow 1, 230, 315, 363, 453, 493, 497; William 268, 332, 338, 363
Godden (Goddin, Godding, Gooden, Goodinge)
Christopher 121; James 355; John 98, 347 (2), 436, 500; Margaret 462; Mark 38; Nathaniel 229; Nicholas 118; Richard 94 (2), 244, 434, 436, 484, 496; Sarah 100; Thomas 94, 505; Walter 100; Widow 355, 434, 448, 462, 503; William 466
Goderfeild
Roger 300; Thomas 300
Godfrey (Godfry)
Barnard 473; Edward 442; Henry 162; John 40, 56, 81; Margaret 162; Mister 512; Richard 506, 507, 514, 529; Robert 364; Widow 192, 355; William 247, 367
Godmeane
John 336
Godsgrace
John 128
Godson
James 356; Mister 229; Thomas 317; Widow 229; William 356, 505
Godwin (Goddwin, Goodwin)
Cornelius 257; Francis 241; Giles 418; Henry 244; John 16, 51, 208, 219, 241, 317, 383 (3); Joseph 38; Peter 241; Philip 1; Richard 12, 22, 29, 42, 193, 206, 208, 298, 503; Robert 236 (2); Simon 46; Thomas 29, 51, 208, 262, 335; Timothy 208; Widow 208, 252, 265; William 1 (2), 56, 193, 243, 254, 267
Goffe (Goff)
John 96, 248, 270, 318; Richard 192; Thomas 192
Goffton
Francis 256
Gold
Barnard 100; Bernard 317; Christopher 103; Edward 104; Henry 420; John 25, 33, 38, 420 (2), 515; Mister 328; Philip 103;

Gold—*cont'd*
Richard 420; Robert 420; Walter 103; Widow 103, 104, 434; William 1, 317, 420, 434, 436
Goldatt
Noah 299; Widow 299
Goldfinch
German 22; Henry 1, 36; John 76 (2); Mister 421; Richard 1, 254; Thomas 26; Widow 21, 56
Golding (Golden, Goldinge)
Arthur 208 (2); John 1, 40, 84, 440; Jonas 347; Richard 418, 440; Thomas 440; Walter 317; Widow 119, 322; William 29, 322, 333, 434, 476
Goldocke
John 332
Goldringe
George 208
Goldsmith
John 76; Richard 235; Thomas 1; William 44, 192
Goldstone
Mister 445
Goldwyre
Edward 130
Goldyer
Elizabeth 135; William 122
Gole
Alexander 526
Golledg
Richard 229
Golley (Goley)
Edward 1; Thomas 29
Gollinge
James 335
Good
Henry 97; John 279 (2); Laurence 29; Richard 261
Goodale (Goodalle)
Alice 449; Francis 436; John 332, 342, 428; Richard 294, 299, 320, 434 (2); Simon 377; Thomas 280; Widow 229, 371, 428, 454; William 434
Goodboddy
Vincent 117 (2)
Goodboy
Henry 113
Goodby
William 279; — 354
Goodchild
Christopher 379; John 362; Richard 191, 397; Thomas 377; Widow 378; William 370, 379
Goodener
William 396
Goodenough
John 436
Goodeve
Edward 29; Richard 80
Goodfaith
Richard 40; Thomas 81
Goodlock
David 332
Goodman
Henry 229; John 6
Goodne
George 317
Goodridge
Arthur 76
Goodyer
Edward 356 (2), 404; Francis 75; George 405; Henry 135, 360, 423; James 407; John 163, 400; Lewis 166; Margaret 122; Mary 67; Stephen 368, 405; Widow 371, 405; William 228, 400, 407
Gookey
Anthony 155; Edward 154; Henry 132; William 126
Gootley
Walter 468
Goppin
— 1
Goringe
William 332
Gorroway
Widow 397
Gosden
George 406; William 406

Gosgill
John 135
Gosler
William 416
Gosling (Goslinge)
George 269; Gilbert 434; James 348; John 103; Richard 279, 324, 396; Robert 20; Thomas 229, 324, 490; Widow 280; William 2, 13, 118
Gosney
Peter 86
Gosse
Ann 101
Gossemer
Anthony 455
Gossoe
Samuel 97
Gost (Goast, Goaste, Goste)
Clement 93; David 1; Henry 141; Richard 91 (2), 108; Widow 86
Gostone
William 127
Gostree
Widow 1
Gourde
Laurence 206 (2)
Gover
John 291; Robert 443; Widow 38
Gowen
John 335; William 333
Goyat
Thomas 450; Widow 450
Grace
John 437, 445, 446; Richard 175; Robert 446; Thomas 434, 445; Widow 485
Gradge
John 252
Gradigge
Isaac 514
Grafton
Anthony 291 (2)
Grainger
Richard 213; Roger 38
Grandum
Mistress 135
Gransome
Christopher 1
Grantham
Edward 1; Richard 362, 417; Thomas 229; Widow 461; William 322
Grantum
Daniel 521
Grasswell
Thomas 68
Graunt (Grant, Grante)
Alexander 263; George 292; Henry 104, 283; John 383; Leonard 263; Nicholas 518, 519 (2), 530; Thomas 1, 72, 96, 118, 289, 380; Widow 263, 391; William 240
Gravett (Graffett)
Christopher 376, 396; Widow 205
Gray (Graye, Grey)
Ambrose 245; Edward 461; Elizabeth 159; Francis 1, 434; Geoffrey 51, 160; Henry 518; James 189; John 1, 148, 159, 339, 463; Joseph 104; Michael 1; Nicholas 226; Thomas 97, 385, 461; Widow 45; William 141, 245; Zacharias 1 (2)
Grayly
Philip 515; Thomas 454
Greatham (Gretham)
Elizabeth 89; Francis 70; Robert 52; Thomas 89; William 36
Gredge
Judith 1
Greene
Ann 340; Christopher 407; Doctor 256; Edward 199, 493; George 393; Henry 2; James 318, 336; John 169, 336, 363, 437, 463, 477, 505 (2); Matthew 157; Maurice 473; Mister 479; Nicholas 118, 418, 476; Peter

Greene—*cont'd*
198; Richard 336, 375, 379; Robert 336, 351, 418; Ruth 343; Stephen 198, 255; Thomas 5 (3), 40, 148, 222, 229, 315, 332, 418, 515; Widow 176, 395; William 5, 162, 176, 183, 254, 255, 270, 332, 337, 357, 408, 418, 434, 488, 503
Greenefeild
William 39
Greenegoe (Gringoe)
John 50; Peter 67; Roger 2
Greenetree
Nicholas 189; Thomas 1
Greeneway (Greenaway, Greenway, Grinaway)
Edward 1; John 1; Robert 1; Samuel 397; Thomas 376, 397
Greenewood
John 122, 271; Nicholas 193; Ralph 38
Greenham
Guy 371
Greensell
Francis 172
Greffitts
John 1
Gregory
Ann 162, 364; Edward 367; Jasper 76; John 163, 197, 367, 374; Peter 366; Philip 387; Richard 38, 136, 143, 195, 197, 217; Robert 32, 398; Thomas 3, 290; Widow 267, 366, 377; William 37, 93, 127, 131, 184, 366, 378
Grenestone
Stephen 401
Grew
Mistress 229
Grice
John 194
Gridge
Joseph 330
Griffin (Griffen)
Arthur 408; Evan 115; John 337, 477, 484, 515; Joseph 418; Richard 291; Robert 493; Roland 434; Stephen 518; Widow 333, 493; William 1
Grigge (Grigg)
Ellen 192; Robert 49; Thomas 83; Widow 40 (2); William 40, 357
Grigson
Alexander 287; Mister 288
Grillingham
Richard 133
Grinedge
William 56
Grinsteed (Grinsted)
John 208; Thomas 227
Griste
James 458; Widow 473
Grivett
Richard 12, 16
Groane
Richard 464
Grobard
William 1
Gross (Groce, Grosse)
Barnard 118; Mister 530; Thomas 125
Grossmith
Andrew 192; Edward 192; Henry 290, 494; John 29, 192
Grove (Groave)
Ambrose 506; Richard 501
Grover
Alexander 424; Anthony 403; Henry 398; Nicholas 213; Thomas 1, 178; Widow 405
Grubb
James 127
Grubbie
William 158
Gruett
Richard 1; William 2
Grunsell (Gruncell)
Charles 503; John 292, 503;

Thomas 465; Walter 252, 493; William 436, 503 (2)
Gubber
Widow 128
Gubbett
Widow 40
Guderidg (Gudgeridge)
Mistress 229; Roger 38
Gudge (Gugge)
Daniel 1; James 293; John 223, 318; Leonard 419; Robert 409; Samuel 299; Susan 285; Thomas 1, 244, 293; Widow 223; William 319; — 1
Gudgeon
Laurence 38
Gudney
Malachi 391
Guidott (Guidatt, Guydott)
Francis 160; Mister 161; William 389
Guilford
Thomas 120
Guillett
Widow 501
Guillum (*see also* Gillum)
Aaron 518; John 518, 530; Peter 527
Gulstone (Gulstons)
Doctor 265; Joseph 29, 292
Gumble
Doctor 292
Gunn (Gunne)
John 1; Widow 1
Gunnell
Widow 384
Gunner
Ambrose 356; Joan 364; John 367, 403; Richard 396; Robert 250; Thomas 396; William 356, 396, 406
Gunning
Robert 164
Gunson
William 256
Gunter
Ralph 192
Guphill (Gupphill)
Frederick 208 (2)
Gurdin
Mister 504
Gusse
William 108
Gutheridge
Thomas 531
Gutter
William 216
Guy (Guye)
Edward 25; Henry 216; James 229; John 16, 83, 216; Peter 441; Richard 40, 189, 376; Thomas 41, 83, 157, 225; Widow 102; William 157
Guyer
Thomas 38; Widow 17 (2)
Guyett
Richard 499; Thomas 434
Gynes
Henry 349; Nicholas 462 (2)
Gyourne
William 59
Habben (Habbin) (*see also* Abbin)
Richard 164 (2), 372; William, 35
Habberly (Haberly)
Anthony 1 (3); James 1; William 1
Hack (Hacke)
Charles 229; Edward 384; Gabriel 473; James 205; Joan 343; John 388, 483, 504; Luke 322; Richard 294, 298; Thomas 418; Widow 411; William 56, 487
Hacker
John 294, 316; Nathaniel 504
Hackett
Edward 35; Francis 29; John 29 (2); Richard 29, 35
Hackman
John 193 (2); William 18
Haddsly
Mister 115

Hadley (Hadly)
George 1; Thomas 236
Hagben
John 1
Hagger (Hager)
James 526; John 233
Hake
Widow 156
Haksford
William 162
Halcope
Simon 1
Hales
Richard 112
Hall (Halle, Halls)
Andrew 301, 333; Ann 375; Benjamin 164; Bridget 368; Christopher 332; Edward 126, 290, 311, 335, 354; Elizabeth 208; George 322, 418; Giles 208; Henry 396, 494; Hugh 285; John 1, 76, 208, 244, 246, 299, 300, 307, 318, 335, 394, 401, 402, 429, 430 (2), 493, 494; Laurence 152; Mary 208; Michael 365; Mister 110, 113; Mordecai 164; Nicholas 208, 249, 339, 340, 473; Peter 165, 494; Philip 428; Richard 108, 279, 332, 366, 379, 416, 418, 494; Robert 6, 331, 332, 374, 419, 428, 429; Roger 449; Stephen 339, 397; Thomas 53, 96, 128 (2), 196, 322, 418 (2), 430; Walter 318; Widow 68, 120, 170, 322, 332, 376, 391, 416, 488; William 85, 89, 112, 221 (2), 227, 332 (2), 339, 347, 357, 374, 383 (3), 396, 414, 423; Zacharias 515; — 405
Halloway
Thomas 434
Halt [ ]
[ ] 54
Ham (Hamm)
John 5, 206, 364; Thomas 5; William 193, 407
Hambleton (*see also* Ambleton)
Henry 395; Robert 418
Hameds
John 126
Hamman
Widow 485
Hammon (Hamon, Hamone)
Edward 95; George 34; Henry 40, 164, 269; John 37, 80, 169, 207, 281, 331, 356, 494, 515; Mister 371; Nathaniel 40; Nicholas 1, 52; Richard 164; Thomas 189, 246, 279; Walter 145; Widow 49, 51, 189, 483, 509; William 6, 38, 80, 163, 253, 472
Hammond (Hamond)
John 219; Mary 164; Richard 243; Sergeant 58; Widow 241
Hampshire
Lancelot 435, 436; William 346
Hampson
Widow 372
Hampton
James 29; John 1, 285; Widow 29
Hanbrough
Saunder 513
Hanbury
Mistress 212
Hancock
Benjamin 401; Elizabeth 38; John 121, 123; Mister 504; Mistress 515; Nicholas 462; Richard 29 (2); Thomas 1, 39 (2); Widow 120; William 96, 108, 123, 229, 292, 517
Handman
Mister 180
Handy
Widow 112
Haniton (Hanniton)
Anthony 303; Barnard 370; Edward 303; John 299, 362; Philip 394; Richard 305, 418; Widow 388

Hankin
Ambrose 318; Richard 318
Hannam
Widow 471
Hannington (Hanington)
John 230; Widow 238, 429; William 506, 515
Hansome
Thomas 170, 189
Hapgood
William 434, 522
Harben
Widow 120
Harber (Harbour)
George 217; Richard 223
Harby
Mister 42
Harding (Hardinge)
Abraham 194 (2); Anthony 460; Arthur 96; Christopher 489; Daniel 507; Francis 449; Henry 163, 315; James 96; John 6, 189, 333, 395, 408 (2), 416, 460, 478, 488, 489; Nicholas 206; Richard 429; Robert 185, 194, 203, 240, 337 (2); Stephen 6, 145, 331; Thomas 231, 244, 489; Widow 100, 127, 150, 189 (2), 244, 249, 290, 305, 332, 335, 396, 456; William 118 (2), 388, 415, 442, 488, 524
Hardly
Thomas 151
Hardman
John 145; Richard 145, 146 (2)
Hardwell
Christopher 339; John 474; Robert 474; Thomas 475, 476
Hardy (Hardye)
Henry 355; William 1, 120
Hardyman
Widow 474
Hare
George 158; Henry 1; Thomas 477
Haregood
Thomas 38; Widow 5
Harfeild
Ambrose 78; John 472; Mister 229; Nicholas 46; Richard 29; Robert 290; Widow 434; William 254, 266
Harfell
Ambrose 229; Christopher 262; John 229, 233, 236, 279; Nicholas 26; Robert 236, 290; Thomas 262; Walter 229; Widow 236, 240, 436; William 229, 244, 484
Harford
Heritage 244; John 76; Robert 1; William 162, 418
Harfsell
Widow 408
Harling
William 227
Harman
Daniel 397; Francis 283 (2); Richard 304; Roger 229; Stephen 38
Harmes
Widow 410
Harmor
John 427
Harmsworth
Edward 336; Francis 57; George 20; John 32; Robert 246; William 37
Harmwood (Harmewood)
Arthur 131; Bartholomew 106, 160; Brian 397; Elizabeth 374; John 160; Nicholas 356; William 131
Harold
Thomas 160
Harper
Alice 339; Guy 40
Harrell
William 298
Harris (Harrice, Harrise, Harriss)
Bartholomew 40; Edward 208,

Harris (Harrice, Harrise, Harriss) —*cont'd*
362; George 192; Henry 159; Hugh 100; James 24, 504; John 80, 82, 86, 100, 112, 117, 148, 163, 229, 376, 383, 418, 440; Mary 159; Matthew 418; Michael 249; Mister 291, 357; Nicholas 51; Philip 332; Richard 52, 191, 229, 292, 355, 465; Robert 29, 112; Samuel 108 (2), 292; Thomas 14, 148, 193, 452, 470; Widow 58, 97, 114, 244, 418, 465; William 148 (2), 267, 324, 418; Woolston 248, 287
Harrison (Harison, Harrisson)
Agnes 214; Bartholomew 40; Christopher 111; George 107, 111; Henry 280; John 405; Mistress 383; Nicholas 206; Peter 405 (2); Ralph 111; Richard 508; Robert 213; Roger 107, 163; Thomas 191; William 107
Hart (Harte)
Edward 83; Eleanor 216; Henry 517; James 331; Jerome 1; John 39, 354, 358; Richard 403; Robert 530; Stephen 403; Thomas 218; Widow 126, 254, 437, 473
Hartford
Widow 59
Hartley (Hartly)
John 12; Robert 290; Thomas 258
Hartwell
John 56
Harvest
Thomas 141
Harvy (Harvie, Harvye)
Andrew 87; Edward 99; John 99, 113; Methuselah 152; Philip 255; Richard 148; Thomas 153, 154
Harwood
David 280; Edward 330; Francis 424; Henry 21, 46, 237; James 424 (2); John 150, 231, 301, 320, 424, 517, 530; Mister 3, 117; Nicholas 28, 299; Peter 241; Richard 18, 46, 60, 193 (2), 328; Thomas 100, 169, 263, 316; Walter 361; Widow 78; William 219, 229, 362, 424
Hascoll
Richard 150
Hase (Hasse)
Ann 494; John 295
Haske
Widow 301
Hasker
James 332; John 499; Richard 418, 429; Thomas 402, 493; Widow 318, 429; William 424, 429
Hasleby
Andrew 252
Hasler
Nicholas 68; Robert 36, 76; Thomas 48, 237, 242; Widow 19, 51; William 42, 51, 76
Haslett (*see also* Aslett)
Joseph 339
Hasling
John 49, 51
Hasman
Walter 332
Haspoole
John 223
Hassell (Hasell)
James 50; John 1
Hasteed (Hasted)
Daniel 197; Henry 197; James 1; John 57, 227; Nicholas 208; Richard 36; Susan 247; Thomas 223, 240; Widow 38; William 247
Hastings
Henry 153 (Sir); Widow 124
Hastler
John 215; Thomas 215
Hastling
John 49

Haswell
Anthony 1; Hugh 244, 292; John 1
Hatch (Hach)
Edward 23; Nicholas 93; Peter 72; Richard 408; Simon 23; Stephen 23 (2); Thomas 1, 76
Hatcher
Richard 462; Thomas 257, 462; Widow 93; William 148
Hatchett (Hatchet, Hattchett)
George 459, 497; James 435, 487; John 235, 434; Nicholas 459; Philip 443; Richard 480, 481; Robert 480; Thomas 244; Widow 470; William 263, 459
Hated
Widow 473
Hatt
Giles 395; John 385; William 397
Hatter
John 21; Widow 51
Hattett
Edward 456
Hattrell (Hatrell, Hatterell)
Edward 72; George 216; Thomas 424; Widow 72, 100 (2); William 76
Hau[ ]
William 1
Hault
John 407
Havery (*see also* Avery)
Peter 1
Hawely
William 1
Hawes
Widow 1
Hawker
Thomas 520, 528
Hawkes
Richard 257, 269; Robert 1 (2)
Hawkins (Hawkens)
Annis 154; Doctor 292; Edward 355 (2); Francis 299, 333; George 110, 177, 299, 368, 392; James 150, 444; John 161, 182 (2), 318, 337, 338, 401, 407, 515; Lewis 1; Matthew 164; Nicholas 444; Richard 263, 317, 418, 478; Robert 355; Roger 391; Thomas 318, 357, 400, 521, 524, 527; Timothy 38; Widow 182, 257, 263, 305, 333, 370, 493; William 160, 346, 383, 407, 418, 425
Hawksworth (Hawkesworth)
Francis 54; Henry 269; Nicholas 37; Peter 30; Richard 76; Widow 37
Hawted
Robert 473
Hawtutt
John 236, 266; Richard 236, 266 (2)
Hay
John 323
Haydon (Heydon)
Widow 439, 445
Hayes *see* Heyes
Hayle
Richard 205; Widow 205
Hayling (*see also* Ayling)
John 229
Haymes
John 332
Haynes (Heynes)
Mary 160; Thomas 56; Widow 216; William 85, 126, 418
Haynewell
Widow 332
Hayter (Heyter)
Daniel 473; Edward 40; Elizabeth 450; John 48, 473; Richard 246; William 49, 115
Head (Hedd)
George 522, 526; John 472; Robert 290; Thomas 1, 418, 451; Widow 131, 320, 441, 454, 459; William 451, 523b, 528
Headland
William 385

Heady
George 521, 527
Heale (Heeles)
Edward 397 (2); Humphrey 397; Matthew 128; Richard 40; Stephen 49; Widow 119, 223
Heaman
Widow 514
Heasley
William 515
Heare
Richard 353; William 355 (2)
Hearecock
Widow 19
Hearly
Joan 66
Hearne
Hugh 38; Nicholas 346; Widow 357; William 331, 333
Heart
Richard 332; Widow 292
Hearth
David 458
Heath
Bartholomew 208; Christopher 241; Edmund 343; Edward 240, 277; George 190, 532a, 524; Henry 193, 523b; Humphrey 488; John 12, 54, 205, 237, 277 (2), 523a; Michael 253; Peter 72; Richard 223, 414, 473, 520, 528; Robert 205; Thomas 1, 194, 234, 324, 519, 522, 523a, 526; Widow 193, 324, 363, 371, 471; William 27, 175, 199, 205, 237, 497
Heather
Anthony 227; Edward 164; George 42; Henry 40 (2), 418 (2); James 418; John 40, 208, 370, 398; Nicholas 418; Peter 208; Ralph 37; Richard 224; Roger 170; Seth 227; Silvanus 418; Stephen 77; Thomas 40, 183, 218, 395; Widow 42, 50, 356, 406; William 47, 184, 208 (2)
Heatherfeild
Widow 29
Hebb (Hebbe)
John 172, 220; Nicholas 220, 243; Philip 92; Thomas 433
Hebberds
Thomas 434
Heberden (Harberden, Hebberden)
Edward 1, 213; Nicholas 223, 247; Peter 161
Hebert
John 158; Nicholas 87
Hedach
John 488; Richard 263
Hedford
John 126
Hedgcock
William 216
Hedger (Headger)
George 96; John 81; Mister 54; Nicholas 1, 194; Richard 81; Robert 81; Thomas 214
Hedges
Ann 342; John 298, 348; Thomas 530
Hedrington
Humphrey 163
Hellender
William 108
Hellhouse
Richard 363; Widow 379
Helliard
Francis 517, 529
Hellier (Helliar, Hellyer)
Anthony 334, 368; Edward 223 (2); Eleanor 8; George 135, 255, 294, 418; Isaac 176; James 316, 450; John 122, 223, 229, 242, 332, 355, 414, 434, 446 (2); Jude 331; Ralph 383; Richard 223, 280, 325, 375, 424, 493; Robert 98, 127, 217, 223, 333, 447; Thomas 79, 122, 239, 298; Walter 334; Widow 20, 176 (2), 193, 197, 298, 332, 355, 472;

William 50, 121, 328, 377, 410, 428; Zacharias 331 (2)
Hellis
John 470; Thomas 360
Helton
Robert 360
Hemist
Richard 258
Hemmings
Goodman 162
Henbest (Henbeast)
Henry 148; John 143
Henbry (Henbery)
Robert 483; William 483, 503
Henchin (Henchen)
Ambrose 267; William 266
Hendly
Widow 255
Hendy (Hendey)
Arthur 112; Roger 130; Thomas 130; Widow 354
Henly (Henley)
Alexander 264; Andrew 374 (Sir), 375 (Sir); Robert 416 (Sir); Thomas 229, 256, 332
Hennam
John 504
Hennard
Joyce 106
Hennen
David 128
Henning
Stephen 122; Widow 86; William 85
Henrys
John 1
Hensen (Hensin)
Mister 363; Thomas 38
Henslow (Henslowe)
Michael 38; Thomas 3, 5 (2), 294
Henstridge
Thomas 527
Henty (Hentey)
Robert 40; Widow 51
Henvill
Christopher 98
Henvist
John 94
Henvy
Widow 96
Henwood
John 202, 319, 364; Robert 366 (2); Thomas 338; Widow 391; William 385; — 202
Herbert
Henry 424; Richard 385; Widow 160
Herd (Heards, Hurd)
Mister 240; Robert 290; Thomas 332
Heringman
Widow 1
Herne
Ambrose 135; Robert 316, 440; Widow 315
Herring
Farmer 503; John 252, 256, 472; Robert 332; Widow 330, 483, 492; William 259, 492
Herrington
Henry 97
Herriott
John 338; Mister 348; Widow 324; William 291
Hersent (Hersnett)
Daniel 517, 529; Peter 20(2), 406 (2)
Hersey (Hearsey)
Jacob 81; Jerome 486; John 223, 486; Richard 221; Thomas 74
Hetchells
Widow 154
Hetton
John 376
Heward
John 317; Thomas 316
Hewell
Widow 396
Hewes (Huse)
Henry 229; Jenkin 523a, 524; John 29, 38, 189, 429, 503;

Hewes (Huse)—*cont'd*
Oswald 321; Richard 170, 181, 294; Stephen 260; Thomas 260, 279; Widow 294, 501; William 252, 418
Hewett (Heuatt, Hewit)
Anthony 530 (2); Henry 442; James 56; John 67 (2), 68, 81, 375; Richard 208; Robert 63, 258; Samuel 373; Thomas 20, 59, 144, 530; Widow 76; William 49, 68
Hewlett (Hewlatt)
Abraham 38; Andrew 529; John 110, 195, 364, 435; Robert 529; William 50
Hewson
James 1; Samuel 236
Heyborne
Edward 250
Heycroft
Henry 218
Heyes (Hayes, Heighes, Heighs, Heys)
Anthony 324; Christopher 362; Edward 184; Henry 189, 333; James 183, 455; John 323, 329; Mary 184; Richard 94, 471; Robert 348 (2), 506; Thomas 434; Widow 94, 188, 400, 455, 501
Heyfor
Richard 419
Heyly
Widow 135
Heyman (Hayman)
Edward 371; John 178, 361; Richard 378
Heyres (*see also* Ayres)
Ralph 442
Heythorne
William 490
Heyward (Hayward, Heywood)
Anthony 1, 240; Charles 94; David 280; Francis 244; Goody 521; John 1 (2), 55, 92, 229 (2), 237, 459, 505 (2); Lancelot 456; Mark 513; Martin 435; Mister 104; Nicholas 527 (2); Robert 292, 418; Samuel 238; Stephen 8; Thomas 104, 434, 505; Widow 119, 240 (2), 459; William 87, 118, 240, 346, 374
Hibbs
John 392
Hickins
John 317
Hickley
Francis 25; John 32 (3), 334
Hickman
Henry 270; John 252 (2), 355; Michael 252; Nicholas 6; Peter 250; Richard 252, 286; Thomas 1, 100, 252 (2); Widow 51, 372
Hickox
William 287
Hicks (Hickes, Hix)
Francis 1 (3); John 93, 249, 434; Robert 281; Thomas 131; Widow 19; William 112
Higgins (Higgens, Higgin)
Edward 218; Henry 95; John 18 (2), 40 (2); Mister 25, 528, 529, 530; Robert 41; Thomas 353 (Sir); Widow 58, 84; William 278, 517
Higgs
Richard 384
Highmore
Benjamin 100
Hildesly
John 124
Hildropp
John 51
Hilken
John 305
Hill (Hills)
Abraham 419 (2); Christopher 202; Edward 38, 357, 369, 418; Elias 81; Goodman 354; Henry 326, 395, 419, 505; James 339,

364; Jasper 339; John 100, 160, 161, 246, 392, 419, 512; Maurice 332; Richard 176, 178, 189, 250, 258, 271; Robert 71, 148, 227, 365; Samuel 39; Thomas 1 (2), 200, 222, 227, 372, 378, 405, 424, 517, 529; Walter 38; Widow 17, 42, 145 (2), 162, 257, 379, 395, 397, 487, 505, 517; William 269, 419, 512; — 68
Hilla
John 136
Hillary
Anthony 473
Hiller
Edward 158; Henry 437
Hillett
Thomas 5
Hilliard
Hugh 324
Hillier
William 128, 219
Hillis
Thomas 357
Hillocke
Widow 276
Hillston
Robert 272
Himbery
William 503
Hinchman
Edward 461
Hincksman (Hinxman)
Joseph 434; Michael 434; Thomas 53; William 436
Hine
John 378
Hinks (Hincks, Hinkes)
Henry 280; Richard 240, 280; Thomas 237, 416; William 229
Hinnon
Widow 122
Hinton
Ann 103; Felix 103; Samuel 332; Thomas 97, 100, 103, 252; Widow 104; William 104, 118, 121
Hinwood
William 362
Hipper
John 266; Thomas 500
Hippitt
John 131
Hiscock (Hescoks, Hiscoke)
Andrew 115; John 155; Robert 95; Thomas 123; Widow 122
Hitchman
Widow 92
Hoare (Hore)
Christopher 513(2); Edward 216(2), 355; Francis 396, 398, 403; George 402, 513; Henry 145, 237; John 72, 257, 270, 272, 281, 322, 392, 405, 526; Nicholas 281; Richard 189, 237, 466, 470; Robert 392; Roger 392; Thomas 1, 216(2), 403; Widow 93, 322; William 280, 322, 398
Hobbs (Hobb, Hoobs)
Christopher 88, 244; Clement 93; Daniel 133; Edward 447; Gunner 44; Henry 269; Jane 89; Joan 89; John 37, 68, 110, 489; Mark 436; Mister 454; Peter 460; Philip 163; Richard 100; Robert 37, 94; Thomas 192(2), 244, 471; Widow 37, 67, 76, 100, 165, 192, 244(2), 460, 493(2); William 93, 195(2), 265; — 100
Hobby
Widow 139
Hobtrick
John 400
Hobtrow
John 398
Hocker
Robert 419
Hockley (Hockly)
Ann 248; Anthony 228; George 49; Henry 237; James 1, 364;

Hockley (Hockly)—*cont'd*
Joan 163; John 20, 29, 79, 163, 192, 250, 283, 353, 365, 386; Michael 334; Nathaniel 45; Nicholas 200; Richard 23, 192, 248; Roger 235; Thomas 248, 249, 257, 353, 515; Widow 248, 368, 410, 495
Hodges
Christopher 290; George 135; Henry 121; John 74, 392, 428; Joseph 370; Richard 38, 177; Robert 135; Widow 38, 342, 348; William 38, 135, 425
Hodman
Gilbert 357; Rose 357
Hodson
Herbert 372; Widow 229, William 192
Hoggard
William 317
Hogges (Hogge)
Edward 38; Henry 379; John 96; Thomas 436; William 324
Hoggis
Widow 292
Hoggsflesh
Nicholas 372; Richard 208; Thomas 398
Holdborne
Barnard 418; Christopher 418
Holder
John 418; Tobias 67
Holding (Holdinge)
Edward 332; Richard 313
Holdipp
Andrew 301; Henry 294; James 316(2), 317; John 317(2); Mister 295, 299; Nicholas 317
Holdropp
William 208
Holdway
Andrew 331; Ann 334; Arthur 334; Elizabeth 337; Henry 440(2); John 292, 331, 337, 346, 444; Richard 303, 349; Ruth 337; Thomas 323, 324, 337, 483; Widow 326, 436; William 333, 334, 337, 349
Hole (Holes, Holle)
Francis 1; Hugh 353; Richard 176; Widow 355; William 179
Holebrooke
Thomas 90
Holladay
Widow 463
Holland
Henry 494; John 42; Richard 163; Robert 493; Thomas 1; William 385
Hollard
Henry 332; William 1
Hollier (Hollyer)
John 114; Roger 89
Hollis
John 361; Mister 371; Samuel 435; Widow 37, 57; William 192
Holloway
Adam 441; Andrew 115; Anthony 100; Brian 231; Catherine 115; Edward 25, 209; Ellis 161; Hugh 459; James 1; Joan 292; John 135, 159, 244, 456, 473, 485, 487, 513(2); Matthew 130, 159; Mistress 176; Nicholas 81; Richard 111, 159, 339, 508; Robert 152; Susan 504; Stephen 156, 508; Thomas 115, 131; Widow 124, 154, 209, 443, 508; William 159, 176
Hollworthy
Sir Matthew 350
Hollyster (Holester)
Henry 1; John 38
Holman
William 436
Holmes (Holmbs, Holms)
John 103, 119, 343, 459; Peter 9; Robert 266; Samuel 436; William 1, 18(2), 442, 502
Holt
Andrew 423; Edward 38, 67;

James 269; John 14, 46, 47, 51, 194, 208, 269; Matthew 60; Mistress 1; Ralph 48, 54; Stephen 242; Thomas 21, 208; Widow 30, 35; William 32, 53, 57, 240, 275
Holton
James 505
Holyday
Ingram 475
Homard
Thomas 1; William 229
Hone
George 369
Honeywell
Richard 434
Honner
Richard 388
Honney
William 171
Honyman
German 23; John 23(2)
Hood
Richard 298, 316; Widow 249, 383
Hooke (Hook)
Edmund 168; John 170; Margaret 170; Richard 431; Widow 57
Hooker
Ann 178; Bartholomew 414; Edward 189, 233, 291, 357; Gregory 76; John 46(2), 227, 234, 318, 355, 395, 414(3), 424, 431; Nicholas 230, 318; Richard 234, 357; Robert 148, 424; Thomas 42, 230, 234, 318, 357; Widow 24, 424, 498; William 93, 95, 114, 238, 257, 266, 271, 398, 424, 433
Hookes
Mister 56
Hookey
Henry 152; Nicholas 128, 153; Richard 153; William 150, 518
Hooper
Edmund 483; Edward 120, 158, 238, 272 (Sir), 521, 527; James 1; John 134, 531; Thomas 38, 138(2), 436; Widow 145, 487
Hoorley
Edward 148
Hopgood
John 437(2), 442; Mister 33; Mistress 526; Richard 334, 483; Robert 434; Thomas 91, 130, 438; William 331, 504
Hopkins
Ann 325; Christopher 434; Henry 119, 135, 156; John 1, 480, 481, 503; Nicholas 1; Richard 50, 118, 119, 121, 150, 483, 494; Robert 324; Thomas 250, 483; Widow 454, 480, 483; William 120, 250, 453, 454(2), 480, 503
Hopley
Widow 59
Hopton
Reuben 316
Hoptree
Arthur 1
Hoptruse
Philip 403
Hopwood
Sir Philip 1
Horbett
Maurice 322
Horde
Matthew 148
Horder
Morgan 112
Horne
Captain 529; George 418; Henry 424, 524, 531; John 352, 383, 418, 443; Laurence 100; Mistress 383; Nicholas 257; Richard 529; Simon 328; Thomas 214, 352; William 25, 67, 257, 332, 517
Hornell
John 334
Horner
John 21, 29, 245; Elizabeth 276;

Horner—*cont'd*
Thomas 241; Widow 29; William 372
Horrell
Joseph 229
Horwood
James 1; John 46, 243
Hosier
Thomas 388
Hoskins (Horskins)
John 160, 507
Hotton
William 86
Houchins (Houchin, Huchens, Huchins, Hutchins, Howchins)
Anthony 260; John 24, 148, 260, 339; Nicholas 162; Richard 117(2), 132, 441; Robert 160, 531; Thomas 1, 472; Widow 418; William 339
Houghton (*see also* Oughton)
Edward 32, 57; John 483(2), 479; Philip 56; Thomas 57; William 55, 56, 57
Hounsham
James 368
Hounsome (Houndsome, Hounsom, Hunsom, Hunsome)
Henry 171, 176; James 184; John 171, 194; Nicholas 25; Robert 74; Widow 194; William 208
House
Elizabeth 436; Ezekiel 436; George 94; James 38; John 194, 301; Richard 115; Thomas 317(2); Widow 94; William 517, 529
Howard
John 133; Nicholas 133; Richard 458(2); Robert 322(Sir), 531
Howe
Widow 99
Howell
Francis 192; James 38; John 269(2); Mister 363; Robert 396
Howers
Robert 298
Howland
John 298
Howorth
John 472
Hoyle
James 135; Samuel 86
Hu[ ]
Thomas 518
Hubbert
John 1; William 299
Hudd
John 112
Hudson
Robert 175
Hudston
John 357
Hughes *see* Hewes
Hugman
Thomas 135
Hull
John 38, 332; Rawleigh 518
Hullpook
Edward 491; John 491
Humber
Catherine 493; George 299; Henry 451; Joan 1; John 412, 478, 479; Robert 473; William 487, 504
Humphry (Humphreys, Humphryes Humphrys)
Andrew 220; Edward 208; James 1; John 317(3), 471; Robert 148, 434; Roger 346; Thomas 192
Hunt
Andrew 115; Barnard 391; Brian 292; Christmas 208(2); Daniel 317; Dorothy 506; Edward 436, 454; Elizabeth 77; George 163, 491; Gregory 256; Henry 1, 333; Hugh 316, 317; Humphrey 418; James 100, 177, 182; Jerome 473(2); Joan 194; John 1(2), 11, 16, 17, 164, 166, 178, 183, 208, 250, 289, 299, 317, 407, 434, 450,

502, 512; Mark 343; Mary 318 Mister 299; Nicholas 168(2), 316, 317; Oliver 1; Peter 194; Ralph 507; Richard 28, 135, 182, 256, 417, 422, 512, 514, 520, 528; Robert 168, 298, 364(2); Sarah 163, 364; Stephen 35, 360, 398, 401(2); Susan 250; Thomas 1, 40, 135, 168(2), 237, 303, 472, 506, 512; Widow 37, 45, 168, 250, 255, 303, 317, 355; William 1, 35, 38, 90, 162, 208, 271, 303, 317(2), 322, 364, 398, 473(2), 475, 518

Hunter
Mistress 292; Philip 1; Widow 371

Huntingford
John 189, 194; William 175, 189

Huntingfre
Eustace 404

Huntly
John 110

Hunton
Andrew 283; Elizabeth 435; Robert 280

Hurd *see* Herd

Hurlock
John 2; Thomas 2, 40

Hurst
Alexander 459; Andrew 160; Edward 68; John 51, 67, 112; Mark 160; Mary 67; Mister 415; Mistress 462; Richard 94, 434(2), 455, 459; Robert 253(2), 443; Stephen 160; Widow 2, 292, 443(2); William 473

Hurt (Hurte)
Elizabeth 11; Nicholas 52

Hussey
James 515; Mister 102; Mistress 229; Widow 24, 229, 277; William 414, 471

Hutchins *see* Houchins

Hyatt
Richard 284

Hyde
Christopher 193; Doctor 240, 292, 443; George 254, 290; Humphrey 197; John 40, 97, 143, 201, 364, 436, 450, 456; Laurence 217, 292; Mister 82; Nathaniel 368; Peter 491; Philip 117(2); Ralph 235; Richard 384(2), 449; Thomas 117, 290; William 442, 455

Hyem
Robert 316

Hymon
Robert 507

Hyne
Richard 311

Illsley (Ilesley, Ilsley)
George 388(2); William 515

Imber
William 128

Imperell
William 338

Implefeild
Richard 92

Ingepenn
Thomas 95

Inges
John 100, 103

Ingram
Anthony 6; Christopher 418; Richard 1; Samuel 1; Widow 38, 97

Inhance
William 436

Inould
Clement 424; William 424

Inwood
Edward 404; John 187, 209, 408; Mary 419; Nicholas 1, 209; Richard 135; Robert 404; Roger 404; Thomas 397; Widow 5, 135; William 236, 404

Ireland
Francis 5; Humphrey 162; John 471; Richard 464; Widow 529; William 229, 471

Iremonger
Christopher 437; John 147, 162, 256, 331, 464, 514; Richard 93, 438; Thomas 464, 514
Irish
Henry 118; Widow 39
Isaack
Abraham 1
Isley
Daniel 317; Matthew 299
Ismonger
Henry 1; Richard 46; Simon 1; Widow 217
Israel
William 517
Isron (Isrone)
James 24, 349; John 229; Philip 476; Thomas 349; Widow 450, 476
Iveman
John 100; Widow 100
Ivemay
James 124; Maurice 117; Robert 126; William 104
Iver
Richard 141
Ives
Edward 418; Matthew 369; Robert 406; Thomas 371; William 380
Ivory
Robert 331
Ivy (Ivye)
Edward 445; John 450, 460; Matthew 255; Richard 456, 460; Robert 27; Widow 96; William 8, 515
Ivyleafe
Widow 504
Jackett
Edward 160
Jackman
Abraham 270; George 464; John 445; Nicholas 192; Peter 1; Widow 93, 470, 509; William 428
Jackson
Clerk 1; Francis 294; Grafton 521; John 182, 235, 418; Thomas 1; Widow 1; William 274, 383, 384
Jacobb (Jacob, Jacobs)
Andrew 247; Christopher 107; Henry 505; John 51, 247; Richard 276, 518; Robert 231; Thomas 1; Widow 111; William 310, 455
James
Christopher 333, 335, 443; Henry 118; Hugh 439; John 208, 351, 418, 472; Mistress 1; Nicholas 310, 346; Peter 437; Philip 1; Reuben 183; Richard 1, 126, 318; Robert 384; Samuel 99; Stephen 164; Thomas 95, 100, 284; Widow 85, 100, 112, 244, 384, 434; William 418, 434
Janverin (Janverine)
Thomas 518, 530; Widow 518, 530
Jaques (Jacques)
Edward 42, 192; John 229; Roger 229; Thomas 208, 434
Jarvis (Jarves, Jarvice, Jarvise, Jervice, Jervis)
John 160; Richard 529; Roland 1; Thomas 389, 517, 529; Walter 337; Widow 531
Jasper (Jesper)
Edward 448; Giles 448
Jay (Jaye, Jayes)
John 299; Jospeh 332; Michael 220; Richard 418
Jeblett
James 363; William 363
Jeckham
James 476
Jeffery (Jefferyes, Jefferys, Jeoffrey)
Christopher 323; Edward 187; George 125; Guy 229; Henry 439; Humphrey 282; James 1, 118; John 1, 119, 256, 268, 397, 484,

526; Margaret 125, 409; Richard 166, 178, 185, 187, 488; Thomas 229, 256, 268, 361; Widow 128, 282; William 2, 125, 260, 268, 282
Jefford (Jeford)
Arthur 94; Mister 509; Robert 461
Jellett
Thomas 1
Jellife (Jellyfe)
Richard 434(2)
Jelman
Widow 37
Jelsen
Widow 298
Jenkins
Anthony 528; Elizabeth 135; Gabriel 1; John 39; Richard 135; Robert 130; Thomas 40; Widow 118, 436; — 269
Jenman
Mister 14; Richard 209; William 1
Jenner
Henry 1; Richard 42; Thomas 1
Jennings (Jennens)
Edward 227, 424; John 96, 213, 378; Mary 284; Nicholas 194, 229, 490; Ralph 29, 227; Richard 436; Robert 363; Thomas 118; Widow 42, 212, 383; William 242, 298
Jenvey (Jenvie)
John 506; Richard 271
Jerman (Jermayne)
Anthony 219; Andrew 244; Edward 21(2); Hugh 219; John 270, 385; Richard 31, 224; Robert 240; Widow 135, 428
Jermye
Widow 390
Jerome
John 229, 458; Widow 229
Jesman (*see also* Gesman)
Widow 504
Jessapp
Widow 170
Jest
Jasper 298
Jewell
John 409; Widow 343
Jewer
William 396
Joardame
Mistress 160
Johns
Tristram 418
Johnson
Benjamin 1; Edward 529; George 106; Henry 1, 159; Humphrey 77; John 38, 161, 356, 434, 512; Richard 192, 317, 477; Robert 371; Thomas 363, 436, 442, 517; Walter 290; Widow 227, 229, 292, 513; William 192, 292, 418(2)
Jolley
Benjamin 51; German 45; Richard 254
Jolliff (Jolleff, Jolleffe, Jolliffe)
Henry 513; Joseph 120; Nicholas 396; Richard 396, 504; William 506(2), 521, 527
Jonas
John 506; Richard 271
Jones (Joanes, Jone)
Alexander 357; Andrew 271; Anthony 163; Bartholomew 371; Edward 257; Francis 38; Giles 418; Goodman 515; Henry 86; Humphrey 1; James 353; John 40, 208, 226, 436, 445, 464; Jospeh 522, 526; Maurice 343; Philip 229, 493; Richard 126, 148, 317; Robert 141, 158, 162, 464, 511; Thomas 1(2), 118, 506; Widow 123, 135, 148, 379(2), 445, 509(2), 515; William 20, 36, 296, 473, 483, 505; — 405

Jordan (Jorden, Jurdan, Jurden)
John 85, 126, 135, 507; Martin 135; William 126
Jourd (Jourde, Jurd)
James 30(2); John 72; Lionel 523a; Thomas 25; Widow 25; William 25; — 35
Jowles
William 450
Joyat
Thomas 449
Joyce
Christopher 317; John 247, 317; Richard 1; Robert 324, 494; Thomas 86, 108; Widow 318
Joye (Joy)
John 164; Richard 206; Widow 299
Joyley
Mister 300
Joylter
Stephen 317
Joyner
Widow 229
Joyte
Edward 333; Thomas 333
Jubber
William 112
Judd
Nicholas 439; Richard 279
Jumper
Daniel 121
Juner
James 371, 397; Robert 396
Justice
John 420; Mister 363; Peter 263; Widow 321
Justigan
John 103
Juward
Robert 1; William 1
Kates
Widow 214
Katterell
Widow 29
Keates (Keate, Keete)
John 434; Simon 219; William 362, 384
Keeffen
Thomas 103
Keele
Richard 434
Keene
John 339; Elizabeth 135
Keepe
Andrew 383; Francis 515(2); Richard 383(2)
Keepen (Keepinge, Kippen, Kipping)
James 100; Joan 92; John 100, 104(2), 120; Richard 118, 524; Robert 523a; Thomas 102
Kellis
John 120
Kellzill
John 172
Kelsey
Edward 470; George 189; Henry 229, 473; John 189, 256, 422, 467, 473; Lambert 355; Mistress 29; Nicholas 189, 390; Richard 465, 506; Robert 258, 483; Roger 269; Thomas 189, 269, 501; Widow 390, 355, 473; William 506
Kemish (*see also* Camish)
John 252; Richard 252, 256
Kemon
Christopher 229
Kempe (Kemp)
Alexander 418; Francis 40; George 175, 189; Henry 40, 72, 260; John 46, 332, 414; Nicholas 163; Richard 407, 443; Robert 326(2), 417, 424; Thomas 332, 408; Widow 219, 260, 326; William 83
Kempster
Bartholomew 520, 528
Kench
John 216

Kendrey
Thomas 357
Kennett
Henry 43(2)
Kent (Kente)
Abraham 508; Alice 506; Andrew 32, 475; Clement 12(2), 50; Edward 504; Ephraim 162; Giles 252; Henry 428; John 1, 34, 141, 148, 299, 384, 428(2), 436, 441, 453, 456(2), 457, 473, 502; Mister 504; Nathaniel 315; Nicholas 257, 339, 483; Peter 112, 460; Philip 459; Ralph 429; Richard 25, 252, 311, 324, 338, 385, 388, 453, 456, 457, 458, 472, 473, 483, 503; Robert 136; Samuel 292; Stephen 376; Thomas 112, 211(2), 137, 336, 442, 454, 456(2), 460; Walter 362; Widow 216, 252(2), 256, 266, 318, 459(2); William 39, 252, 258, 324, 331, 402; — 139
Kenton
William 441
Kenwood
Edward 23
Keny
John 124
Kerby (Kerbye, Kirby)
Anthony 223; Elizabeth 22; Henry 160; John 162, 396; Lancelot 229; Parnel 22; Robert 26; Thomas 1, 135, 394, 396; Widow 122, 270, 365; William 1, 497(2)
Kercher
Mister 284
Kerly (Kerley) (*see also* Cerly)
George 157(2); John 118; Peter 157; Richard 118; Robert 120; William 112
Kernell
Walter 19
Kernes
Mistress 529
Kernett
John 292, 416
Kerrill
Andrew 92
Kersley
Richard 422
Kerver (Kirver)
Ann 226; William 205
Kervill (Kirvill)
Hayden 515; John 470
Kettlewell (Kittlewell)
George 195; Mary 75
Kew
Obadiah 418; Richard 418; Robert 418(2); Thomas 293, 418
Kewen
William 252
Kibelitte
Widow 332
Kidgar
Widow 332
Kidgell
John 231, 482; Thomas 483; Widow 352, 474
Kidler
Francis 317
Kiffen
Thomas 104
Kiftall (Kiftell)
John 416; Richard 418; Thomas 526
Kifte
John 445; William 445
Kill
Moses 206; Widow 202
Kimber (Kember) (*see also* Cimber)
Alice 156; Clement 299; Dorothy 453; Giles 531; Henry 156(2), 298; Joan 378, 431; John 97, 299, 356; Leonard 356; Mary 453; Richard 156; Stephen 135; Thomas 97, 155, 298, 378; Valentine 299; Widow 93, 96, 365
Kinchin (Kinchen)
Abraham 353; Austin 289; John

Kinchin (Kinchen)—*cont'd*
193, 418; Richard 289; Robert 366; Roland 290; William 239, 357, 478
Kindley
John 70
Kingate
Thomas 35
Kinge (King)
Ambrose 102; Anthony 113; Catherine 442; Charles 428; Chloe 168; Christopher 157, 194; Edward 38, 113, 165, 283; Elizabeth 164; Ellen 456; Giles 19; Henry 93, 157(2), 433; Humphrey 223; James 40, 121, 130, 229; John 27, 57, 92, 117, 119, 122, 149, 160, 218, 223, 252, 332, 365, 371, 400, 434, 497; Kemberlin 85; Mister 203; Nathaniel 531; Richard 30, 158, 160, 232, 283, 423, 451, 455; Robert 38, 102, 115, 286, 420, 440, 531; Roger 127, 130, 472; Stephen 229, 442; Thomas 1, 43, 94, 102, 130, 324, 353, 355, 368, 391, 392, 442, 447, 463; Widow 1, 25, 49, 100, 120, 165, 215, 290, 339, 371, 404, 442; William 57, 75, 85, 113, 118, 154, 155, 165, 323, 364, 395, 442, 456
Kingman
Nicholas 468; Robert 1; William 37
Kingsmill (Kingsmell)
Daniel 440; John 331, 434; Lady 320
Kinnell
William 265
Kipson
Richard 332
Kirber
Anthony 225
Kirby *see* Kerby
Kirke
Thomas 38
Kirver *see* Kerver
Kirvil *see* Kervill
Kitch
Anthony 119, 121; Charity 132; Elizabeth 323; James 121; John 119, 135; Thomas 194; Walter 123; Widow 131, 135
Kitchener (Kitchiner)
Samuel 418; Thomas 418; William 188
Kite (Kyte)
Robert 27, 147; Widow 445
Kittyer
Evan 127; George 134; Henry 134; Widow 134; William 134
Knaper
Thomas 294, 299
Knapp (*see also* Napp)
John 45
Knapton
Albin 89; Bartholomew 89; Mister 517; Ralph 518; Richard 89; Thomas 95; William 89, 520
Knell
Henry 71; John 134
Knight
Abraham 208(2); Alexander 290, 436; Barnard 166; Christopher 513; Clement 40(2); Daniel 206; Edward 23, 64, 229; Francis 182; George 206; Henry 88, 103, 196; Isaac 504, 505, 511, 513; James 185, 189, 309, 314, 317(3), 332(2), 334, 431, 487; Joan 327; John 1(2), 26, 31, 76, 96, 167, 191, 202, 206(2), 209, 223, 228, 246, 247, 317, 333, 334, 368, 490, 506, 508, 515, 523b; Mary 434; Mister 185, 362; Mistress 527; Nathaniel 523a; Nicholas 164, 173, 206, 208(2), 316, 317, 379, 402; Peter 23, 303, 317, 357; Philip 223; Richard 21, 76, 177, 188, 191(3), 215, 220, 229(2), 250(2), 313, 447; Robert 72, 191, 312, 317, 406, 442, 460; Samuel

1; Sarah 375; Simon 163; Stephen 332; Thomas 6, 17, 18, 31(2), 58, 60, 191, 223, 229, 289, 332, 334, 346, 401, 418; Walter 343; Widow 5, 36, 42, 77, 221, 244, 311, 317, 332, 342, 405, 418, 434; William 1(3), 58, 68, 206(3), 208, 312, 317, 339, 391, 407, 418, 438, 442, 521

Knightingall (*see also* Nitinghall)
Nicholas 97

Knightlin
Thomas 434; Tobias 436

Knott
Thomas 257; Widow 515

Knowen
Widow 10

Knowler
Edward 523a, 524; Henry 246; James 530; Thomas 23; Widow 519

Knowles
Edmund 274; Edward 157; Henry 446; John 436, 446; Mister 8; Mistress 273; Thomas 258; Widow 436; William 436

Knowlton
William 216

Kyles
Widow 98

Labourer
Widow 177

Labrane
Widow 193

Lacie (Lacey, Lacy, Lacye)
Bethlem 160; Edward 239; John 317, 256, 279; Peter 241; Richard 196, 250 (Sir), 299, 334; Thomas 322; Widow 112, 241; William 242

Ladd
Henry 219

Lake (Lakes)
Arthur 529, 530; Edward 529; Joan 101; John 67, 86, 193, 299; Robert 337, 346; William 229, 332

Lale
Francis 38

Lalle
John 89

Lambe (Lamb)
James 518; Mister 229; Robert 17; Thomas 82; Widow 94, 461; William 283, 418

Lambert
Alexander 273; John 1; Nicholas 91; Richard 162; Robert 88, 96, 326; Thomas 229; William 269

Lamboll (Lambole, Lambolle)
Daniel 524; Edward 306; Francis 523a; James 257(2), 293; John 388; Philip 182; Richard 42; Robert 523a, 524; Thomas 142, 177, 184, 425; Widow 370; William 407

Lamborne
Richard 332; Thomas 332

Lampard
John 229; Laurence 229; Nicholas 229; William 414

Lampart
John 171

Lampe
William 334

Lampert
John 160

Lamphier
Widow 229

Lamport
Edward 424; Francis 164; John 161, 419, 424, 431; Laurence 164; Peter 418; Robert 163; Thomas 317; William 317

Lampson
Andrew 1

Lancaster
Thomas 446; William 250

Lanckfell
Richard 451

Landon
John 348
Lane (Layne)
Christopher 334; Edward 265; George 72; Henry 112; James 316; John 244, 246, 273, 277, 362, 408, 490; Mary 100, 125; Richard 128, 229, 249; Robert 218, 316, 385; Roger 229, 252; Samuel 339; Stephen 100; Thomas 100, 118, 124, 130, 159, 316, 462; Widow 100, 119, 128, 408; William 29, 72, 81, 144, 229, 231, 348, 434
Langard (Langhard)
Anthony 133
Langdew
John 272
Langester
John 418; Richard 418
Langfeild
William 493
Langford
Edward 83, 178; Nicholas 489; Richard 139; Stephen 522; Thomas 229, 237, 530; Widow 5, 493; William 27
Langley (Langly)
Roger 522; Thomas 38; Widow 470; William 112, 518, 529
Langridge (Langradge, Langridg)
Alexander 493; Austin 472; George 461; Peter 219; Silvester 468(2)
Langrish (*see* Longrish)
Laninge
Widow 114
Lansdale (Lansdall, Lansdalle)
John 100; Robert 111; William 95
Lany
James 512
Lapp
Gabriel 115
Larby (Larbee)
Edward 201; Goodman 171; James 201; John 206; Richard 206; Widow 201; William 194
Lardner
John 488; Richard 340; William 229
Larman
James 1
Larmor (Laremoore)
John 316; Richard 375
Larnam
Simon 1
Lasham
Widow 205
Lashfourd
John 381
Lashley
John 503
Lassam
John 182
Lathum
George 38
Latter
Simon 46
Laud (Lawd, Lawde)
John 333; Thomas 46; Widow 508
Lauder (Lawder)
Peter 418; Widow 119
Laughtry
John 93
Launder (Laundres)
Andrew 324; Christopher 192; Richard 1; Samuel 281; William 121, 124
Launston
John 296; Thomas 231; William 252(2)
Lavender
Francis 531; William 123
Lavington
Edward 205; Francis 512; John 236; Thomas 512; — 229
Lawes
Ann 157; Henry 107; John 90, 338, 342, 387; Thomas 38, 299; Widow 38; William 476

Lawrence (Laurence, Laurens)
Edward 316; John 144, 161, 229, 235, 269, 272, 375(2), 422; Mary 89; Mister 367, 441; Philip 205; Richard 229(3), 503, 505; Robert 143, 332, 434, 451; Samuel 39; — 290
Lawson
Francis 92
Layding
Henry 150
Layman
John 38
Layte
Edward 517
Leach
Arthur 115; Edward 436; Giles 55, 58; James 397, 483; John 1, 255, 459, 487; Joseph 352; Laurence 118; Mary 442; Stephen 457; Thomas 266, 436; Widow 56, 471, 503 (2); William 346, 483, 487
Leadwell
Thomas 56
Leaffe (Leafe)
Austin 471; John 1, 471; William 473(2)
Leagrave
John 362
Leates
Francis 369
Leather
Robert 192; Thomas 299; Widow 299; Zacharias 38
Leawood
John 252
Lecar
Robert 122
Leckford
Robert 395
Lee (Lea, Leigh)
Barnard 179; Catherine 55; Daniel 23; George 251; Harman 258; Henry 55, 391; James 251, 418, 424; John 29, 51, 299, 522, 526; Mister 530; Mistress 1; Philip 145(2); Ralph 418; Richard 29, 194, 258, 270; Robert 38, 530; Roger 38; Thomas 29, 368, 531; Widow 56; William 51, 172, 250, 348, 355, 357, 424
Leece
Thomas 96
Leedes
Paul 471; Thomas 473
Leekeblade
Henry 19; Widow 19
Leeman
Thomas 192
Leffe
John 118
Legatt (Legat, Legatte, Leigatt)
Edward 226, 316; George 245; Henry 55, 62; John 64, 81(2); Richard 90, 422; Robert 187; Widow 285; William 437
Legey
Mister 257
Legg (Legge)
Ellis 419; John 38, 118, 200, 208, 404, 457, 513; Mister 453; Mistress 208; Robert 208; Thomas 385; Widow 334, 493; William 169, 385, 398
Legith
Barnard 96
Leighborne
Robert 138; Thomas 146, 147; William 144
LeLandre (Lelaunder)
Daniel 520, 529
Lellaby
John 487
Lemmett
Joseph 271
LeMotte (*see also* De La Motte)
Captain 530
Lempster
John 351

Lennox
Widow 512
Lentall
Mister 429
Leonard
Henry 51; Richard 122; Robert 250; Thomas 1; Widow 122
Le Page
Robert 527
Lerrick
John 276
Lester
Andrew 110; John 122, 135
Leucar
Widow 119
Leversuch
Richard 229
Leves
John 1; Thomas 1
Levett
William 1
Lewden
George 333(2)
Lewenton
Thomas 434
Lewes
Jasper 158; John 158(2); Widow 1
Lewin (Lewyn)
Edward 119; John 1
Lewington
Edward 437; Thomas 438
Lewis
John 260, 434, 446, 473; Richard 260, 363, 447; Robert 492; William 102, 228(Sir), 440
Lews
John 518
Leywood
John 458; Thomas 458(2)
Liberd
John 29
Ligge
Thomas 80
Light
Christopher 515; Elizabeth 270; John 95; Richard 144, 527; Robert 108, 270; Thomas 118, 252(2), 270, 515; Widow 252, 515; William 1(2), 113, 138, 394, 416
Lilly
John 38
Lillywhite
Peter 392; Richard 200; Thomas 485; William 205
Limbers
William 334
Limery
Edward 316
Liminge (Limming, Limynge)
James 315; John 357; Thomas 163; Widow 163
Limingham
Widow 369
Limington (Lymington)
Richard 357; Roger 244; Thomas 108
Limlock (Limelooke)
Adam 332; Thomas 324
Limpas
Widow 445
Lincefeild
Richard 103
Linckhorne
James 273
Lindsey (Linsey)
Thomas 1, 158
Lingham
Widow 95
Linney
Austin 473; William 317
Linshott
Thomas 200
Linston
William 357
Linter
Peter 72; Thomas 355
Linton (Lynton)
Alexander 468; William 473
Lipputt
Richard 37

Lipscombe (Lipscomb)
Arthur 248; Charles 192; Henry 1; John 193, 330, 424; Margaret 366; Mary 366; Robert 366, 394; Thomas 193, 291; William 165
Lisle
Mistress 117; Peter 526; William 104
Litchfeild
John 35; Richard 122
Little
Widow 255
Littlefeild
Ann 42; Arthur 465; Edward 29; James 270; John 69, 77, 468; Mister 371; Nicholas 69; Richard 478, 490; William 56
Littleworth
Richard 336; Robert 362
Livelong
Henry 100; John 100; Margaret 102; Richard 100, 102, 112; Thomas 113
Lively
John 437; William 437
Lloyd (Lloyde)
Christopher 222; James 1; Thomas 252
L[o]
Thomas 524
Loaden
Widow 469
Loader (Loder)
Mister 5; Nicholas 40; Widow 504
Loaght
Richard 461
Lock (Locke)
Alice 93, 178; Dorothy 38; Edward 246, 474; Francis 37, 56; Henry 194(2); James 1, 5, 252; John 182(2), 209, 272, 324; Oliver 261; Richard 228; Robert 70, 342, 408; Thomas 93, 170; Widow 2, 154, 265, 331, 474; William 1, 65, 124, 187, 231, 265, 484
Locker
Richard 1
Lockett
James 229; John 29; Thomas 97
Locksum
Francis 172
Lockyer (Lockier)
Andrew 161; Christopher 190; John 218; Richard 120; Robert 189; Widow 118; William 120
Lodger
Arthur 214
Lomday
Elizabeth 56
Londay
Francis 29
Long (Longe)
Ann 418; Anthony 219, 220; Blewett 208; Dennis 339; Elizabeth 434; Francis 39; Henry 434; John 161, 193, 436, 465, 515; Joseph 81; Mary 339; Maurice 334; Michael 317; Nathaniel 221; Nicholas 219; Philip 135; Postumus 102; Richard 40, 56, 60, 218, 488; Robert 434, 515; Sidrach 135; Thomas 208, 226, 322, 339, 448; Timothy 86; Widow 55, 217(2), 317, 398, 473; William 83, 134, 408
Longland
Humphrey 495; John 142, 294; Richard 299; Robert 25; Thomas 142, 258; Widow 258; William 252
Longman
John 324, 331; Robert 349; Thomas 458; William 458
Longrish (Langrish)
Anthony 221; Edward 223; John 42; Nicholas 222; Widow 221
Longrove *see* Lovegrove

Longworth
Mister 205(2)
Loope
John 317
Lopham
Gilbert 317
Lord
Thomas 90
Lording
Mister 300; Thomas 335
Loringe
William 436
Lotter
Thomas 1
Louse
George 72
Love
Barnard 229, 263; James 196; John 176; Mary 6; Mister 429; Richard 176, 244; Widow 37; William 252
Lovedidge
Widow 112
Lovedy
Widow 100
Lovegrove (Longrove, Lovegrowe)
John 436; Richard 436; William 435
Loveing (Loving)
John 279; Mister 529; Richard 267; Widow 279(2)
Lovelett
Widow 501
Lovell
Felix 143; Richard 141, 299; Stephen 299, 302; Thomas 24(2), 95, 162, 282, 299; Widow 493
Lovelock
James 317
Lovey
John 255
Lowder
Widow 216
Lowe (Lowes)
Francis 201; John 38, 124
Lowell
John 125
Lower
Francis 332; William 206
Lowman
Edward 87; Francis 291; Hugh 394(2); John 193; Ralph 398
Lowmer
Edward 473; John 76(2), 252; Richard 252; Thomas 19, 252
Lucas (Luces)
David 1; Francis 1; Robert 125; Thomas 38; William 85, 89, 290
Luce
William 332
Lucey (Lewcy, Lucy)
Thomas 385; Widow 206; William 322, 337
Luckeham
John 101
Ludley
Edward 358
Ludwell
William 527
Luess
William 424
Luffder
William 53
Luffe (Luff)
Jane 95; John 44(2), 169, 220, 529; Mister 14; Nicholas 57; Widow 55; William 99, 222
Luke
George 530; James 229; Mister 126; Richard 521; Robert 330; William 45
Lukenor
Sir John 427
Lukin
Robert 203
Lumbard
William 110
Lumford
Widow 193
Lunn (Lunne)
Francis 56; Henry 51, 67, 75;

John 40, 398, 404, 405; Richard 185, 189; Thomas 30; William 1(2)
Lunston
Richard 357
Luscock
Walter 317
Lush
John 134
Lusse
William 424
Luter (Lutter)
Robert 88; Thomas 142
Luttman
Richard 189, 227; William 46
Lyant
Henry 142; Widow 142
Lydalle (Lyddell)
Edward 521; Peter 23; Widow 23
Lyddiard
Mister 494
Lyde (Lidd)
Christopher 38; Richard 25; Robert 190
Lyewood (Lywood)
Hugh 457; Richard 457; Thomas 457; Widow 457
Lylewhite
Thomas 398
Lymborner (Lymeburner)
James 515; John 1; Thomas 515
Lymeger
Widow 491
Lynam (Lynhm)
Joan 462; Richard 353
Lyne (Line, Lynne)
Andrew 162; Charles 87; Christopher 104; Edward 98, 162(2); Henry 100(2), 103, 160, 201; Holden 100; Hugh 100; James 256, 512; John 100(3), 104, 201, 283, 496; Maurice 104; Mister 99; Peter 317; Philip 104(3); Samuel 38; Shadrack 229; Thomas 100, 151, 175, 412; Ursula 496; Widow 104, 128, 150, 285, 499, 528; William 100, 150, 159, 266, 387, 496, 522, 526
Lyon
John 76; William 54
Mabbancke
Widow 356
Mabbutt
Thomas 356
Macco
Cornelius 88
Macham
Cornelius 528; Richard 151; William 517, 529
Mackerell (Mackerill)
Dorothy 325; John 329; Thomas 418; William 128, 155
Madgwick
Elizabeth 414; George 364; Thomas 364
Madhead
Richard 513
Mafey (Maffey, Maphey, Maphy)
Dorothy 473; Goodman 515; John 469; Widow 72, 266(2); William 473
Magbin
Philip 398
Mahew (Mayhew)
Edward 405; John 193(2), 194; Thomas 193, 299(2)
Maidlow (Maydlow)
Ann 222; Peter 222; Thomas 43
Mainor
John 48
Major (Majors)
Avery 504; Henry 177, 279; James 177; John 2, 112, 229; Nicholas 1; Richard 462, 505; Roland 134; Widow 112; William 392, 504
Mallard
Martha 518; Thomas 404
Mance
William 398
Mancey
Henry 403

Manger
Edward 298
Mann (Man)
Charles 530; George 149; Giles 59; Jonathan 229; John 123, 154; Richard 120, 153, 156, 229; Ursula 521; Widow 527; William 29, 68
Mannell
Ellen 181
Manner (Manners, Mannor)
Margaret 104; Obadiah 524; Thomas 103(2)
Manneringe (Mannering)
John 374; Mister 357, 376
Mannery
John 192
Manningham
Mister 256
Mannings (Manninge)
Edward 524; John 165, 418, 524
Mannington
Thomas 366
Mansack
William 229
Mansbridge (Mansbridg)
Andrew 62; Anthony 260; Henry 145, 408; John 44, 49, 145, 258; Philip 1; Richard 257, 260, 290; Robert 145; Stephen 137, 138; Thomas 413; Widow 257, 270, 291; William 134
Mansell
John 55, 310
Manser
Thomas 81, 83
Mansfeild (Mandfeild, Mandfild, Mansfield)
Esther 281; George 434; John 521, 527, 418; Joseph 418; Robert 435; William 522, 526
Mantle
Henry 135, 155; James 155; John 156; Maurice 332; Richard 155; William 155
Maphew
Edward 473(2), 493; Henry 473; Widow 473; William 296
Mapp
John 178
Mappleton
Jonathan 357
March
George 97; Henry 14; Mister 5
Marcham
Edward 217
Mardell
William 299
Markett
John 135
Marks (Marke)
Ann 86; Edward 27, 283; James 30, 35; John 59, 317, 476; Richard 1; Thomas 342, 442; William 397
Marlow
Edward 383; John 376; Widow 371; William 363
Marman
John 212
Marrimer
Widow 135
Marriner (Mariner)
Brian 408, 409; Francis 29; Joan 106; John 41, 46, 105, 219, 343; Matthew 80, 237, 244; Richard 40, 41, 236; Robert 298; Widow 40; William 223
Marris
Mister 504
Marsey
John 376
Marsh
John 459; William 494
Marshall
Anthony 219; Barnaby 463; Francis 170; George 358, 398; Joan 392; John 37, 42, 104, 163, 223, 272, 362, 392, 398, 400; Joseph 392; Mister 283; Moses 257; Richard 169; Robert 185;

Roger 185; Thomas 383, 417, 418, 434, 471; Widow 38, 185; William 123, 183
Martin (Marten, Matine, Martyn, Martyne)
Brian 284; Christopher 378; Edward 162, 339; George 102; Giles 229; Henry 372; James 29, 385, 479; Joan 335; John 1, 94, 102, 113, 115, 194, 215, 257, 332, 345, 370, 376, 462, 504, 508; Jonas 311; Maurice 22; Mister 229; Philip 317; Revell 298(2); Richard 42, 63, 80(2), 298, 335, 412, 436, 487; Robert 102, 282, 378; Saunder 513; Sibyl 254; Stephen 100(2); Thomas 40, 42, 45, 94, 100, 158(2), 254, 255, 422, 508; Widow 5, 100, 128, 194, 333(2), 396, 420, 447, 462, 508; William 1, 25, 102, 217, 311, 332(2), 384, 397, 476
Martindale
John 29
Martle
Robert 40
Marwick (Marwicke)
Mister 192; William 208
Marys
George 257
Masey (Massey)
Christopher 334; Mister 257; Mistress 143; Nicholas 104; Richard 136; Thomas 94
Maskell
Edward 333
Mason
Charles 378; George 308; James 299; John 1, 40, 298, 379; Richard 266, 324, 472; Robert 229 (Sir); Thomas 271; Widow 257, 299, 318, 331, 529; William 257, 318, 502, 517
Masters
Francis 49; Hercules 89; Nicholas 100; Walter 382; Widow 49, 382
Mathew (Mathewes, Mathews, Matthews)
Arthur 229; Benjamin 1, 98, 189, 190, 420, 421; Daniel 392; Doctor 72; Edward 418; George 177, 392, 483; Henry 3, 164, 168, 194, 309; James 163, 251(2); John 189, 190, 223, 231, 237, 272, 273, 301, 317, 355, 368, 385, 394, 404, 460, 506; Joseph 158; Laurence 368; Mister 208; Nathaniel 178; Nicholas 462; Philip 245; Richard 38, 168, 505; Simpson 434; Thomas 100, 163(2), 194, 199, 205, 212, 230, 251(2), 292, 356; Widow 189, 205(2), 252, 272, 298, 299, 309, 316, 371, 392, 420; William 191, 201, 246, 251, 279, 371, 385, 418, 471, 505
Matten (Matton)
Fabler 418; Robert 454
Mattersfeild
John 407
Mattocke (Mattox)
William 36, 80
Maudlin
Richard 222
Maulter
William 323
Maunder
Robert 252
May
Anthony 338; Benjamin 404; Christopher 423; Edward 357(2); Francis 317; George 163; Henry 269, 305; Humphrey 397; Ingram 491; James 316, 336; John 191, 223, 279, 321, 334, 356, 375, 378, 385(2); Lewis 5; Mary 299; Michael 237, 316; Richard 356; Robert 395; Thomas 305, 316, 338, 378, 397; Widow 1, 36, 378, 483; William 5, 305, 355, 397(2); — 378

Maybancke
Robert 189
Maydley
Thomas 4
Maydman
Thomas 281; Widow 40, 103
Mayham
Thomas 20
Mayhew *see* Mahew
Mayle
Clement 54; John 32, 56(2); Robert 49; Thomas 56
Mayleigh
Widow 257
Maymore
John 378
Maynard
Christopher 362; Thomas 377, 397(3)
Mayne
Anthony 379; Mister 418
Mayweather
Thomas 483
Meacham
Thomas 475
Meade
William 1, 115
Meadkirke
Mistress 208
Meakens
Widow 1
Meales
John 440; William 444
Meature
John 464
Meden
John 126
Medever
Widow 298
Medhouse
John 112
Medhurst
Thomas 436
Medley
John 515
Mee
John 221
Meeres (Meare, Meares, Meere, Meires)
James 404; John 383, 523a, 524; Richard 269, 368, 392; Thomas 282, 368, 450; Widow 371, 422; William 32, 254
Meggs
Christopher 292; Mister 380
Melledge
John 100; Josias 100; Phineas 157; Thomas 101
Mellendey
John 85
Mellis
Thomas 46
Mells
Richard 1
Melsome
Luke 56
Melton
James 370
Menshew (Menshaw)
Henry 146; John 124; Simon 139
Merchant
George 168; James 356(2); William 356
Merefield
Henry 517
Merrett
Francis 160; Henry 152; John 106; Seth 148; Widow 1, 76
Merrick
Edward 38; George 434, 436
Merricott
Richard 99
Merriott (Merrott)
Andrew 193; Gregory 76; Humphrey 286; Isaac 367; James 249; John 1, 135, 285; Michael 365, 390; Mister 421, 456; Nicholas 390; Robert 367; Thomas 285, 390; Widow 76, 120, 250; William 249

Merriweather
David 1; Goodwife 162
Merry
William 348
Merser (Mercer)
Henry 323; John 323(2), 404, 445; Peter 323; Richard 258; Stephen 439; Widow 323; William 258
Mersh
Catherine 269; George 38, 56, 163; Guy 84; Henry 3, 462; John 229, 242(2), 266, 472, 473, 512; Nathaniel 182; Nicholas 229; Quinbanner 38; Richard 213, 362(2), 462, 473; Thomas 164, 224, 462, 469, 473; Widow 229(2), 336, 471, 473; William 2, 55, 56, 462, 473
Mersham
Arthur 192(2); Austin 237; Ebden 215; Thomas 192; Walter 292; William 476
Mersom
John 322
Mertham
Widow 324
Merven
Widow 51
Meservice
Roger 130; William 128
Mesey
Richard 316
Mesher
Robert 100
Meshman
John 94
Messor
Christopher 323; William 323
Meux
Robert 160
Mew
Andrew 266; Doctor 392; Ellis 229; John 181, 229; Richard 276(2); Thomas 84; Widow 266
Mewsellwheat
William 136
Michaell
Mister 89
Michell (Michells, Michill, Mitchell)
Ambrose 270; Christian 270; Edward 408; Francis 93; George 428; Henry 132; James 110; Joan 394; John 38, 83, 112, 189, 250, 252, 270, 272; Nicholas 515; Peter 367; Richard 241; Robert 229; Sibyl 67; Stephen 246; Thomas 182, 252, 366, 506; Widow 42, 94, 208, 229(2), 270, 394(2), 531; William 1, 42, 89, 92
Michen (Michin)
John 397, 418; Richard 418; Robert 418; Stephen 388
Middleton (Midleton)
Henry 371; Mister 229; Roger 230; Widow 235; William 1; — 240
Mifflin
Thomas 86
Mikes
William 470
Mildmay
Henry 236, 237
Miles (*see also* Mills)
Edward 449; Elizabeth 445; John 330; Nicholas 506
Milland
Edmund 371
Millard
Clement 84; Edward 40; Gilbert 58; Humphrey 397; John 213, 397; Thomas 84; Widow 428
Millberry (Milbery, Millbery)
Edward 518; John 518; Mister 530; William 518, 530
Miller
Francis 211; Henry 521(2), 527; Humphrey 494; John 100, 179, 434; Ralph 100; Richard 378, 473; Robert 100(2); Thomas 311, 434, 448; Widow 97, 229, 322(2),

Miller—*cont'd*
410, 434(2); William 109
Millesh
Thomas 217
Millett
Geoffrey 378; James 378; Matthew 339; Nicholas 454; Thomas 3, 317, 371, 488; Widow 420; William 378
Millham
William 375
Mills (Mill, Milles) (*see also* Miles)
Andrew 30, 68; Anthony 212; Bartholomew 40; David 92, 457; Edward 189, 331; Elizabeth 199; Giles 193; Henry 208; Humphrey 317; James 25, 33; Joan 157; John 1(2), 83, 93, 136 (Sir), 317, 332, 379, 385, 414, 418, 475, 478, 483, Knappen 135; Lukenour 89; Matthew 39; Michael 1, 162, 164; Mister 25; Nathaniel 246(2); Richard 1, 176, 180, 185, 195, 301, 317, 436, 458, 474; Robert 68, 157, 227, 255, 385; Stephen 294; Thomas 1, 164, 194, 213, 229, 246, 323, 378, 404, 414, 476, 484; Widow 29, 38, 190, 316, 332, 474, 513; William 291, 318, 331, 342, 372
Milton
John 370; Nicholas 433
Minchin
John 227, 281; Thomas 436
Miner
Henry 200
Mingham
David 214; Robert 195
Minkes
Elizabeth 244
Mintron
Thomas 123
Minty (Mintey)
George 115; Roger 115
Mislebrooke (Mislebrook)
Browman 299; Edward 299; Richard 265; Robert 299; Widow 265; William 299(2)
Misling
Thomas 272
Missa
Richard 451(2)
Missinge
William 60
Missingham
Daniel 1; John 175; Thomas 181; William 361
Misson
Samuel 332
Mist
John 112; Nicholas 113; William 98
Mitchener (Michener, Michenor, Michiner)
Clement 216; Edward 418; Edmund 418; Henry 395; James 498; John 44; Richard 216, 503, 512; Samuel 418; Thomas 1; Widow 354, 398
Mitchenell
William 407
Miths
Robert 354
Mittens
Richard 1
Mobery
William 1
Mogg
James 418; John 418
Moggeridg
Widow 229
Moiden
Widow 363
Moncke
John 446; Richard 332; Widow 38; William 481
Mondey, Moundy, Mundy *see* Mundey
Money
Edward 182; James 37; Robert 357; Thomas 66, 70; Widow 183, 193; William 203

Monson
Andrew 1
Moody (Moodey)
Ann 447; John 1(2); Nicholas 519, 530; Stephen 257; Thomas 522, 526
Moone
Edward 92; John 92; Richard 226; Widow 404
Moore (Moores, More, Morre)
Abraham 482; Bartholomew 407; Edmund 124; Edward 19; Francis 332, 418; George 1; Henry 150, 361; Hercules 241; John 35, 81, 89, 108, 164, 265, 353, 357(2), 397; Philip 89; Richard 85, 108, 127, 154, 237, 265; Rickman 133; Robert 50, 265; Thomas 134, 273, 299, 342; Walter 236; Widow 103, 119, 135, 150(2), 342, 354, 390, 396; William 81, 133, 159(2), 244, 342, 348, 432
Moorer
John 194(2); William 194
Moorey (Moory, Morey, Mory)
Edward 408, 415; John 183, 284; Joseph 227; Richard 36, 213; Robert 218; Thomas 184, 191; William 191
Mooten
John 96
Mordant
Thomas 3
Morden
Widow 25
Morecroft
James 254
Moreing (Mooreing, Mooreinge, Mooringe, Moring)
Andrew 436; Anthony 436; Edward 422, 493; George 436; John 465; Richard 29(2); Robert 434; Widow 408, 434, 465
Moreneing
Widow 146
Morgan
Francis 267; Godfrey 1; James 267; John 38, 168; Susan 27; Theophilus 354; Thomas 473(2); Widow 476, 504; William 181
Morlen (Morlin)
Gervase 38; John 420
Morles
John 93
Morlett
Thomas 45
Morley (Morely)
Giles 29; James 252, 256; John 1, 178, 252(2); Richard 252, 264(2), 379; Robert 252; Thomas 1, 191, 230, 269; Widow 250
Morlow
Widow 435
Morrant
Henry 252; Mark 252; John 475; Richard 474; Robert 265; Widow 231, 443; William 252(2)
Morrell (Morrill)
Benjamin 477; Edmund 450; John 38; Peter 522, 526; Richard 450; Widow 332, 342; William 163, 418, 425, 450; — 442
Morris (Maurice, Morrice)
Clement 94; Dorothy 38; Edward 177; John 96, 117, 219; Richard 24, 122, 183, 265, 317; Thomas 24, 372; William 429(2), 465
Morrison
Mister 29
Morrock (Morrack)
John 76; Widow 468
Morrow
Charles 206
Mortimer (Mortemore, Mortimore)
John 96, 164, 418, 507; William 363
Morton (Moreton, Morten)
Edmund 483; John 227, 435; Nicholas 194; Robert 24

Mosdell
John 338; Maurice 338; Thomas 338
Mosden
William 375
Mosell
Gregory 161; John 317
Moser
Henry 1
Mosey
Widow 119
Moss (Mosse)
Alexander 424; Edward 472; Henry 184; Richard 83; Thomas 1, 8; Widow 229
Moth
George 1; James 428; John 428; Richard 428; Robert 417; Widow 246; William 332, 428
Mott
Robert 1(2)
Mould
Richard 209
Moule
Thomas 100
Moulen
Henry 114
Moulton
Elizabeth 283; John 112, 283; Richard 503; Susan 283; Widow 94, 198; William 238, 290
Mounger
George 407
Mountague
Francis Lord Viscount 226
Mountayne (Mounteine)
Goody 434; John 504; Robert 436; Widow 436
Mourne
Daniel 76; Edward 418; James 418; John 72; Thomas 50
Mowdy (Mowday, Mowdey)
John 68, 76; Richard 292(2); Robert 473; Sarah 283; Thomas 117, 442, 482; Widow 494
Mowland
Andrew 107; Edward 159; Henry 159; Jasper 157; John 134, 159; Robert 109; Widow 130; William 115, 159
Mowle
Goody 256; Richard 249; Thomas 487; William 125
Mowrton
Thomas 32
Moxom
John 461
Moyle
Christopher 118; Widow 104, 118; William 128
Mudge
James 520; William 1
Mufford
John 391
Mulford
James 382; John 424; Richard 379(2); Thomas 1; William 191
Mullenox
Nicholas 104
Mullins (Mullings)
Henry 527; Simon 42; Thomas 1; Widow 42; William 42, 276
Mumford
John 276; Richard 208, 229
Mundey (Mondey, Mondy, Moundy, Munday, Mundy, Mundye)
Alexander 308; Andrew 75, 332; Anthony 490; Austin 458; Francis 352; George 208, 500; Henry 212; James 528; Jasper 331, 446; John 228, 229(2), 331, 332(2), 355, 429, 437, 441, 473, 493; Nathaniel 440; Paul 523a, 524; Richard 256, 292, 434, 436, 452, 499; Robert 452, 461(2), 493, 500; Thomas 331, 437, 439, 445, 504, 531; Tristram 462; Widow 75, 299, 500(2); William 26, 29, 227, 332(2), 437, 438, 446, 452, 455, 493, 504

Munges
Richard 494; Robert 494
Murrell
John 418; Robert 302; Thomas 76; Widow 390
Musgrave
John 38; Judith 1; Mister 252, 336; Simon 1; Widow 219
Muspratt
Thomas 229
Mutcher
Dorothy 160
Mywater
Nicholas 298
Naish
Robert 431; Widow 420
Namier
Widow 100
Napp (*see also* Knapp)
Edward 229(2)
Napper
George 434; John 385
Nash (Nashe)
Christopher 370; Edward 76; George 392; Henry 76, 87, 247, 294; Joan 355; John 126, 299, 361, 379; Nicholas 361; Richard 391; Robert 370, 492; Thomas 29(2), 173; Widow 361, 370; William 316, 323, 353, 356
Natts
Jerome 354
Naule
George 50
[Nawes]
Francis 1
Nayder
John 324
Nayle
Henry 141; Robert 456
Nayler (Naylor)
Henry 460(2); John 142; Thomas 148
Naynow
Thomas 208; William 208
Neale (Neales, Neele)
Ann 229; Christopher 513; Humphrey 68; James 299; John 169, 397, 438, 513; Nicholas 396(2); Peter 206, 334; Richard 293, 316, 388; Robert 1, 434, 521(2); Thomas 75, 418; Widow 206, 280, 317; William 334(2), 337, 339
Neate
Goodman 515
Neave (Neeve)
Benjamin 163; Elizabeth 178; James 216; John 420; Moses 163; Thomas 163, 339
Needle
Mister 521
Needler
Thomas 1
Neigh
John 40
Neller
John 163
Nellier
William 357
Nelson
John 504(2); Mister 6, 14
Nepper
John 13
Netherleft
John 202
Netter
Daniel 164(2)
Nevell (Nevill)
John 192(2); Richard 286(2); Robert 343; Thomas 317
Nevey
Mister 257
New (Newe)
Andrew 436(2); Edward 1; Elizabeth 128; Henry 96; James 498; John 159, 181; Maurice 463; Richard 1; Robert 436; Thomas 363; Widow 51, 54
Newbery
Edward 49; John 29; Mister 235;

Newbery—*cont'd*
Old 51; Thomas 1; Widow 282
Newbolt
Charles 164; Jerome 254; John 229; Mark 265; Widow 229; William 229
Newbone
Richard 1
Newby
Widow 244; William 471; — 244
Newell (Newall)
Daniel 380; George 106, 355; John 161, 164, 181, 183, 269, 355, 442; Richard 2, 248; Robert 238; Tristram 106; Widow 191, 371; William 208, 362
Newen (Newne)
Francis 118; Jane 135; John 89, 130; Thomas 135; Toby 128; Widow 87, 123, 156
Newham
George 416; Lionel 200
Newhooke
Edward 1; Thomas 270
Newland (Newlands)
Edward 192; Elizabeth 506; Henry 218, 227; John 223, 244, 284, 404, 485; Newton 38; Peter 244; Richard 514; Stephen 218, 463, 514; Thomas 72, 244
Newlin (Newling, Newlinge)
George 176; Henry 175(2); John 175, 176, 200, 237; Richard 176; Thomas 189, 190, 200, 247; William 202
Newlock
John 1
Newman (Numan)
Alexander 462; Andrew 355; Anthony 115(2); Edward 72, 139, 170, 172, 257; Francis 473; Henry 128, 195; James 334; John 49, 115, 128, 159, 177, 192, 194, 307, 364, 504, 507, 515(2); Joseph 506; Leonard 473; Lewe 160; Mary 1; Mister 42; Peter 339; Ralph 356; Richard 27, 77, 271; Robert 106, 115, 182; Thomas 46, 95, 115, 177, 229, 238, 250; Walter 89; Widow 1, 84, 177, 229, 236(2), 273, 283, 285, 290, 316, 324, 471, 530; William 15, 42, 83(2), 84, 97, 112, 177, 217, 240, 339(2), 504, 506, 507, 515, 519
Newport
George 157; John 100
Newsham
Widow 135
Newton
Richard 211; Robert 245; Thomas 290; William 447
Newtor
Thomas 148
Nexon
Widow 227
Ney
Ann 135
Nicholas
John 218, 342; Michael 487; Mister 266; Peter 1; William 518, 530
Nicholls (Nichols)
John 160; Thomas 343; Widow 229; William 346
Nichollson (Nicholson)
George 213; John 164, 172; Thomas 163; Nicholas 197
Nicklin
Henry 168; John 188
Nitinghall (Nightinghall) (*see also* Knightingall)
Humphrey 422; John 1; Nicholas 361; Ralph 429
Noble
Roger 471
Noell
Thomas 24
Norborne
Henry 528
Norden
Josias 133, 160

Norgrove
William 389
Normand (Norman, Normond)
Francis 383; John 407, 424; Thomas 362; Widow 7; William 40, 177
Normanton
William 163(2), 164
Norris (Norice, Noris, Norrice)
Anthony 119; Daniel 194; Edward 110, 453; Francis 223, 302; Henry 107; John 6, 111, 418; Nicholas 108, 125(2); Richard 434; Robert 107, 112(2); Thomas 38, 107, 118, 125; Widow 37, 76, 97, 332; William 125, 194, 448
North
Edward 68, 244; Francis 331; George 74; James 229; Jerome 229(2); John 100, 269, 324; Mister 25(2); Ralph 418; Richard 229; Robert 324; Thomas 120, 200, 217, 328, 397; Widow 418, 487, 493; William 68, 245, 397, 488
Northcott
George 1
Northfolk
Mister 378
Northgate
Giles 229
Northover
William 102
Norton
James 192; John 1, 208(Sir), 372(Sir); Mistress 181; Richard 2, 3, 248; Widow 89; William 1
Norwood
Peter 158
Nose
Richard 229
Nosse
Arthur 42; Goodman 223; Henry 46; Richard 271
Note
Mister 498
Nottam
Richard 17
Notten
John 119
Noyes (Noyse)
Ann 435; Daniel 475; Edward 455; George 434, 442; John 436, 445, 470; Michael 427; Mister 439; Mistress 438; Nicholas 470; Richard 255, 446, 447; Robert 370, 438, 445(2), 458, 495; Thomas 151(2), 365, 435, 475; Widow 437, 454, 460; William 445, 470, 482
Noysh
Robert 423
Nunn
John 60; Richard 49(2)
Nurse
John 481(2)
Nutcher
Robert 495; Thomas 273
Nuttby
Mister 423
Nutter
David 493; Thomas 493
Nuttgrave
Peter 256
Nuttier (Nuttyer)
John 229; Robert 16
Nuttingham
Widow 203
Nuttkin (Nuttkins)
James 332; John 441
Oades
Daniel 379; John 223, 378, 394; Mary 394; Nicholas 419; Richard 378; Roger 291(2); Thomas 229; Widow 376, 418; William 378
Oakey (Okee, Okey)
John 518; Samuel 205; Widow 530
Oasteler
Thomas 461

Oates (Oats)
Ambrose 115; John 324; Richard 324; Robert 115; Widow 115; William 115
Oaty
William 248
Oborne
Robert 448
Ockleford
Alexander 531; Hugh 527; John 529
Odber
Edward 156; Widow 113, 117
Odison
Laurence 163
Odums
Widow 6, 15
Ogborne
Peter 434
Ogle
Sir Thomas 311
Okeford (Ockford)
Nicholas 101; Widow 100
Okehurst
John 397; William 397
Okely
John 75, 193, 197, 249; Joseph 223; Richard 249; William 249
Okeshott
Benjamin 1; John 189; Philip 372
Oldfeild
John 354
Olding (Oldinge)
Abraham 148; John 266; Robert 148; Stephen 1; Vitall 493; William 94, 148
Oldman
Richard 333, 522, 526
Olis
Simon 136
Oliver
Ann 244; George 46, 368; Jerome 39; John 1, 80, 89, 106, 161, 193, 223, 230; Merrell 160; Nathaniel 200; Richard 80, 148; Thomas 193(2); Widow 38, 98, 161, 193
Omedee
William 490
Oneey
Henry 338
Ong
William 396
Oram
Alexander 229; Edward 112; Richard 108; Thomas 442; William 229, 436, 442
Orchard
Adam 476(2); Joseph 498; Thomas 276, 503; Widow 498; William 15
Orpington
Ralph 489; Widow 2
Orpwood
John 317; Mister 427; William 269
Orred
Joseph 348
Osborne (Osbone, Osbourne)
Charles 171; Edward 331; James 98; John 38, 54, 331, 424; Mister 424; Thomas 35, 38; Widow 227
Osey
Andrew 90; James 24, 87; Mister 87, 483; William 87
Osgood
Bartholomew 134; David 456; Edward 1; John 332; Peter 456; Richard 292, 332, 456; Robert 112; Stephen 446; Thomas 256; Walter 371(2); William 113, 460
Osier
William 14
Osland
Thomas 518
Oslinge
Francis 55(2)
Osmond (Osman, Osmand, Osmon)
James 339; John 55(2), 87, 317; Joseph 317; Peter 339; Richard 229; Robert 257, 316; Thomas 317; Widow 94, 95, 271; William 66, 70, 349

Othen (Oathen, Othon)
John 365; Robert 75, 391
Oughton (Owten) (*see also* Houghton)
Edward 80; Robert 283
Oven
John 242(2)
Over
Anthony 371; Henry 168; John 182; Robert 95, 148; William 343
Overton
Jerome 229; John 283, 436; Thomas 254
Overy
John 52; Thomas 1
Oviatt
William 520
Owder
Richard 530
Owen
Mister 208; Widow 208
Owting
Henry 104; Widow 103
Oxenbridge
Robert 347
Oxford
Thomas 38; William 58
Oyliffe (Oleife)
Anthony 52; John 38
Pace
James 208
Pack (Packe, Packs)
Edward 203; Henry 135; Martin 122; Moses 124; Nicholas 494; Richard 96; Stephen 122, 156 (2); Thomas 119; Widow 119; William 170
Padden
William 6
Padding
George 1
Paddock
John 79
Padner
John 102
Padwick (Padwicke)
Humphrey 46; Nicholas 216 (2); Robert 46; Roger 217; Widow 46, 216 (2); William 42, 45
Pafford (Paford)
John 3, 7; Thomas 64; Widow 65; William 64
Page (Paige)
Edmund 37; Elizabeth 124; George 36, 164, 194, 225; Henry 322; James 518, 530; John 37, 41, 56 (2), 185, 189, 191, 192, 193, 208, 244, 248, 324, 367, 523a, 524; Jonas 262, 484; Leonard 162; Michael 523a; Peter 372; Philip 144, 321; Ralph 279; Richard 216, 225, 241; Robert 51, 442; Sibyl 267; Thomas 189, 194, 208, 220; Widow 51, 367, 439, 484; William 38, 164, 212, 249, 267, 334, 434
Paine *see* Payne
Painter *see* Paynter
Palladay
William 1
Pallington
Robert 168
Pallter
Widow 332
Palmer
Alice 335; Ananias 256; Andrew 338; Ann 163; Anthony 486; Edward 37, 520, 528 (2); Geoffrey 252; George 106; Gilbert 440; James 38; John 40, 54, 134, 141, 193, 322, 335, 338, 434 (3), 456, 470 (2), 523a; Laurence 418; Mary 189; Mister 169, 208, 225; Nicholas 18, 334, 370; Richard 164, 332, 334, 338, 464, 466, 504, 515; Robert 118, 199, 208; Stephen 40; Thomas 51, 177, 199, 283, 310, 317, 504, 513, 515, 531; Widow 163, 256, 324, 333, 515; William 35, 40,

Palmer—*cont'd*
81, 102, 208, 256, 270, 299, 331, 434, 464, 466, 504, 521, 527 (2), 531
Palmeter
Elizabeth 130
Pamons
Laurence 38
Pamplin
Thomas 184
Panford
William 418
Pannell
Edward 38; Philip 80; William 40, 41, 80
Panter
Henry 483
Parcher
George 252
Pare
Thomas 193
Parford
Edward 76; Philip 76
Pargett
Joseph 198
Pargiter
Mister 190 (2)
Paringe
John 339
Parke (Parks)
Michael 152; Robert 396; Thomas 1,160, 404
Parker
Alexander 212; Andrew 249; Ann 197, 326, 355; Christopher 332; Elizabeth 326; Edmund 363; George 363; Goodman 531; James 142, 229, 518, 530; John 35, 68, 74, 94, 119, 208, 294, 318, 332; Nicholas 197 (3), 242; Peter 237, 338; Richard 40, 244, 250, 283, 330; Robert 1, 58, 208, 290 (2), 326, 332, 340, 358; Thomas 1, 38, 223, 283, 431; Widow 244, 298, 300, 342; William 1, 37, 159, 197, 212 (2), 247, 310, 339, 346
Parkhurst
James 418; Mister 362; Roger 163
Parkins
Alice 118; William 118
Parlott (Parlett)
Sarah 27; Stephen 27
Parlter
John 49
Parmon
Robert 456
Parnell
Edward 122; James 127; Philip 127; Richard 24; William 127 (2)
Parner
John 134
Parr
Alexander 362; Anthony 227; James 317; John 1, 130, 479, 487; Moses 27, 418; Oliver 268; Philip 430; Richard 269; Robert 1; Thomas 128, 259, 260, 382; Valentine 414; Widow 40, 260, 304, 411
Parrett
Richard 1; William 257
Parrick (Parrock)
Henry 416; John 413; Joseph 471; Richard 287, 456; Thomas 418; Widow 451
Parris
Henry 332
Parry (Parrey)
Christopher 320; Edward 315; George 395; John 354, 421; Rebecca 229; Richard 273; Thomas 128, 339; Valentine 320; Widow 339; William 321
Parsley
James 375
Parsonage
Thomas 24
Parsons
Christopher 152 (2), 153; James

36, 128, 129; Joan 128; John 127, 128, 135, 227, 513, 522, 526 (2); Peter 56; Richard 161, 221, 519; Stephen 11; Thomas 38, 77, 87, 119, 473; Widow 72, 128, 158; William 56 (2), 128
Parvin
William 219
Pascall
Richard 448; Robert 451; William 451
Pascue
John 112; Widow 107
Paskett
Edward 155; Widow 153, 154
Paskins
Thomas 33
Pasmore
William 530
Passenger
Henry 10
Passingham
William 197
Patience
John 487; William 427
Patinton
Andrew 466
Patrick (Patricke)
Edward 1, 208; John 358; Thomas 212, 363 (2); Widow 212; William 369
Pattee
Edward 490
Patten (Patterne)
John 37, 72
Pattfall
Thomas 404
Paulle
Widow 38
Pave
Thomas 519
Pawfoot
John 215
Pawlter
Ann 67
Pawson (Pawsons)
Richard 135; William 155
Pay (Paye, Pey)
Mistress 208 (2); Ralph 54; Richard 214; Stephen 84; Thomas 1, 39; William 81, 84
Payle
Robert 512
Payne (Paine, Paynes)
Alexander 439; Brian 370; Edward 363; Elizabeth 523b, Esquire 487; George 363, 434 (2); Gilbert 434; John 322, 493; Mary 439; Richard 150, 323; Robert 453; Roger 91; Thomas 158; William 239, 317, 363 (2), 434
Paynter (Painter)
George 338; Henry 141; Humphrey 435; Joan 497; John 89, 104, 447, 464; Robert 214, 435; Widow 141, 322
Payse (Paice, Paise, Payce)
Edward 429; Francis 418; Henry 370; James 353; John 189, 336, 361, 371, 383 (2), 384, 385, 490, 512; Nicholas 384, 504; Richard 424, 512; Robert 363; Thomas 362, 383, 397, 504; Widow 515; William 362 (2), 378
Peace (Pease, Peaze)
Richard 117, 282, 444, 512; Thomas 158 (2), 512
Peacey (Peacy)
Widow 435; William 436
Peach
Henry 27, 530; William 530
Peacher
William 385
Peachy
Gregory 38
Peacock (Pacock)
Mister 210, 227; Philip 203; William 407; — 200
Peade (Peades)
Andrew 333; John 333, 490

Peale
Henry 392; Peter 24, 90
Pearce (Peirce)
Christopher 330; Edward 339 (2); Elizabeth 56; George 106; James 229, 340; John 94, 256 (3), 340, 519, 530; Luke 437; Peter 229; Richard 97; Robert 120, 332; Thomas 324, 332, 434, 462, 518, 530; Widow 256 (2), 319, 322; William 151, 317, 324, 333, 462, 470, 531
Pearcy
James 434; William 352
Peare
Richard 256
Pearle
John 94 (2)
Pearman (Peareman, Pereman)
Edmund 353; James 353; Mary 5; Mistress 5; Richard 5, 353; Thomas 353; Widow 332
Peate
Mister 151; William 217
Peck (Pecke)
Christopher 1; Daniel 1; Edward 398; George 177; Mister 376; — 1
Peckett
Elizabeth 189; Richard 207; Widow 163; William 189
Peckham
Anthony 208; Robert 94; Thomas 94; William 100, 146
Pecotte
Thomas 473
Pedley
Henry 283; Mistress 521
Peeke (Peake)
Ellis 135; Henry 38, 121, 122, 155; James 155; Richard 437; Simon 155; Widow 51, 122 (2), 156, 530; William 119, 120, 128 (2), 135
Peinock
Henry 472
Pelley
Edward 517
Pelten
Henry 1
Penbrooke (Penbrook)
Lancelot 392; Margery 419
Penfold
Abraham 38; James 197; John 39; Thomas 49
Penford (Penforde)
Cuthbert 29; Elizabeth 51; John 35; Thomas 29; Widow 29 (2), 35, 51
Penfull
Samuel 96
Penke
John 117
Penn
Laurence 209
Pennington
Isaac 290
Penny (Penney)
Henry 115; Jerome 255; John 85, 121; Mary 139; Nicholas 128; Peter 91; Richard 89, 115; Thomas 132; Widow 103, 145; William 89, 115, 127, 132
Pennyatt
John 245
Penruddock
Sir John 107
Pentford
Thomas 38
Penton
Drew 94; Edward 93, 322, 348; George 267, 271, 340; Godson 229; John 338, 483, 505, 518; Peter 504; Richard 293, 388; Robert 434, 476; Thomas 256, 258, 437, 483, 508; Walter 160; Widow 286; William 332, 437
Penvell
Jerome 419
Penycott (Penicott, Penicoate, Pennycott)
Charles 291; Edward 242;

Hannibal 132; James 12; John 72
People
Elizabeth 93
Peperinge
Henry 29; John 29; Thomas 29; William 29
Peppersele
Ralph 29
Pepson
Thomas 84; William 83, 84
Percivall
James 115 (2); Philip 100; Samuel 100
Percy (Pirsey)
Henry 418; Nicholas 97; Philip 418; Stephen 47; Thomas 97
Perdock
Christopher 193
Perfect
Noah 294
Perkins (Pirkins)
Francis 93; John 104, 118, 283; Nicholas 38; Richard 1, 84; Thomas 83, 84 (2); Widow 94, 104, 120; William 157, 229
Perkinson
Richard 92
Permine (Permyn)
Widow 488; William 428
Perne
Widow 38; William 38
Perrier (Perriour, Perryer, Peryer)
Edward 208, 465 (2); John 94, 462, 472; William 208
Perrum
John 162
Perry
Alexander 110; Edward 378; John 164; Stephen 130; Walter 1; Widow 49, 378, 411; William 435
Perryn (Perrin, Perringe, Perryne, Peryn, Perynn)
Barnard 67; Henry 1, 248; John 1, 208; Nicholas 83; Robert 1, 17; Thomas 408; Widow 194, 459; William 8
Persons (Person)
Christopher 100; Edmund 49; Elizabeth 1; George 342; Joan 67; John 51, 67, 168; Nicholas 1; Pernasses 118; Robert 335; Thomas 67, 335; Widow 46
Perton
Edmund 322
Pescod (Pescodd)
Edmund 162; Henry 162; John 208, 209; Joseph 208; Mister 49; Richard 183; Robert 229; Widow 485; William 217
Peskins
Stephen 279
Pest
Thomas 515
Pestle
Thomas 229
Pether
Thomas 380
Petre
James 292
Petteford
George 3
Petter
John 398; William 376
Pettis
John 162
Pettman
Thomas 130
Pettoe (Petoe)
John 423, 433; William 189
Pettwyne
Bartholomew 120
Petty
Dorothy 227; Elizabeth 292; Henry 323; John 55, 252; Joseph 397; Mister 158; Richard 428; Thomas 158; Widow 362, 418, 425, 465
Pew (Pewe)
Francis 292; William 57

Pewsey
John 100, 387, 443, 473; Philip 473; Richard 473; Thomas 450; Widow 434, 443
Pewton
Jane 505
Phelipps
James 143; Lady 261
Phelps (Phelpes)
Ambrose 106; Anthony 112; James 104, 148; Thomas 205; Widow 113, 130
Phetiplace (Phettiplace)
Edward 100; James 100; Widow 108
Phey
William 163
Philipps (Philip, Philipp, Philippe, Philips, Phillips, Phillipps, Philpps Philps)
Bridger 183; Doctor 517, 529; Edward 240; Henry 272; Hugh 280, 397, 513; James 94, 96, 340, 398; Joan 499; John 162, 285, 427, 473; Michael 35; Mister 229; Nicholas 96; Philip 38; Richard 56, 512; Robert 1, 2, 162, 229 (2), 293, 398; Stephen 35; Susan 256, 493; Thomas 51, 190, 207(2), 281, 299, 372, 504; Ursula 449; Widow 96, 207, 229, 277, 294, 354, 376; William 231 (2), 418
Philpott (Phillpott, Philpot)
Christopher 334; Francis 333; George 346; Henry 85; John 97; Nicholas 349; Richard 97; Thomas 342, 349; Widow 111, 112, 349; William 346, 440
Phinn
Ralph 216
Phipps
John 162
Phripp
John 120
Pickering (Pickeringe)
Mister 357; Thomas 487; William 252
Pickernell
Edward 287, 419, 456; John 472; Richard 506
Pickerney
Edward 374
Pickett
Ann 246; Roger 38
Pickland
Richard 506
Pike
Edward 405; Robert 462; Simon 332; Thomas 462
Pildrim (Pildrin)
John 58; Michael 229; Richard 229 (2); Widow 42; William 257
Pile (Pyle)
Andrew 163; Captain 456; George 458; Humphrey 367; John 299, 456 (2), 495; Joseph 495; Mister 299; Nicholas 494 (2); Richard 434, 444, 504; Robert 456, 457; Thomas 456; Widow 332; William 472 (2)
Pilgrim
John 123; William 122
Pilkin
James 333
Piller
William 323
Pillian
John 89
Pincer
John 332
Pinchin
Christopher 51
Pincke (Pinck)
Christopher 205; David 2; Dorothy 415; Edmund 394; Francis 46; George 202; James 490; Jane 223; Joan 293; John 193, 227, 240, 293, 394, 418; Mister 421; Nicholas 220, 222,

Plinnell
Richard 97
Plipott
John 434
Plott
John 433
Plover
James 1
Plowden
Mister 367
Plower
Thomas 1
Plowman
Ambrose 156; Henry 448; James 86; John 527; Michael 155; Richard 85; Walter 531; Widow 440
Ployden
Lady 11
Plumbly
Nicholas 102
Plumer
Edward 289
Plumpton
Robert 442; William 442
Plympton
John 480; Widow 480; William 480 (2)
Poate
John 1, 219; Richard 217; Robert 223; Thomas 1, 212; William 216
Pocock
Henry 85; James 333; John 1, 96, 292; Mister 486; Philip 96, 200 (2); Thomas 246, 247, 298; W 531; Widow 218, 318; William 96, 112, 528
Podd
Nicholas 38
Poett
Thomas 177
Pointdexter
Thomas 523a
Pointlett
Charles 331
Pollard
George 168; Richard 466; Robert 1; Thomas 466; William 281
Pollentine
Thomas 7
Polling (Pollinge)
Richard 174; William 208
Pollington
Adam 316; Elizabeth 246; Thomas 13; William 135
Polson
Gilbert 395
Ponfrey
William 378
Ponte
Thomas 1
Pooke
Crews 165; John 136, 208, 220, 227, 367; Thomas 220
Poole
Ann 115; Barnaby 102; George 192, 229; James 100; John 489; Philip 102; Robert 198, 520, 529; Stephen 479; Thomas 246, 378; Widow 100, 123, 192, 436, 489; William 102, 267
Poore
Alexander 503; Alice 475; Arthur 159; Catherine 159; John 305, 440, 472; Richard 128, 347; Rigell 342; Robert 226, 442, 480 (2); Samson 72; Simon 193; Thomas 472, 479, 493; Widow 290, 480; William 331, 339, 349 442, 494, 497 (2)
Pope
Andrew 108; Arthur 465; George 465; Gilbert 115; Isaac 465; James 1, 100; John 1, 38, 85, 229; Mary 118; Nicholas 117; Peter 283; Ralph 504; Rebecca 38; Robert 292; Roger 465; Thomas 118; Walter 115; Widow 115, 409, 429; William 18, 96, 108

Popinay
John 434
Porbery
William 8
Porter
Alice 5; Christopher 203; Esardes 1; Ferdinand 178; John 164, 355, 362; Nicholas 169; Richard 184, 190; Robert 214; Stephen 251, 401; Thomas 168; Widow 190, 223; William 175, 203, 240, 405, 414
Portsmouth
Benjamin 479; Henry 384; John 331, 384 (2); Joseph 331; Margaret 384; Richard 376, 384; Thomas 384; Widow 418; William 298, 384, 420
Post (Poste)
Daniel 162; Thomas 513
Poticary
John 483
Potte
Richard 1
Potter
Edward 378; Hugh 402; John 283 (2), 337, 363, 378; Nicholas 99, 240; Richard 10, 336; Robert 72, 431; William 1, 52 (2), 125, 440
Potterne
John 23
Pottle
William 152
Poulter (Powlter)
Bartholomew 433; Henry 56; Isaac 396; Richard 376; Thomas 363, 433; Widow 397
Pounds (Pound)
Henry 6; John 3; Thomas 3
Powell
Edward 38; George 529 (2); John 37, 148 (2), 212, 239; Michael 148; Nicholas 99, 407; Thomas 1, 450 (2), 519, 530; Widow 89, 229, 277, 507
Powlett (Pawlett, Powlet)
Charles 440; Edward 506; Essex 292; Henry 448, 457 (2); Hercules 405; Lady 286; Mister 229; William 95
Powling
Edward 7
Pownell
Israel 1
Powsely
Thomas 51
Poyle
Nicholas 133
Poynter (Pointer, Poyntter)
George 338, 414; John 339, 388, 457; Mister 445, 446; Thomas 378, 457; William 72, 339
Pragnell (Prangnell)
George 462; Henry 159, 456; John 159, 462, 466, 470, 471, 473, 517; Widow 471, 506; William 81, 473
Pransell
Austin 144
Prater
Edward 472; William 256
Pratt
Ellen 42, 217; Francis 76; Henry 355; John 42, 79, 244; Mister 308; Nicholas 37, 245; Richard 2, 178; Robert 187; Thomas 44, 217; William 2, 44, 45, 191, 308
Preist
Matthew 363
Premlish (Primlish)
Mister 286; William 290
Prenton
John 38
Present
John 392
Presse
John 337
Pressey (Precy, Pressy)
Edward 159; Henry 1; John 523a(2); Robert 457, 459

Prestford
Robert 276
Preston
Henry 122; John 121; Joseph 121; Thomas 201, 207 (2), 407; Widow 207
Pretty
Widow 38
Price (Prise)
Ann 37; Athey 135; Christopher 35; Edmund 397; James 96; John 40, 57, 67, 135, 390; Peter 56, 57; Thomas 94, 135; Widow 135, 473; William 49
Prickler
William 220
Pricklowe
Thomas 437
Pricksmall (Prismall, Prixmell)
Andrew 317; Edward 338; John 144, 335, 398; Nicholas 343; Robert 141
Primer
Anthony 299; John 322; Paul 338; Richard 317; Widow 332
Primier
Margery 493; Robert 493
Prince
Ann 279; Edward 24; George 418, 522(2), 529; John 229, 434, 435 (2), 443; Michael 503; Mistress 526; Philip 100; Richard 317, 335; Thomas 431; Widow 322, 517; William 229, 422, 503
Princke
John 52; William 50
Priseman
Robert 188
Pritcherd (Prichard)
Widow 472; William 1
Pritchett
Edward 100; John 465
Privett
John 5; Mary 197; Peter 193; Richard 193; Thomas 196; William 195
Procter
William 292
Proper
Widow 38
Prover
Richard 115
Provitt
Richard 524
Provo (Provoe)
Nathaniel 522, 530; Peter 529
Prowling
John 2
Prowte
Ellis 120
Prowtinge (Prowting)
David 26; Elizabeth 15; Henry 21, 368; John 23, 271, 430; Richard 21 (2), 29, 50; Robert 271; Roland 191; Thomas 40, 69, 82; Widow 21, 219; William 33, 189, 397
Pryaulx
Mistress 520
Pryor (Prior, Pryer, Pryers, Pryors)
Barbara 77; Barnard 385; Edmund 46, 246; Edward 317; Guy 249; Henry 6, 249, 334; John 29, 191, 241, 249; Nicholas 1; Richard 75, 249, 385; Robert 298, 388; Roger 215; Thomas 29, 45, 191 (2), 248, 527; Widow 29, 248 (2), 397, 429; William 249 (2), 378, 529
Puckeridge (Puckeridg, Puckridg, Puckridge)
Andrew 505; Barnard 515; Edward 383; James 513; John 376, 418, 424, 508; Richard 513; Simon 163; Thomas 163, 376; Widow 362, 384, 397; William 163
Pucknell
Joan 252; John 252; Richard 252
Pudsey
John 292

Pullen (Pullin)
Richard 122, 124; Thomas 356; Widow 122; William 124
Puller
James 139
Pullinger
Arthur 213; Giles 27; John 246, 247; Robert 247
Pullington
James 246
Pummell
William 169
Puntice
Richard 123; Thomas 123; Widow 123
Purbeck
William 521, 529
Purcas
John 95 (2); Widow 117, 135
Purchase (Purchis)
Alexander 98; Peter 456; Simon 90
Purchill
John 331, 414; Richard 414; Robert 306
Purdue
Andrew 331, 504; Edward 515; George 434; James 457; John 44, 169, 181, 229, 299, 434, 456, 459, 475, 476; Matthew 473; Nicholas 229; Thomas 303; Widow 181, 260, 266, 515; William 162, 170, 252, 266
Purnell
Mister 1
Purse (Perce, Perse, Pirce)
Henry 390; James 104, 205; Richard 133, 353; Robert 418; Stephen 68; Thomas 198, 236, 407, 487; Widow 291, 294; William 20
Purser
Ambrose 252; Catherine 255; Peter 270; Ralph 252
Pusse
Peter 96
Puttland
John 1
Pyatt
Widow 531
Pyball (Piball, Piboll)
Ann 95; Hugh 95; Leonard 412; Thomas 494
Pydgeon
Thomas 1
Pye
John 29, 257; Thomas 49; Widow 51; William 92, 257, 397
Quallett
Ann 244; Henry 244; John 244(2); Richard 38, 168, 216, 227, 244; Widow 242; William 244
Quayte (Quaite)
Thomas 418; William 168
Quint
Michael 160
Quittance
John 517
Rabbetts (Rabett, Rabetts)
Andrew 408; John 162; Nicholas 418; Thomas 301, 417; Widow 118, 135
Rabnett (Rabinett, Rabnutt)
John 230, 418; Richard 193; Widow 206; William 206
Rachbond
John 435
Radford
William 480
Ragett
Thomas 158; Widow 398
Raines
Simon 285
Rainger (Raynger)
Edward 163; Henry 434; John 355; Matthew 229; Widow 494
Ralph (Ralfe)
George 256; Philip 256; Richard 290; Thomas 38; William 290 (2)
Rammer
John 1

Rampkin
Patrick 1
Rampton
Edward 318; John 318; Richard 353 (2); Thomas 353; Widow 216; William 353
Ramsdeane
Stephen 174
Randford
Edward 390; Matthew 1
Randoll (Randall, Randell)
Alexander 100, 115 (2); Anthony 120; Edward 120; Francis 211; Henry 55, 96; James 98; Jasper 384; John 98, 194, 215, 339, 418; Joseph 339; Nicholas 81; Peter 74; Richard 29, 372; Robert 219; Thomas 1, 97, 98 (2), 120, 149, 219, 324; Widow 159, 229; William 74, 149, 171, 219
Ranfeild (Ranffeild)
John 51; Thomas 1
Rann
William 131
Ransom (Ransome, Ramson)
Courteous 219; John 114; Widow 1
Ransteed
Henry 1; Richard 212 (2), 229
Rapier
George 34
Rapkin
James 306
Rapley (Raply)
John 147, 148
Rashbridg
William 86
Rashley
Nathaniel 309
Ratchell
William 75
Rathwell
Mister 473; Thomas 243; William 244
Rattcliffe (Ratclife, Ratcliff, Ratcliffe)
Ezekiel 208; Moses 196; Robert 530; Thomas 208; William 210
Ratte
Francis 269; Peter 515; Widow 269
Rattey
Edmund 346; Thomas 346
Rattue
Edward 437; George 506; John 437, 443; Mary 434; Sydrack 437; Thomas 437
Ravell
John 158
Rawlins (Rawlings)
Edward 162 (2); John 519, 530; Richard 455, 483; Stephen 254, 406; Thomas 241, 283; Widow 162 (2), 365, 451, 455; William 519
Rawton
William 378
Ray (Raye, Rey)
John 1, 42, 484, 506 (2); Margaret 44; Mistress 18; Thomas 397
Raynscroft
James 490
Readall
Widow 56
Reade (Read, Reads, Reed, Reede)
Charles 108; Edward 6, 112; Francis 299; Griffin 1; Henry 93 (2), 104, 335, 446; Hugh 455; John 45, 84, 94, 117, 189, 210, 234, 244, 404, 437; Joseph 317, 518, 530; Margaret 108, 150, 330; Mister 362; Nicholas 112 (2); Philip 46, 106; Richard 358, 404, 434; Robert 103, 109, 428, 447, 490; Stephen 335; Thomas 1, 294; Widow 100, 189 (2), 229, 299, 318, 446; William 61, 120, 229, 282, 354, 397, 404, 436, 486
Reading (Readinge)
Ann 353; Anthony 208; James 353; John 1, 209, 212, 353, 355;

Richard 72; Thomas 355; Timothy 212; Widow 202, 397; William 78, 210
Reamen
John 294
Reanes
Francis 318
Reddhead
Peter 112
Reddway
Thomas 221
Redford
John 455; Thomas 122; William 455
Redhouse
Nicholas 276
Redman
Barnard 1
Redney
George 96
Reeks (Reekes)
Elizabeth 128; Farmer 98; Henry 154; Joan 124; John 122; Joseph 531; Richard 113, 121, 152; Robert 121, 153, 154, 156; Stephen 155; Thomas 98; Widow 122, 153; William 98, 122, 156, 188
Reeves (Reeve, Reves)
Bridget 258; Cosine 93; Edward 86 (2), 473; Hugh 283; John 355, 435, 460, 473; Lionel 256; Ralph 416; Richard 192, 370; Robert 252, 260, 368; Thomas 29, 256, 260, 509; Valentine 256; Widow 256, 270; William 1, 29, 277, 400, 465, 494
Reggs
Thomas 383
Remington
Edward 429; John 385
Remnant
Stephen 418
Renger
William 95
Renn
Widow 252; William 128
Renney
William 299
Renouf
Widow 520
Renwood
Edward 213; Henry 486; Widow 213
Reresby
Sir Thamo 362
Restall
John 192, 227; Richard 192, 227; Widow 29
Restler
George 188
Revell
Andrew 83, 84
Rew
William 223
Rewell
Richard 339; Widow 252
Reyley
Robert 229
Reymand
Thomas 56 (2)
Reynolds
Aaron 513; Carew 168; Edward 488; Geoffrey 513; George 38; Henry 50, 208; John 39, 40, 41, 453; Matthew 89; Mister 470; Richard 189, 434; Robert 1 (2), 41, 263, 369 (Sir), 371, (2, Sir); Widow 290
Ribread
Widow 5
Rice
Peter 46; Rannell 428; Richard 515 (2); Robert 490; Stephen 513; Thomas 249; Widow 513
Rich
Nicholas 40
Richards
Ann 371; Brian 379; Christopher 378; Edward 517; Henry 1, 46, 76; Honor 191; Humphrey 135;

Richards—*cont'd*
John 58, 127, 201, 244, 334, 374; Lionel 512; Mary 290; Nicholas 216; Paul 1(2); Philip 79; Robert 376, 490; Stephen 355; Thomas 80, 100, 159, 204, 205, 219, 378, 513; Widow 192, 256, 290, 397; William 72, 208

Richardson (Richardsons)
Christopher 335; Edward 229; John 155, 229, 390; Thomas 434; Widow 38, 153, 354, 435

Richbell (Richbill)
Robert 33, 517, 529, 530

Richman (Rickman)
Andrew 107; Anthony 77; David 209; Grace 86; Henry 135, 505; James 133; John 107, 119, 208 (2); Joseph 74; Nicholas 103, 133; Richard 77, 100, 101, 142; Robert 100; Roger 505; Thomas 100, 117; Widow 301, 505; William 103, 107

Richmond
Francis 515; Venis 332; William 508

Rickers
John 339

Rickett (Ricketts)
Ann 126; James 38; John 152; Widow 149

Rider (Ryder)
Jacob 252; John 88, 90, 142, 270 (2); Philip 252; Richard 240, 280; Thomas 355; Widow 364; William 523a, 531

Ridge (Ridges)
Edward 1; John 8 (3); Mister 17; Nathaniel 8; William 378

Ridgers
— 183

Riggett
Edward 158; William 158

Riggs
John 142; Laurence 395 (3); Mister 54; Ogle 36; Widow 383

Right (Righte)
Edward 94; John 94; Richard 162, 513; William 170

Rigors
William 324

Rill
Richard 24

Rilley
Nicholas 246

Ringe (Ring)
Edward 277; John 44, 277; Richard 77, 527; Stephen 44; Thomas 44; Widow 77; William 44

Ringwood
Mister 108

Rippin
Widow 2

Risbrige
John 96

Risden
Widow 38

Rise
Widow 368

Risord
John 324

Rivers (River)
Ann 407; Bartholomew 356; John 359, 361, 434; Michael 248; Richard 181, 260; Robert 368; Thomas 181, 188, 399; Widow 181, 398, 405

Rives (Ryve, Ryves)
Andrew 38; Barnard 418; James 394; John 37, 208, 259, 334, 343, 394, 407, 412; Lionel 76; Robert 21, 473; Widow 25, 418; William 1, 60, 200, 286 (2)

Rivett
Francis 493; William 163

Roach
George 1; John 29, 517

Roades (Roade)
Bartholomew 127; John 189; Widow 89

Roake
Francis 227; Widow 227
Roaker (Roker)
John 194; Widow 1, 54
Roates
Ford 148
Robbins (Robins)
Henry 91; John 38 (2); Philip 418; Thomas 38; Widow 98
Roberts (Robertts)
John 270, 301, 317 (2); Mistress 208; Nathaniel 290; Richard 1, 497; Robert 208; Thomas 1, 370
Robertson
James 292; John 326, 507
Robinson
Edward 194; George 404; Henry 371; Hugh 189; John 194; Laurence 163; Mister 527; Nathaniel 521; Ralph 24; Walter 434; Widow 194, 404; William 402, 421, 437
Robson
John 334 (2)
Rockwell
John 1
Roe (Rowe)
Daniel 266; Edward 471; Goodman 162; Henry 106; John 1, 188, 461; Richard 89, 183, 266, 464, 466; Robert 42, 501; Roger 266; William 19, 159, 461
Rogers (Roger)
Ann 128; Catherine 208; Edward 97; Francis 461; George 1; Harud 406 (2); Henry 103 (2), 112, 135, 396 (2), 449; John 113 (Sir), 256, 395, 406, 479; Peter 103, 104; Richard 83, 124, 128, 213, 335, 396; Robert 113 (Sir); Stephen 410; Susan 236; Thomas 98, 256, 465; Widow 84, 124, 256, 272, 434, 485, 509; William 94, 95 (2), 124, 148, 309, 315
Rolfe (Rolphe)
Edward 393; Elias 141; Elizabeth 162; Francis 284; George 152; Guy 208; Henry 227; James 132; John 227, 478; Martin 135; Richard 86, 162; Robert 2, 141; Ruth 162 (2); Stephen 513; Thomas 148, 431, 530; Widow 121, 142, 478, 509; William 5, 37, 54, 351, 372, 478 (2)
Roman
John 1; Ralph 5; Thomas 84
Romboll (*see also* Rumbold)
Francis 487 (2); William 303
Romey
Thomas 531
Roode (Roodes)
Alexander 22; Robert 76; Thomas 14; William 37
Rooder
Richard 30
Rooke (Rook, Rookes)
Ann 159; Edward 117, 208; Ew 208; Henry 97, 112, 159; John 104, 117, 124, 198, 247; Joyce 159; Ogden 97, 112; Richard 198, 208; Robert 92; Thomas 1, 159, 247, 332; Widow 13, 208; William 97, 98, 112, 115, 208, 223
Rookeford
Henry 285
Rookely (Rookley)
Edith 124; John 135; Simon 158; Thomas 135; Widow 162
Rooker
Widow 208
Rosbludd
Joan 480
Rose
Elizabeth 113; John 208, 316; Richard 1, 462 (2); Thomas 462; Widow 160, 512
Rossiter (Rositer)
James 91; Joan 89; Michael 89; Philip 89; Widow 148
Rosswell
Elizabeth 439

Roude (Rowde)
Edward 465; Richard 465; Widow 465; William 493
Roudway
Richard 44
Rowden
Henry 133, 473; John 41; Widow 473
Rowell
Daniel 368
Rowland
Edmund 160; Edward 81, 89; John 193, 517; Nicholas 38; Robert 395; Widow 317; William 529
Rowle (Rowles)
Francis 468; James 119
Rowse (Rouse)
Griffin 482; Richard 177; Thomas 526; William 67, 83
Rowte (Route, Rowt, Rowtt)
Annis 300; Francis 5; John 5 (2), 517 (2), 528; Mister 290, 523a; Peter 292; Robert 177, 208; Thomas 37, 208; Walter 520, 528; Widow 165; William 54
Rowter
Thomas 1
Roy
Henry 56; John 76; Mister 363; Nicholas 76 (2); Petronella 56; Widow 51; William 76 (2)
Royall
Peter 162; William 94
Ruben
William 205
Rudd
Henry 27
Rudley (Ruddley)
Baskfeild 435; Thomas 229
Rudsby
Philip 229
Rudyard
Benjamin 354
Ruffen (Ruffin)
John 208; Richard 1
Ruffold
Widow 244
Ruggatt
Christopher 363; John 369
Rule
Richard 57; Thomas 51
Ruman
Ralph 1
Rumbold (Rumboll, Rumbolt) (*see also* Romboll)
Anthony 326; George 450 (2); Henry 472; John 324, 332, 338; Matthew 346; Nicholas 333; Robert 326 (2), 340; Thomas 330, 335, 501; William 331, 450, 453
Rumey
Mary 299; William 332
Rumpton
Edward 298
Rumsey
John 342; Stephen 1; Thomas 110, 450; Widow 342; William 229
Rungar (Runeger)
Arthur 379; William 418
Russell
Alice 293; Ann 244; Arthur 422; Edmund 146; Edward 76; Elizabeth 89; Francis 227 (2); George 499; Jacob 192; Joan 160; John 57, 390, 417, 493; Joseph 394; Michael 493; Mister 331, 446; Nicholas 1, 76; Oliver 227; Peter 35; Philip 422; Richard 144, 379, 417; Robert 346; Samuel 252; Thomas 3, 178, 333, 434; Widow 76, 79, 148, 263, 383, 420, 443, 480, 483, 518; William 252, 483, 503
Russen
Ann 266; Austin 462; Mistress 530; Richard 507; Widow 271; William 340
Rutter
Adieno 505; Christopher 236; George 407; John 25; Nicholas

343; Richard 30; Widow 137, 481; William 245
Ruttley
Michael 436
Rybeard
Thomas 32
Ryman
Thomas 447
Rymes (Rimes)
John 332; Peter 290; Richard 258, 312; Thomas 289; Widow 369, 414; William 418 (2)
Sabine (Sabin)
Henry 56; Robert 1; Widow 397; William 51
Sadler
Joan 437; Richard 510
Saige
Samson 335
Saings
John 483(2); Richard 483
Saint
William 1
St Barbe (St Barb)
George 517; John 521; Mister 526, 529
St John
Oliver 493, 495
Saintlow
John 38
Salisbery
Hugh 1(2)
Salmies
Widow 447
Salmon
John 437; Peter 435; Richard 342; William 437
Salt (Salte)
John 141, 506; Richard 470; Widow 256, 514; William 128
Salter
Francis 249; Mary 208; Thomas 92; Widow 40, 286; William 447
Samber
Edward 85; Thomas 160(2); William 130
Samborne
James 434
Sambrough
Widow 122
Samms
Widow 521
Sampson
Edward 27; Richard 85
Sanckey
Widow 470
Sandall (Sandale, Sandell)
John 168, 308; William 182
Sandford
Giles 108; Peter 244; Thomas 56(2); William 97
Sandham (Sandam)
John 490; Philip 298
Sands
Widow 94
Sandwich
Richard 361
Sandys (Sandy)
John 157; Widow 332; William Lord 295, 472
Sangar
John 100
Sanley
Mister 138
Sansbery
Jonathan 507
Sapp
John 39
Saunders
Anthony 125, 135; George 504; Henry 125; James 101; John 97, 112, 118(2), 119, 123, 434, 465; Joseph 457; Luke 118; Martin 86; Mister 428; Nicholas 1, 338; Richard 118, 457, 504; Robert 513(2); Thomas 7, 79, 118, 317, 513; Walter 280; Widow 118, 513; William 98
Saunderson
Mister 445
Savage (Savadge)
Edward 397; George 473(2);

Savage (Savadge)—*cont'd*
John 473; Jona 38; Richard 25; Robert 316, 440
Savery
— 290
Savin
Richard 290
Savis
John 348
Sawcer
Thomas 490
Sawer
Robert 116
Sawyer
James 334
Saxey
Henry 58; Widow 59
Say
Francis 518, 530; Giles 530
Sayer
John 334; Nicholas 337
Sayte
Christopher 265; Thomas 37; Widow 265
Saywell
Widow 380
Scamell (Scamull)
John 1; William 108
Scapland
Philip 100
Scarbrough
Christopher 357
Scardefeild
William 40
Scarlett
Nathaniel 1; Widow 493
Scarvill
Widow 56
Scodsden
John 434
Scotcher
Nicholas 97
Scott
Catherine 246; Daniel 355, 371, 423; Edward 121; George 131, 132; Henry 1, 72; James 118, 490; John 102, 132, 133(2), 136; Joseph 118; Mary 115; Michael 1; Richard 135, 418; Widow 136, 161, 379, 420; William 32, 97, 126
Scottshall
John 483
Scovell
John 97; Thomas 507; William 507
Scragle
Edward 507(2)
Scragnell
George 29
Scrimpton
Michael 340
Scriven (Screven, Screvin)
Anthony 248; James 287, 416; Nicholas 176, 192; Peter 219; Thomas 425; William 7, 394
Scrutton
John 229
Scullard
Brock 513; Edward 437; Widow 436; William 434(3); Zacharias 436(2)
Sculler
Edward 528
Scutt (Scutts)
Richard 205; — 112
Seager
George 236; Henry 112; John 63; Roger 68; Widow 236, 431
Seagrove (Seagrave, Seygrave)
Barnard 418; John 434; Richard 418, 436
Seale
John 340, 531; Richard 29; Widow 531; William 340
Seaman
Robert 347
Searle (Searlle, Searles)
Ann 229, 355; Edward 23, 380, 522, 526; Ellen 355; Francis 358; George 356; Henry 355; James 418; John 40, 164, 212, 354, 357, 371, 380, 405; Lambert 404;

Lambourne 423; Matthew 72; Nicholas 354, 371; Randal 212; Richard 164(2), 212(3), 377, 483; Stephen 229; Thomas 246, 356, 397; Widow 40, 282, 430; William 45, 212, 354
Seaser (*see also* Cesar)
John 363
Seazon
Robert 1
Seddall
Humphrey 1
Sedwick
Widow 208
See
Richard 355
Seeds (Seedes)
Michael 290; William 233
Seely (Seelye)
John 348; Richard 357
Seire
Thomas 84
Seladen
Anthony 1
Selfe
Batten 98; George 438, 445; John 330; Peter 331
Sellan (Seland)
Nicholas 1; Robert 325; Widow 369
Seller
William 396
Selling
Elizabeth 77
Sellwood
Richard 460(2)
Selward
Henry 5
Senex
Widow 456
Senior
John 524
Sentilo
Joan 99
Sentwell
Robert 177
Serjeant
Richard 366
Serrell
John 99
Sershall
Richard 292
Serwood
Matthew 336
Sessions
Mister 266
Sessoe
Henry 229
Seston
Mister 354
Setter
Edward 332
Severton
George 24
Seward (Sewarde)
Richard 195, 218, 290, 292; Thomas 195; William 227, 463
Sewell (*see also* Cewell)
John 87; Robert 388
Sewett *see* Suett
Sex
Henry 377; John 112, 397, 431; Philip 112; Richard 112; Widow 424
Sexton
Henry 316; Nicholas 202; Robert 316; Thomas 307, 314, 317, 350; Widow 298, 316
Seymore (Seimor, Seimore, Semor)
Henry 86; Richard 152; Thomas 38, 332; Widow 86, 175; William 152
Seynall
Thomas 357
Seyward (Seywood)
Mister 445; Robert 434; Widow 440(2)
Shackleford
Charles 197; Richard 3, 192; John 192, 363; Thomas 419

Shaffling (Shaflin)
Robert 461; Widow 483
Shaffte
John 246
Shakeblade
John 245
Shalle (Shale)
John 112, 192; Widow 60
Shallett
Edward 245; William 211
Shambler
John 121
Shanke
Widow 448
Shannbler
Mary 51
Sharfe
Widow 530
Sharke
John 1
Sharlock
Henry 472; Richard 472
Sharpe (Sharp, Sharpp)
Andrew 512; Edmund 264; Francis 209; Henry 280; Humphrey 442; John 122, 424, 425; Richard 58, 474; Thomas 19, 82, 122; Widow 21, 362; William 164, 443, 465, 515
Shath
Widow 480
Shaulle
Widow 58
Shaw (Shawe)
Edward 96; Robert 514; Thomas 487; Toby 218; Widow 40
Sheare
Widow 229
Shearethorne
Widow 349
Shellwood
John 331; Richard 324
Shelly
Elizeas 184
Shepdam
Thomas 38
Shepherd (Shephard, Shepheard, Sheppard)
Edward 95; George 115, 160; Henry 14; John 27, 106, 161, 252; Margaret 267; Nicholas 456; Patience 92; Richard 87, 464; Robert 87; Thomas 256, 499; Widow 161, 229, 232, 260, 266, 291, 499; William 161, 252, 499(3)
Shereman (Sheerman)
Edward 330; John 330, 394; Matthew 330; Thomas 394
Sherfeild
Mister 459; Richard 244
Sherly
Mister 451
Sherrick
Robert 291
Sherryer (Sharrier, Sherrier, Sherrior)
Daniel 44; Edward 78; Gregory 212; John 72, 139, 244; Philip 214; Robert 193; Thomas 195; Widow 17; William 21
Sherton
Widow 332
Sherwood (Sherrwood)
Edward 318; Widow 290
Shesey
William 331
Shewell
Robert 335
Shidley
Susannah 106
Shilly
Widow 96
Shinell
Widow 134
Shingle
Thomas 294; Widow 348
Shipman
John 388
Shipton
Maurice 434, 436

Shoale
Philip 148
Shone
Robert 256
Shonke
John 357; Nicholas 384; Widow 263, 397
Shore
William 179
Shorier
William 246, 454
Shorling
Widow 484
Short (Shorte)
John 470; Nicholas 115; Paul 436; Richard 100; Thomas 2; William 2
Shory
William 1
Shottbolt
Mister 300
Shotter
Henry 247; William 226
Shoulders
Philip 212
Shoule
John 323
Showell
John 1
Showler
Richard 372; Thomas 240
Shrimps
Thomas 361
Shrimpton
Francis 354; Widow 370
Shrubb
Anthony 194; Edmund 194; John 361; Richard 194; Stephen 206; William 194
Shutt
Richard 530
Shywell
John 334
Sibbers
James 333
Sibbott
Martin 125
Sibley
Catherine 120; James 120; John 104; Martin 120; Roger 156; Stephen 527; Widow 100, 112, 120(2)
Sidford
Anthony 530; Widow 507
Sidmore
— 508
Siferwest
Michael 135
Sifte
John 237
Silence
John 436
Silley
Thomas 1
Silrey
Widow 333
Silver
Arthur 501; Henry 144; James 476; John 292(2), 293, 351, 420, 478(2); Nicholas 263, 412; Robert 145; Thomas 138, 412, 474; William 390, 488, 490
Silvester
Ann 222; Edward 222; Francis 177; Henry 251; Hugh 223; James 391, 392; Jesse 224; John 223, 224, 348, 407; Joseph 242; Michael 205; Richard 224; Robert 402; Roger 223; Stephen 434; Thomas 201, 208, 342, 414; Widow 208, 229, 305, 352; William 222, 225
Simons *see* Symons
Simpson (Sempson, Sympson, Symson)
Anthony 490; Barnard 298; James 51; John 192, 388; Margaret 417; Richard 490; Thomas 148, 316, 322
Sims *see* Symes

Singleton
Nicholas 20; Thomas 236
Sish
Henry 92
Sivell
John 418
Sivyer (Seevier, Siveor)
John 108; Richard 434; William 6
Skeate (Sceate, Skeat)
Alice 453; Henry 453, 455; John 450, 453, 477, 479; Magdalen 453; Nicholas 450, 487; Richard 339, 474, 475, 483; Thomas 478, 480(2); Tristram 290, 453; Widow 25, 477, 483; William 451, 478(2)
Skeele
Ellen 414; John 229, 284; Thomas 284; Widow 229
Skeene (Skeane)
Henry 492; John 448; Robert 457
Skilton
Goodwife 198; John 465; Nicholas 205; Richard 190, 205; Walter 504; Widow 462; William 205
Skinner (Skynner)
Abraham 292; George 66; John 249, 292; Nicholas 29; Robert 29, 140, 188, 249, 524; Thomas 29, 164; Widow 43, 176; William 55
Skipper
Roger 24
Skirvill
John 229
Slade
Anthony 49; John 101; Nicholas 135; Robert 246
Slader
Richard 100
Slanden
Widow 466
Slann
William 157(2)
Slaskett
Widow 94
Slatford
Thomas 292; William 134(2)
Slatterforde
Thomas 1
Slaw
Walter 298
Slawter (Slaughter)
Widow 177; William 52(2)
Sleate
John 152; Mary 153; Richard 152; Robert 120
Slefeild
Henry 208
Sley (Slye)
Henry 253; John 335; Jonathan 164; Richard 164
Sleydon
Arthur 466
Slide
Widow 164
Slidle (Slidles, Slydle)
Hugh 100, 150; John 104; Widow 86, 103, 120
Slinger
John 245
Slithurst
Vincent 396
Slonn
Thomas 37
Sloper
Widow 324
Slothfull
James 316
Slowe
William 324
Slugnells
Widow 299
Small
Andrew 158; Edward 192; George 301; John 200, 321; Philip 311; Robert 38; Thomas 427; Widow 371, 434; William 301, 322

Smallpese
Richard 395
Smart (Smarrt, Smartt)
Adam 332; Henry 24; John 332, 504(2); Richard 61, 427; Thomas 38, 404; Widow 504; William 333
Smerehead
Edward 324
Smith (Smeathe)
Ann 67, 220, 244, 353; Anthony 1, 46, 81; Arthur 1; Barnard 290, 390; Bartholomew 45; Benjamin 189, 229, 343, 357; Brian 395; Catherine 124; Christopher 192, 335, 518, 529; Clement 25; Desire 164; Edmund 513; Edward 1, 6, 11, 276, 308, 332(2), 440; Francis 49, 81, 229, 279, 506; George 236, 240, 324, 434; Giles 119; Henry 30, 179, 196, 211, 240, 278, 344, 357, 370, 418, 420; Hugh 312, 317; James 388; Jasper 193, 195, 450; Joan 515; John 25, 27, 35, 39, 40, 42, 67, 81, 89, 128(2), 129, 138, 144, 145, 161, 171, 177, 193, 195, 197, 198, 240, 244, 258, 269, 307, 317(4), 318, 321, 330, 332, 339, 370, 414, 436, 441, 444, 448, 456, 473(2), 498, 523a; Joseph 67; Julian 356; Mary 338; Michael 310; Mister 168, 240, 266, 290, 451, 457, 529; Mistress 388; Nicholas 75, 317, 410, 495; Peter 303; Philip 31, 332; Ralph 287; Rebecca 115; Richard 12, 23, 56, 89, 162, 163(2), 176, 183, 189, 244, 319, 340, 377, 395, 397, 406, 409, 417, 418, 434(2), 442, 498; Robert 1, 8, 23, 67, 76, 88, 163, 252, 308, 320, 324, 341, 434, 493, 494; Roger 219, 420; Samuel 1(2), 326; Sarah 37; Simon 285; Solomon 223; Stephen 67, 99, 162, 490; Thomas 1, 2, 33, 37, 41(2), 58, 62, 80, 81, 91, 93, 108, 126, 162(2), 168, 192, 240(2), 248, 255, 283, 287(2), 291, 303, 304, 305, 317(3), 332, 336, 338(2), 395, 405, 436, 441, 487, 495, 497; Timothy 192; Vincent 428; Warner 361; Widow 7, 40, 81, 89, 92, 120, 135, 181, 217, 229, 236, 240, 252, 286, 291, 292, 299, 317, 324, 332, 363(2), 397, 418, 422, 434, 472, 481, 483, 487, 498, 503(2), 507, 515(2); William 10, 23, 38, 42, 49, 56, 83, 89, 163, 178, 192, 213(3), 214, 229, 235, 237, 244, 269, 272, 285, 313, 317(2), 333(2), 343, 363, 383, 408, 418(2), 431(2), 446, 476, 484, 494, 513, 517, 529(2)
Smither
Barnard 39; Isaac 194; John 51; Thomas 6; William 194, 405(2)
Smuggs
Widow 349
Sneade
Widow 351
Snelling (Snellen)
Henry 104; John 118, 420; Nicholas 171
Snellor (Sniller)
John 488; Widow 1
Snooks (Snooke)
Laurence 256; Nicholas 482
Snossell
Widow 483
Snow (Snowe)
John 252; Nicholas 476; Richard 493; Robert 395; Thomas 494; Widow 216, 461, 483
Snuggs (Snugg)
Edmund 227; John 78; Thomas 142; Widow 414; William 418
Soafe
Robert 94; Thomas 94
Soare
Ellen 396

Softly
John 38; Richard 39(2); William 40
Solmes
George 397; Mister 397
Solsby
Richard 298
Somerset(t) *see* Sumersett
Sommers *see* Summers
Somredge
Henry 371
Sone (Soane, Soone, Sowne)
Andrew 405; Bartholomew 80; Christopher 357; Edward 237; Geoffrey 38; John 39, 46, 77, 287; Peter 38, 56; Robert 25, 357; Thomas 80, 83, 208, 237; William 182
Soper
John 302; Mister 295; Peter 388; Philip 388; Richard 307; Robert 416; William 344, 387, 388(2)
Sopp
Robert 226; Widow 473
South (Southt)
Ambrose 318; John 311; Mister 357, 481; Peter 518; Richard 355; Robert 428, 490; Thomas 298; Widow 418, 423, 431; William 1, 363
Southampton
Thomas Earl of 414
Southen
Thomas 298
Southwell
Roger 461; Thomas 461
Southwoods
Mister 481
Sowter (Souter)
Christopher 226; John 1; William 226
Spadwell
Widow 445
Spanell
Sidrach 437
Sparfeild
Edward 54
Sparkfeild
Thomas 338; Widow 338
Sparkman
Andrew 283; George 283; James 40(2), 229(2); Leonard 434; Stephen 35, 283, 323; Widow 323; William 315
Sparks
Francis 164; George 392; John 4, 18, 217, 392; Nathaniel 83; Richard 1, 18, 166, 531; Robert 5; Thomas 164
Sparrow
Robert 206
Sparsment
Richard 163
Sparvell (Sparvill, Sparwell)
Edward 47, 50; — 354
Speed (Speede)
Doctor 528; George 529; Richard 517, 529; Thomas 29; — 25
Speere
Richard 255
Speering (Speereing, Speeringe)
Christopher 229; Henry 1; John 416, 436, 517; Mister 529; Richard 229(2); Thomas 11, 13(3), 17; Widow 229, 416, 435
Spegg (Spegge)
Henry 273; John 279; Richard 283
Spelke
Widow 128
Spelt
William 124, 130
Spencer
Elizabeth 151; Francis 263; Henry 123, 135, 252, 317, 324; Joan 223, 336; John 38, 45, 135, 249, 305, 458, 460, 487, 530; Margaret 304; Nicholas 29; Richard 53, 362; Robert 75, 487; Samuel 287; Thomas 5, 17(2), 53, 148, 269, 291, 397(2); Widow

252, 304, 317, 318, 322, 460, 487; William 268, 362, 418(2)
Spershott (Sparshott, Spersholt)
Alexander 56; John 17, 23, 56; Richard 30, 276; Robert 56, 69; Thomas 283; Widow 71, 208, 276, 282; William 276(2)
Spett
William 91
Spicer
Edward 185; Elias 141; Giles 317
Spickernell
Richard 112
Spire (Spyre)
John 418(2); Richard 353, 362, 424; Robert 418; Thomas 428; Widow 418; William 418
Spittle
Nathaniel 434; Richard 418
Spittsberg
Edward 214
Sponder
John 471; William 497
Spooner
Thomas 38
Spr[ ]
Widow 1
Sprackborne
John 317
Spragg (Spragge)
Edward 461, 462; James 461; Widow 135, 515
Sprangler
Widow 94
Spranklen
John 135
Spratt
Adam 503; Arthur 113; Henry 104; Humphrey 134; John 440; Luke 448; Thomas 503; Widow 104, 443, 503
Spreadborough (Spradborowe, Spredbrowe)
Goody 434; Henry 453; John 400; Thomas 403
Spriggs
Henry 81; James 81; Simon 81; William 81(2)
Sprince
Richard 209
Spring (Springe)
Edward 192; Widow 139, 480; William 434
Spurrier
Ann 178; John 164; Widow 187
Squibb
George 513; Henry 505
Squire
James 339; Nicholas 339
Stace
William 265
Stacy (Stacie, Stacye)
Edward 160; Henry 380; John 178, 229, 317, 489; Robert 363, 367; Roger 346; Thomas 357; Walter 385; Widow 192, 317, 339; William 177, 317(2), 442
Stafferton
Mister 378; Thomas 363
Stagg
John 422; William 151
Staignell
John 32
Staingmore (Staingemore)
John 508; Robert 213
Stainsmore
Edward 112; Stephen 68
Stakes
William 38
Stallard
Edward 100
Stalter
Widow 218
Stanbrooke (Standbrooke)
John 296; Richard 413
Standard
Elizabeth 123; Jesse 135
Standbridg (Standbridge)
John 418(2); Richard 322
Standen
Thomas 192

Standford (Stanford)
Ambrose 1; John 434; Robert 208; Thomas 214(2); William 208
Stane
Ralph 14
Stanley (Stanly)
George 520; John 163; Nicholas 229; Widow 161, 394; William 88, 517(2), 529, 530
Stansby (Stansbery)
Jonathan 508; Richard 229, 408
Stanter
Thomas 93
Stanton
George 357; Henry 51; John 339
Staples (Staple, Staplle)
Christopher 418; Margaret 335; Nicholas 520; Thomas 160; Widow 527
Stares (Stare, Starres, Stayres, Steares)
Edmund 384; Edward 317; George 384; James 63; John 9, 401; Nicholas 50; Peter 317; Richard 361; Robert 1, 71, 384; Widow 37, 361, 384; William 35, 59, 60; — 1
Starke (Starks)
John 96, 103, 115; Thomas 271
Starkey
Francis 206
Start
Robert 1; Roger 1; William 357
Starvill
Richard 1
Stead
Thomas 163
Stedman (Steedman)
Joshua 1; Richard 38
Steele
George 503(2); Henry 193, 245; John 2, 217, 285(2); Robert 229, 316; Thomas 47, 87, 218, 503; Walter 19; William 222, 299, 473(2); Zacharias 87
Steggen
Peter 1
Stemp
Henry 92
Stent
Andrew 405; George 213; John 97, 188, 388, 468; Joseph 168; Nicholas 187; Richard 39, 42, 106, 163, 170; Thomas 173, 384; Widow 54, 102, 168, 179, 405, 468; William 134
Stepney
John 38
Stepto (Steptoe, Steptow)
John 521, 527, 530; Nicholas 334; Simon 333; Thomas 1, 345; Widow 333
Stevens (Stephens)
Ann 130; Catherine 102; Edmund 121; Elizabeth 128; Francis 49; Henry 92; Jacob 1; John 130, 163, 310, 445, 506; Joseph 163; Laurence 163(2), 418; Matthew 112; Mister 445, 515, 527; Mistress 1; Richard 92, 212, 292; Robert 5; Silvester 337; Susan 130, 134, 153; Thomas 1, 89, 104, 128, 135(2), 236, 253; Widow 97, 102, 128, 130, 195, 260, 383; William 23, 130, 229, 252, 290, 292
Steventon
John 1 (Sir); Mistress 1; William 1
Steward
Sir Nicholas 173, 190
Stewkely (Stewkly)
Hugh 241 (baronet); John 78
Sticker
Giles 208
Stickings
John 299
Stiff (Stiffe)
John 384; Richard 298, 336; Thomas 429; William 316, 317(2)

Streape (Streep)
John 192, 231, 499
Streater
Widow 171
Street (Streate, Streete, Streets)
Francis 117; George 369, 493; Isaac 474; John 100, 115, 484; Matthew 40; Mister 40; Nicholas 100; Peter 112; Richard 104; Robert 75, 208; Thomas 100(2), 192, 406; Widow 127
Stride
Christopher 94; Edward 96; John 94, 311; Joseph 94; Nicholas 113; Roger 512; Thomas 148, 158, 512; Widow 94, 113(2), 258; William 94, 95, 148, 317
Stringer
John 317
Stripe
John 214; Richard 504
Stroake
Nicholas 154
Strode (Stroade)
Edward 142; George 136; Richard 90
Strong (Stronge)
John 291, 335, 511; Nicholas 24, 237; Richard 24, 148, 283, 434(2); Thomas 290; Widow 98, 456, 481, 504; William 229, 263
Stropp
Richard 89
Strowde (Stroude)
Henry 431; John 257, 355, 419; Thomas 324; Widow 248, 303; William 308, 416
Strowder
Widow 219
Struddick
Stephen 203; Thomas 205
Strugnell
Andrew 21, 27, 162; Edward 23; John 246; Philip 30; Thomas 35; Widow 21, 42
Stubber
Widow 1
Stubbington (Stubington)
David 26; Henry 240; John 20, 26, 28, 42; Nicholas 19; Richard 240; Thomas 290; Widow 29, 240; William 237
Stubbs (Stubb)
Joan 493; John 269, 493; Richard 335; William 259
Stucke
George 1
Studd
Philip 240
Stude
John 256
Studley
James 161; John 161; Widow 161
Studman
William 384
Studwick
Mister 376
Stulby
Robert 450
Sturridg
Thomas 473
Sturt (Stirte, Sturte)
Edward 119; Guy 493; John 119; Thomas 357; Widow 405
Styles
Edward 455; John 79; William 530
Suckett
John 195; Robert 219; Thomas 219; Widow 206
Suckley
Edward 339, 340
Suett (Suatt, Sewett)
Henry 22, 50; Richard 21, 25, 26
Suffeild (Suffild)
John 517; Richard 158; Simon 127
Suggett
Anthony 221
Sumersett (Somersett, Summersett)
Duchess of 281; James 436;

Stephen 127; Thomas 261; Widow 156; — 377

Summers (Sommers, Sumer, Summer, Sumner)
Arthur 420; Charles 9; George 108; Henry 416(2); Joan 420; John 135, 317, 362, 372, 420(2); Richard 16; Robert 397; Thomas 420; Widow 56, 148, 209, 420; William 420, 456

Suscor
John 362

Sutton
George 75; John 5, 57(2), 229, 339, 341, 418; Luke 268; Mister 305; Nathaniel 480; Richard 318, 322; Robert 42, 324, 347, 442; Roger 481, 482; Ruth 343; Stephen 483; Thomas 494; Walter 260, 266, 501; Widow 351, 436, 481, 483, 499; William 332(2), 434, 497

Swagg
John 513

Swann (Swanne)
Anthony 50; Geoffrey 54; James 1; John 47; Nicholas 51, 194; Richard 47, 217; Robert 24(2), 54; Thomas 14, 41, 64; William 48, 56, 356

Swayne (Swaine)
Benjamin 229; James 397; Joan 100; Robert 99, 168; Roger 100, 101; Thomas 383, 395; Widow 119, 229; William 229

Sweet (Sweat, Sweete)
Thomas 30; William 36, 57

Sweetapple (Swetapple, Swettapple)
Andrew 299; George 163; John 418, 435, 439, 440; Widow 447; William 192, 434, 437, 447, 448

Sweetland
Richard 100

Swettingham (Swetingham)
Henry 98, 118; Richard 112

Swettman
Thomas 65; Widow 509; William 160

Swift (Swifte)
Thomas 502; Widow 455; William 494

Swinden
Alexander 50

Swithingham
John 38; Richard 38

Swyer
Thomas 530

Symes (Symmes, Syms)
Alice 252; Catherine 254; Edmund 252, 343; Edward 265; Geoffrey 515; Henry 267; James 29, 317; John 112, 252, 256; Margery 68; Mary 252; Matthew 428; Mister 456; Ralph 390, 470; Richard 1, 237, 252, 271, 523b, 525; Thomas 1, 112, 146, 164, 252(2), 270, 286, 324, 497; Widow 240, 252(4), 265, 316, 515, 525; William 1, 229, 252, 333

Symons (Simons, Symmonds, Symonds)
Alexander 452; Edward 357; Elizabeth 357; Hugh 530; James 513; John 208, 305, 384, 514; Matthew 1; Mister 2, 45, 77; Owen 1; Peter 229; Richard 38; Simon 489; Thomas 292; Widow 102, 411, 445, 491, 503; William 208

Symson, Sympson *see* Simpson

Tabbet (Tabut)
Edward 93; John 471

Tabor
Mister 330

Tackell
Samuel 1

Tadborow
Widow 390

Talbott (Talbot, Talbutt)
Elizabeth 471; Francis 362; John 117; Widow 117
Talke
Mister 112
Tallman
John 209
Talmage
Edmund 285; Edward 337(2), 437; Henry 260; John 330; Peter 330; Richard 476; Robert 461; Thomas 260; Widow 260, 324
Tanner
Andrew 339; Gregory 227; Henry 290; Hugh 36; Joan 317; John 241, 494; Nicholas 338; Paul 306; Richard 99, 305; Robert 395; Widow 332, 421; William 324, 435, 436, 478
Taphurst
Richard 437
Taplin (Taplyn)
Benjamin 342; John 89, 386, 397; Thomas 294; Widow 490; William 428, 490
Tapner
Thomas 342; Widow 443
Tapp
John 100; Silvester 131; Widow 316; William 100
Targett
George 520, 528
Tarleton
Benjamin 434; George 229; John 435; Peter 229; Robert 434; Thomas 229; Widow 229(2)
Tarman
John 298; Mister 342
Tarrant
Benjamin 442; David 445; Elizabeth 152; George 442; Henry 1, 442(2), 445; Hercules 445; James 493; John 445; Richard 445; Samuel 445(2); Thomas 131, 145, 339, 442, 445, 448; — 256
Tarry
Widow 98
Tarver
John 89(2), 117; Joseph 158; Mary 98; Nicholas 91; Richard 117; Widow 89, 130; William 117
Tasker
Alice 38; John 5
Tassell
Widow 1
Tatwell
Anthony 436
Taunt
Richard 2, 3
Taunton
Richard 526
Tawke
Arthur 208; John 1
Taylor (Tailor, Tayler)
Alexander 504(2); Arthur 78, 229; Doctor 229; Edward 298, 332, 426, 473; George 1, 128, 397, 418; Henry 122; James 38, 92; John 93, 193, 229, 263, 300, 334, 378, 418, 487, 517; Joseph 1; Martin 100; Mary 42; Michael 1; Mister 254, 292, 529; Mistress 528; Nicholas 229; Philip 16(2), 229, 279; Richard 17, 229, 317, 418; Robert 219, 306; Thomas 103, 193, 246, 316, 355, 473, 520, 528(2), 529; Widow 1, 38, 212, 229(2), 418, 473; William 80, 212, 229, 339, 356, 406, 418, 500
Tayste
Mistress 357
Teane
Edward 515
Tee
James 240(2); John 429; Thomas 92, 216
Teever
Robert 122
Tefferd
Thomas 87

Tegg
John 115; William 115
Tellew
Peter 334
Tellier
William 160
Teme
John 505; Robert 505
Templer (Templar)
Richard 436(2)
Terme
Richard 311
Terrer
Robert 512; Thomas 515
Terrill (Terryll)
Anthony 219; Richard 247; Widow 219
Terry
Anthony 405; James 211, 391; John 223, 391, 401; Mister 357, 501; Mistress 388; Moses 403, 404, 405, 407; Richard 372, 405(3); Robert 90, 177, 399, 402(3), 461; Stephen 402; Thomas 391; Widow 35, 396, 405, 418; William 283, 368
Tevell
Richard 203
Tewes
James 237
Tewksbery
Frances 135
Thackham
Francis 182; John 520, 529; William 396
Tharpe
John 418
Thayne
John 98
Thayre
William 395
Theare
Widow 396
Therle
Edward 131
Thernell
William 132
Thextone
John 140
Thire
William 383
Thistlethwaite (Thistlewayt)
Mister 462; Widow 461
Thomas (Thomes)
Alexander 461; Anthony 357; Cicely 159; Elizabeth 506; Henry 159, 473, 513; Humphrey 141; John 1, 40, 91, 208, 255, 357, 502, 507; Mister 459; Nicholas 100, 116; Richard 1, 100(2), 466, 507, 508, 509; Simon 270; Stephen 38; Thomas 133; Walter 471; Widow 116, 443, 457, 504; William 116, 506, 507; — 1, 523b
Thombs
Widow 418
Thornberry
John 520
Thorne
Edward 151, 160, 523a, 524; George 108; Henry 98, 123; John 1, 160, 286; Richard 460; Thomas 38, 355; William 96
Thornebrough (Thorneburgh)
John 528; Mistress 436
Thorner
Edward 40; John 428
Thorneton (Thornton)
Henry 493; John 357; Nicholas 357; Robert 493
Thorngate (Thornegate)
John 269; Robert 342; Widow 500
Thorpe
George 383; Henry 394; Hugh 383; Walter 394
Thridge
John 335
Throllopp
John 434

Throughgood
— 1
Thurborne
Thomas 376
Thurman
Mary 434; Mistress 434; Sarah 480; Walter 1
Thurston (Thirston)
John 160, 473
Tibbs
Richard 1
Tibby
Joseph 527
Tibley
Peter 104
Tidall
Widow 290
Tidwell
Ann 249
Tilbery
Christopher 366
Tilborowe (Tilborrowe)
Francis 390; Isaac 394; Oliver 390; Robert 390; Thomas 422; William 390(3)
Tilbrow
William 200
Tilden
Henry 38
Tiler *see* Tyler
Tille
John 81, 184; Mister 56; Richard 431; Thomas 81
Tiller (Tyller)
Hugh 98; John 161
Tilly (Tylly)
Barnard 134; Daniel 118; Edward 118; George 118; Henry 376; Richard 118; Tristram 163
Timbrill (Timbrell)
John 1(2); Mistress 1
Tindall
Widow 163
Tinker
John 1
Tinley
Francis 370
Tipper
Henry 372; John 74, 229; Richard 229(2); Widow 372; William 74, 209
Tippetts (Tippitts)
John 1; Robert 1
Tippin
Thomas 357
Tisteed
Christopher 331
Titchborne (Titchbourne)
Benjamin 196 (Sir); Francis 404; Henry 118(2) (Sir), 244, 485 (Sir); Mister 221; William 465
Titheridge (Titheridg, Tytheridg)
John 248; Widow 238; William 292
Tittcombe (Titcombe)
John 245; Margaret 327; Richard 440
Tivito
Joan 132; Thomas 132
Tocock (Tococke)
Richard 371; Thomas 223, 362
Todd
John 236; Mister 201; Thomas 49, 192, 229; Widow 76, 192
Todey
Stephen 518
Togge
Widow 442
Tolefrey (Tolefry)
Jane 261; John 267, 270, 318; Martin 270; Nicholas 484; Robert 498; Thomas 263; Widow 324, 484, 498; William 498
Tombs
Edward 118; John 84, 229; Widow 1, 456; William 436
Tomer
Thomas 97
Tomes (Toms)
John 91; Robert 120; Widow 120
Tomlins
Mister 33

Tompkins (Tomkins)
Charles 435; Giles 436; John 436, 523a, 524; Thomas 160; Widow 192; William 530
Tompson (Tompsone, Tomsone)
Albery 194; Anthony 413; John 46, 434; Matthew 229; Richard 256; Robert 103, 343; Stephen 106; Widow 1, 229, 504; William 265
Tongs (Tonges)
Daniel 494; Widow 292, 494
Tooke
John 118; Thomas 382
Tooker
Thomas 1; Widow 332
Tookey
Mistress 292
Toomer
George 120
Toote
William 252, 270
Toppes
Widow 442
Tovery
Moses 407
Tovey (Toovey, Tovye)
Henry 1, 24; John 86
Towch
Daniel 290; Widow 291
Towers
Daniel 418; William 177
Towler
William 452
Towleton
Thomas 515
Towlman
Ann 119
Towne
Ambrose 318; John 318; Thomas 298
Townsend (Townesend)
Austin 473; Philip 494; William 473
Towton
Philip 458; Richard 458; Simon 443; Widow 443; William 443
Traffells
Edward 229
Travis
John 490; Nicholas 490; Robert 397(2)
Trebett
William 119
Treddle (Treadle)
Thomas 434; Widow 1, 290
Tredge
John 165
Tredgold (Tredgall, Tredgoll)
Edward 134; John 434(2), 440, 498; Simon 270; Thomas 437, 440; William 437
Treherne
Richard 158; William 158
Tremaine (Tremany, Tremone)
Gowen 100; John 103, 104; Peter 100; Widow 481
Trench
William 335
Tresler
John 226
Trevise
William 100
Trew
Widow 135
Trewliff
Edward 414
Trewlove (Trewelove)
Giles 252; Richard 252; Widow 446; William 442
Trewman
Widow 290
Tribb
Anthony 171; Edward 195; Jacob 81; John 206, 222; Ralph 212, 223; Richard 42, 77, 171, 177; Robert 211; Thomas 42; William 170, 171, 227
Tribbick (Trebeck, Tribbicke)
Elizabeth 61; Nicholas 46; Widow 58

Triblecock (Triblock)
Francis 1(2)
Trickhup
Bartholomew 97
Trigg (Trigge, Triggs)
Abraham 361; Edward 208; Henry 189; John 200, 208, 371, 395, 405; Richard 189, 223; Solomon 247; Thomas 404; Widow 208, 375; William 355, 403, 431; — 1
Trigoll (Triggall)
James 429; John 135; William 135
Trill
Avis 124; Matthew 124; Richard 122; Thomas 125, 128, 132; William 122
Trim
Henry 153; Richard 80; Thomas 118, 120
Trimer (Trimmer, Trymer)
Christopher 87; Daniel 375; Edmund 178(2); Edward 392; John 178, 311, 418; Richard 178, 407; Robert 179; Thomas 490(2); Widow 222, 376, 379
Triminge
Jerome 390
Trimnell
Philip 229
Trininge
Widow 192
Triphooke (Triphook, Trippick, Trippocke)
Ambrose 115; Bartholomew 115; Edward 108, 115(2), 121, 159; John 115
Trippett
John 58
Triver
John 38
Trivett
William 56
Troake
Joseph 154; Mary 153
Trodd (Trod)
Andrew 26; Edward 26, 252; Francis 19, 36; John 26, 52; Richard 26(2), 29; Thomas 26, 48, 252(2), 521; Widow 244
Troth
John 126
Trott
Sir John 295, 296(2), 436
Trublefeild
William 235
Truddle (Trudle)
Thomas 214(2), 241; Widow 38, 51; William 51
Trunby
William 93
Trusler
John 159, 367; Richard 177; Robert 182; Thomas 249; Widow 256, 367; William 112
Trussell
Edward 237; Widow 229
Trye
Thomas 164
Tryman
William 55
Tubb
John 356; Ralph 462
Tucker
James 5; John 29; Robert 25(2), 124; Thomas 25, 27, 104; Widow 1, 515
Tuckes
Thomas 164
Tuckey
George 199(2)
Tuckle
Widow 96; William 119
Tuffing
Roger 473
Tuffy
Robert 91
Tufton
Richard 292, 334
Tugfeild
Barnard 383

Tuggey
William 252
Tull
Edward 527(2); John 334(2); Robert 189; Widow 175
Tullatt
John 214
Tulse
William 118(2)
Tunton
Richard 522
Tunworth
Thomas 200
Turfeild
William 338
Turgis
Francis 100; Tristram 100
Turkas
Widow 357
Turke
Thomas 171
Turkett
Thomas 81
Turman
William 501
Turner
Edward 194; Francis 490; Gilbert 19; Henry 397, 473; James 418; Jerome 397; John 28, 37, 205(2), 213, 267, 291(2), 369, 417, 418, 512; Joseph 434; Mary 199; Matthew 1; Mistress 528; Nicholas 198, 363, 504; Procter 374; Richard 19, 247, 375; Robert 199, 202, 241, 471; Roger 34, 163; Thomas 8, 21, 198, 252, 367, 374, 397, 436; Ursula 44; Widow 369, 403, 434; William 1, 163, 369, 370, 375, 376, 414, 418(2), 471, 528
Turnham (Turneham)
John 137; Widow 141
Turton
Sarah 333; Thomas 418
Turvill (Turvell)
Edward 182; Thomas 189
Tutchin (Tuchin)
Mister 357; Robert 89
Tutt
Goody 408; John 379; Thomas 244; Widow 229; William 408
Tuttson
Thomas 471
Twine (Twyne)
Francis 445; Henry 355; James 481; John 263, 293, 366, 394, 446; Margaret 417; Peter 414; Richard 263(2), 476; Thomas 209; Widow 38, 263, 481; William 192, 264
Twiner (Twinner, Twyner)
John 418; Richard 256; Robert 249; Widow 249
Twinney (Twinny)
Henry 231; John 523b, 524
Twitchen
Andrew 93
Twitt
John 193
Twynham (Twinham)
Henry 76; Thomas 237; William 76
Tyball
Silas 454
Tyler (Tiler)
Edward 112; John 229, 357; Julia 363; Richard 518, 530; Stephen 229; Widow 225; William 108
Tyre (Tire, Tyer)
John 43; Stephen 43; Thomas 413; Widow 37, 49; William 1(3)
Undee
John 473; Richard 473; Robert 473
Underwood
Edward 404; Richard 181(2), 270(2)
Upden
Edward 456
Uphen
Robert 298

Uphill
Giles 229; John 160; Richard 161; Robert 24
Upjohn
Thomas 158(2)
Upman
Robert 1; William 40
Uppery
Thomas 447
Upsdale (Upsdall, Upsdell)
Isaac 207; John 8, 487; Thomas 228, 493
Upton
George 327; James 431; Jasper 418; John 178, 431, 434, 483; Matthew 424; Widow 424; William 164, 229
Urry
John 91; Mister 148; Thomas 160
Usher
William 318
Uvedale
John 51; Lady 68; Richard 23 (Sir); Widow 38; William 229
Vaine
Widow 504
Valence
Nicholas 513
Valenter
Bartholomew 336
Vallett
Henry 318, 530
Vallines
John 505
Vallor (Valler, Valor)
Christopher 163; Goodman 212; Henry 194; John 194(2), 213, 227; Raphael 171, 189; Robert 194, 208; Thomas 208, 213; Widow 194; William 189
Vandell
Widow 193
Vander
Adam 229; Humphrey 229; Richard 229(2); William 229
Vanderplanke
William 513
Vanderslatt
Andrew 292
Vanner
Goody 515
Varndell
Robert 194
Varneham
Widow 529
Vate
Elizabeth 317
Vaughan (Vaugham)
Clement 9; George 208; John 40; Widow 229, 252, 404
Vaukes (Vakes, Vauks)
Ambrose 318; John 318; Mary 318; Widow 318
Vause (Vaus, Vawse)
Edward 310; Mistress 357(2); Widow 515
Veale
Daniel 529; George 529; John 102, 134; Nicholas 127; Roger 38
Veare
Andrew 279; James 436; John 279; Leonard 269; Mister 320; Richard 279; Thomas 9, 279; William 193, 198, 279
Vecke
Daniel 192
Vedinge
Widow 454
Veeke (Veake)
John 118, 192; Widow 118
Veltum
Joan 471
Venables (Venable, Vennables)
Barbara 195; John 42; Nicholas 435; William 193
Vengon (Vengen)
Thomas 83(2); Widow 46
Venn
Henry 189
Vennor
Thomas 93

Ventham
Abraham 434; Edward 472; Elizabeth 468; George 468; Giles 504; Henry 513; Joan 465; John 256(2), 462, 465, 472; Nicholas 256, 468, 473(2); Peter 256; Richard 256, 434, 472(2); Robert 468; Thomas 498; Widow 472; William 457, 465
Verndell
John 189, 222
Verrell
Alexander 1; Widow 291
Verse
Stephen 299
Vertue
John 315
Verundell
Widow 308
Viccary (Vicary)
James 182; Jerome 182; John 361, 431; Richard 163; Robert 165, 173, 182, 392; Thomas 172
Vice
William 357
Vidler
Anthony 398; Stephen 366; Widow 259; Zacharias 223, 390
Vildew
James 67
Villers (Viller)
Philip 332; Widow 292
Vince
John 503
Vincent (Vinsent, Vinson)
George 493, Henry 133, 418; John 1, 115, 177, 515; Matthew 115; Richard 473; Thomas 89, 229, 349; William 114, 329
Vincorne
Thomas 1
Vinden
John 222(2), 223, 285, 369; Robert 407; Thomas 376; Widow 31, 357
Vine (Vines)
Christopher 466; Henry 1
Vinecourte
Henry 133
Vining (Vinning)
Francis 1; William 1
Vinn (Vinne)
John 229; Richard 506, Thomas 229; Widow 68, 229, 236; William 229
Vinnerye
Thomas 374
Vinon
John 238
Vinren
Thomas 160
Vipant
Anthony 285
Virge
Widow 135
Vittery
William 356, 400
Viveash
Hugh 100
Voakes (Voak, Voake, Vooke, Vox)
Arthur 84; Edmund 472; Henry 39; Jacob 211; John 1, 8, 10; Joseph 1; Richard 489(2); Widow 84, 256
Voller
John 246; Widow 335
Vosse
William 530
Vovert
John 521; Mister 527
Vye
William 152
Wackfeild (Wakfeild)
Edward 424; John 424; Mister 424
Wade
Christopher 118; Henry 262; John 227, 248, 418; Richard 6, 75, 254; Thomas 133 (2), 265; Widow 192; William 192, 253

Wademan
John 87; Widow 87
Wademore
Christopher 99
Waden
John 333
Wafferer
Doctor 292; Mirth 19
Wagg (Wagge)
John 125; Maurice 104 (2); Robert 104; Thomas 104; William 103
Waight *see* Weight
Wake (Wakes)
Henry 177, 205; John 138, 232, 412, 487; Nicholas 263; Richard 249, 484; Robert 484; Thomas 206; Wellinough 293; Widow 164, 206; William 163, 379
Wakeford
David 226; George 183; James 88; John 226; Richard 124
Waker
John 209
Walcott
John 1
Walden (Waldon)
John 103, 104; Robert 355; Widow 135 (2)
Walder
Widow 1
Waldron (Waldren)
Andrew 515; Brian 140; Edmund 464; Edward 436, 442; Henry 455; Jonathan 476; John 1; Martin 504; Moses 504; Nicholas 513; Richard 229 (2), 455; Robert 442; Thomas 1, 310; Widow 464; William 229
Waldropp
Mistress 313; Peter 338; Simon 419; Widow 338
Wale
George 445; Henry 528; Peter 517, 529; Richard 445; Thomas 445
Walker
Cuthbert 418; Edward 357, 375; George 405, 419; Henry 229; Nicholas 46; Richard 54, 208, 517; Roger 522; Simon 163; Thomas 29, 208, 249, 355 (2); Widow 266; William 35
Wall (Walle, Walles)
Andrew 171; Edward 296, 445; Henry 160; John 331; Thomas 127, 229; Widow 117; William 403; [s] 523b
Wallbank
Matthew 403
Waller (Waler)
Elizabeth 434; Francis 61; John 55, 57; Martha 436; Robert 57; Stephen 57; Widow 68; William 1, 63, 436
Walleston (Wallistone)
Dorothy 518; Mistress 530; William 518, 530
Wallington
Giles 494; Widow 368
Wallis
James 376; John 374; Peter 363, 448; Richard 448; Thomas 117, 269, 376, 518 (2), 530; Widow 448, 456; William 255
Wallopp (Wallop)
Henry 250, 343, 386
Walsdeane
John 332
Waltensis
Mister 192
Walter (Walters)
Alexander 456; Edward 501; John 118, 334, 338; Nicholas 334, 338; Richard 320, 503; Robert 442, 445; Thomas 30, 338; Walter 503; Widow 339; William 338; — 100
Walteridge (Waltheridge)
John 418; Thomas 418
Waltham
Mary 342

Walwin
Mister 208
Wansey
Thomas 161
Ward (Warde, Wards)
Daniel 317; Edward 226; Francis 293; Jacob 517, 529; John 11, 89, 305; Matthew 93; Richard 383; Widow 56; William 450 (2)
Warden
George 38; Martin 407; Mary 93; Richard 46; Robert 88; Thomas 511; Widow 93
Warder
Henry 128
Ware
Widow 317, 376; William 284, 428
Wareham (Warham)
John 119, 255, 418, 442; Maurice 306; Paul 157; Richard 115, 117, 307; Robert 102; Simon 157; Widow 157; William 273, 479
Warford
Robert 530
Warne
Andrew 94; Bartholomew 160; Henry 118 (2); Hugh 101; James 100, 104; Jane 98; Joan 157; John 98, 100 (3), 101, 102, 118, 157; Joseph 100; Ralph 104 (2); Richard 131, 213; Thomas 92, 103, 104 (2); Widow 100, 104, 150; William 102, 104 (2)
Warner
Darby 177; Doctor 517; Francis 465; George 357; Henry 177; Joan 133; John 161, 229, 240, 388; Laurence 357; Margaret 162; Mister 161; Mistress 405; Nicholas 163; Richard 26, 316; Robert 355; Simon 163; Stephen 283; Thomas 2, 55, 177; Widow 51, 55, 163; William 25, 367 (2), 418 (2); — 354
Warre
Roger 10
Warrell
David 129; Widow 38
Warren (Warrene, Warrin)
Benjamin 192; Clement 504; Henry 1, 135; John 29; Nyatt 29; Richard 119, 394; Thomas 120, 504; Widow 120, 122, 397; William 122 (3), 332, 515
Warterne
William 164
Warthington
James 193
Warwick (Warrick)
Catherine 148; James 91, 159; John 151, 159; Nicholas 464; Ralph 128; Stephen 316; Thomas 148, 464; Widow 24, 89, 128; William 124
Wash
Robert 192
Washbeard
William 450
Wassell
Edward 283; Goodman 162; John 38, 39, 265, 283; Margaret 47; Thomas 21, 31; Widow 48; William 59
Wastell
John 70
Waterman (Watterman)
Anthony 96; Christopher 378, 430; Dorothy 323; Edward 108; Elizabeth 98; Elton 96; George 412; Henry 258; Hugh 257, 323; James 305; John 14, 118 (2), 257, 292, 298, 371; Mary 334; Mister 387; Nicholas 25, 229; Philip 317; Ralph 365; Reynold 162; Richard 86, 108, 317, 331, 430, 463; Robert 341, 343, 463; Thomas 323, 341, 354, 477, 527; Timothy 412; Widow 118, 257, 331, 463, 477; William 96, 108, 118, 319, 333, 334, 342, 387, 394

Waters
Widow 85, 357; William 1
Watkins (Wattkins)
Alexander 1; Jerome 283; Richard 240; Widow 5 (2); William 156
Watridge (Wartridge, Wateridge, Watridg)
Anthony 322; John 299, 322, 511; Richard 299; Robert 169, 257, 258; Thomas 324; Widow 322
Watten
John 104
Wattmer (Wattmore)
Richard 418; Robert 318; Walter 429; William 385 (2)
Watts
Abraham 86; Arthur 86; Elizabeth 178; Farden 86; Francis 332; George 363, 428; Harmand 370; Henry 98; John 330, 358, 378, 406, 409, 418 (2); Laurence 322; Martha 86; Mister 395; Nicholas 371, 397, 406; Peter 404; Robert 37, 378, 395, 406; Stephen 376; Thomas 1, 324, 332, 357, 378, 490; Walter 113 (2), 148; Widow 252, 318, 331, 332, 362, 395, 437, 527; William 252, 331, 371, 376, 378, 406; [ ]astine 1
Wattson (Watson)
John 1, 406 (2); Mister 40; Mistress 441; Richard 396; William 54, 229
Wavell
David 106; John 126, 132, 134; Robert 132, 133; Thomas 229
Wayes
Thomas 344
Weale
Martin 24; Thomas 35; William 106
Weames
— 29
Weare
William 316
Wearham
Richard 319
Wearing
Widow 331
Weary
John 334
Weaver
Humphrey 403
Webb
Abbott 317; Alexander 370; Andrew 344, 484; Arthur 335; Bartholomew 229; Christopher 317; Cornelius 415, 489; Daniel 253, 292; Edward 266, 316, 418; George 518; Henry 30, 317; James 339; John 1, 93, 227, 229, 231, 414, 415, 476; Mister 102; Nathaniel 471; Nicholas 266, 428; Noye 391; Richard 25, 284, 292, 412; Robert 419; Roger 266, 317; Samuel 164; Silvester 468; Thomas 1 (2), 229, 287, 319, 324, 395, 498; Widow 100, 375, 471, 484; William 1, 24, 229, 286, 303, 324, 351, 471, 523b, 525
Webber
Matthew 464
Weckham
Robert 292
Wedge
Thomas 164
Wedmer
George 158
Weeden
John 14
Weekes (Weeke, Weeks)
Edward 192, 243; Francis 518; George 515; John 6, 15, 118, 218, 428; Joseph 198; Richard 238, 244, 426; Rigmell 244; Thomas 248, 317; Widow 214; William 193, 214, 218, 429

Weekham (Weekam)
Henry 518, 530; Thomas 263
Weels
George 233
Weene
John 193, 486; Nicholas 202; Richard 193, 486; Robert 193; Thomas 193, 433
Weight (Waight, Waite, Wayte)
Abraham 435; Andrew 236; Anthony 357; Daniel 215; Deborah 195: Edward 339; Francis 316; Henry 1, 299; Hugh 332; James 267; Jerome 488; John 149, 317, 415, 508, 515; Joseph 434; Mark 357; Michael 236; Richard 252, 317 (2), 434, 500; Thomas 38, 263, 409, 491; Widow 29, 229, 252, 267, 303 (2), 357; William 252, 415, 434, 458; — 415
Weilder
John 97; Nicholas 17
Weith
Edward 374; William 379
Welch (Welsh)
Edmund 192; Edward 96; James 117; Joan 150; John 1 (2), 162, 236; Joseph 100; Lucy 192; Nicholas 162; Richard 227; Thomas 1, 162, 378; William 100
Welchman
John 135
Wellbred
Peter 1
Wellenough
John 256
Weller
Alexander 208
Welling (Wellings)
Richard 472; Thomas 428
Wellman
Widow 197
Welloway
John 458; Robert 458
Wells
Bridget 447; Charles 236; Christopher 526; John 219, 348, 383, 408, 418; Mister 500; Peter 205; Richard 178, 436; Robert 98, 299; Swithun 93; Thomas 1, 488; Widow 163, 418; William 299, 447
Welsted (Welsteed)
Henry 327; Humphrey 122; John 126, 390; Simon 123; Stephen 229; Susan 129; Widow 100
Werndell
Andrew 361
Weshman
John 94
West
Ann 269; Benjamin 528; Charles 92; Dorothy 269; Edward 30; George 434; Gilbert 38; James 1, 317; John 72, 163, 193, 197, 269, 283, 300, 418; Mister 229, 495; Richard 1, 27, 298; Robert 483; Thomas 21, 24, 298 (2), 361, 530; Widow 229, 280, 339; William 57, 418
Westbery
Edward 119; James 135; Richard 459; William 119
Westbrooke
Ann 41; Christopher 54; Henry 406; John 40, 190, 208, 227, 228, 404; Richard 190; Robert 40; Thomas 164, 208 (2); Widow 40; William 196
Westcombe (Wescombe)
George 282; Jerome 290; John 25; Nicholas 280; Thomas 436; Widow 291
Westcott
Bartholomew 27
Westend
Stephen 370
Westerton
Samuel 192; William 192

Westhook
Francis 372
Weston (Westen)
Ann 388; David 269; Henry 343; John 418; Margaret 335; Nicholas 48; Richard 269, 339; Thomas 2 (2), 269; Widow 388, 418; William 435
Westover
William 213
Westwood
Mister 378; Widow 299
Wey
William 414
Weyler
Stephen 306
Weyman
John 434; Thomas 139
Whale (Wale, Whalle)
George 445, 511; Henry 528; John 252, 443; Mister 504; Nicholas 177; Peter 331, 517, 529; Richard 320, 445 (3), 455, 515; Thomas 231, 339, 394, 445, 455; Widow 256, 320, 437; William 531
Wharford
Robert 518
Wharton
John 504; Widow 277
Wheable
Andrew 266; Richard 252, 256 (2), 493; Robert 256; Thomas 252; William 462
Wheaden
William 1
Wheate (Wheat)
John 521; Joseph 1; Joshua 1; Nicholas 37; Randal 385; Samuel 298, 429, 490
Wheatland
Cuthbert 468; John 1, 175, 434, 492; Philip 287; Richard 338 (2); Thomas 339; Widow 76, 303, 316, 412, 434
Wheatly (Whatley, Wheatley)
Chidick 280; Henry 479; John 434, 466; Mister 363; Richard 107 (2), 434; Thomas 434; Widow 488; William 193; — 107
Wheatstone
Thomas 407
Wheele
William 403
Wheeler (Weeler)
Abraham 112, 380; Benjamin 273; Christopher 158; Edward 29, 190; Elizabeth 158; Francis 308; George 404; Guy 223; Henry 164, 168, 269, 504 (3); Hugh 29; James 130, 355, 518, 530; John 23, 81, 117, 158 (2), 182, 276, 299, 333, 364, 370, 395, 431, 451; Mister 454; Nicholas 46, 182, 269, 276; Richard 317, 333; Robert 129, 134, 158, 276; Simon 158; Stephen 99, 118; Thomas 38, 81 (2), 118, 429; Widow 38, 81, 168, 189, 276, 380, 460; William 99, 118, 163, 181, 271, 317, 339, 404 (3); — 1
Wheeles
Richard 332
Whelpdell
Andrew 431
Whelpe
Richard 317
Whetter
James 68
Whettman
Richard 504
Whichelow
Thomas 294
Whisladd (Whislad)
Widow 530; William 518, 530
Whistler (Whisler)
Laurence 491; Mister 384
Whitaker
Andrew 157; Charles 338
Whitcher (Whicher, Witcher)
Alexander 468; George 480;

Widley
Thomas 331
Widmore (Widmoore)
John 208, 297, 317
Wieth
John 357
Wigge (Wigg, Wiggs)
Andrew 357; Edward 320, 322; John 61, 377, 394 (2); Joseph 27; Mary 27 (2); Philip 380; Richard 363, 394; Robert 57, 494; Thomas 4, 57, 58, 357, 394; Widow 48, 370
Wiggens
Austin 259
Wigley
John 429; William 113, 356
Wigmore
Edward 1; John 294; Joseph 317; Richard 303, 316; Thomas 437; Walter 316; Widow 339; William 324
Wild (Wilde)
Alice 408; John 100, 120, 299; Reuben 434; Richard 332; Robert 342; Widow 93, 299, 428, 434 (2); William 318, 333
Wilkins (Wilkin, Willkins)
Andrew 51; Anthony 100; Francis 296 (2); Gilbert 174; Giles 317; Henry 100; Hugh 471; John 256, 316; Nicholas 256, 462; Richard 252, 256, 339; Robert 1; Roger 423; Samuel 283; Stephen 477; Thomas 229, 252, 316; Widow 25, 100, 151, 241, 267, 348, 487; William 151, 160, 252, 290, 294, 328, 478; — 51
Wilkinson
Edward 207; James 178; Widow 177
Wilks (Wilkes)
Ambrose 391; Gilbert 397; Henry 40; Nathaniel 379; Richard 60, 65; William 394
Willard
Thomas 1; — 1
Willcott
Thomas 209
Willcox
John 96
Willer
Robert 178
Williams (William)
Andrew 16; Ann 394; Barnard 1; Dorothy 418; Edward 450, 503; Eleanor 135; George 229; Henry 89, 160, 273; Isaac 56 (2); Jane 2; Jasper 1; John 1, 38, 41, 120, 244, 255, 277, 448; Michael 139; Samuel 1 (2); Thomas 51, 89, 448; Widow 29, 531; William 255, 468
Williamson
John 1; Widow 257; — 194
Willinott
Robert 361
Willis
Henry 229, 391; James 100; John 244, 266, 330 (2), 331, 368; Laurence 205, 207; Richard 110; Robert 1; Samuel 277, 281; Thomas 323; Widow 144; William 1, 255, 363
Willmott (Willmett)
Edward 293; Goodwife 208; John 67, 92, 150, 293, 368; Richard 303, 355; Robert 68; Thomas 229; William 208
Willts
John 158; Thomas 158 (2); William 158
Wilson (Willson)
An 89; George 256; Jerome 276; John 24, 127, 229; Matthew 92; Mister 150; Nathaniel 49; Thomas 38, 255; Widow 255, 512; William 29, 255
Wilton
John 512

Nicholas 316; Widow 299; William 316
Woodyer
Thomas 404
Wooldridge (Wooldridg, Woolldridge, Woollridge)
George 274; John 357, 403 (2); Widow 1; William 208
Woolfrey (Woolfreys)
George 1; Mister 113
Woolgar (Woolger, Woollgar)
Arthur 39; Henry 39; John 3, 53; Richard 74, 208; Robert 47; John 1, 59, 227; Widow 81; William 40 (2), 50, 227
Wooll (Wool, Woolles, Woolls)
Andrew 505; John 51, 100 (2), 237, 252, 509; Ralph 235; Richard 235, 236, 252; Widow 235; William 29
Woollman
Edward 317
Woolmay
Mister 170
Woolston
Widow 40
Wooly
William 434
Woort (Woorte)
George 108, 161; John 161 (2); Richard 107
Wootheridge
William 77
Wordlinge
Edward 59
Worland
Widow 150
Worlidge (Worlidg)
Ann 208; Francis 208; Henry 192; Joan 192; Samuel 1; Stephen 1
Wormstall (Wormestall)
Mistress 530; — 528
Worsham
John 148, 205; Robert 192
Worsley
Sir Henry 126, 254, 288
Worten
John 397 (2); Widow 317
Worth
Ellis 1; Philip 335
Worthington
James 193; John 193; William 193
Wotte
William 250
Woway
Widow 398
Wren
George 89
Wrestler
Robert 193
Wright
Barnard 418; Edward 292; Garrett 1; Henry 85, 290, 418; Isaac 424; John 94, 280, 418; Mister 290; Richard 281, 415; Thomas 85, 258, 354, 356, 384; Widow 6, 56, 94, 209, 290; William 94
Writh
Widow 227
Wroth
Robert 520, 528
Wy[ ]
Grantham 1
Wyatt (Wiatt, Wyat, Wyate)
Benjamin 42; Edward 75; Henry 75, 322; John 1 (2), 21, 35, 212, 245, 299, 322, 331, 377, 405; Justinian 1; Postumous 418; Richard 27, 42; Robert 78, 120; Samuel 48; Thomas 19, 35, 91, 245, 299, 418; Widow 76 (2), 78, 95, 299; William 72, 120
Wye
John 396; William 356
Wykes
Bridget 102
Wyman
Thomas 335

Wynn
William 357, 361
Yalden
Anthony 252; Edward 452; John 226; Mister 170, 229 (3), 230; Robert 193 (2), 372
Yarrington
Dorothy 192
Yeames
Richard 256
Yeare
John 340
Yearly (Yarly, Yeareley)
Edward 331; John 394; Mister 421
Yeatman
John 158; Mary 158; Widow 146
Yeatmay
Samuel 103
Yeats (Yates, Yeate)
Anthony 123; George 293; James 419; Mister 178; Widow 122, 428
Yeeles
William 418
Yeoman (Yeomans)
Anthony 229, 292, 372; Edward 36, 93; Frances 255; George 471; John 93; Richard 36, 237; Thomas 318; Widow 506; William 526
Yorke
John 38
Younge (Young, Younges, Youngs)
Anthony 226; Edmund 504; Edward 213 (2); George 1; Henry 125, 178; Hugh 301; James 6; Joan 335; John 98, 103, 112, 118, 192, 208 (2), 236, 245, 299, 317, 332, 335, 336, 358; Jonathan 103, 118; Joseph 103, 418; Major 527; Matthew 128; Mister 138, 416; Mistress 252; Peter 209; Richard 229, 359, 367, 403; Robert 191; Roger 522; Thomas 1, 18, 91, 298, 434; Widow 38, 40, 98, 332, 418; William 1, 24, 240, 317, 462
Younger
Widow 332
Zaines
John 520, 527, 528; Mary 530; Thomas 519 (2)
Zanger
Ralph 108
Zankey
Mister 383
Zealy
Widow 100
Zebutt
John 118
Zelman
John 99
Zoffe
Ann 149
[ ]alloway
Thomas 42
[ ]e
Zacharias 51
[fold]
Henry 517
[ ]icas
Widow 190
[ ]imple
Edward 2
[ ]inder
— 1
[ ]irker
— 200
[or]ling
— 1
[osbolt]
Anthony 372
[ ]rd
Thomas 51
[ ]tall
Mister 483
[ ]te
Richard 54

INDEX OF PLACES

All places are in Hampshire unless otherwise stated. The names of places are given in their modern form. Original spellings are given as footnotes in the main text. Division and hundred names are in capitals. Tithing or township names are indexed both in their own alphabetical place (with the parish identified in brackets), and under the name of the parish. The structure of parishes current at the time is used. All references are to section numbers.

INDEX OF NAMED PROPERTIES

INDEX OF OCCUPATIONS AND TITLES

Goodman, Goodwife, Mister, Mistress and Widow occur frequently and have not been indexed.